TSUBASA
THOSE WITH WINGS

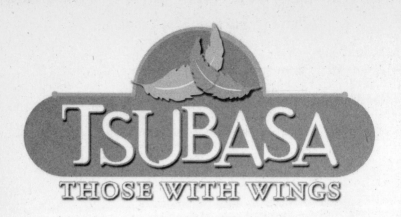

Volume: 3

By Natsuki Takaya

TOKYOPOP®

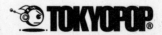

HAMBURG // LONDON // LOS ANGELES // TOKYO

Tsubasa: Those with Wings Volume 3
Created by Natsuki Takaya

Translation - Adrienne Beck
English Adaptation - Soo-Kyung Kim
Retouch and Lettering - Star Print Brokers
Production Artist - Rui Kyo
Graphic Designer - Louis Csontos

Editor - Cindy Suzuki
Print Production Manager - Lucas Rivera
Managing Editor - Vy Nguyen
Senior Designer - Louis Csontos
Associate Publisher - Marco F. Pavia
President and C.O.O. - John Parker
C.E.O. and Chief Creative Officer - Stu Levy

A  Manga

TOKYOPOP and  are trademarks or registered trademarks of TOKYOPOP Inc.

TOKYOPOP Inc.
5900 Wilshire Blvd. Suite 2000
Los Angeles, CA 90036

E-mail: info@TOKYOPOP.com
Come visit us online at www.TOKYOPOP.com

ISBN: 978-1-4278-1430-2

First TOKYOPOP printing: November 2009
10 9 8 7 6 5 4 3 2 1
Printed in the USA

CONTENTS

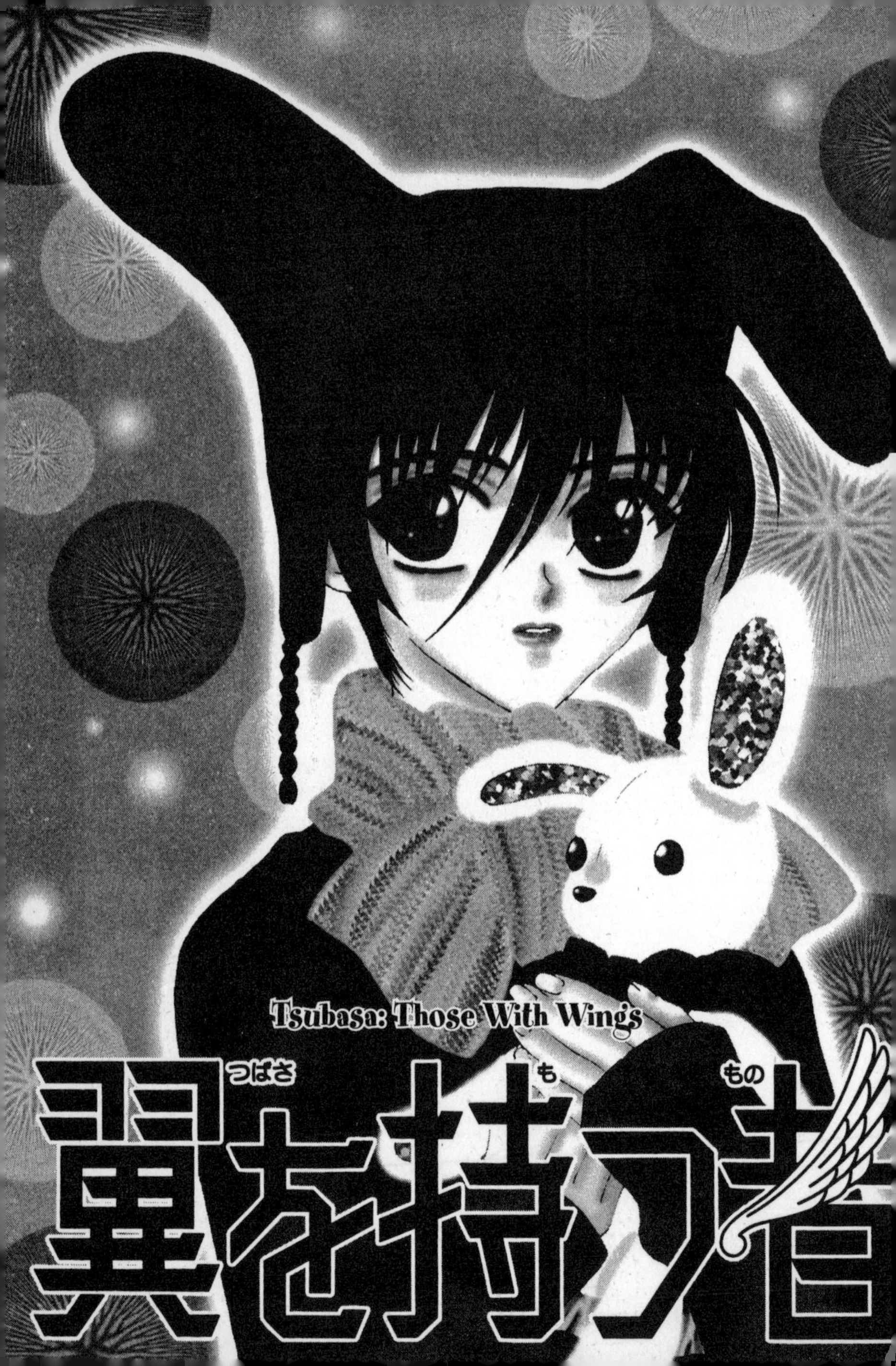
Tsubasa: Those With Wings
翼(つばさ)を持(も)つ者(もの)

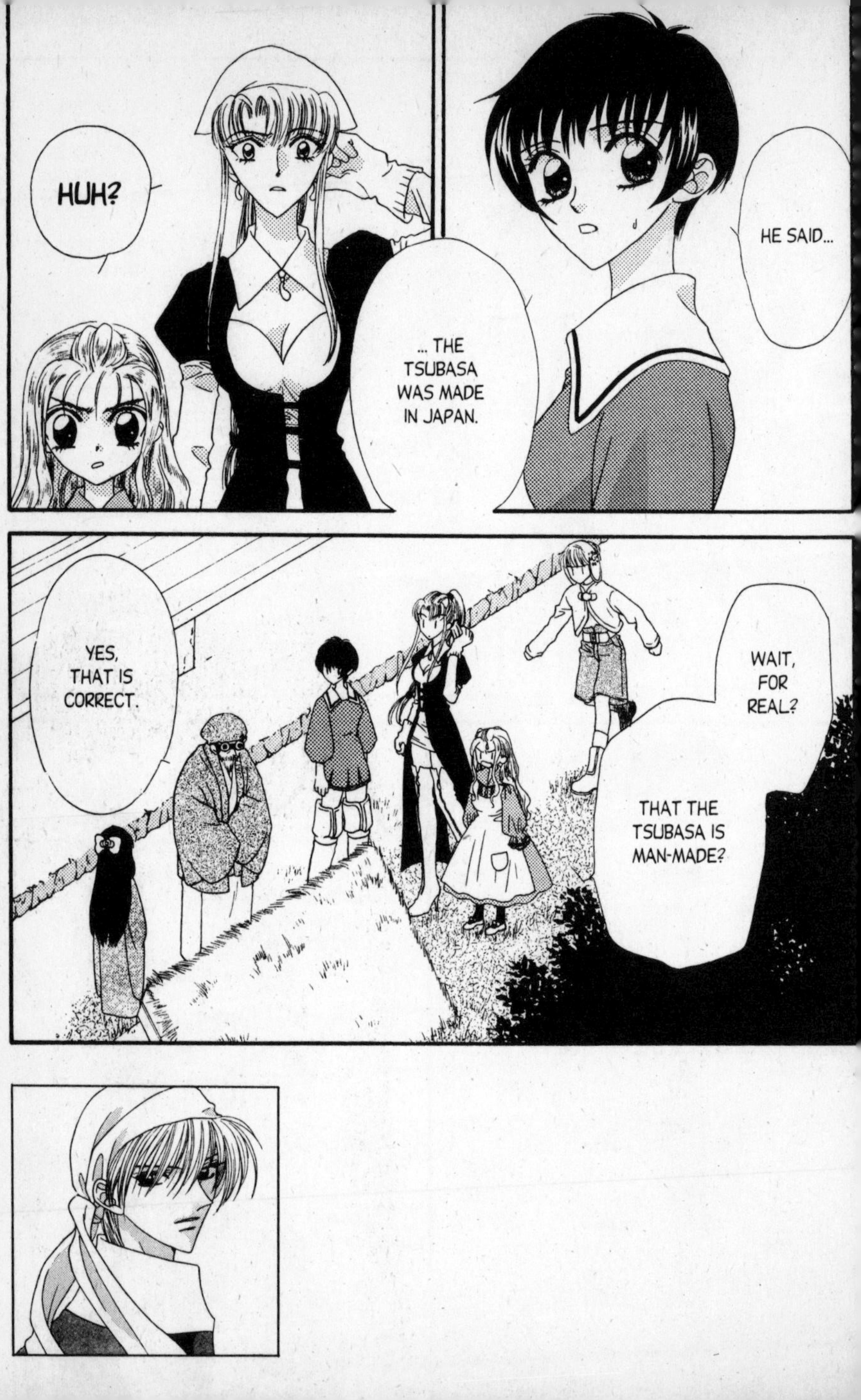
HE SAID...
... THE TSUBASA WAS MADE IN JAPAN.
HUH?
WAIT, FOR REAL?
THAT THE TSUBASA IS MAN-MADE?
YES, THAT IS CORRECT.

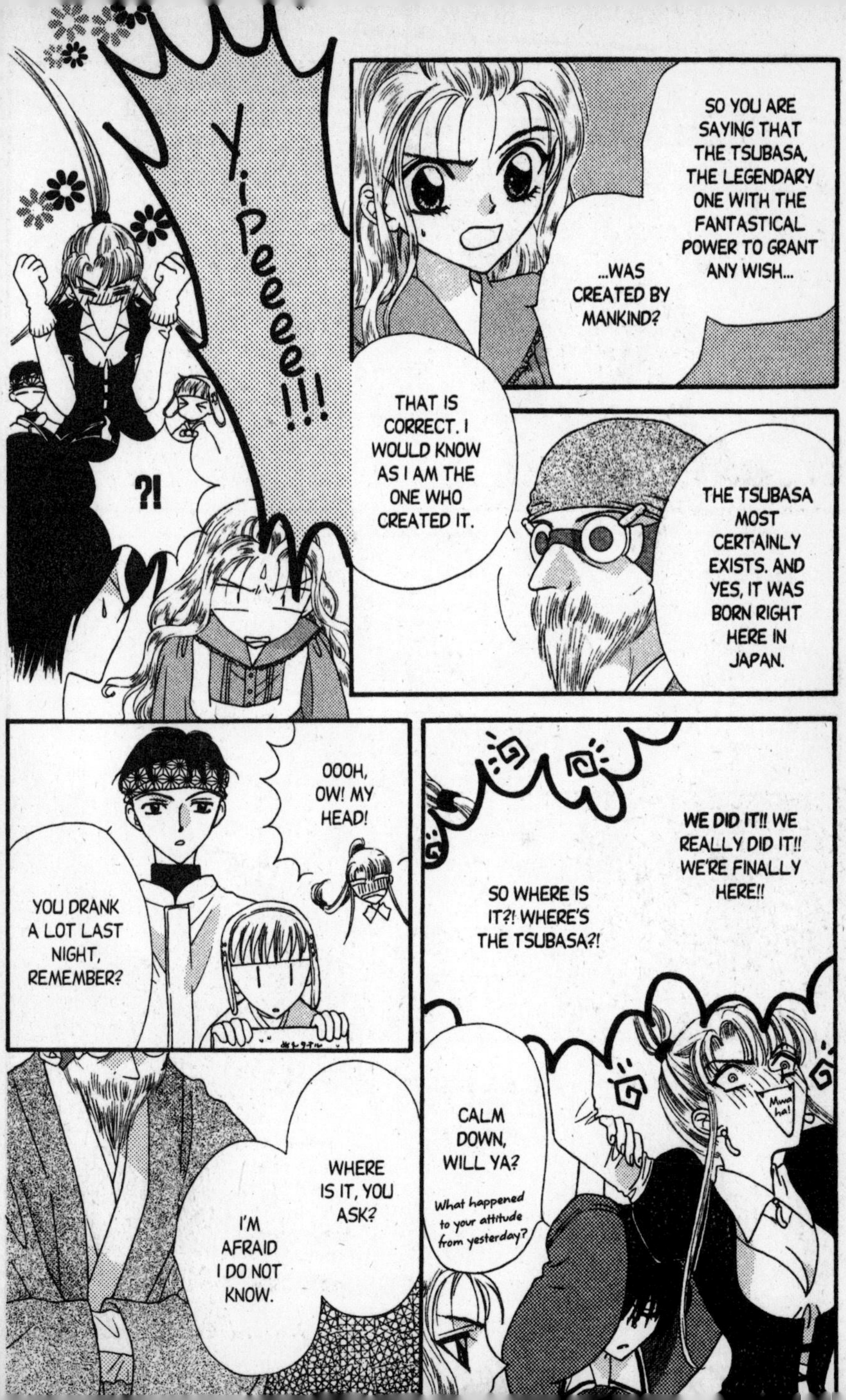

SO YOU ARE SAYING THAT THE TSUBASA, THE LEGENDARY ONE WITH THE FANTASTICAL POWER TO GRANT ANY WISH...
...WAS CREATED BY MANKIND?
THAT IS CORRECT. I WOULD KNOW AS I AM THE ONE WHO CREATED IT.
THE TSUBASA MOST CERTAINLY EXISTS. AND YES, IT WAS BORN RIGHT HERE IN JAPAN.
YiPeeeee!!!
?!
WE DID IT!! WE REALLY DID IT!! WE'RE FINALLY HERE!!
SO WHERE IS IT?! WHERE'S THE TSUBASA?!
OOOH, OW! MY HEAD!
YOU DRANK A LOT LAST NIGHT, REMEMBER?
Mwa ha!
CALM DOWN, WILL YA?
What happened to your attitude from yesterday?
WHERE IS IT, YOU ASK?
I'M AFRAID I DO NOT KNOW.

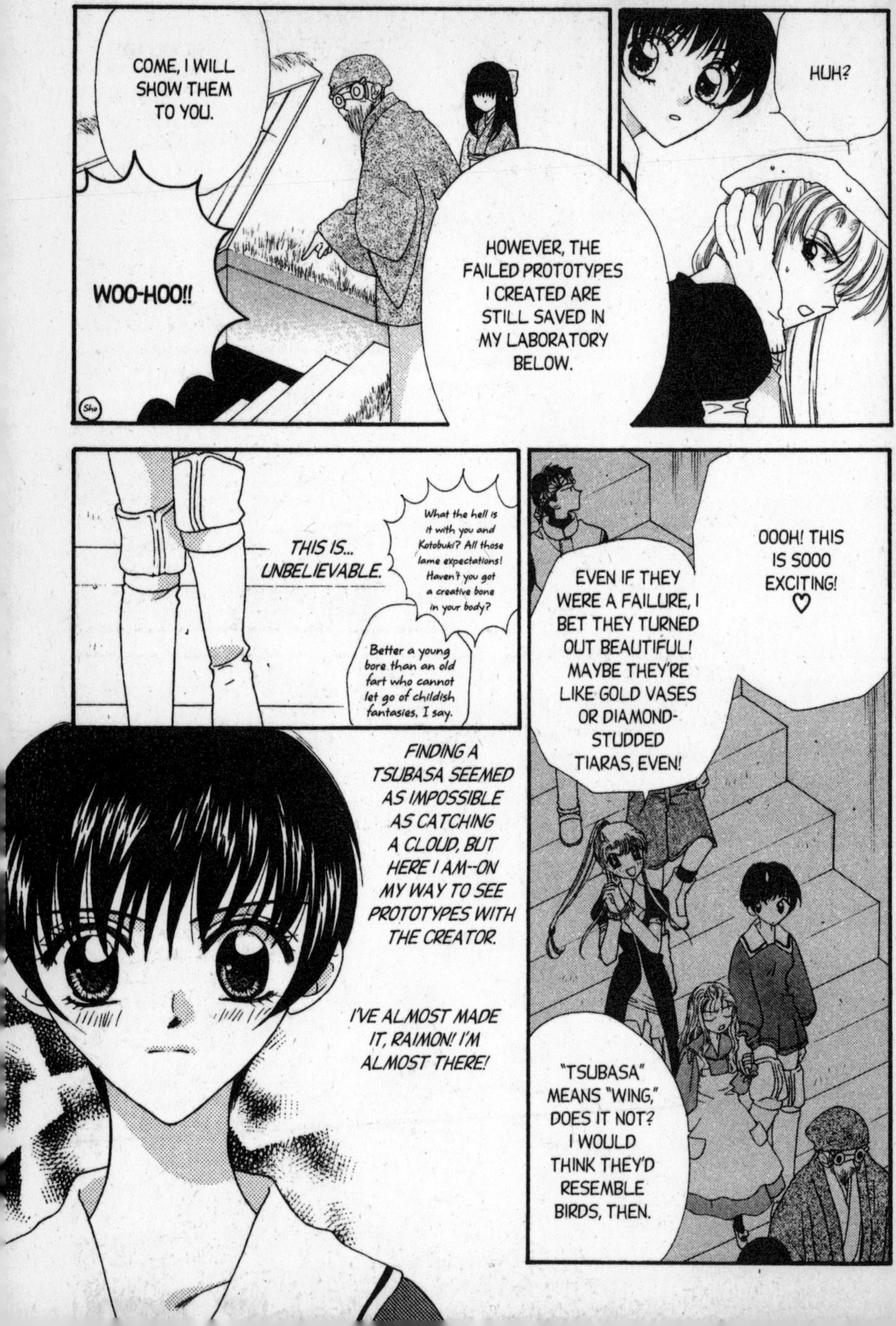
HUH?
HOWEVER, THE FAILED PROTOTYPES I CREATED ARE STILL SAVED IN MY LABORATORY BELOW.
COME, I WILL SHOW THEM TO YOU.
WOO-HOO!!
Sho
OOOH! THIS IS SOOO EXCITING! ♡
EVEN IF THEY WERE A FAILURE, I BET THEY TURNED OUT BEAUTIFUL! MAYBE THEY'RE LIKE GOLD VASES OR DIAMOND-STUDDED TIARAS, EVEN!
"TSUBASA" MEANS "WING," DOES IT NOT? I WOULD THINK THEY'D RESEMBLE BIRDS, THEN.
THIS IS... UNBELIEVABLE.
What the hell is it with you and Kotobuki? All those lame expectations! Haven't you got a creative bone in your body?
Better a young bore than an old fart who cannot let go of childish fantasies, I say.
FINDING A TSUBASA SEEMED AS IMPOSSIBLE AS CATCHING A CLOUD, BUT HERE I AM--ON MY WAY TO SEE PROTOTYPES WITH THE CREATOR.
I'VE ALMOST MADE IT, RAIMON! I'M ALMOST THERE!

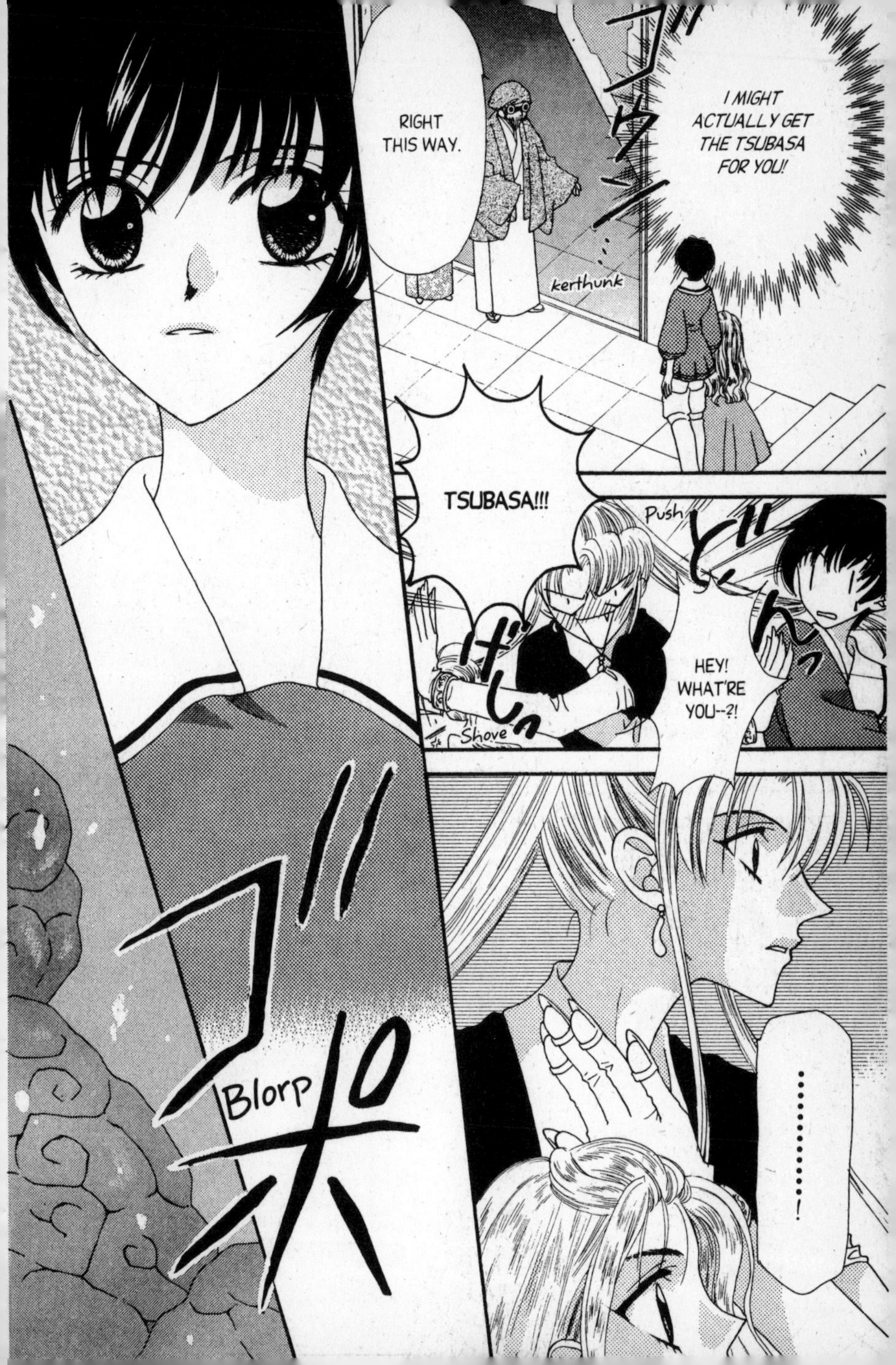

I MIGHT ACTUALLY GET THE TSUBASA FOR YOU!
RIGHT THIS WAY.
kerthunk
TSUBASA!!!
Push
Shove
HEY! WHAT'RE YOU--?!
.........!
Blorp

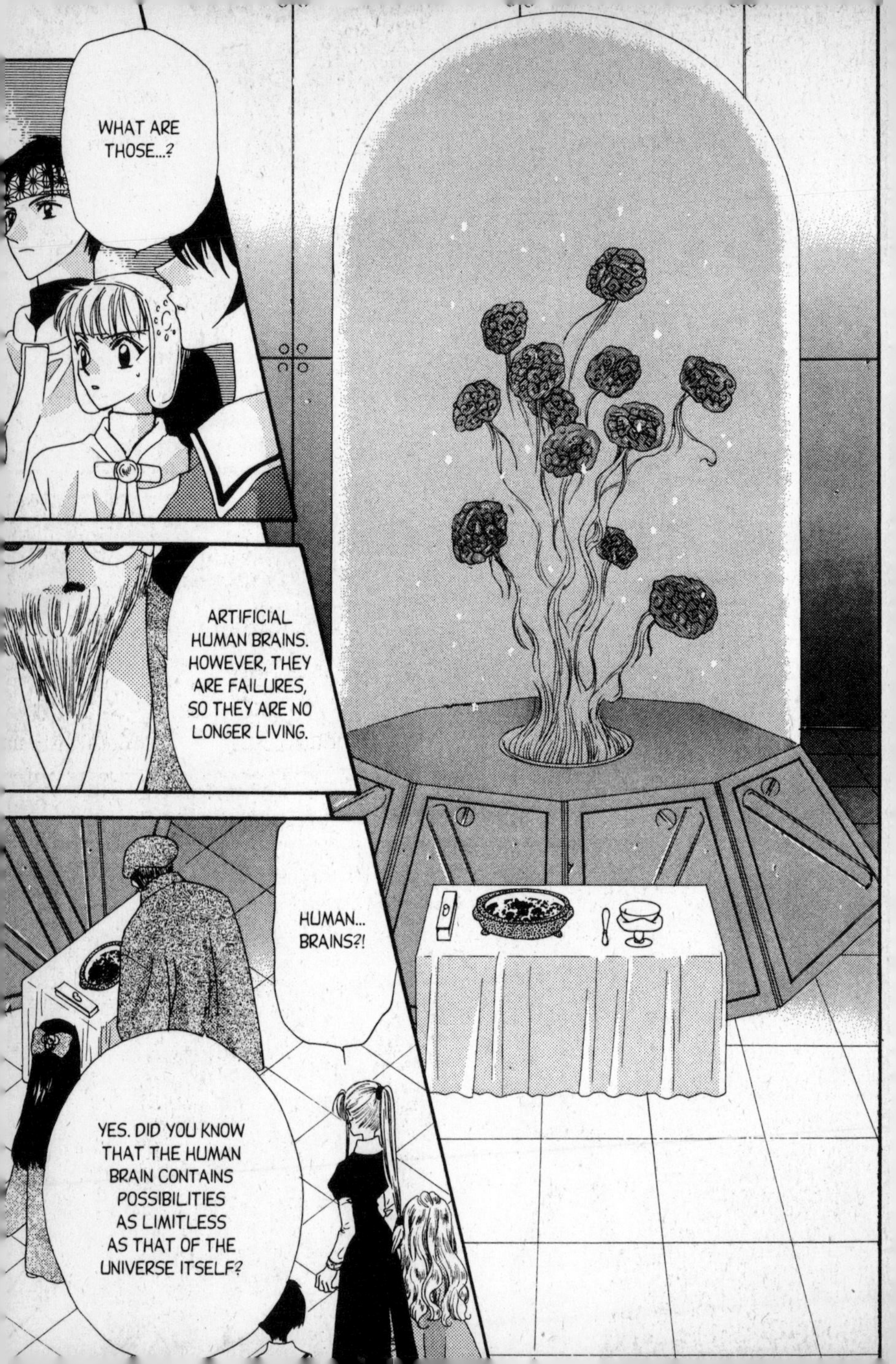
WHAT ARE THOSE...?
ARTIFICIAL HUMAN BRAINS. HOWEVER, THEY ARE FAILURES, SO THEY ARE NO LONGER LIVING.
HUMAN... BRAINS?!
YES. DID YOU KNOW THAT THE HUMAN BRAIN CONTAINS POSSIBILITIES AS LIMITLESS AS THAT OF THE UNIVERSE ITSELF?

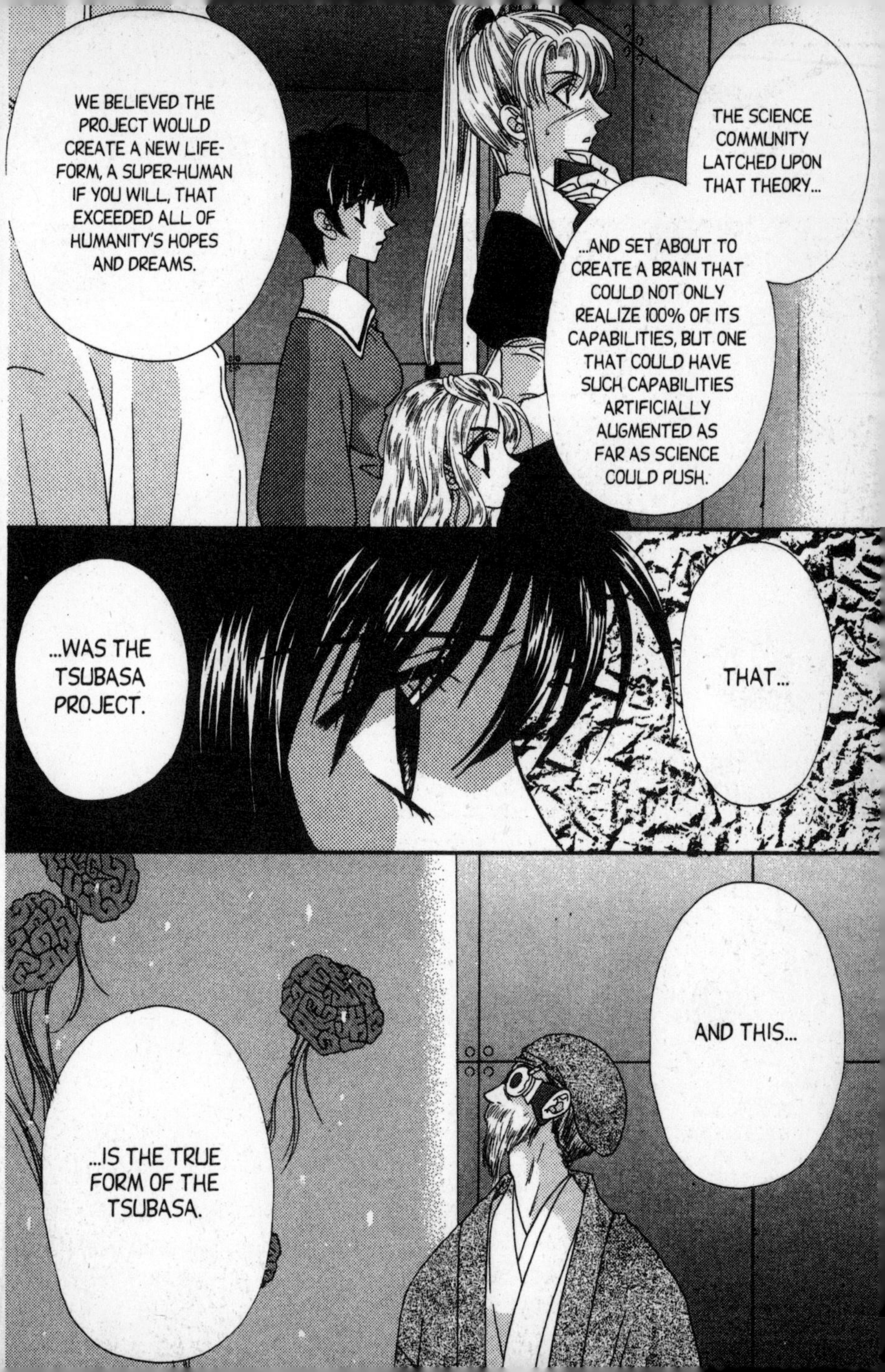
THE SCIENCE COMMUNITY LATCHED UPON THAT THEORY...
...AND SET ABOUT TO CREATE A BRAIN THAT COULD NOT ONLY REALIZE 100% OF ITS CAPABILITIES, BUT ONE THAT COULD HAVE SUCH CAPABILITIES ARTIFICIALLY AUGMENTED AS FAR AS SCIENCE COULD PUSH.
WE BELIEVED THE PROJECT WOULD CREATE A NEW LIFE-FORM, A SUPER-HUMAN IF YOU WILL, THAT EXCEEDED ALL OF HUMANITY'S HOPES AND DREAMS.
THAT...
...WAS THE TSUBASA PROJECT.
AND THIS...
...IS THE TRUE FORM OF THE TSUBASA.

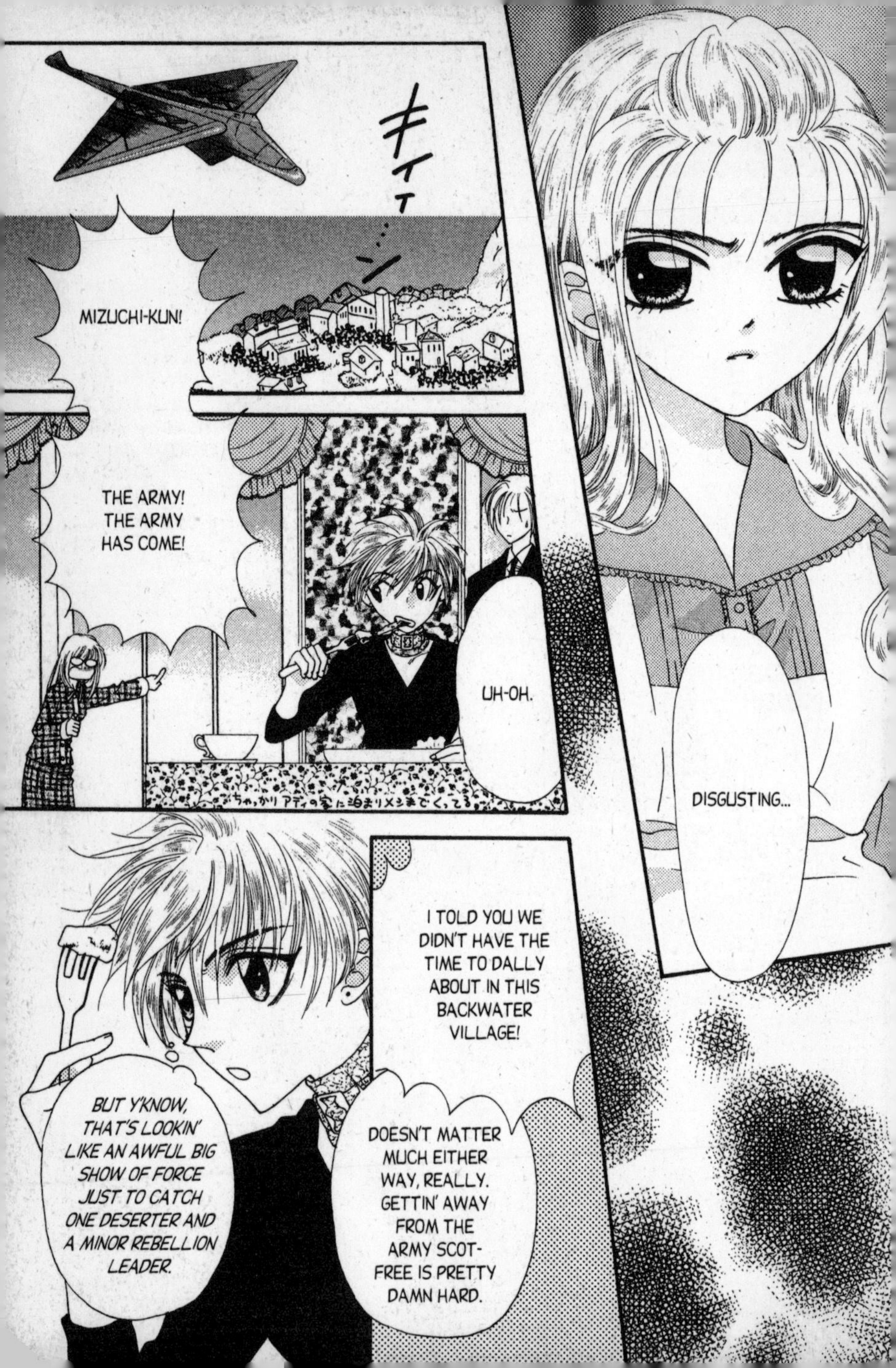
DISGUSTING...
キィィ…ン
MIZUCHI-KUN!
THE ARMY! THE ARMY HAS COME!
UH-OH.
ちゃっかりアディの家に泊まりメシまでくってる
I TOLD YOU WE DIDN'T HAVE THE TIME TO DALLY ABOUT IN THIS BACKWATER VILLAGE!
DOESN'T MATTER MUCH EITHER WAY, REALLY. GETTIN' AWAY FROM THE ARMY SCOT-FREE IS PRETTY DAMN HARD.
BUT Y'KNOW, THAT'S LOOKIN' LIKE AN AWFUL BIG SHOW OF FORCE JUST TO CATCH ONE DESERTER AND A MINOR REBELLION LEADER.

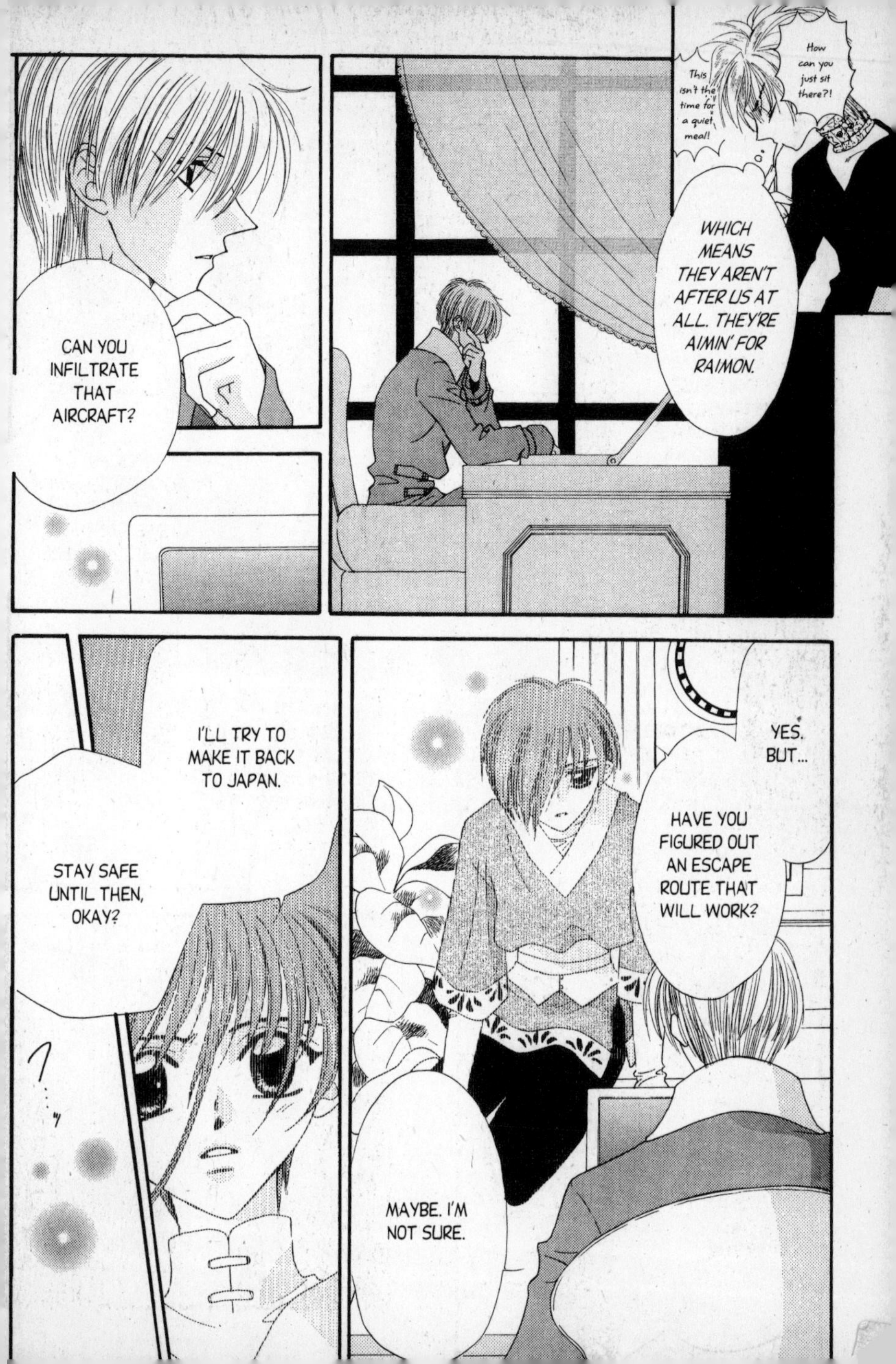
How can you just sit there?!
This isn't the time for a quiet meal!
WHICH MEANS THEY AREN'T AFTER US AT ALL. THEY'RE AIMIN' FOR RAIMON.
CAN YOU INFILTRATE THAT AIRCRAFT?
YES. BUT...
HAVE YOU FIGURED OUT AN ESCAPE ROUTE THAT WILL WORK?
MAYBE. I'M NOT SURE.
I'LL TRY TO MAKE IT BACK TO JAPAN.
STAY SAFE UNTIL THEN, OKAY?

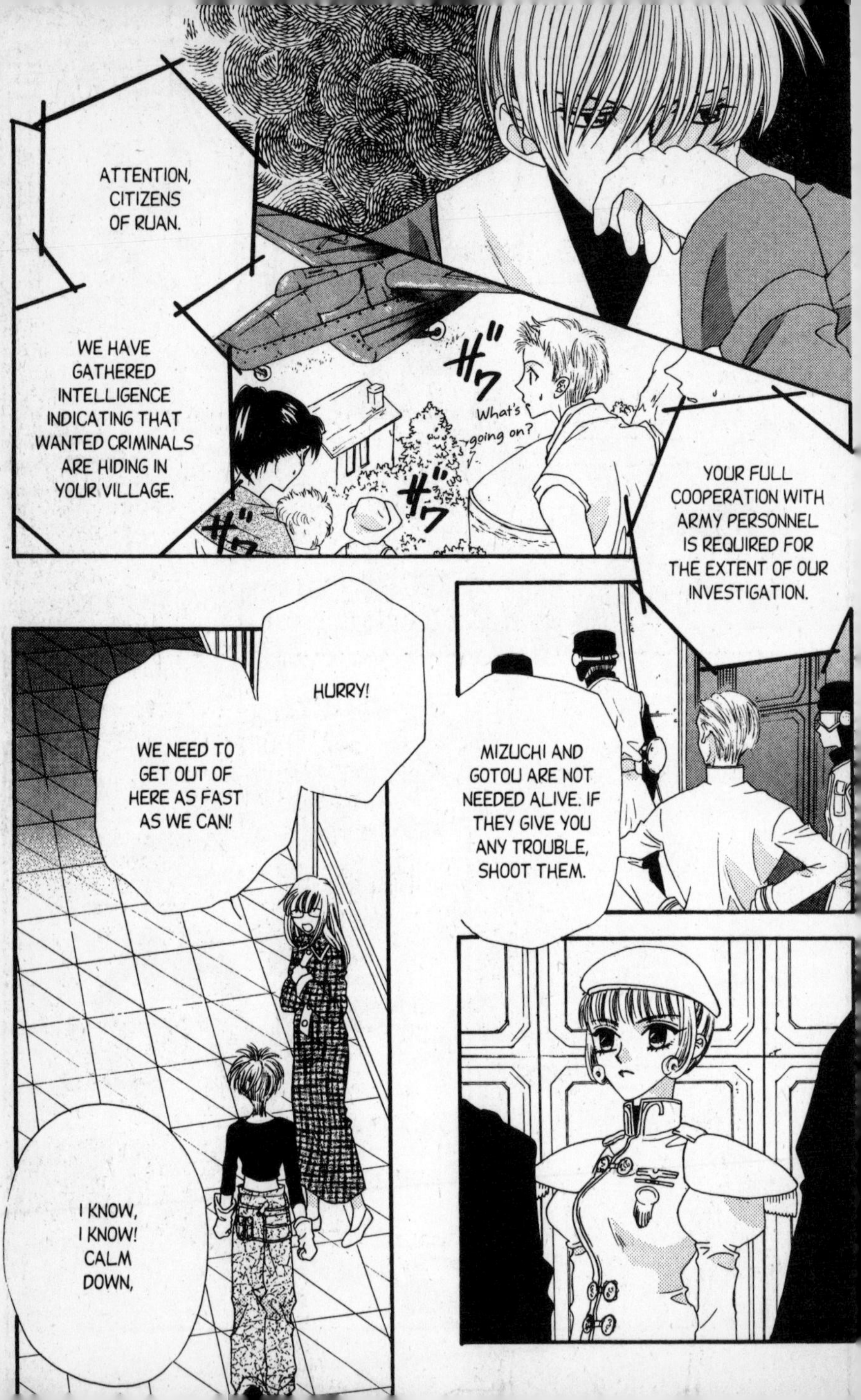
ATTENTION, CITIZENS OF RUAN.
WE HAVE GATHERED INTELLIGENCE INDICATING THAT WANTED CRIMINALS ARE HIDING IN YOUR VILLAGE.
ザワ
What's going on?
ザワ
ザワ
YOUR FULL COOPERATION WITH ARMY PERSONNEL IS REQUIRED FOR THE EXTENT OF OUR INVESTIGATION.
MIZUCHI AND GOTOU ARE NOT NEEDED ALIVE. IF THEY GIVE YOU ANY TROUBLE, SHOOT THEM.
HURRY!
WE NEED TO GET OUT OF HERE AS FAST AS WE CAN!
I KNOW, I KNOW! CALM DOWN,

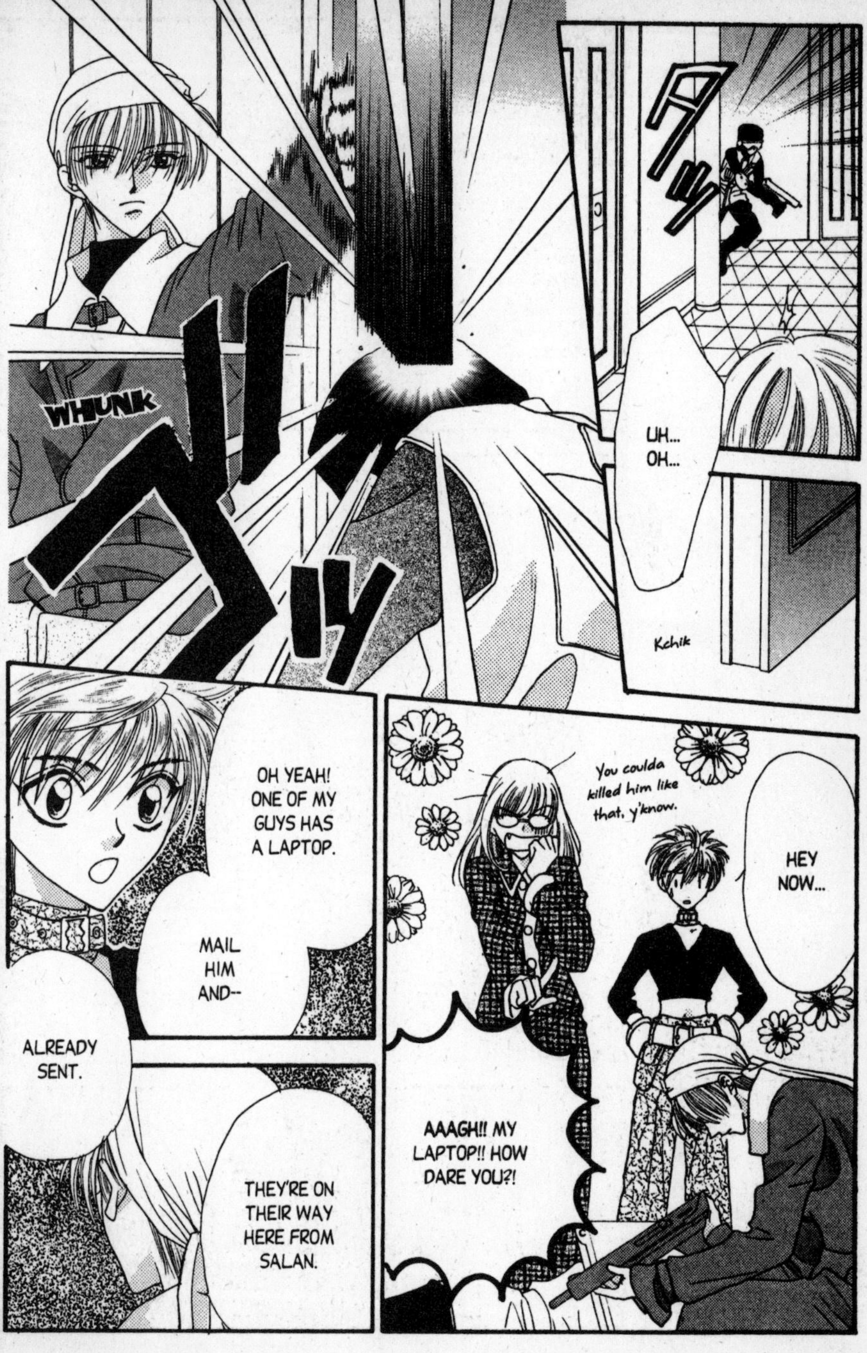
UH... OH...
Kchik
WHUNK
HEY NOW...
You coulda killed him like that, y'know.
AAAGH!! MY LAPTOP!! HOW DARE YOU?!
OH YEAH! ONE OF MY GUYS HAS A LAPTOP.
MAIL HIM AND--
ALREADY SENT.
THEY'RE ON THEIR WAY HERE FROM SALAN.

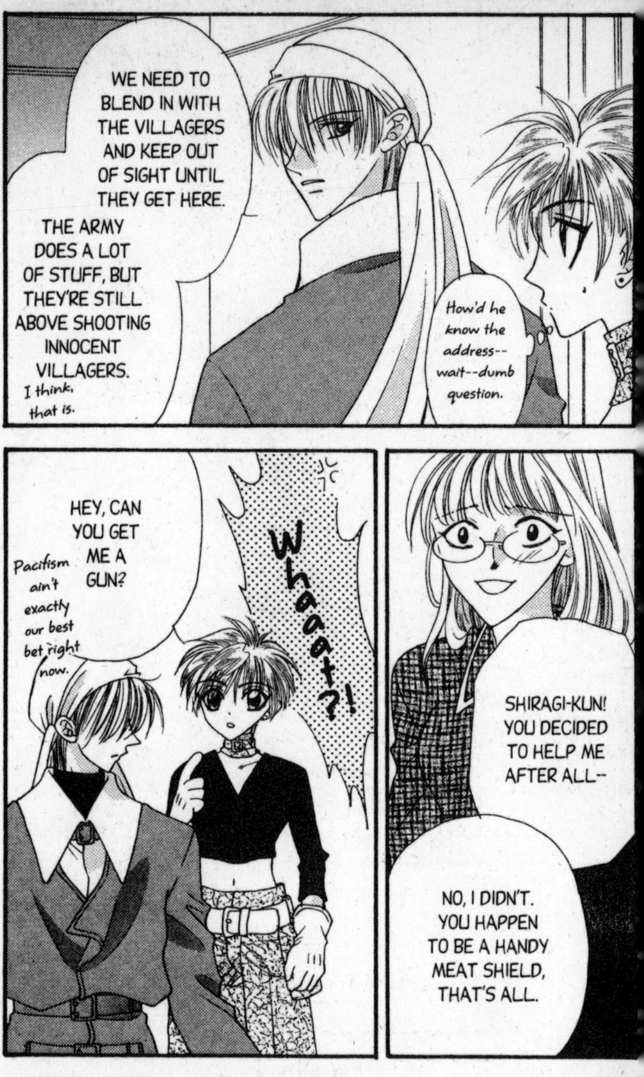
WE NEED TO BLEND IN WITH THE VILLAGERS AND KEEP OUT OF SIGHT UNTIL THEY GET HERE.
THE ARMY DOES A LOT OF STUFF, BUT THEY'RE STILL ABOVE SHOOTING INNOCENT VILLAGERS.
I think, that is.
How'd he know the address-- wait--dumb question.
SHIRAGI-KUN! YOU DECIDED TO HELP ME AFTER ALL--
NO, I DIDN'T. YOU HAPPEN TO BE A HANDY MEAT SHIELD, THAT'S ALL.
HEY, CAN YOU GET ME A GUN?
Pacifism ain't exactly our best bet right now.
Whaaat?!
THERE!!
FUGITIVES SPOTTED!!
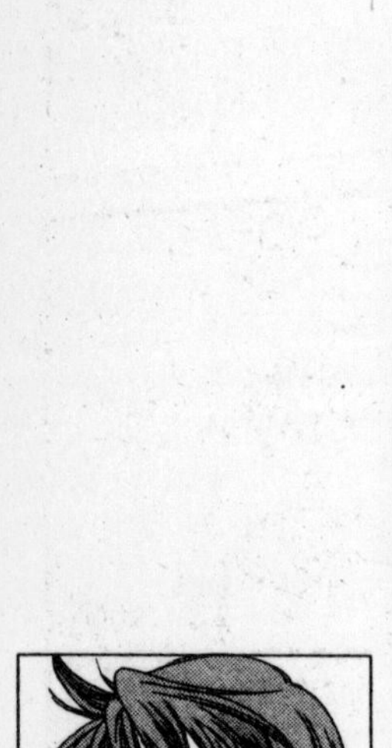

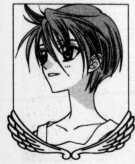

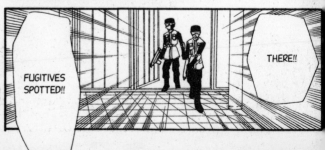

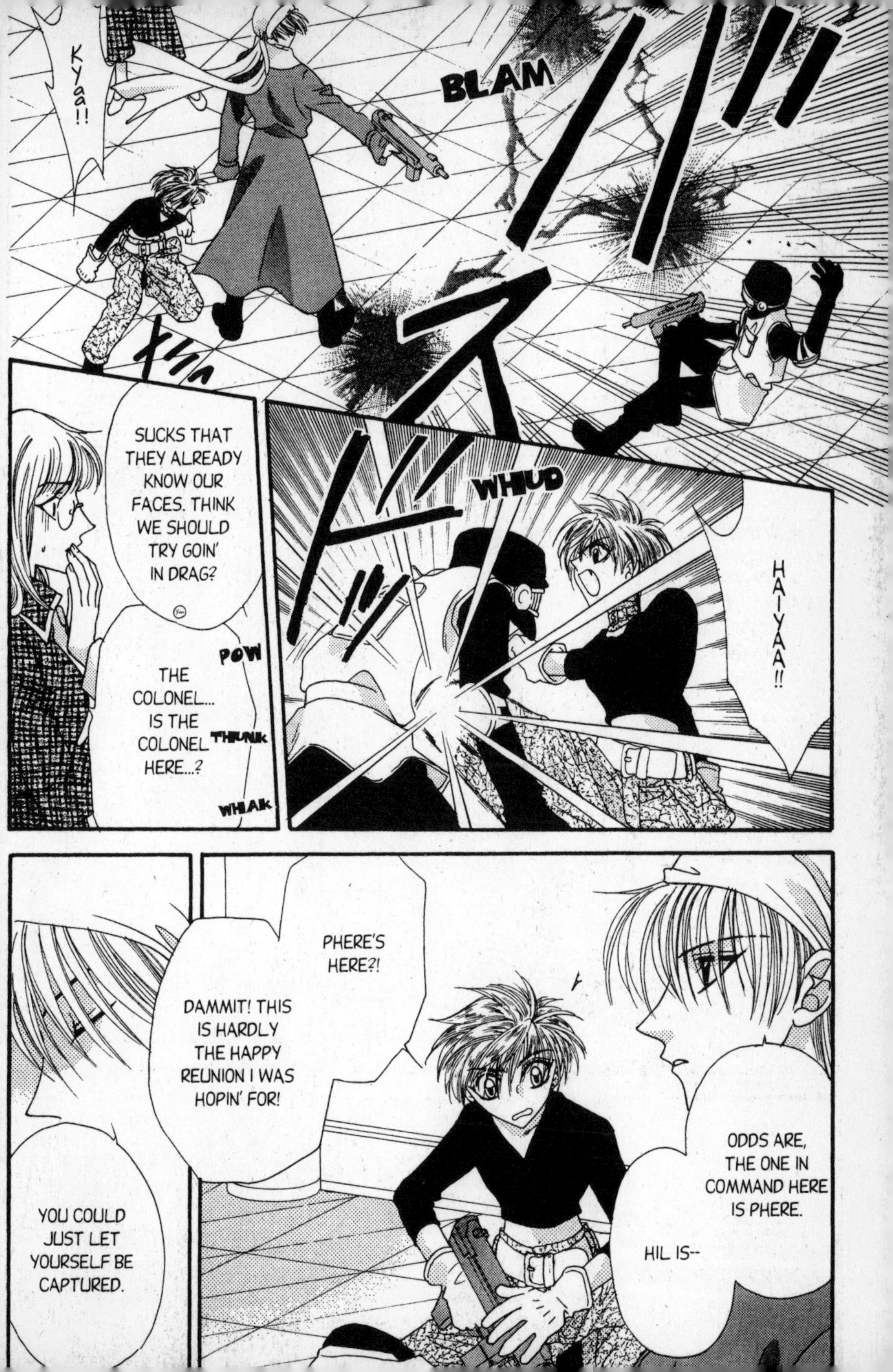
BLAM
Kyaa!!
WHUD
HAIYAA!!
SUCKS THAT THEY ALREADY KNOW OUR FACES. THINK WE SHOULD TRY GOIN' IN DRAG?
POW
THE COLONEL... IS THE COLONEL HERE...?
THUNK
WHAK
ODDS ARE, THE ONE IN COMMAND HERE IS PHERE.
HIL IS--
PHERE'S HERE?!
DAMMIT! THIS IS HARDLY THE HAPPY REUNION I WAS HOPIN' FOR!
YOU COULD JUST LET YOURSELF BE CAPTURED.

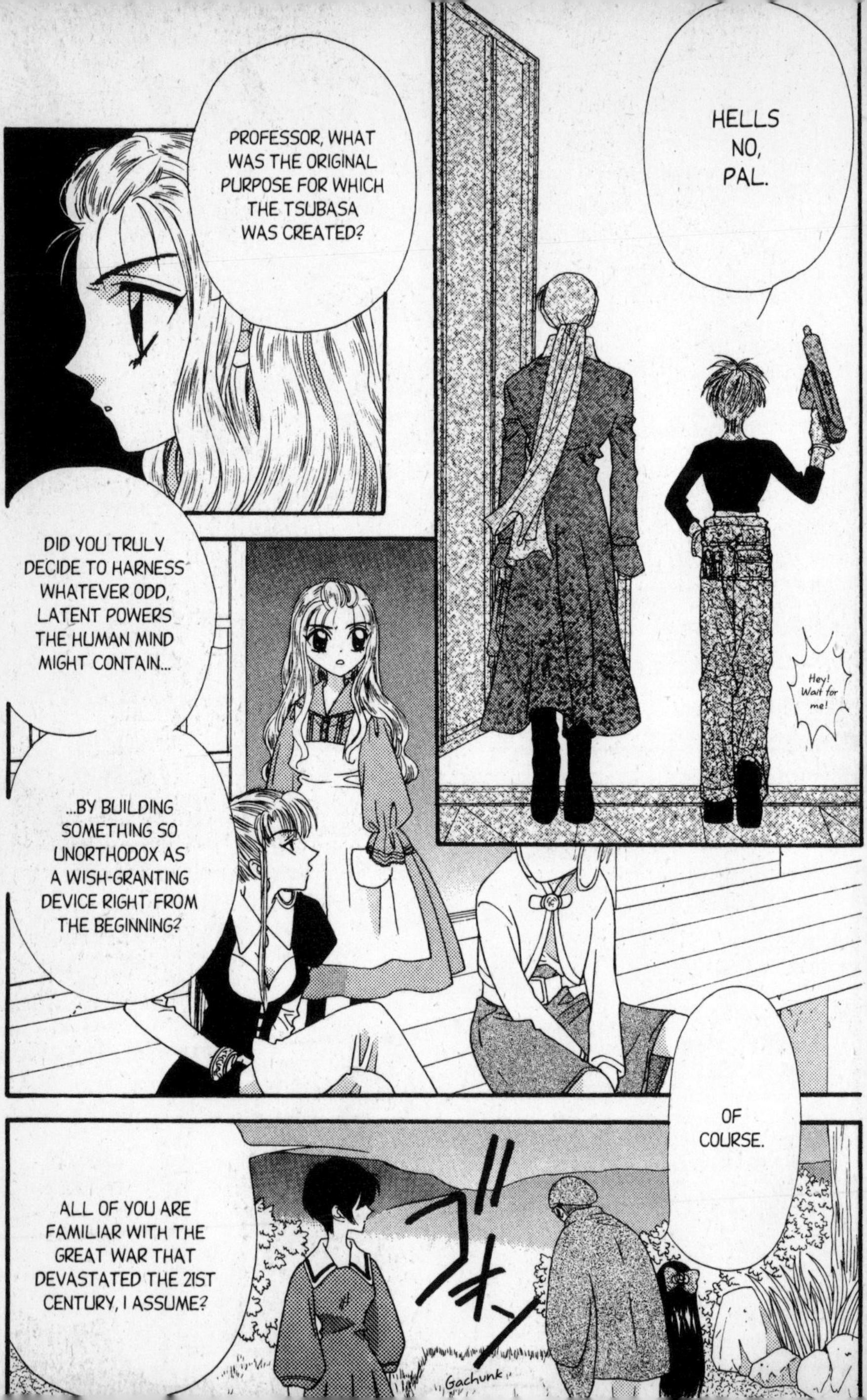
HELLS NO, PAL.
Hey! Wait for me!
PROFESSOR, WHAT WAS THE ORIGINAL PURPOSE FOR WHICH THE TSUBASA WAS CREATED?
DID YOU TRULY DECIDE TO HARNESS WHATEVER ODD, LATENT POWERS THE HUMAN MIND MIGHT CONTAIN...
...BY BUILDING SOMETHING SO UNORTHODOX AS A WISH-GRANTING DEVICE RIGHT FROM THE BEGINNING?
OF COURSE.
ALL OF YOU ARE FAMILIAR WITH THE GREAT WAR THAT DEVASTATED THE 21ST CENTURY, I ASSUME?
Gachunk

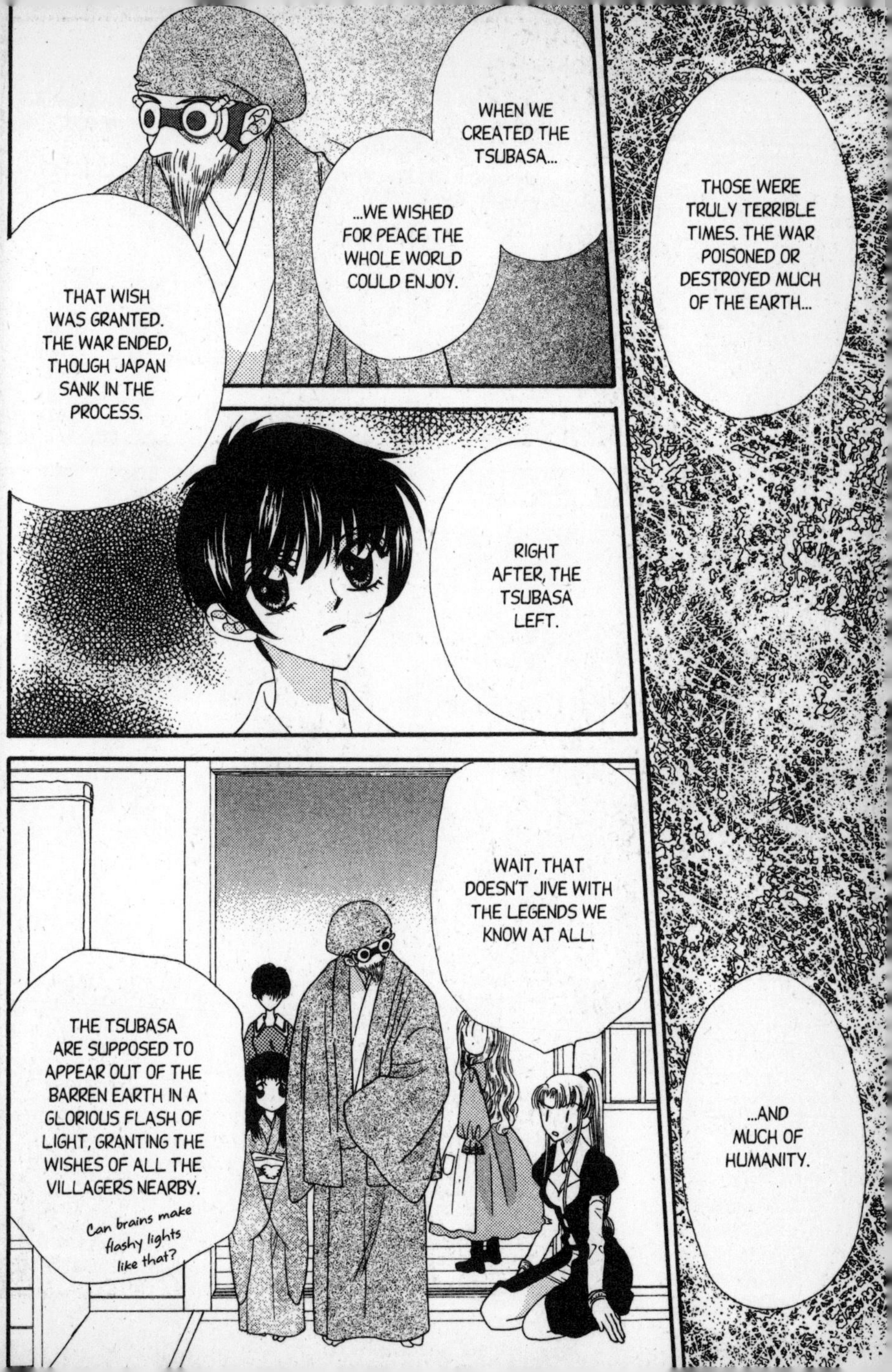
THOSE WERE TRULY TERRIBLE TIMES. THE WAR POISONED OR DESTROYED MUCH OF THE EARTH...
...AND MUCH OF HUMANITY.
WHEN WE CREATED THE TSUBASA...
...WE WISHED FOR PEACE THE WHOLE WORLD COULD ENJOY.
THAT WISH WAS GRANTED. THE WAR ENDED, THOUGH JAPAN SANK IN THE PROCESS.
RIGHT AFTER, THE TSUBASA LEFT.
WAIT, THAT DOESN'T JIVE WITH THE LEGENDS WE KNOW AT ALL.
THE TSUBASA ARE SUPPOSED TO APPEAR OUT OF THE BARREN EARTH IN A GLORIOUS FLASH OF LIGHT, GRANTING THE WISHES OF ALL THE VILLAGERS NEARBY.
Can brains make flashy lights like that?

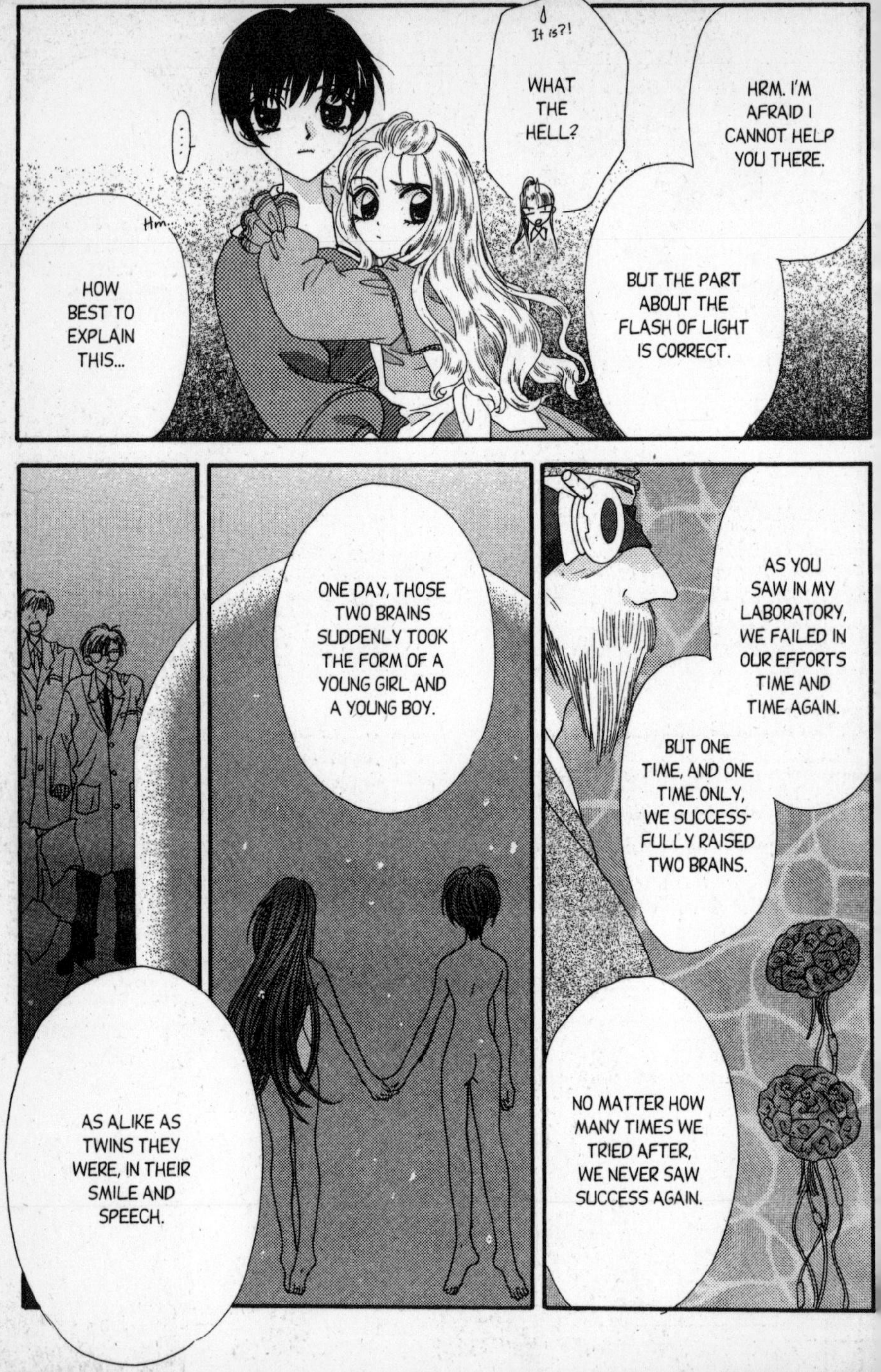
HRM. I'M AFRAID I CANNOT HELP YOU THERE.
BUT THE PART ABOUT THE FLASH OF LIGHT IS CORRECT.
It is?!
WHAT THE HELL?
...
Hm...
HOW BEST TO EXPLAIN THIS...
AS YOU SAW IN MY LABORATORY, WE FAILED IN OUR EFFORTS TIME AND TIME AGAIN.
BUT ONE TIME, AND ONE TIME ONLY, WE SUCCESS-FULLY RAISED TWO BRAINS.
NO MATTER HOW MANY TIMES WE TRIED AFTER, WE NEVER SAW SUCCESS AGAIN.
ONE DAY, THOSE TWO BRAINS SUDDENLY TOOK THE FORM OF A YOUNG GIRL AND A YOUNG BOY.
AS ALIKE AS TWINS THEY WERE, IN THEIR SMILE AND SPEECH.

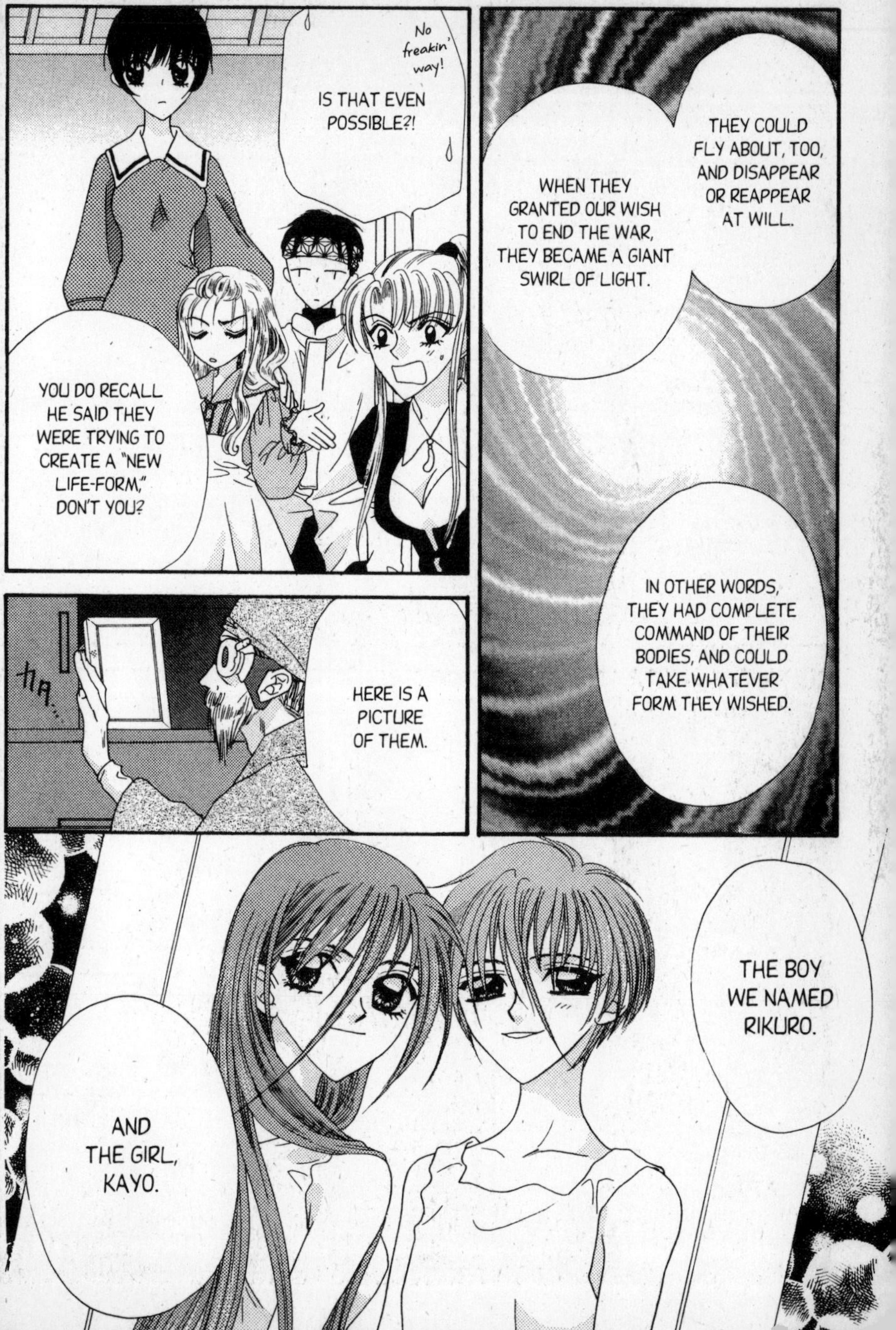
THEY COULD FLY ABOUT, TOO, AND DISAPPEAR OR REAPPEAR AT WILL.
WHEN THEY GRANTED OUR WISH TO END THE WAR, THEY BECAME A GIANT SWIRL OF LIGHT.
IN OTHER WORDS, THEY HAD COMPLETE COMMAND OF THEIR BODIES, AND COULD TAKE WHATEVER FORM THEY WISHED.
No freakin' way!
IS THAT EVEN POSSIBLE?!
YOU DO RECALL HE SAID THEY WERE TRYING TO CREATE A "NEW LIFE-FORM," DON'T YOU?
HERE IS A PICTURE OF THEM.
THE BOY WE NAMED RIKURO.
AND THE GIRL, KAYO.

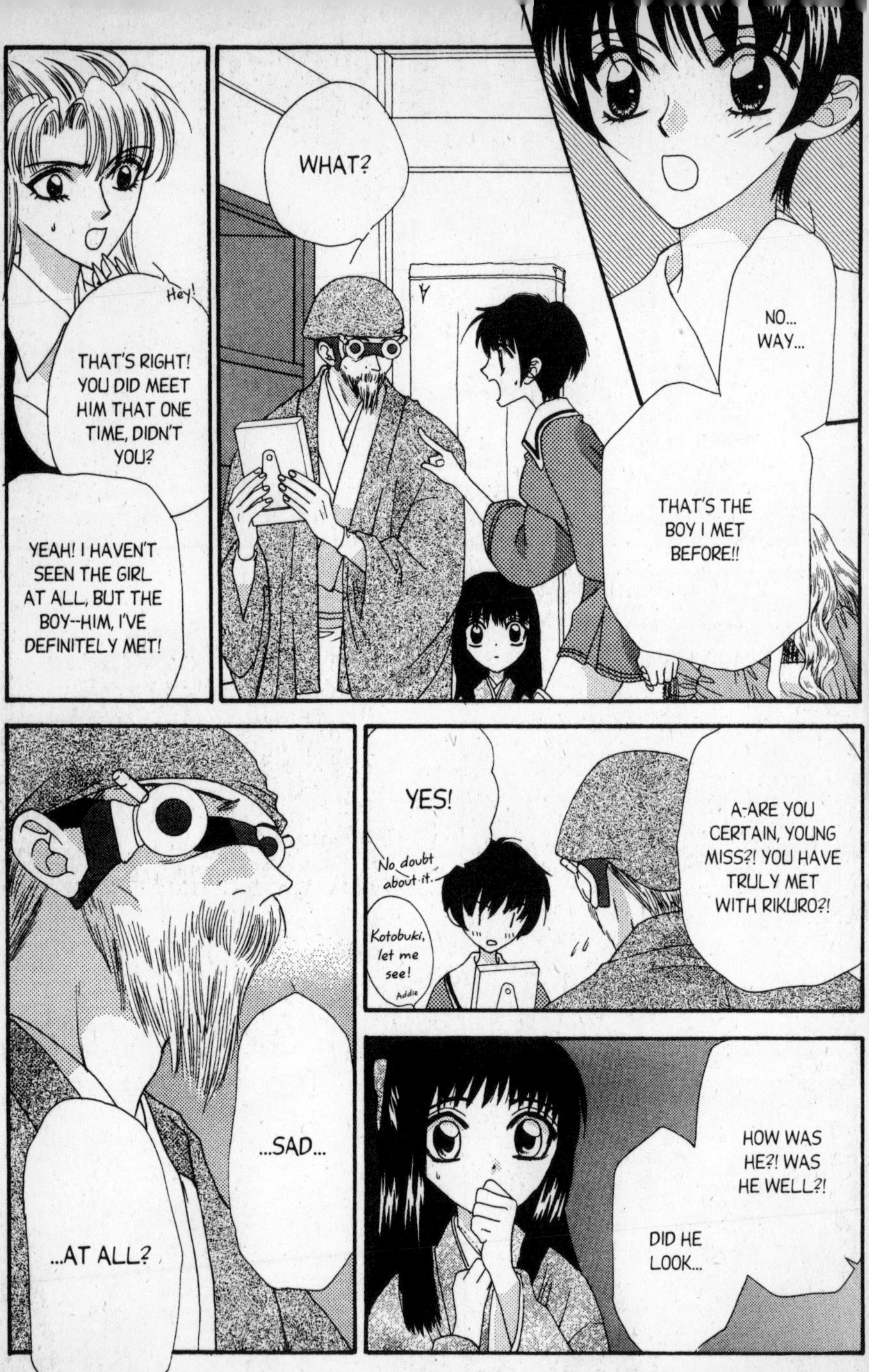
NO... WAY...
THAT'S THE BOY I MET BEFORE!!
WHAT?
Hey!
THAT'S RIGHT! YOU DID MEET HIM THAT ONE TIME, DIDN'T YOU?
YEAH! I HAVEN'T SEEN THE GIRL AT ALL, BUT THE BOY--HIM, I'VE DEFINITELY MET!
A-ARE YOU CERTAIN, YOUNG MISS?! YOU HAVE TRULY MET WITH RIKURO?!
YES!
No doubt about it.
Kotobuki, let me see!
Addie
HOW WAS HE?! WAS HE WELL?!
DID HE LOOK...
...SAD...
...AT ALL?

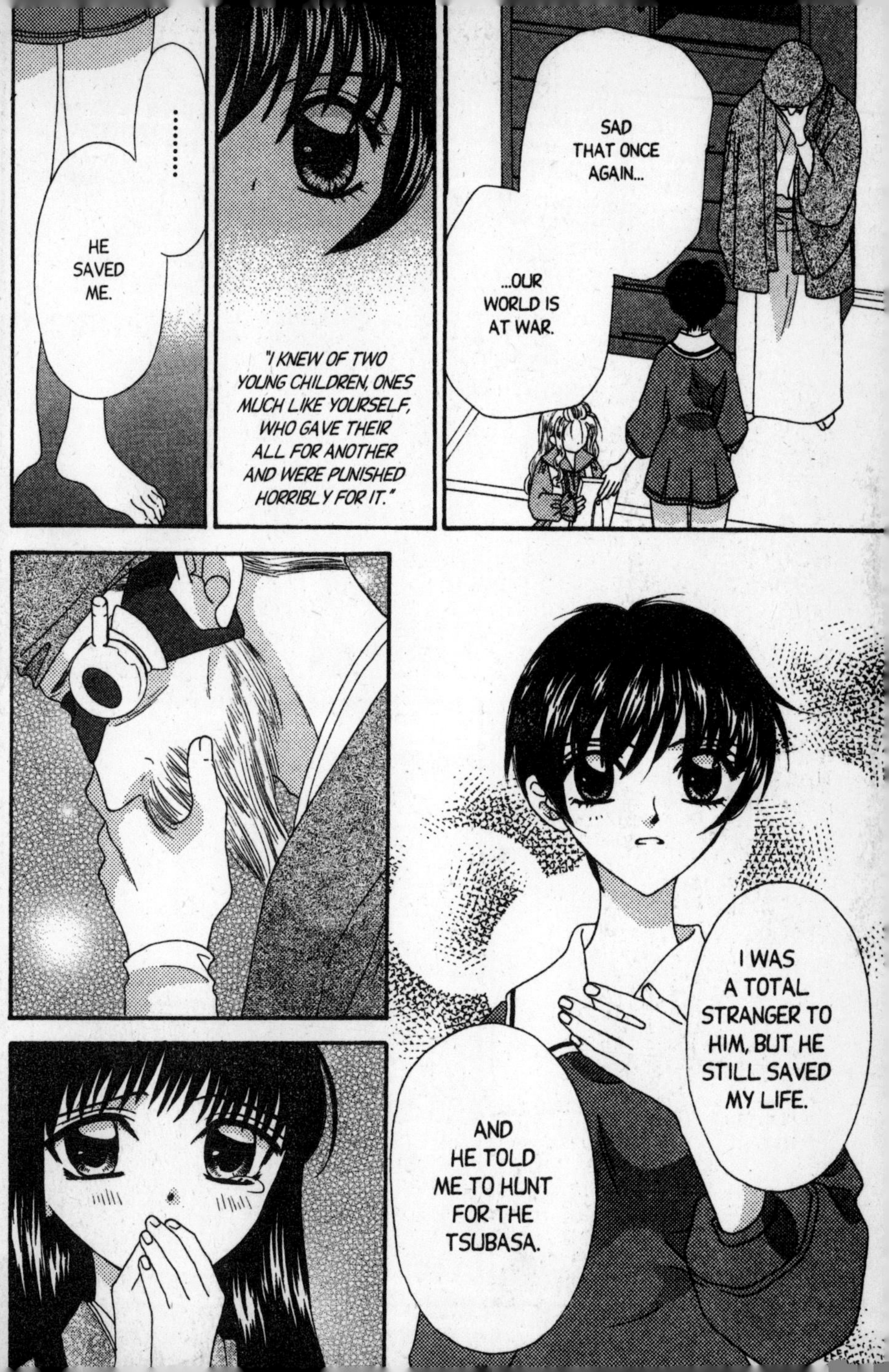
SAD THAT ONCE AGAIN...
...OUR WORLD IS AT WAR.
"I KNEW OF TWO YOUNG CHILDREN, ONES MUCH LIKE YOURSELF, WHO GAVE THEIR ALL FOR ANOTHER AND WERE PUNISHED HORRIBLY FOR IT."
......
HE SAVED ME.
I WAS A TOTAL STRANGER TO HIM, BUT HE STILL SAVED MY LIFE.
AND HE TOLD ME TO HUNT FOR THE TSUBASA.

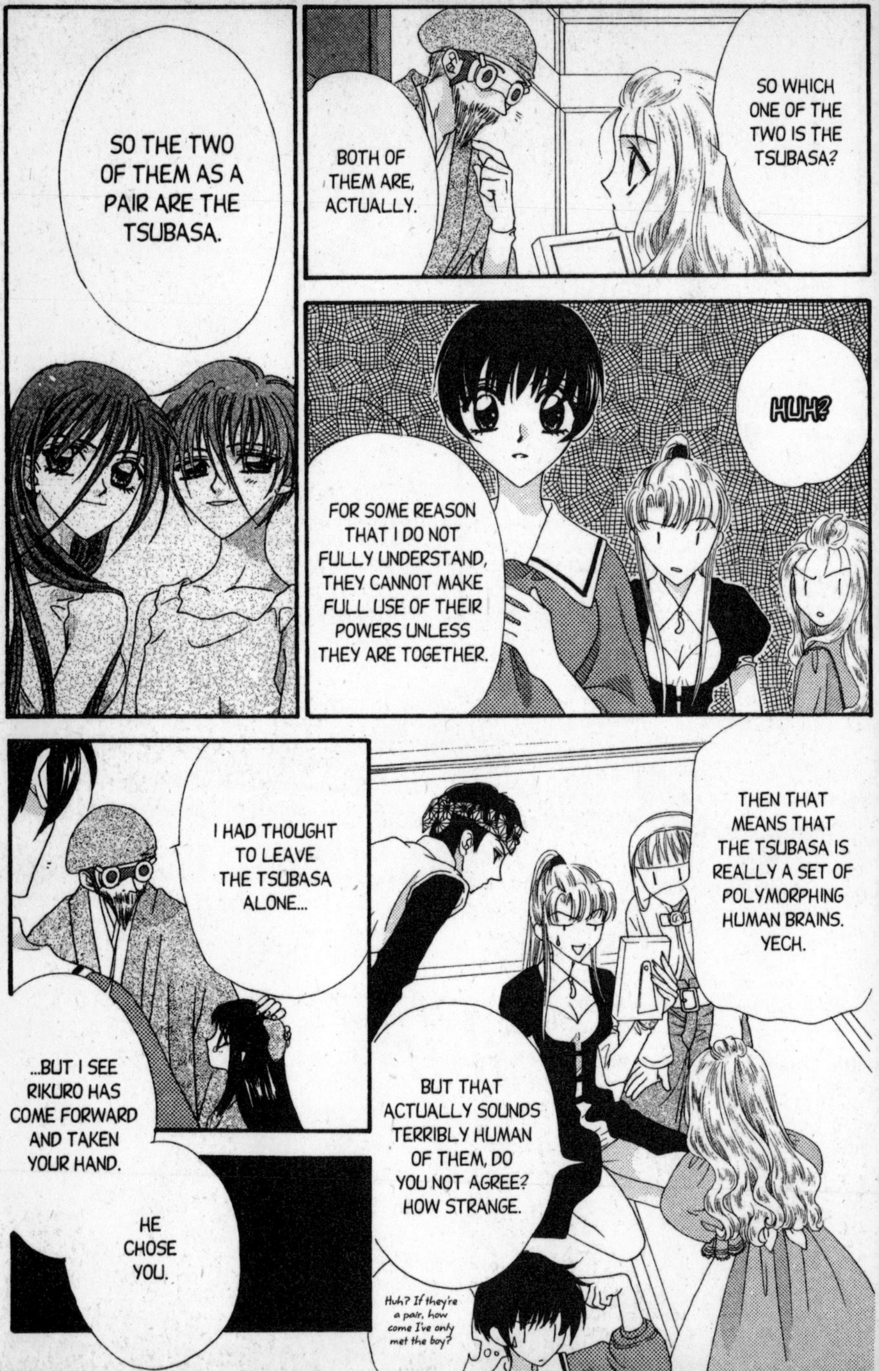
SO WHICH ONE OF THE TWO IS THE TSUBASA?
BOTH OF THEM ARE, ACTUALLY.
HUH?
FOR SOME REASON THAT I DO NOT FULLY UNDERSTAND, THEY CANNOT MAKE FULL USE OF THEIR POWERS UNLESS THEY ARE TOGETHER.
SO THE TWO OF THEM AS A PAIR ARE THE TSUBASA.
THEN THAT MEANS THAT THE TSUBASA IS REALLY A SET OF POLYMORPHING HUMAN BRAINS. YECH.
BUT THAT ACTUALLY SOUNDS TERRIBLY HUMAN OF THEM, DO YOU NOT AGREE? HOW STRANGE.
Huh? If they're a pair, how come I've only met the boy?
I HAD THOUGHT TO LEAVE THE TSUBASA ALONE...
...BUT I SEE RIKURO HAS COME FORWARD AND TAKEN YOUR HAND.
HE CHOSE YOU.

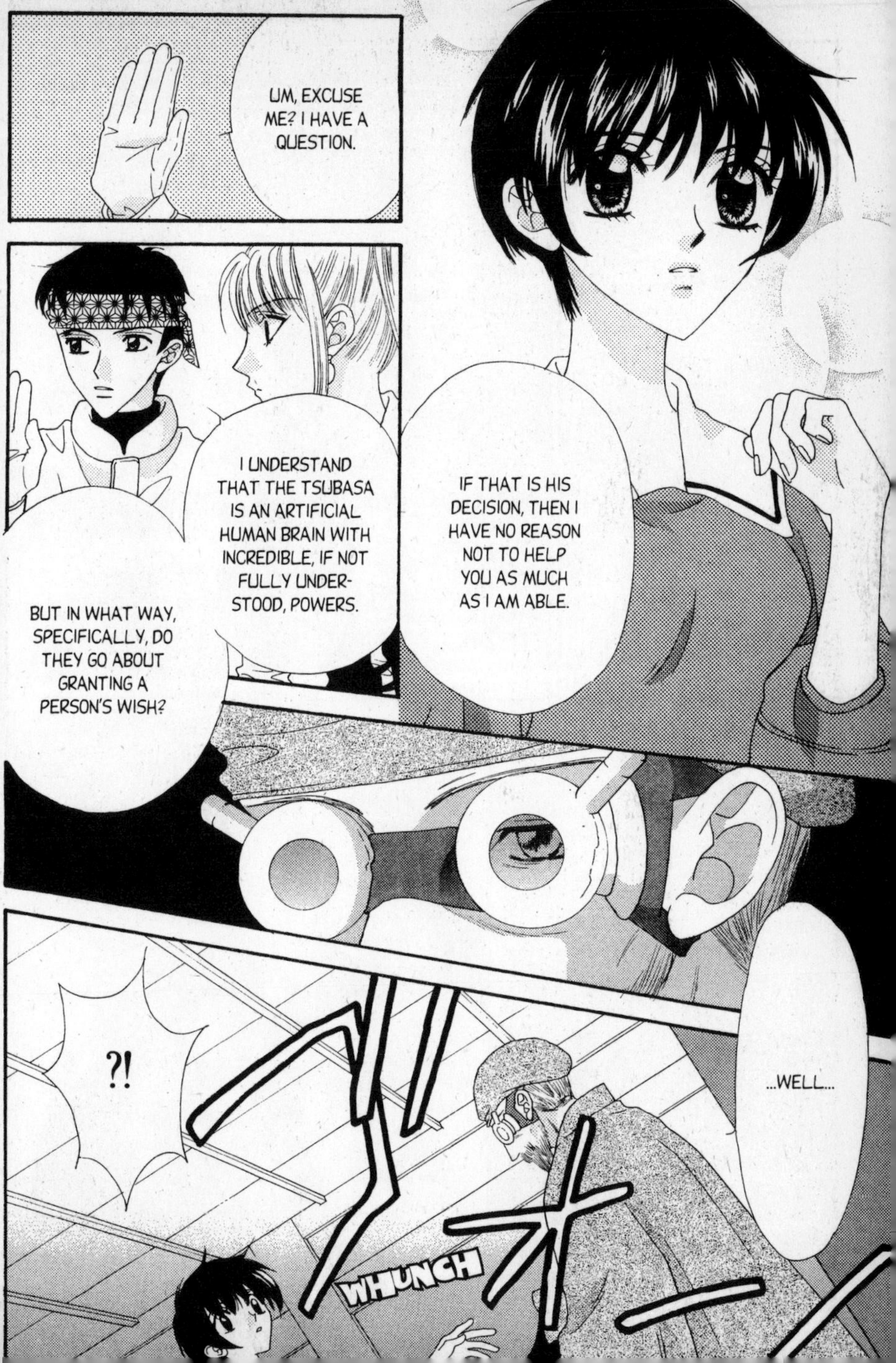
IF THAT IS HIS DECISION, THEN I HAVE NO REASON NOT TO HELP YOU AS MUCH AS I AM ABLE.
UM, EXCUSE ME? I HAVE A QUESTION.
I UNDERSTAND THAT THE TSUBASA IS AN ARTIFICIAL HUMAN BRAIN WITH INCREDIBLE, IF NOT FULLY UNDER-STOOD, POWERS.
BUT IN WHAT WAY, SPECIFICALLY, DO THEY GO ABOUT GRANTING A PERSON'S WISH?
...WELL...
?!
WHUNCH

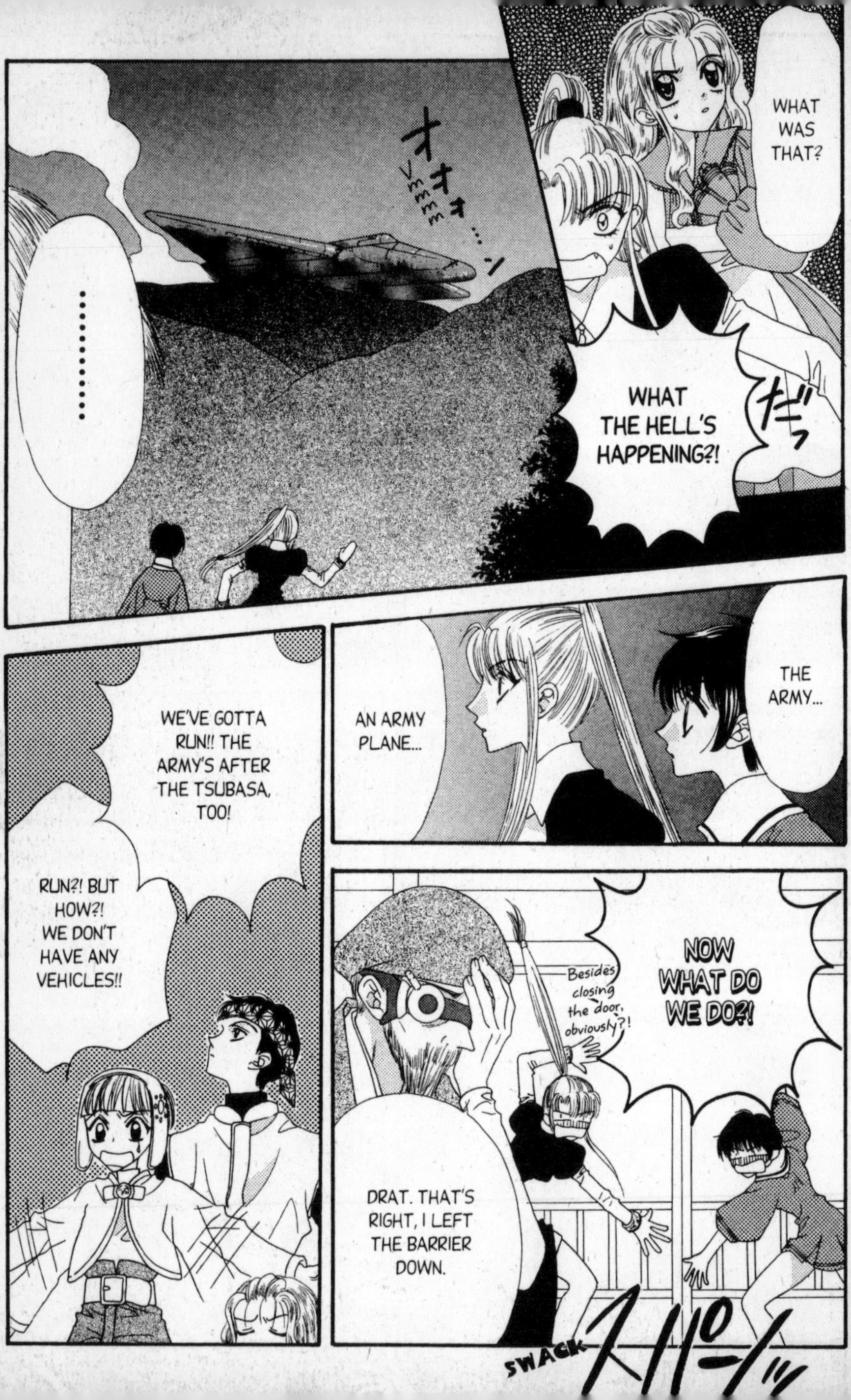

WHAT WAS THAT?
WHAT THE HELL'S HAPPENING?!
Vmmmm
......
THE ARMY...
AN ARMY PLANE...
NOW WHAT DO WE DO?!
Besides closing the door, obviously?!
DRAT. THAT'S RIGHT, I LEFT THE BARRIER DOWN.
SWACK
WE'VE GOTTA RUN!! THE ARMY'S AFTER THE TSUBASA, TOO!
RUN?! BUT HOW?! WE DON'T HAVE ANY VEHICLES!!

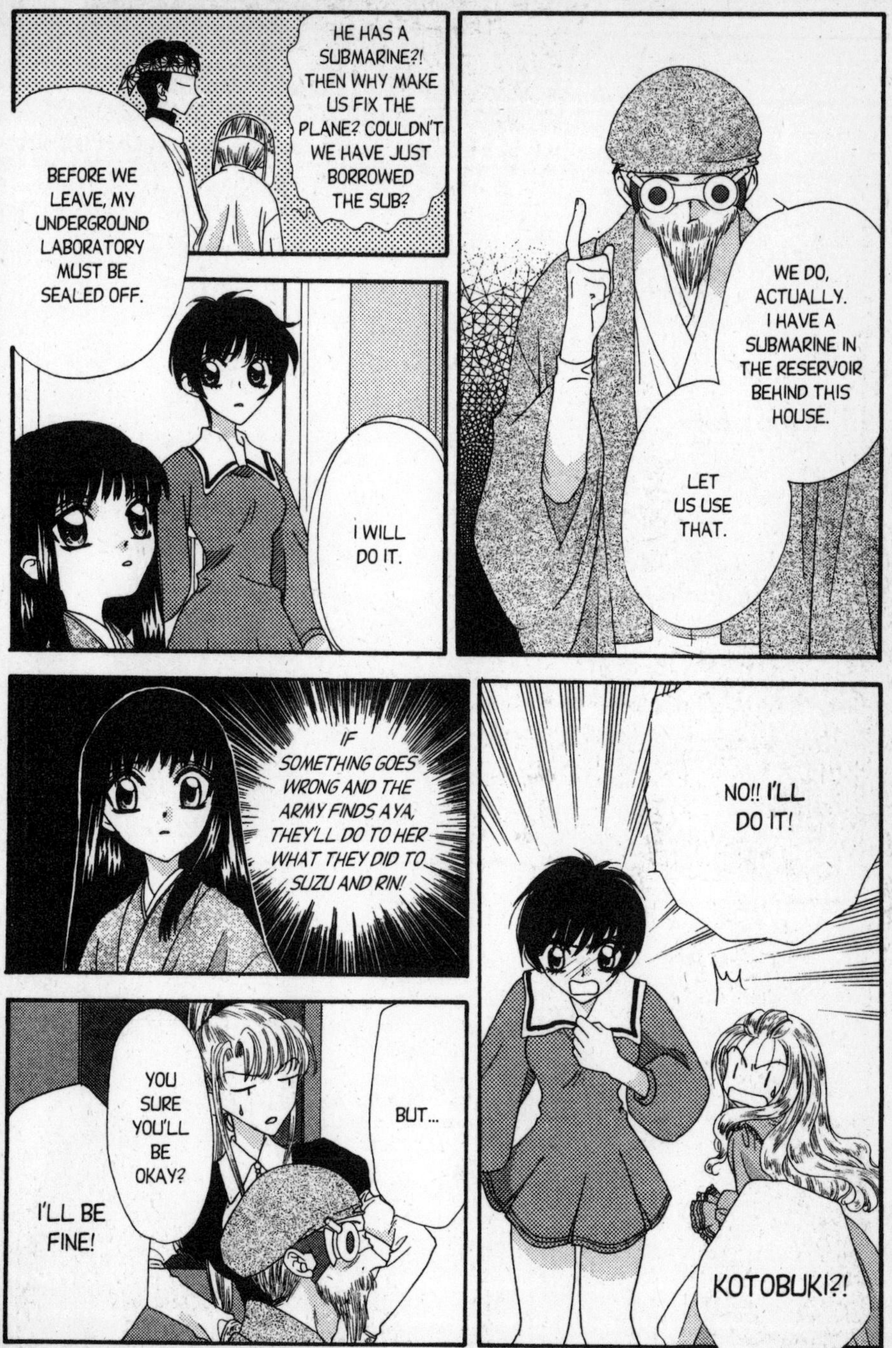
WE DO, ACTUALLY. I HAVE A SUBMARINE IN THE RESERVOIR BEHIND THIS HOUSE.
LET US USE THAT.
HE HAS A SUBMARINE?! THEN WHY MAKE US FIX THE PLANE? COULDN'T WE HAVE JUST BORROWED THE SUB?
BEFORE WE LEAVE, MY UNDERGROUND LABORATORY MUST BE SEALED OFF.
I WILL DO IT.
NO!! I'LL DO IT!
KOTOBUKI?!
IF SOMETHING GOES WRONG AND THE ARMY FINDS AYA, THEY'LL DO TO HER WHAT THEY DID TO SUZU AND RIN!
BUT...
YOU SURE YOU'LL BE OKAY?
I'LL BE FINE!

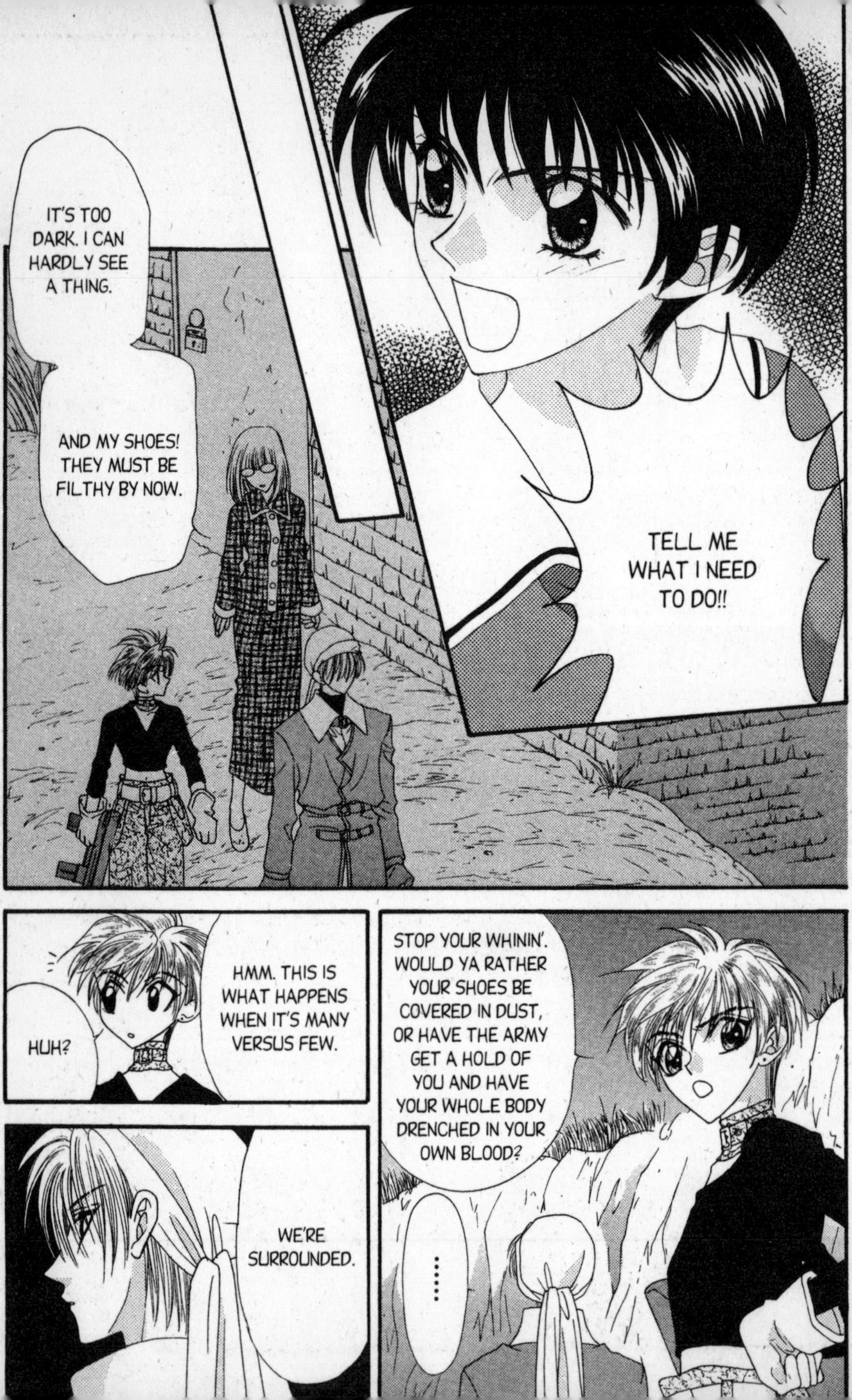
TELL ME WHAT I NEED TO DO!!
IT'S TOO DARK. I CAN HARDLY SEE A THING.
AND MY SHOES! THEY MUST BE FILTHY BY NOW.
STOP YOUR WHININ'. WOULD YA RATHER YOUR SHOES BE COVERED IN DUST, OR HAVE THE ARMY GET A HOLD OF YOU AND HAVE YOUR WHOLE BODY DRENCHED IN YOUR OWN BLOOD?
......
HMM. THIS IS WHAT HAPPENS WHEN IT'S MANY VERSUS FEW.
HUH?
WE'RE SURROUNDED.

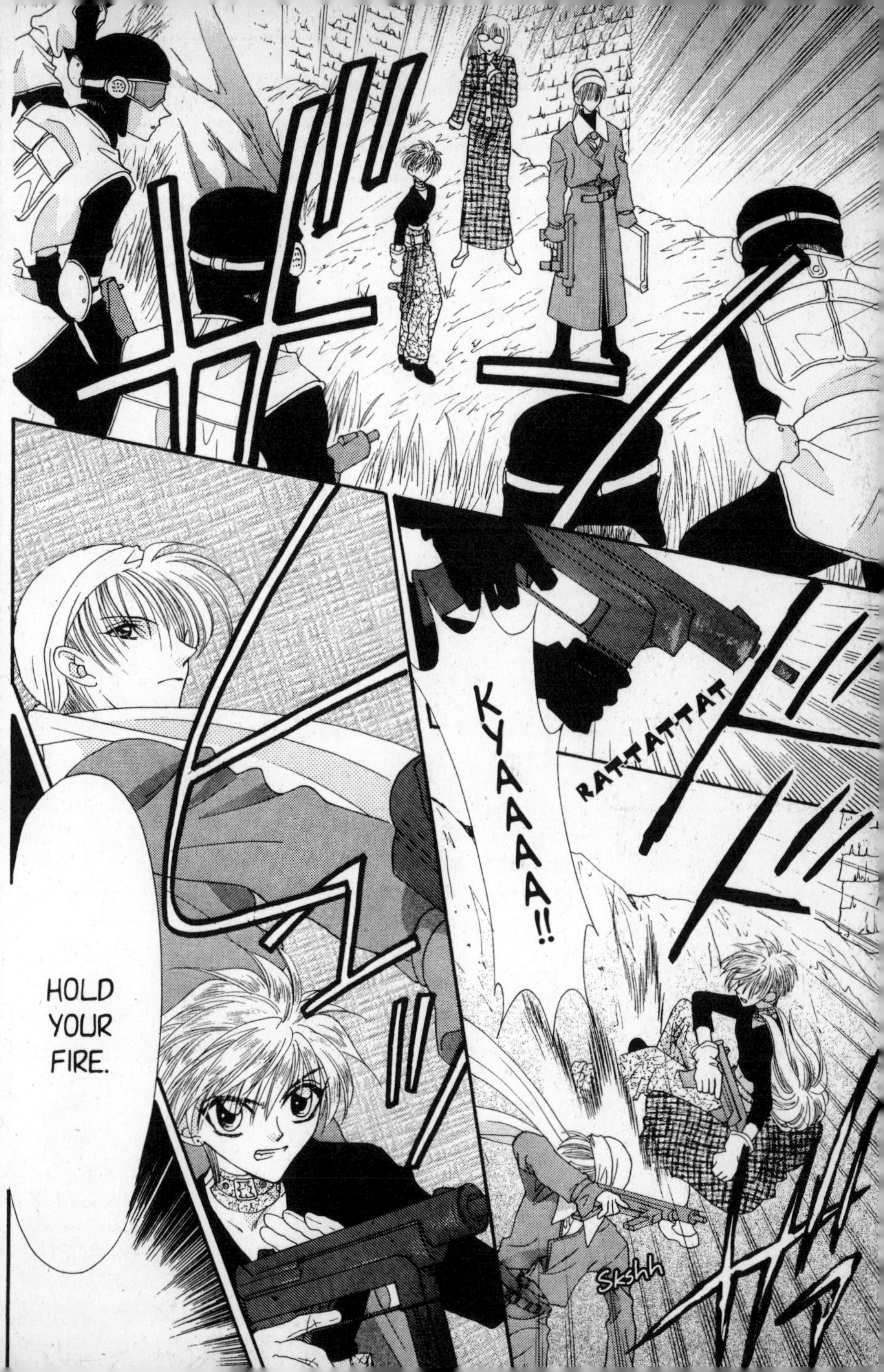
RATTATTAT
KYAAAAA!!
Skshh
HOLD YOUR FIRE.

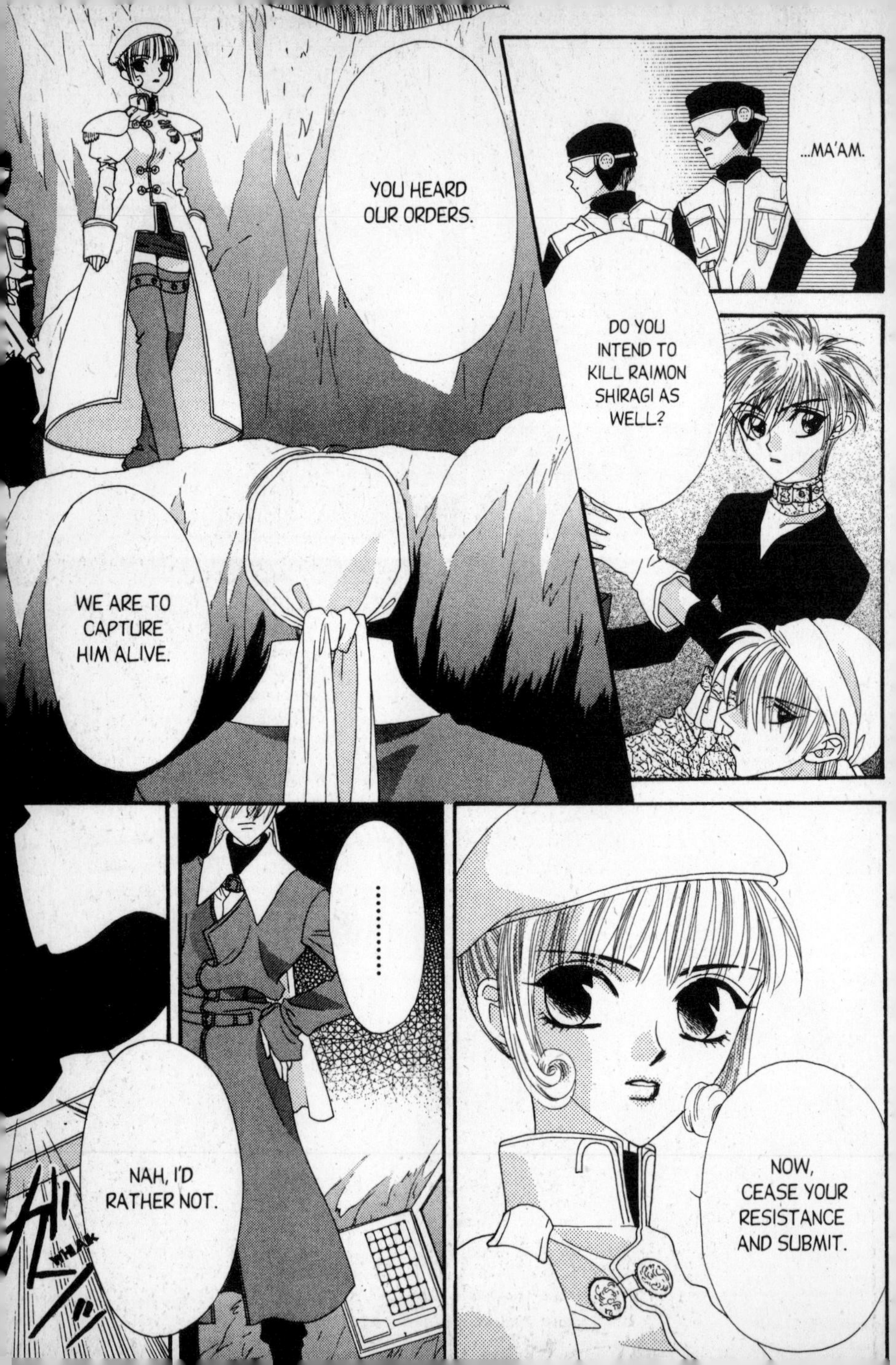
...MA'AM.
DO YOU INTEND TO KILL RAIMON SHIRAGI AS WELL?
YOU HEARD OUR ORDERS.
WE ARE TO CAPTURE HIM ALIVE.
NOW, CEASE YOUR RESISTANCE AND SUBMIT.
....
NAH, I'D RATHER NOT.
WHAK

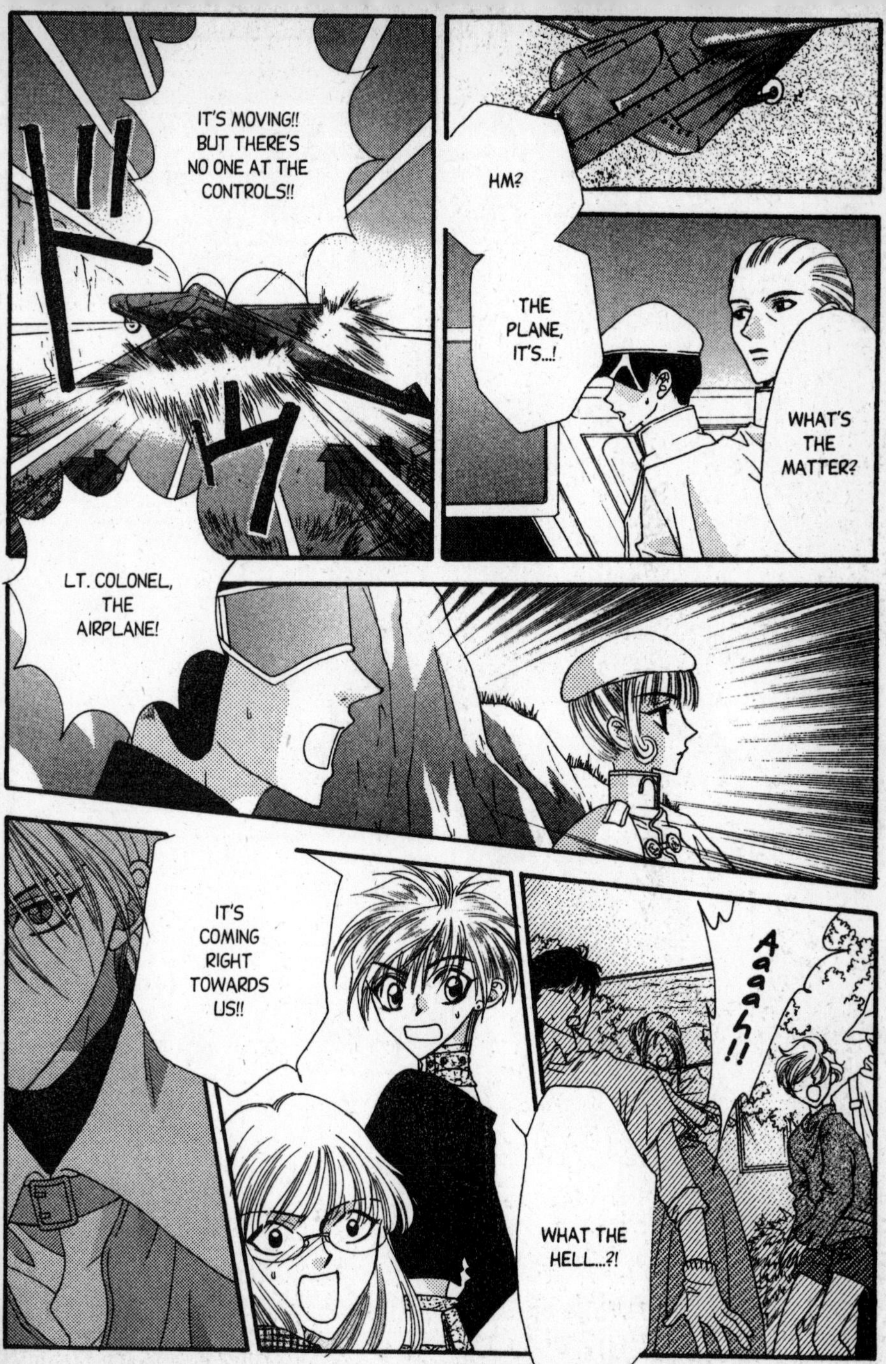
HM?
WHAT'S THE MATTER?
THE PLANE, IT'S...!
IT'S MOVING!! BUT THERE'S NO ONE AT THE CONTROLS!!
LT. COLONEL, THE AIRPLANE!
Aaaah!!
WHAT THE HELL...?!
IT'S COMING RIGHT TOWARDS US!!

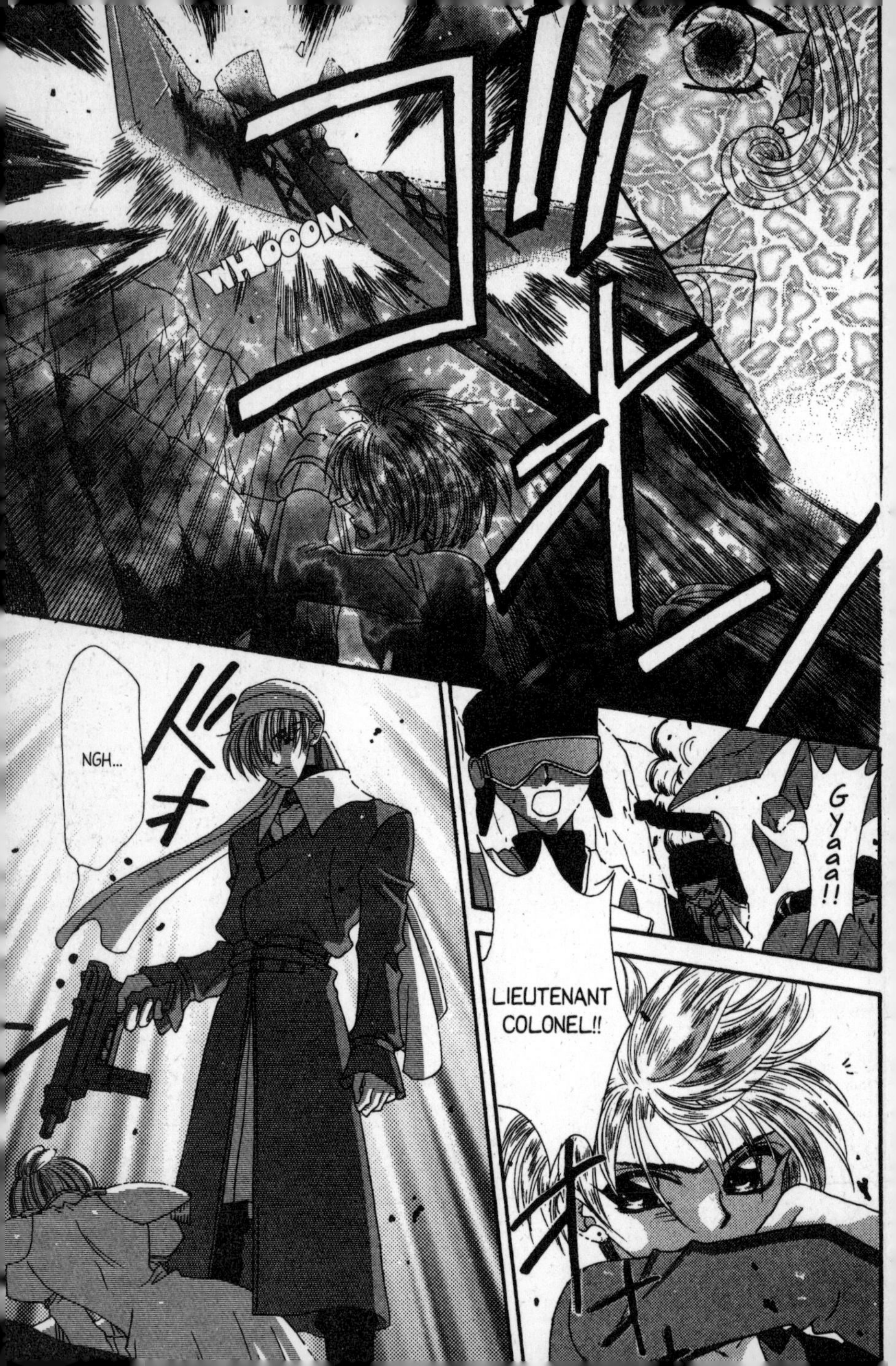
WHOOOM
Gyaaa!!
LIEUTENANT COLONEL!!
NGH...

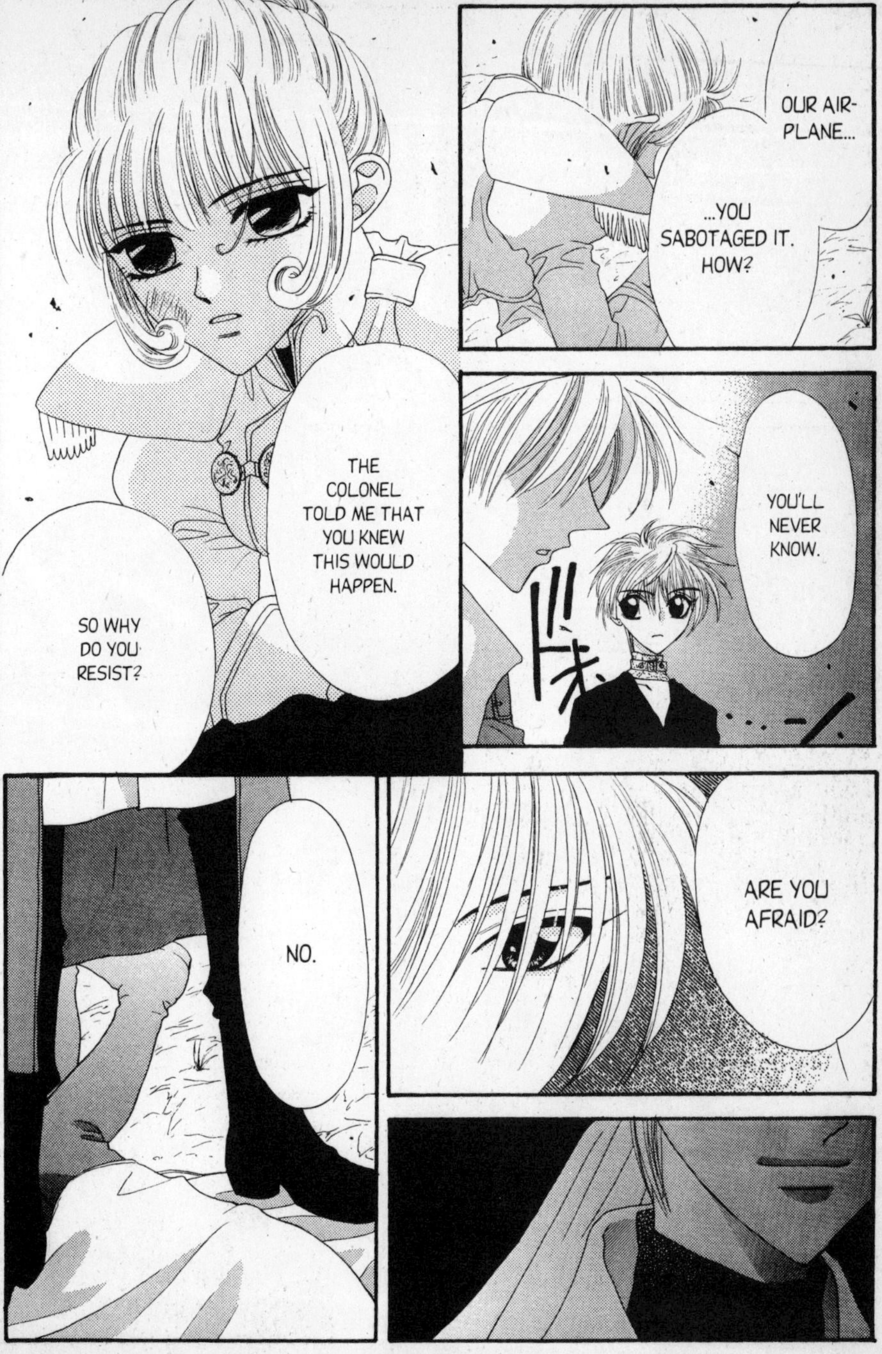
OUR AIR-PLANE...
...YOU SABOTAGED IT. HOW?
YOU'LL NEVER KNOW.
ドキ
THE COLONEL TOLD ME THAT YOU KNEW THIS WOULD HAPPEN.
SO WHY DO YOU RESIST?
ARE YOU AFRAID?
NO.

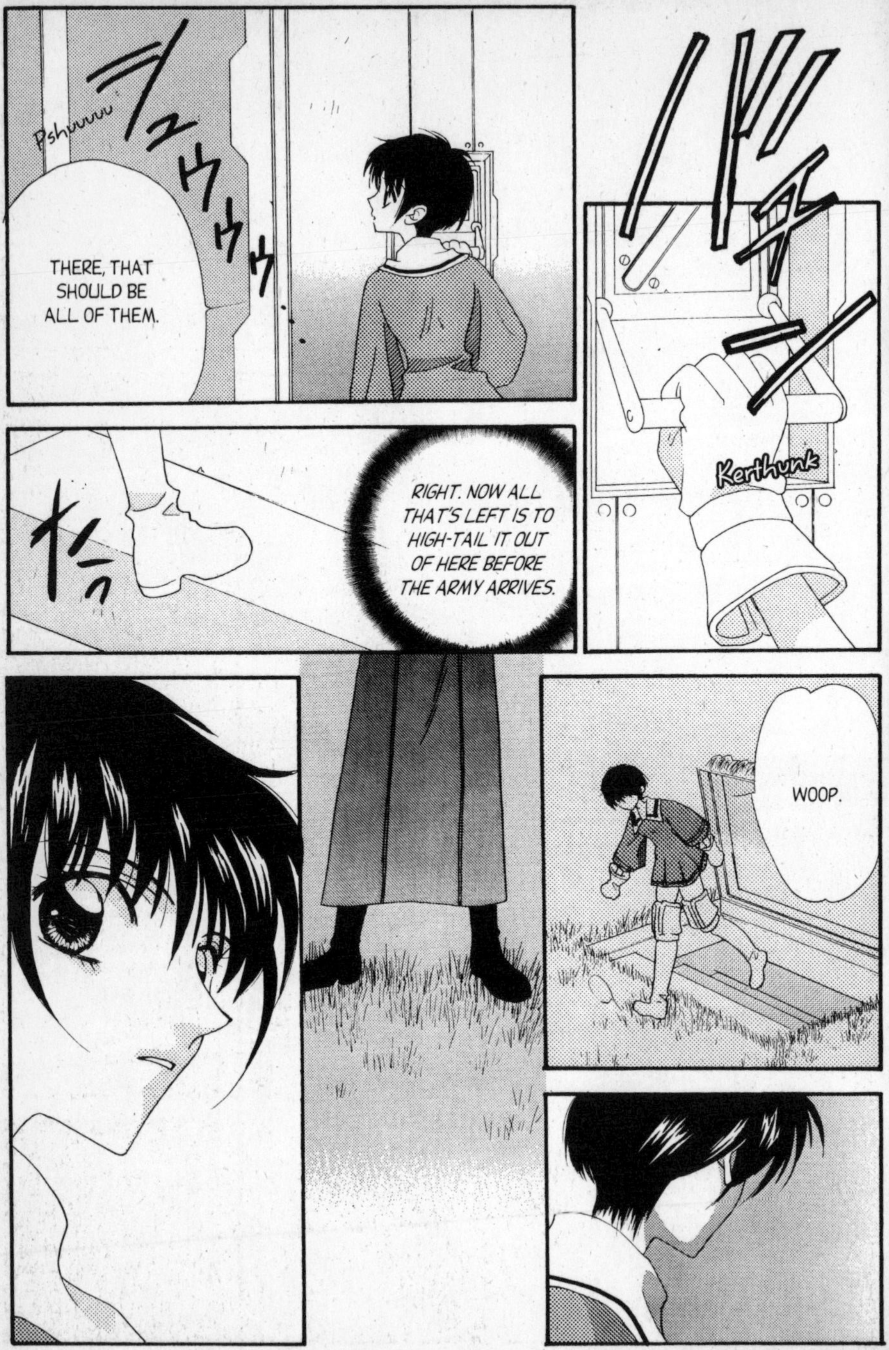
Kerthunk
Pshuuuu
THERE, THAT SHOULD BE ALL OF THEM.
RIGHT. NOW ALL THAT'S LEFT IS TO HIGH-TAIL IT OUT OF HERE BEFORE THE ARMY ARRIVES.
WOOP.

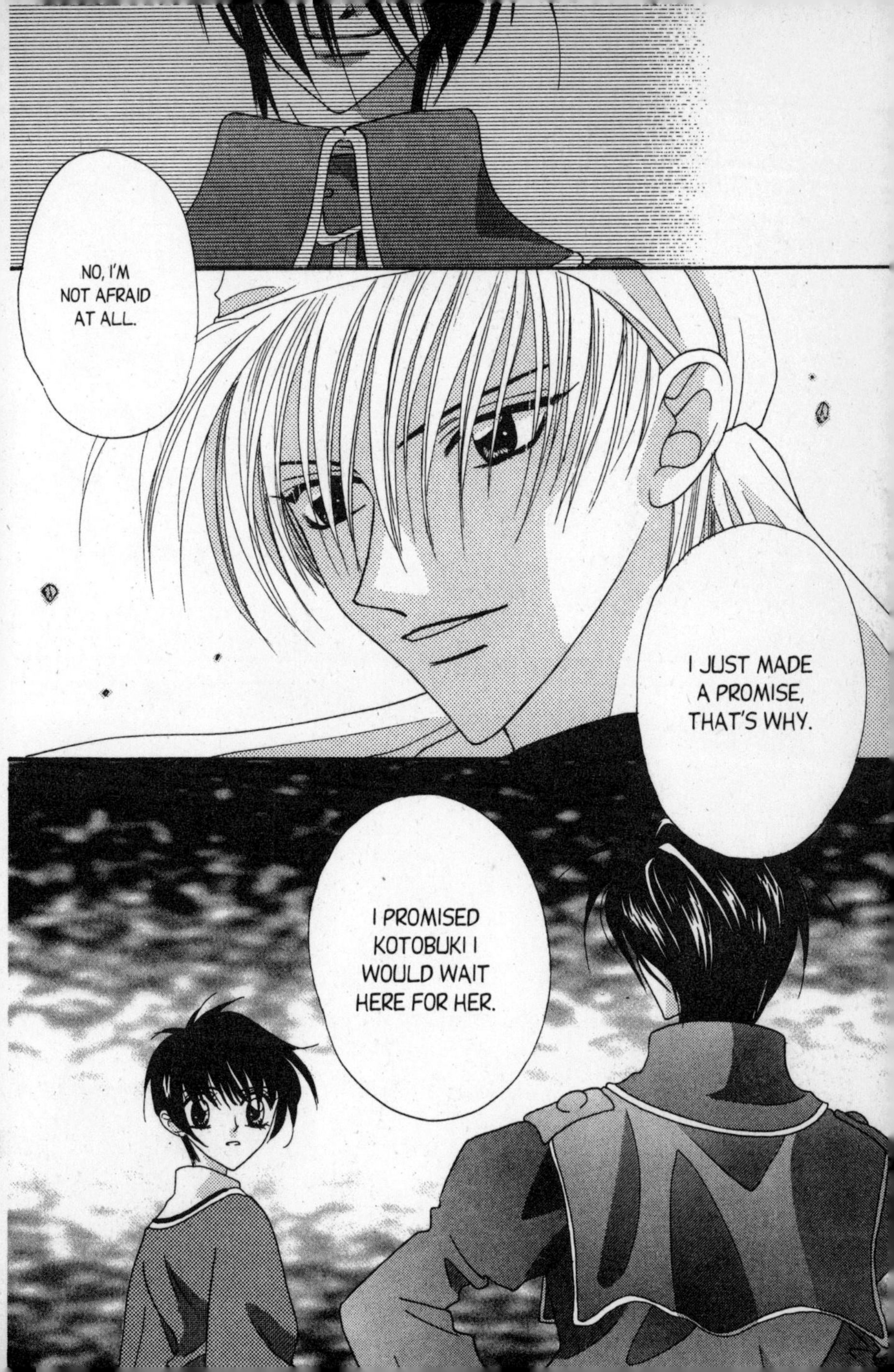
NO, I'M NOT AFRAID AT ALL.
I JUST MADE A PROMISE, THAT'S WHY.
I PROMISED KOTOBUKI I WOULD WAIT HERE FOR HER.

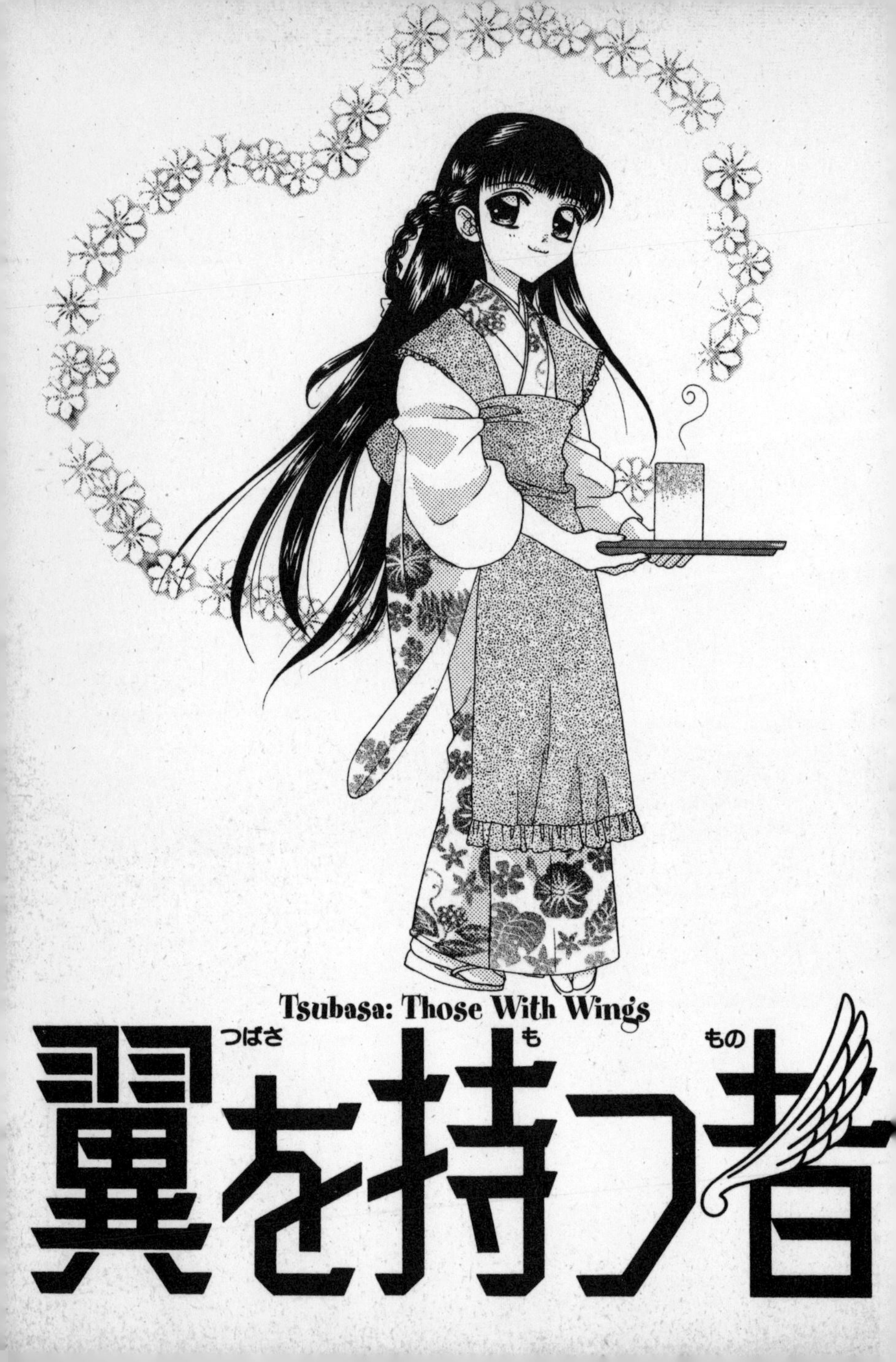

Tsubasa: Those With Wings

翼を持つ者

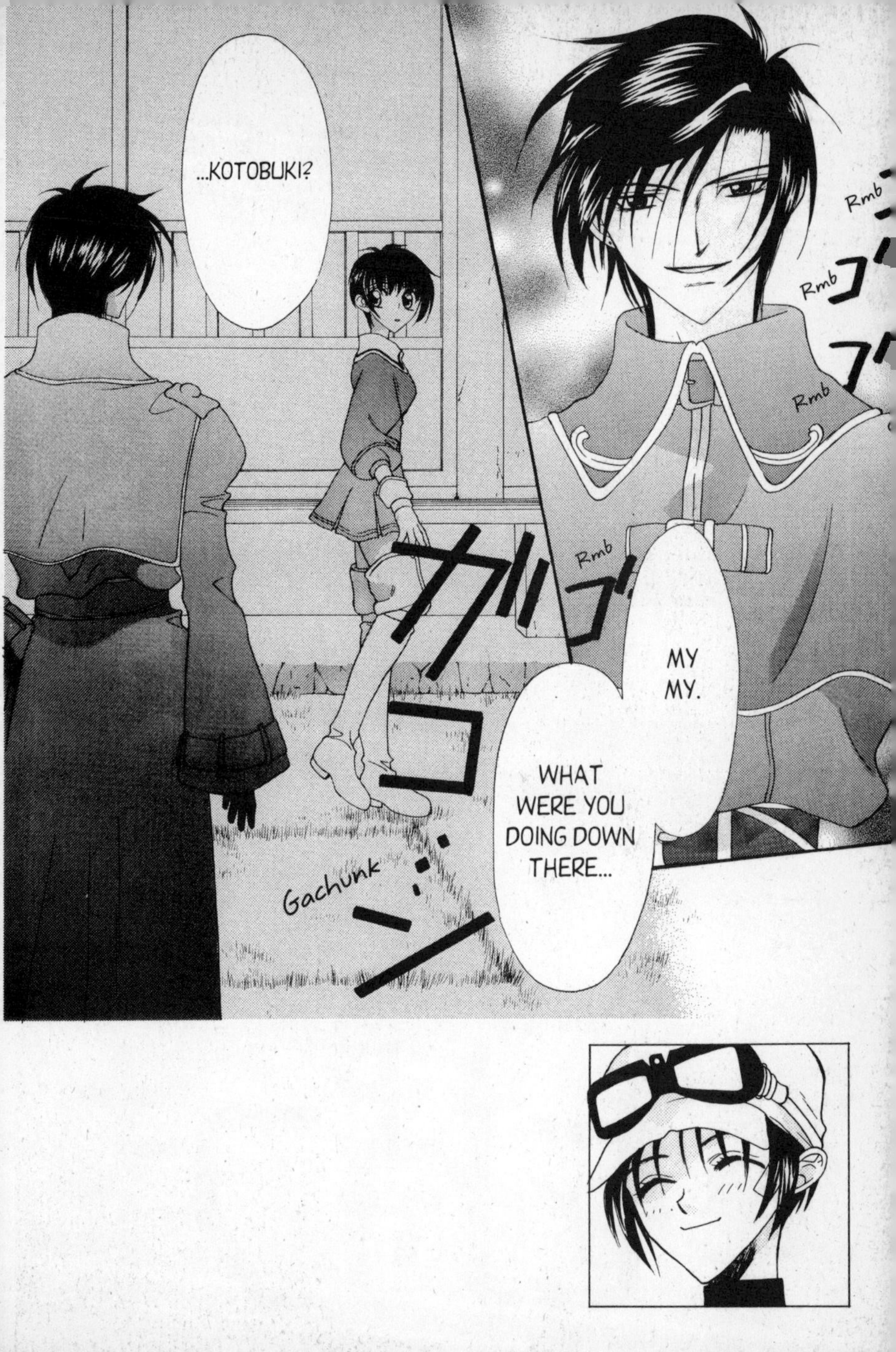

Rmb
Rmb
Rmb
Rmb
MY MY.
WHAT WERE YOU DOING DOWN THERE...
...KOTOBUKI!?
Gachunk

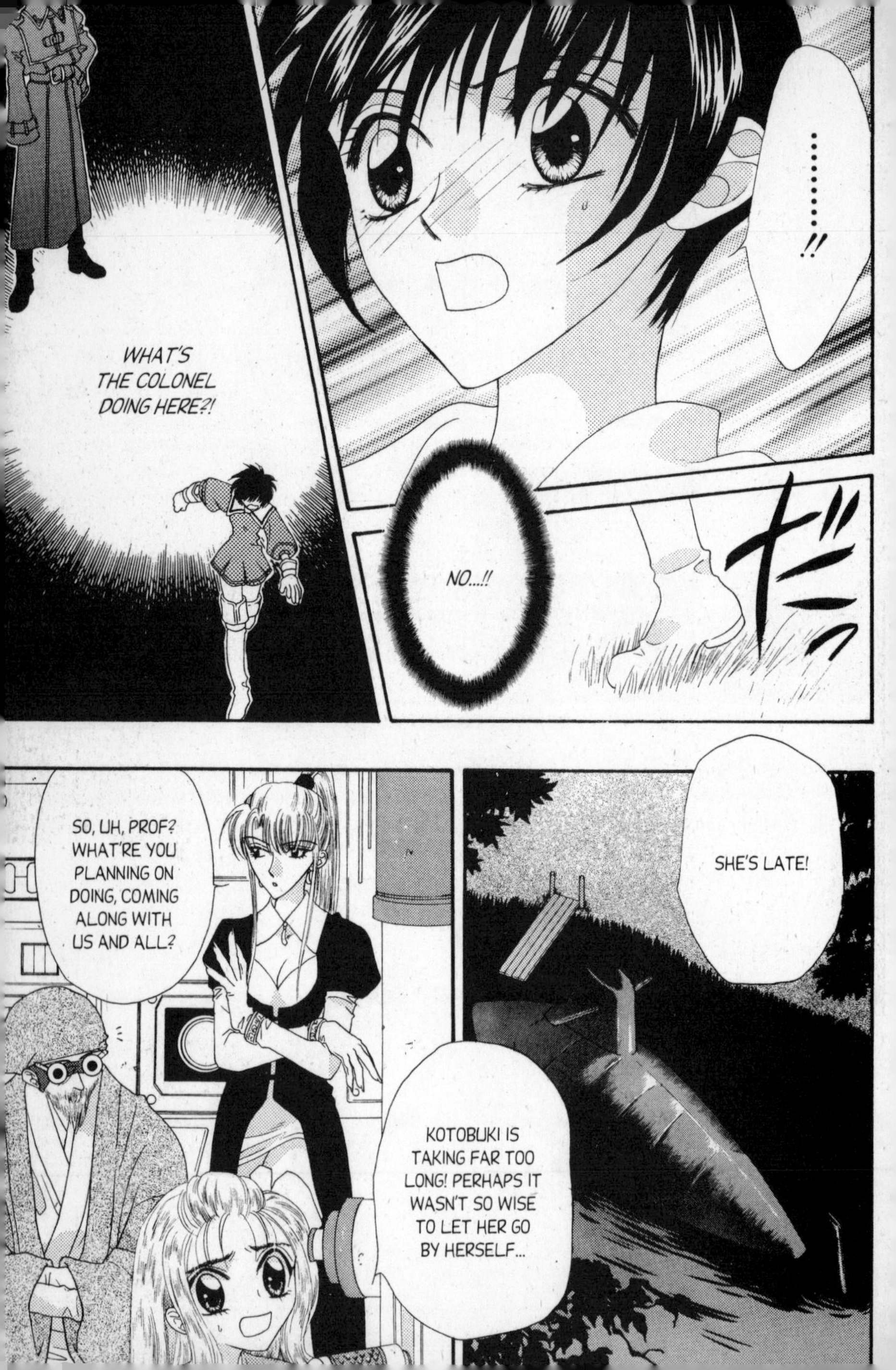
......!!
NO...!!
ダッ
WHAT'S THE COLONEL DOING HERE?!
SHE'S LATE!
KOTOBUKI IS TAKING FAR TOO LONG! PERHAPS IT WASN'T SO WISE TO LET HER GO BY HERSELF...
SO, UH, PROF? WHAT'RE YOU PLANNING ON DOING, COMING ALONG WITH US AND ALL?

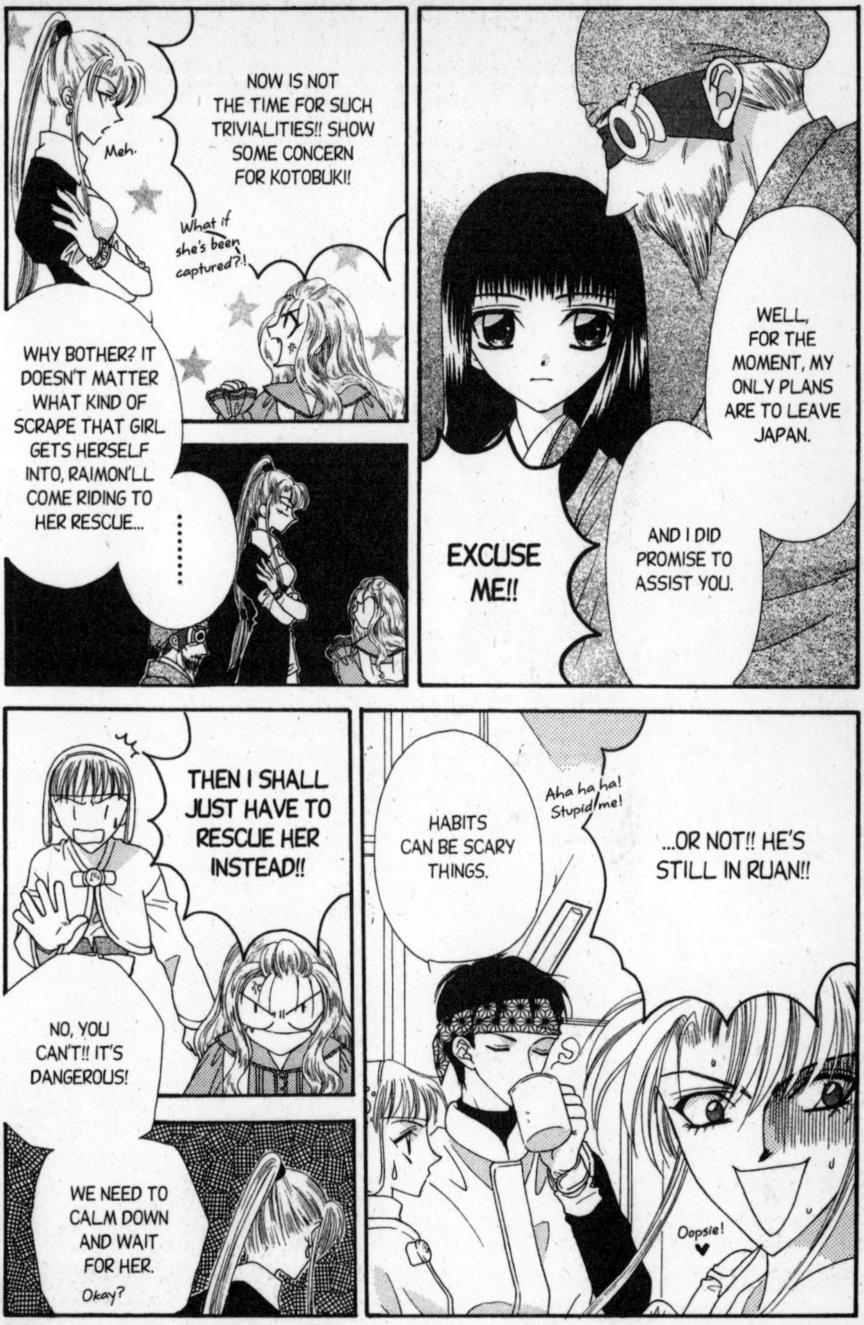
WELL, FOR THE MOMENT, MY ONLY PLANS ARE TO LEAVE JAPAN.
AND I DID PROMISE TO ASSIST YOU.
EXCUSE ME!!
NOW IS NOT THE TIME FOR SUCH TRIVIALITIES!! SHOW SOME CONCERN FOR KOTOBUKI!!
Meh.
What if she's been captured?!
WHY BOTHER? IT DOESN'T MATTER WHAT KIND OF SCRAPE THAT GIRL GETS HERSELF INTO, RAIMON'LL COME RIDING TO HER RESCUE...
....
...OR NOT!! HE'S STILL IN RUAN!!
Aha ha ha! Stupid me!
HABITS CAN BE SCARY THINGS.
Oopsie! ♥
THEN I SHALL JUST HAVE TO RESCUE HER INSTEAD!!
NO, YOU CAN'T!! IT'S DANGEROUS!
WE NEED TO CALM DOWN AND WAIT FOR HER.
Okay?

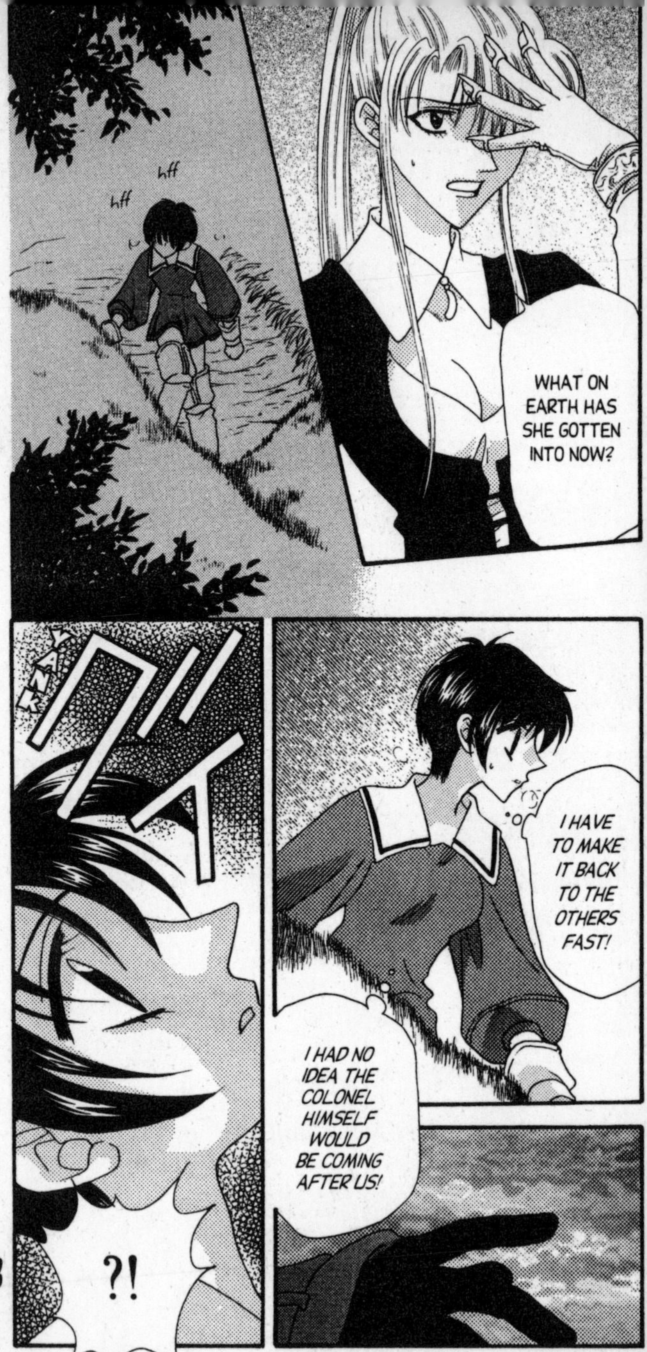
WHAT ON EARTH HAS SHE GOTTEN INTO NOW?
hff
hff
I HAVE TO MAKE IT BACK TO THE OTHERS FAST!
I HAD NO IDEA THE COLONEL HIMSELF WOULD BE COMING AFTER US!
YANK
?!

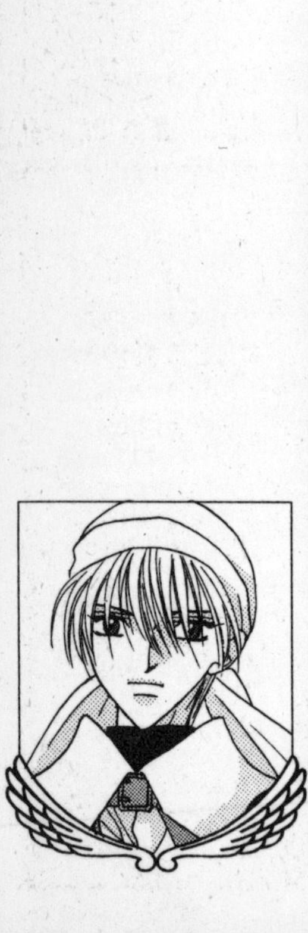

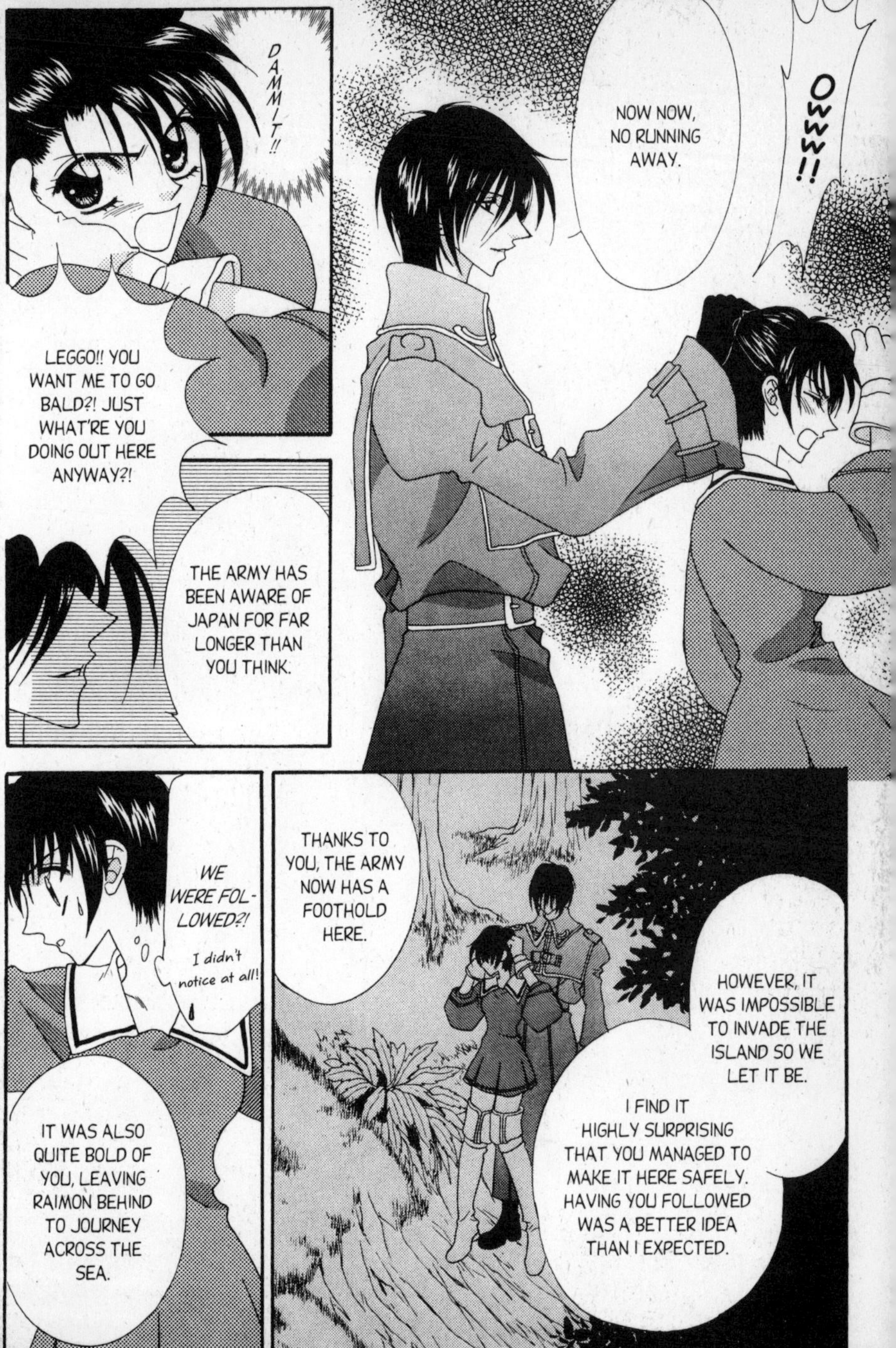
OWWW!!
NOW NOW, NO RUNNING AWAY.
DAMMIT!!
LEGGO!! YOU WANT ME TO GO BALD?! JUST WHAT'RE YOU DOING OUT HERE ANYWAY?!
THE ARMY HAS BEEN AWARE OF JAPAN FOR FAR LONGER THAN YOU THINK.
THANKS TO YOU, THE ARMY NOW HAS A FOOTHOLD HERE.
HOWEVER, IT WAS IMPOSSIBLE TO INVADE THE ISLAND SO WE LET IT BE.
I FIND IT HIGHLY SURPRISING THAT YOU MANAGED TO MAKE IT HERE SAFELY. HAVING YOU FOLLOWED WAS A BETTER IDEA THAN I EXPECTED.
WE WERE FOL-LOWED?!
I didn't notice at all!
IT WAS ALSO QUITE BOLD OF YOU, LEAVING RAIMON BEHIND TO JOURNEY ACROSS THE SEA.

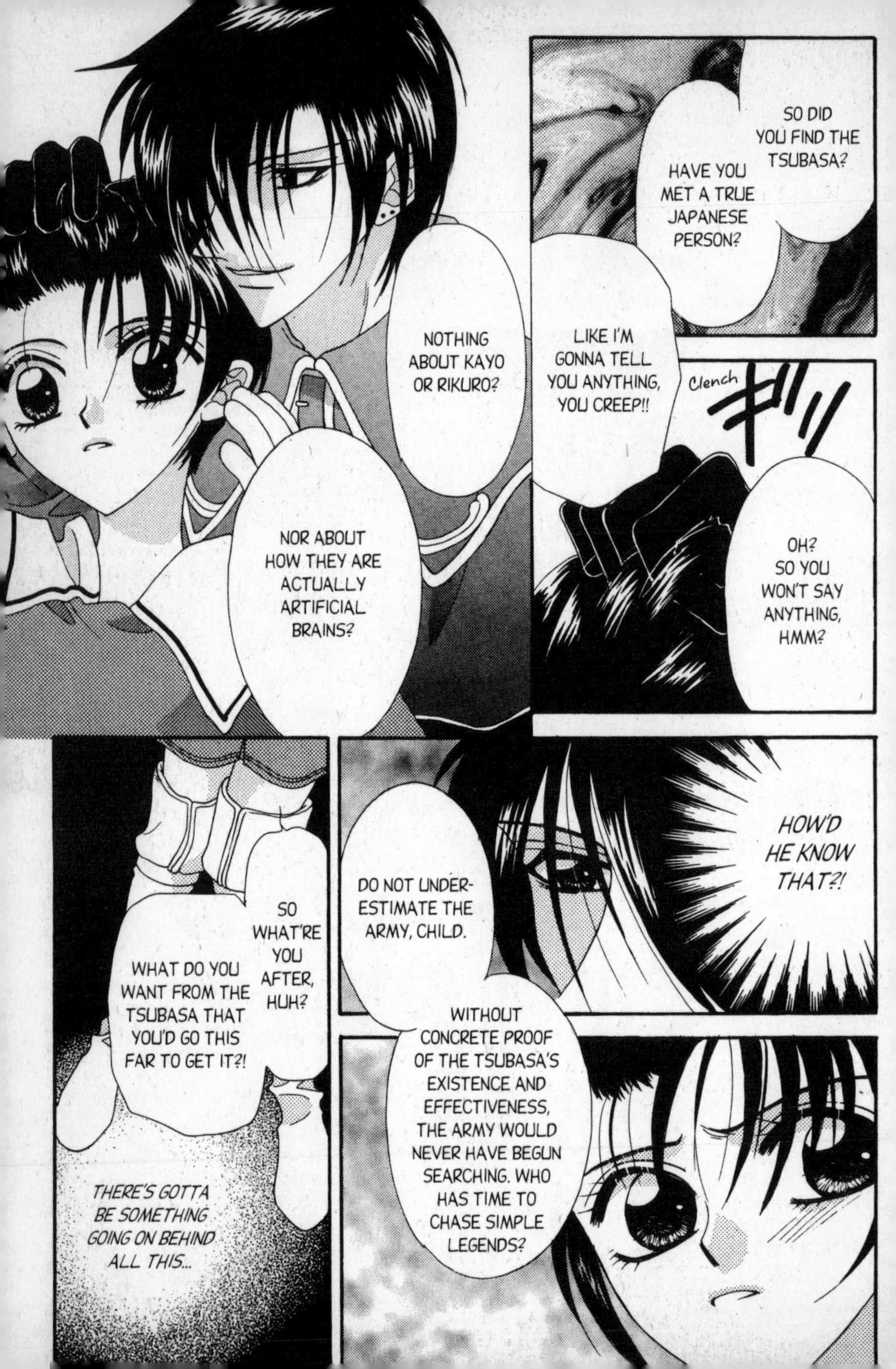
SO DID YOU FIND THE TSUBASA?
HAVE YOU MET A TRUE JAPANESE PERSON?
LIKE I'M GONNA TELL YOU ANYTHING, YOU CREEP!!
Clench
OH? SO YOU WON'T SAY ANYTHING, HMM?
NOTHING ABOUT KAYO OR RIKURO?
NOR ABOUT HOW THEY ARE ACTUALLY ARTIFICIAL BRAINS?
HOW'D HE KNOW THAT?!
DO NOT UNDER-ESTIMATE THE ARMY, CHILD.
WITHOUT CONCRETE PROOF OF THE TSUBASA'S EXISTENCE AND EFFECTIVENESS, THE ARMY WOULD NEVER HAVE BEGUN SEARCHING. WHO HAS TIME TO CHASE SIMPLE LEGENDS?
SO WHAT'RE YOU AFTER, HUH?
WHAT DO YOU WANT FROM THE TSUBASA THAT YOU'D GO THIS FAR TO GET IT?!
THERE'S GOTTA BE SOMETHING GOING ON BEHIND ALL THIS...

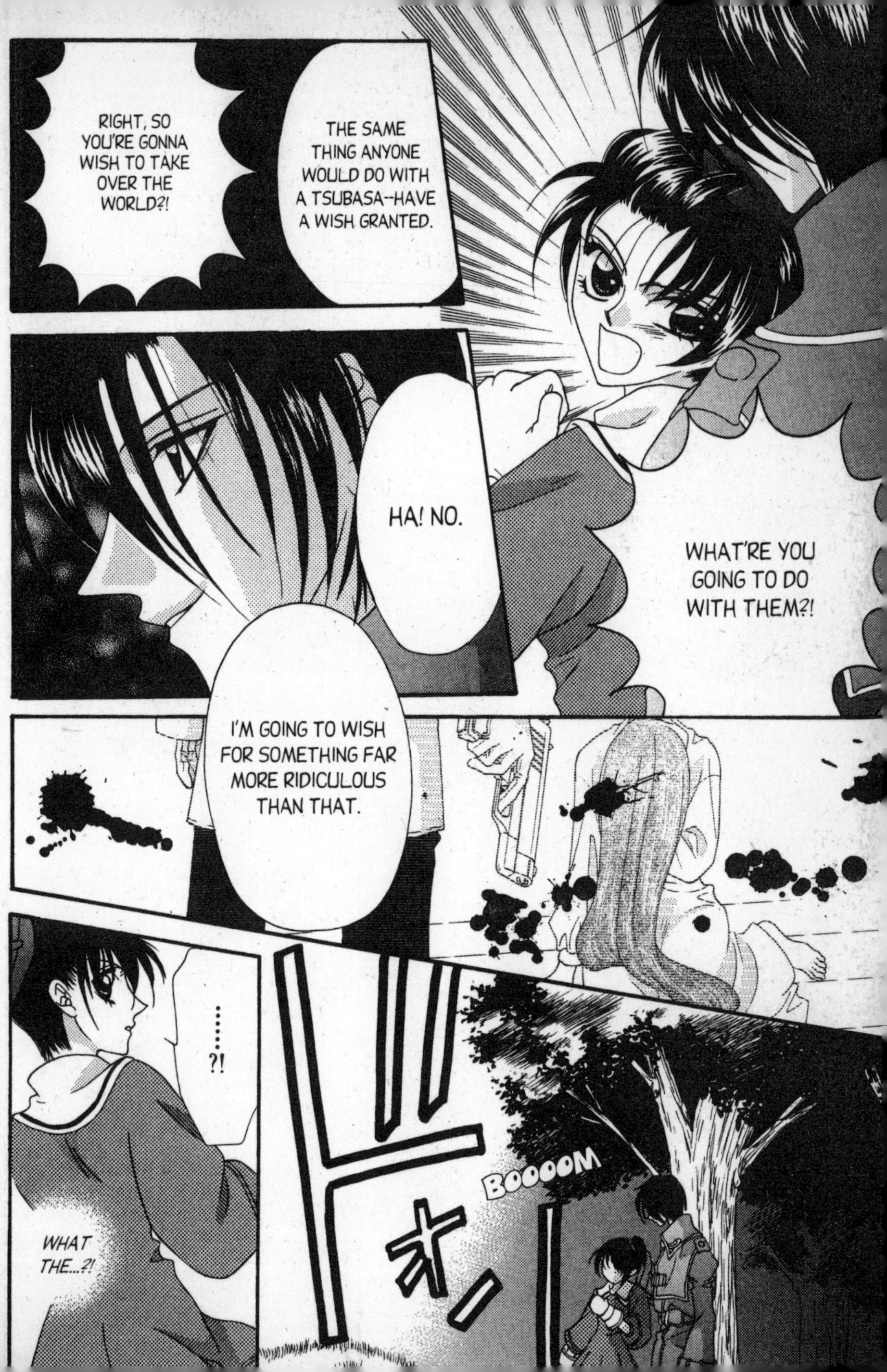
WHAT'RE YOU GOING TO DO WITH THEM?!
THE SAME THING ANYONE WOULD DO WITH A TSUBASA--HAVE A WISH GRANTED.
RIGHT, SO YOU'RE GONNA WISH TO TAKE OVER THE WORLD?!
HA! NO.
I'M GOING TO WISH FOR SOMETHING FAR MORE RIDICULOUS THAN THAT.
BOOOOM
......?!
WHAT THE...?!

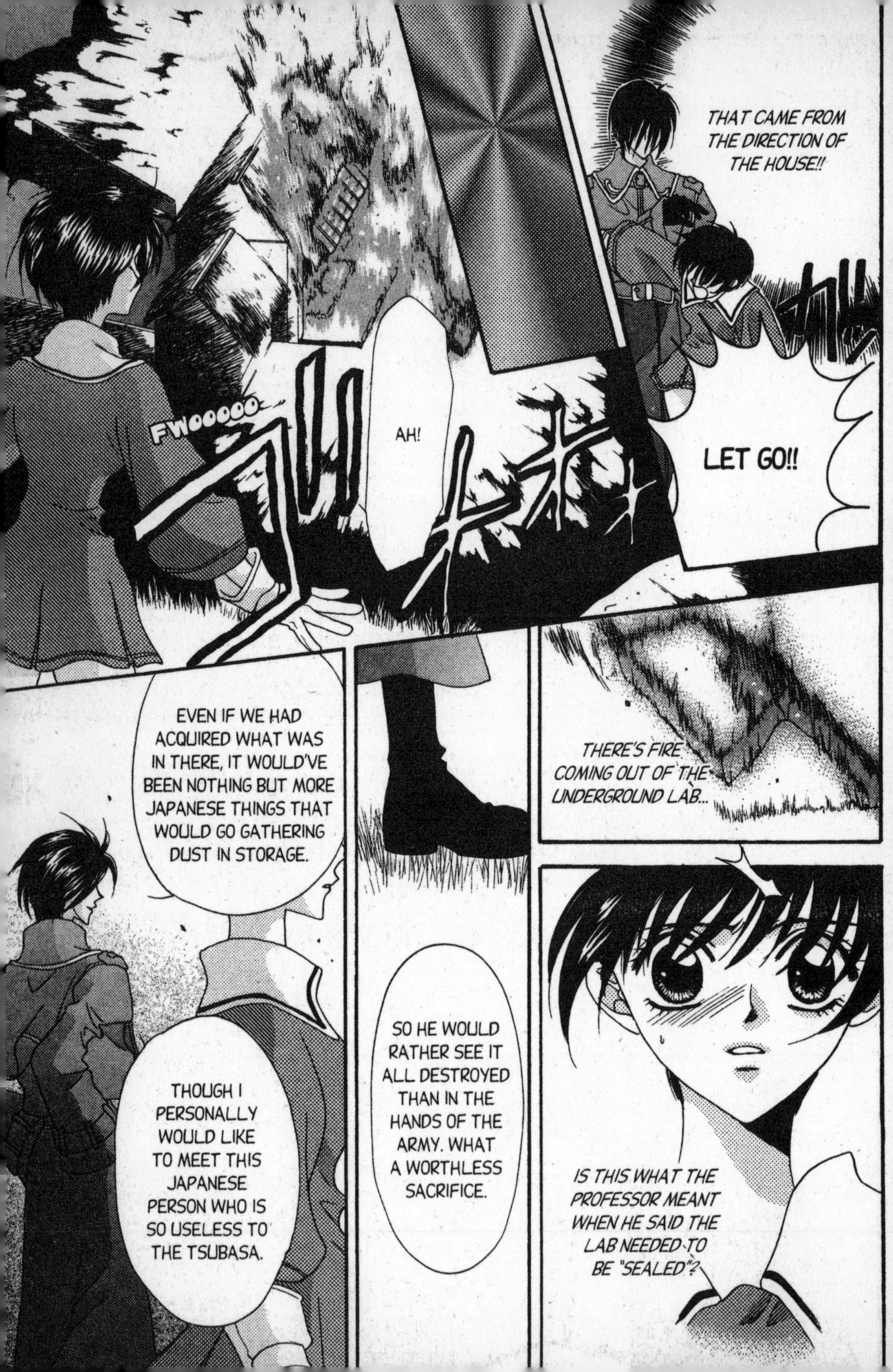
THAT CAME FROM THE DIRECTION OF THE HOUSE!!
LET GO!!
AH!
FWOOOOO
THERE'S FIRE COMING OUT OF THE UNDERGROUND LAB...
IS THIS WHAT THE PROFESSOR MEANT WHEN HE SAID THE LAB NEEDED TO BE "SEALED"?
SO HE WOULD RATHER SEE IT ALL DESTROYED THAN IN THE HANDS OF THE ARMY. WHAT A WORTHLESS SACRIFICE.
EVEN IF WE HAD ACQUIRED WHAT WAS IN THERE, IT WOULD'VE BEEN NOTHING BUT MORE JAPANESE THINGS THAT WOULD GO GATHERING DUST IN STORAGE.
THOUGH I PERSONALLY WOULD LIKE TO MEET THIS JAPANESE PERSON WHO IS SO USELESS TO THE TSUBASA.

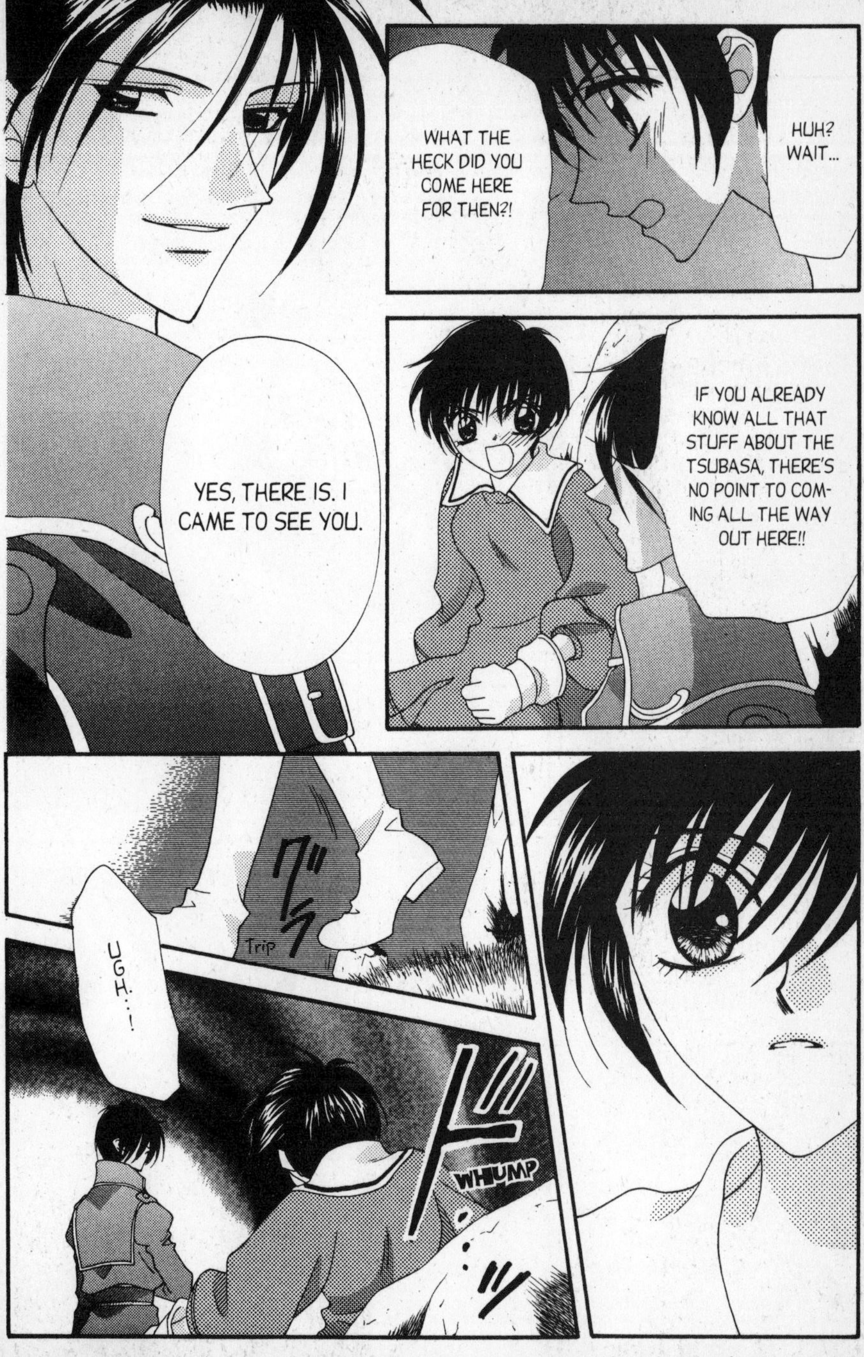
HUH? WAIT...
WHAT THE HECK DID YOU COME HERE FOR THEN?!
IF YOU ALREADY KNOW ALL THAT STUFF ABOUT THE TSUBASA, THERE'S NO POINT TO COMING ALL THE WAY OUT HERE!!
YES, THERE IS. I CAME TO SEE YOU.
UGH..!
Trip
WHUMP

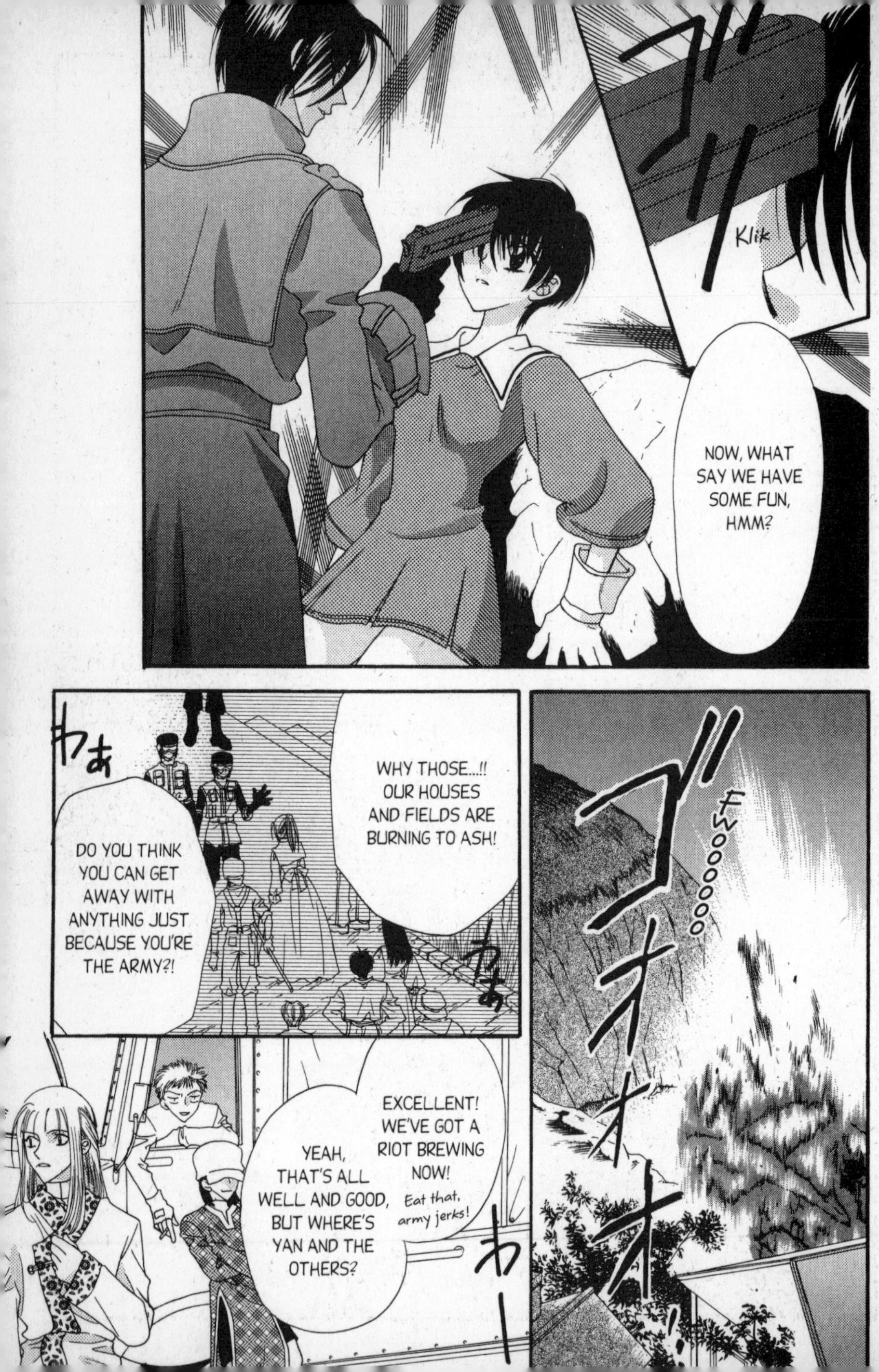
Klik
NOW, WHAT SAY WE HAVE SOME FUN, HMM?
FWOOOOOOO
WHY THOSE...!! OUR HOUSES AND FIELDS ARE BURNING TO ASH!
わぁ
DO YOU THINK YOU CAN GET AWAY WITH ANYTHING JUST BECAUSE YOU'RE THE ARMY?!
わぁ
EXCELLENT! WE'VE GOT A RIOT BREWING NOW!
Eat that, army jerks!
YEAH, THAT'S ALL WELL AND GOOD, BUT WHERE'S YAN AND THE OTHERS?

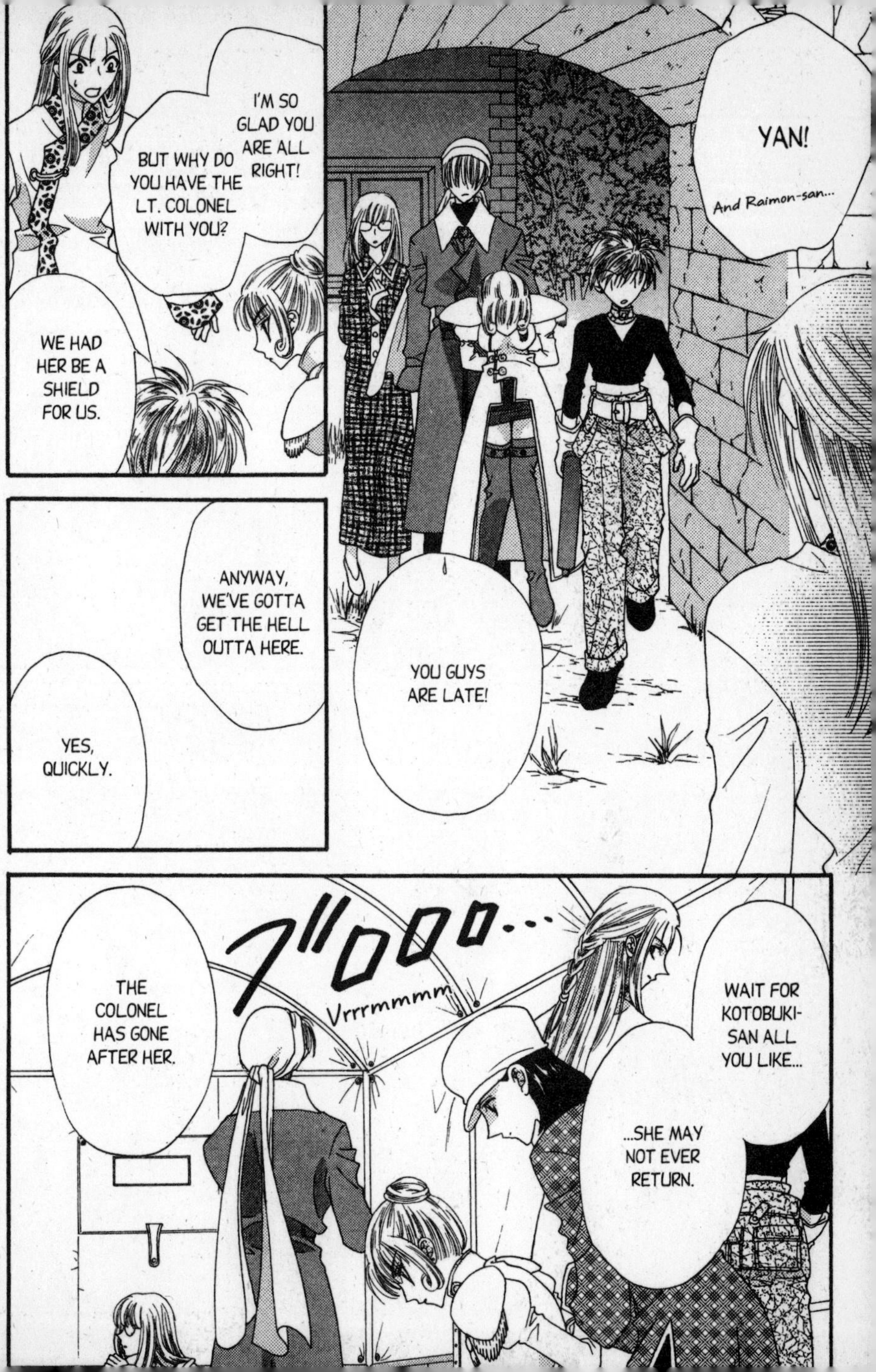
YAN!
And Raimon-san...
YOU GUYS ARE LATE!
I'M SO GLAD YOU ARE ALL RIGHT!
BUT WHY DO YOU HAVE THE LT. COLONEL WITH YOU?
WE HAD HER BE A SHIELD FOR US.
ANYWAY, WE'VE GOTTA GET THE HELL OUTTA HERE.
YES, QUICKLY.
WAIT FOR KOTOBUKI-SAN ALL YOU LIKE...
...SHE MAY NOT EVER RETURN.
ブロロロ...
Vrrrmmmm
THE COLONEL HAS GONE AFTER HER.

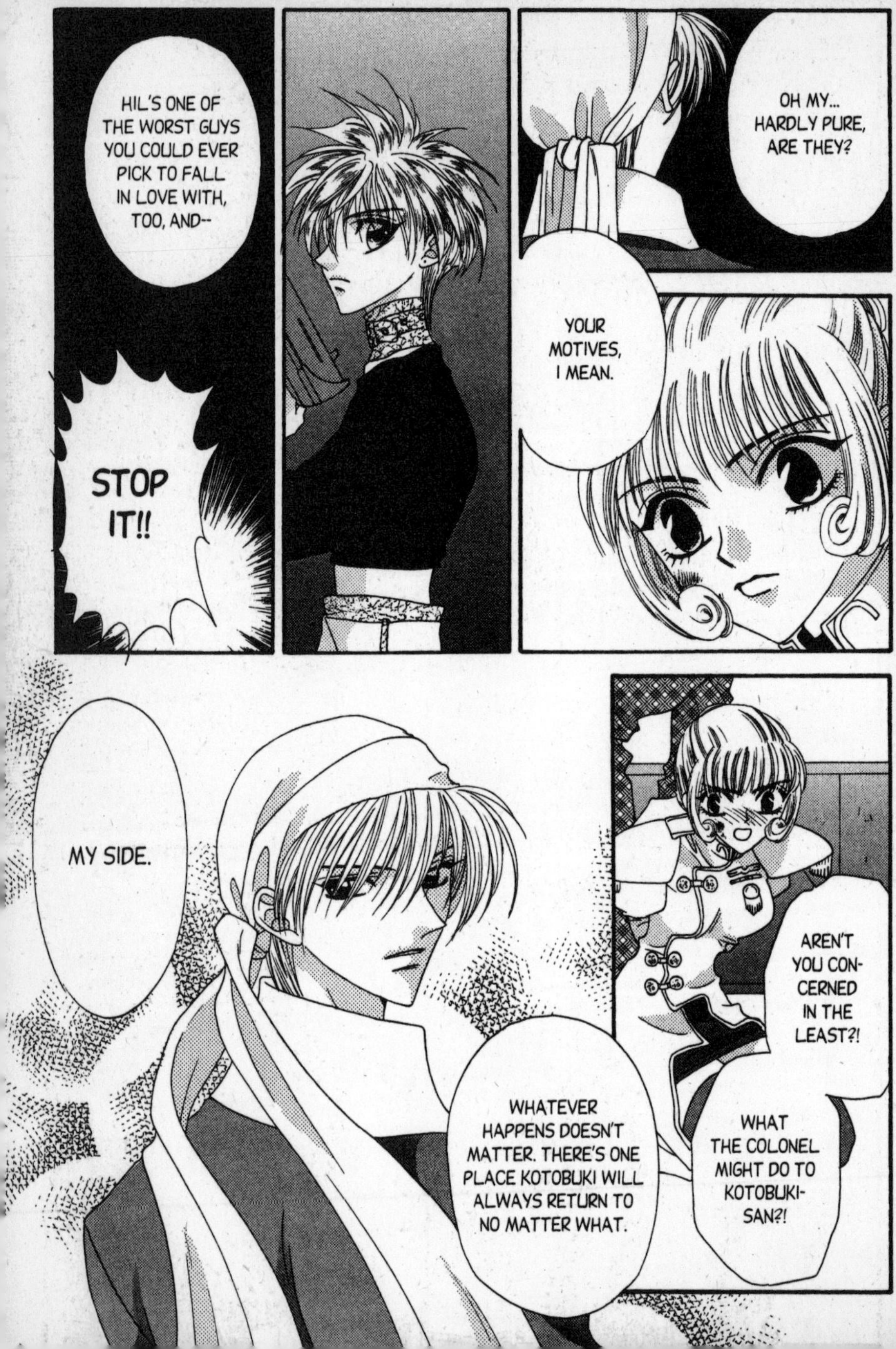
OH MY... HARDLY PURE, ARE THEY?
YOUR MOTIVES, I MEAN.
HIL'S ONE OF THE WORST GUYS YOU COULD EVER PICK TO FALL IN LOVE WITH, TOO, AND--
STOP IT!!
AREN'T YOU CONCERNED IN THE LEAST?!
WHAT THE COLONEL MIGHT DO TO KOTOBUKI-SAN?!
WHATEVER HAPPENS DOESN'T MATTER. THERE'S ONE PLACE KOTOBUKI WILL ALWAYS RETURN TO NO MATTER WHAT.
MY SIDE.

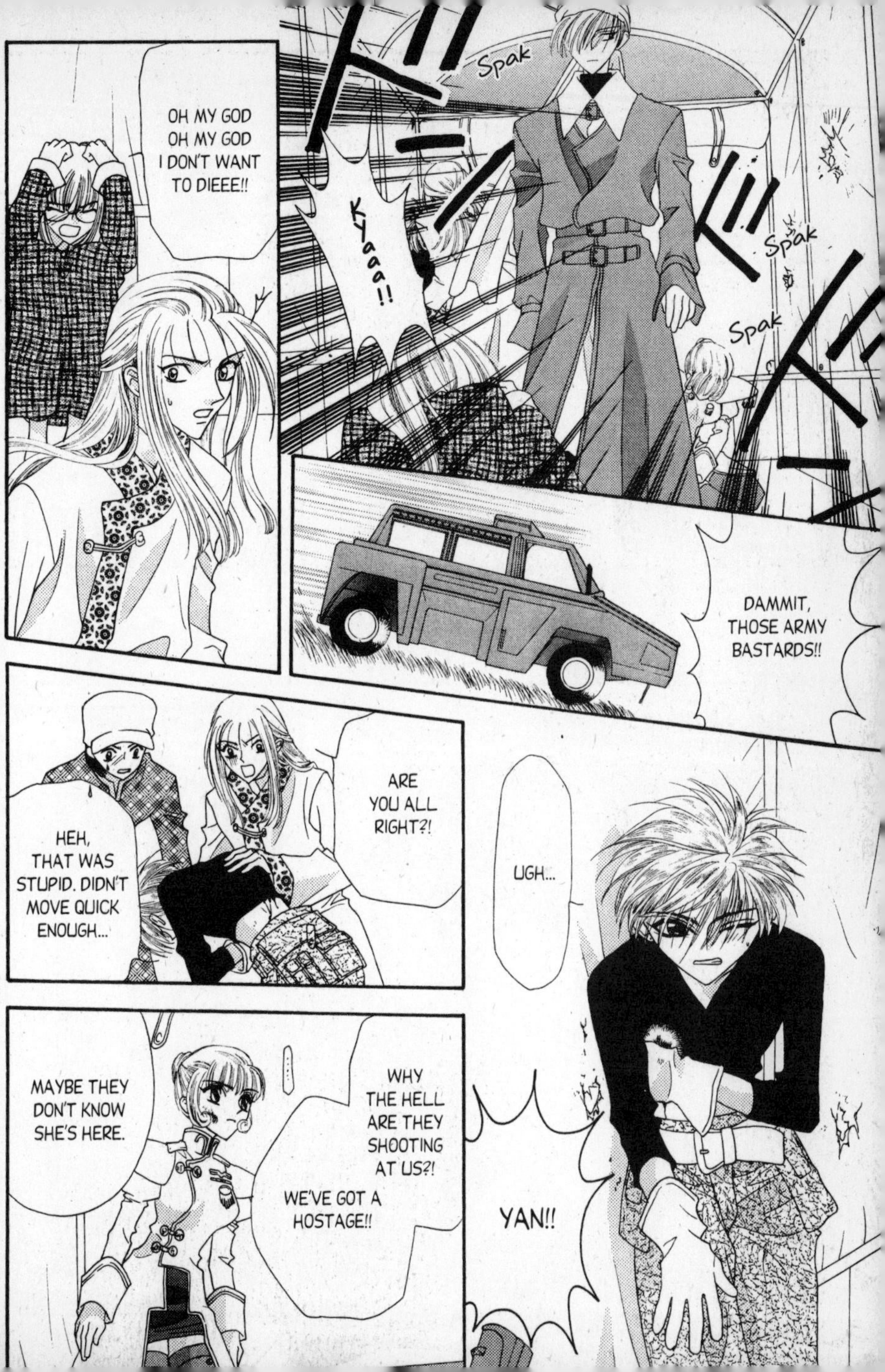
Spak
Kyaaa!!
Spak
Spak
DAMMIT, THOSE ARMY BASTARDS!!
OH MY GOD OH MY GOD I DON'T WANT TO DIEEE!!
UGH...
YAN!!
ARE YOU ALL RIGHT?!
HEH, THAT WAS STUPID. DIDN'T MOVE QUICK ENOUGH...
...
WHY THE HELL ARE THEY SHOOTING AT US?!
WE'VE GOT A HOSTAGE!!
MAYBE THEY DON'T KNOW SHE'S HERE.

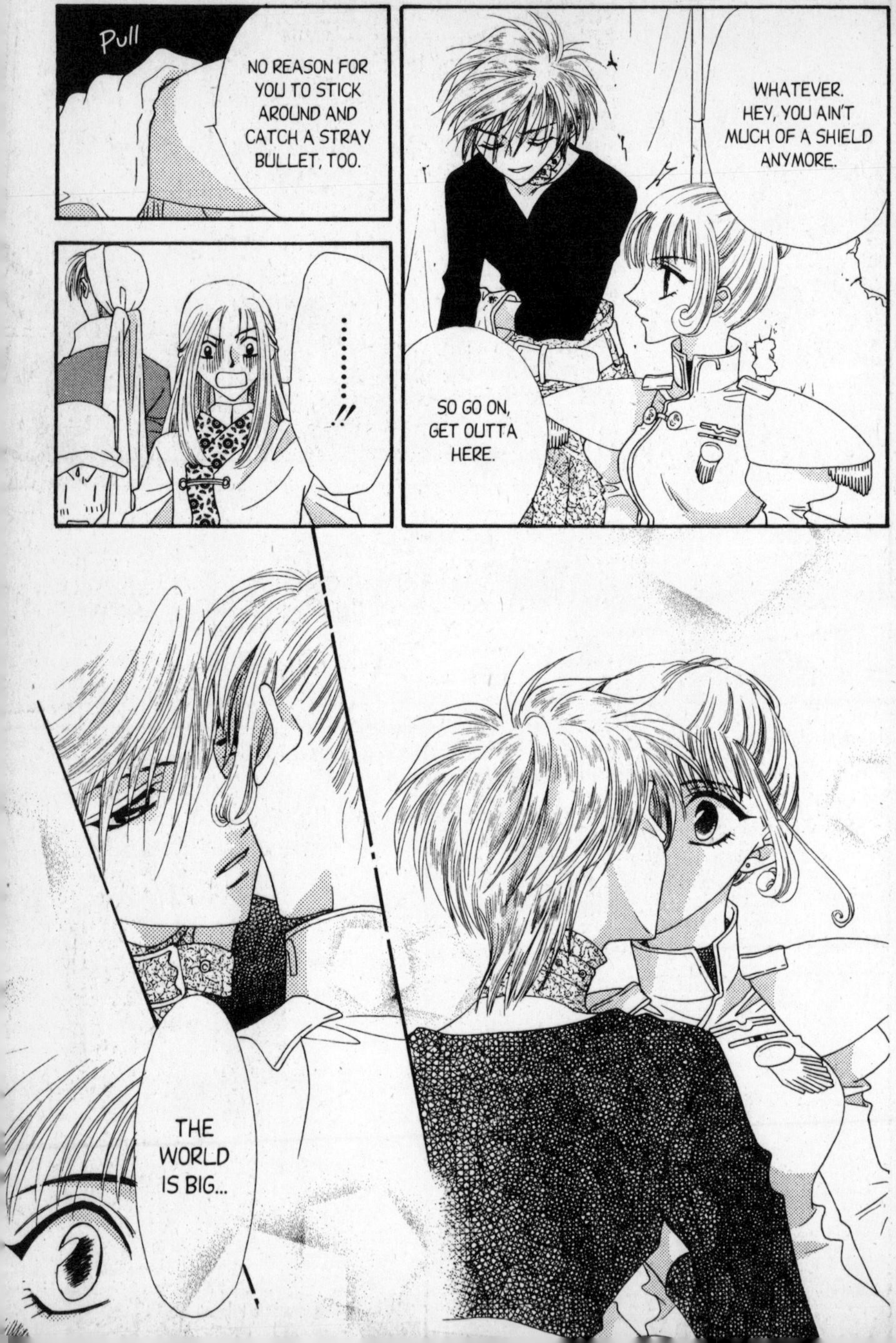
WHATEVER. HEY, YOU AIN'T MUCH OF A SHIELD ANYMORE.
SO GO ON, GET OUTTA HERE.
Pull
NO REASON FOR YOU TO STICK AROUND AND CATCH A STRAY BULLET, TOO.
........!!
THE WORLD IS BIG...

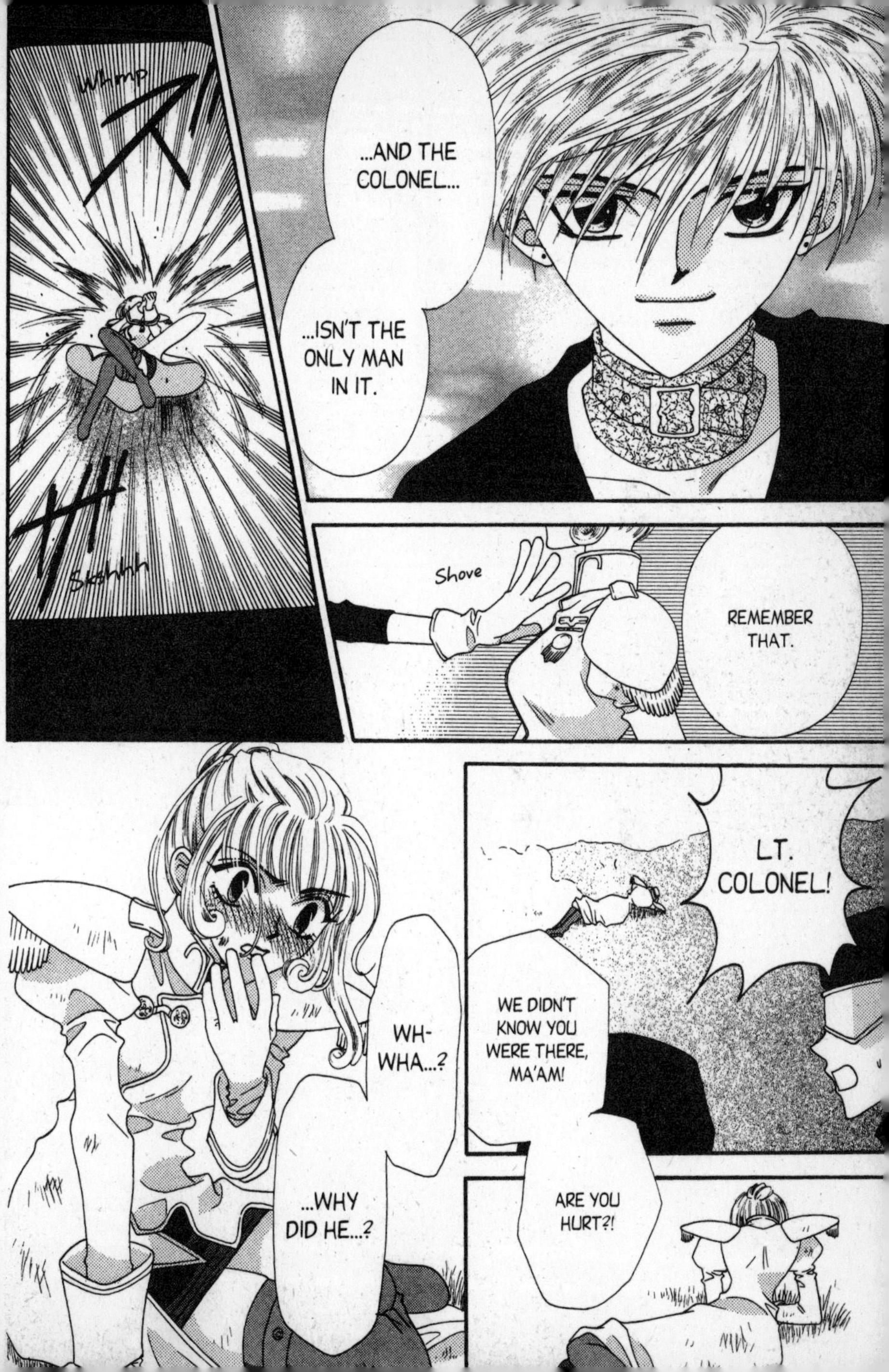
...AND THE COLONEL...
...ISN'T THE ONLY MAN IN IT.
REMEMBER THAT.
Shove
Whmp
Skshhh
LT. COLONEL!
WE DIDN'T KNOW YOU WERE THERE, MA'AM!
ARE YOU HURT?!
WH- WHA...?
...WHY DID HE...?

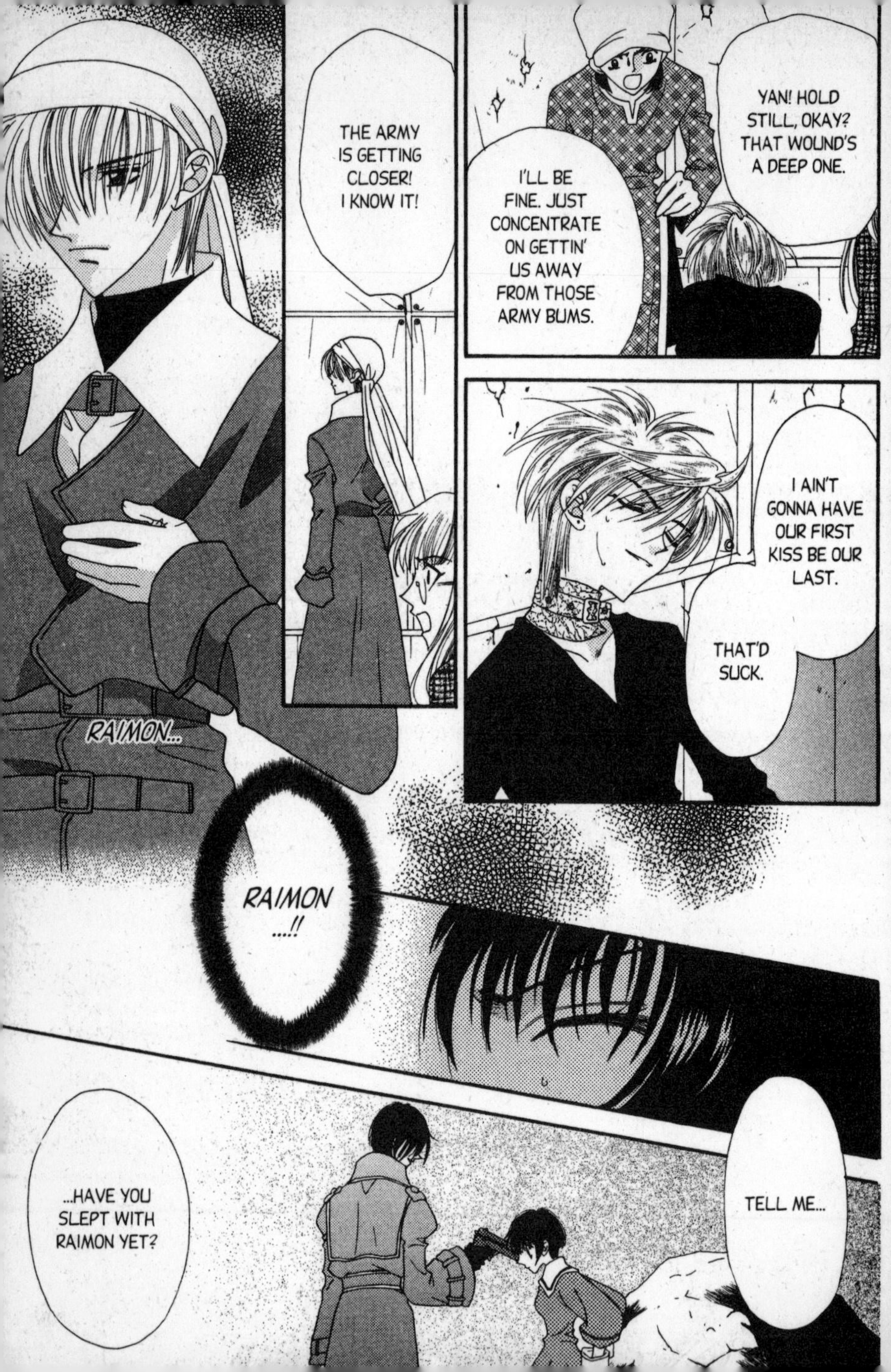
YAN! HOLD STILL, OKAY? THAT WOUND'S A DEEP ONE.
I'LL BE FINE. JUST CONCENTRATE ON GETTIN' US AWAY FROM THOSE ARMY BUMS.
I AIN'T GONNA HAVE OUR FIRST KISS BE OUR LAST.
THAT'D SUCK.
THE ARMY IS GETTING CLOSER! I KNOW IT!
RAIMON...
RAIMON ...!!
TELL ME...
...HAVE YOU SLEPT WITH RAIMON YET?

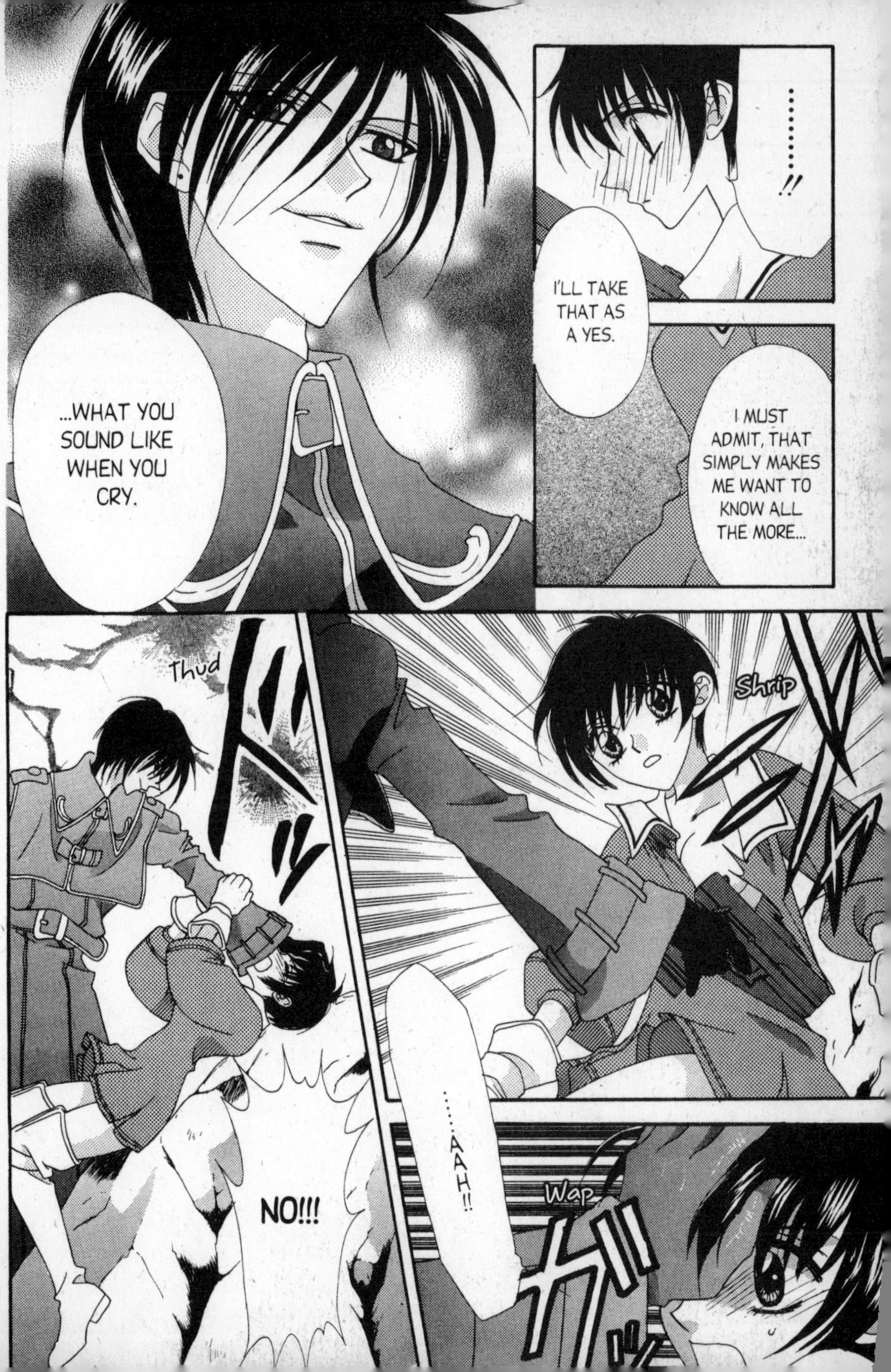

......!!
I'LL TAKE THAT AS A YES.
I MUST ADMIT, THAT SIMPLY MAKES ME WANT TO KNOW ALL THE MORE...
...WHAT YOU SOUND LIKE WHEN YOU CRY.
Shrip
......AAH!!
Wap
Thud
NO!!!

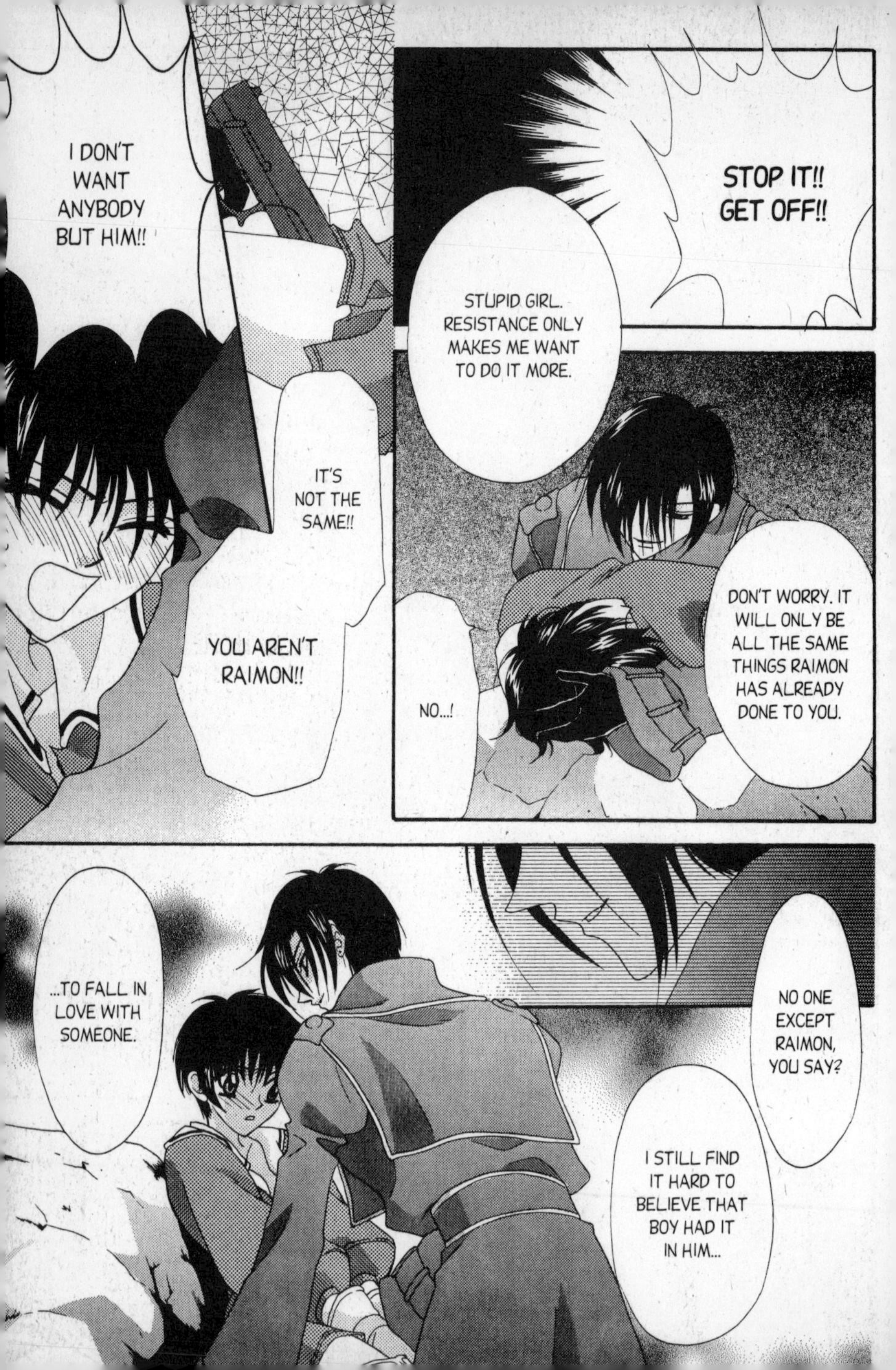
STOP IT!! GET OFF!!
STUPID GIRL. RESISTANCE ONLY MAKES ME WANT TO DO IT MORE.
DON'T WORRY. IT WILL ONLY BE ALL THE SAME THINGS RAIMON HAS ALREADY DONE TO YOU.
NO...!
IT'S NOT THE SAME!!
YOU AREN'T RAIMON!!
I DON'T WANT ANYBODY BUT HIM!!
NO ONE EXCEPT RAIMON, YOU SAY?
I STILL FIND IT HARD TO BELIEVE THAT BOY HAD IT IN HIM...
...TO FALL IN LOVE WITH SOMEONE.

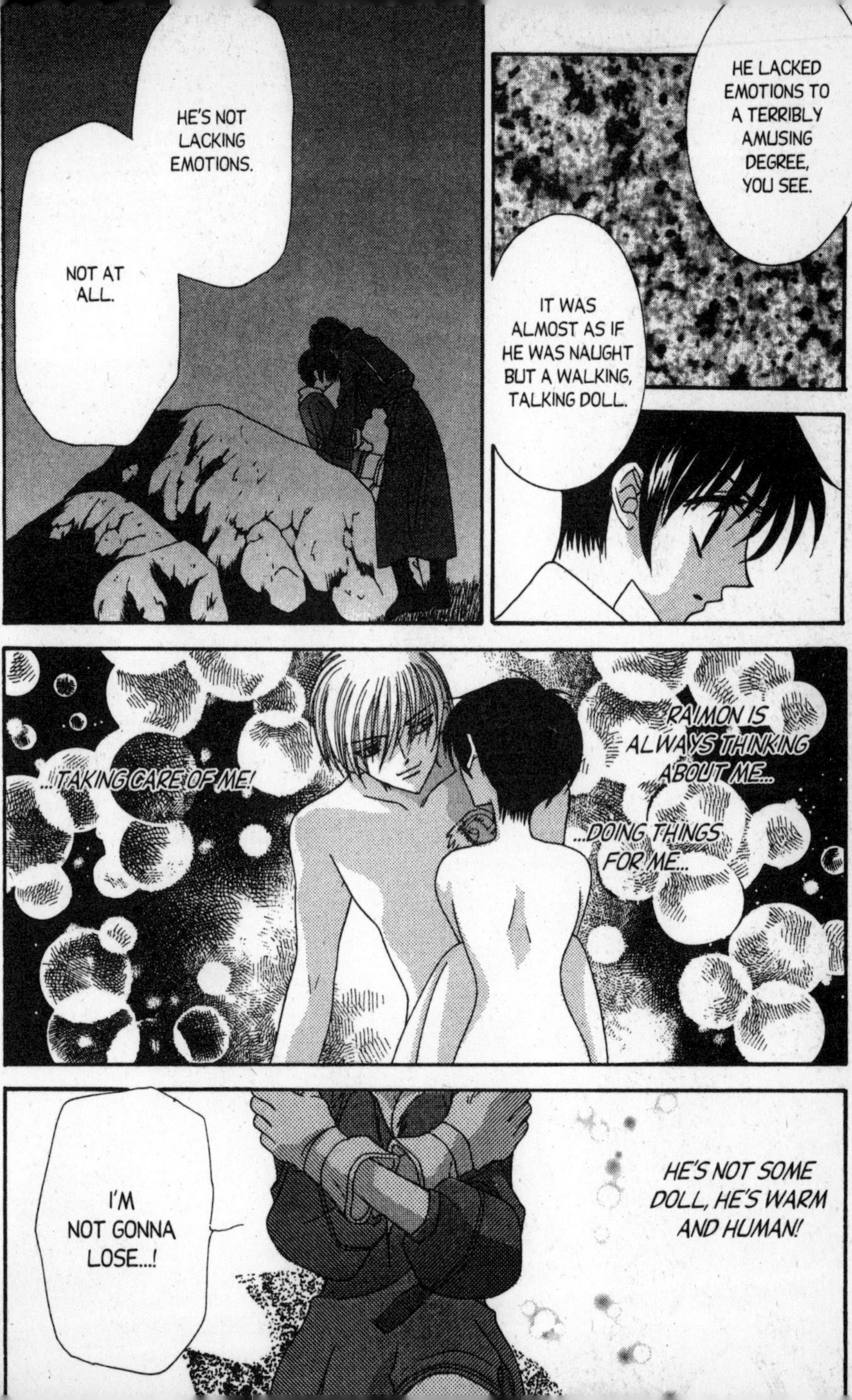
HE LACKED EMOTIONS TO A TERRIBLY AMUSING DEGREE, YOU SEE.
IT WAS ALMOST AS IF HE WAS NAUGHT BUT A WALKING, TALKING DOLL.
HE'S NOT LACKING EMOTIONS.
NOT AT ALL.
RAIMON IS ALWAYS THINKING ABOUT ME...
...DOING THINGS FOR ME...
...TAKING CARE OF ME!
HE'S NOT SOME DOLL, HE'S WARM AND HUMAN!
I'M NOT GONNA LOSE...!

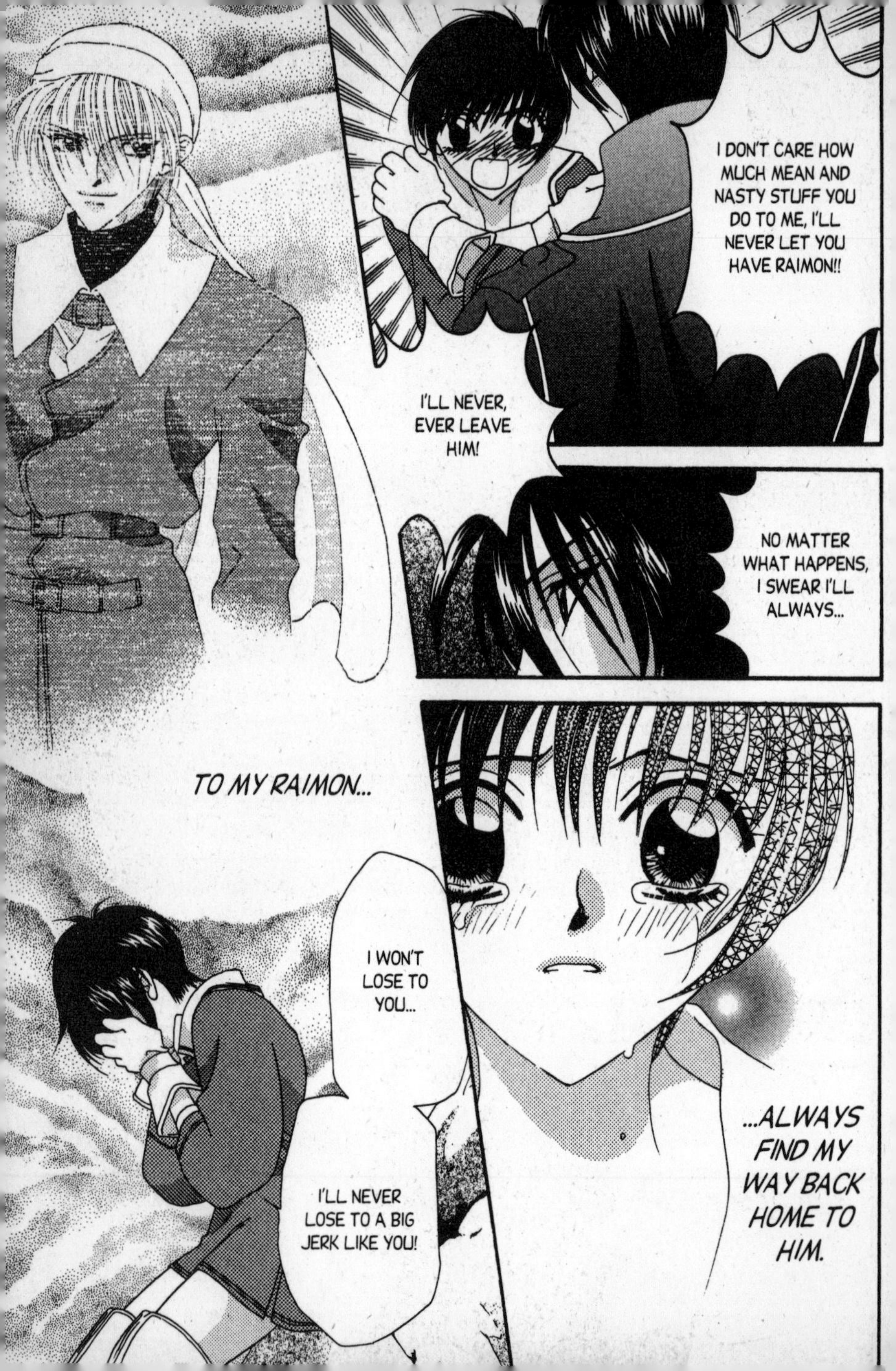
I DON'T CARE HOW MUCH MEAN AND NASTY STUFF YOU DO TO ME, I'LL NEVER LET YOU HAVE RAIMON!!
I'LL NEVER, EVER LEAVE HIM!
NO MATTER WHAT HAPPENS, I SWEAR I'LL ALWAYS...
...ALWAYS FIND MY WAY BACK HOME TO HIM.
TO MY RAIMON...
I WON'T LOSE TO YOU...
I'LL NEVER LOSE TO A BIG JERK LIKE YOU!

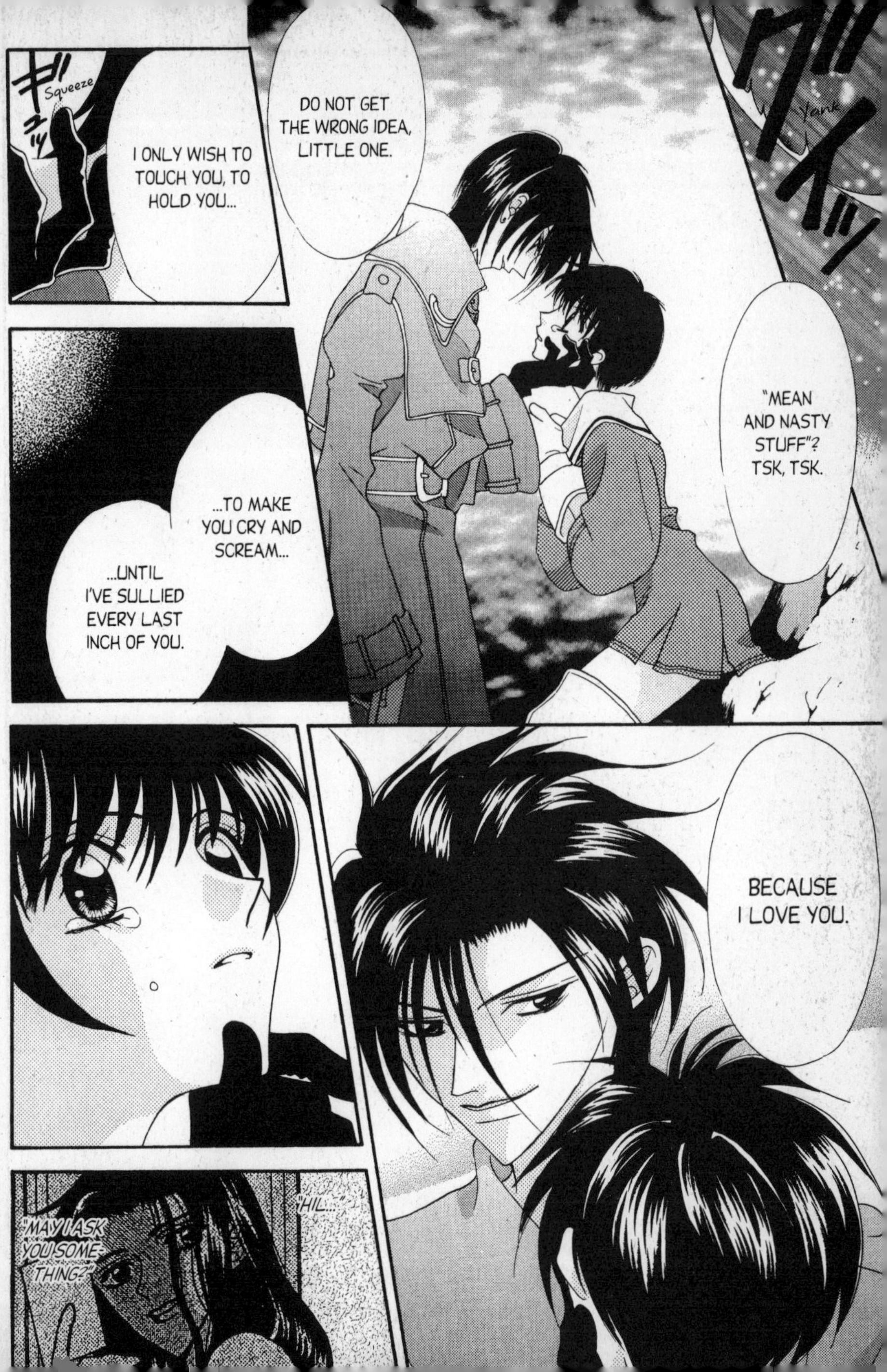
Yank
"MEAN AND NASTY STUFF"? TSK, TSK.
DO NOT GET THE WRONG IDEA, LITTLE ONE.
Squeeze
I ONLY WISH TO TOUCH YOU, TO HOLD YOU...
...TO MAKE YOU CRY AND SCREAM...
...UNTIL I'VE SULLIED EVERY LAST INCH OF YOU.
BECAUSE I LOVE YOU.
"HIL..."
"MAY I ASK YOU SOMETHING?"

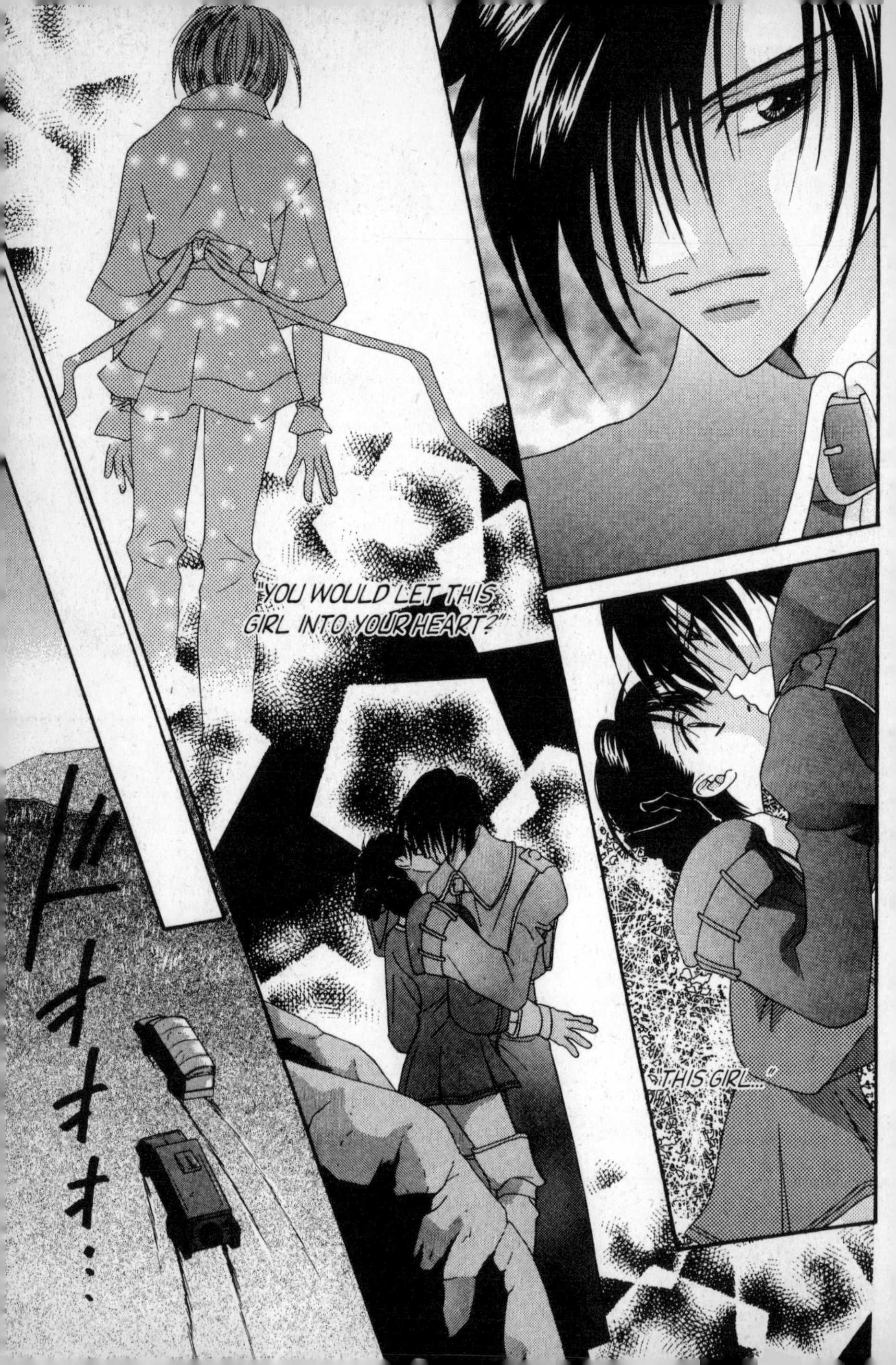
"THIS GIRL..."
"YOU WOULD LET THIS GIRL INTO YOUR HEART?"
ドオオオ…

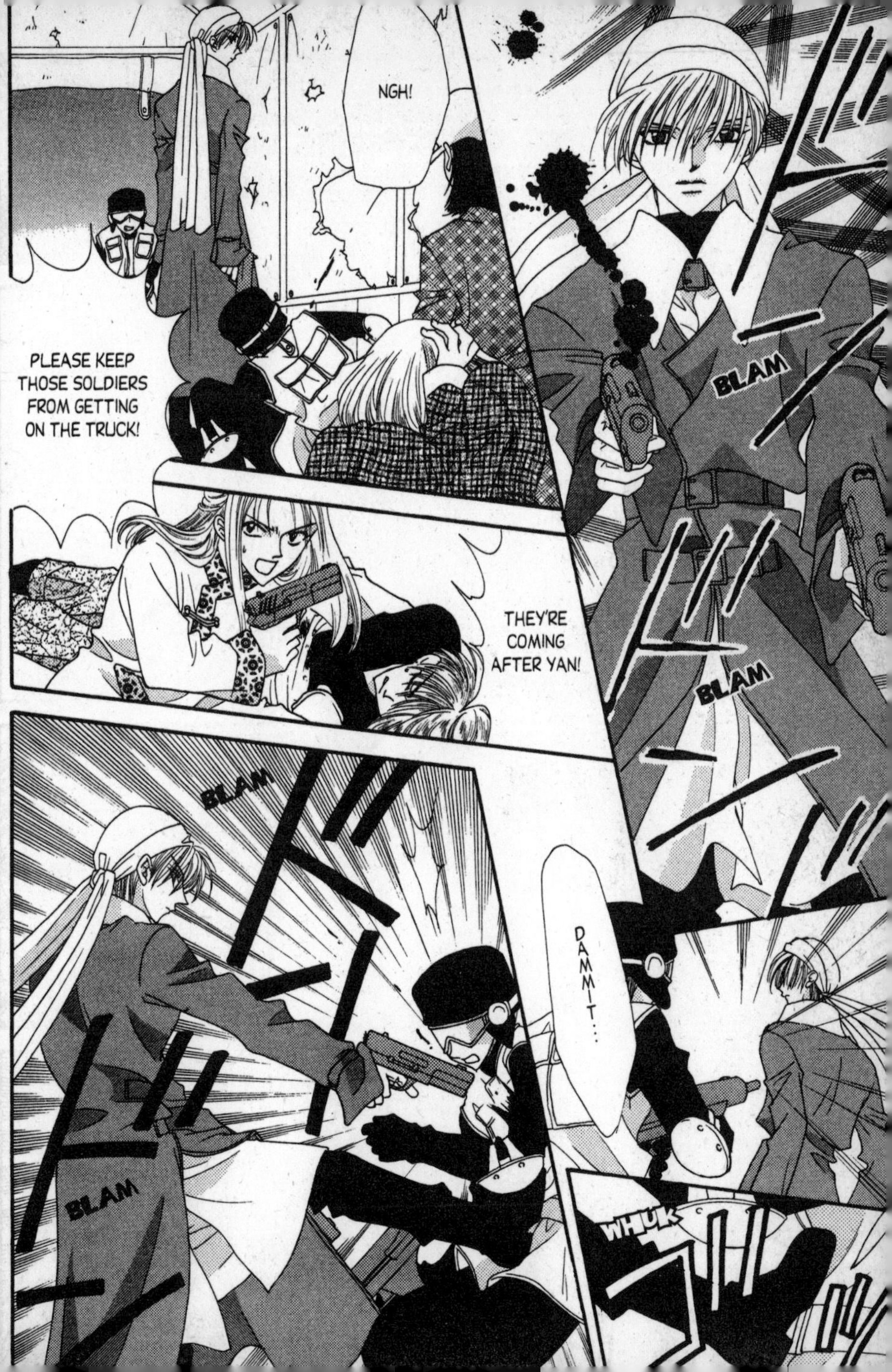
BLAM
BLAM
NGH!
PLEASE KEEP THOSE SOLDIERS FROM GETTING ON THE TRUCK!
THEY'RE COMING AFTER YAN!
DAMMIT...
WHUK
BLAM
BLAM

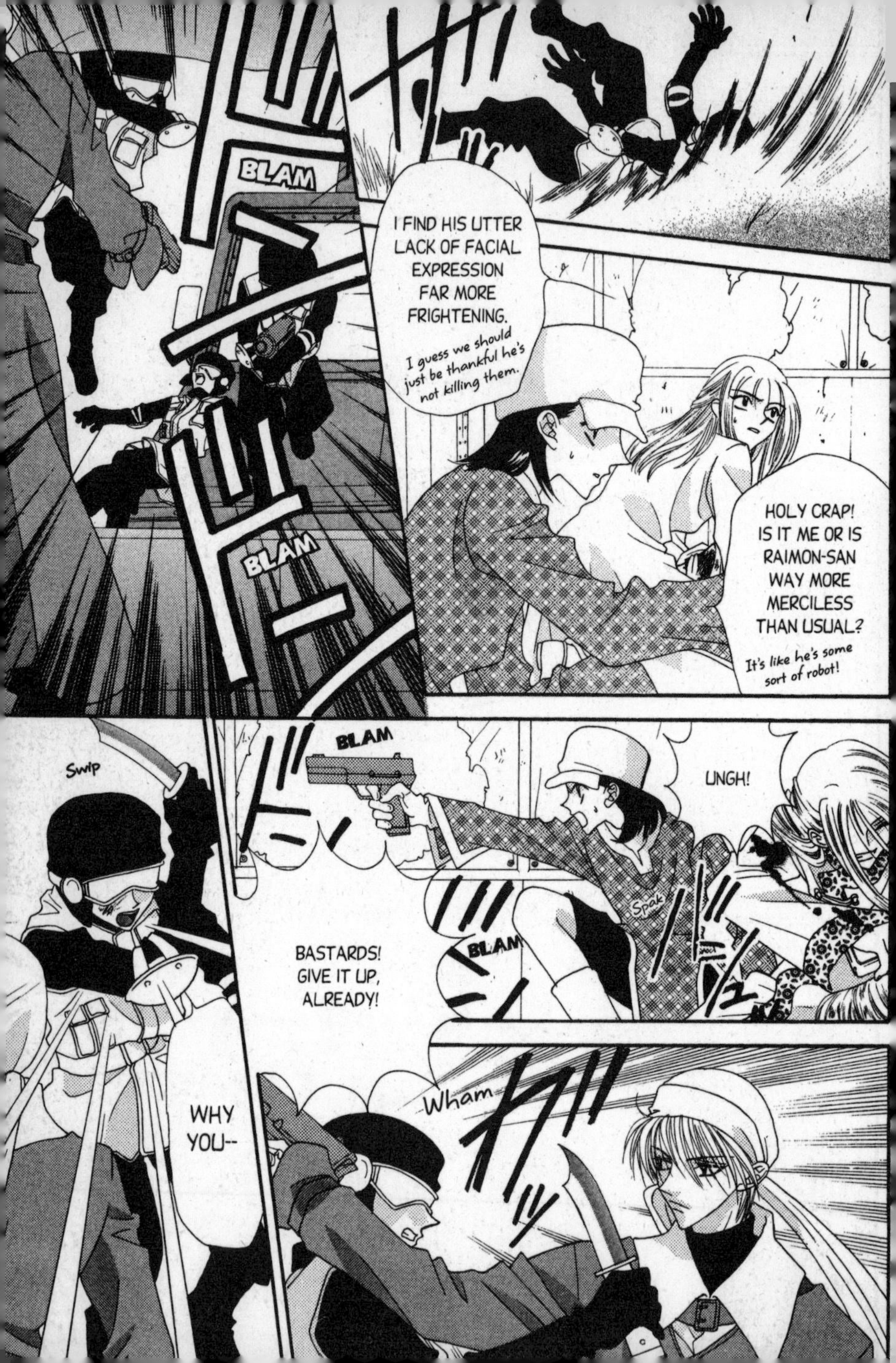
HOLY CRAP! IS IT ME OR IS RAIMON-SAN WAY MORE MERCILESS THAN USUAL?
It's like he's some sort of robot!
I FIND HIS UTTER LACK OF FACIAL EXPRESSION FAR MORE FRIGHTENING.
I guess we should just be thankful he's not killing them.
BLAM
BLAM
UNGH!
BLAM
Spak
BLAM
BASTARDS! GIVE IT UP, ALREADY!
Wham
Swip
WHY YOU--

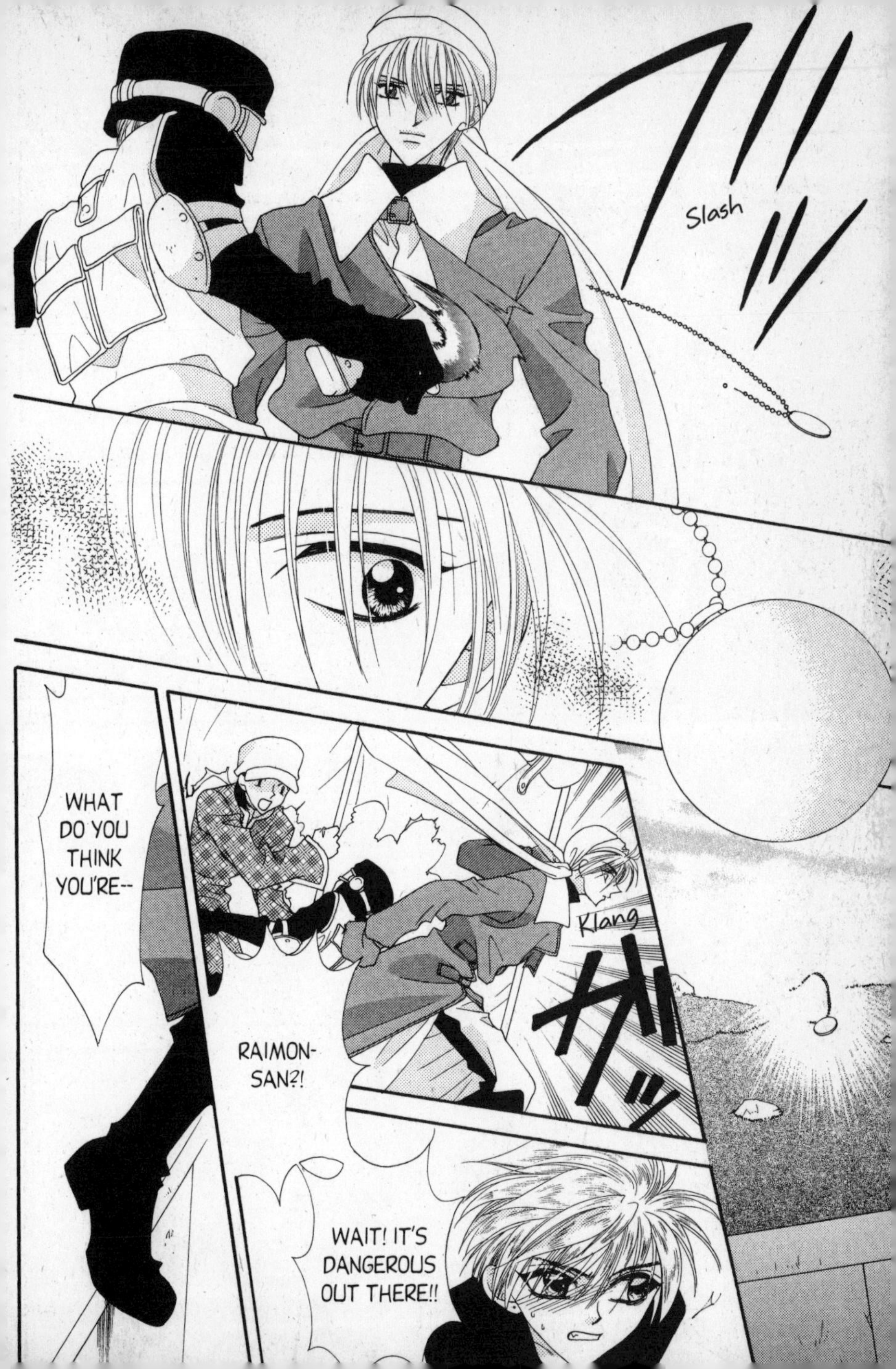
Slash
Klang
RAIMON-SAN?!
WAIT! IT'S DANGEROUS OUT THERE!!
WHAT DO YOU THINK YOU'RE--

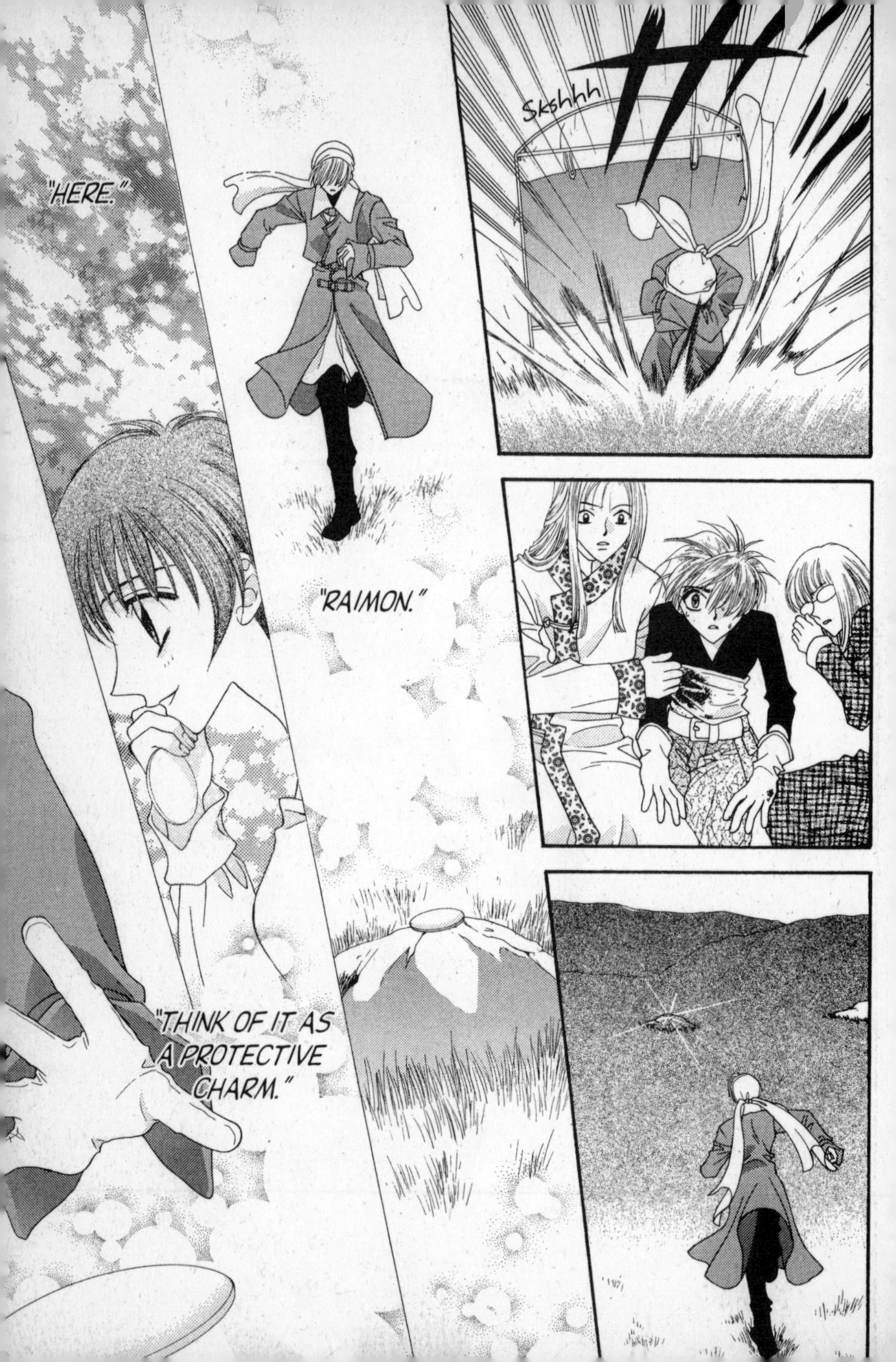

Skshhh
"HERE."
"RAIMON."
"THINK OF IT AS A PROTECTIVE CHARM."

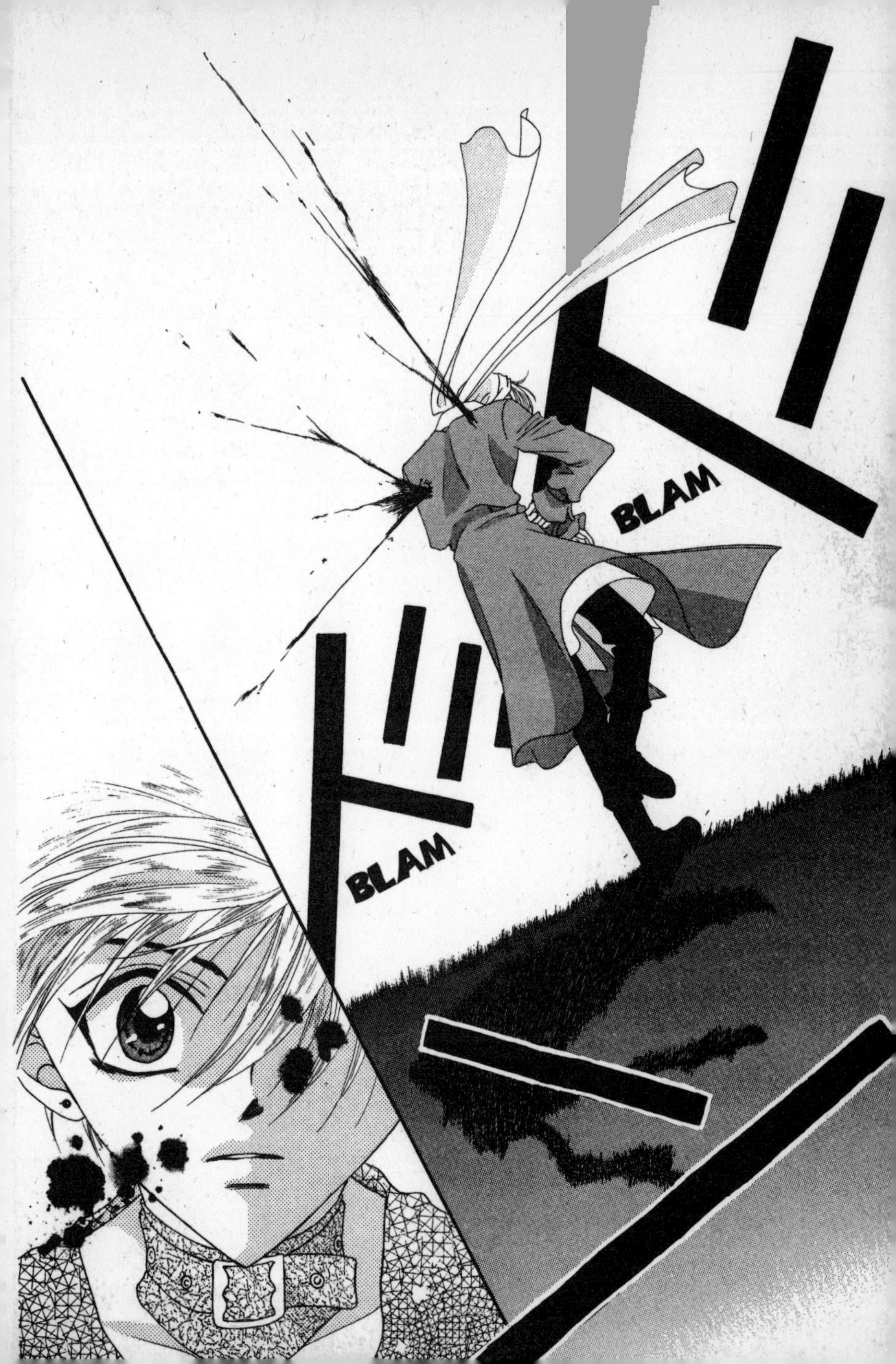
BLAM
BLAM

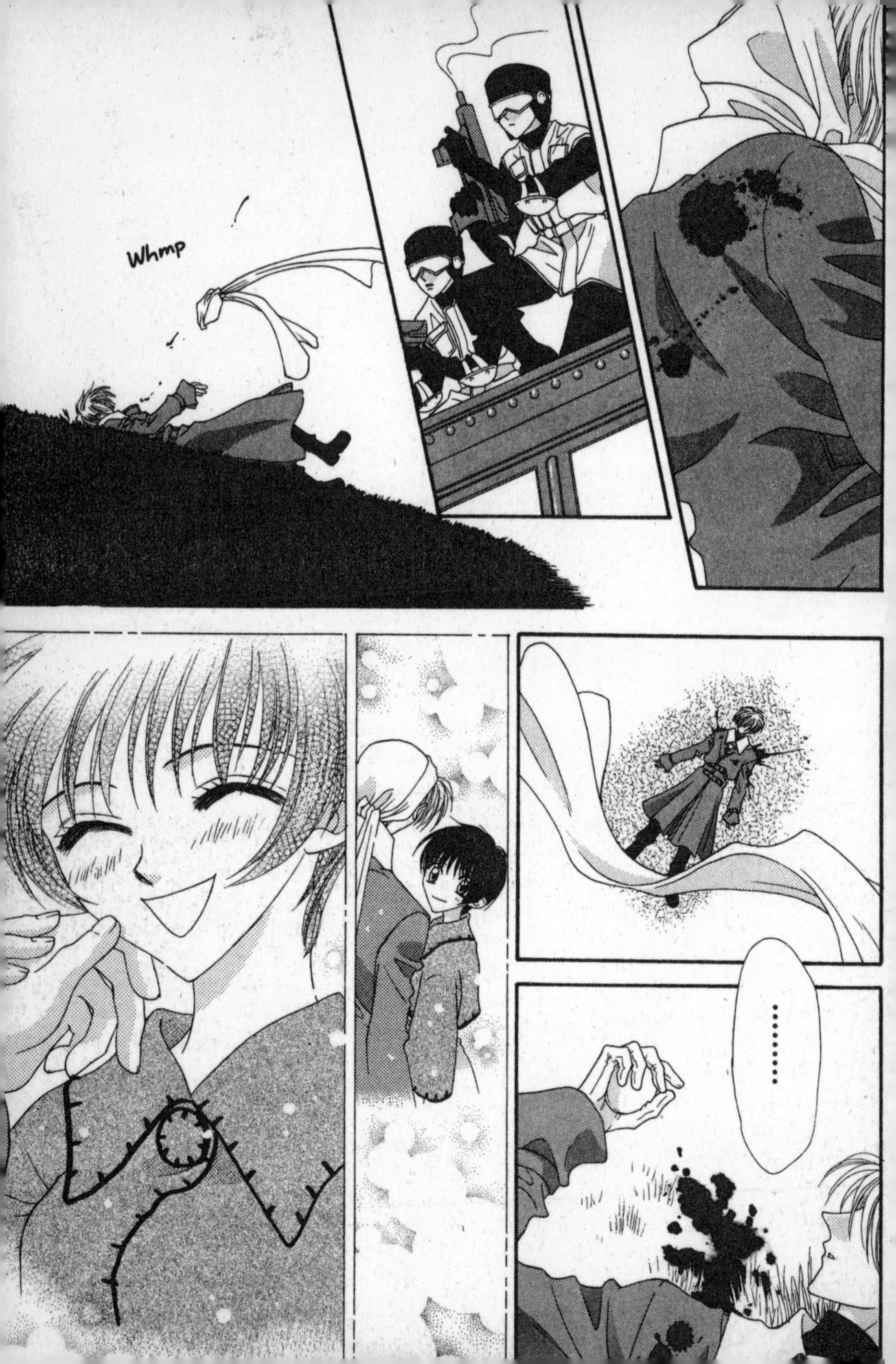
Whmp
....

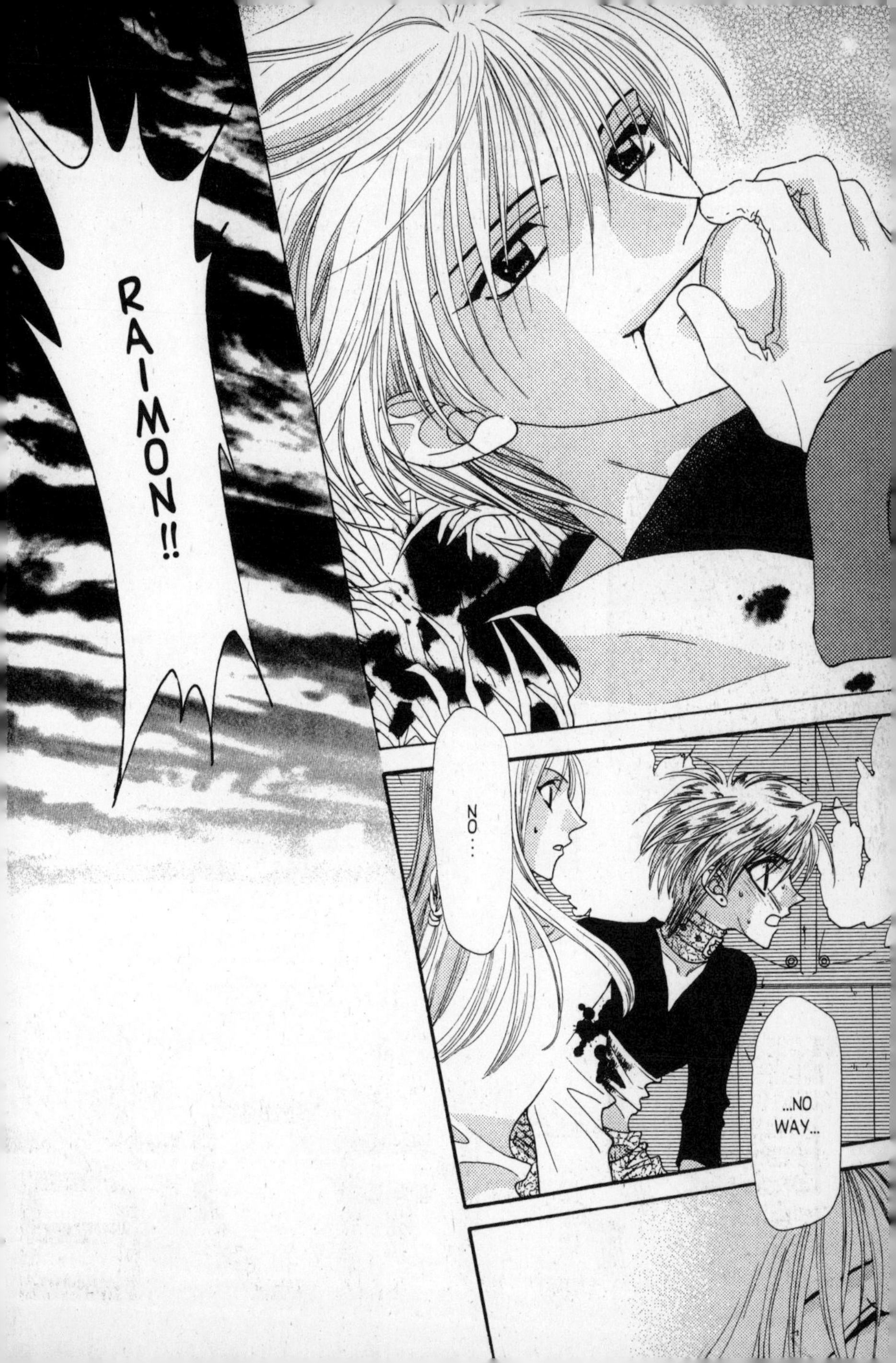
RAIMON!!
NO...
...NO WAY...

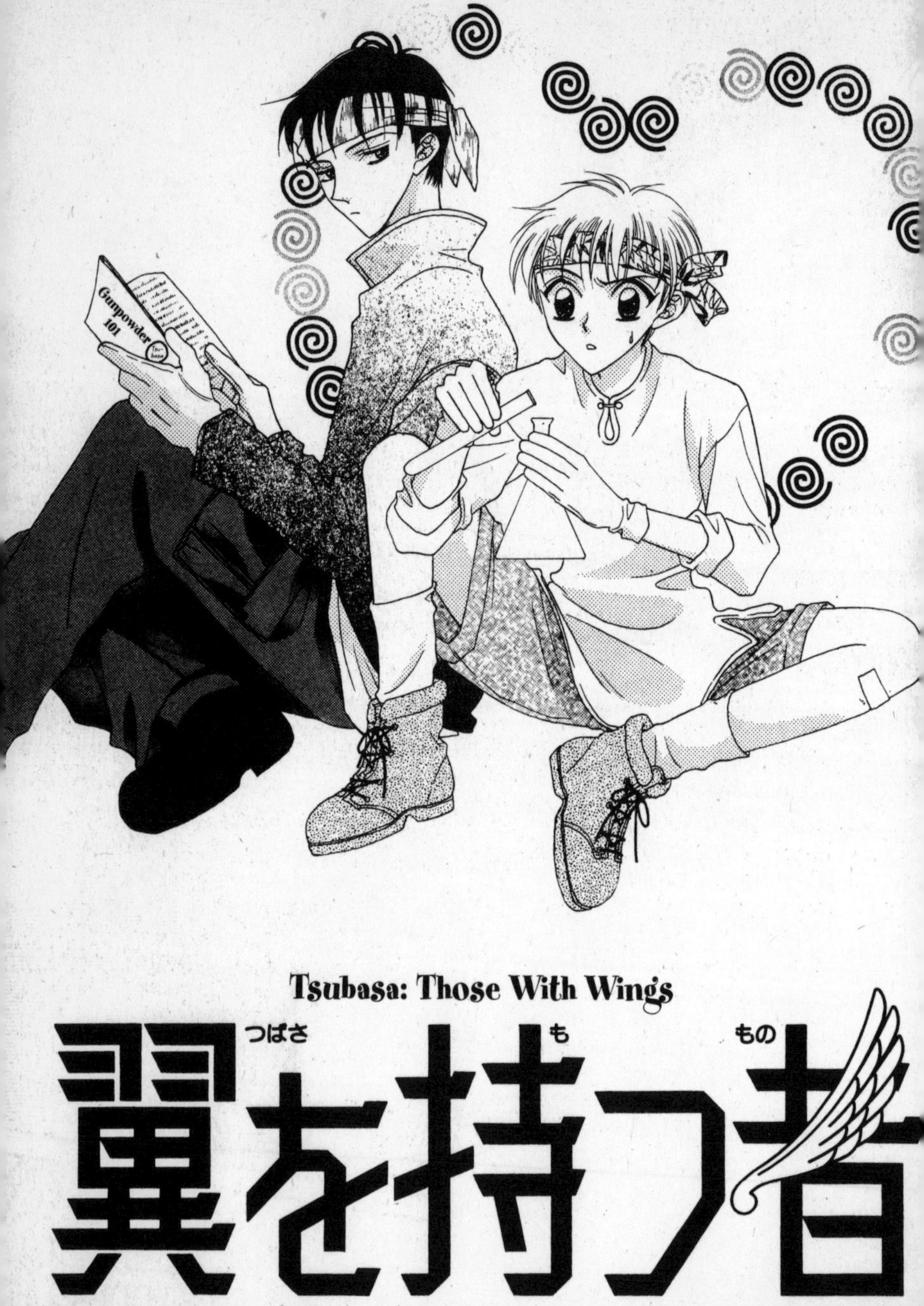
Gunpowder 101

Tsubasa: Those With Wings

翼(つばさ)を持(も)つ者(もの)

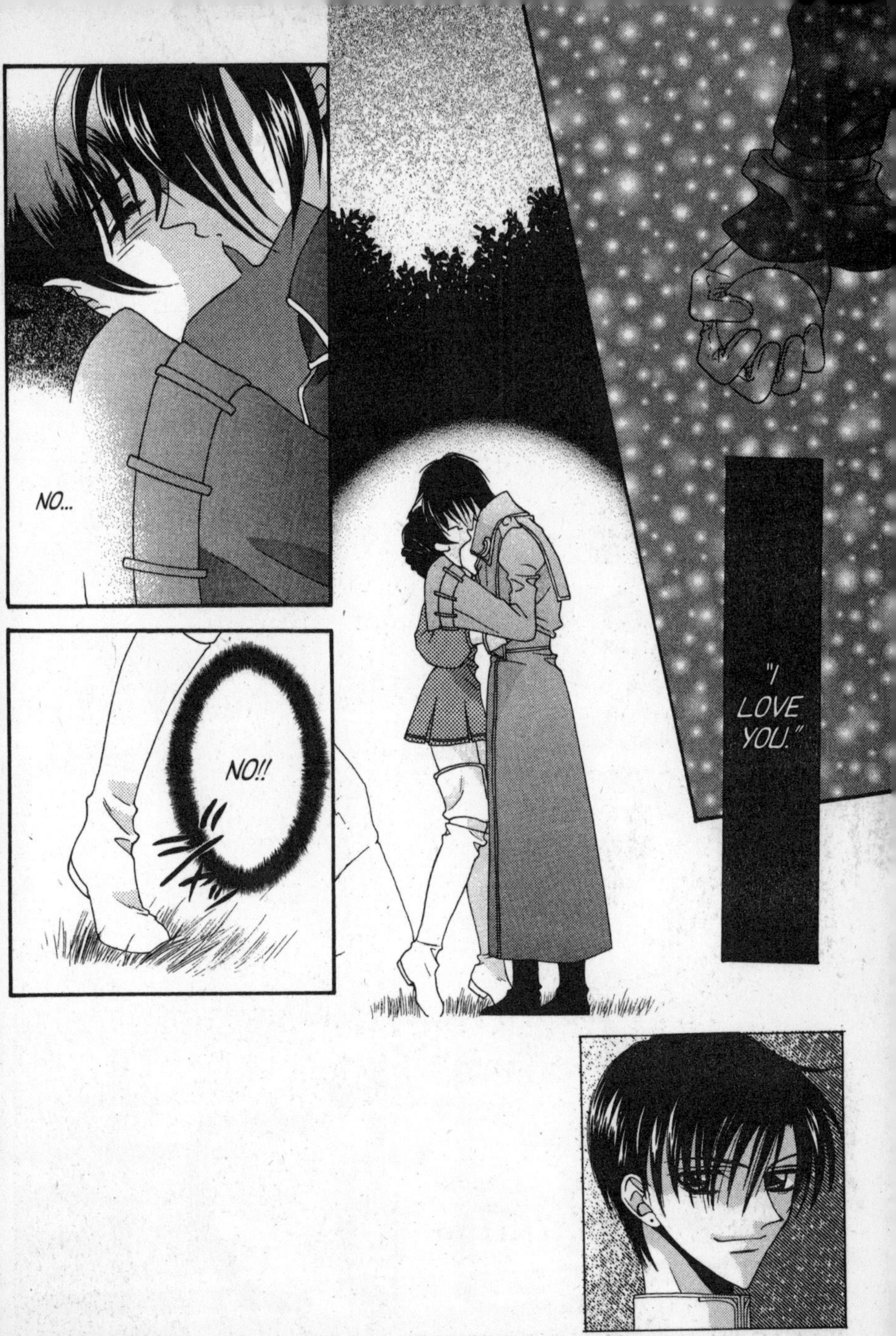
"I LOVE YOU."
NO...
NO!!

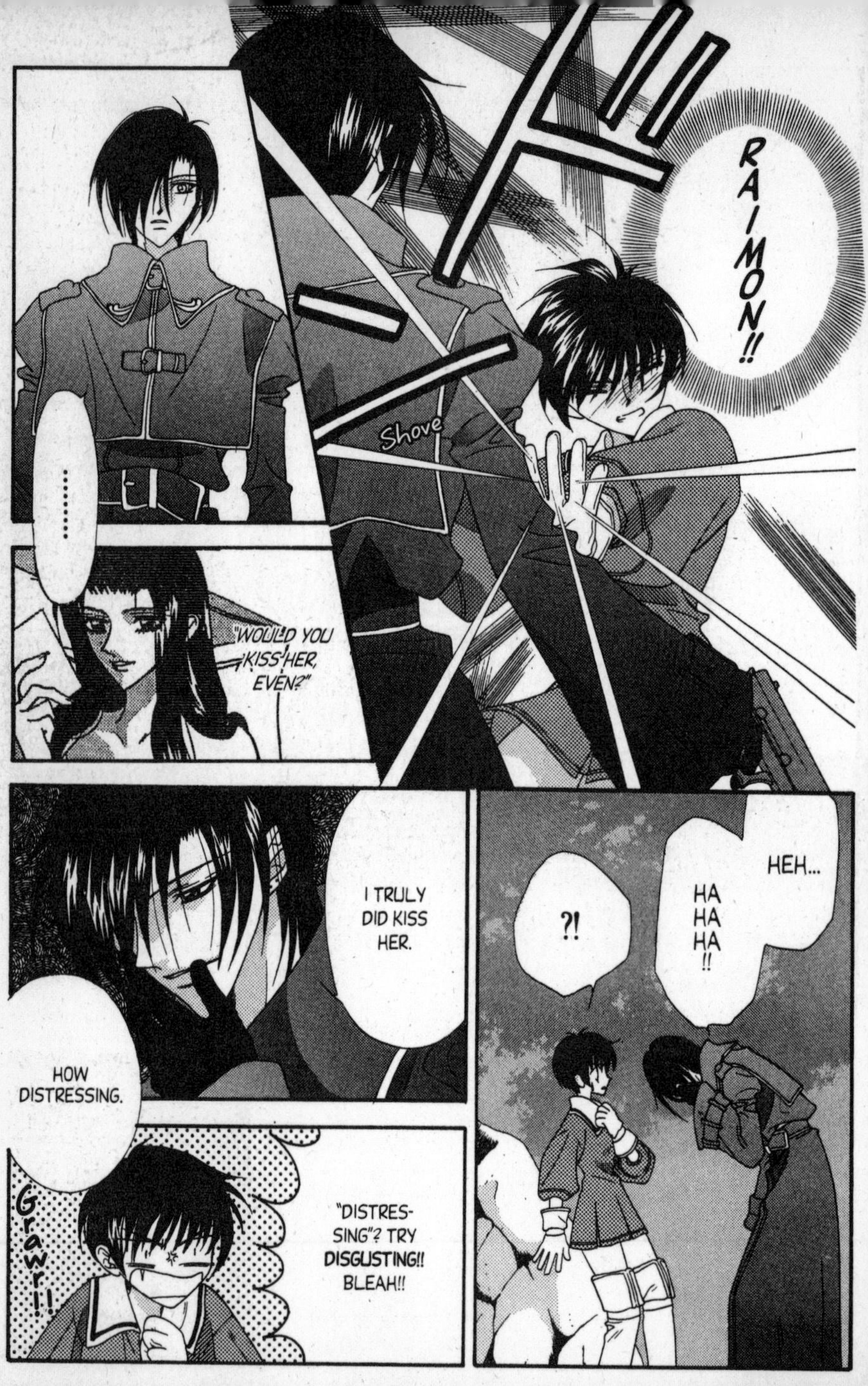
RAIMON!!
Shove
......
"WOULD YOU KISS HER, EVEN?"
HEH...
HA HA HA!!
?!
I TRULY DID KISS HER.
HOW DISTRESSING.
"DISTRES-SING"? TRY DISGUSTING!! BLEAH!!
Grawr!!

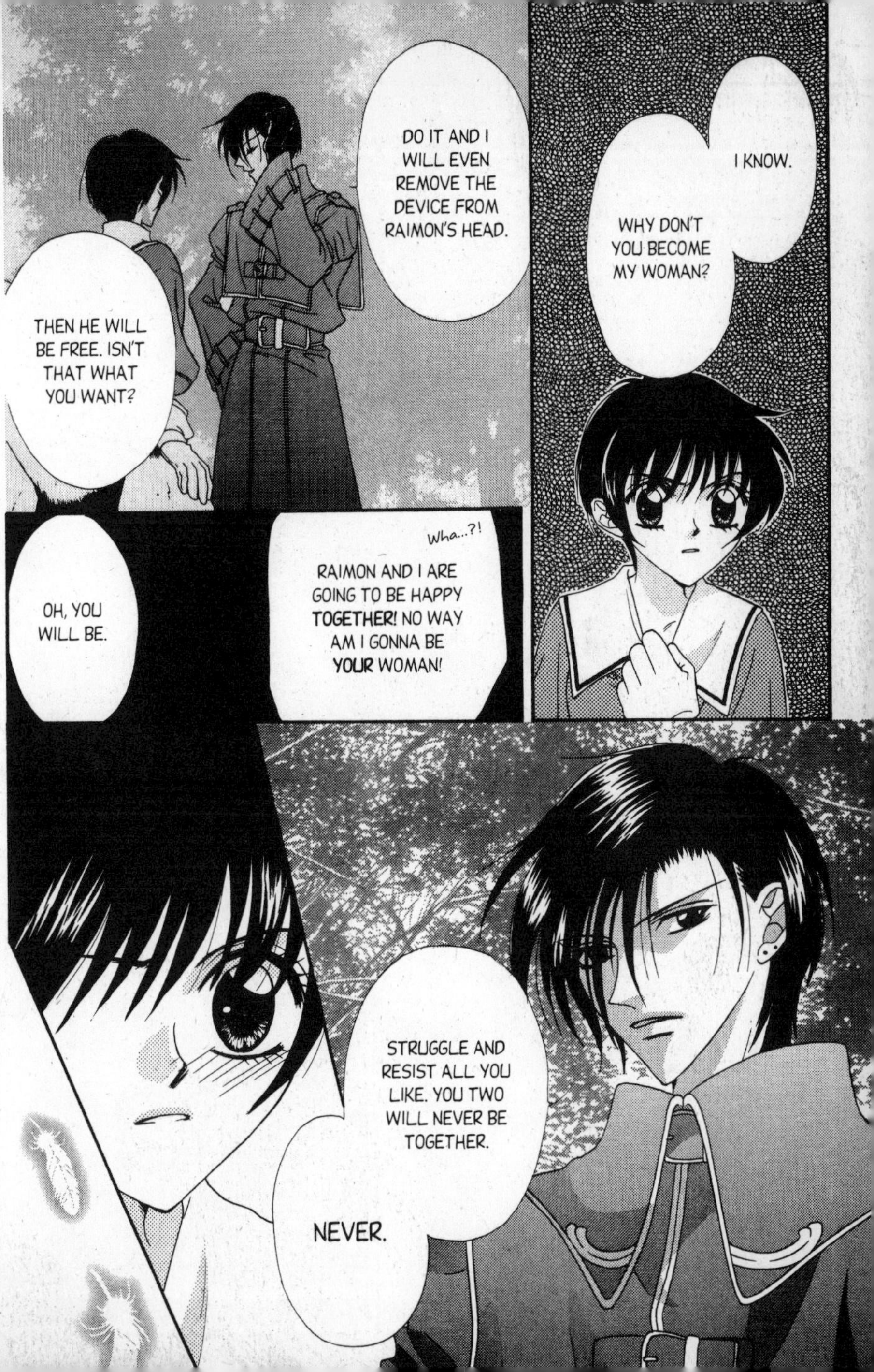
I KNOW.
WHY DON'T YOU BECOME MY WOMAN?
DO IT AND I WILL EVEN REMOVE THE DEVICE FROM RAIMON'S HEAD.
THEN HE WILL BE FREE. ISN'T THAT WHAT YOU WANT?
Wha...?!
RAIMON AND I ARE GOING TO BE HAPPY **TOGETHER!** NO WAY AM I GONNA BE **YOUR** WOMAN!
OH, YOU WILL BE.
STRUGGLE AND RESIST ALL YOU LIKE. YOU TWO WILL NEVER BE TOGETHER.
NEVER.

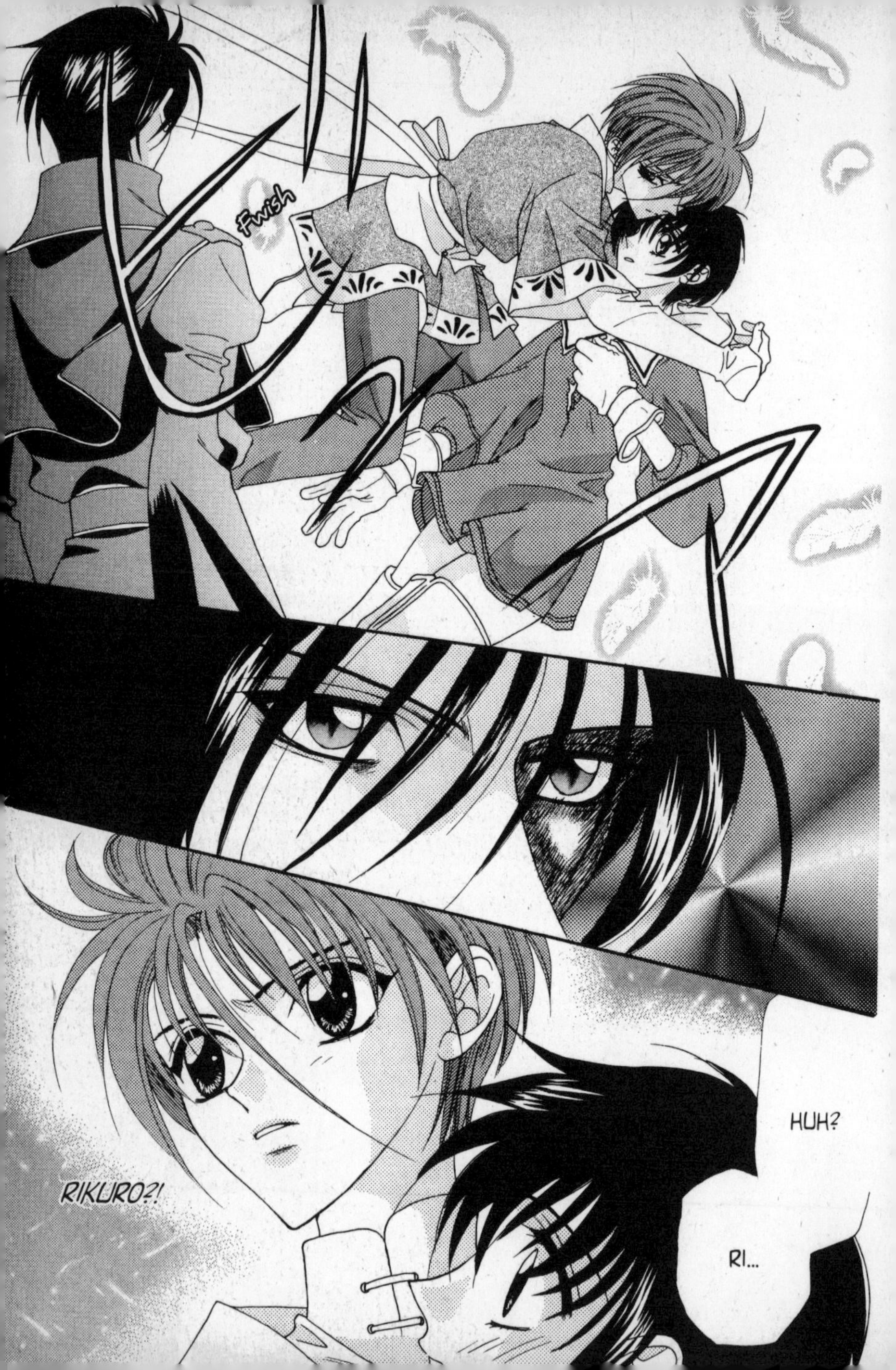
Fwish
HUH?
RI...
RIKURO?!

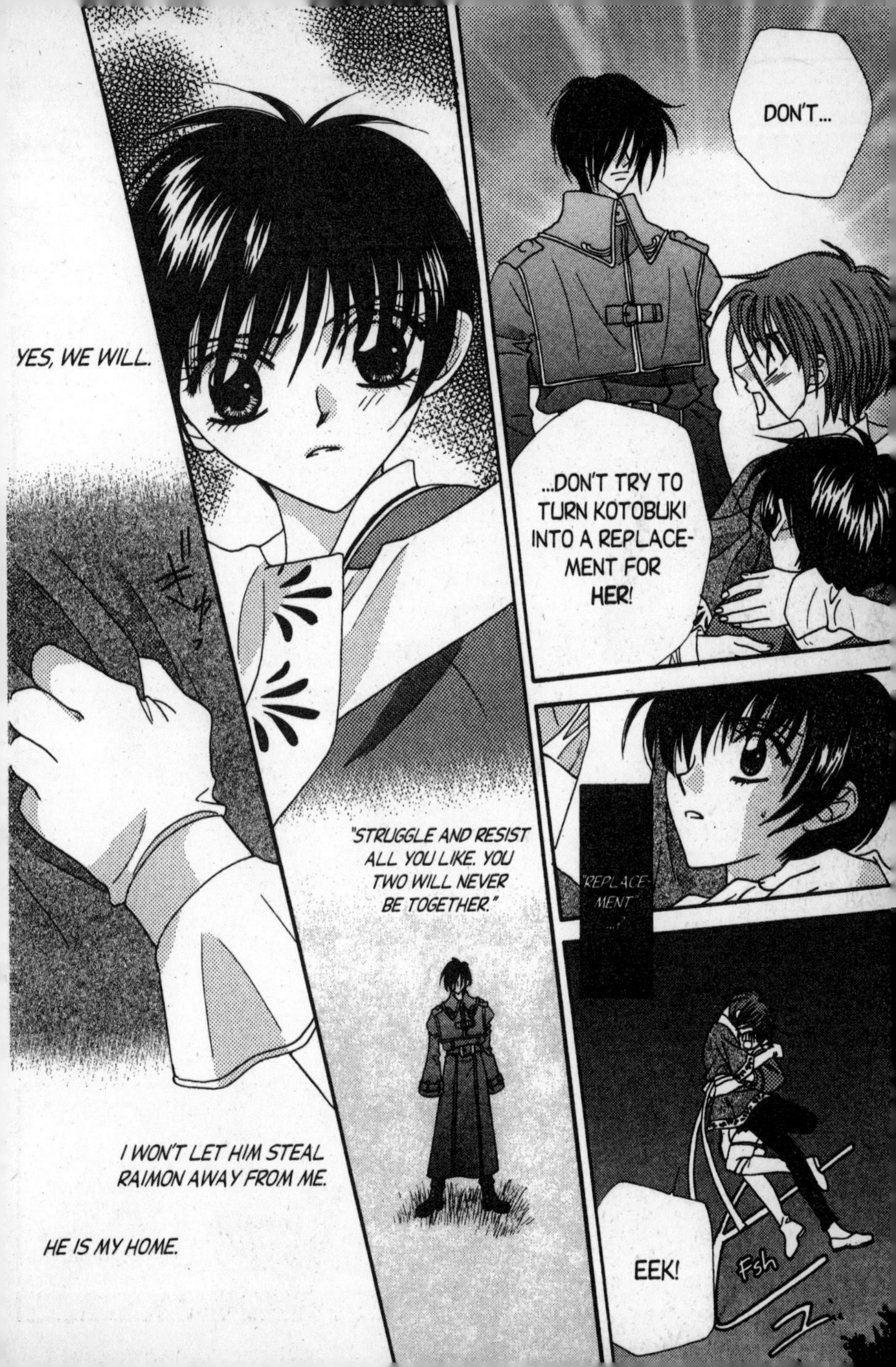

DON'T...
...DON'T TRY TO TURN KOTOBUKI INTO A REPLACE-MENT FOR HER!
"REPLACE-MENT" ...?
EEK!
Fsh
YES, WE WILL.
"STRUGGLE AND RESIST ALL YOU LIKE. YOU TWO WILL NEVER BE TOGETHER."
I WON'T LET HIM STEAL RAIMON AWAY FROM ME.
HE IS MY HOME.

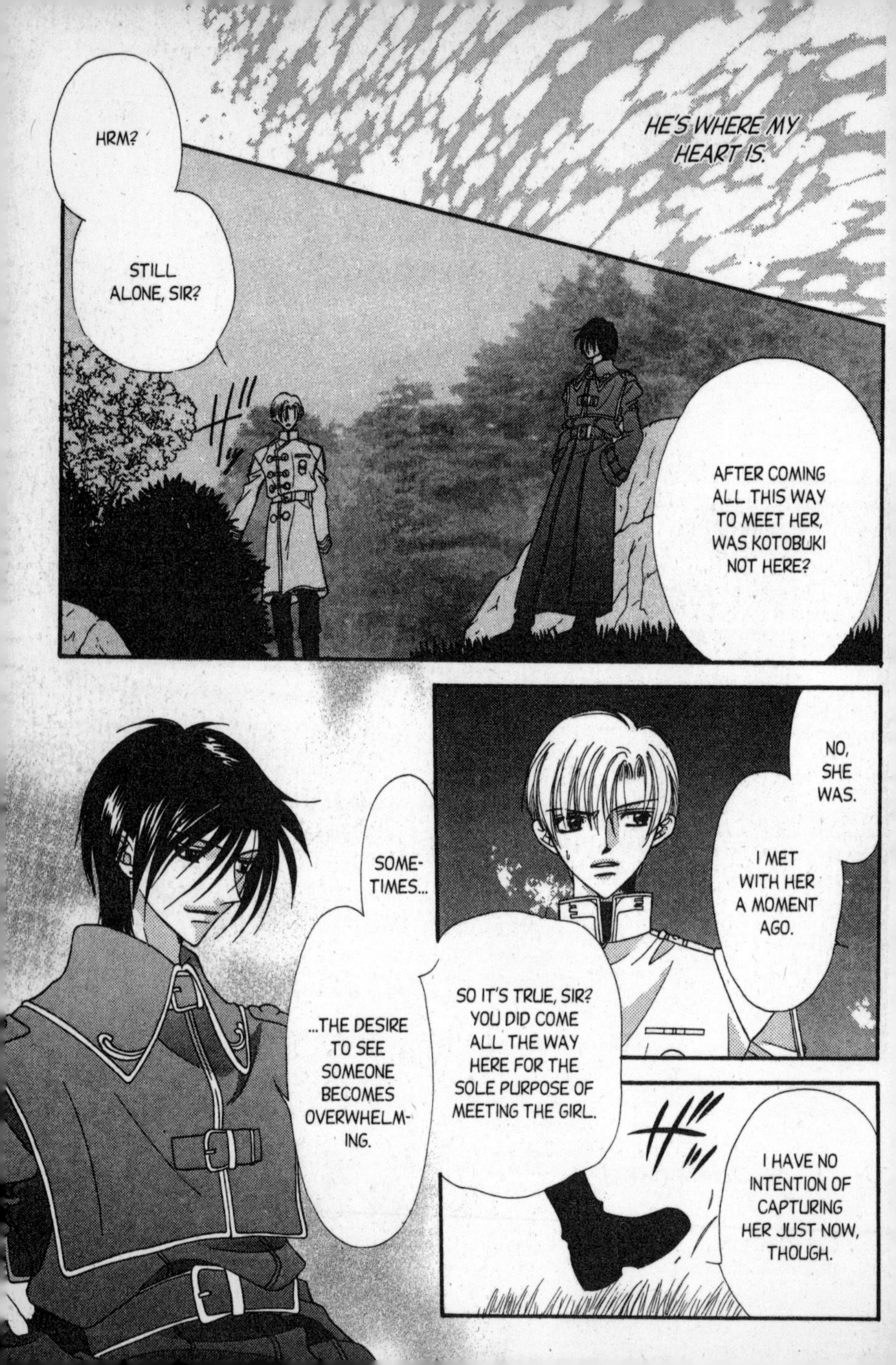
HE'S WHERE MY HEART IS.
HRM?
STILL ALONE, SIR?
AFTER COMING ALL THIS WAY TO MEET HER, WAS KOTOBUKI NOT HERE?
NO, SHE WAS.
I MET WITH HER A MOMENT AGO.
I HAVE NO INTENTION OF CAPTURING HER JUST NOW, THOUGH.
SO IT'S TRUE, SIR? YOU DID COME ALL THE WAY HERE FOR THE SOLE PURPOSE OF MEETING THE GIRL.
SOME-TIMES...
...THE DESIRE TO SEE SOMEONE BECOMES OVERWHELM-ING.

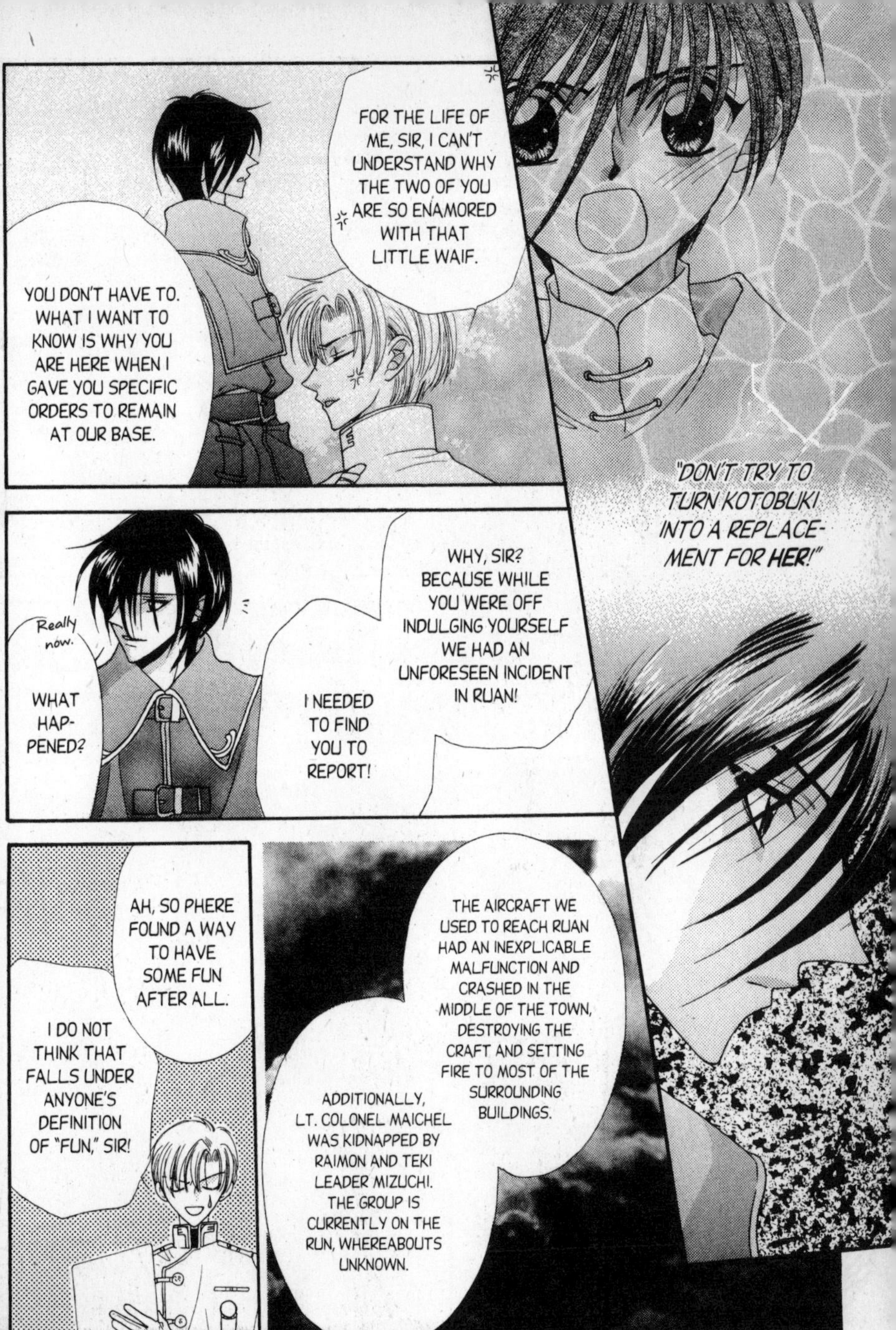
"DON'T TRY TO TURN KOTOBUKI INTO A REPLACEMENT FOR **HER**!"
FOR THE LIFE OF ME, SIR, I CAN'T UNDERSTAND WHY THE TWO OF YOU ARE SO ENAMORED WITH THAT LITTLE WAIF.
YOU DON'T HAVE TO. WHAT I WANT TO KNOW IS WHY YOU ARE HERE WHEN I GAVE YOU SPECIFIC ORDERS TO REMAIN AT OUR BASE.
WHY, SIR? BECAUSE WHILE YOU WERE OFF INDULGING YOURSELF WE HAD AN UNFORESEEN INCIDENT IN RUAN!
I NEEDED TO FIND YOU TO REPORT!
Really now.
WHAT HAPPENED?
THE AIRCRAFT WE USED TO REACH RUAN HAD AN INEXPLICABLE MALFUNCTION AND CRASHED IN THE MIDDLE OF THE TOWN, DESTROYING THE CRAFT AND SETTING FIRE TO MOST OF THE SURROUNDING BUILDINGS.
ADDITIONALLY, LT. COLONEL MAICHEL WAS KIDNAPPED BY RAIMON AND TEKI LEADER MIZUCHI. THE GROUP IS CURRENTLY ON THE RUN, WHEREABOUTS UNKNOWN.
AH, SO PHERE FOUND A WAY TO HAVE SOME FUN AFTER ALL.
I DO NOT THINK THAT FALLS UNDER ANYONE'S DEFINITION OF "FUN," SIR!

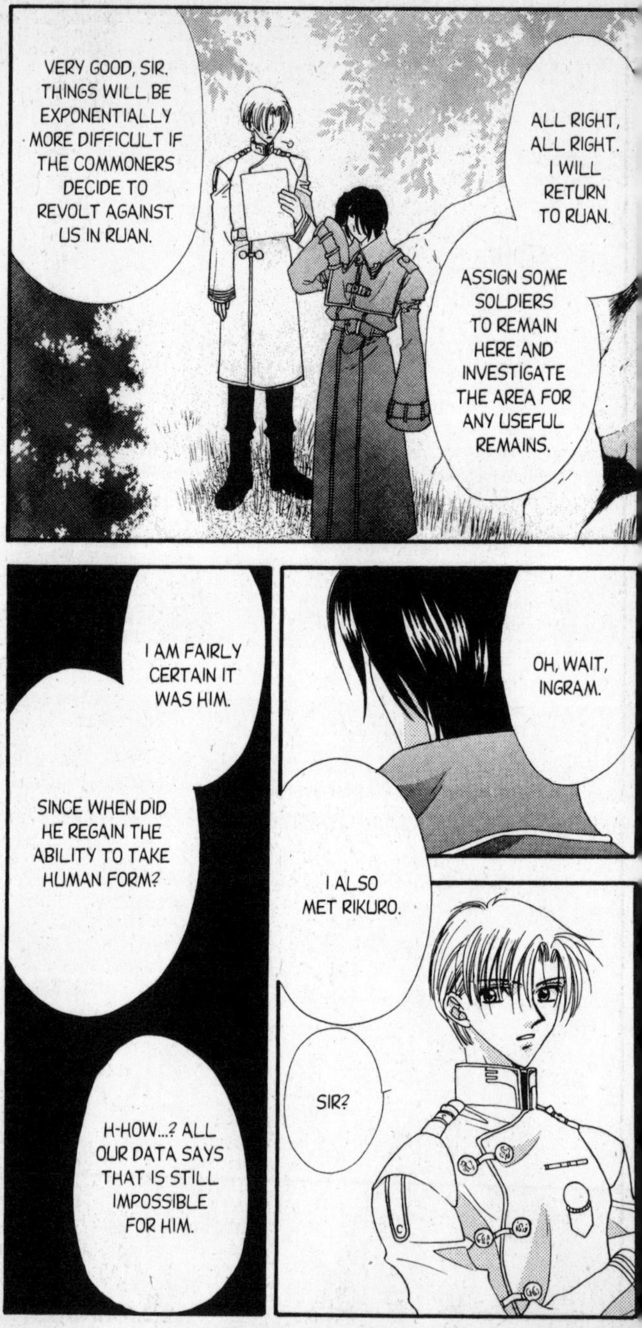
ALL RIGHT, ALL RIGHT. I WILL RETURN TO RUAN.
ASSIGN SOME SOLDIERS TO REMAIN HERE AND INVESTIGATE THE AREA FOR ANY USEFUL REMAINS.
VERY GOOD, SIR. THINGS WILL BE EXPONENTIALLY MORE DIFFICULT IF THE COMMONERS DECIDE TO REVOLT AGAINST US IN RUAN.
OH, WAIT, INGRAM.
I ALSO MET RIKURO.
SIR?
I AM FAIRLY CERTAIN IT WAS HIM.
SINCE WHEN DID HE REGAIN THE ABILITY TO TAKE HUMAN FORM?
H-HOW...? ALL OUR DATA SAYS THAT IS STILL IMPOSSIBLE FOR HIM.

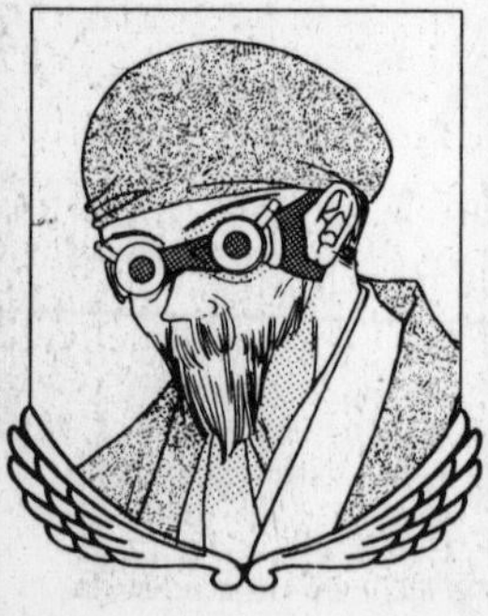

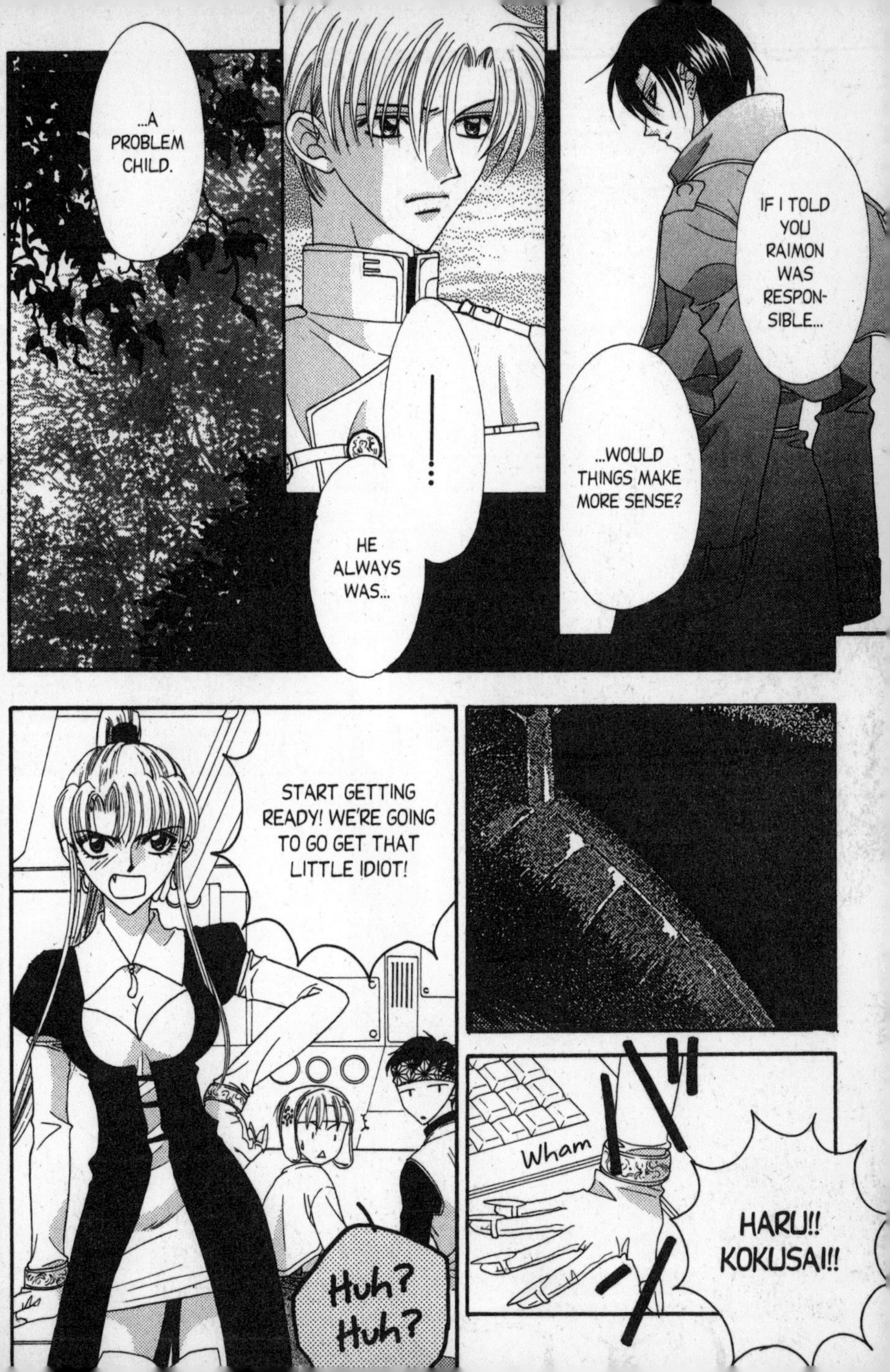

IF I TOLD YOU RAIMON WAS RESPONSIBLE...
...WOULD THINGS MAKE MORE SENSE?
...
HE ALWAYS WAS...
...A PROBLEM CHILD.
Wham
HARU!! KOKUSAI!!
START GETTING READY! WE'RE GOING TO GO GET THAT LITTLE IDIOT!
Huh? Huh?

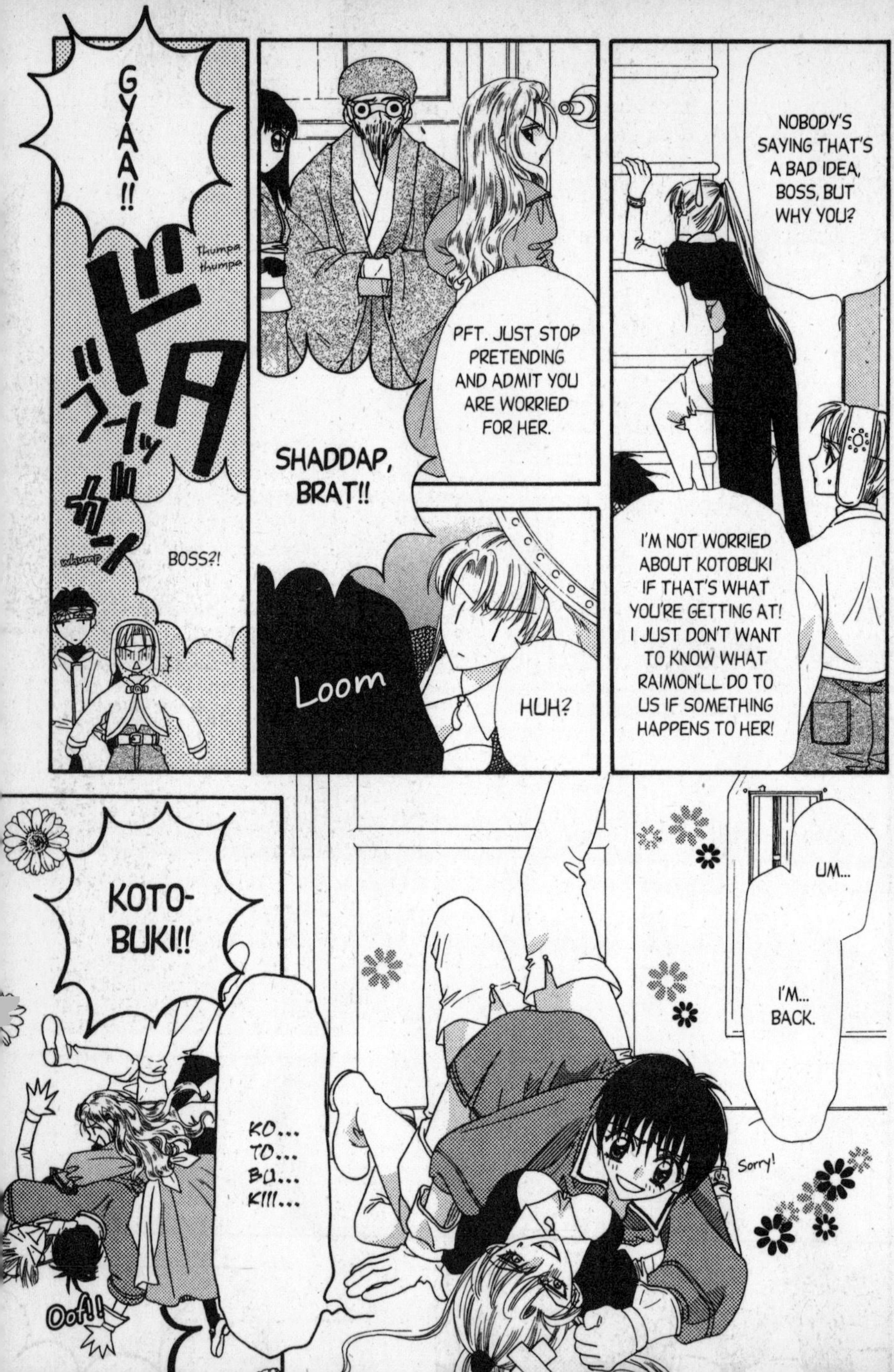
NOBODY'S SAYING THAT'S A BAD IDEA, BOSS, BUT WHY YOU?
I'M NOT WORRIED ABOUT KOTOBUKI IF THAT'S WHAT YOU'RE GETTING AT! I JUST DON'T WANT TO KNOW WHAT RAIMON'LL DO TO US IF SOMETHING HAPPENS TO HER!
PFT. JUST STOP PRETENDING AND ADMIT YOU ARE WORRIED FOR HER.
HUH?
Loom
SHADDAP, BRAT!!
GYAA!!
Thumpa thumpa
whump
BOSS?!
UM...
I'M... BACK.
Sorry!
KOTO-BUKI!!
KO... TO... BU... KI!!...
Oof!!

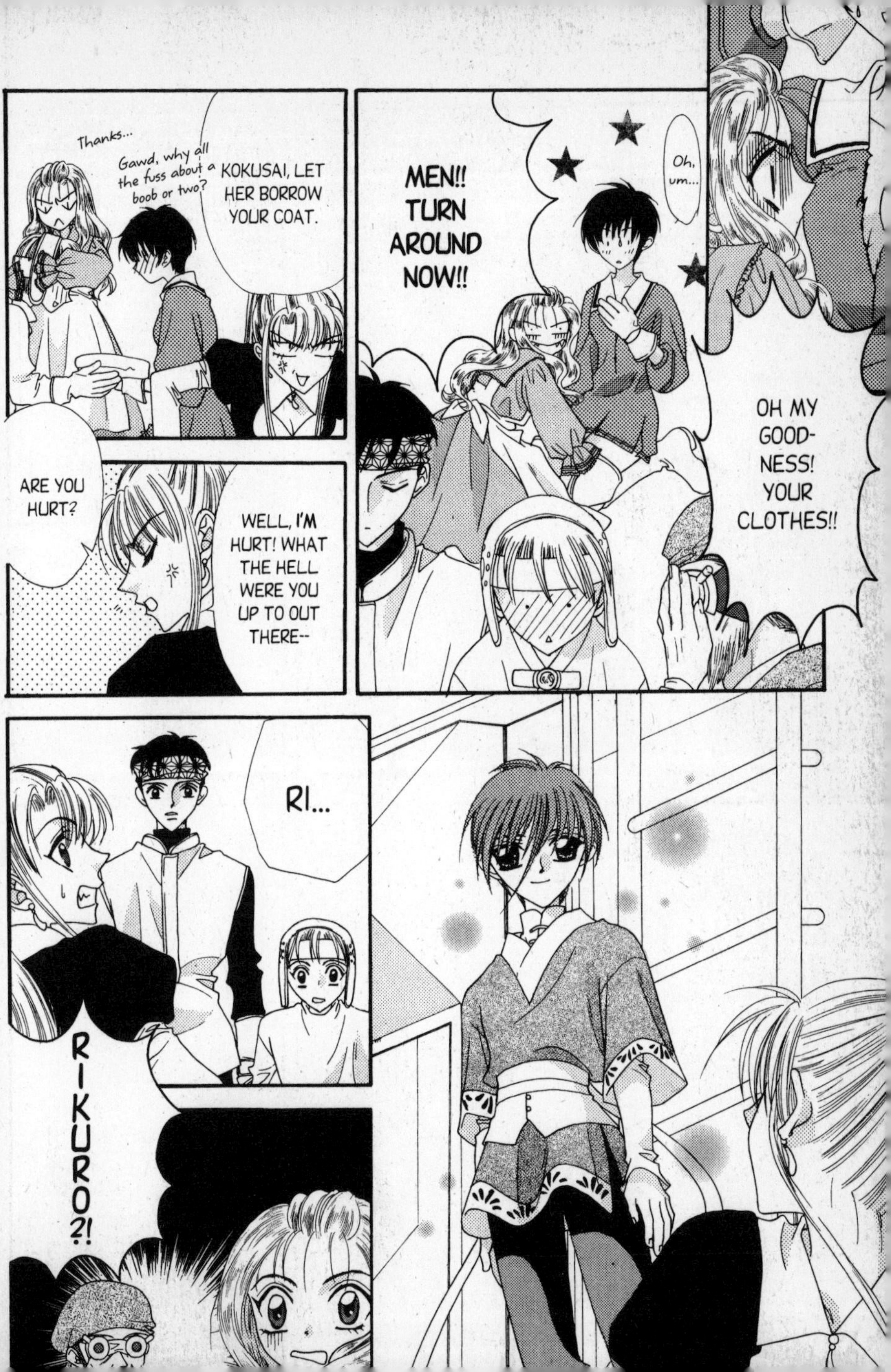
OH MY GOODNESS! YOUR CLOTHES!!
Oh, um...
MEN!! TURN AROUND NOW!!
KOKUSAI, LET HER BORROW YOUR COAT.
Gawd, why all the fuss about a boob or two?
Thanks...
WELL, I'M HURT! WHAT THE HELL WERE YOU UP TO OUT THERE--
ARE YOU HURT?
RI...
RIKURO?!

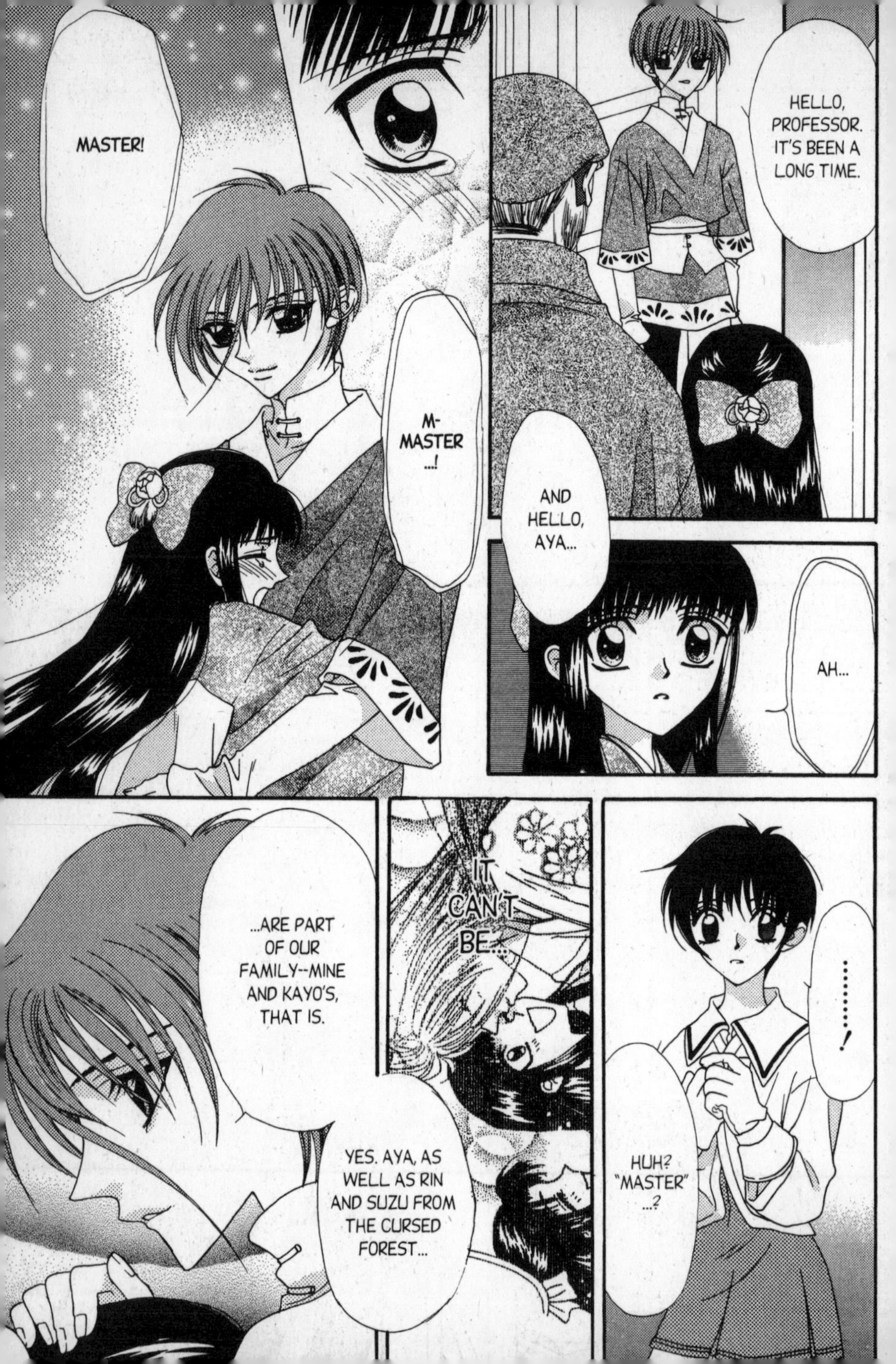
HELLO, PROFESSOR. IT'S BEEN A LONG TIME.
AND HELLO, AYA...
AH...
MASTER!
M-MASTER ...!
......!
HUH? "MASTER" ...?
IT CAN'T BE...
YES. AYA, AS WELL AS RIN AND SUZU FROM THE CURSED FOREST...
...ARE PART OF OUR FAMILY--MINE AND KAYO'S, THAT IS.

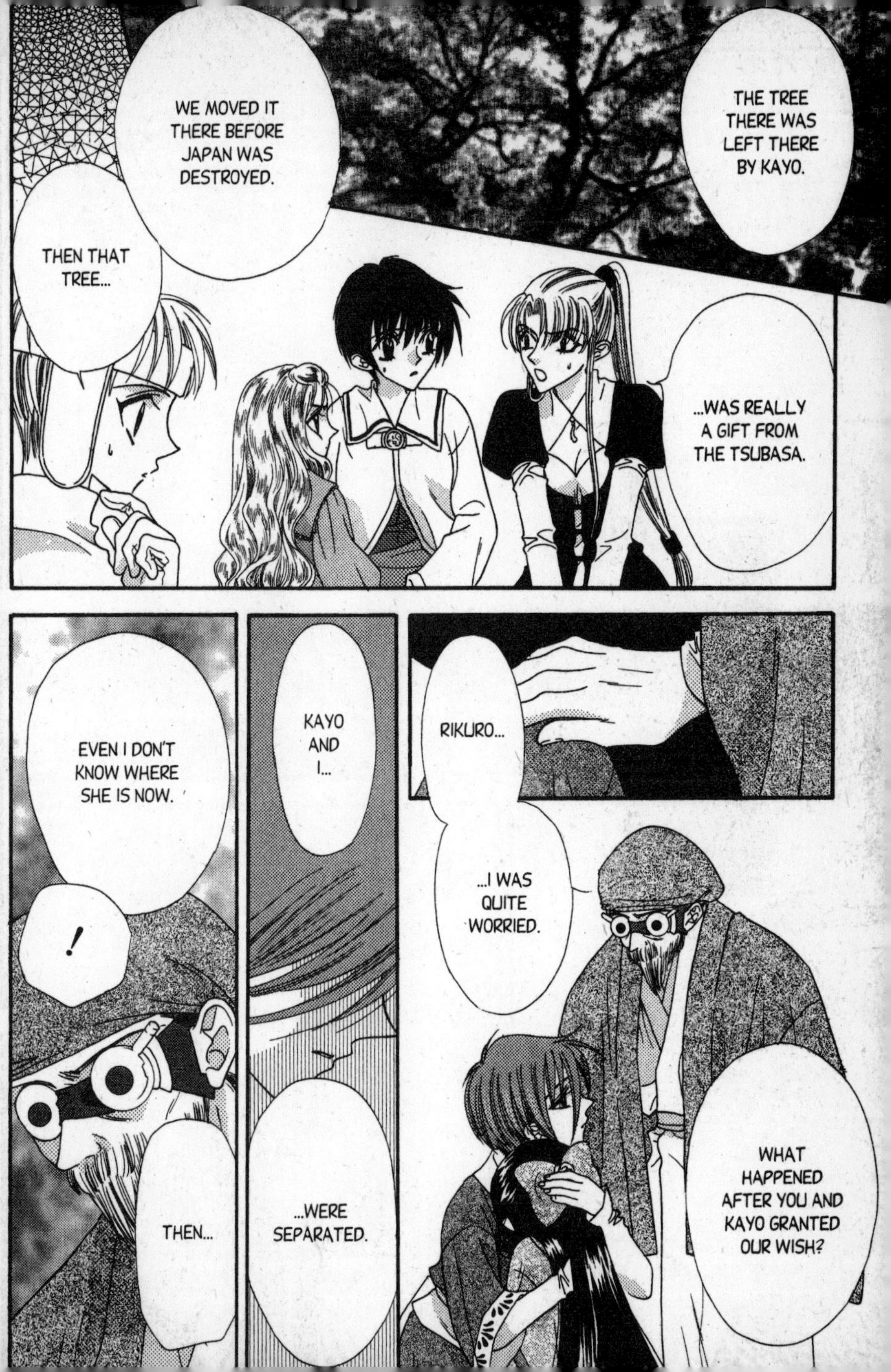
THE TREE THERE WAS LEFT THERE BY KAYO.
WE MOVED IT THERE BEFORE JAPAN WAS DESTROYED.
THEN THAT TREE...
...WAS REALLY A GIFT FROM THE TSUBASA.
RIKURO...
...I WAS QUITE WORRIED.
WHAT HAPPENED AFTER YOU AND KAYO GRANTED OUR WISH?
KAYO AND I...
...WERE SEPARATED.
EVEN I DON'T KNOW WHERE SHE IS NOW.
!
THEN...

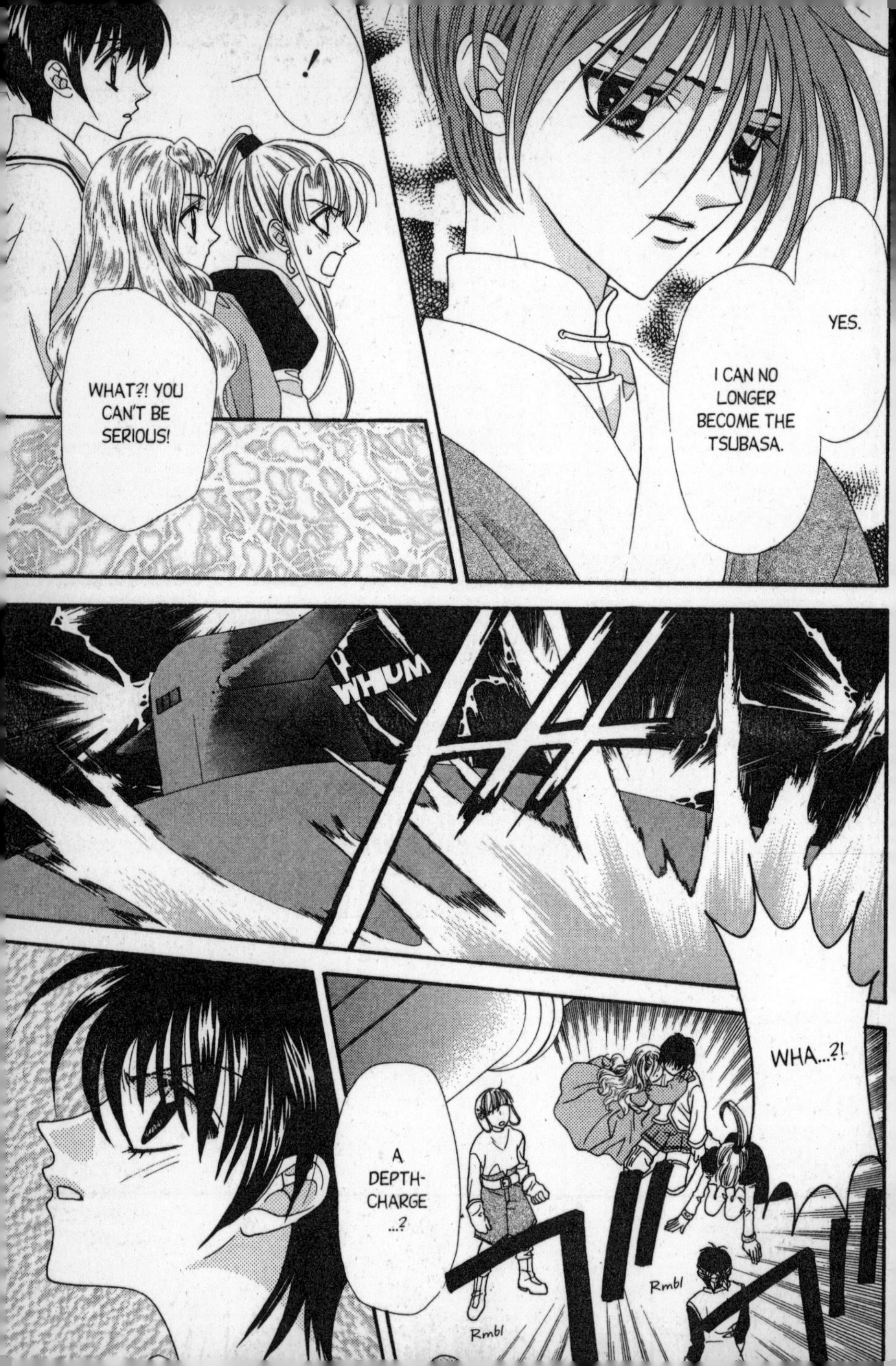
YES.
I CAN NO LONGER BECOME THE TSUBASA.
!
WHAT?! YOU CAN'T BE SERIOUS!
WHUM
WHA...?!
Rmbl
Rmbl
A DEPTH-CHARGE ...?

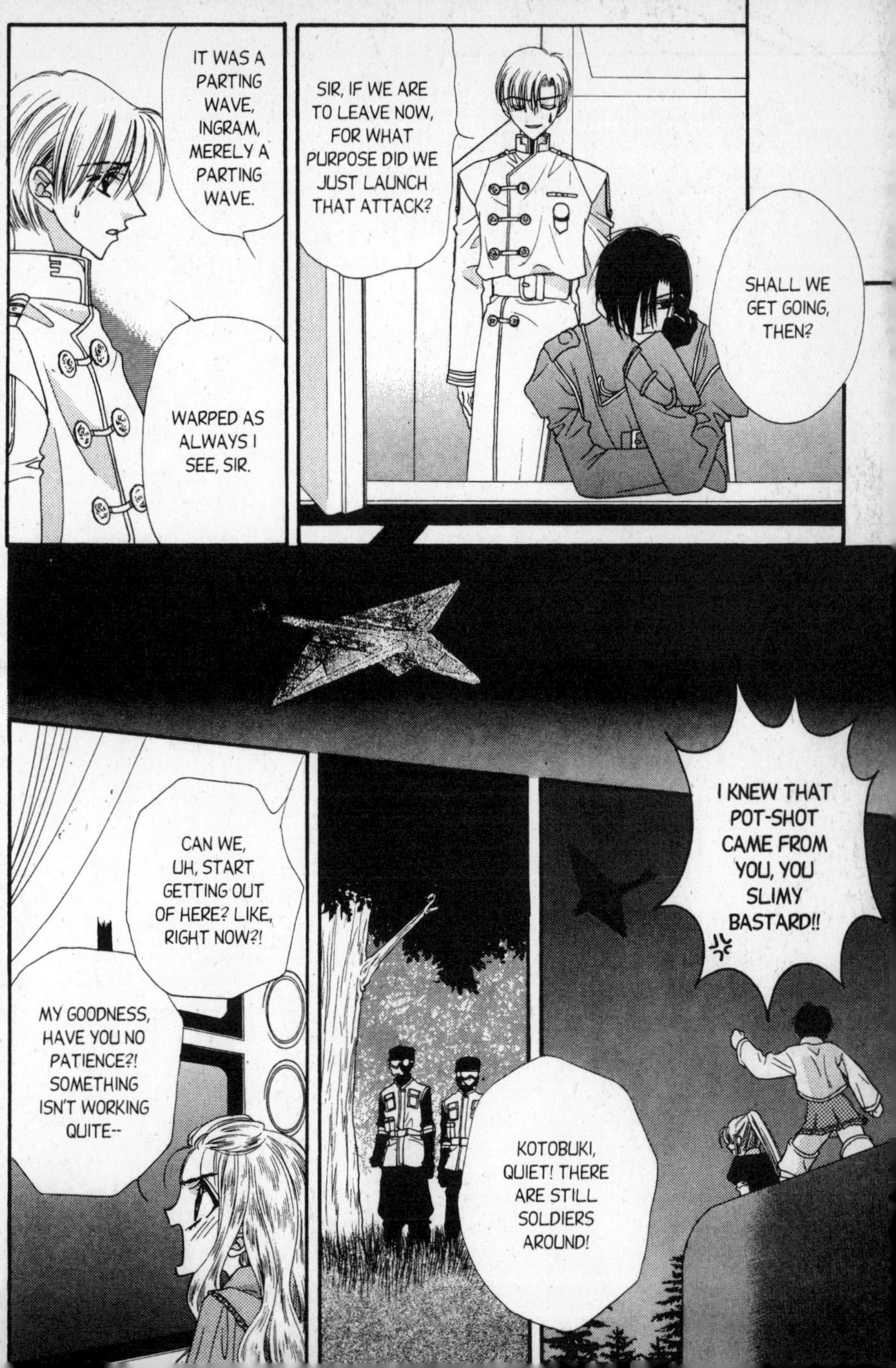
SHALL WE GET GOING, THEN?
SIR, IF WE ARE TO LEAVE NOW, FOR WHAT PURPOSE DID WE JUST LAUNCH THAT ATTACK?
IT WAS A PARTING WAVE, INGRAM, MERELY A PARTING WAVE.
WARPED AS ALWAYS I SEE, SIR.
I KNEW THAT POT-SHOT CAME FROM YOU, YOU SLIMY BASTARD!!
KOTOBUKI, QUIET! THERE ARE STILL SOLDIERS AROUND!
CAN WE, UH, START GETTING OUT OF HERE? LIKE, RIGHT NOW?!
MY GOODNESS, HAVE YOU NO PATIENCE?! SOMETHING ISN'T WORKING QUITE--

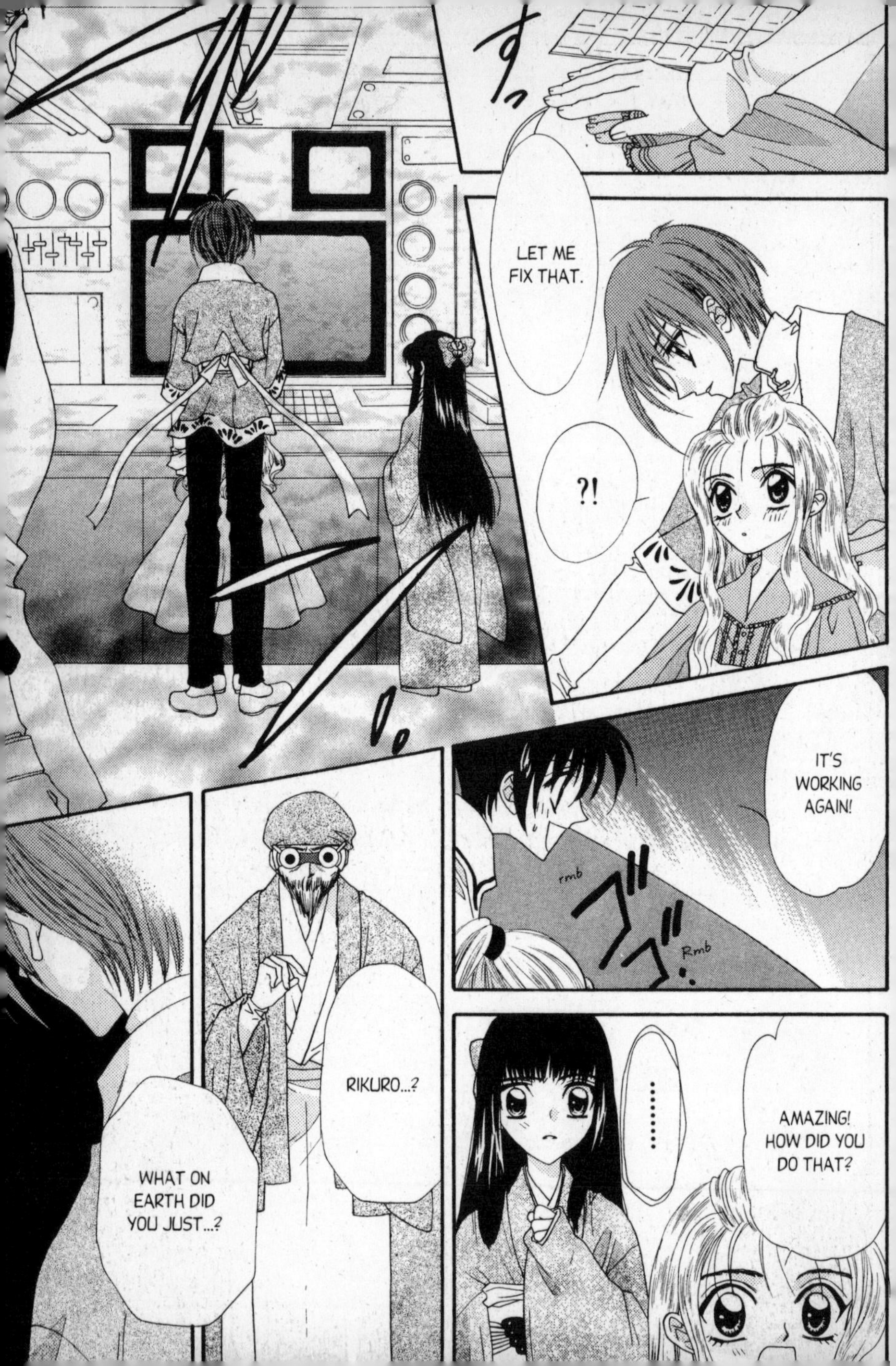
すっ
LET ME FIX THAT.
?!
IT'S WORKING AGAIN!
rmb
Rmb
AMAZING! HOW DID YOU DO THAT?
......
RIKURO...?
WHAT ON EARTH DID YOU JUST...?

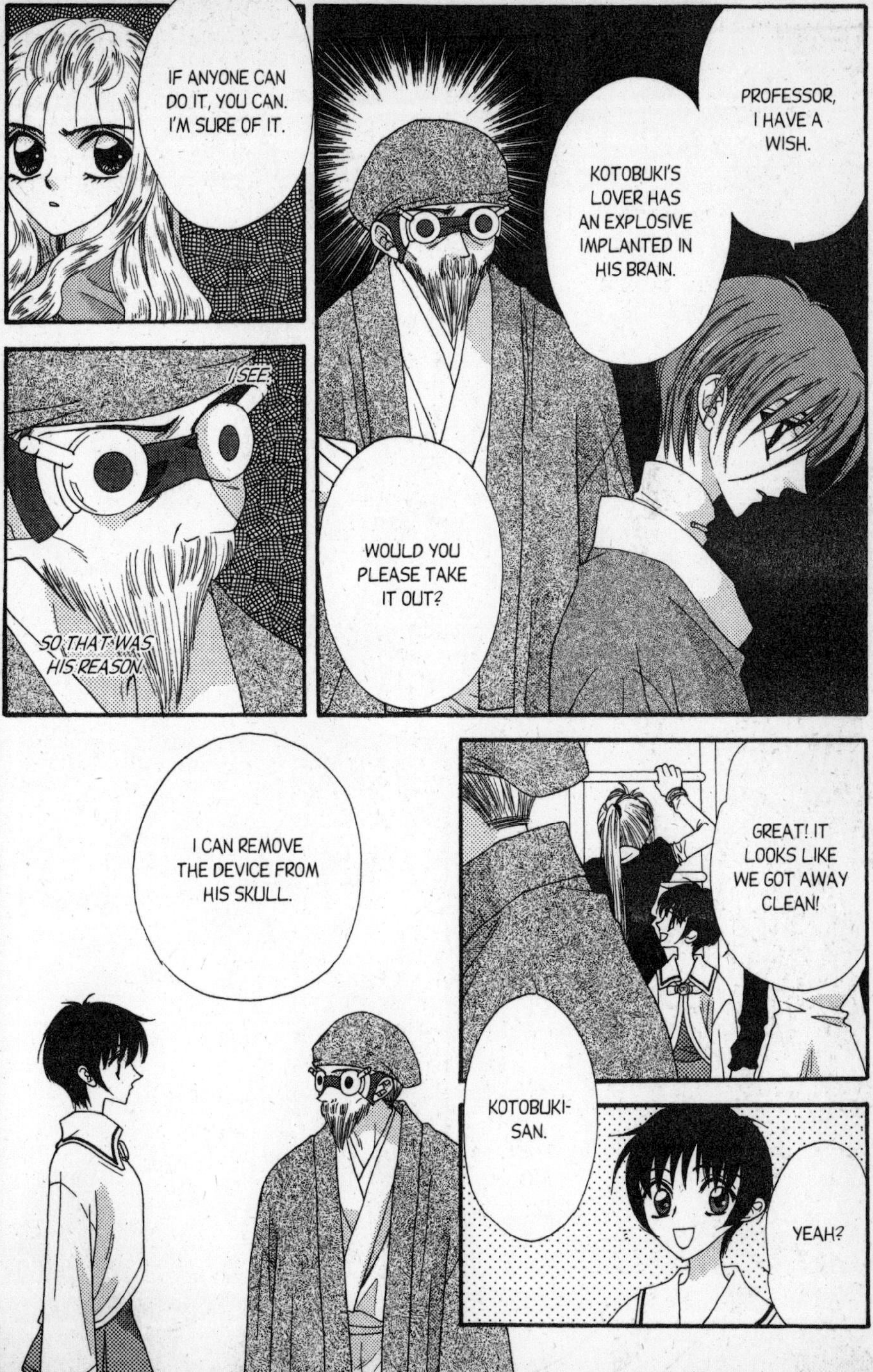
PROFESSOR, I HAVE A WISH.
KOTOBUKI'S LOVER HAS AN EXPLOSIVE IMPLANTED IN HIS BRAIN.
WOULD YOU PLEASE TAKE IT OUT?
IF ANYONE CAN DO IT, YOU CAN. I'M SURE OF IT.
I SEE.
SO THAT WAS HIS REASON.
GREAT! IT LOOKS LIKE WE GOT AWAY CLEAN!
KOTOBUKI-SAN.
YEAH?
I CAN REMOVE THE DEVICE FROM HIS SKULL.

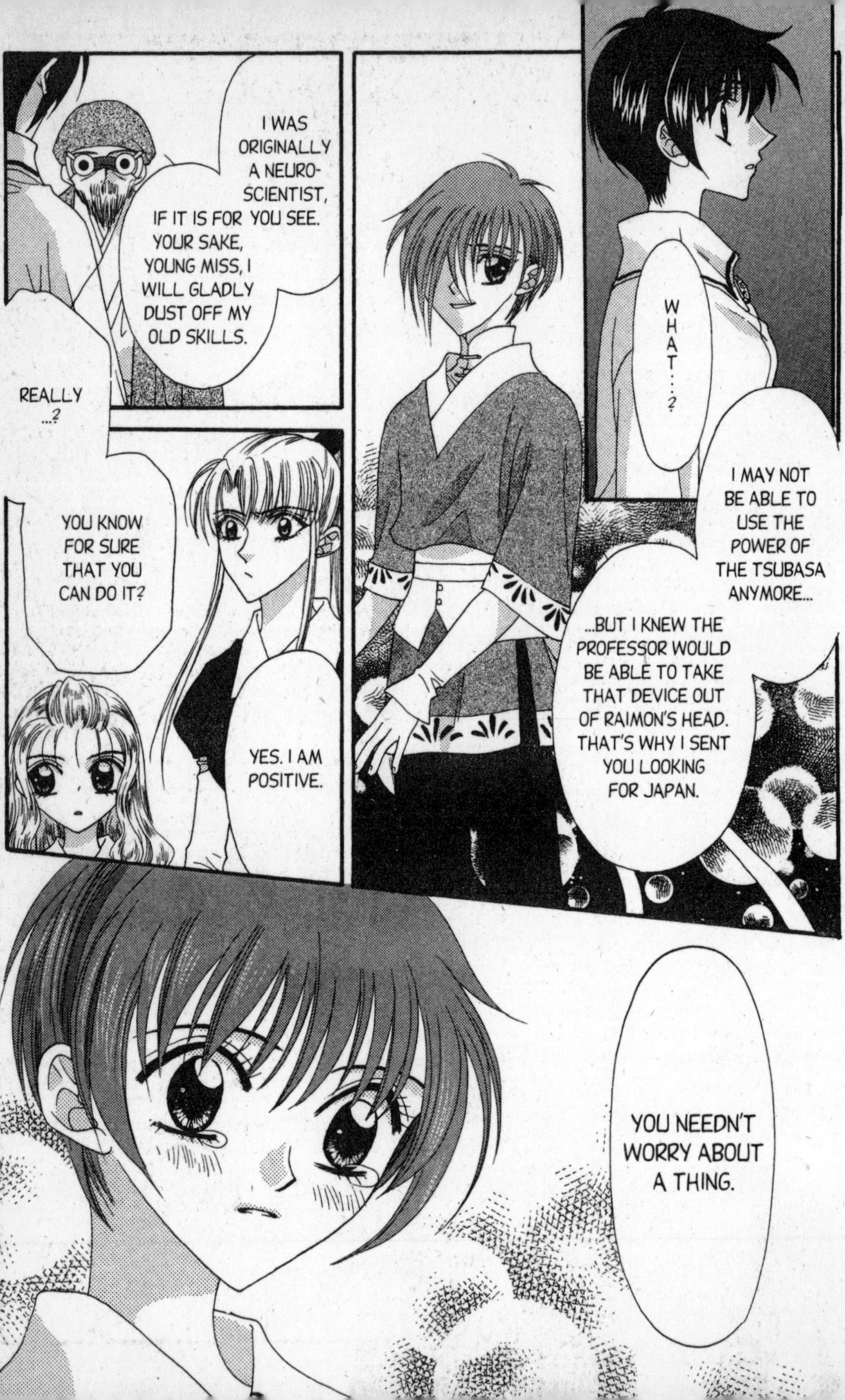
WHAT...?
I MAY NOT BE ABLE TO USE THE POWER OF THE TSUBASA ANYMORE...
...BUT I KNEW THE PROFESSOR WOULD BE ABLE TO TAKE THAT DEVICE OUT OF RAIMON'S HEAD. THAT'S WHY I SENT YOU LOOKING FOR JAPAN.
I WAS ORIGINALLY A NEURO-SCIENTIST, YOU SEE.
IF IT IS FOR YOUR SAKE, YOUNG MISS, I WILL GLADLY DUST OFF MY OLD SKILLS.
REALLY ...?
YOU KNOW FOR SURE THAT YOU CAN DO IT?
YES. I AM POSITIVE.
YOU NEEDN'T WORRY ABOUT A THING.

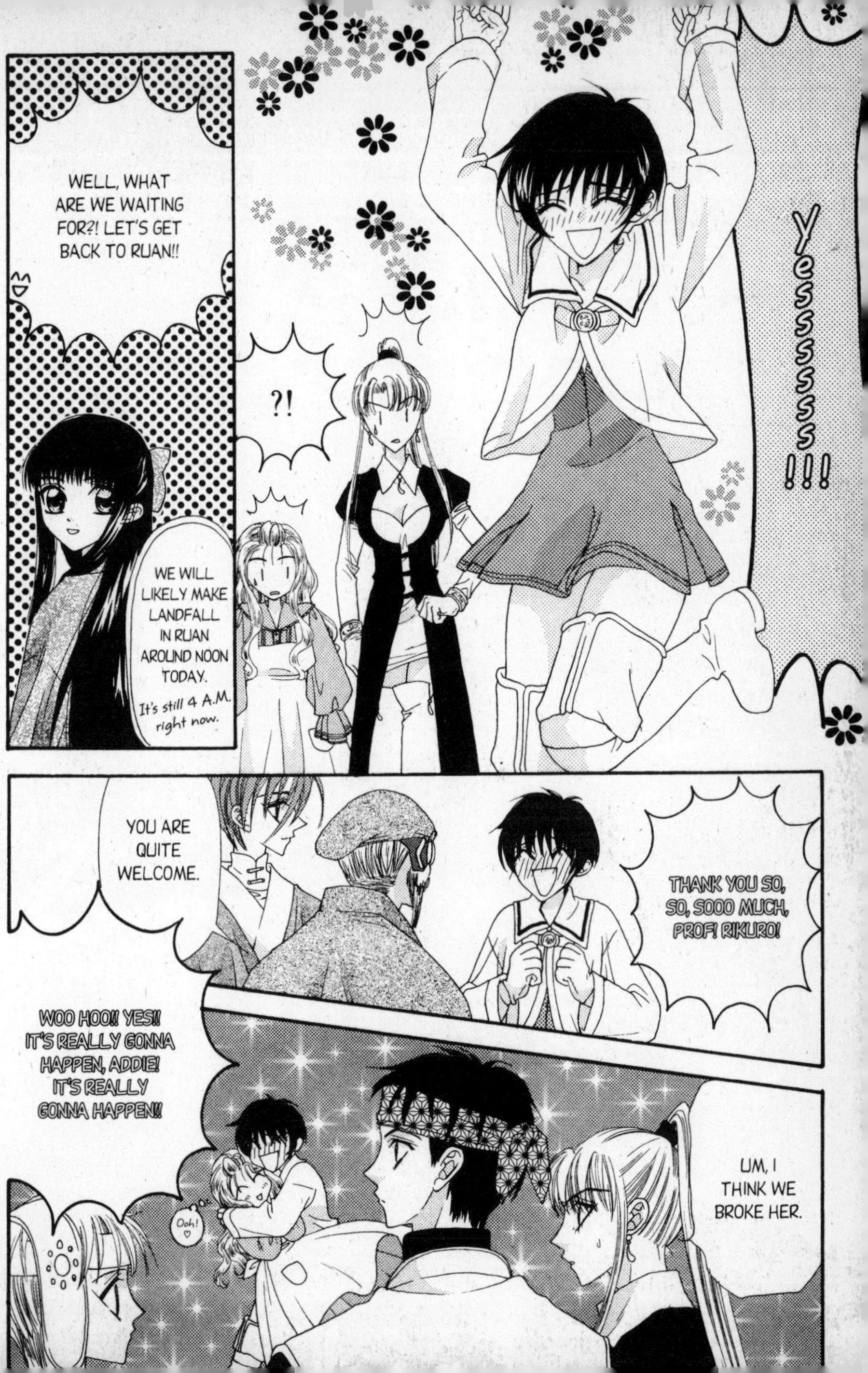
Yessssss!!!
?!
WELL, WHAT ARE WE WAITING FOR?! LET'S GET BACK TO RUAN!!
WE WILL LIKELY MAKE LANDFALL IN RUAN AROUND NOON TODAY.
It's still 4 A.M. right now.
THANK YOU SO, SO, SOOO MUCH, PROF! RIKURO!
YOU ARE QUITE WELCOME.
UM, I THINK WE BROKE HER.
WOO HOO!! YES!! IT'S REALLY GONNA HAPPEN, ADDIE! IT'S REALLY GONNA HAPPEN!!
Ooh! ♥

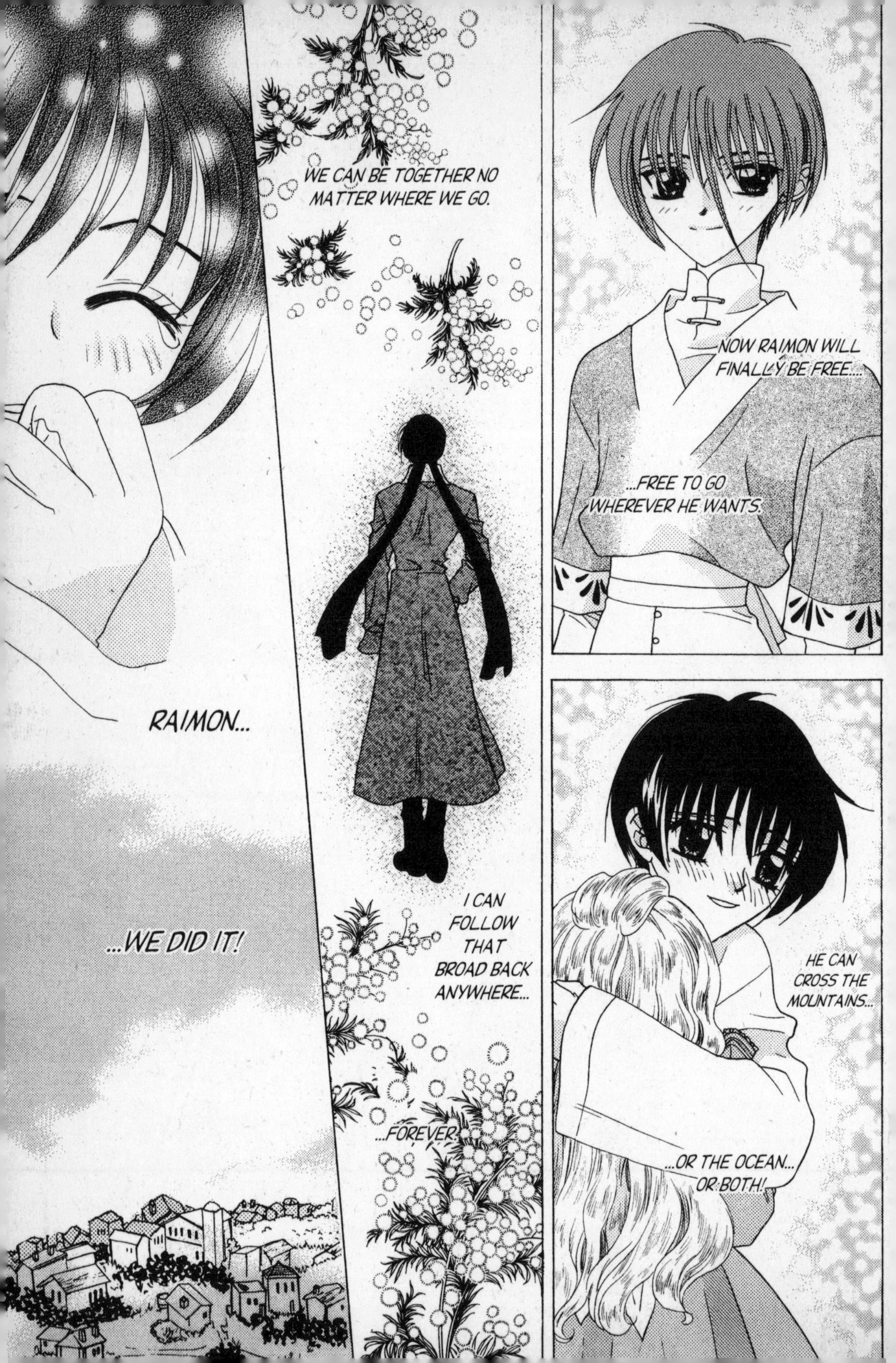
NOW RAIMON WILL FINALLY BE FREE...
...FREE TO GO WHEREVER HE WANTS.
HE CAN CROSS THE MOUNTAINS...
...OR THE OCEAN... OR BOTH!
WE CAN BE TOGETHER NO MATTER WHERE WE GO.
I CAN FOLLOW THAT BROAD BACK ANYWHERE...
...FOREVER.
RAIMON...
...WE DID IT!

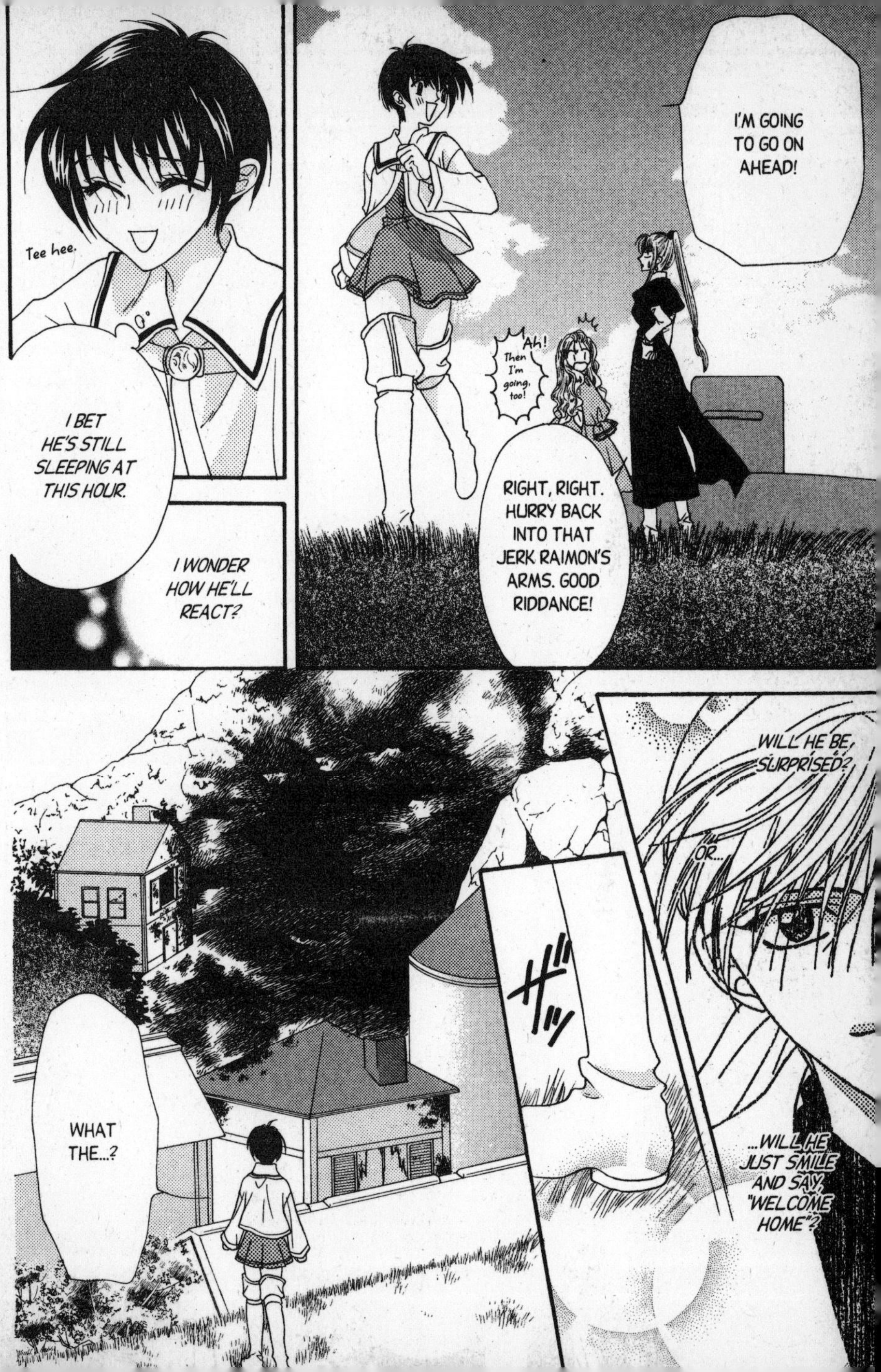
I'M GOING TO GO ON AHEAD!
Ah! Then I'm going, too!
RIGHT, RIGHT. HURRY BACK INTO THAT JERK RAIMON'S ARMS. GOOD RIDDANCE!
Tee hee.
I BET HE'S STILL SLEEPING AT THIS HOUR.
I WONDER HOW HE'LL REACT?
WILL HE BE SURPRISED?
OR...
...WILL HE JUST SMILE AND SAY, "WELCOME HOME"?
ザッ
WHAT THE...?

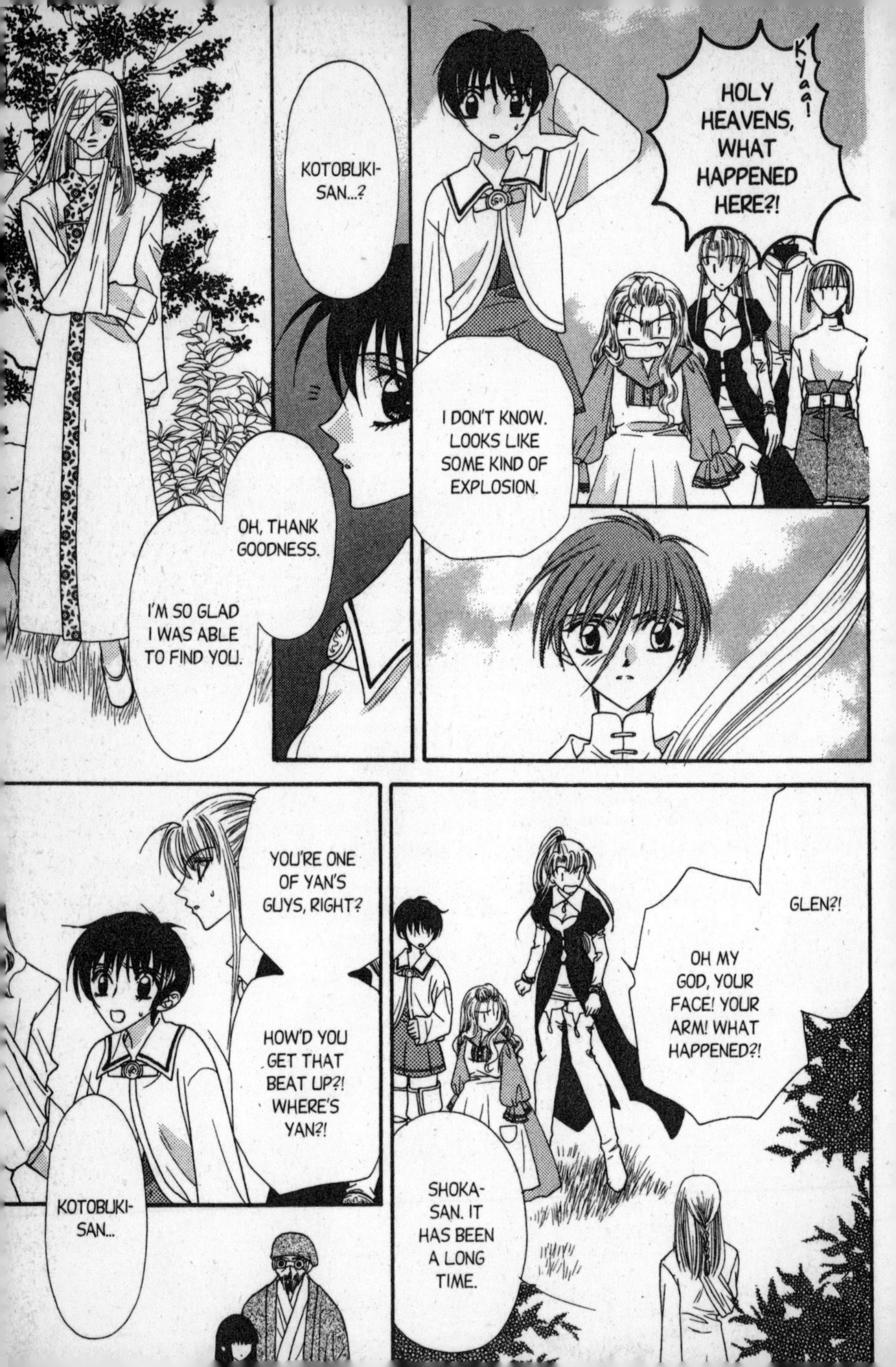
KYaa!
HOLY HEAVENS, WHAT HAPPENED HERE?!
I DON'T KNOW. LOOKS LIKE SOME KIND OF EXPLOSION.
KOTOBUKI-SAN...?
OH, THANK GOODNESS.
I'M SO GLAD I WAS ABLE TO FIND YOU.
GLEN?!
OH MY GOD, YOUR FACE! YOUR ARM! WHAT HAPPENED?!
SHOKA-SAN. IT HAS BEEN A LONG TIME.
YOU'RE ONE OF YAN'S GUYS, RIGHT?
HOW'D YOU GET THAT BEAT UP?! WHERE'S YAN?!
KOTOBUKI-SAN...

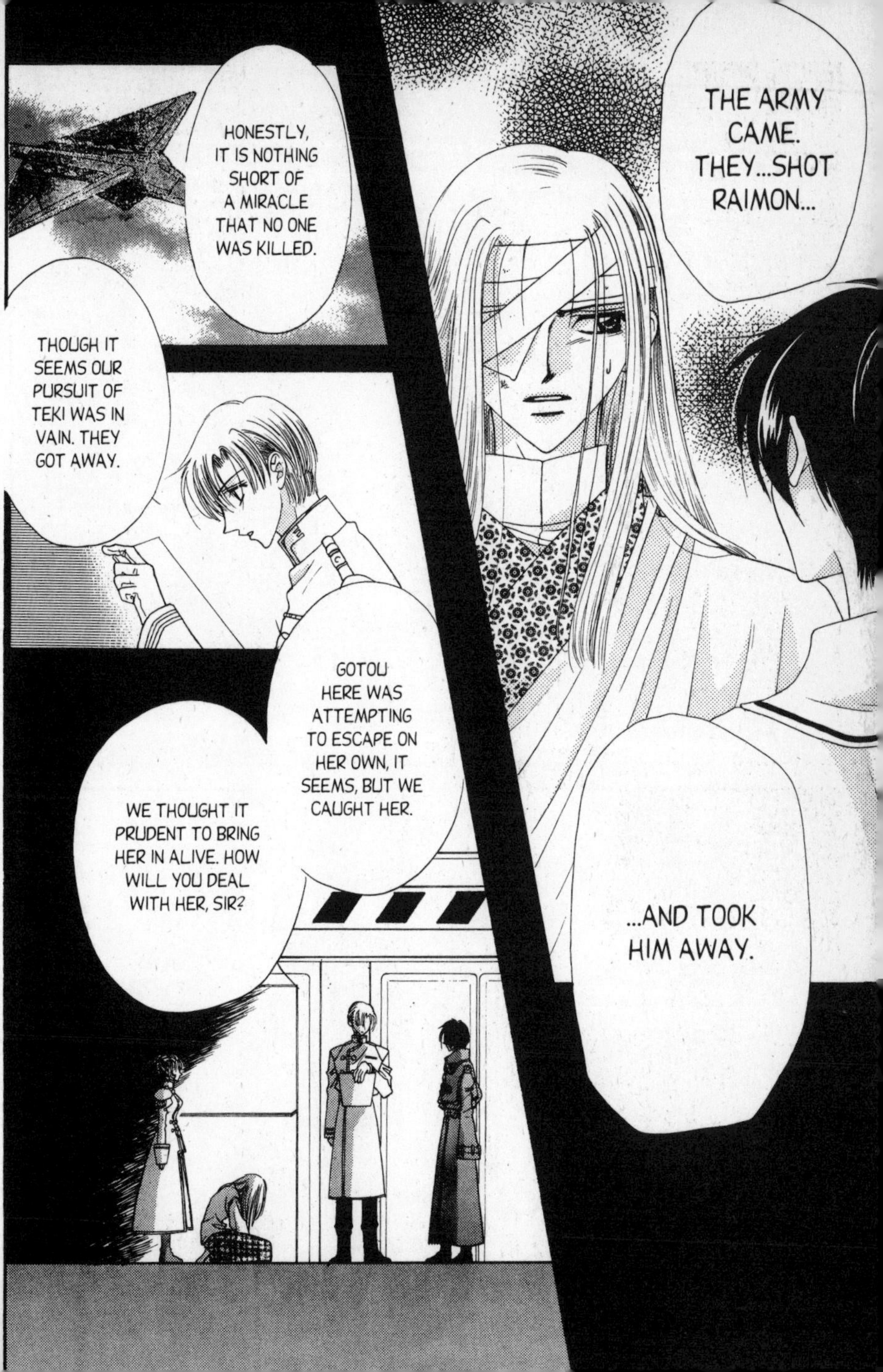
THE ARMY CAME. THEY...SHOT RAIMON...
...AND TOOK HIM AWAY.
HONESTLY, IT IS NOTHING SHORT OF A MIRACLE THAT NO ONE WAS KILLED.
THOUGH IT SEEMS OUR PURSUIT OF TEKI WAS IN VAIN. THEY GOT AWAY.
GOTOU HERE WAS ATTEMPTING TO ESCAPE ON HER OWN, IT SEEMS, BUT WE CAUGHT HER.
WE THOUGHT IT PRUDENT TO BRING HER IN ALIVE. HOW WILL YOU DEAL WITH HER, SIR?

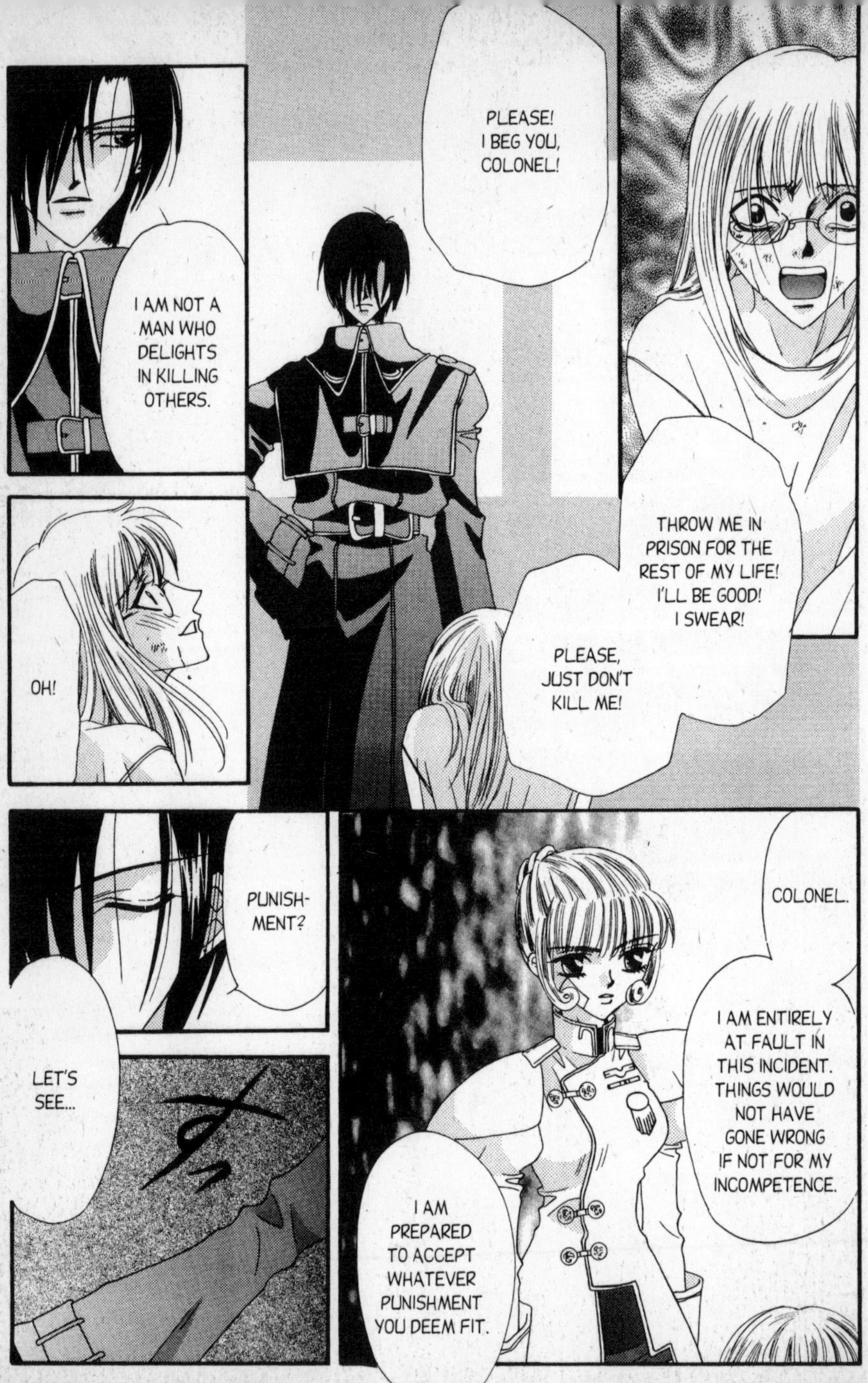
PLEASE! I BEG YOU, COLONEL!
THROW ME IN PRISON FOR THE REST OF MY LIFE! I'LL BE GOOD! I SWEAR!
PLEASE, JUST DON'T KILL ME!
I AM NOT A MAN WHO DELIGHTS IN KILLING OTHERS.
OH!
COLONEL.
I AM ENTIRELY AT FAULT IN THIS INCIDENT. THINGS WOULD NOT HAVE GONE WRONG IF NOT FOR MY INCOMPETENCE.
I AM PREPARED TO ACCEPT WHATEVER PUNISHMENT YOU DEEM FIT.
PUNISH-MENT?
LET'S SEE...

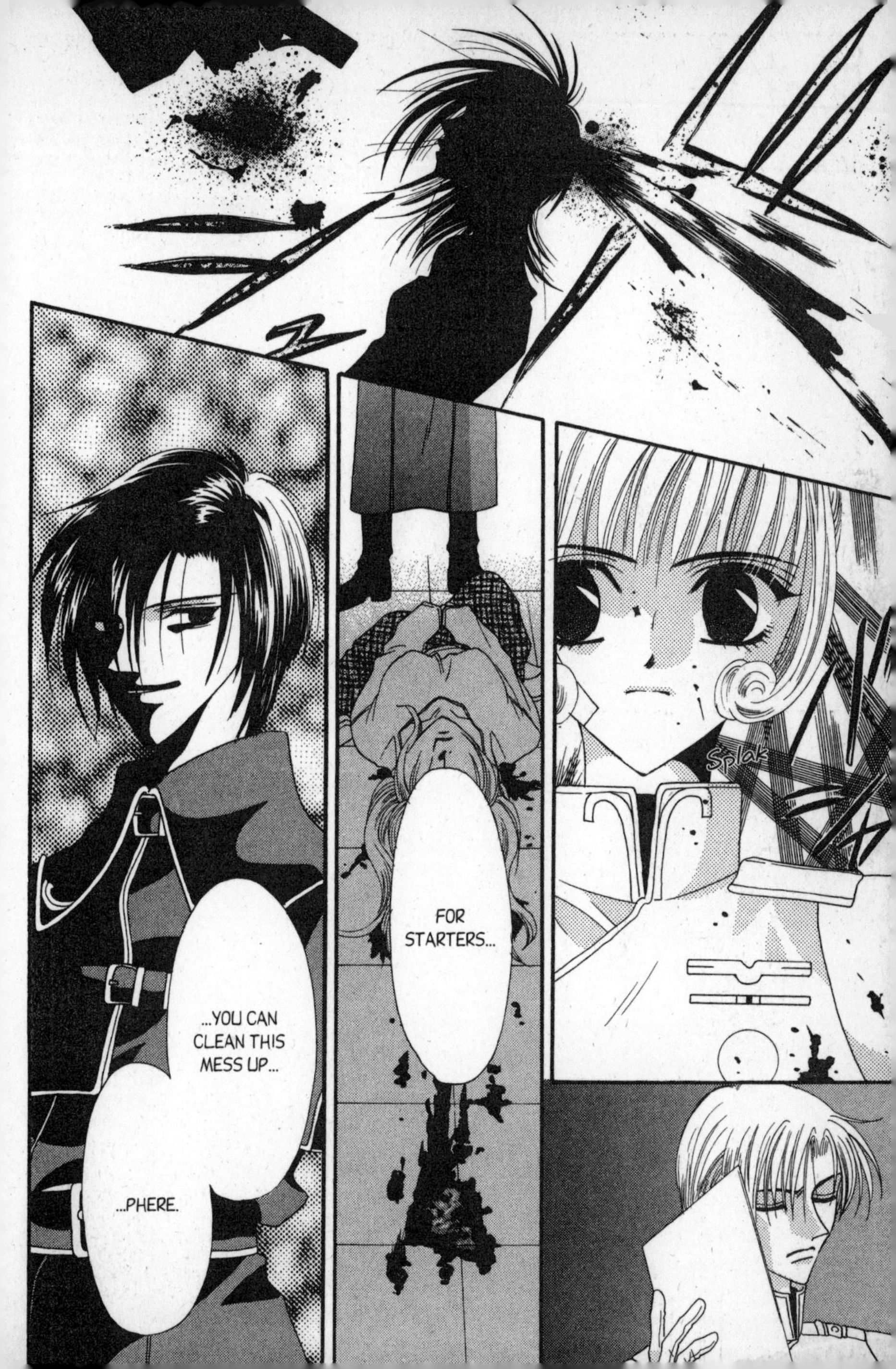
Splak
FOR STARTERS...
...YOU CAN CLEAN THIS MESS UP...
...PHERE.

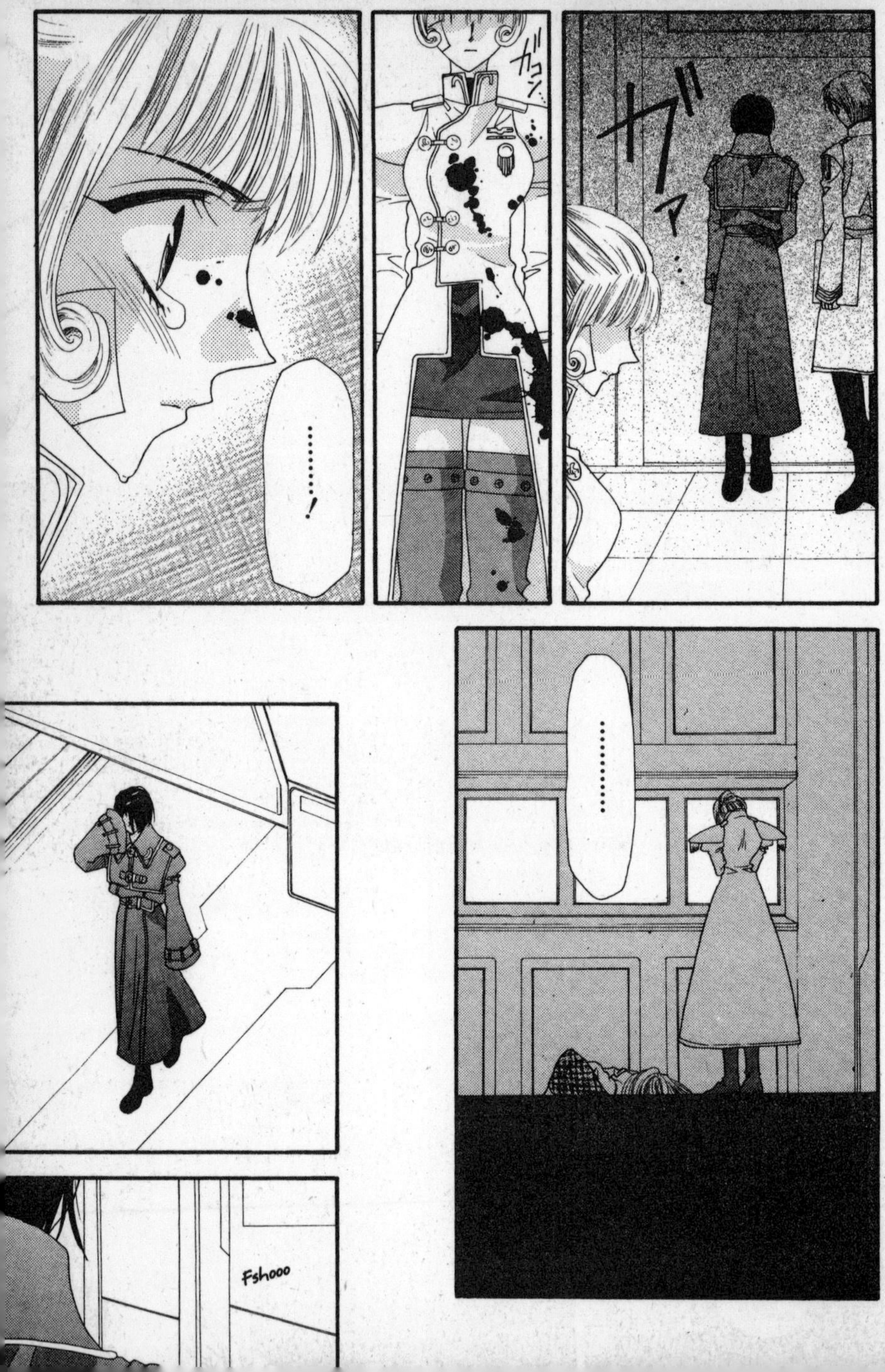
ザア…
ガコン…
......!
....
Fshooo

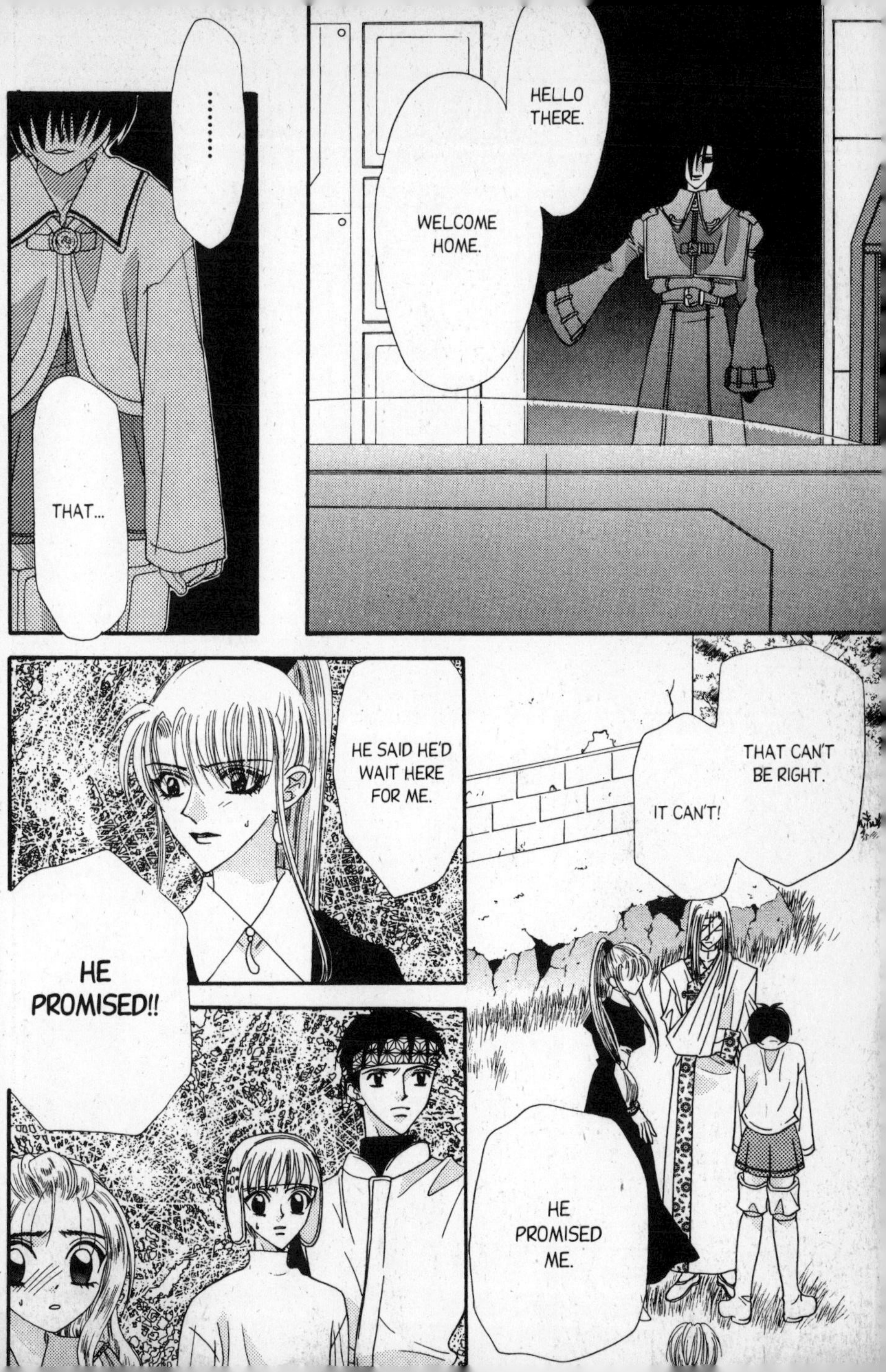
HELLO THERE.
WELCOME HOME.
......
THAT...
THAT CAN'T BE RIGHT.
IT CAN'T!
HE PROMISED ME.
HE SAID HE'D WAIT HERE FOR ME.
HE PROMISED!!

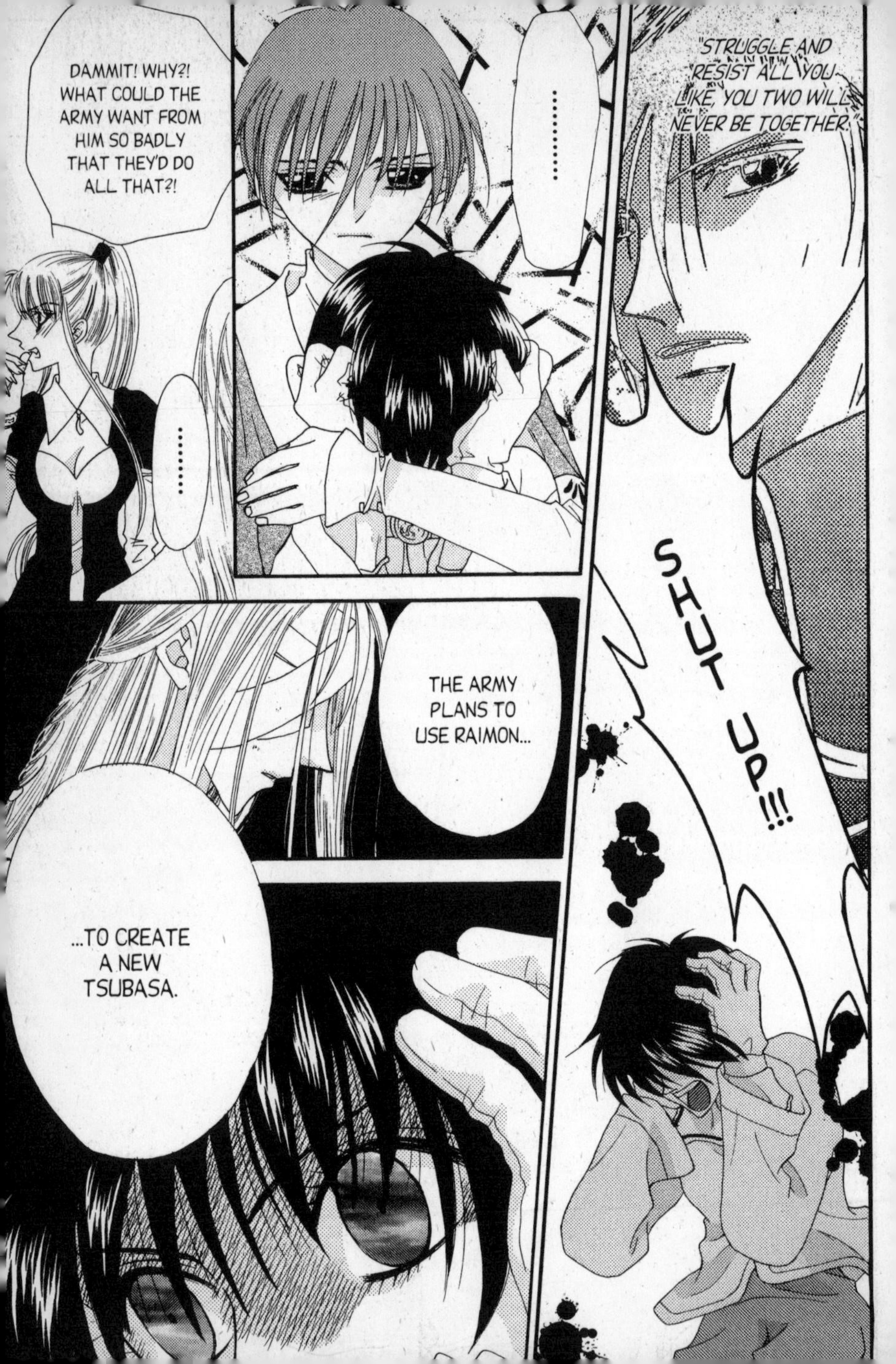
"STRUGGLE AND RESIST ALL YOU LIKE, YOU TWO WILL NEVER BE TOGETHER."
SHUT UP!!!
......
DAMMIT! WHY?! WHAT COULD THE ARMY WANT FROM HIM SO BADLY THAT THEY'D DO ALL THAT?!
......
THE ARMY PLANS TO USE RAIMON...
...TO CREATE A NEW TSUBASA.

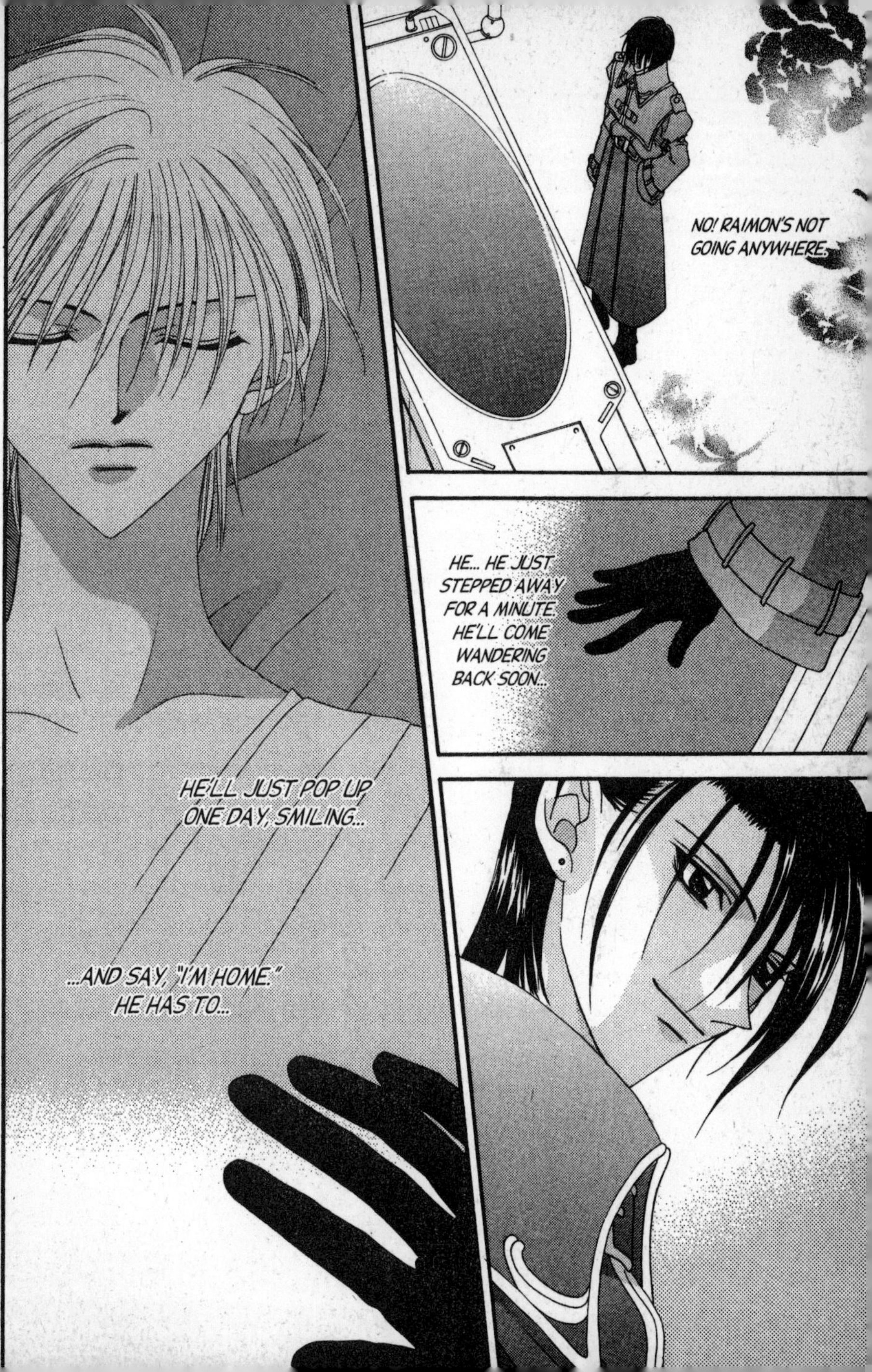
NO! RAIMON'S NOT GOING ANYWHERE.
HE... HE JUST STEPPED AWAY FOR A MINUTE. HE'LL COME WANDERING BACK SOON...
HE'LL JUST POP UP ONE DAY, SMILING...
...AND SAY, "I'M HOME." HE HAS TO...

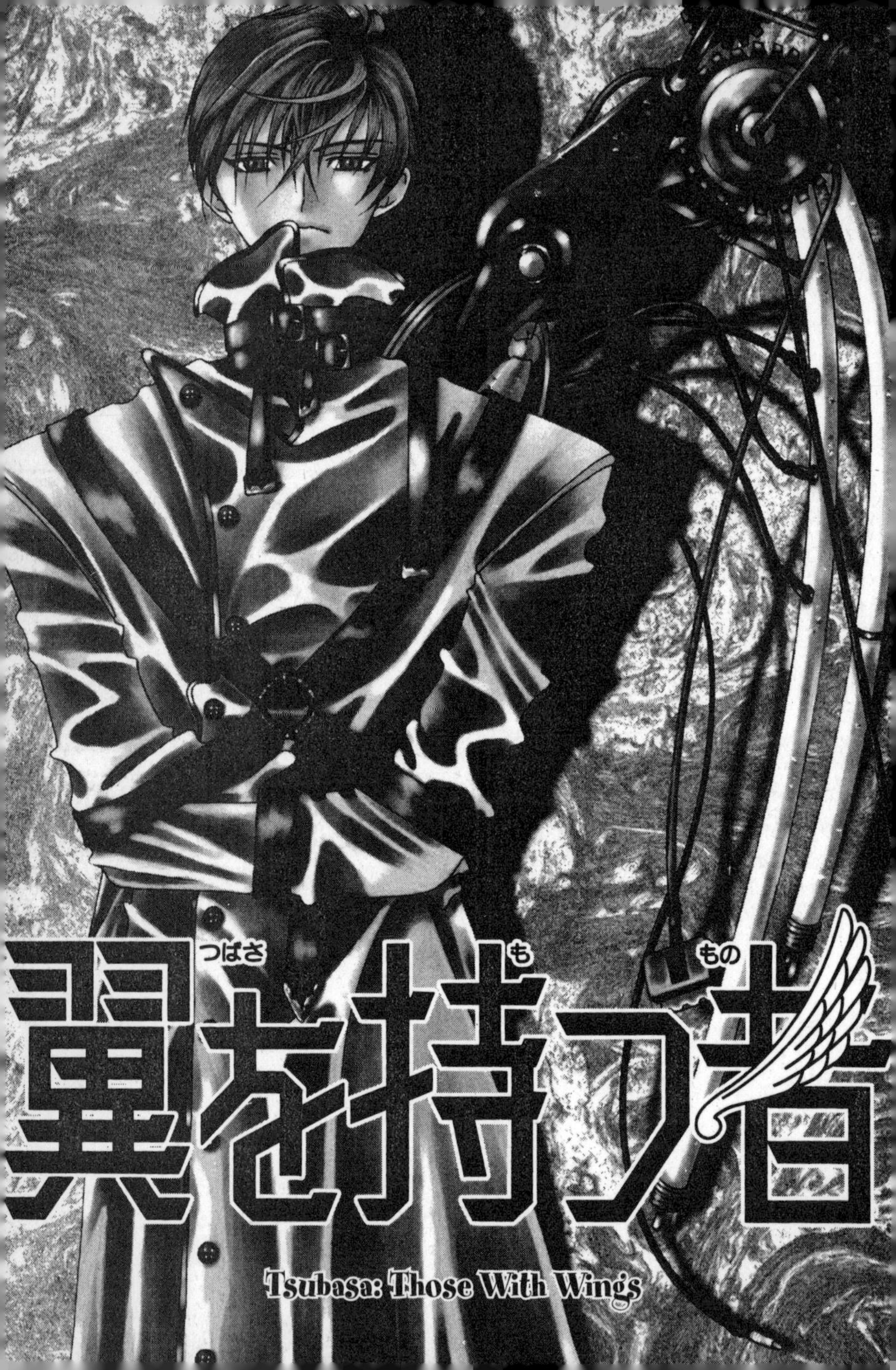
翼を持つ者
つばさ も もの
Tsubasa: Those With Wings

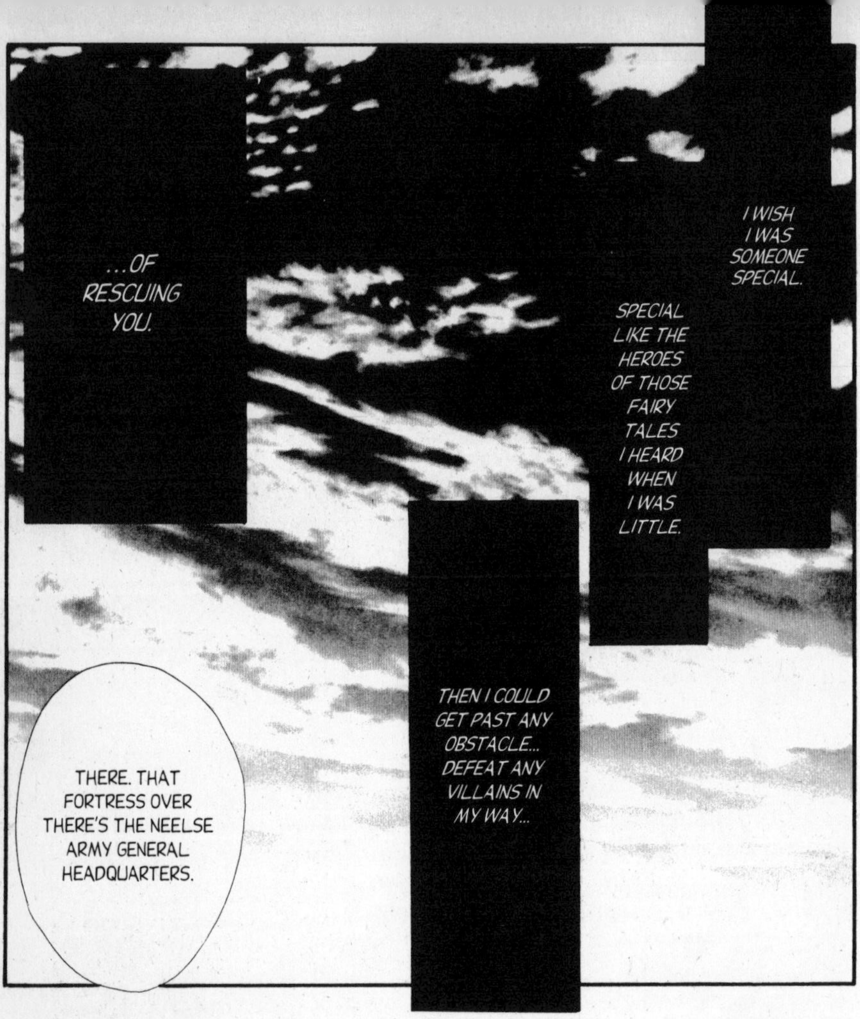
I WISH I WAS SOMEONE SPECIAL.
SPECIAL LIKE THE HEROES OF THOSE FAIRY TALES I HEARD WHEN I WAS LITTLE.
...OF RESCUING YOU.
THEN I COULD GET PAST ANY OBSTACLE... DEFEAT ANY VILLAINS IN MY WAY...
THERE. THAT FORTRESS OVER THERE'S THE NEELSE ARMY GENERAL HEADQUARTERS.

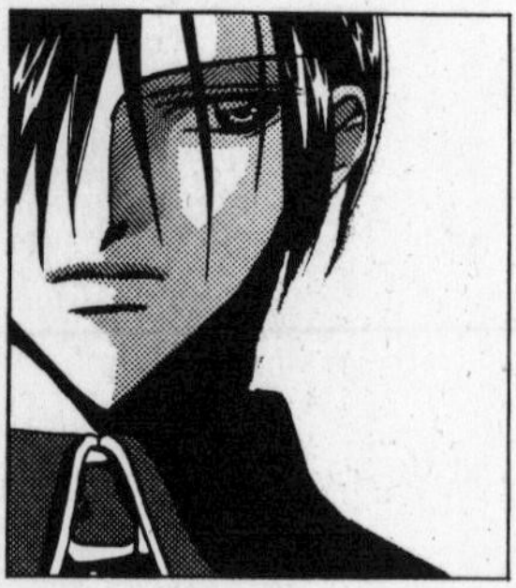

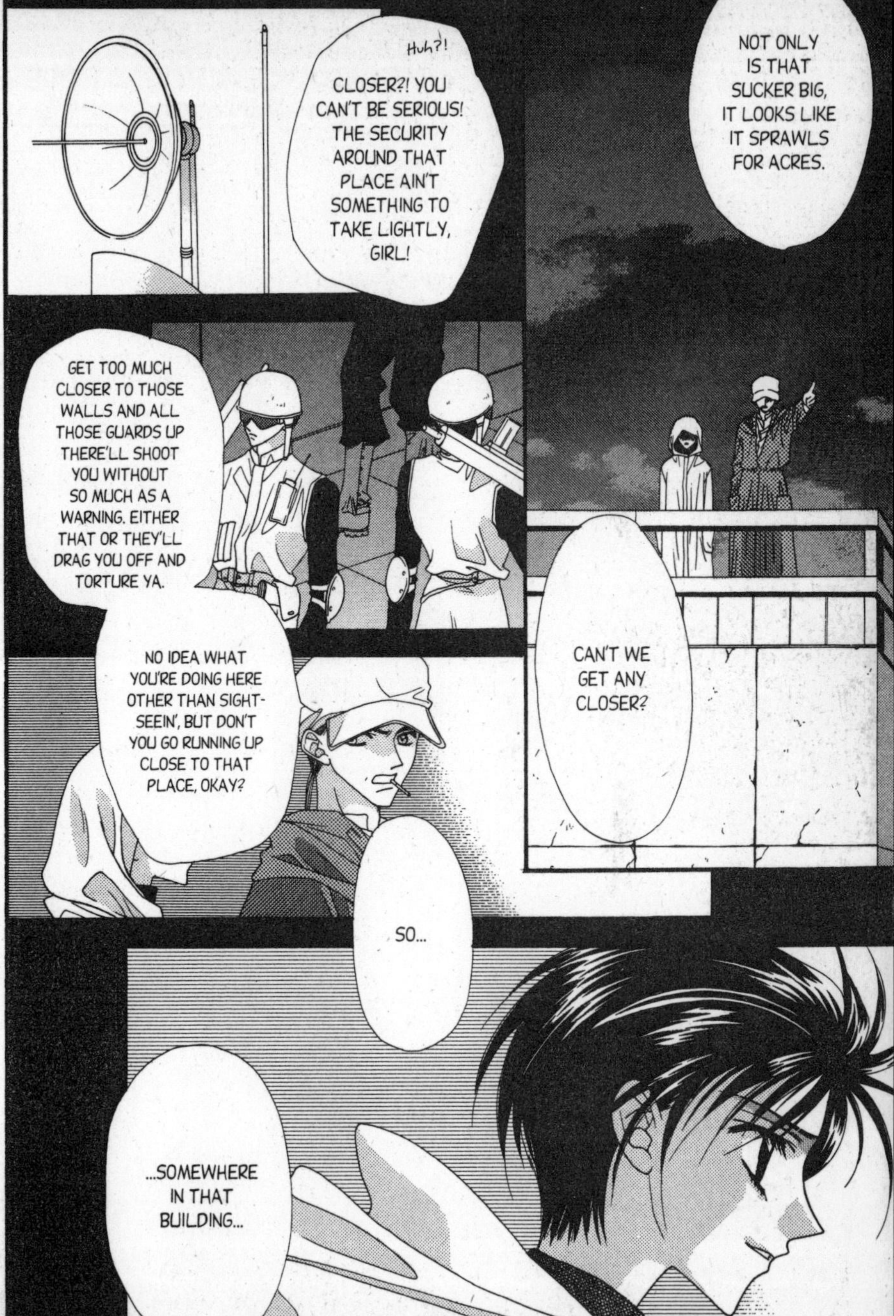
NOT ONLY IS THAT SUCKER BIG, IT LOOKS LIKE IT SPRAWLS FOR ACRES.
CAN'T WE GET ANY CLOSER?
Huh?!
CLOSER?! YOU CAN'T BE SERIOUS! THE SECURITY AROUND THAT PLACE AIN'T SOMETHING TO TAKE LIGHTLY, GIRL!
GET TOO MUCH CLOSER TO THOSE WALLS AND ALL THOSE GUARDS UP THERE'LL SHOOT YOU WITHOUT SO MUCH AS A WARNING. EITHER THAT OR THEY'LL DRAG YOU OFF AND TORTURE YA.
NO IDEA WHAT YOU'RE DOING HERE OTHER THAN SIGHT-SEEIN', BUT DON'T YOU GO RUNNING UP CLOSE TO THAT PLACE, OKAY?
SO...
...SOMEWHERE IN THAT BUILDING...

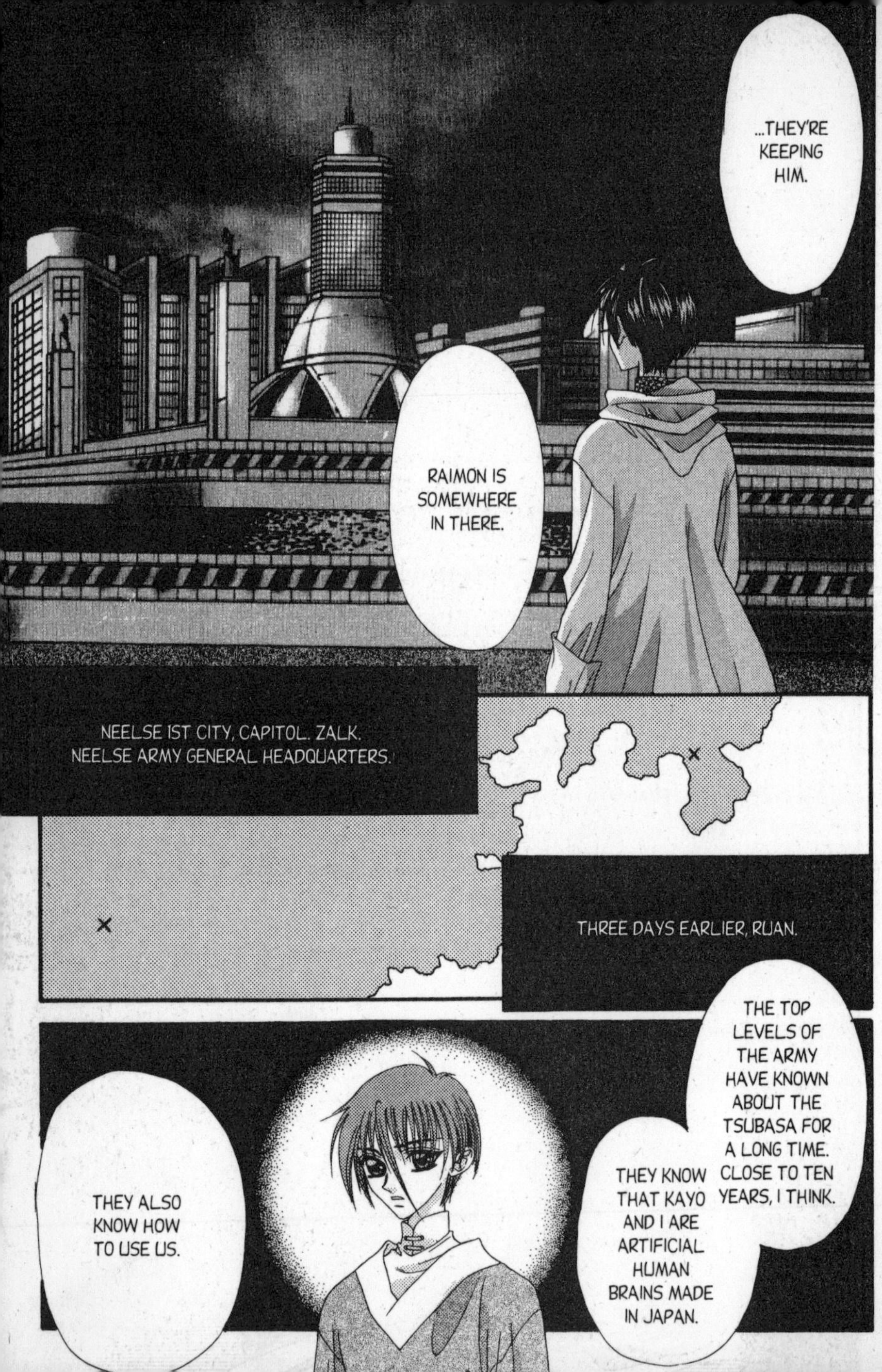
...THEY'RE KEEPING HIM.
RAIMON IS SOMEWHERE IN THERE.
NEELSE 1ST CITY, CAPITOL. ZALK. NEELSE ARMY GENERAL HEADQUARTERS.
THREE DAYS EARLIER, RUAN.
THE TOP LEVELS OF THE ARMY HAVE KNOWN ABOUT THE TSUBASA FOR A LONG TIME. CLOSE TO TEN YEARS, I THINK.
THEY KNOW THAT KAYO AND I ARE ARTIFICIAL HUMAN BRAINS MADE IN JAPAN.
THEY ALSO KNOW HOW TO USE US.

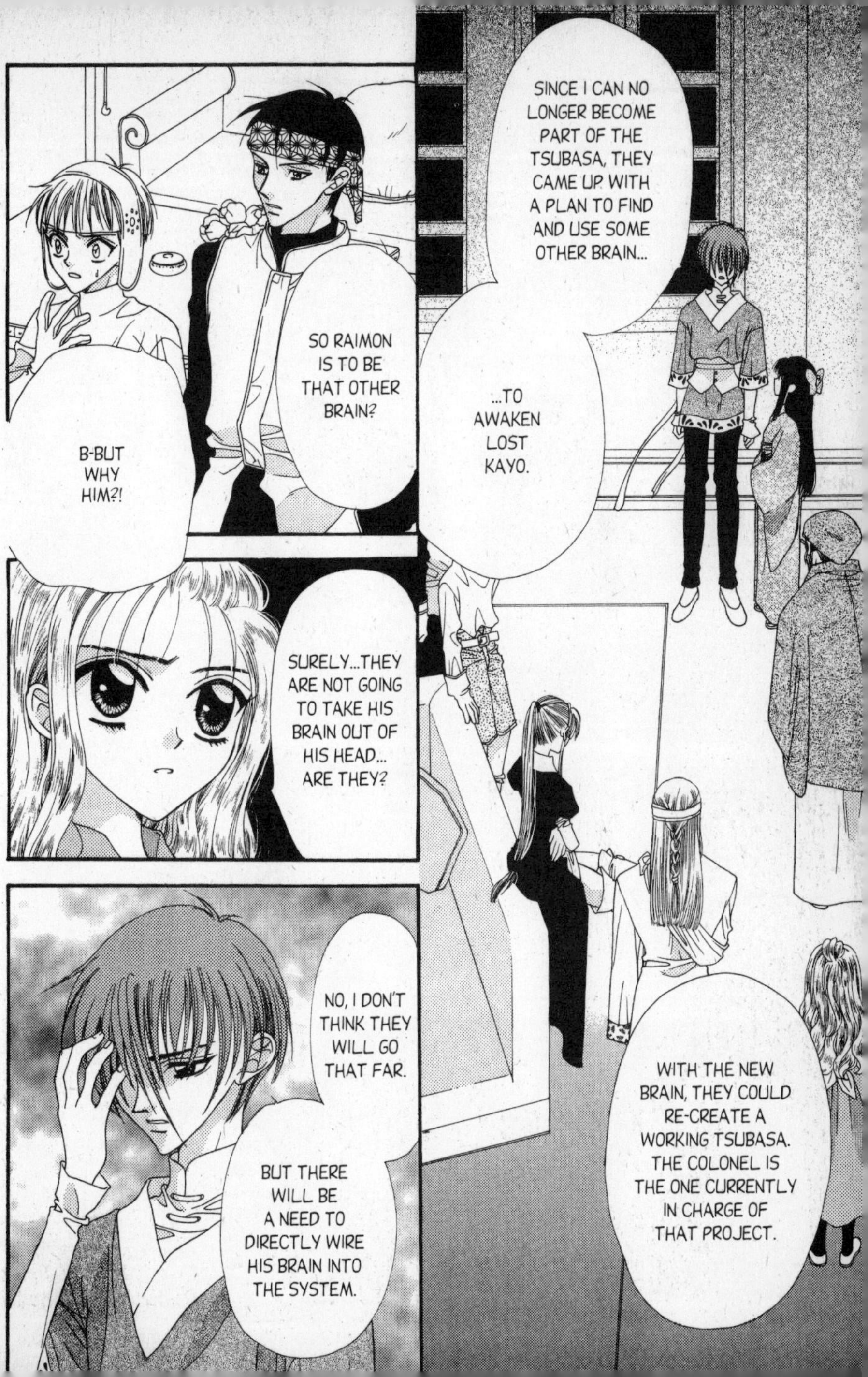
SINCE I CAN NO LONGER BECOME PART OF THE TSUBASA, THEY CAME UP WITH A PLAN TO FIND AND USE SOME OTHER BRAIN...
...TO AWAKEN LOST KAYO.
WITH THE NEW BRAIN, THEY COULD RE-CREATE A WORKING TSUBASA. THE COLONEL IS THE ONE CURRENTLY IN CHARGE OF THAT PROJECT.
SO RAIMON IS TO BE THAT OTHER BRAIN?
B-BUT WHY HIM?!
SURELY...THEY ARE NOT GOING TO TAKE HIS BRAIN OUT OF HIS HEAD... ARE THEY?
NO, I DON'T THINK THEY WILL GO THAT FAR.
BUT THERE WILL BE A NEED TO DIRECTLY WIRE HIS BRAIN INTO THE SYSTEM.

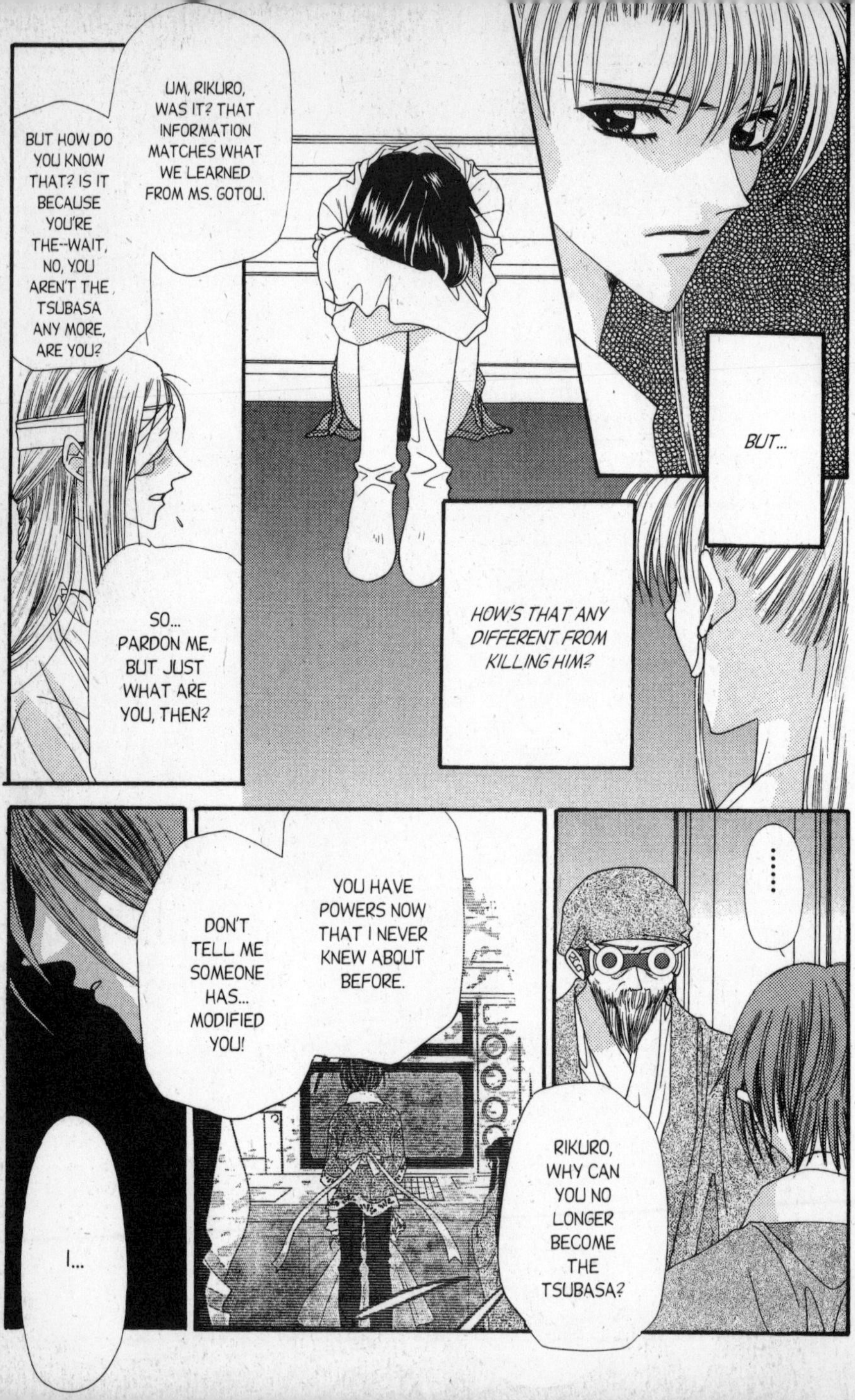
BUT...
HOW'S THAT ANY DIFFERENT FROM KILLING HIM?
UM, RIKURO, WAS IT? THAT INFORMATION MATCHES WHAT WE LEARNED FROM MS. GOTOU.
BUT HOW DO YOU KNOW THAT? IS IT BECAUSE YOU'RE THE--WAIT, NO, YOU AREN'T THE TSUBASA ANY MORE, ARE YOU?
SO... PARDON ME, BUT JUST WHAT ARE YOU, THEN?
......
RIKURO, WHY CAN YOU NO LONGER BECOME THE TSUBASA?
YOU HAVE POWERS NOW THAT I NEVER KNEW ABOUT BEFORE.
DON'T TELL ME SOMEONE HAS... MODIFIED YOU!
I...

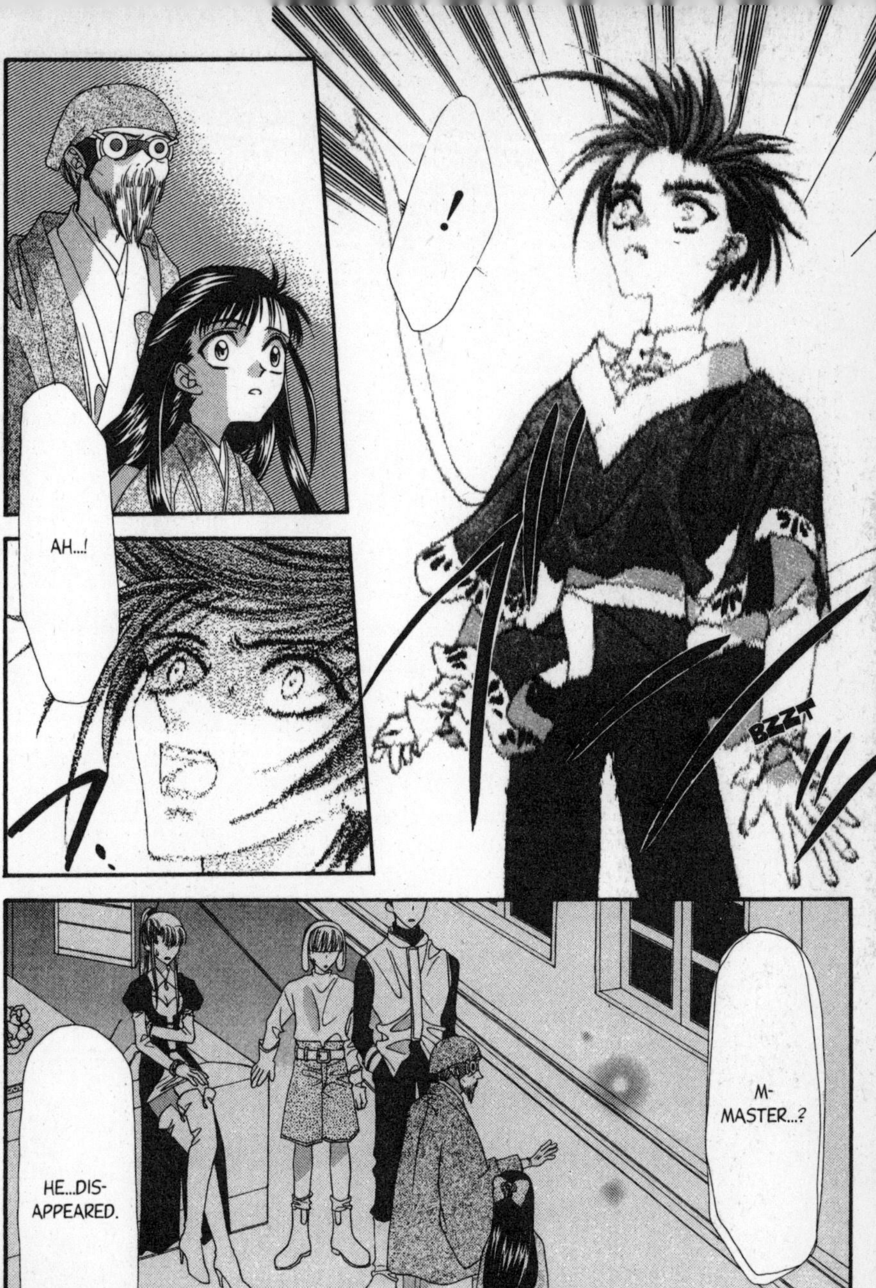
!
BZZT
AH...!
M-
MASTER...?
HE...DIS-
APPEARED.

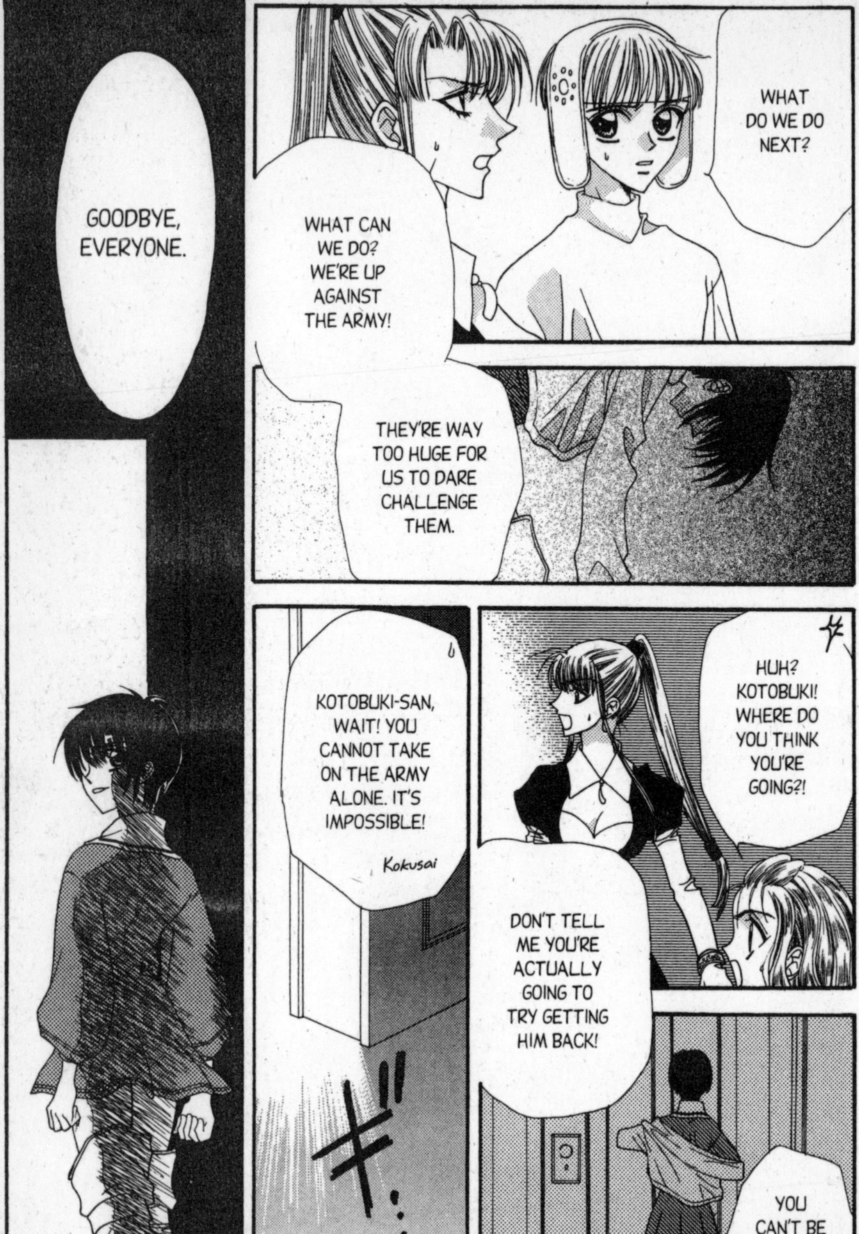
WHAT DO WE DO NEXT?
WHAT CAN WE DO? WE'RE UP AGAINST THE ARMY!
THEY'RE WAY TOO HUGE FOR US TO DARE CHALLENGE THEM.
HUH? KOTOBUKI! WHERE DO YOU THINK YOU'RE GOING?!
DON'T TELL ME YOU'RE ACTUALLY GOING TO TRY GETTING HIM BACK!
YOU CAN'T BE SERIOUS!!
KOTOBUKI-SAN, WAIT! YOU CANNOT TAKE ON THE ARMY ALONE. IT'S IMPOSSIBLE!
Kokusai
Kreee
GOODBYE, EVERYONE.

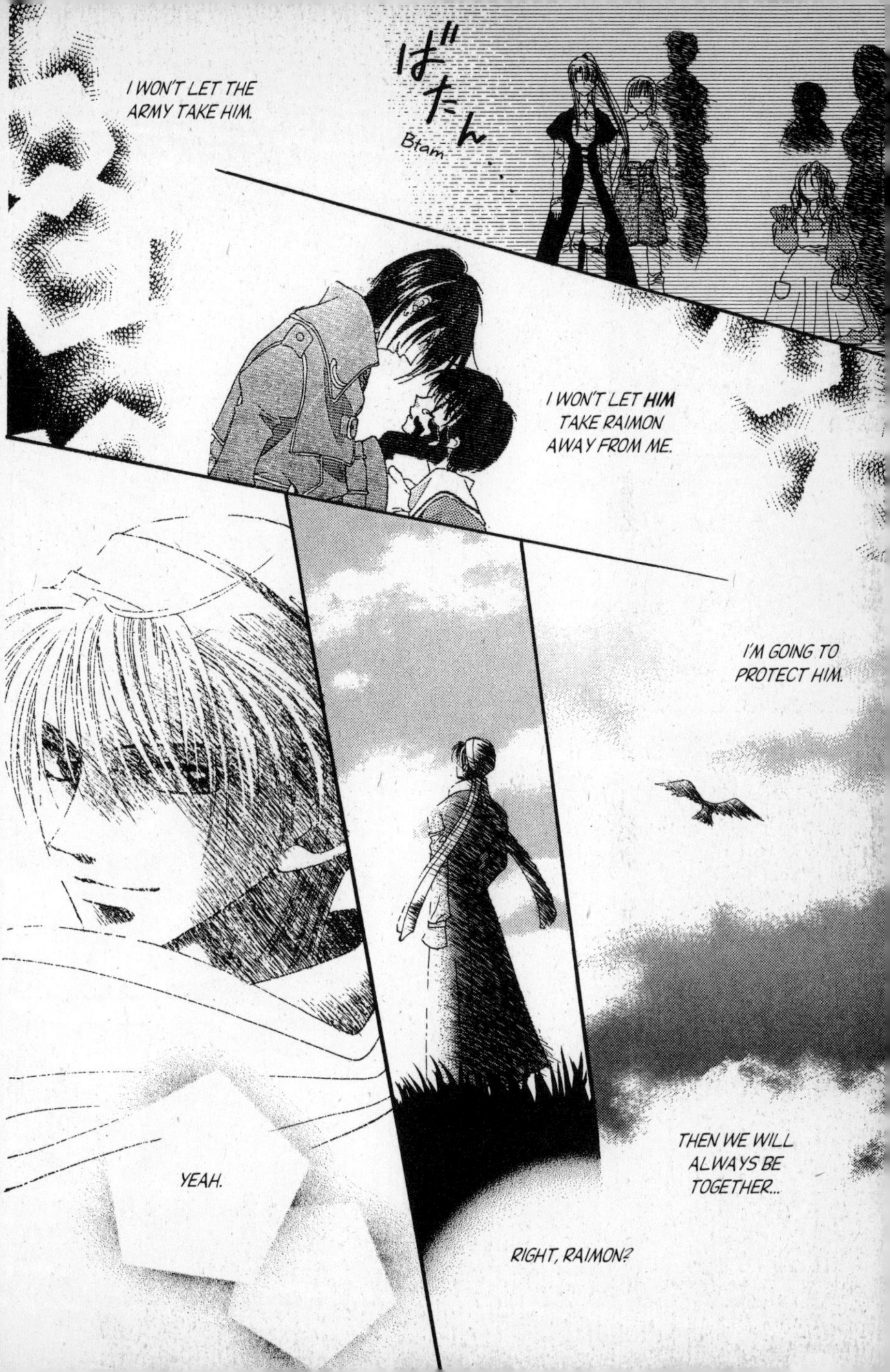

ばたん
Btam
I WON'T LET THE ARMY TAKE HIM.
I WON'T LET HIM TAKE RAIMON AWAY FROM ME.
I'M GOING TO PROTECT HIM.
THEN WE WILL ALWAYS BE TOGETHER...
RIGHT, RAIMON?
YEAH.

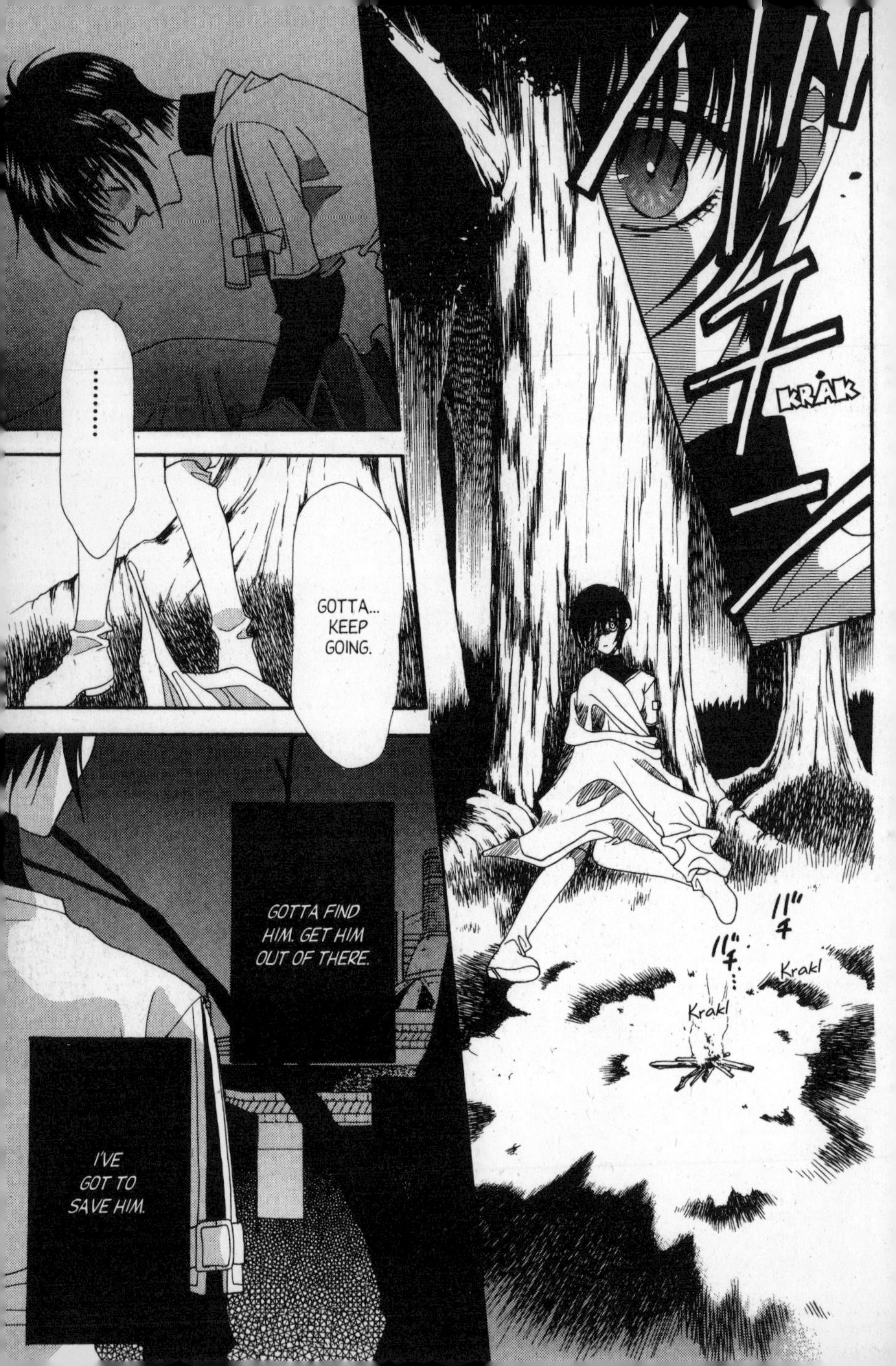

KRAK
Krakl
Krakl
......
GOTTA... KEEP GOING.
GOTTA FIND HIM. GET HIM OUT OF THERE.
I'VE GOT TO SAVE HIM.

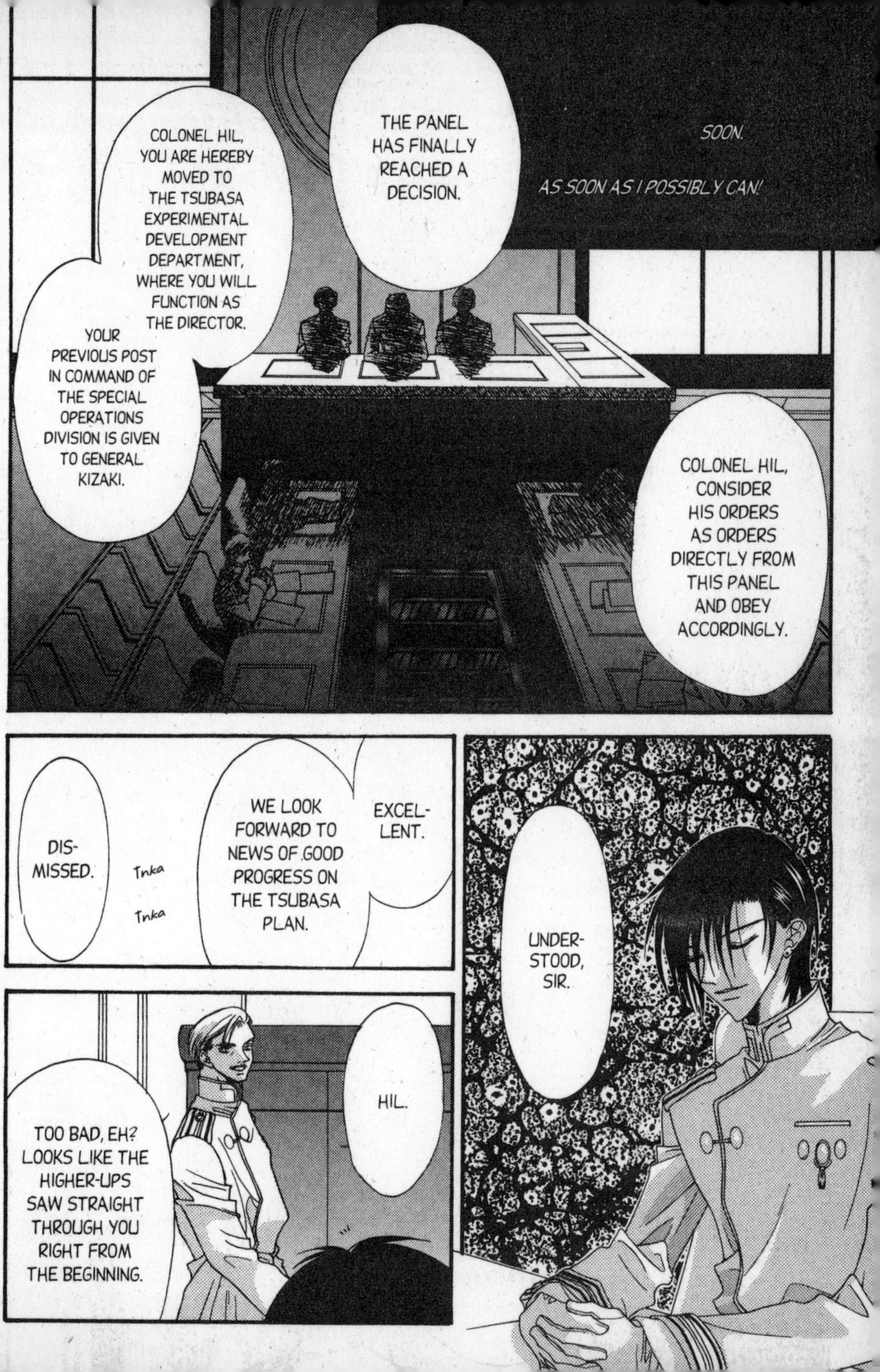
SOON.
AS SOON AS I POSSIBLY CAN!
THE PANEL HAS FINALLY REACHED A DECISION.
COLONEL HIL, YOU ARE HEREBY MOVED TO THE TSUBASA EXPERIMENTAL DEVELOPMENT DEPARTMENT, WHERE YOU WILL FUNCTION AS THE DIRECTOR.
YOUR PREVIOUS POST IN COMMAND OF THE SPECIAL OPERATIONS DIVISION IS GIVEN TO GENERAL KIZAKI.
COLONEL HIL, CONSIDER HIS ORDERS AS ORDERS DIRECTLY FROM THIS PANEL AND OBEY ACCORDINGLY.
UNDER-STOOD, SIR.
EXCEL-LENT.
WE LOOK FORWARD TO NEWS OF GOOD PROGRESS ON THE TSUBASA PLAN.
Tnka
Tnka
DIS-MISSED.
HIL.
TOO BAD, EH? LOOKS LIKE THE HIGHER-UPS SAW STRAIGHT THROUGH YOU RIGHT FROM THE BEGINNING.

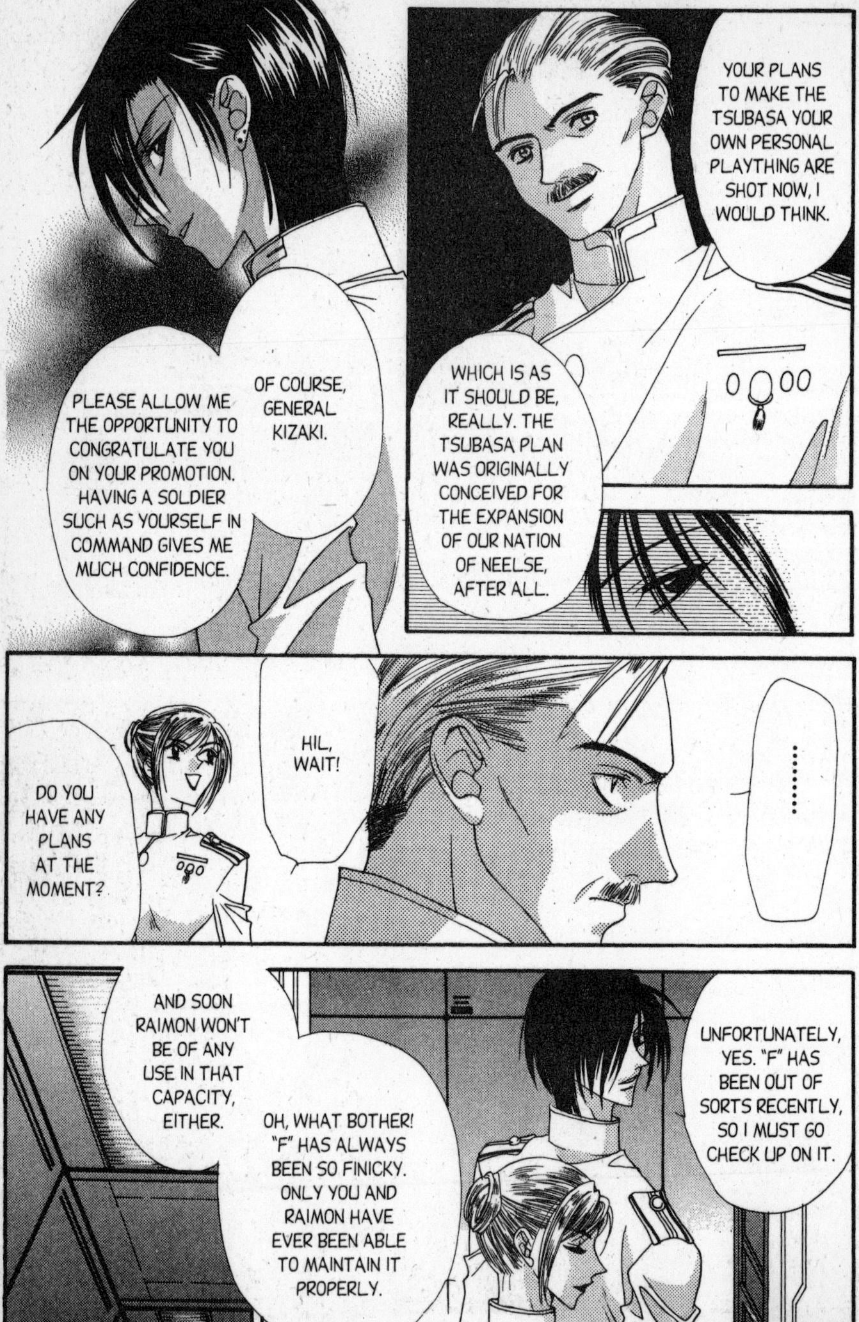

YOUR PLANS TO MAKE THE TSUBASA YOUR OWN PERSONAL PLAYTHING ARE SHOT NOW, I WOULD THINK.
WHICH IS AS IT SHOULD BE, REALLY. THE TSUBASA PLAN WAS ORIGINALLY CONCEIVED FOR THE EXPANSION OF OUR NATION OF NEELSE, AFTER ALL.
OF COURSE, GENERAL KIZAKI.
PLEASE ALLOW ME THE OPPORTUNITY TO CONGRATULATE YOU ON YOUR PROMOTION. HAVING A SOLDIER SUCH AS YOURSELF IN COMMAND GIVES ME MUCH CONFIDENCE.
....
HIL, WAIT!
DO YOU HAVE ANY PLANS AT THE MOMENT?
UNFORTUNATELY, YES. "F" HAS BEEN OUT OF SORTS RECENTLY, SO I MUST GO CHECK UP ON IT.
OH, WHAT BOTHER! "F" HAS ALWAYS BEEN SO FINICKY. ONLY YOU AND RAIMON HAVE EVER BEEN ABLE TO MAINTAIN IT PROPERLY.
AND SOON RAIMON WON'T BE OF ANY USE IN THAT CAPACITY, EITHER.

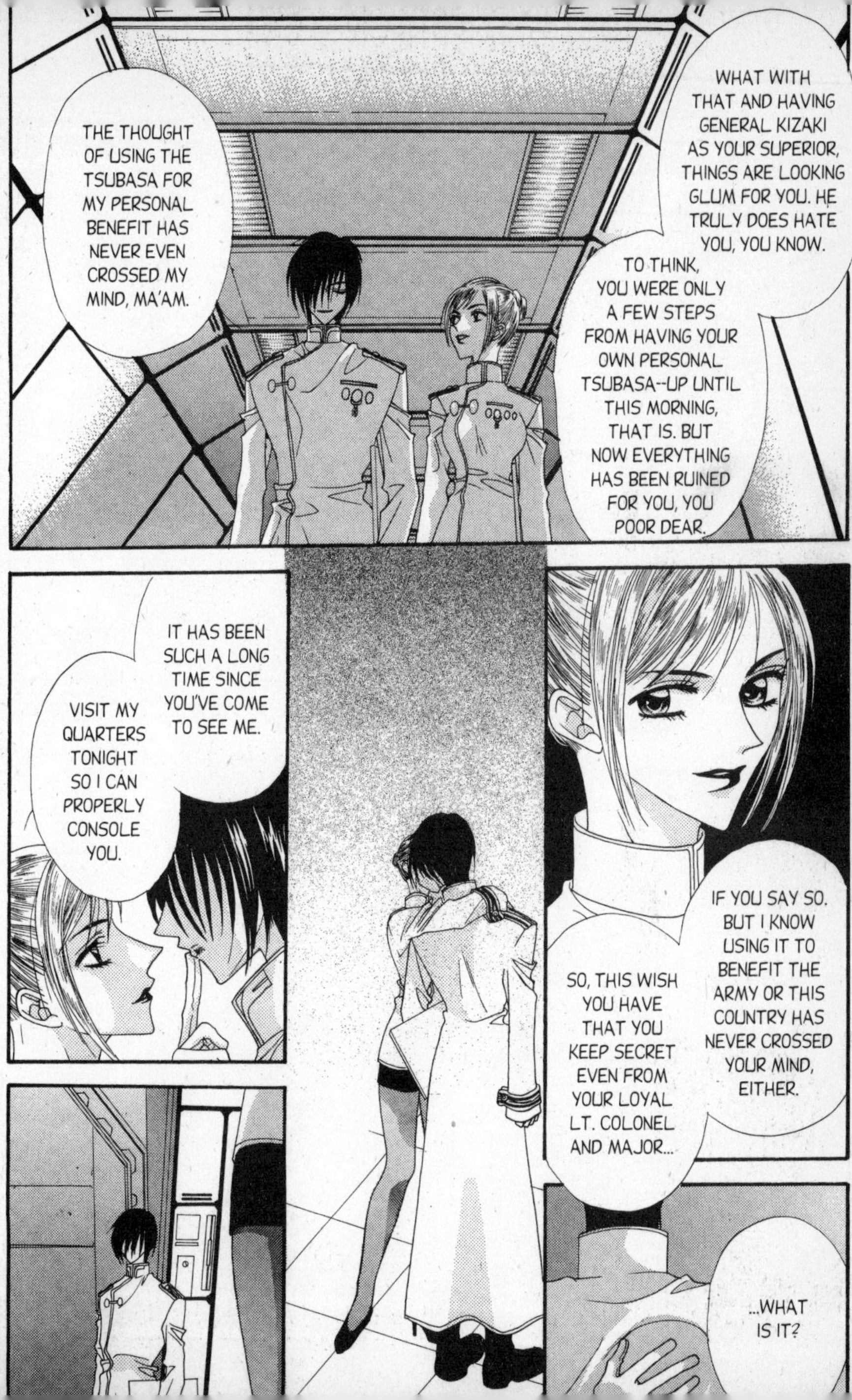
WHAT WITH THAT AND HAVING GENERAL KIZAKI AS YOUR SUPERIOR, THINGS ARE LOOKING GLUM FOR YOU. HE TRULY DOES HATE YOU, YOU KNOW.
TO THINK, YOU WERE ONLY A FEW STEPS FROM HAVING YOUR OWN PERSONAL TSUBASA--UP UNTIL THIS MORNING, THAT IS. BUT NOW EVERYTHING HAS BEEN RUINED FOR YOU, YOU POOR DEAR.
THE THOUGHT OF USING THE TSUBASA FOR MY PERSONAL BENEFIT HAS NEVER EVEN CROSSED MY MIND, MA'AM.
IF YOU SAY SO. BUT I KNOW USING IT TO BENEFIT THE ARMY OR THIS COUNTRY HAS NEVER CROSSED YOUR MIND, EITHER.
SO, THIS WISH YOU HAVE THAT YOU KEEP SECRET EVEN FROM YOUR LOYAL LT. COLONEL AND MAJOR...
...WHAT IS IT?
IT HAS BEEN SUCH A LONG TIME SINCE YOU'VE COME TO SEE ME.
VISIT MY QUARTERS TONIGHT SO I CAN PROPERLY CONSOLE YOU.

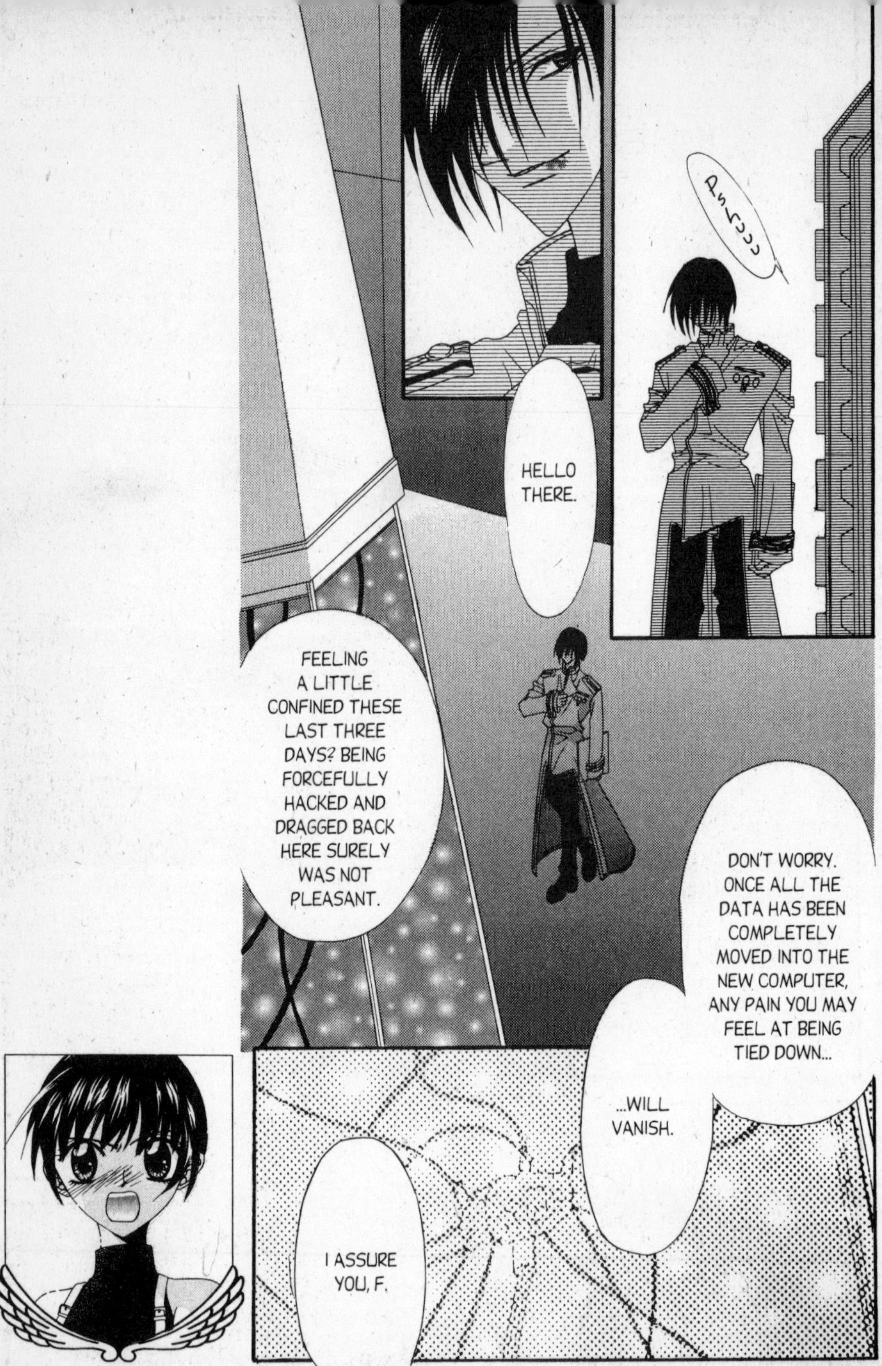
Pshuuu
HELLO THERE.
FEELING A LITTLE CONFINED THESE LAST THREE DAYS? BEING FORCEFULLY HACKED AND DRAGGED BACK HERE SURELY WAS NOT PLEASANT.
DON'T WORRY. ONCE ALL THE DATA HAS BEEN COMPLETELY MOVED INTO THE NEW COMPUTER, ANY PAIN YOU MAY FEEL AT BEING TIED DOWN...
...WILL VANISH.
I ASSURE YOU, F.

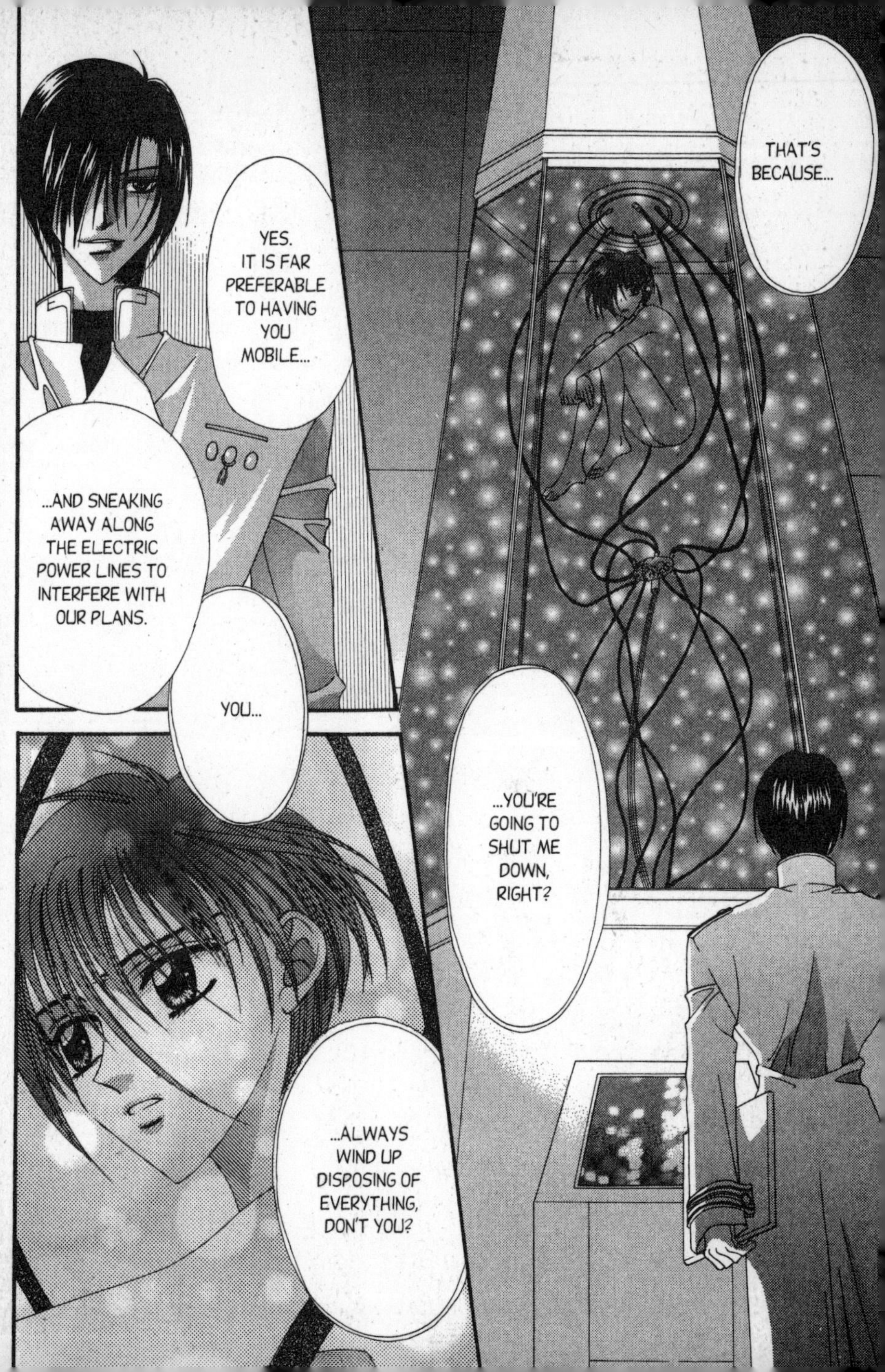

THAT'S BECAUSE...
...YOU'RE GOING TO SHUT ME DOWN, RIGHT?
YES. IT IS FAR PREFERABLE TO HAVING YOU MOBILE...
...AND SNEAKING AWAY ALONG THE ELECTRIC POWER LINES TO INTERFERE WITH OUR PLANS.
YOU...
...ALWAYS WIND UP DISPOSING OF EVERYTHING, DON'T YOU?

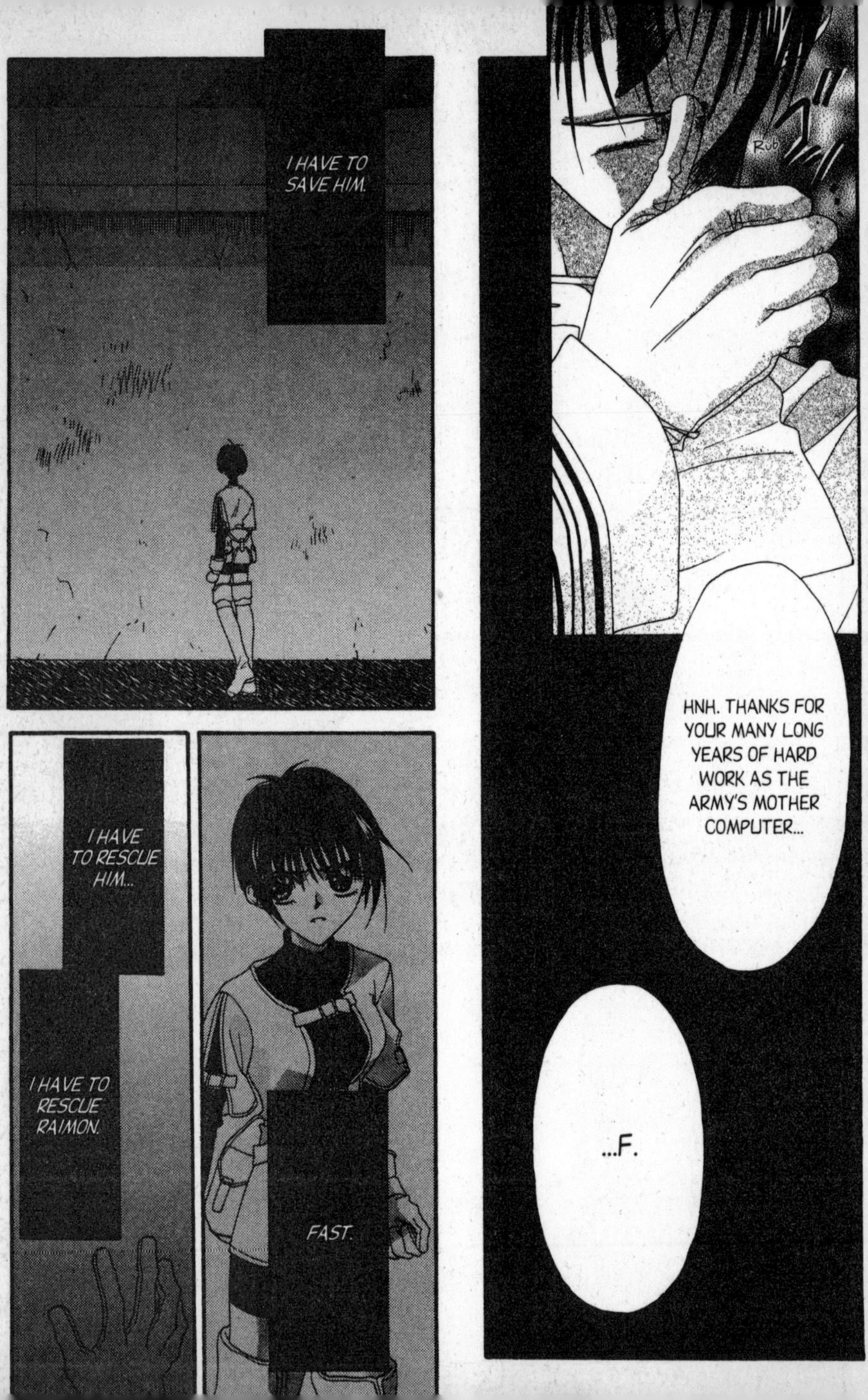
Rub
HNH. THANKS FOR YOUR MANY LONG YEARS OF HARD WORK AS THE ARMY'S MOTHER COMPUTER...
...F.
I HAVE TO SAVE HIM.
FAST.
I HAVE TO RESCUE HIM...
I HAVE TO RESCUE RAIMON.

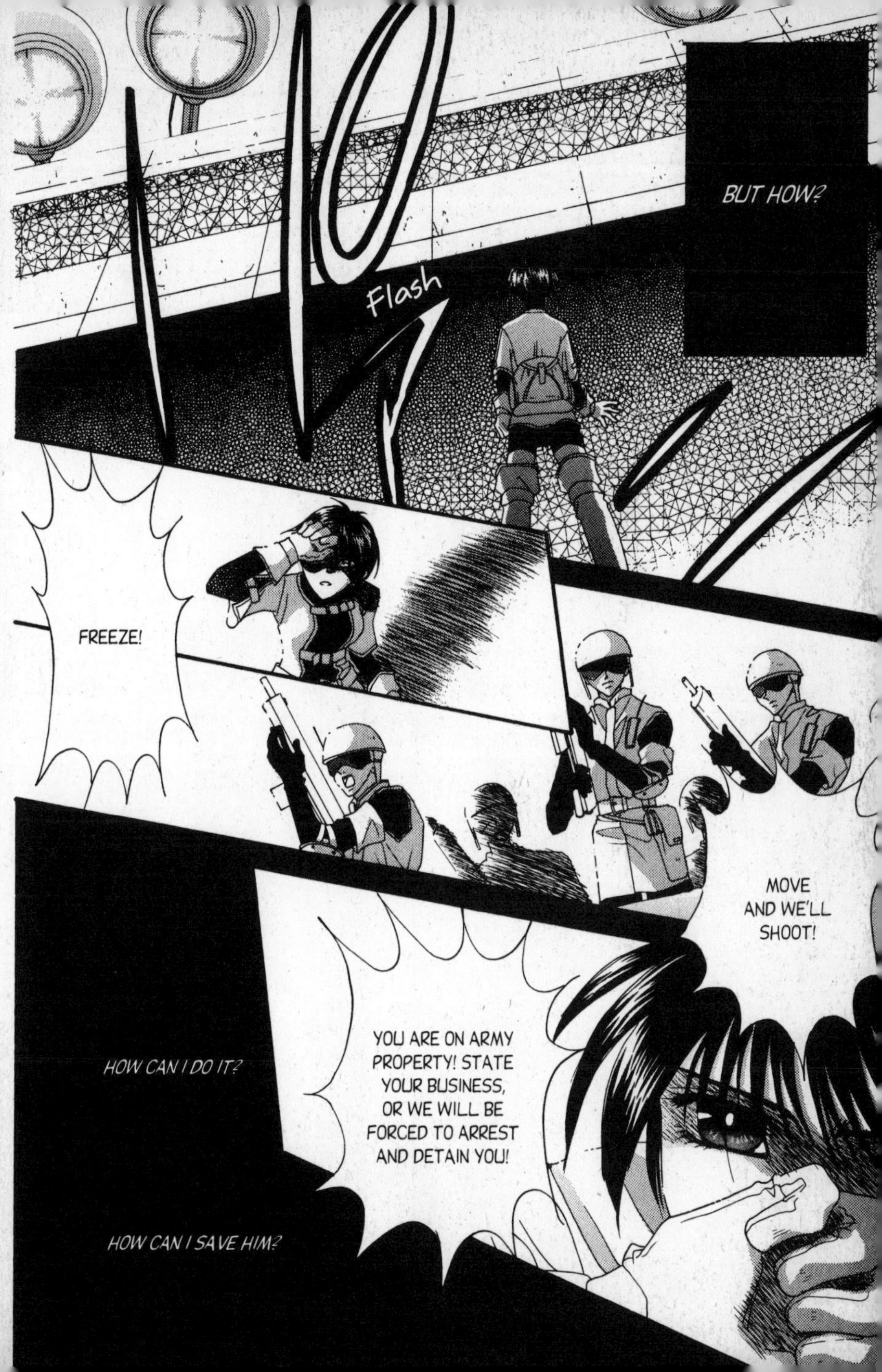
BUT HOW?
Flash
FREEZE!
MOVE AND WE'LL SHOOT!
YOU ARE ON ARMY PROPERTY! STATE YOUR BUSINESS, OR WE WILL BE FORCED TO ARREST AND DETAIN YOU!
HOW CAN I DO IT?
HOW CAN I SAVE HIM?

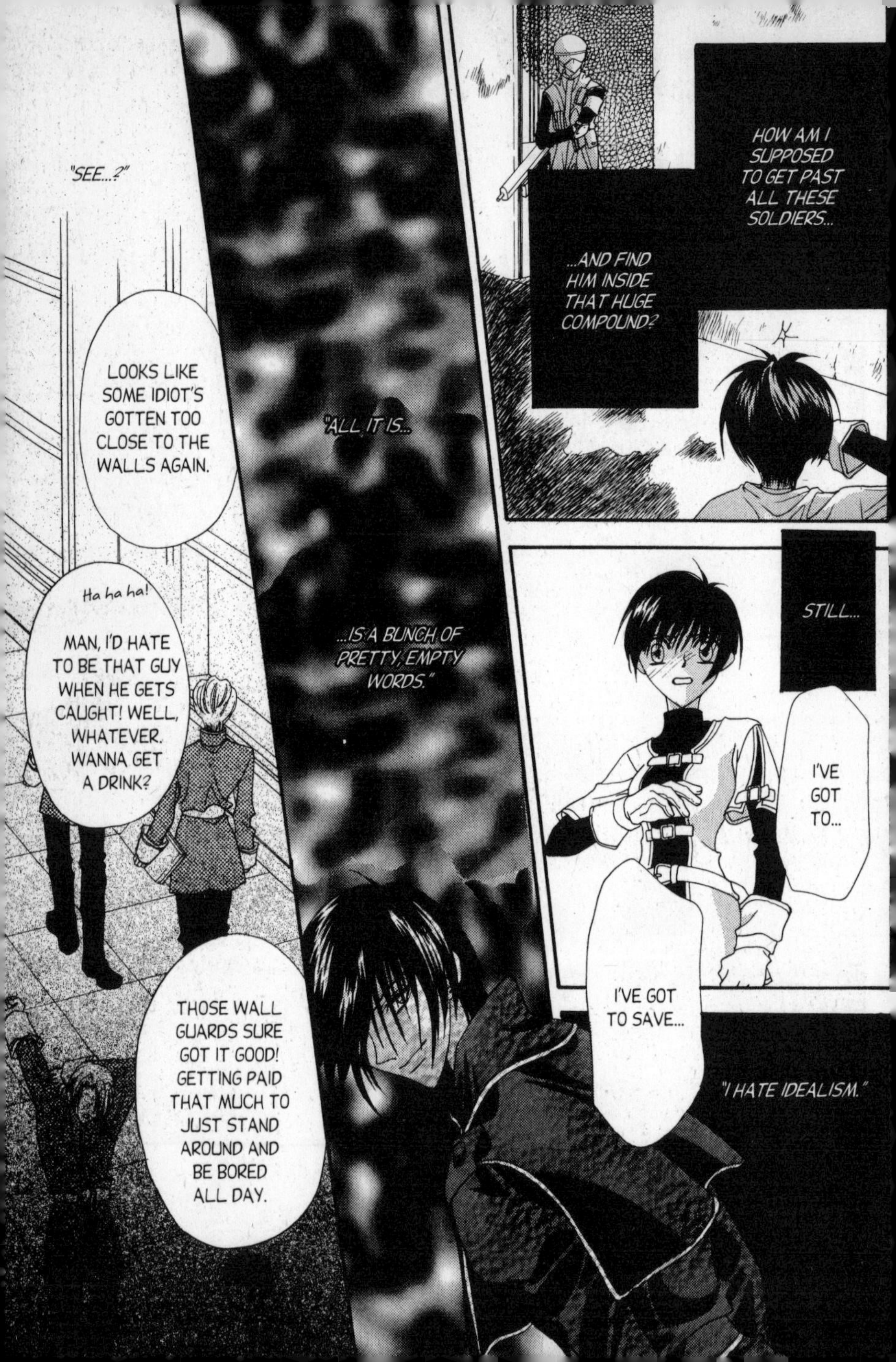
HOW AM I SUPPOSED TO GET PAST ALL THESE SOLDIERS...
...AND FIND HIM INSIDE THAT HUGE COMPOUND?
STILL...
I'VE GOT TO...
I'VE GOT TO SAVE...
"I HATE IDEALISM."
"ALL IT IS...
...IS A BUNCH OF PRETTY, EMPTY WORDS."
"SEE...?"
LOOKS LIKE SOME IDIOT'S GOTTEN TOO CLOSE TO THE WALLS AGAIN.
Ha ha ha!
MAN, I'D HATE TO BE THAT GUY WHEN HE GETS CAUGHT! WELL, WHATEVER. WANNA GET A DRINK?
THOSE WALL GUARDS SURE GOT IT GOOD! GETTING PAID THAT MUCH TO JUST STAND AROUND AND BE BORED ALL DAY.

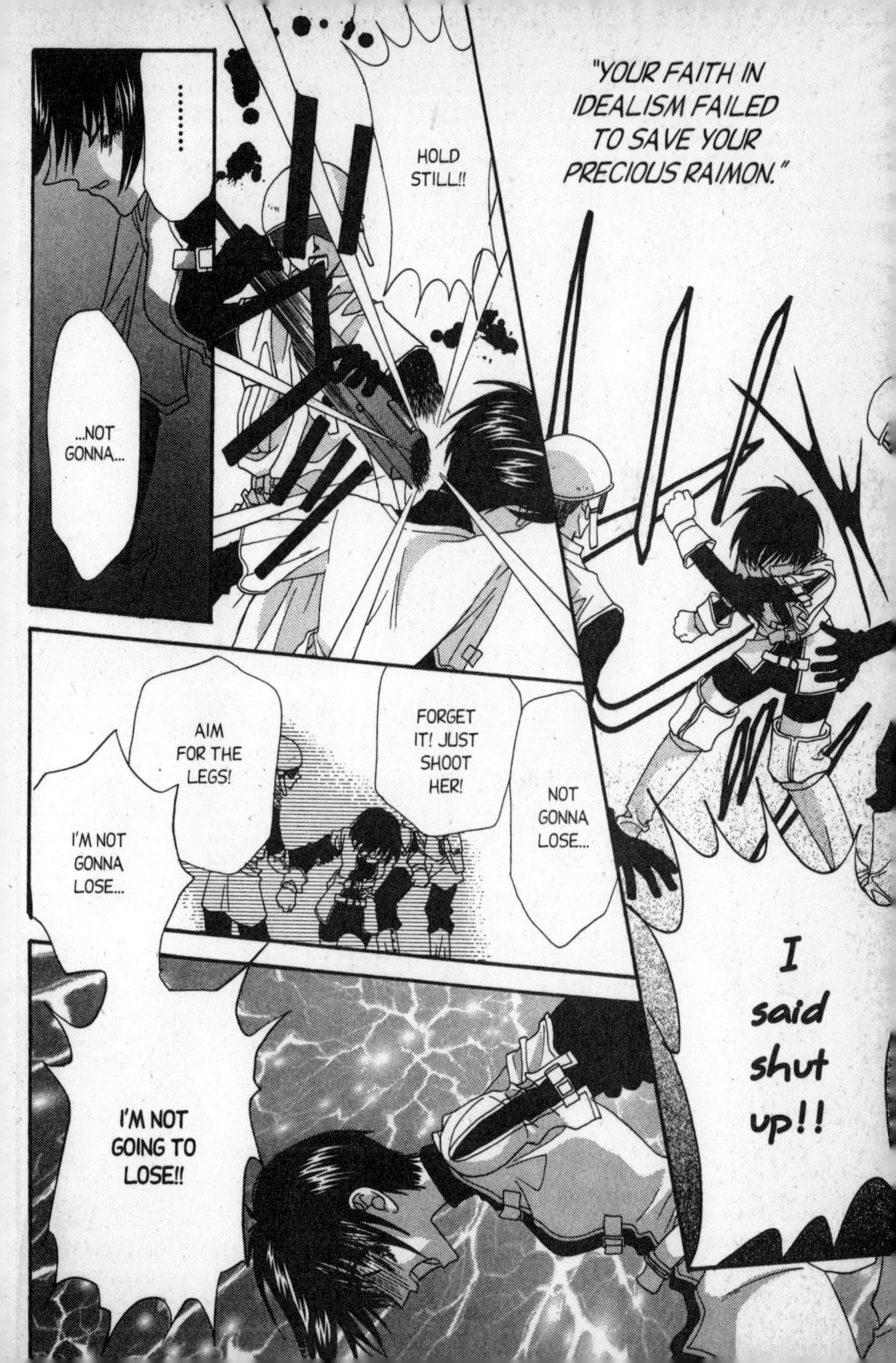
"YOUR FAITH IN IDEALISM FAILED TO SAVE YOUR PRECIOUS RAIMON."
HOLD STILL!!
......
...NOT GONNA...
FORGET IT! JUST SHOOT HER!
AIM FOR THE LEGS!
NOT GONNA LOSE...
I'M NOT GONNA LOSE...
I said shut up!!
I'M NOT GOING TO LOSE!!

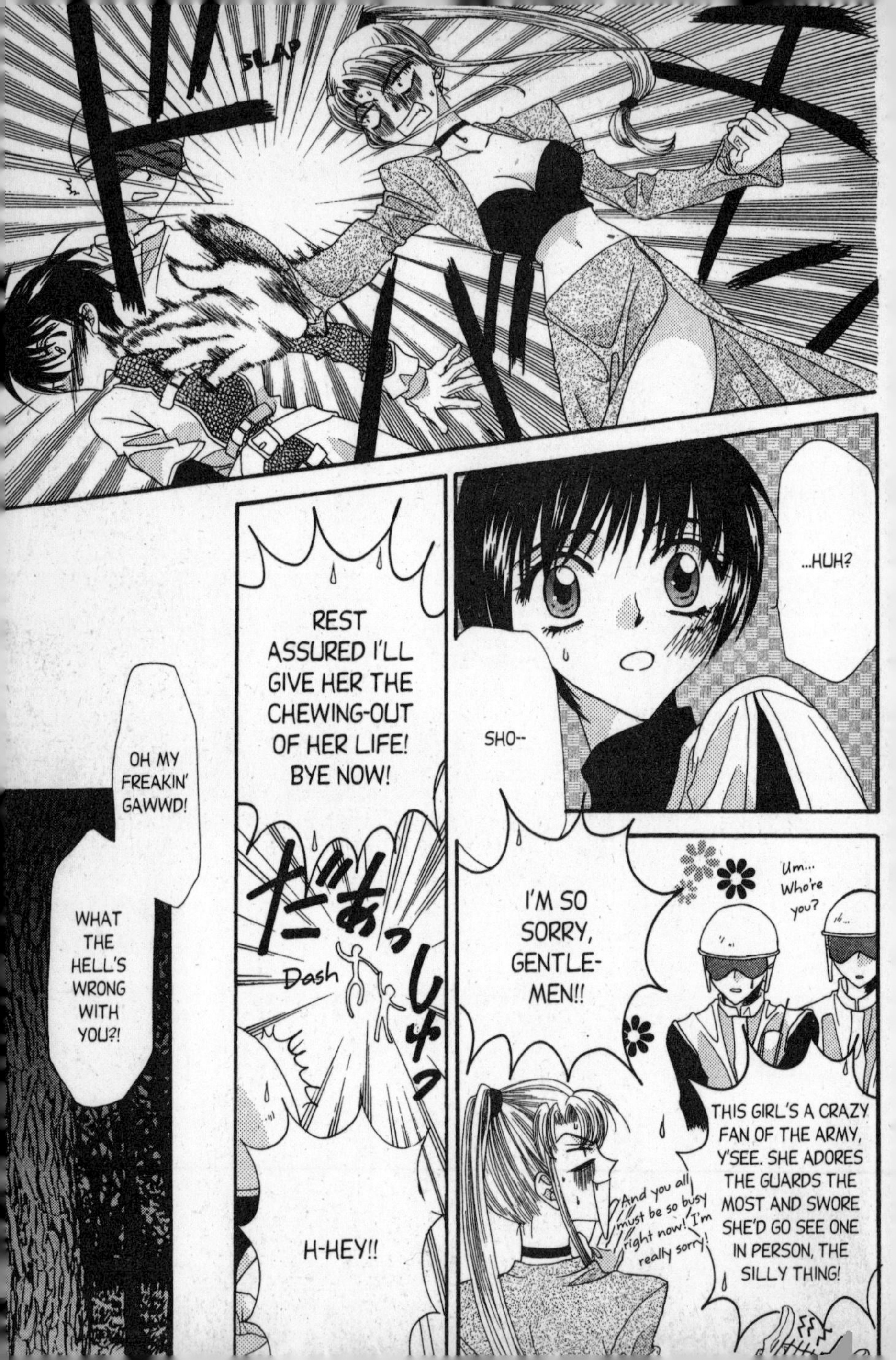
SLAP
...HUH?
SHO--
I'M SO SORRY, GENTLEMEN!!
Um... Who're you?
THIS GIRL'S A CRAZY FAN OF THE ARMY, Y'SEE. SHE ADORES THE GUARDS THE MOST AND SWORE SHE'D GO SEE ONE IN PERSON, THE SILLY THING!
And you all must be so busy right now! I'm really sorry!
REST ASSURED I'LL GIVE HER THE CHEWING-OUT OF HER LIFE! BYE NOW!
だあっしゅっ
Dash
H-HEY!!
OH MY FREAKIN' GAWWD!
WHAT THE HELL'S WRONG WITH YOU?!

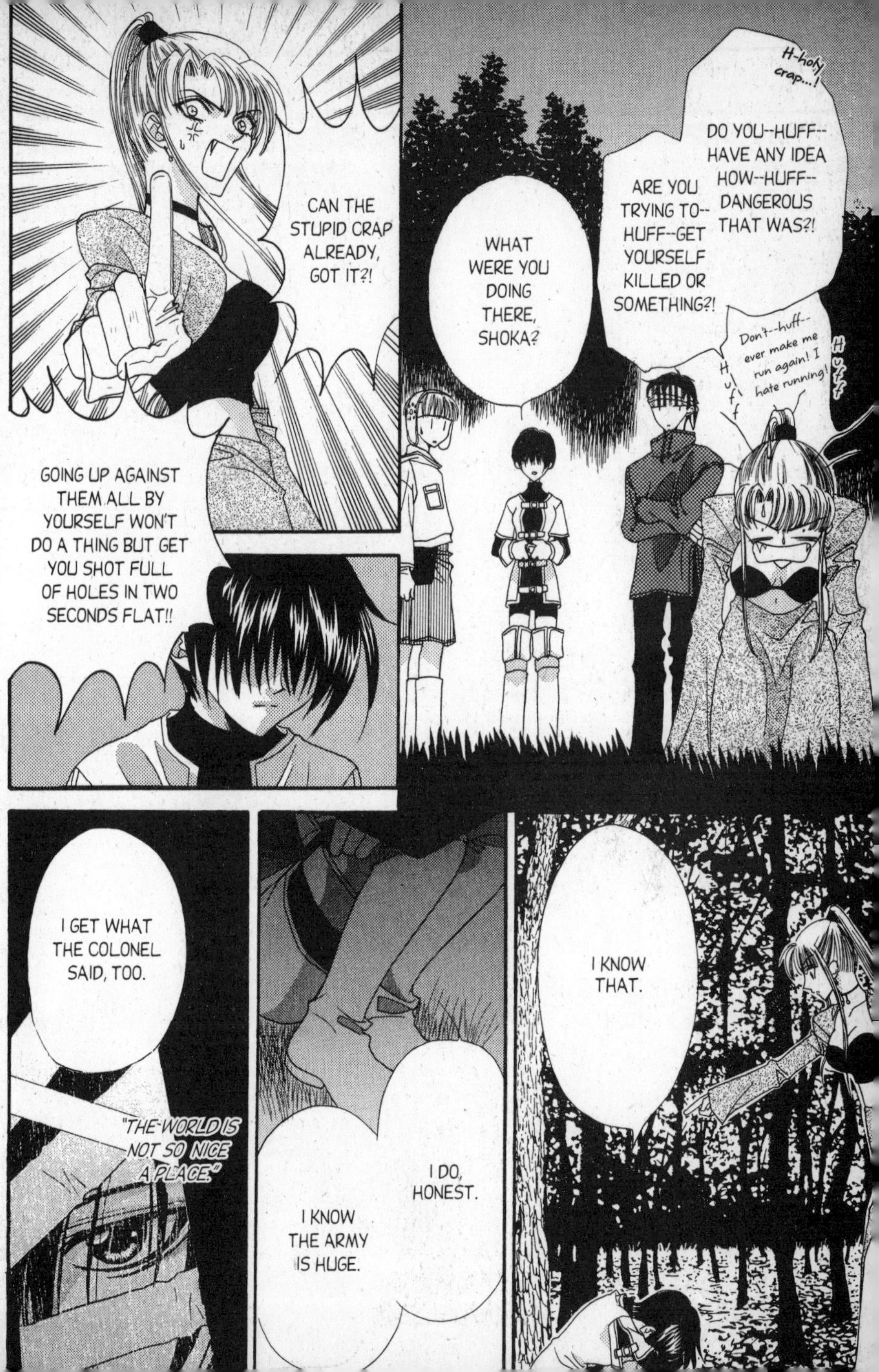

H-holy crap...!
DO YOU--HUFF--HAVE ANY IDEA HOW--HUFF--DANGEROUS THAT WAS?!
ARE YOU TRYING TO--HUFF--GET YOURSELF KILLED OR SOMETHING?!
Huff
Don't--huff--ever make me run again! I hate running!
Huff
WHAT WERE YOU DOING THERE, SHOKA?
CAN THE STUPID CRAP ALREADY, GOT IT?!
GOING UP AGAINST THEM ALL BY YOURSELF WON'T DO A THING BUT GET YOU SHOT FULL OF HOLES IN TWO SECONDS FLAT!!
I KNOW THAT.
I DO, HONEST.
I KNOW THE ARMY IS HUGE.
I GET WHAT THE COLONEL SAID, TOO.
"THE WORLD IS NOT SO NICE A PLACE."

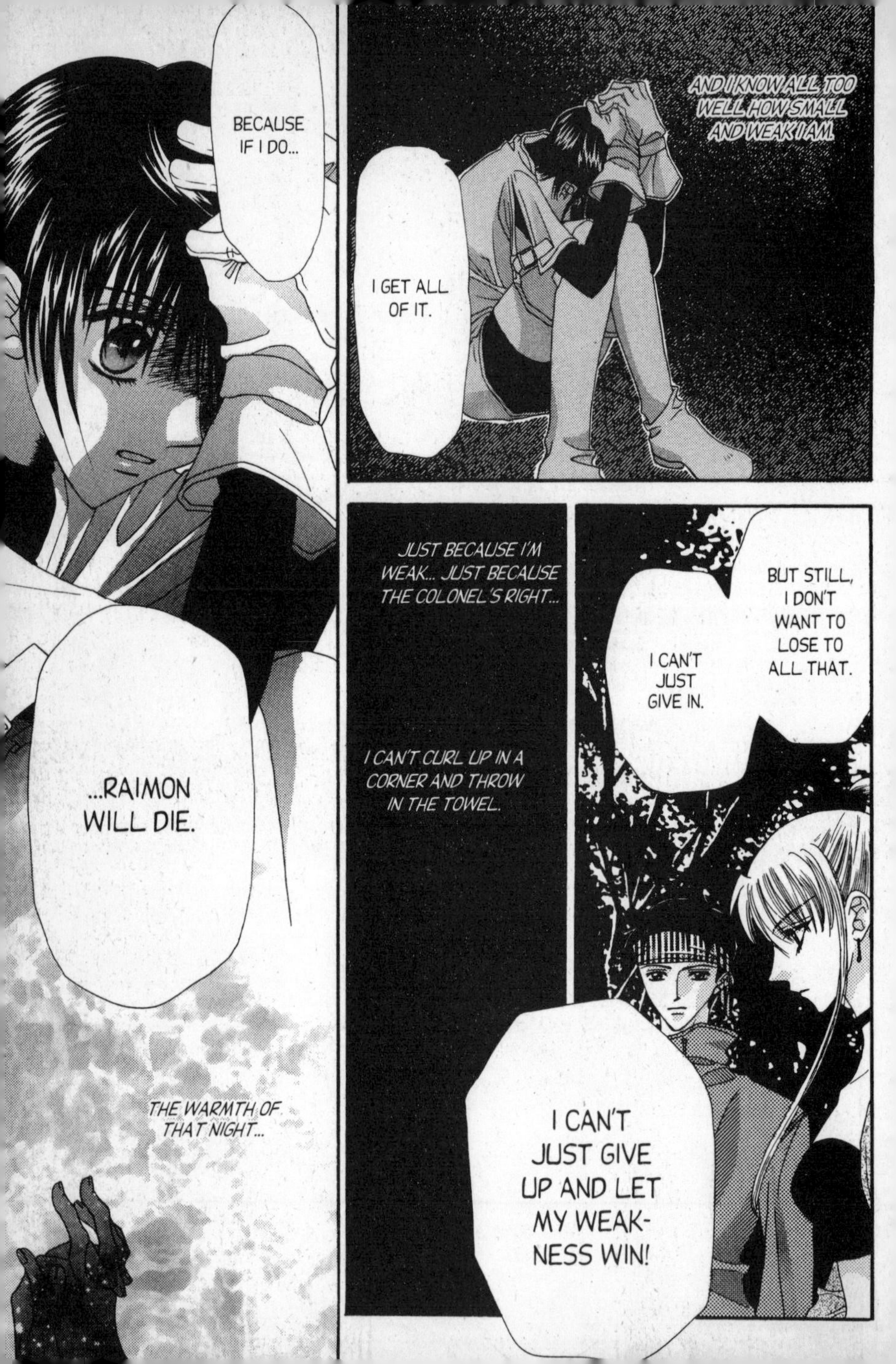
AND I KNOW ALL TOO WELL HOW SMALL AND WEAK I AM.
I GET ALL OF IT.
BUT STILL, I DON'T WANT TO LOSE TO ALL THAT.
I CAN'T JUST GIVE IN.
I CAN'T JUST GIVE UP AND LET MY WEAK-NESS WIN!
JUST BECAUSE I'M WEAK... JUST BECAUSE THE COLONEL'S RIGHT...
I CAN'T CURL UP IN A CORNER AND THROW IN THE TOWEL.
BECAUSE IF I DO...
...RAIMON WILL DIE.
THE WARMTH OF THAT NIGHT...

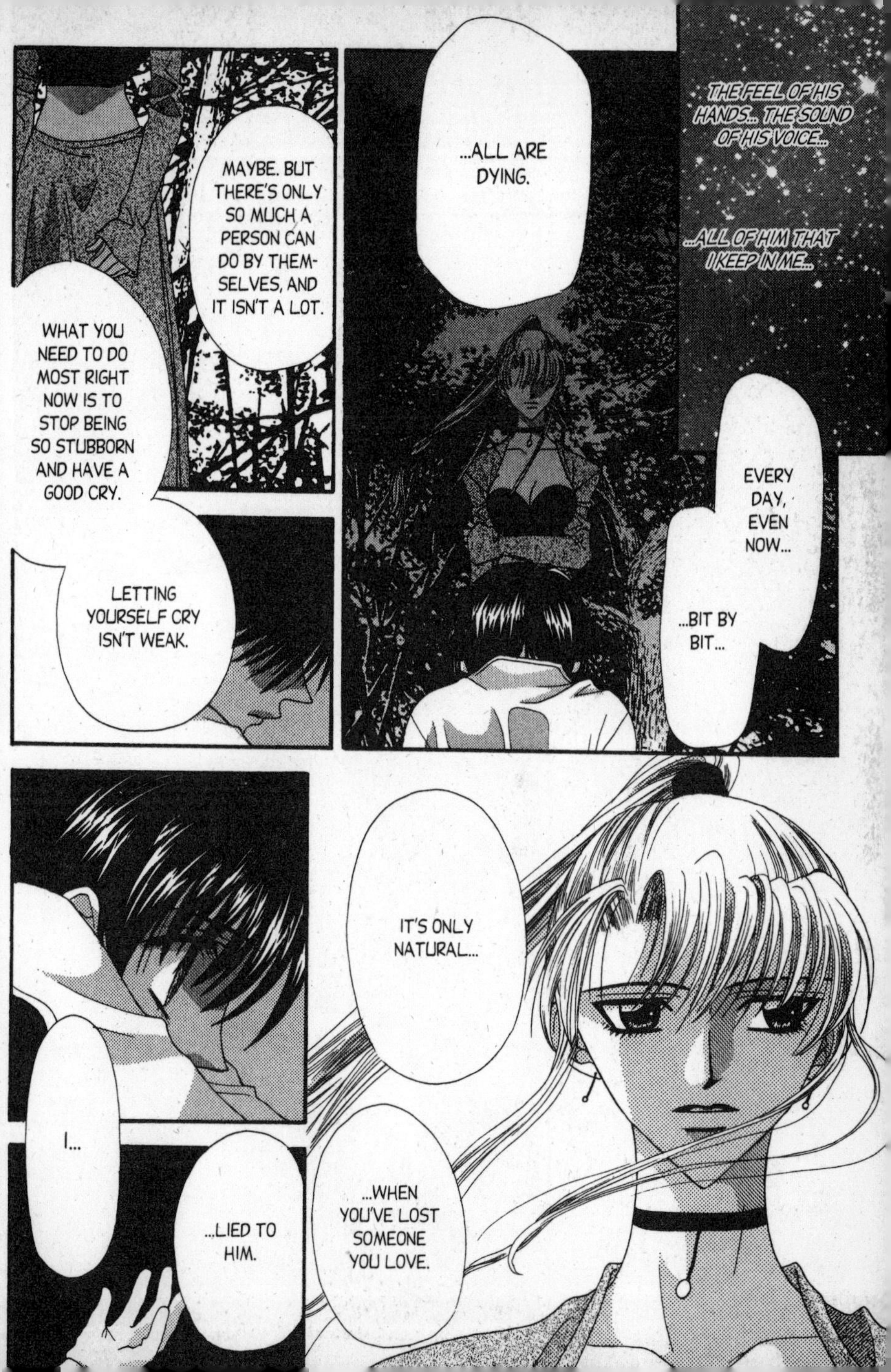
THE FEEL OF HIS HANDS... THE SOUND OF HIS VOICE...
...ALL OF HIM THAT I KEEP IN ME...
EVERY DAY, EVEN NOW...
...BIT BY BIT...
...ALL ARE DYING.
MAYBE. BUT THERE'S ONLY SO MUCH A PERSON CAN DO BY THEMSELVES, AND IT ISN'T A LOT.
WHAT YOU NEED TO DO MOST RIGHT NOW IS TO STOP BEING SO STUBBORN AND HAVE A GOOD CRY.
LETTING YOURSELF CRY ISN'T WEAK.
IT'S ONLY NATURAL...
...WHEN YOU'VE LOST SOMEONE YOU LOVE.
I...
...LIED TO HIM.

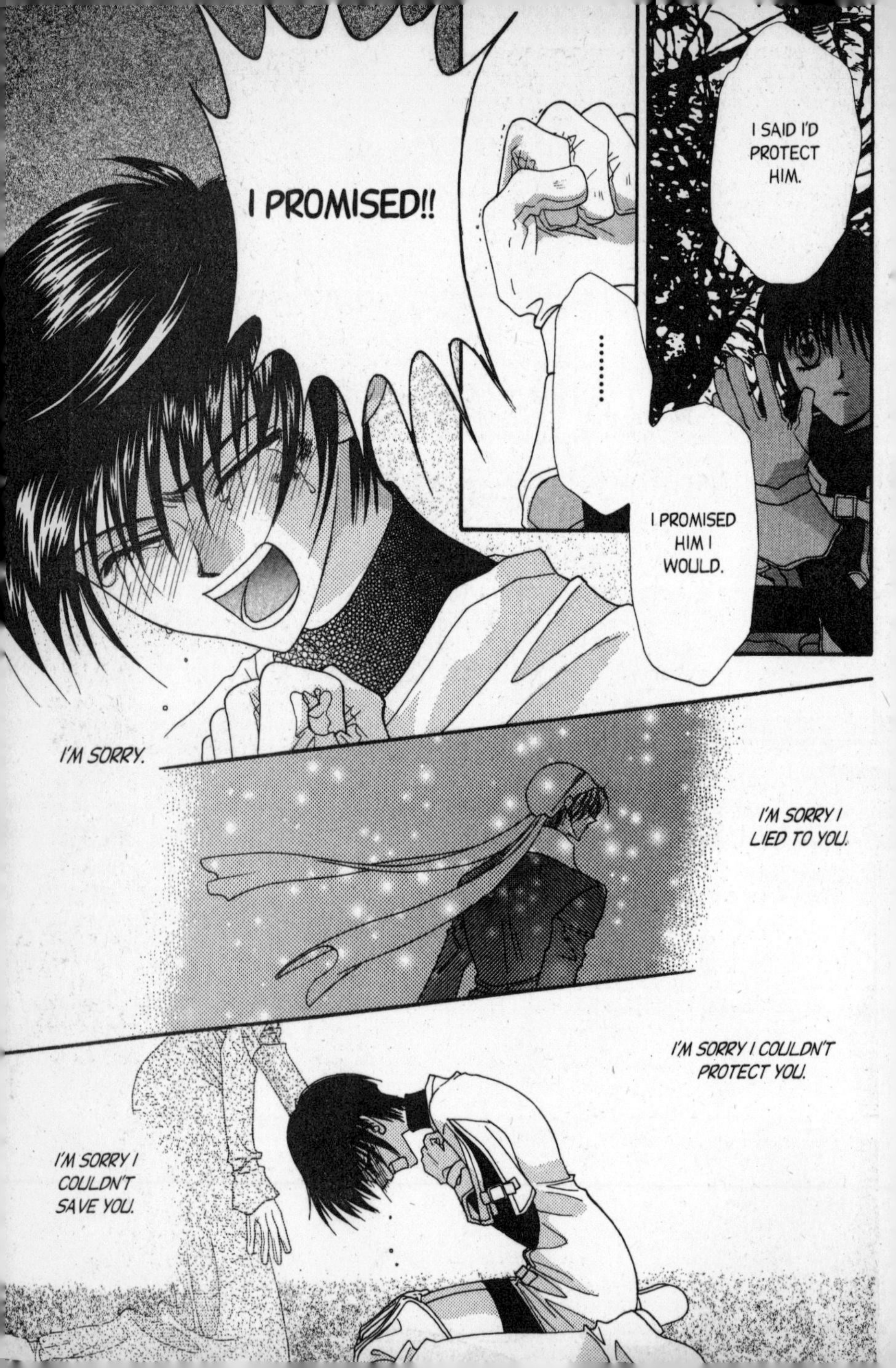
I SAID I'D PROTECT HIM.
......
I PROMISED HIM I WOULD.
I PROMISED!!
I'M SORRY.
I'M SORRY I LIED TO YOU.
I'M SORRY I COULDN'T PROTECT YOU.
I'M SORRY I COULDN'T SAVE YOU.

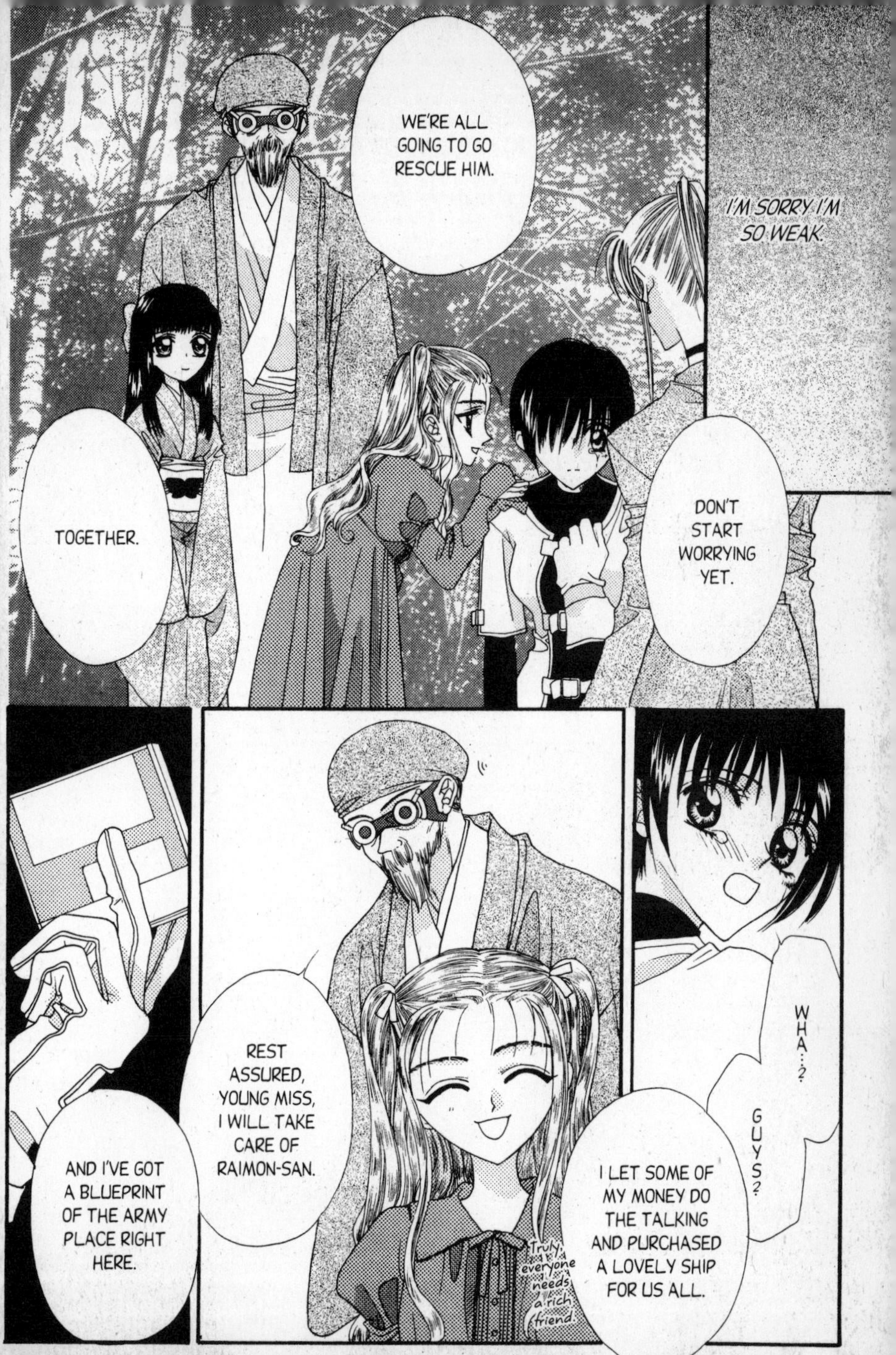
I'M SORRY I'M SO WEAK.
WE'RE ALL GOING TO GO RESCUE HIM.
DON'T START WORRYING YET.
TOGETHER.
WHA...?
GUYS?
REST ASSURED, YOUNG MISS, I WILL TAKE CARE OF RAIMON-SAN.
I LET SOME OF MY MONEY DO THE TALKING AND PURCHASED A LOVELY SHIP FOR US ALL.
Truly, everyone needs a rich friend.
AND I'VE GOT A BLUEPRINT OF THE ARMY PLACE RIGHT HERE.

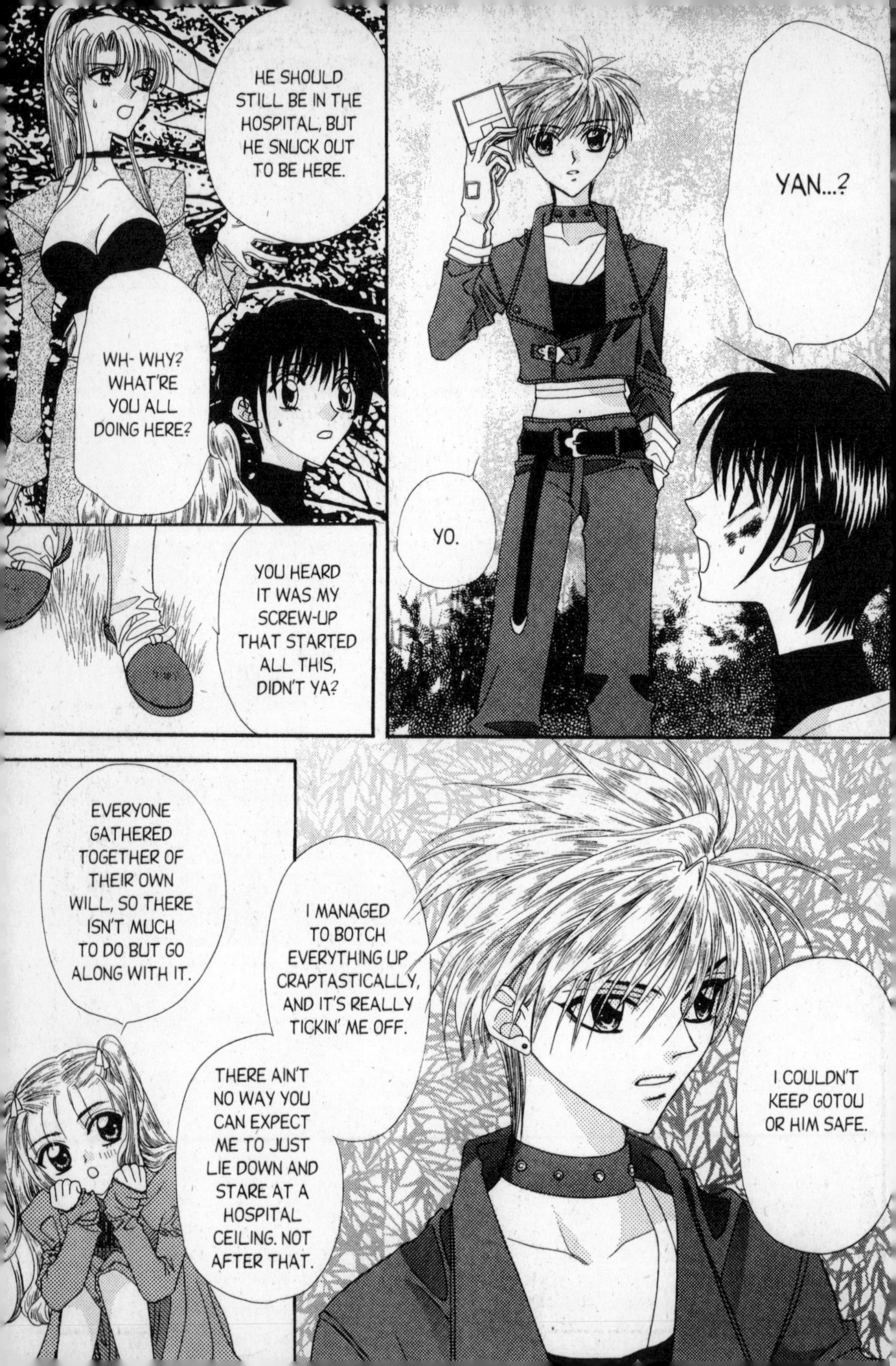
YAN...?
YO.
HE SHOULD STILL BE IN THE HOSPITAL, BUT HE SNUCK OUT TO BE HERE.
WH- WHY? WHAT'RE YOU ALL DOING HERE?
YOU HEARD IT WAS MY SCREW-UP THAT STARTED ALL THIS, DIDN'T YA?
I COULDN'T KEEP GOTOU OR HIM SAFE.
I MANAGED TO BOTCH EVERYTHING UP CRAPTASTICALLY, AND IT'S REALLY TICKIN' ME OFF.
THERE AIN'T NO WAY YOU CAN EXPECT ME TO JUST LIE DOWN AND STARE AT A HOSPITAL CEILING. NOT AFTER THAT.
EVERYONE GATHERED TOGETHER OF THEIR OWN WILL, SO THERE ISN'T MUCH TO DO BUT GO ALONG WITH IT.

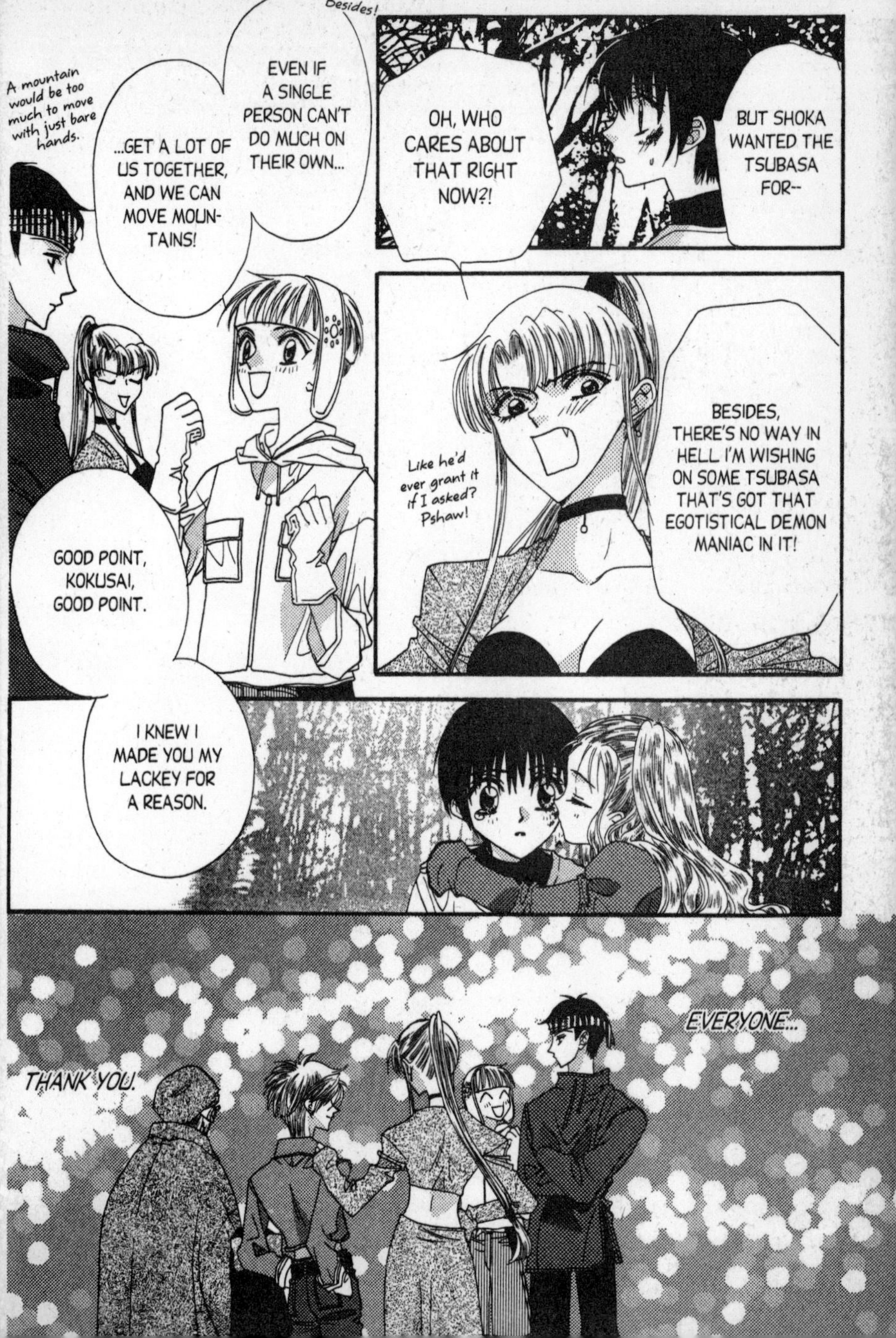

BUT SHOKA WANTED THE TSUBASA FOR--
OH, WHO CARES ABOUT THAT RIGHT NOW?!
BESIDES, THERE'S NO WAY IN HELL I'M WISHING ON SOME TSUBASA THAT'S GOT THAT EGOTISTICAL DEMON MANIAC IN IT!
Like he'd ever grant it if I asked? Pshaw!
Besides!
EVEN IF A SINGLE PERSON CAN'T DO MUCH ON THEIR OWN...
...GET A LOT OF US TOGETHER, AND WE CAN MOVE MOUN-TAINS!
A mountain would be too much to move with just bare hands.
GOOD POINT, KOKUSAI, GOOD POINT.
I KNEW I MADE YOU MY LACKEY FOR A REASON.
EVERYONE...
THANK YOU.

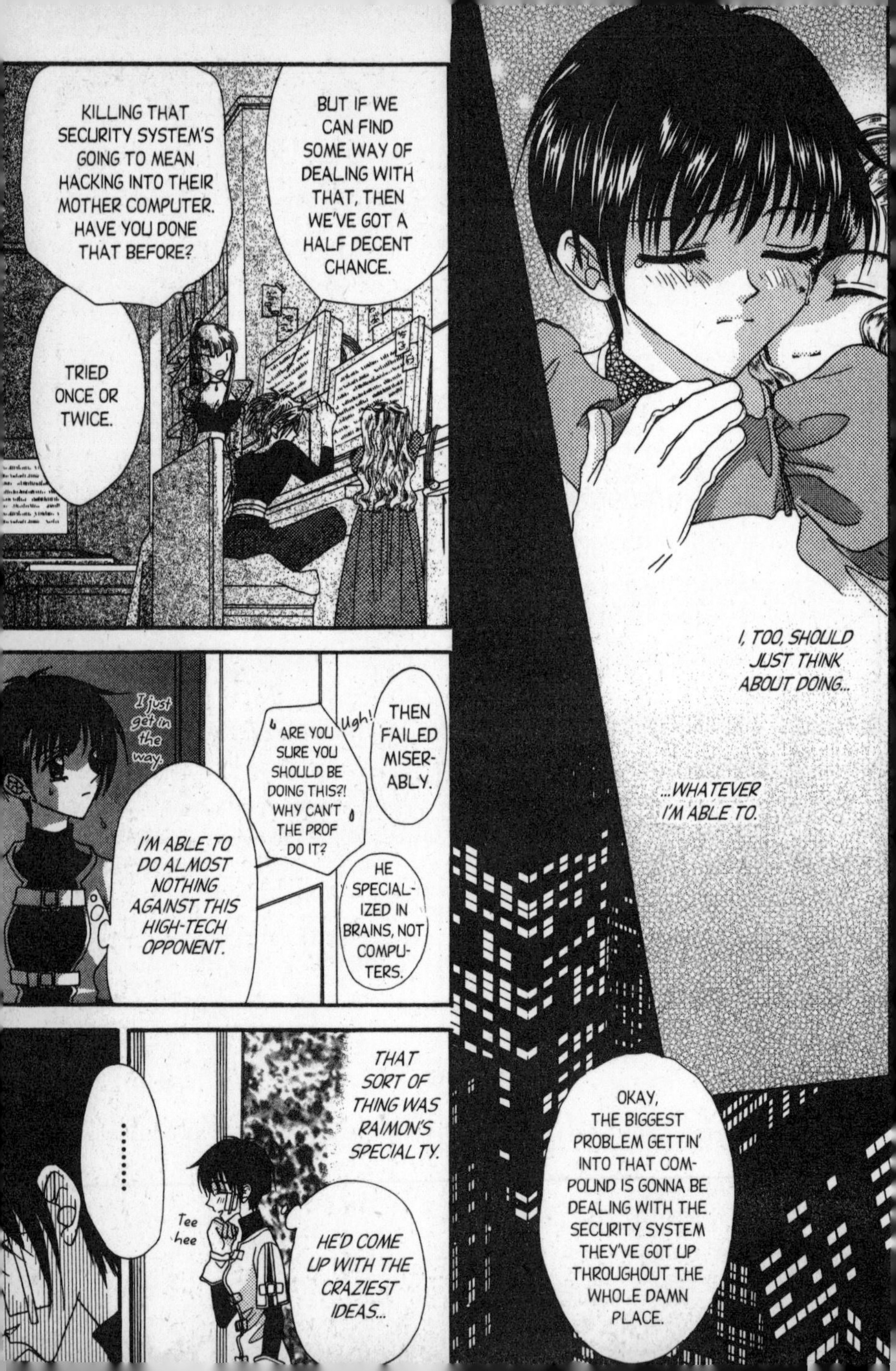
I, TOO, SHOULD JUST THINK ABOUT DOING...
...WHATEVER I'M ABLE TO.
OKAY, THE BIGGEST PROBLEM GETTIN' INTO THAT COMPOUND IS GONNA BE DEALING WITH THE SECURITY SYSTEM THEY'VE GOT UP THROUGHOUT THE WHOLE DAMN PLACE.
BUT IF WE CAN FIND SOME WAY OF DEALING WITH THAT, THEN WE'VE GOT A HALF DECENT CHANCE.
KILLING THAT SECURITY SYSTEM'S GOING TO MEAN HACKING INTO THEIR MOTHER COMPUTER. HAVE YOU DONE THAT BEFORE?
TRIED ONCE OR TWICE.
THEN FAILED MISERABLY.
Ugh!
ARE YOU SURE YOU SHOULD BE DOING THIS?! WHY CAN'T THE PROF DO IT?
HE SPECIALIZED IN BRAINS, NOT COMPUTERS.
I'M ABLE TO DO ALMOST NOTHING AGAINST THIS HIGH-TECH OPPONENT.
I just get in the way.
THAT SORT OF THING WAS RAIMON'S SPECIALTY.
HE'D COME UP WITH THE CRAZIEST IDEAS...
Tee hee
......

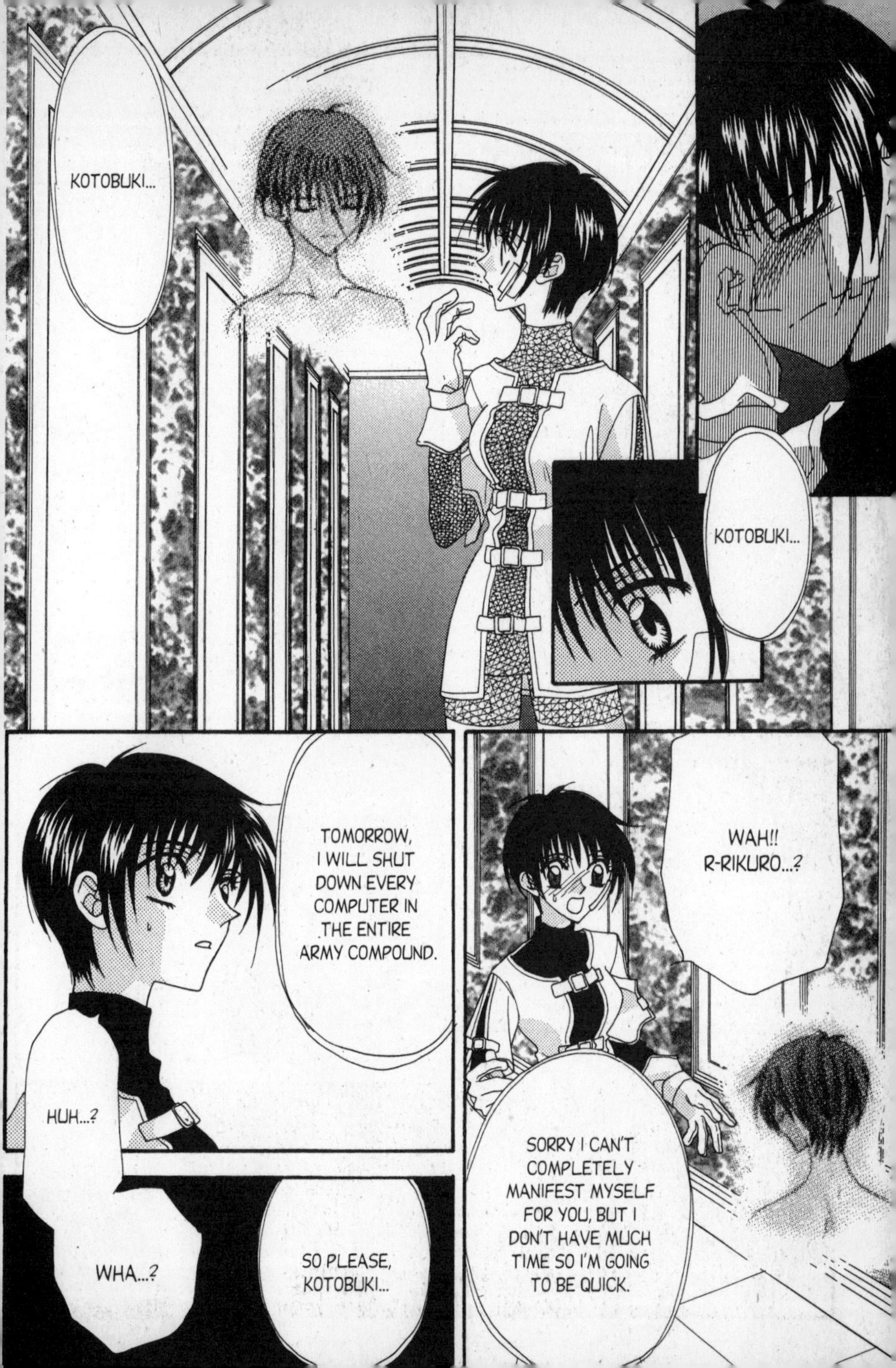

KOTOBUKI...
KOTOBUKI...
WAH!! R-RIKURO...?
SORRY I CAN'T COMPLETELY MANIFEST MYSELF FOR YOU, BUT I DON'T HAVE MUCH TIME SO I'M GOING TO BE QUICK.
TOMORROW, I WILL SHUT DOWN EVERY COMPUTER IN THE ENTIRE ARMY COMPOUND.
HUH...?
SO PLEASE, KOTOBUKI...
WHA...?

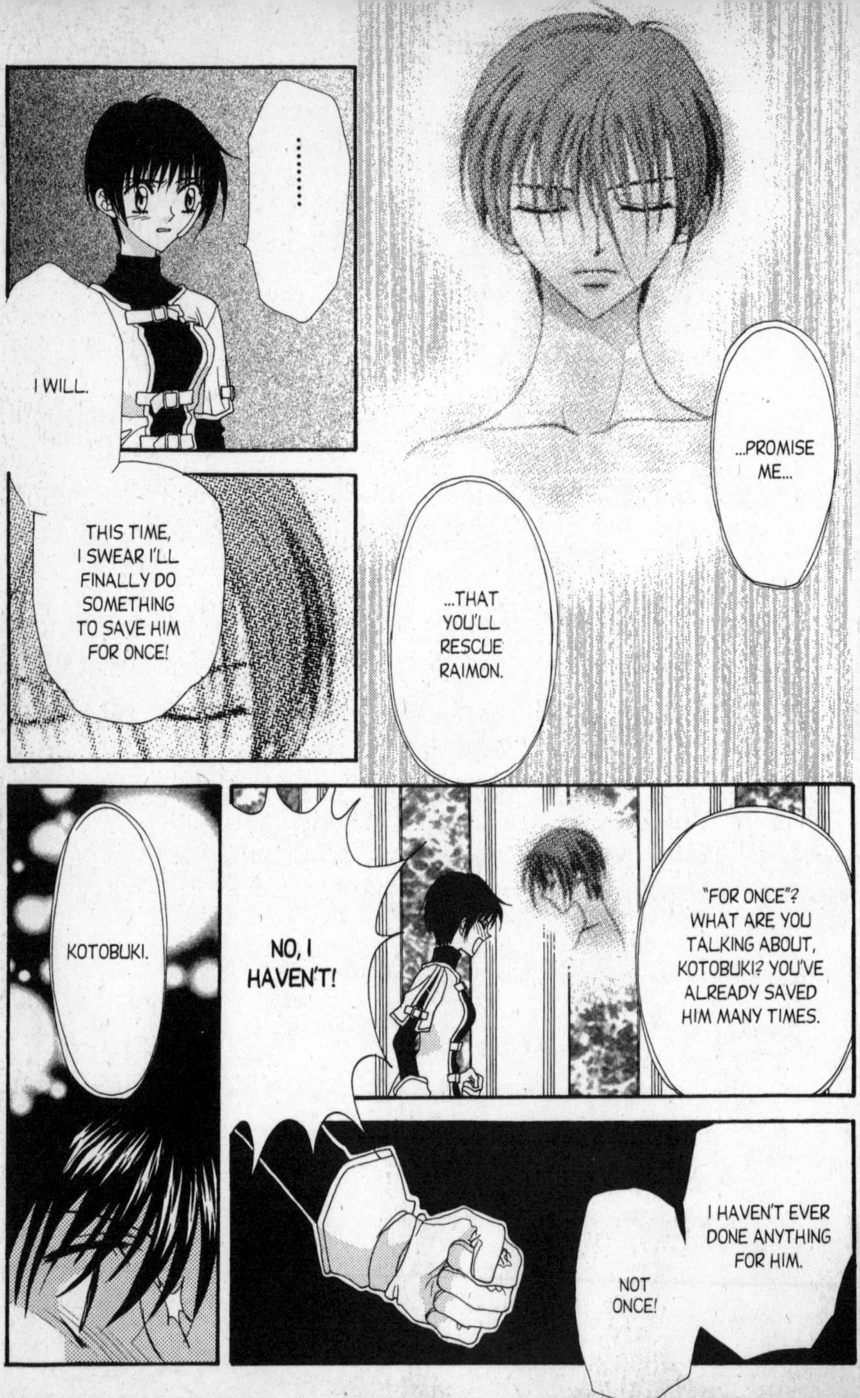
...PROMISE ME...
...THAT YOU'LL RESCUE RAIMON.
......
I WILL.
THIS TIME, I SWEAR I'LL FINALLY DO SOMETHING TO SAVE HIM FOR ONCE!
"FOR ONCE"? WHAT ARE YOU TALKING ABOUT, KOTOBUKI? YOU'VE ALREADY SAVED HIM MANY TIMES.
NO, I HAVEN'T!
I HAVEN'T EVER DONE ANYTHING FOR HIM.
NOT ONCE!
KOTOBUKI.

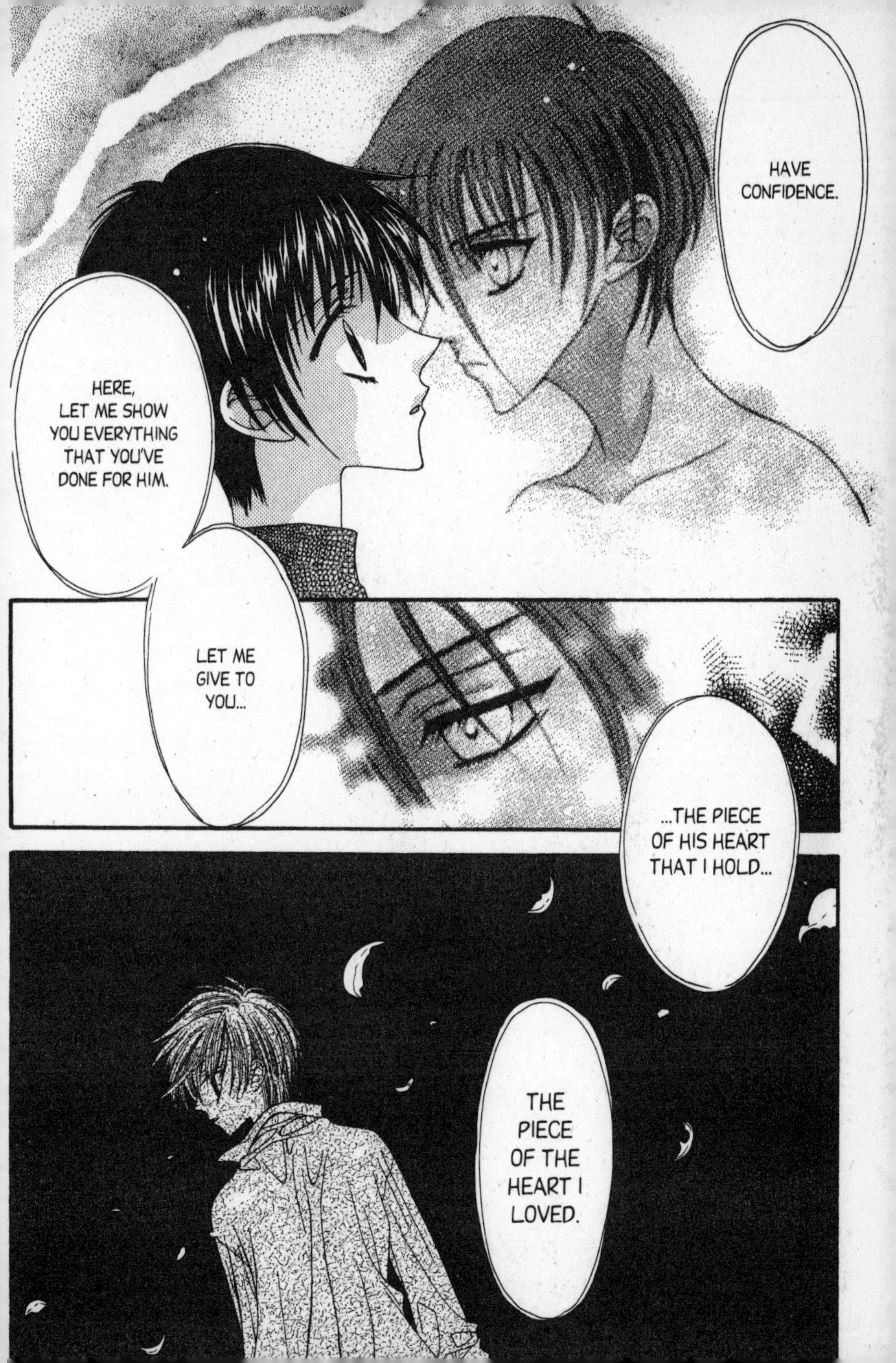
HAVE CONFIDENCE.
HERE, LET ME SHOW YOU EVERYTHING THAT YOU'VE DONE FOR HIM.
LET ME GIVE TO YOU...
...THE PIECE OF HIS HEART THAT I HOLD...
THE PIECE OF THE HEART I LOVED.

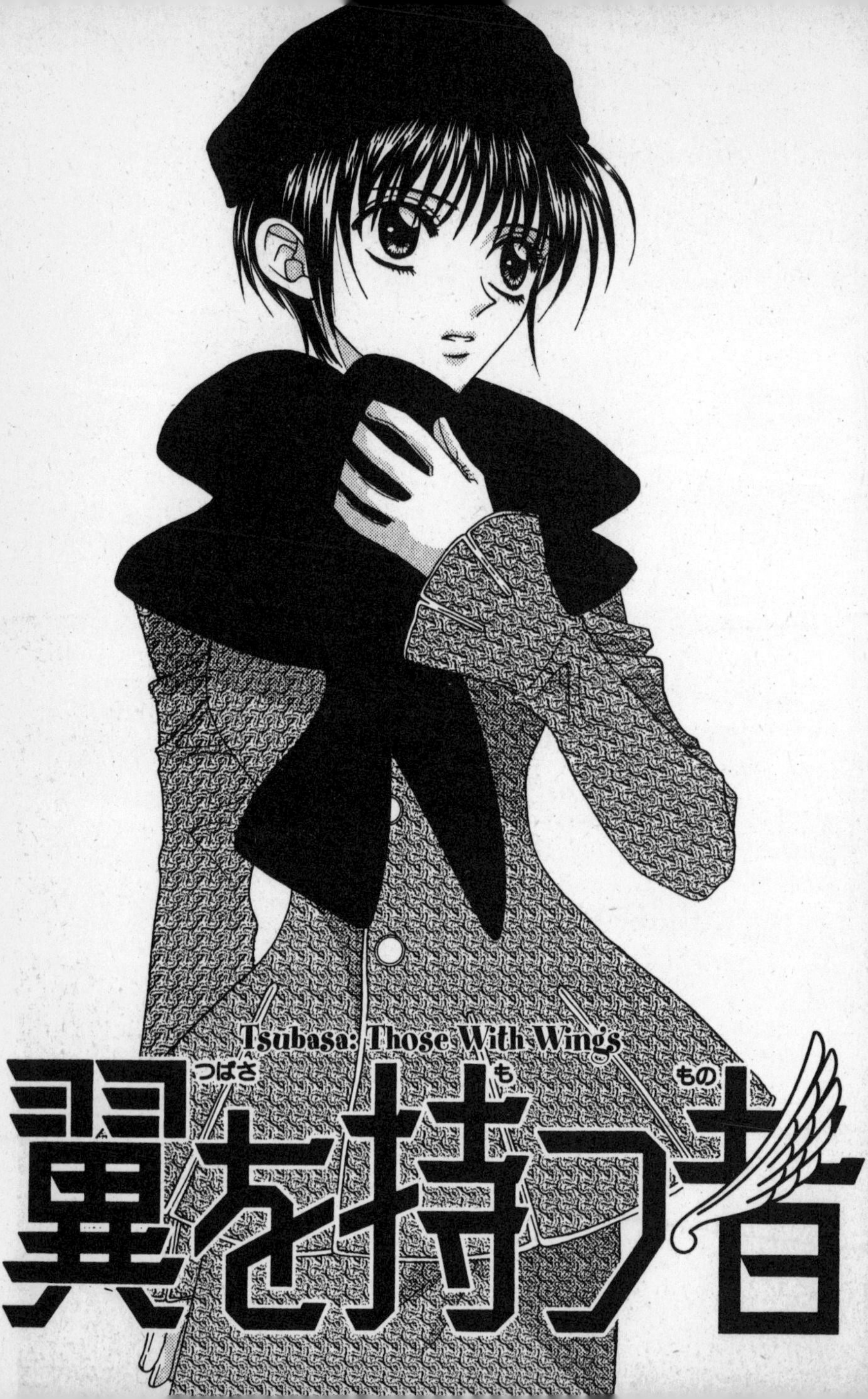
Tsubasa: Those With Wings
翼を持つ者
つばさ も もの

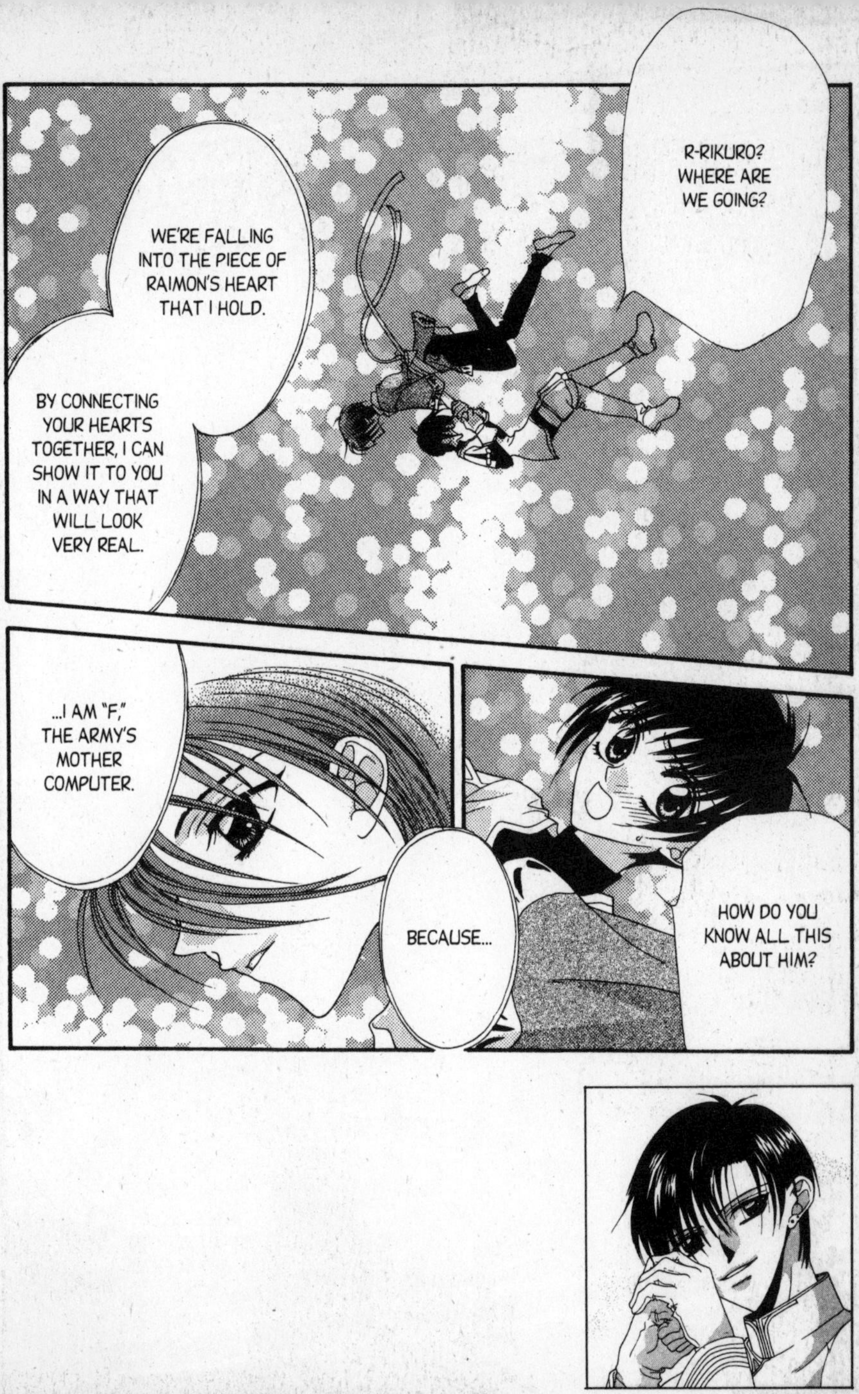
R-RIKURO? WHERE ARE WE GOING?
WE'RE FALLING INTO THE PIECE OF RAIMON'S HEART THAT I HOLD.
BY CONNECTING YOUR HEARTS TOGETHER, I CAN SHOW IT TO YOU IN A WAY THAT WILL LOOK VERY REAL.
HOW DO YOU KNOW ALL THIS ABOUT HIM?
BECAUSE...
...I AM "F," THE ARMY'S MOTHER COMPUTER.

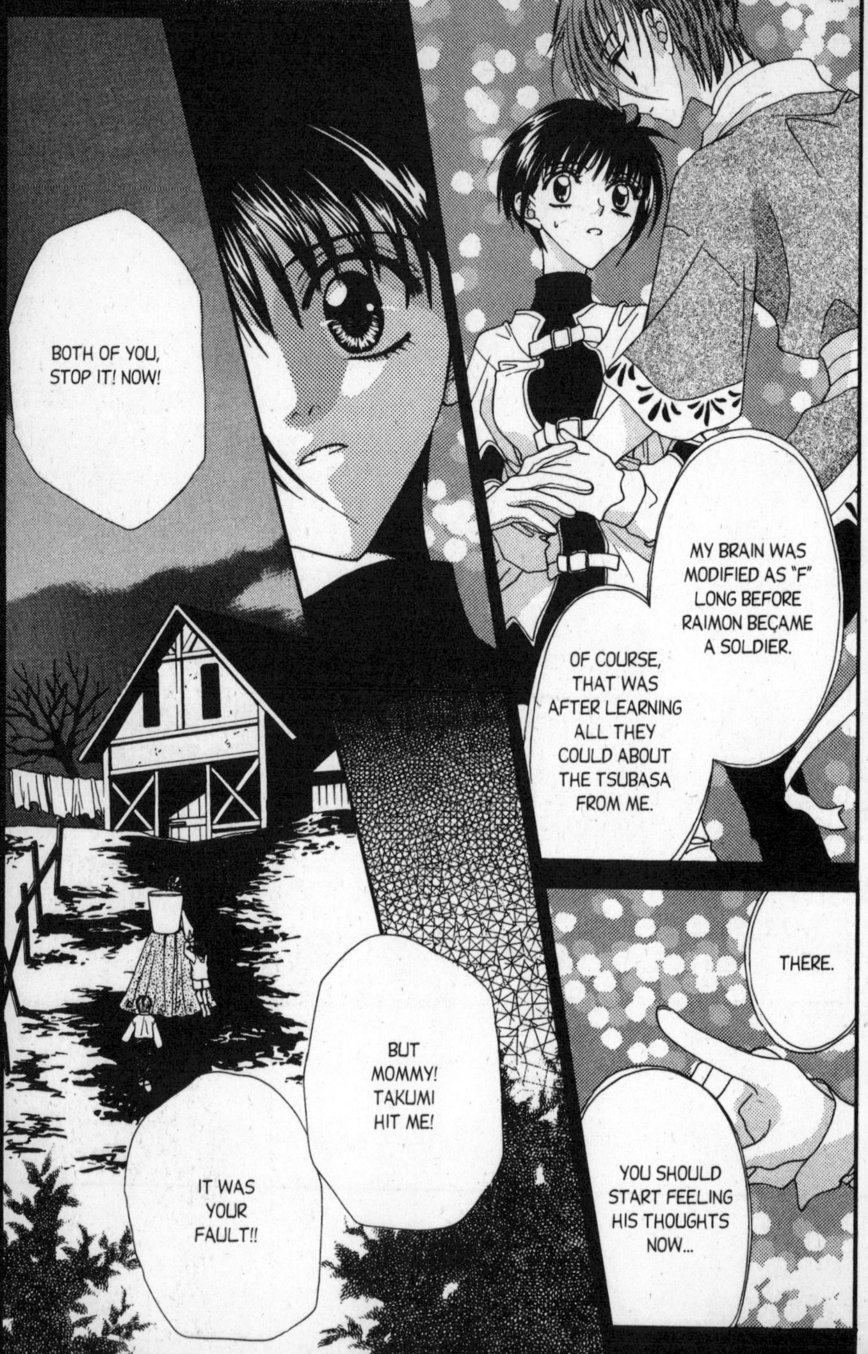
MY BRAIN WAS MODIFIED AS "F" LONG BEFORE RAIMON BECAME A SOLDIER.
OF COURSE, THAT WAS AFTER LEARNING ALL THEY COULD ABOUT THE TSUBASA FROM ME.
THERE.
YOU SHOULD START FEELING HIS THOUGHTS NOW...
BOTH OF YOU, STOP IT! NOW!
BUT MOMMY! TAKUMI HIT ME!
IT WAS YOUR FAULT!!

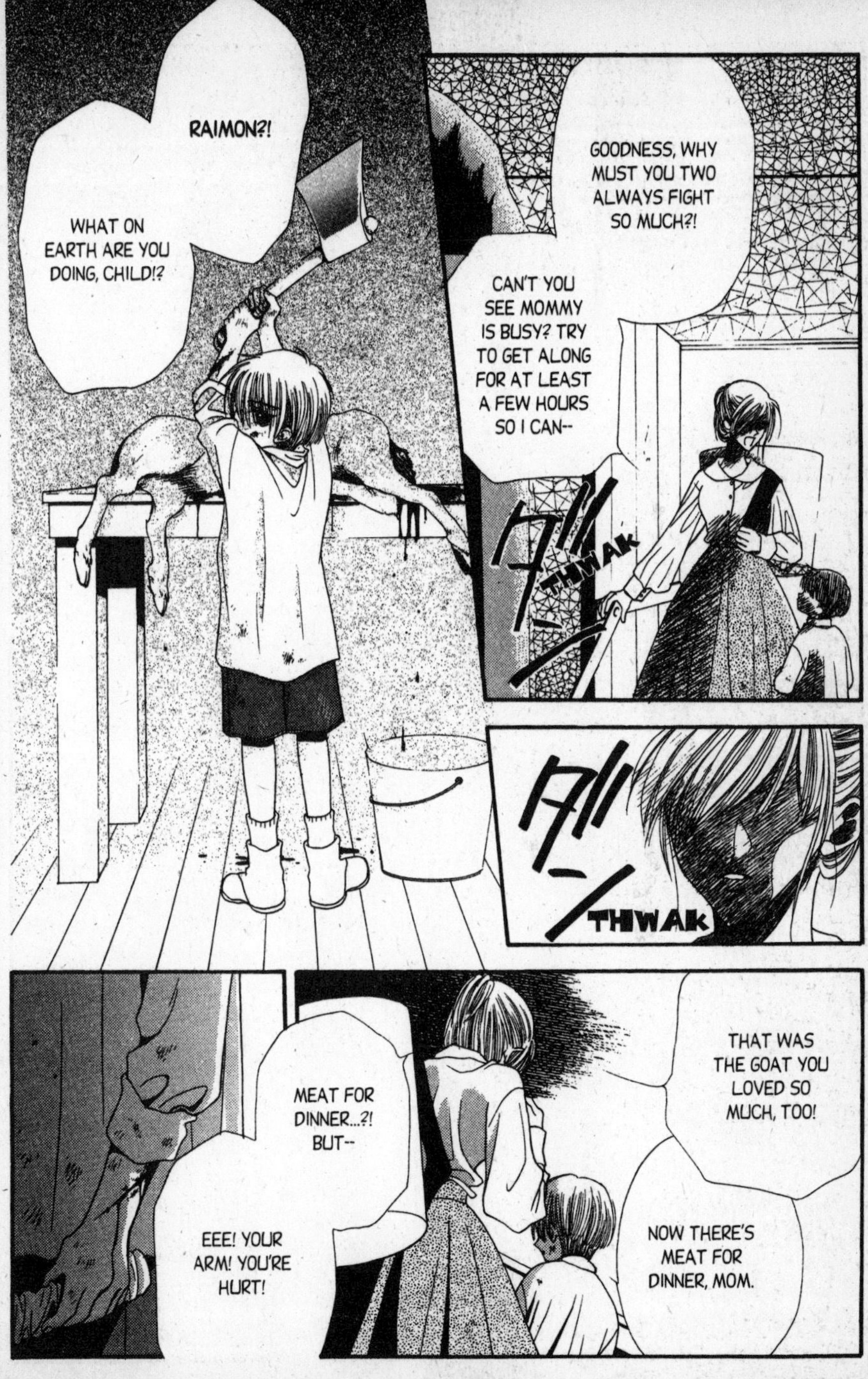
GOODNESS, WHY MUST YOU TWO ALWAYS FIGHT SO MUCH?!
CAN'T YOU SEE MOMMY IS BUSY? TRY TO GET ALONG FOR AT LEAST A FEW HOURS SO I CAN--
THWAK
THWAK
RAIMON?!
WHAT ON EARTH ARE YOU DOING, CHILD!?
THAT WAS THE GOAT YOU LOVED SO MUCH, TOO!
NOW THERE'S MEAT FOR DINNER, MOM.
MEAT FOR DINNER...?! BUT--
EEE! YOUR ARM! YOU'RE HURT!

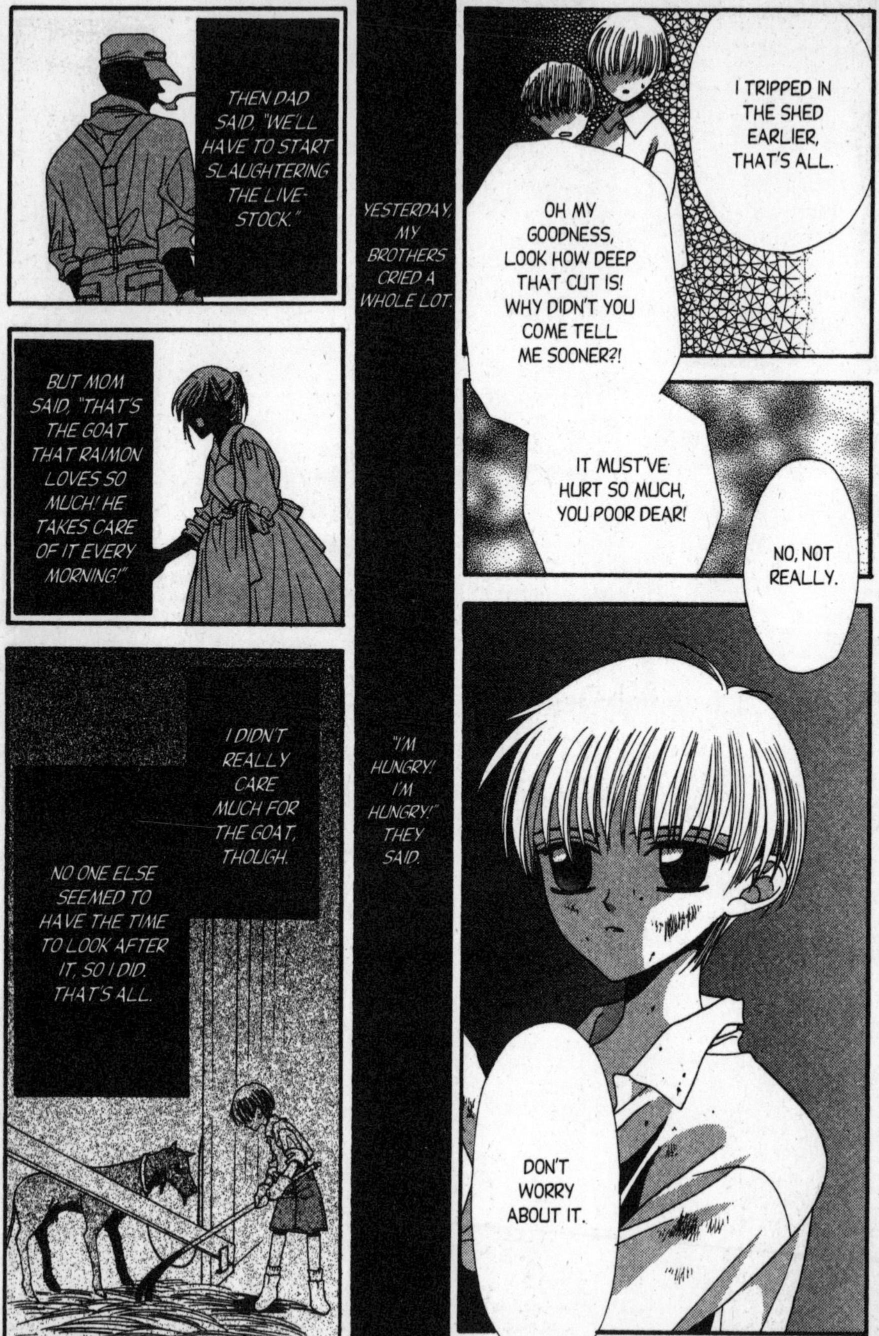
I TRIPPED IN THE SHED EARLIER, THAT'S ALL.
OH MY GOODNESS, LOOK HOW DEEP THAT CUT IS! WHY DIDN'T YOU COME TELL ME SOONER?!
IT MUST'VE HURT SO MUCH, YOU POOR DEAR!
NO, NOT REALLY.
DON'T WORRY ABOUT IT.
YESTERDAY, MY BROTHERS CRIED A WHOLE LOT.
"I'M HUNGRY! I'M HUNGRY!" THEY SAID.
THEN DAD SAID, "WE'LL HAVE TO START SLAUGHTERING THE LIVE-STOCK."
BUT MOM SAID, "THAT'S THE GOAT THAT RAIMON LOVES SO MUCH! HE TAKES CARE OF IT EVERY MORNING!"
I DIDN'T REALLY CARE MUCH FOR THE GOAT, THOUGH.
NO ONE ELSE SEEMED TO HAVE THE TIME TO LOOK AFTER IT, SO I DID. THAT'S ALL.

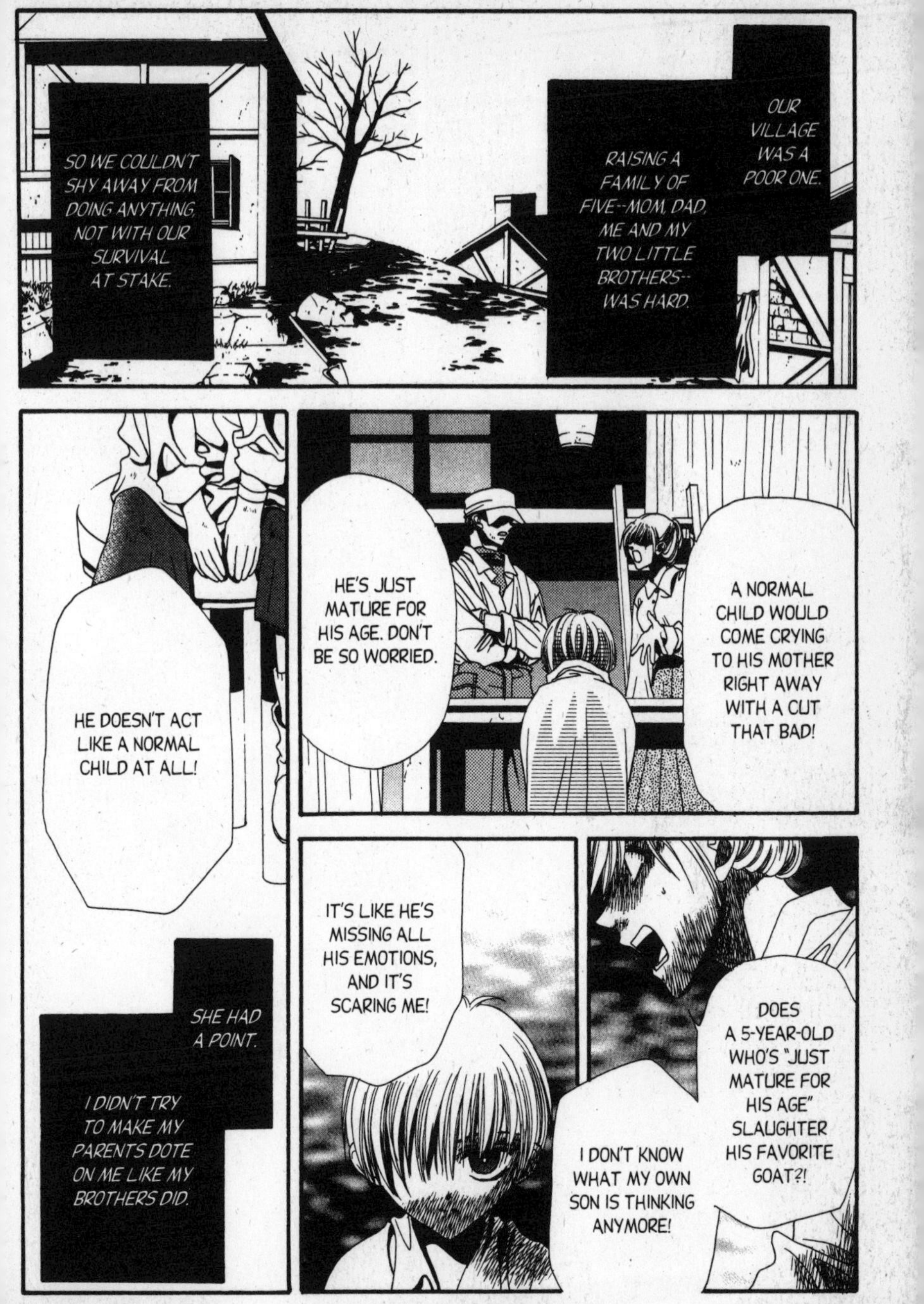
OUR VILLAGE WAS A POOR ONE.
RAISING A FAMILY OF FIVE--MOM, DAD, ME AND MY TWO LITTLE BROTHERS--WAS HARD.
SO WE COULDN'T SHY AWAY FROM DOING ANYTHING, NOT WITH OUR SURVIVAL AT STAKE.
A NORMAL CHILD WOULD COME CRYING TO HIS MOTHER RIGHT AWAY WITH A CUT THAT BAD!
HE'S JUST MATURE FOR HIS AGE. DON'T BE SO WORRIED.
DOES A 5-YEAR-OLD WHO'S "JUST MATURE FOR HIS AGE" SLAUGHTER HIS FAVORITE GOAT?!
I DON'T KNOW WHAT MY OWN SON IS THINKING ANYMORE!
IT'S LIKE HE'S MISSING ALL HIS EMOTIONS, AND IT'S SCARING ME!
HE DOESN'T ACT LIKE A NORMAL CHILD AT ALL!
SHE HAD A POINT.
I DIDN'T TRY TO MAKE MY PARENTS DOTE ON ME LIKE MY BROTHERS DID.

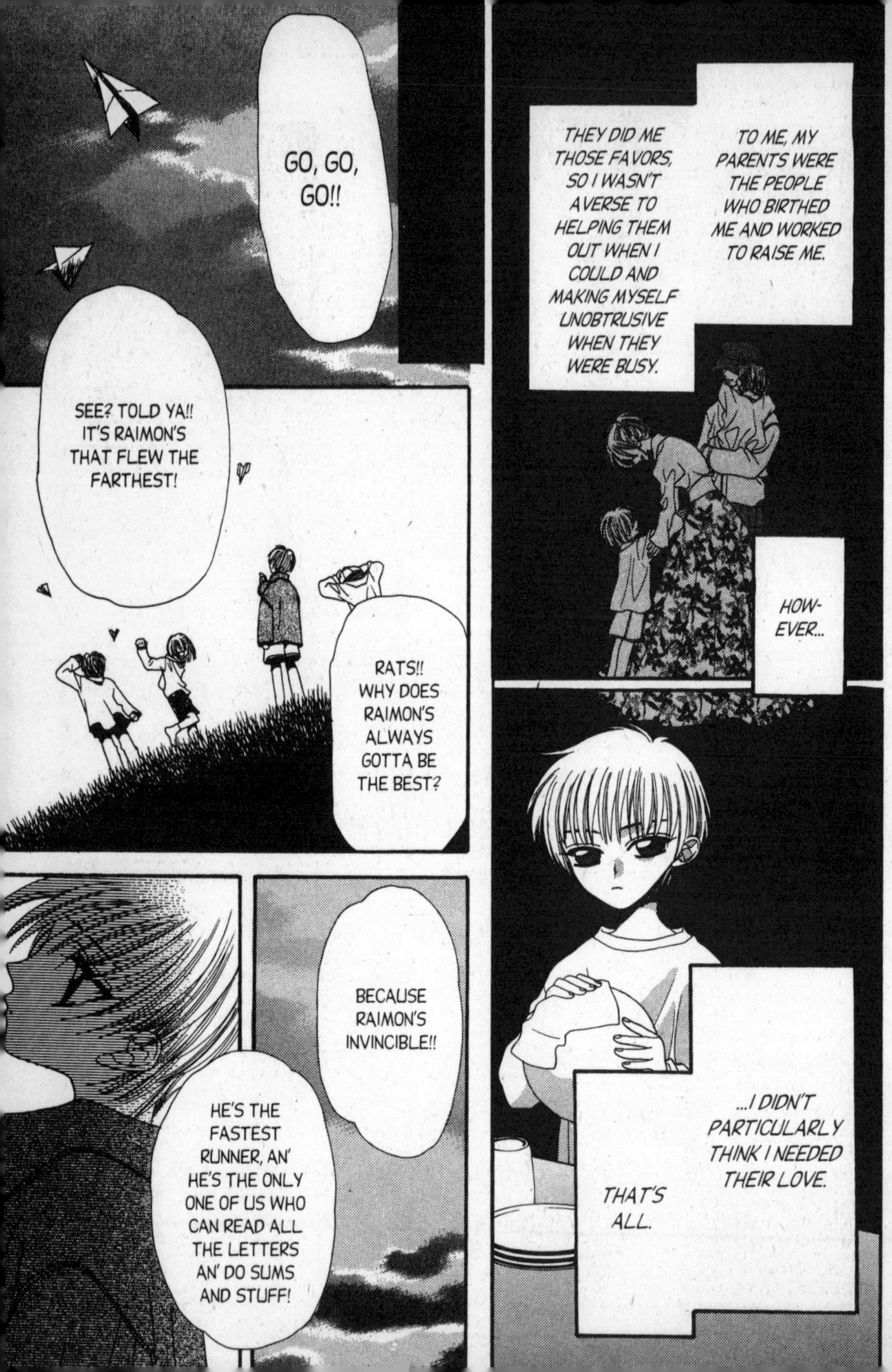
TO ME, MY PARENTS WERE THE PEOPLE WHO BIRTHED ME AND WORKED TO RAISE ME.
THEY DID ME THOSE FAVORS, SO I WASN'T AVERSE TO HELPING THEM OUT WHEN I COULD AND MAKING MYSELF UNOBTRUSIVE WHEN THEY WERE BUSY.
HOW-EVER...
...I DIDN'T PARTICULARLY THINK I NEEDED THEIR LOVE.
THAT'S ALL.
GO, GO, GO!!
SEE? TOLD YA!! IT'S RAIMON'S THAT FLEW THE FARTHEST!
RATS!! WHY DOES RAIMON'S ALWAYS GOTTA BE THE BEST?
BECAUSE RAIMON'S INVINCIBLE!!
HE'S THE FASTEST RUNNER, AN' HE'S THE ONLY ONE OF US WHO CAN READ ALL THE LETTERS AN' DO SUMS AND STUFF!

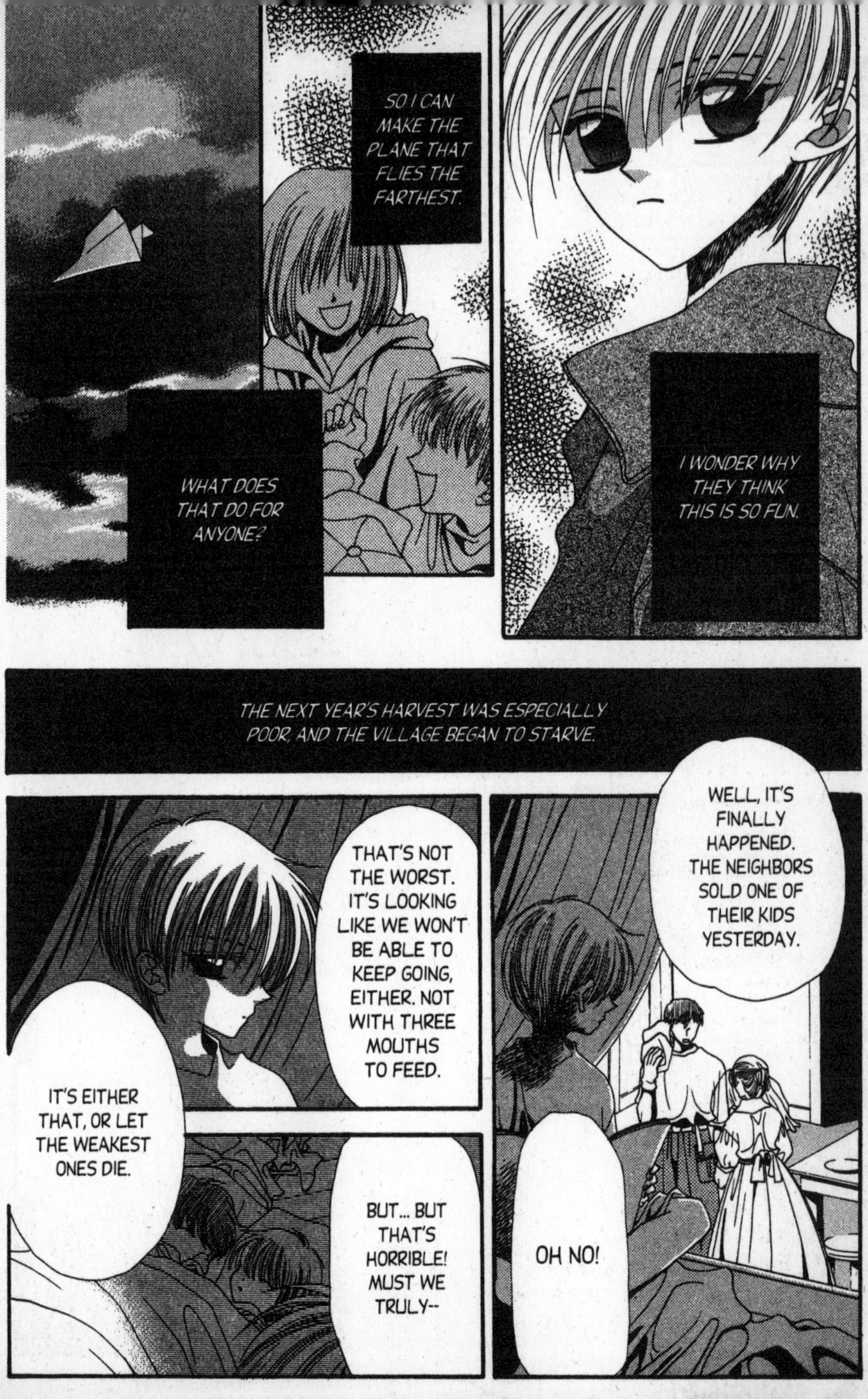
I WONDER WHY THEY THINK THIS IS SO FUN.
SO I CAN MAKE THE PLANE THAT FLIES THE FARTHEST.
WHAT DOES THAT DO FOR ANYONE?
THE NEXT YEAR'S HARVEST WAS ESPECIALLY POOR, AND THE VILLAGE BEGAN TO STARVE.
WELL, IT'S FINALLY HAPPENED. THE NEIGHBORS SOLD ONE OF THEIR KIDS YESTERDAY.
OH NO!
THAT'S NOT THE WORST. IT'S LOOKING LIKE WE WON'T BE ABLE TO KEEP GOING, EITHER. NOT WITH THREE MOUTHS TO FEED.
IT'S EITHER THAT, OR LET THE WEAKEST ONES DIE.
BUT... BUT THAT'S HORRIBLE! MUST WE TRULY--

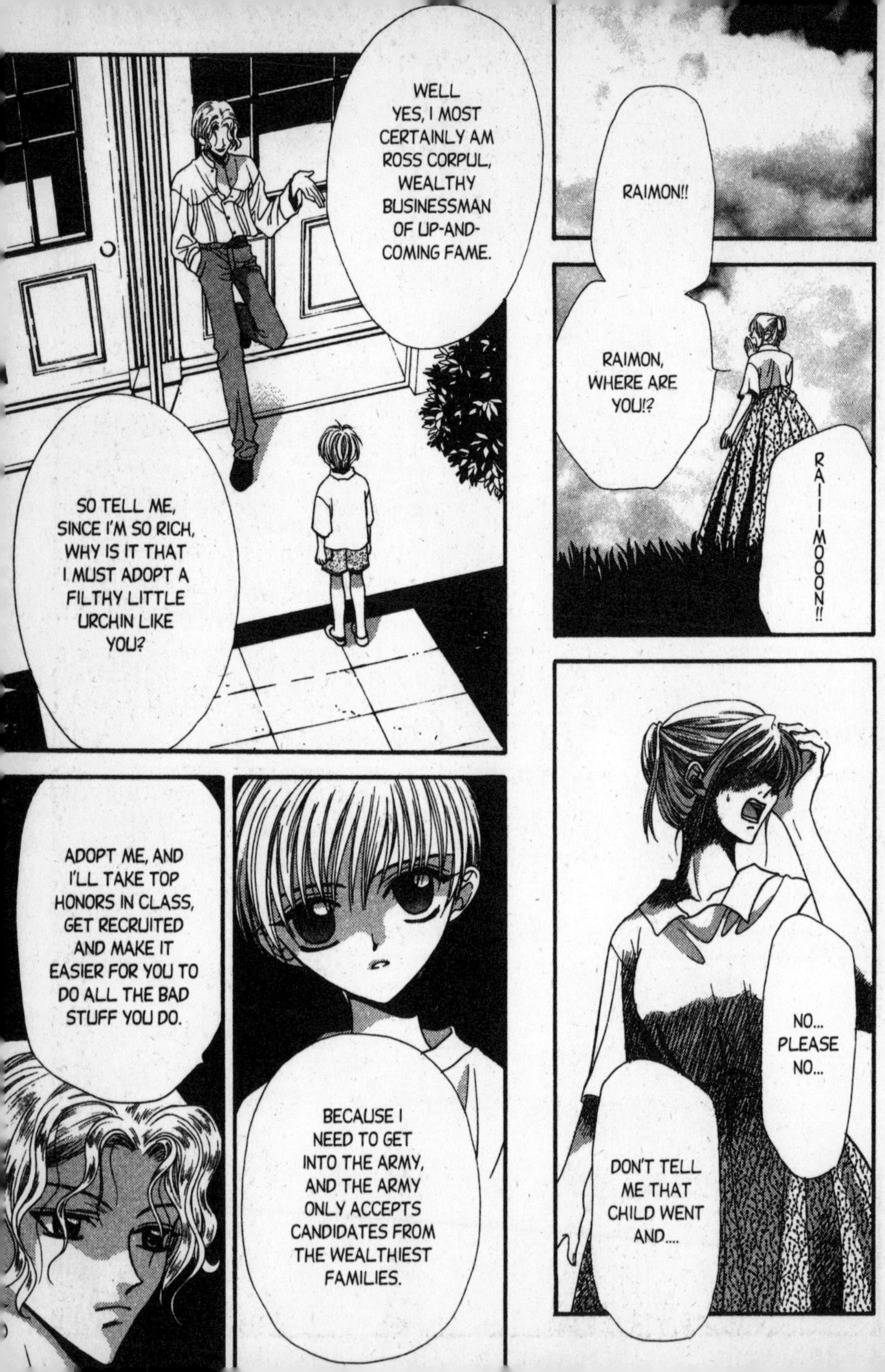
RAIMON!!
RAIMON, WHERE ARE YOU!?
RAIIMOOON!!
NO... PLEASE NO...
DON'T TELL ME THAT CHILD WENT AND....
WELL YES, I MOST CERTAINLY AM ROSS CORPUL, WEALTHY BUSINESSMAN OF UP-AND-COMING FAME.
SO TELL ME, SINCE I'M SO RICH, WHY IS IT THAT I MUST ADOPT A FILTHY LITTLE URCHIN LIKE YOU?
BECAUSE I NEED TO GET INTO THE ARMY, AND THE ARMY ONLY ACCEPTS CANDIDATES FROM THE WEALTHIEST FAMILIES.
ADOPT ME, AND I'LL TAKE TOP HONORS IN CLASS, GET RECRUITED AND MAKE IT EASIER FOR YOU TO DO ALL THE BAD STUFF YOU DO.

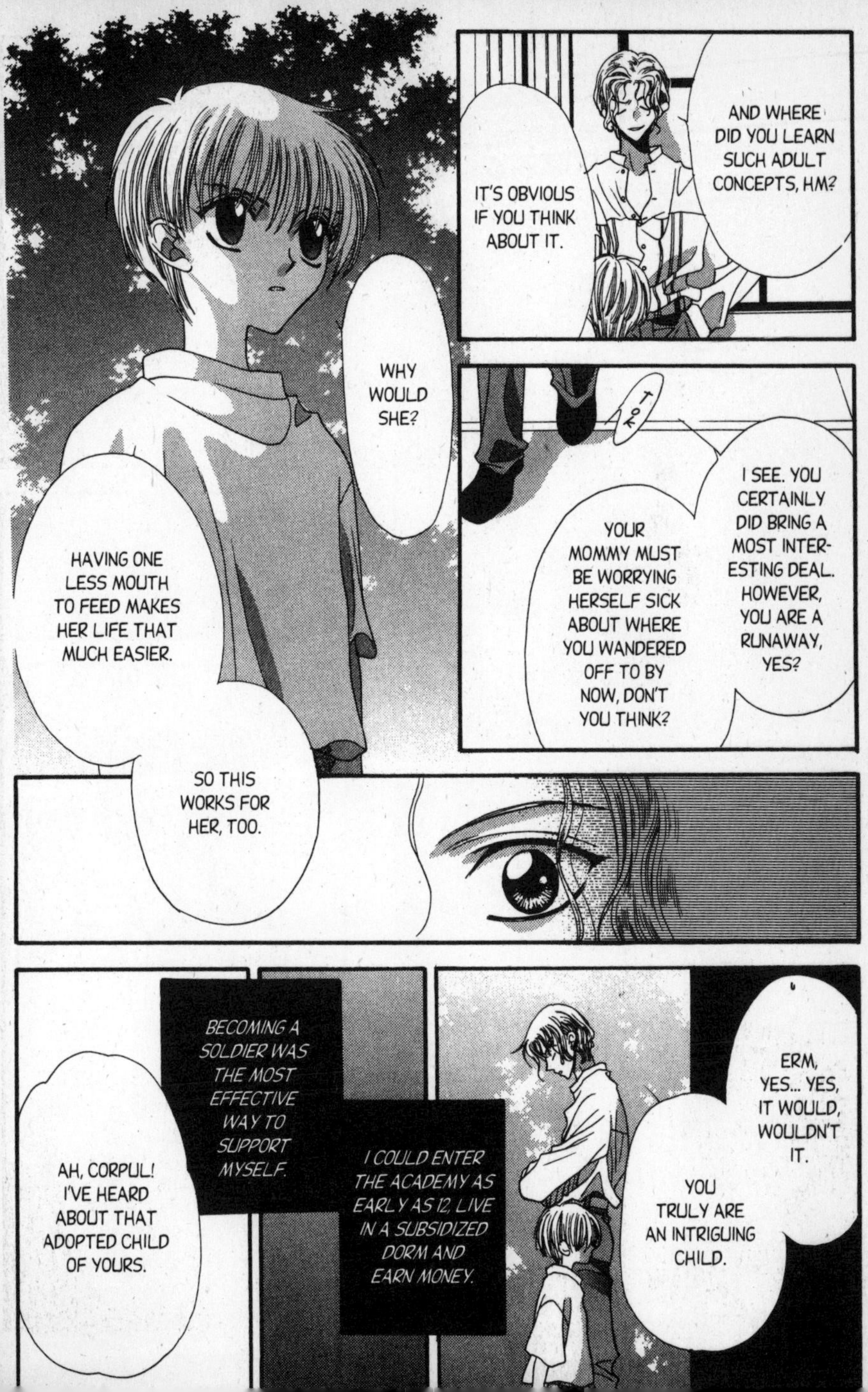
AND WHERE DID YOU LEARN SUCH ADULT CONCEPTS, HM?
IT'S OBVIOUS IF YOU THINK ABOUT IT.
TOK
I SEE. YOU CERTAINLY DID BRING A MOST INTER-ESTING DEAL. HOWEVER, YOU ARE A RUNAWAY, YES?
YOUR MOMMY MUST BE WORRYING HERSELF SICK ABOUT WHERE YOU WANDERED OFF TO BY NOW, DON'T YOU THINK?
WHY WOULD SHE?
HAVING ONE LESS MOUTH TO FEED MAKES HER LIFE THAT MUCH EASIER.
SO THIS WORKS FOR HER, TOO.
ERM, YES... YES, IT WOULD, WOULDN'T IT.
YOU TRULY ARE AN INTRIGUING CHILD.
BECOMING A SOLDIER WAS THE MOST EFFECTIVE WAY TO SUPPORT MYSELF.
I COULD ENTER THE ACADEMY AS EARLY AS 12, LIVE IN A SUBSIDIZED DORM AND EARN MONEY.
AH, CORPUL! I'VE HEARD ABOUT THAT ADOPTED CHILD OF YOURS.

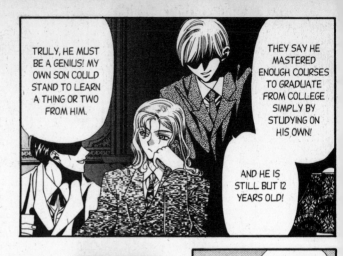

THEY SAY HE MASTERED ENOUGH COURSES TO GRADUATE FROM COLLEGE SIMPLY BY STUDYING ON HIS OWN!
AND HE IS STILL BUT 12 YEARS OLD!
TRULY, HE MUST BE A GENIUS! MY OWN SON COULD STAND TO LEARN A THING OR TWO FROM HIM.
IT DOES MAKE HIM TERRIBLY, AH...**PRICKLY** TO DEAL WITH, HOWEVER.
OH WELL. SHOULD HE PASS THE ARMY ENTRANCE EXAMINATIONS WITH A PERFECT SCORE...
...NO ONE WILL BE ABLE TO GAINSAY HIS INTELLIGENCE.
I JOINED THE ARMY WHEN I WAS 12.
SHIRAGI! WELCOME, MY BOY! YOUR GENIUS IS DRAWING EYES FROM ALL OVER, LET ME TELL YOU!

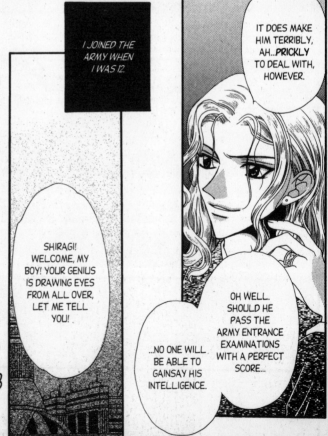

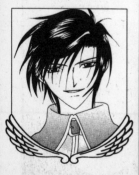

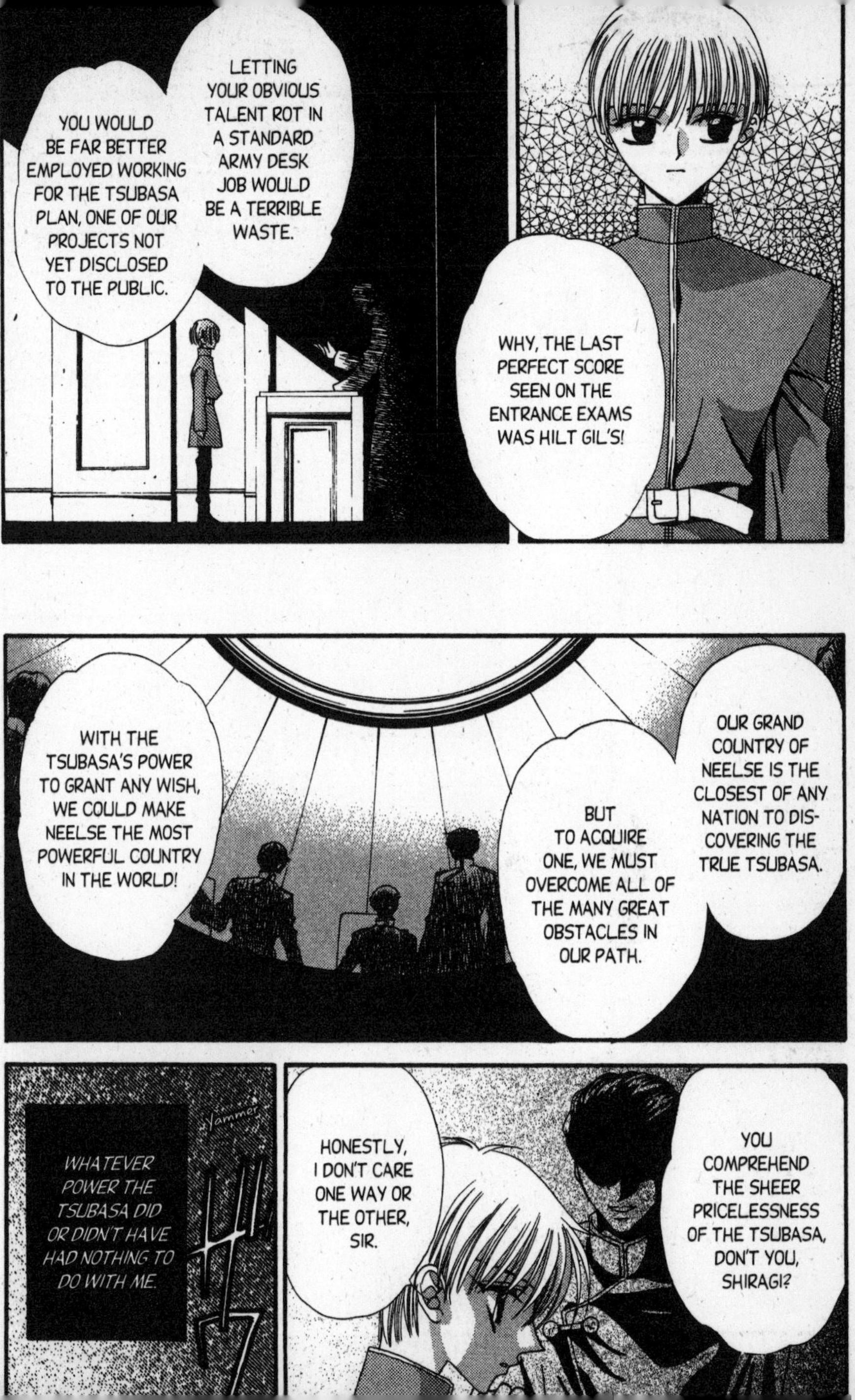
WHY, THE LAST PERFECT SCORE SEEN ON THE ENTRANCE EXAMS WAS HILT GIL'S!
LETTING YOUR OBVIOUS TALENT ROT IN A STANDARD ARMY DESK JOB WOULD BE A TERRIBLE WASTE.
YOU WOULD BE FAR BETTER EMPLOYED WORKING FOR THE TSUBASA PLAN, ONE OF OUR PROJECTS NOT YET DISCLOSED TO THE PUBLIC.
OUR GRAND COUNTRY OF NEELSE IS THE CLOSEST OF ANY NATION TO DIS-COVERING THE TRUE TSUBASA.
BUT TO ACQUIRE ONE, WE MUST OVERCOME ALL OF THE MANY GREAT OBSTACLES IN OUR PATH.
WITH THE TSUBASA'S POWER TO GRANT ANY WISH, WE COULD MAKE NEELSE THE MOST POWERFUL COUNTRY IN THE WORLD!
YOU COMPREHEND THE SHEER PRICELESSNESS OF THE TSUBASA, DON'T YOU, SHIRAGI?
HONESTLY, I DON'T CARE ONE WAY OR THE OTHER, SIR.
Yammer
WHATEVER POWER THE TSUBASA DID OR DIDN'T HAVE HAD NOTHING TO DO WITH ME.

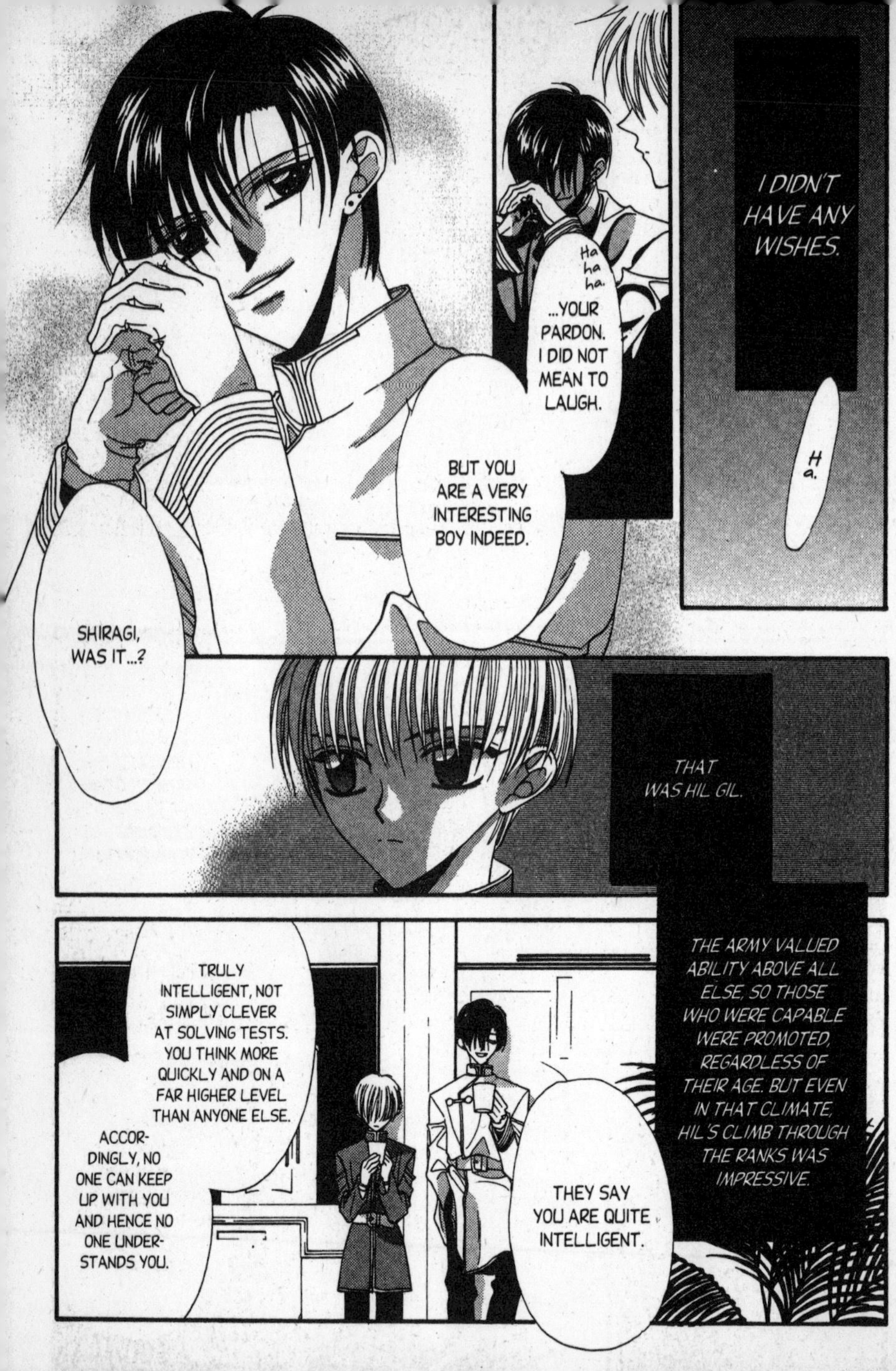
I DIDN'T HAVE ANY WISHES.
Ha.
Ha ha ha.
...YOUR PARDON. I DID NOT MEAN TO LAUGH.
BUT YOU ARE A VERY INTERESTING BOY INDEED.
SHIRAGI, WAS IT...?
THAT WAS HIL GIL.
THE ARMY VALUED ABILITY ABOVE ALL ELSE, SO THOSE WHO WERE CAPABLE WERE PROMOTED, REGARDLESS OF THEIR AGE. BUT EVEN IN THAT CLIMATE, HIL'S CLIMB THROUGH THE RANKS WAS IMPRESSIVE.
THEY SAY YOU ARE QUITE INTELLIGENT.
TRULY INTELLIGENT, NOT SIMPLY CLEVER AT SOLVING TESTS. YOU THINK MORE QUICKLY AND ON A FAR HIGHER LEVEL THAN ANYONE ELSE.
ACCORDINGLY, NO ONE CAN KEEP UP WITH YOU AND HENCE NO ONE UNDERSTANDS YOU.

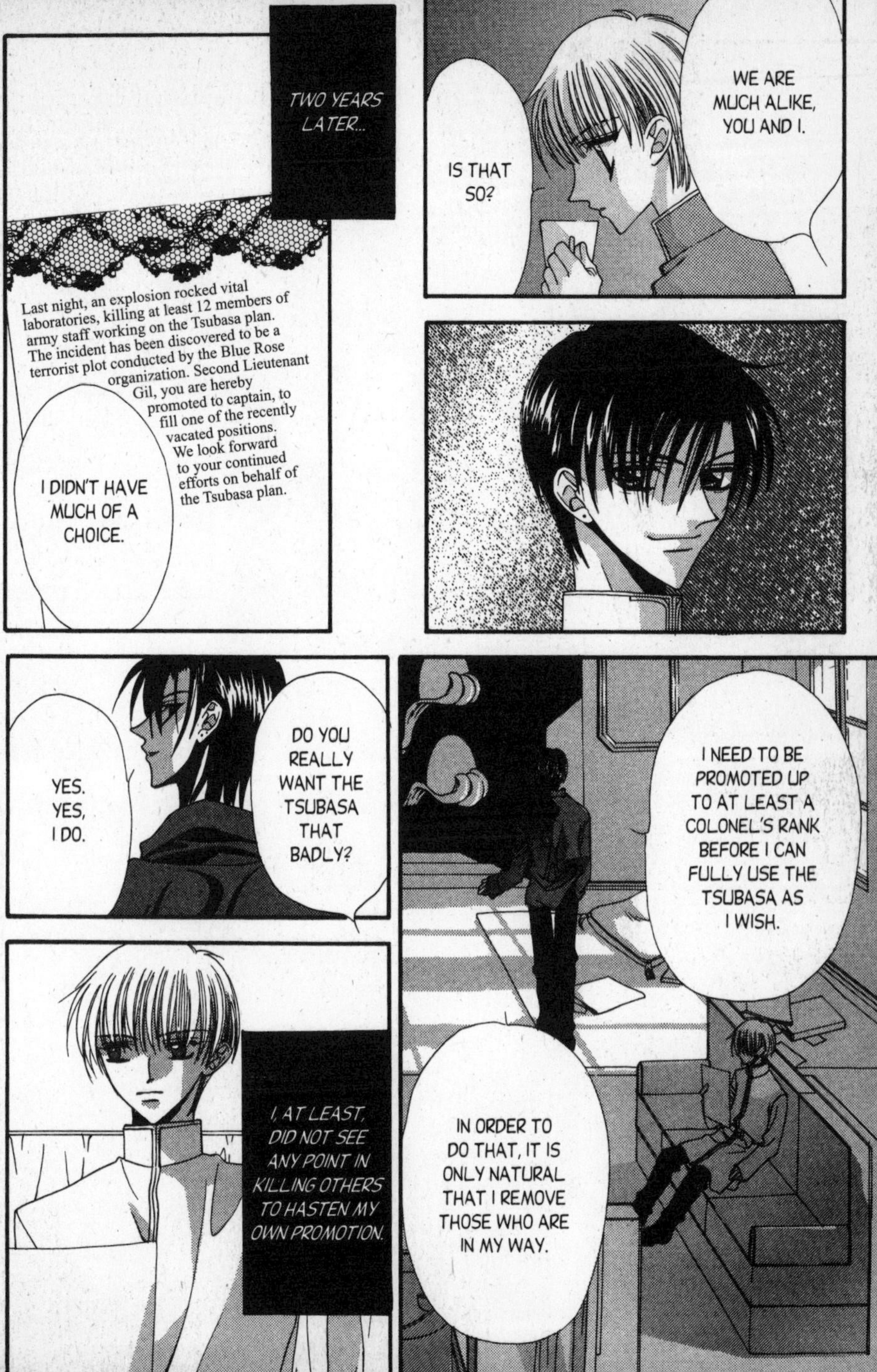
WE ARE MUCH ALIKE, YOU AND I.
IS THAT SO?
TWO YEARS LATER...
Last night, an explosion rocked vital laboratories, killing at least 12 members of army staff working on the Tsubasa plan. The incident has been discovered to be a terrorist plot conducted by the Blue Rose organization. Second Lieutenant Gil, you are hereby promoted to captain, to fill one of the recently vacated positions. We look forward to your continued efforts on behalf of the Tsubasa plan.
I DIDN'T HAVE MUCH OF A CHOICE.
I NEED TO BE PROMOTED UP TO AT LEAST A COLONEL'S RANK BEFORE I CAN FULLY USE THE TSUBASA AS I WISH.
IN ORDER TO DO THAT, IT IS ONLY NATURAL THAT I REMOVE THOSE WHO ARE IN MY WAY.
DO YOU REALLY WANT THE TSUBASA THAT BADLY?
YES. YES, I DO.
I, AT LEAST, DID NOT SEE ANY POINT IN KILLING OTHERS TO HASTEN MY OWN PROMOTION.

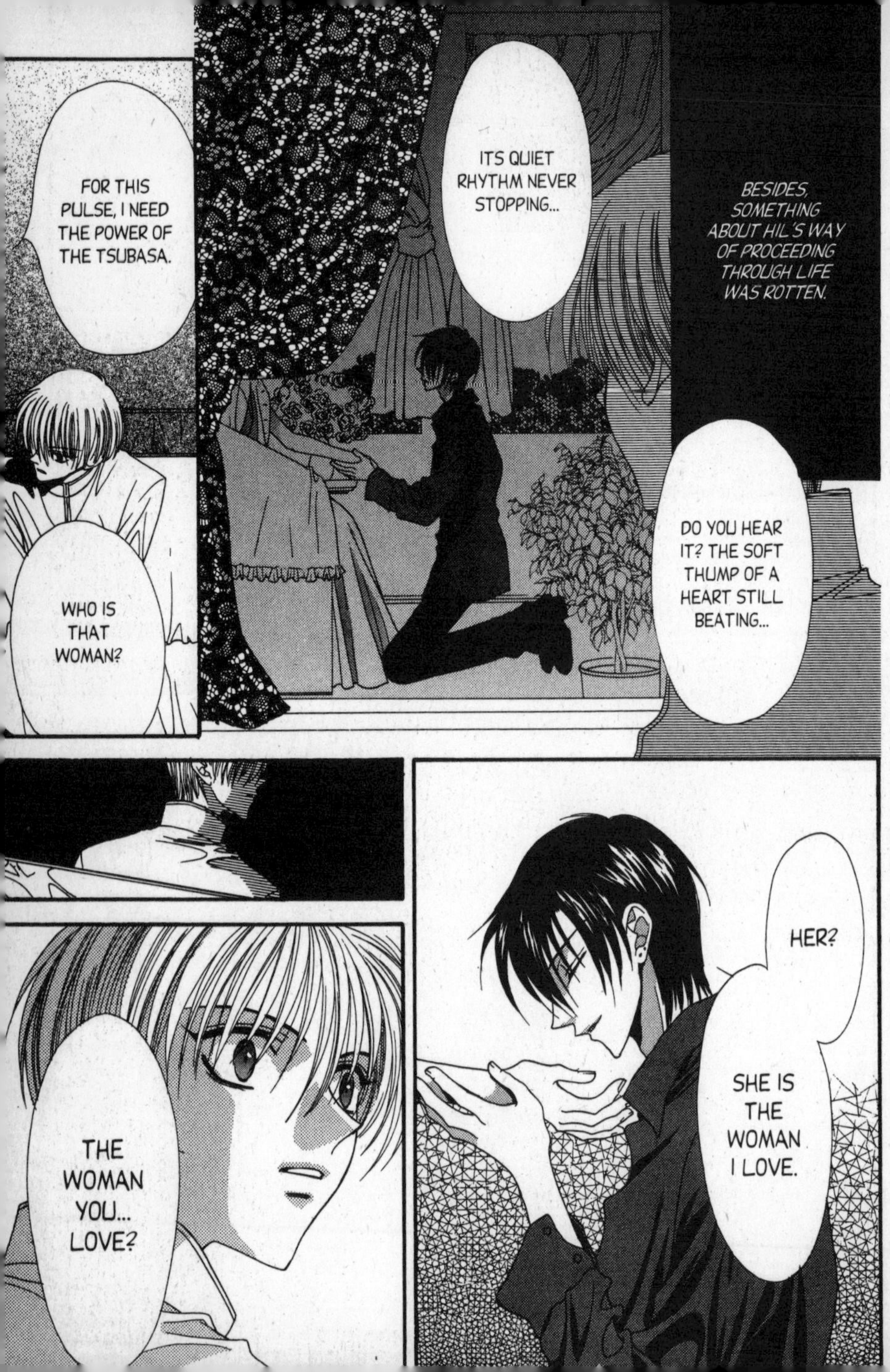
BESIDES, SOMETHING ABOUT HIL'S WAY OF PROCEEDING THROUGH LIFE WAS ROTTEN.
DO YOU HEAR IT? THE SOFT THUMP OF A HEART STILL BEATING...
ITS QUIET RHYTHM NEVER STOPPING...
FOR THIS PULSE, I NEED THE POWER OF THE TSUBASA.
WHO IS THAT WOMAN?
HER?
SHE IS THE WOMAN I LOVE.
THE WOMAN YOU... LOVE?

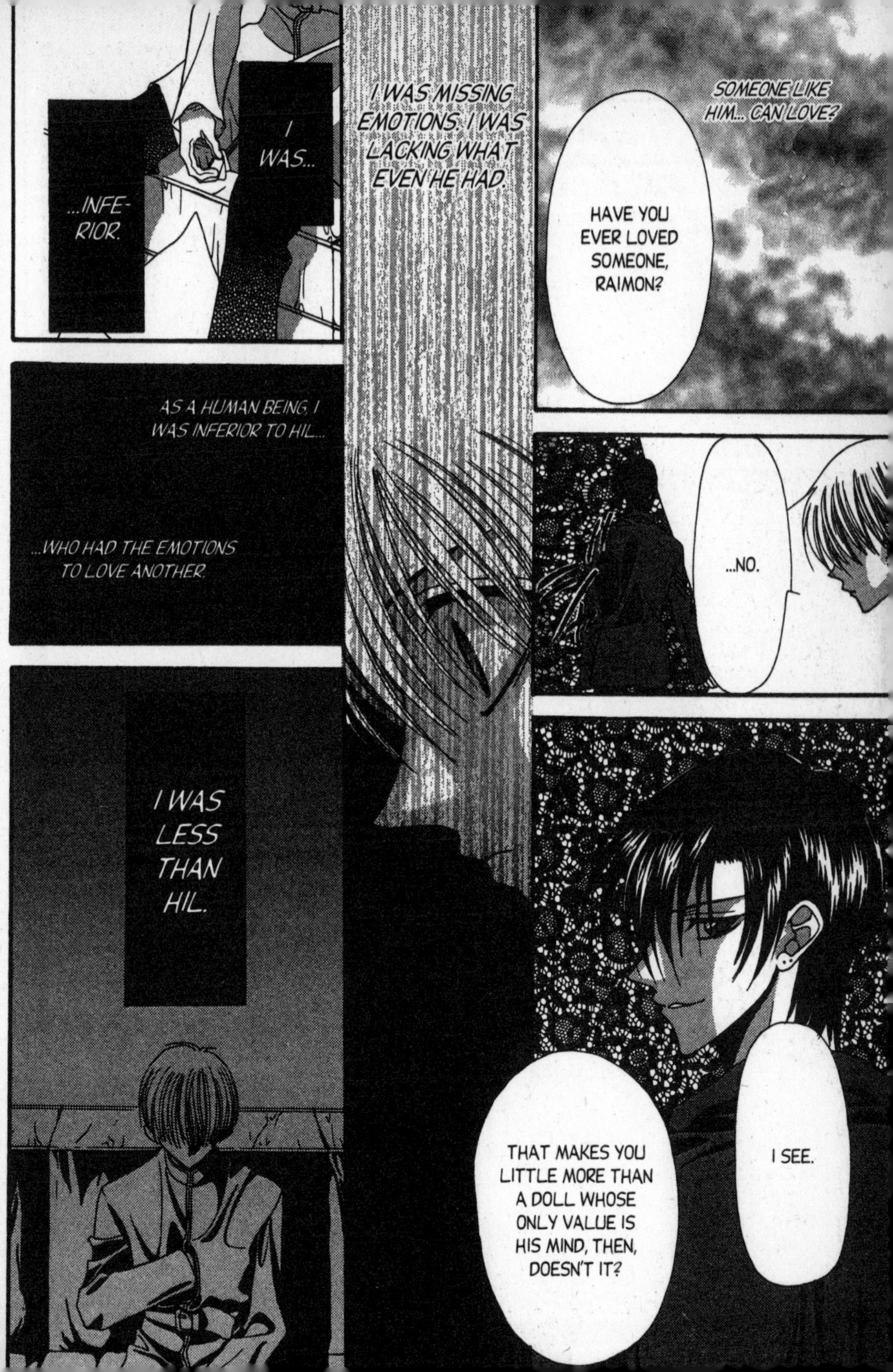
SOMEONE LIKE HIM... CAN LOVE?
HAVE YOU EVER LOVED SOMEONE, RAIMON?
...NO.
I SEE.
THAT MAKES YOU LITTLE MORE THAN A DOLL WHOSE ONLY VALUE IS HIS MIND, THEN, DOESN'T IT?
I WAS MISSING EMOTIONS. I WAS LACKING WHAT EVEN HE HAD.
I WAS...
...INFE-RIOR.
AS A HUMAN BEING, I WAS INFERIOR TO HIL...
...WHO HAD THE EMOTIONS TO LOVE ANOTHER.
I WAS LESS THAN HIL.

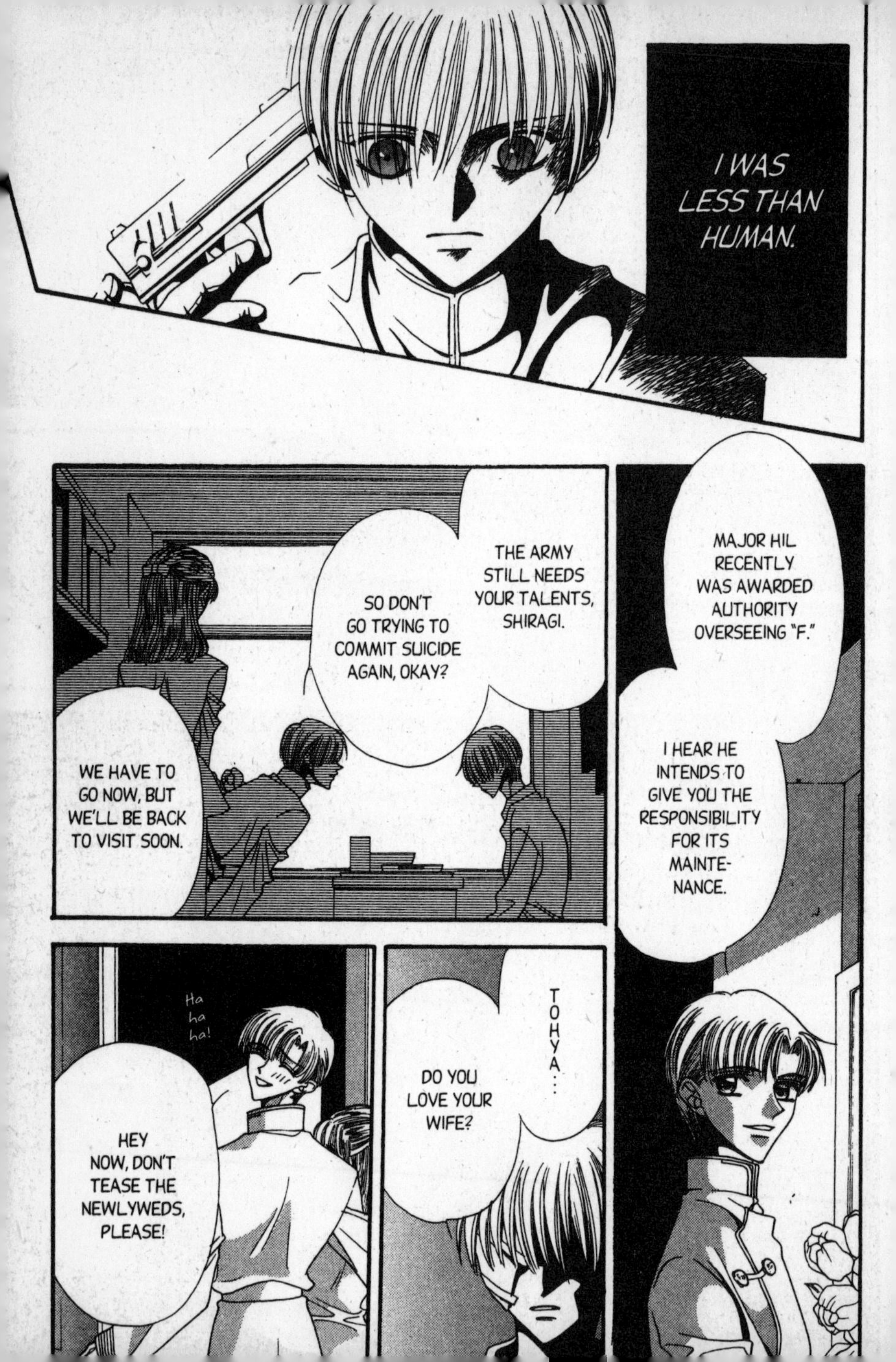
I WAS LESS THAN HUMAN.
MAJOR HIL RECENTLY WAS AWARDED AUTHORITY OVERSEEING "F."
I HEAR HE INTENDS TO GIVE YOU THE RESPONSIBILITY FOR ITS MAINTE-NANCE.
THE ARMY STILL NEEDS YOUR TALENTS, SHIRAGI.
SO DON'T GO TRYING TO COMMIT SUICIDE AGAIN, OKAY?
WE HAVE TO GO NOW, BUT WE'LL BE BACK TO VISIT SOON.
TOHYA...
DO YOU LOVE YOUR WIFE?
Ha ha ha!
HEY NOW, DON'T TEASE THE NEWLYWEDS, PLEASE!

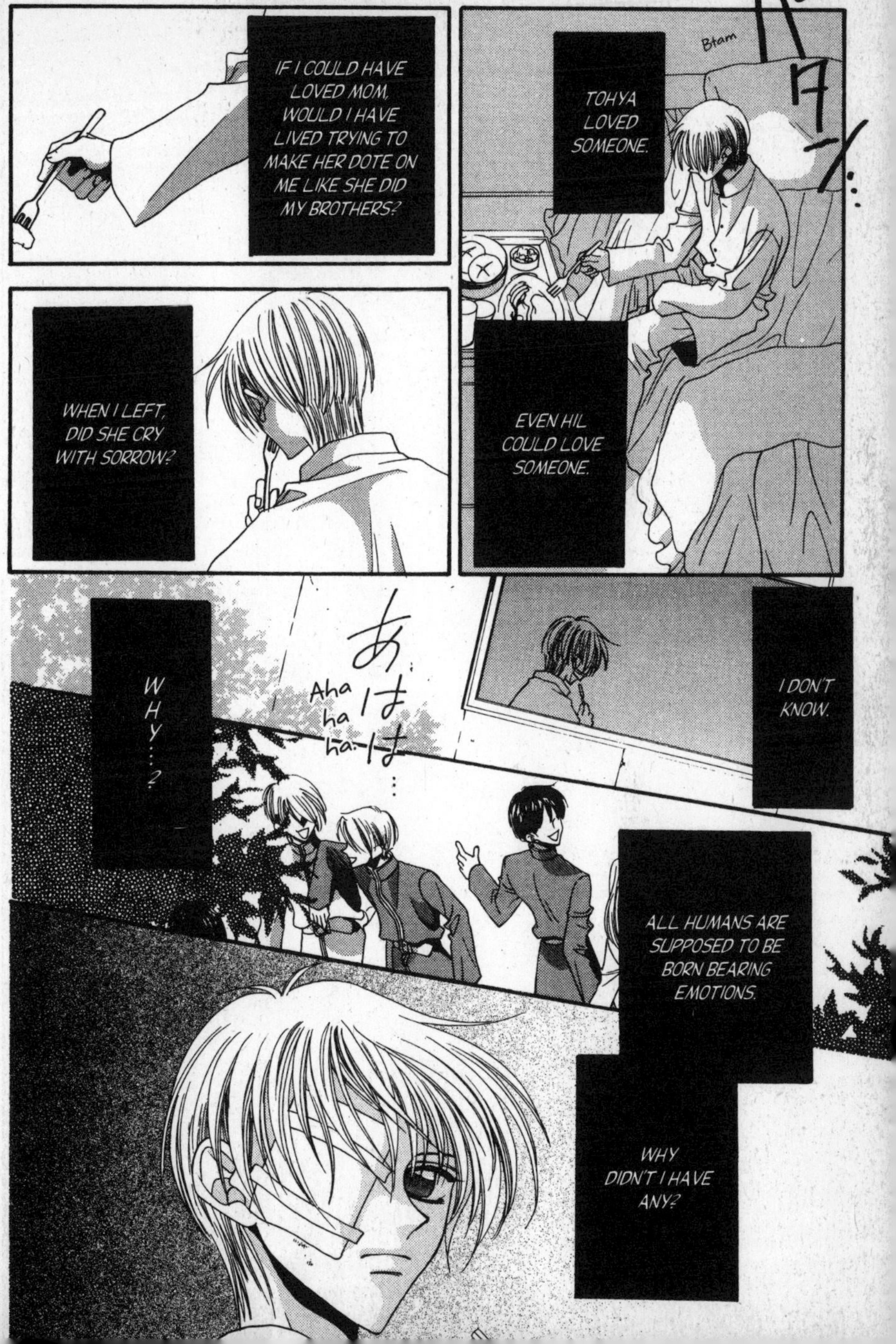

Btam
TOHYA LOVED SOMEONE.
EVEN HIL COULD LOVE SOMEONE.
IF I COULD HAVE LOVED MOM, WOULD I HAVE LIVED TRYING TO MAKE HER DOTE ON ME LIKE SHE DID MY BROTHERS?
WHEN I LEFT, DID SHE CRY WITH SORROW?
I DON'T KNOW.
あはは…
Aha ha ha.
WHY...?
ALL HUMANS ARE SUPPOSED TO BE BORN BEARING EMOTIONS.
WHY DIDN'T I HAVE ANY?

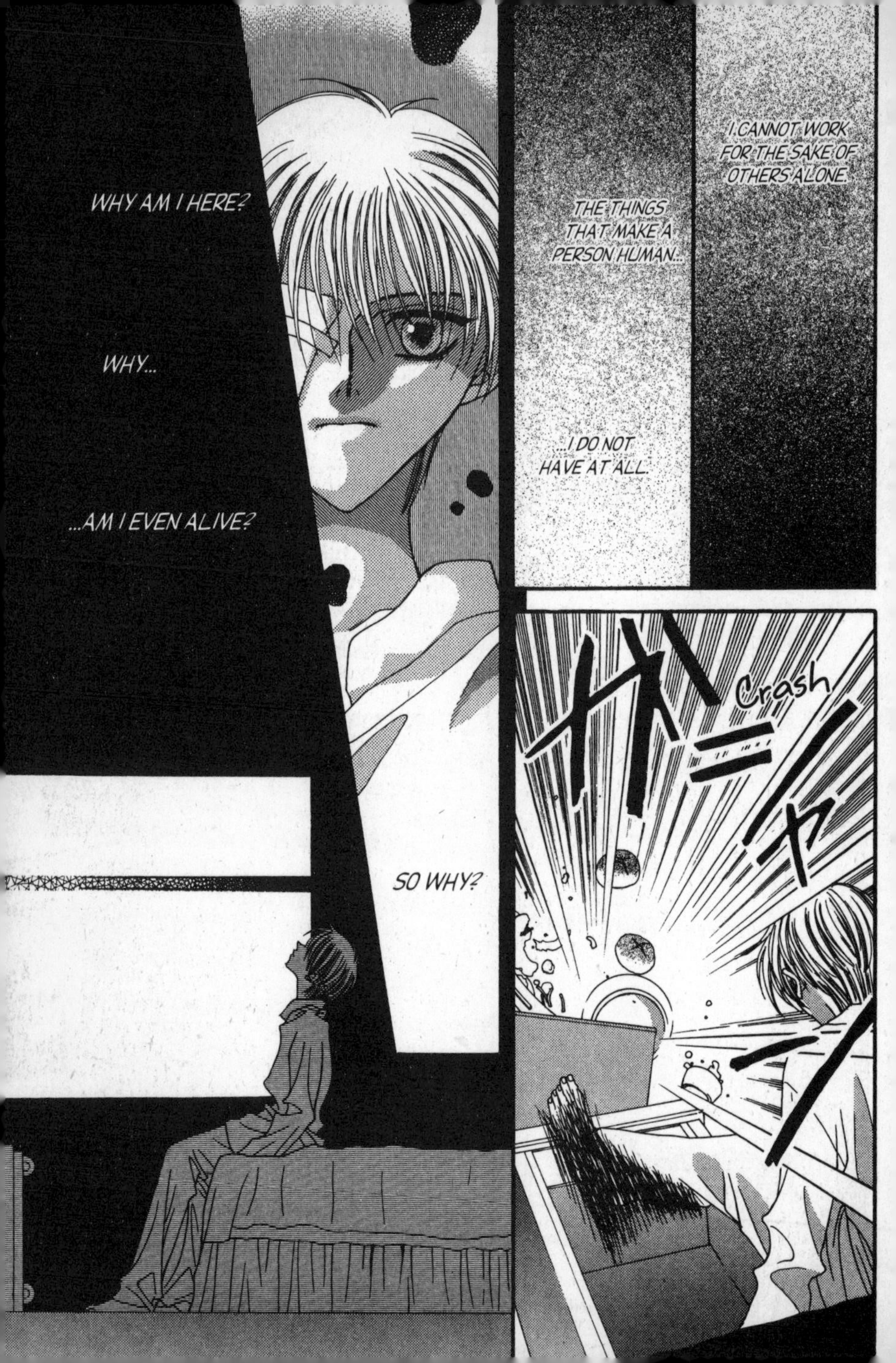
I CANNOT WORK FOR THE SAKE OF OTHERS ALONE.
THE THINGS THAT MAKE A PERSON HUMAN...
...I DO NOT HAVE AT ALL.
Crash
WHY AM I HERE?
WHY...
...AM I EVEN ALIVE?
SO WHY?

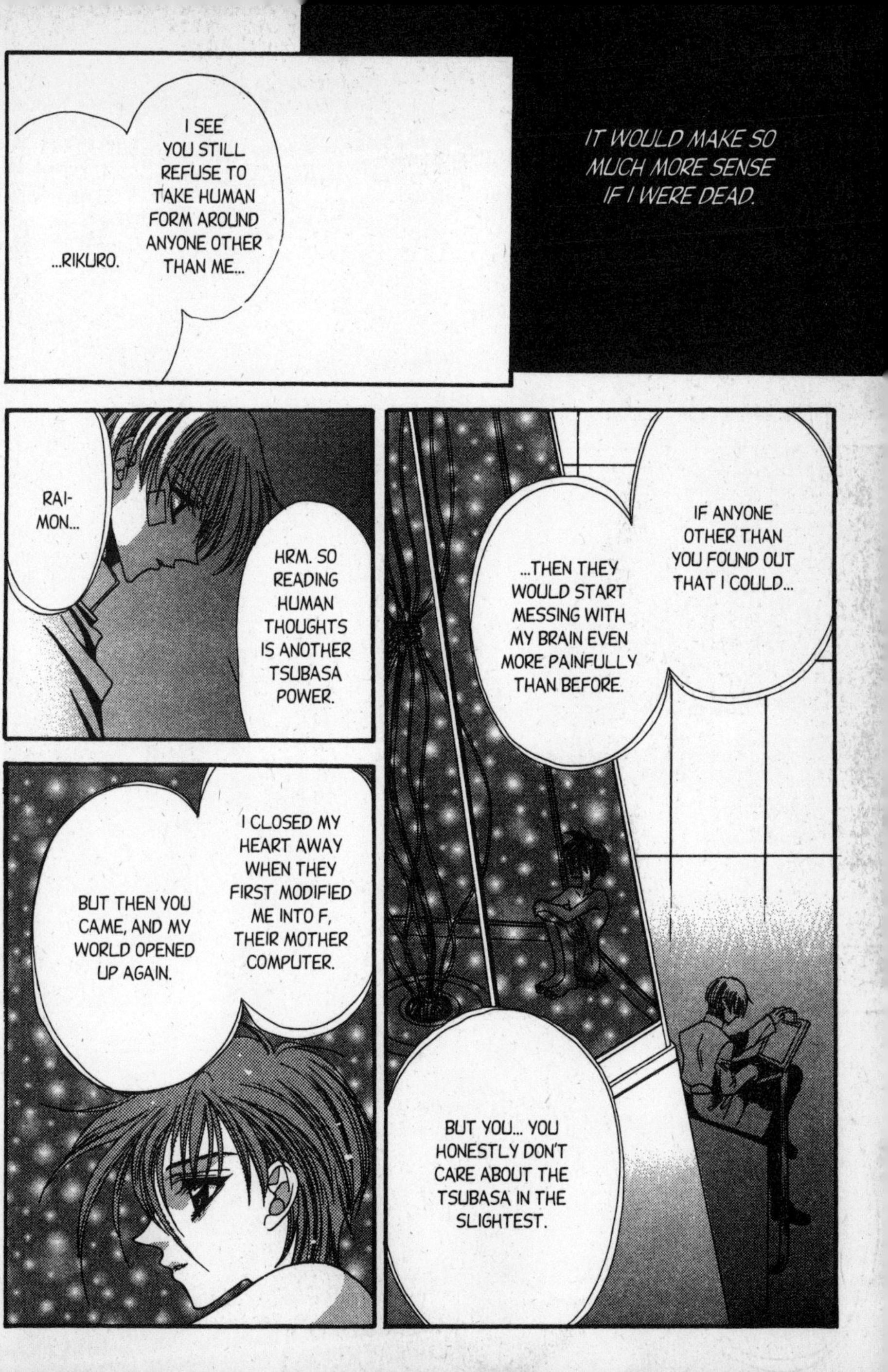

IT WOULD MAKE SO MUCH MORE SENSE IF I WERE DEAD.
I SEE YOU STILL REFUSE TO TAKE HUMAN FORM AROUND ANYONE OTHER THAN ME...
...RIKURO.
IF ANYONE OTHER THAN YOU FOUND OUT THAT I COULD...
...THEN THEY WOULD START MESSING WITH MY BRAIN EVEN MORE PAINFULLY THAN BEFORE.
BUT YOU... YOU HONESTLY DON'T CARE ABOUT THE TSUBASA IN THE SLIGHTEST.
HRM. SO READING HUMAN THOUGHTS IS ANOTHER TSUBASA POWER.
RAI-MON...
I CLOSED MY HEART AWAY WHEN THEY FIRST MODIFIED ME INTO F, THEIR MOTHER COMPUTER.
BUT THEN YOU CAME, AND MY WORLD OPENED UP AGAIN.

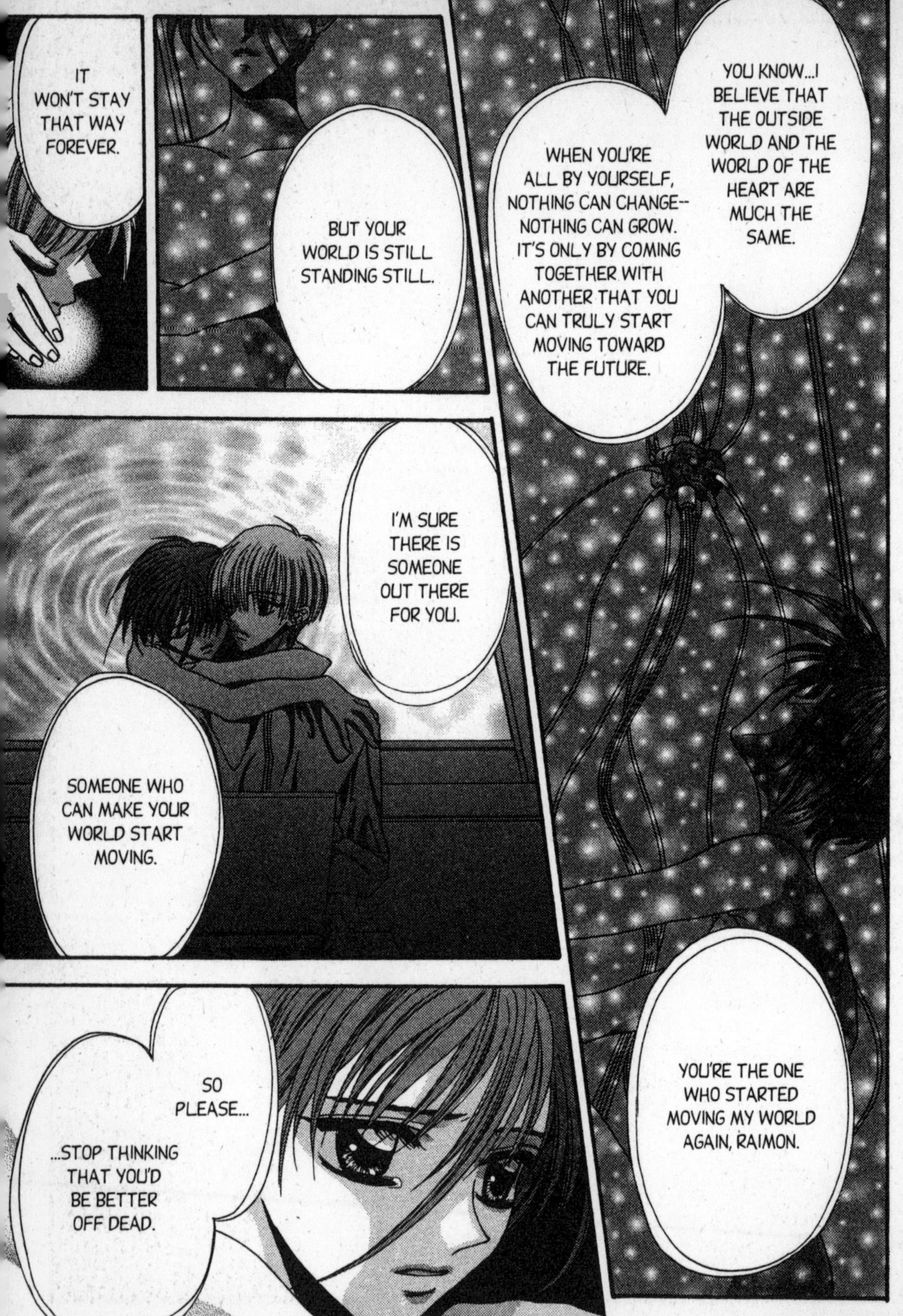
YOU KNOW...I BELIEVE THAT THE OUTSIDE WORLD AND THE WORLD OF THE HEART ARE MUCH THE SAME.
WHEN YOU'RE ALL BY YOURSELF, NOTHING CAN CHANGE-- NOTHING CAN GROW. IT'S ONLY BY COMING TOGETHER WITH ANOTHER THAT YOU CAN TRULY START MOVING TOWARD THE FUTURE.
YOU'RE THE ONE WHO STARTED MOVING MY WORLD AGAIN, RAIMON.
BUT YOUR WORLD IS STILL STANDING STILL.
IT WON'T STAY THAT WAY FOREVER.
I'M SURE THERE IS SOMEONE OUT THERE FOR YOU.
SOMEONE WHO CAN MAKE YOUR WORLD START MOVING.
SO PLEASE...
...STOP THINKING THAT YOU'D BE BETTER OFF DEAD.

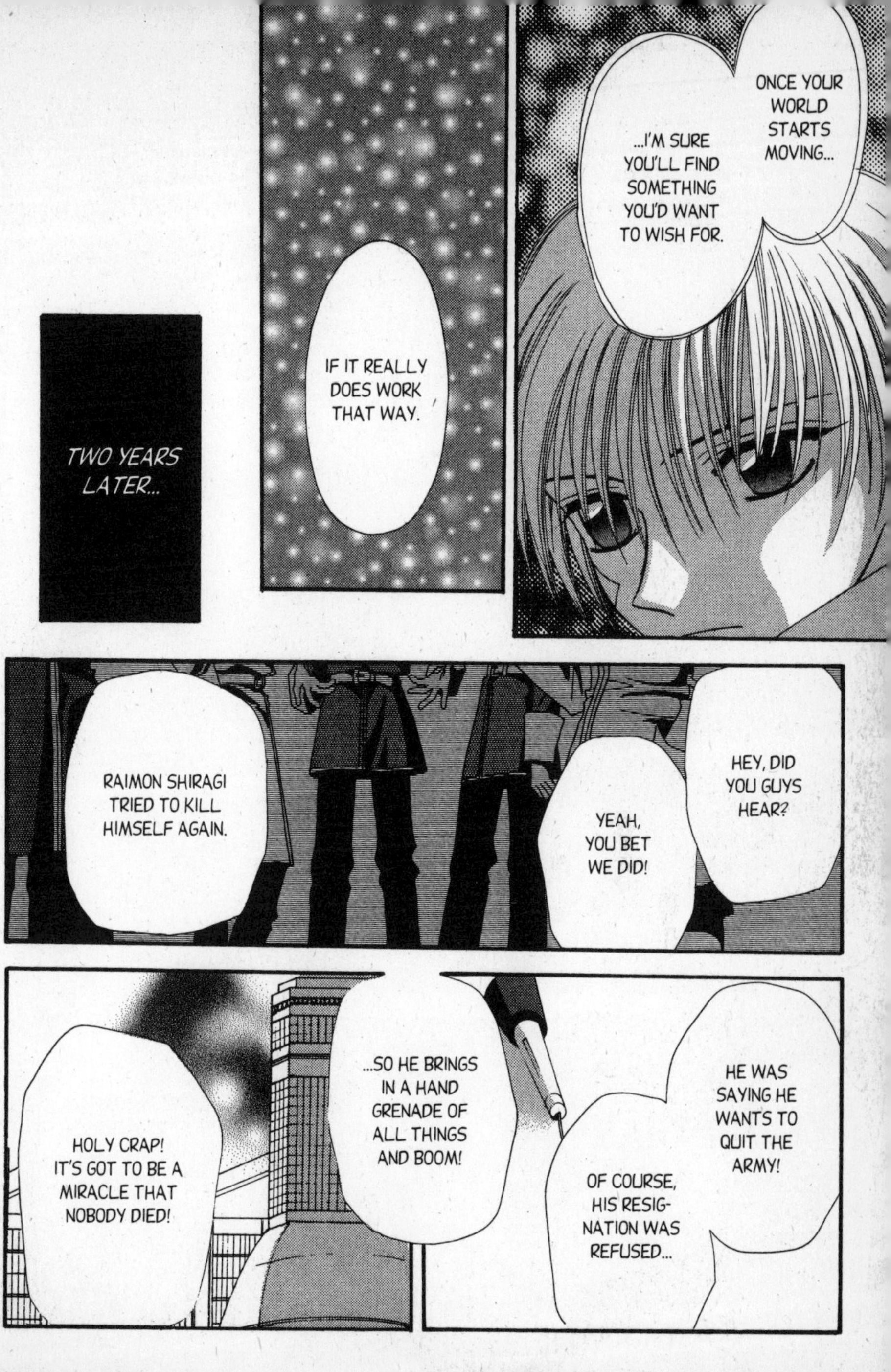
ONCE YOUR WORLD STARTS MOVING...
...I'M SURE YOU'LL FIND SOMETHING YOU'D WANT TO WISH FOR.
IF IT REALLY DOES WORK THAT WAY.
TWO YEARS LATER...
HEY, DID YOU GUYS HEAR?
YEAH, YOU BET WE DID!
RAIMON SHIRAGI TRIED TO KILL HIMSELF AGAIN.
HE WAS SAYING HE WANTS TO QUIT THE ARMY!
OF COURSE, HIS RESIGNATION WAS REFUSED...
...SO HE BRINGS IN A HAND GRENADE OF ALL THINGS AND BOOM!
HOLY CRAP! IT'S GOT TO BE A MIRACLE THAT NOBODY DIED!

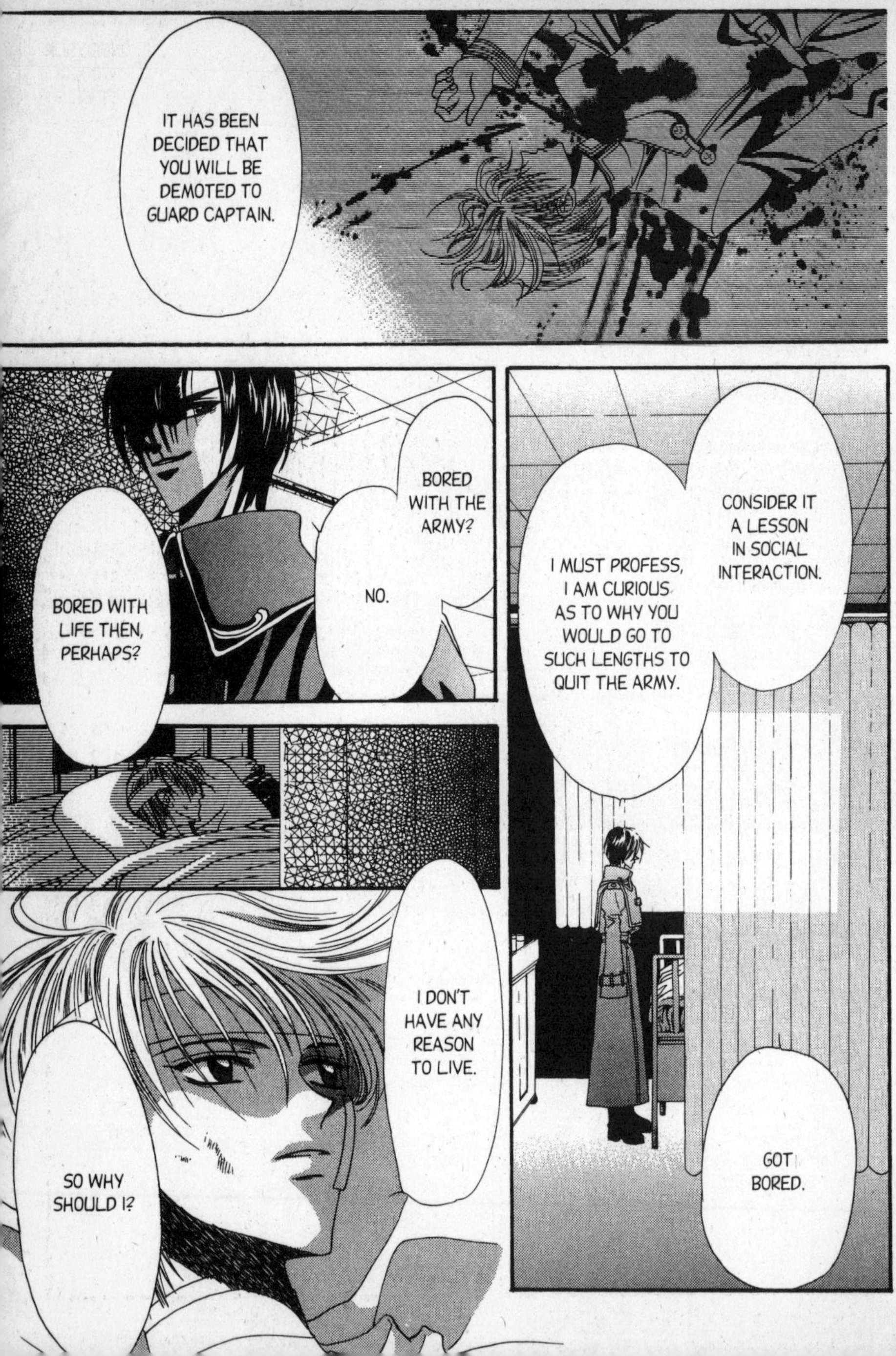
IT HAS BEEN DECIDED THAT YOU WILL BE DEMOTED TO GUARD CAPTAIN.
CONSIDER IT A LESSON IN SOCIAL INTERACTION.
I MUST PROFESS, I AM CURIOUS AS TO WHY YOU WOULD GO TO SUCH LENGTHS TO QUIT THE ARMY.
GOT BORED.
BORED WITH THE ARMY?
NO.
BORED WITH LIFE THEN, PERHAPS?
I DON'T HAVE ANY REASON TO LIVE.
SO WHY SHOULD I?

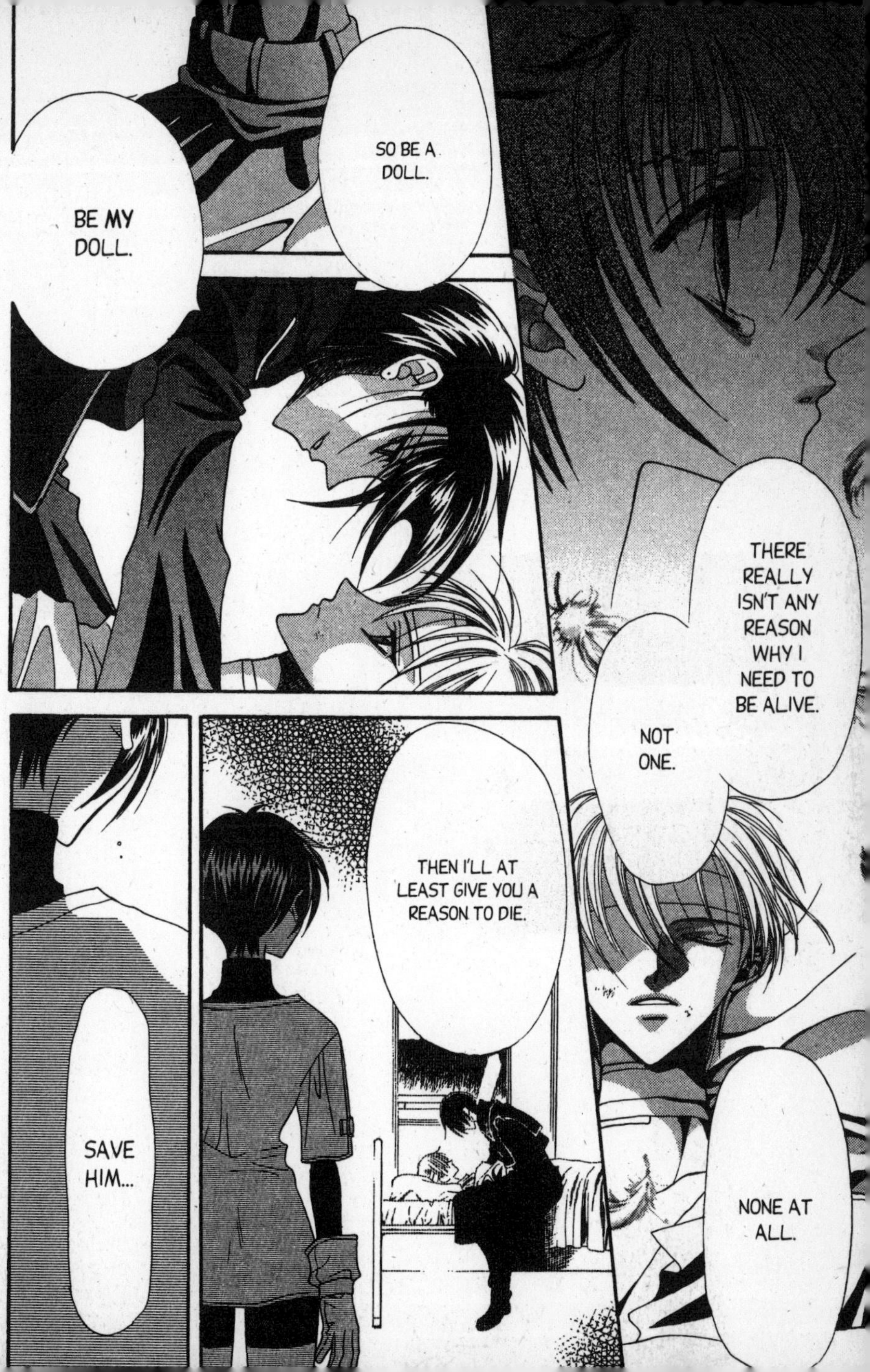

THERE REALLY ISN'T ANY REASON WHY I NEED TO BE ALIVE.
NOT ONE.
NONE AT ALL.
SO BE A DOLL.
BE MY DOLL.
THEN I'LL AT LEAST GIVE YOU A REASON TO DIE.
SAVE HIM...

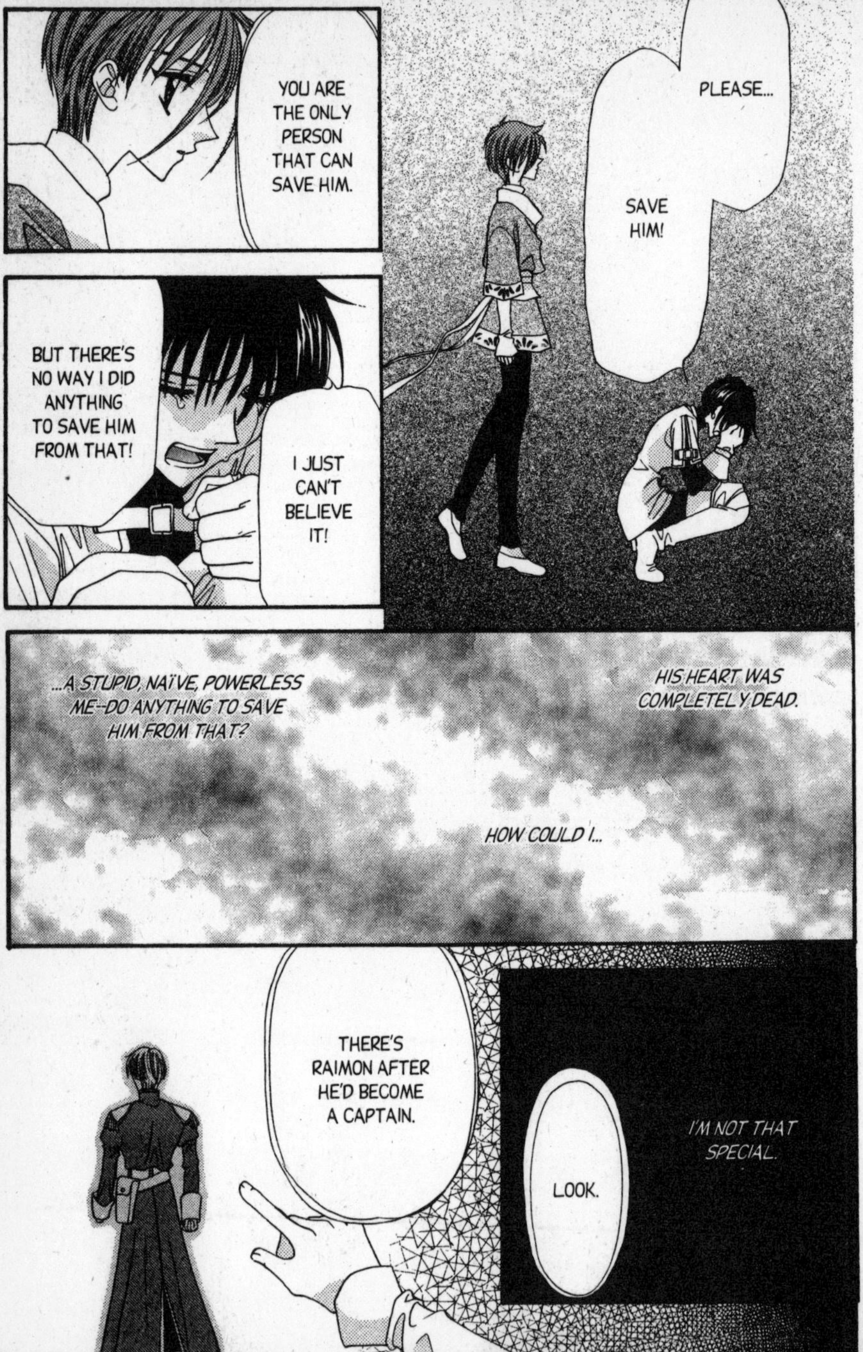
PLEASE...
SAVE HIM!
YOU ARE THE ONLY PERSON THAT CAN SAVE HIM.
BUT THERE'S NO WAY I DID ANYTHING TO SAVE HIM FROM THAT!
I JUST CAN'T BELIEVE IT!
HIS HEART WAS COMPLETELY DEAD.
HOW COULD I...
...A STUPID, NAÏVE, POWERLESS ME--DO ANYTHING TO SAVE HIM FROM THAT?
I'M NOT THAT SPECIAL.
LOOK.
THERE'S RAIMON AFTER HE'D BECOME A CAPTAIN.

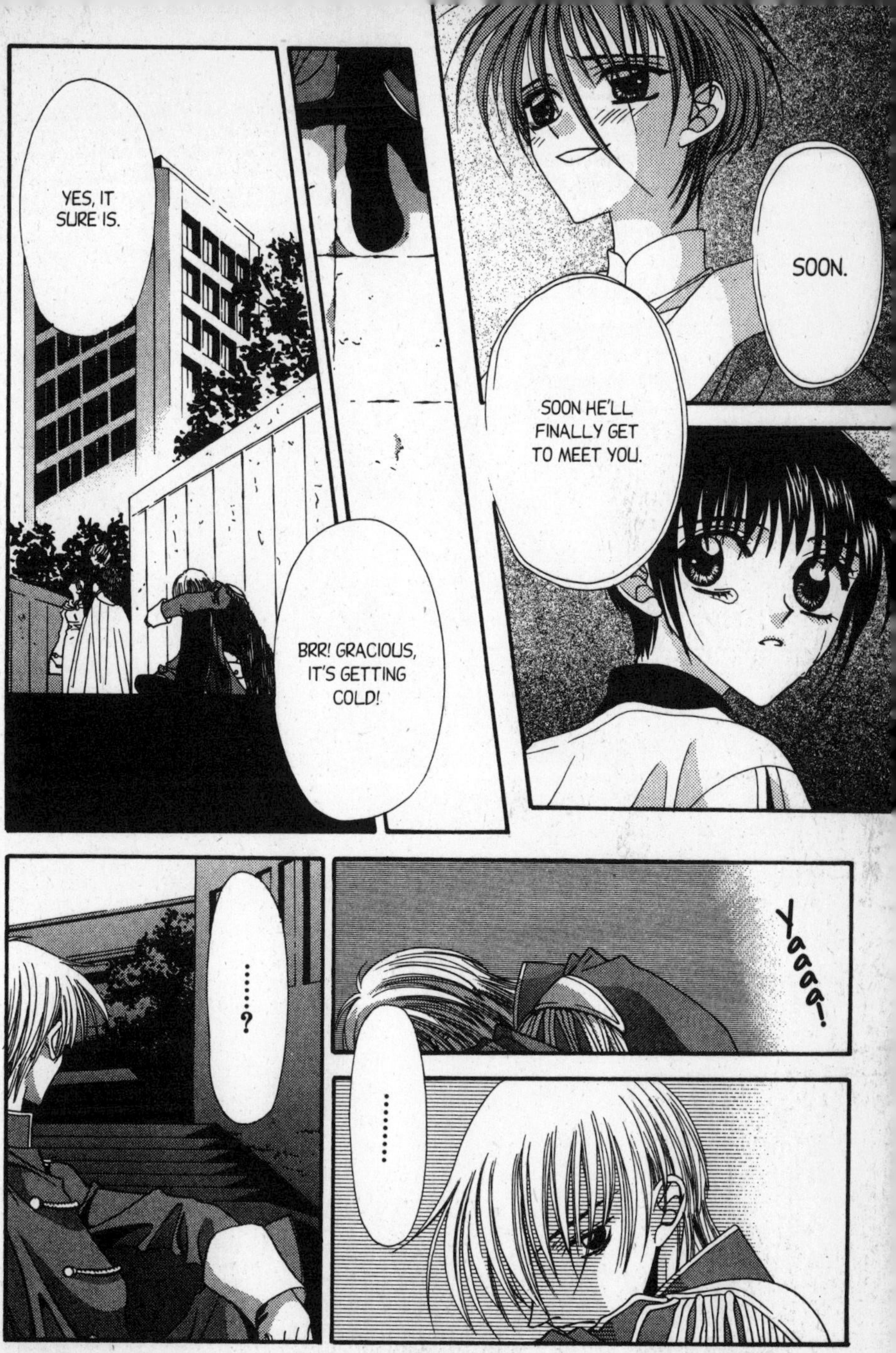
SOON.
SOON HE'LL FINALLY GET TO MEET YOU.
BRR! GRACIOUS, IT'S GETTING COLD!
YES, IT SURE IS.
Yaaaa!
……
……?

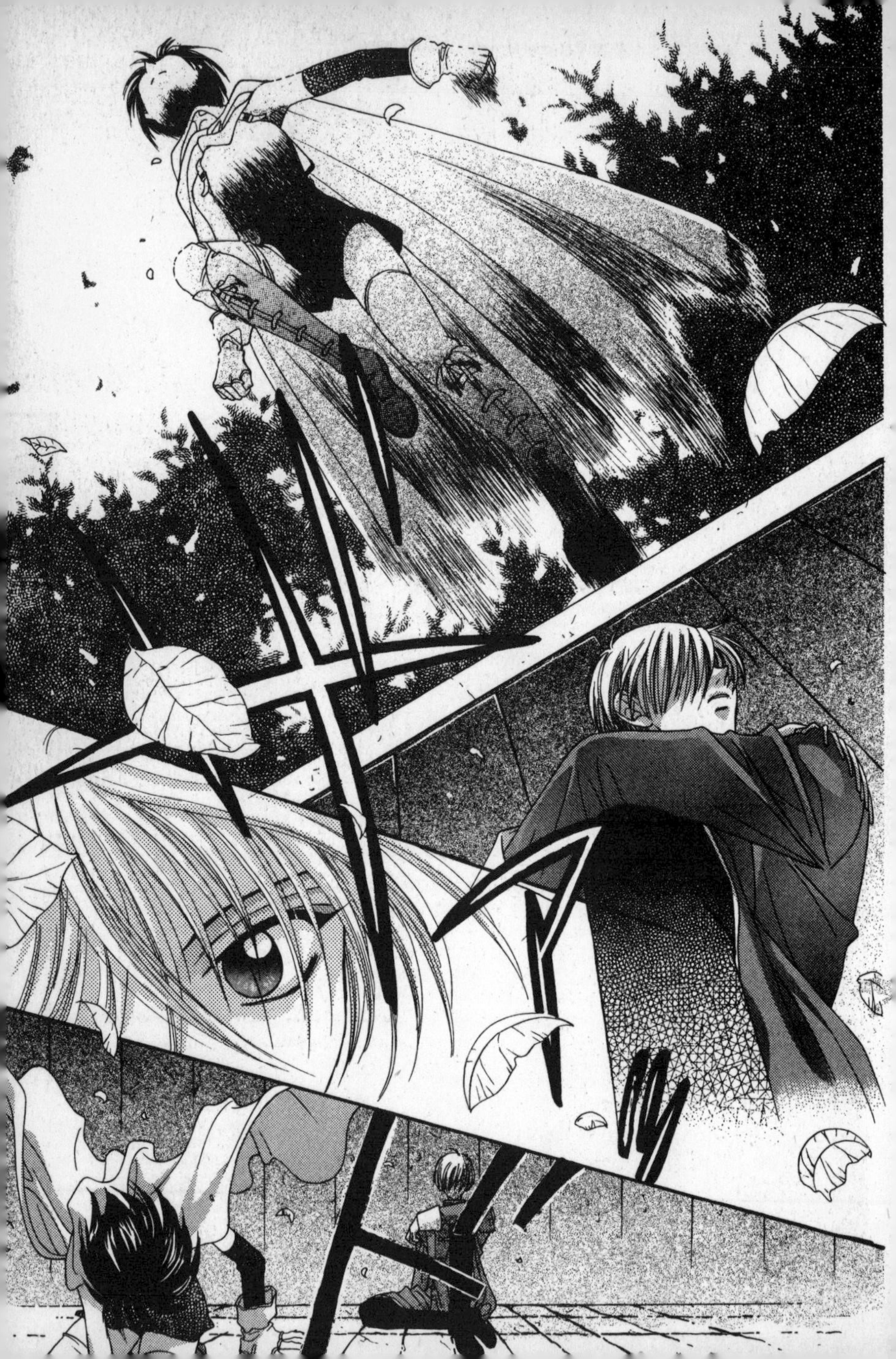

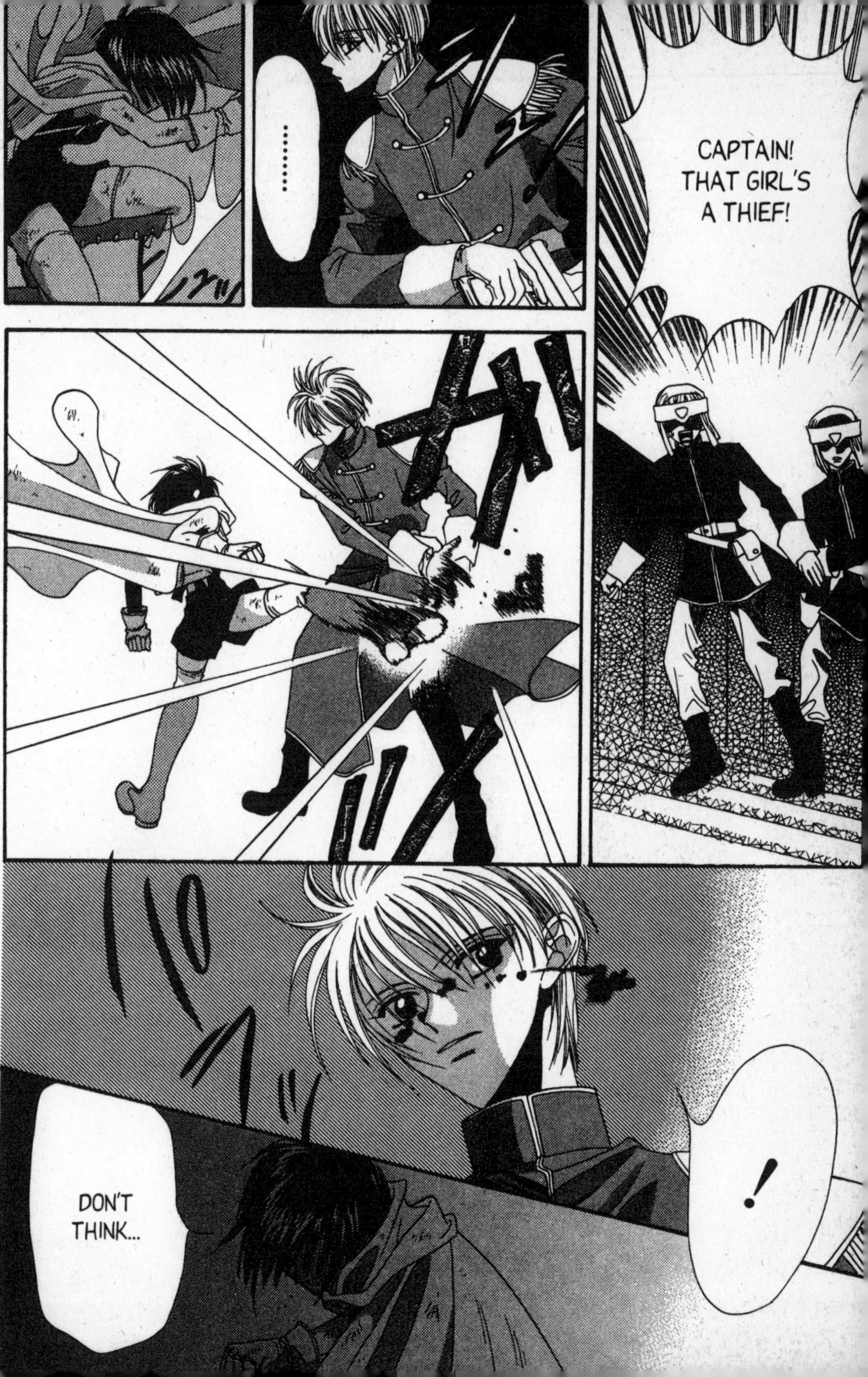
CAPTAIN! THAT GIRL'S A THIEF!
......
!
DON'T THINK...

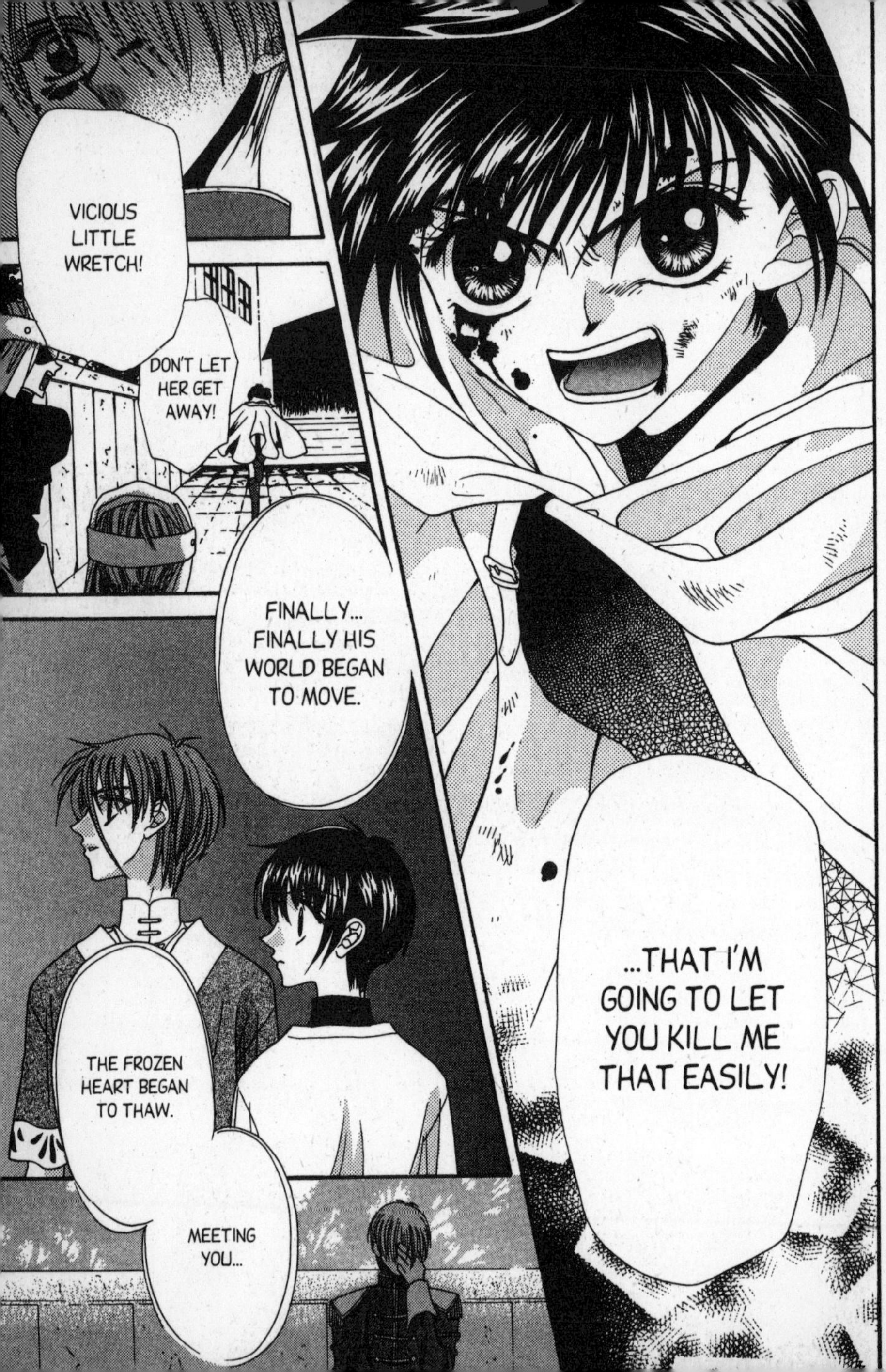
...THAT I'M GOING TO LET YOU KILL ME THAT EASILY!
VICIOUS LITTLE WRETCH!
DON'T LET HER GET AWAY!
FINALLY... FINALLY HIS WORLD BEGAN TO MOVE.
THE FROZEN HEART BEGAN TO THAW.
MEETING YOU...

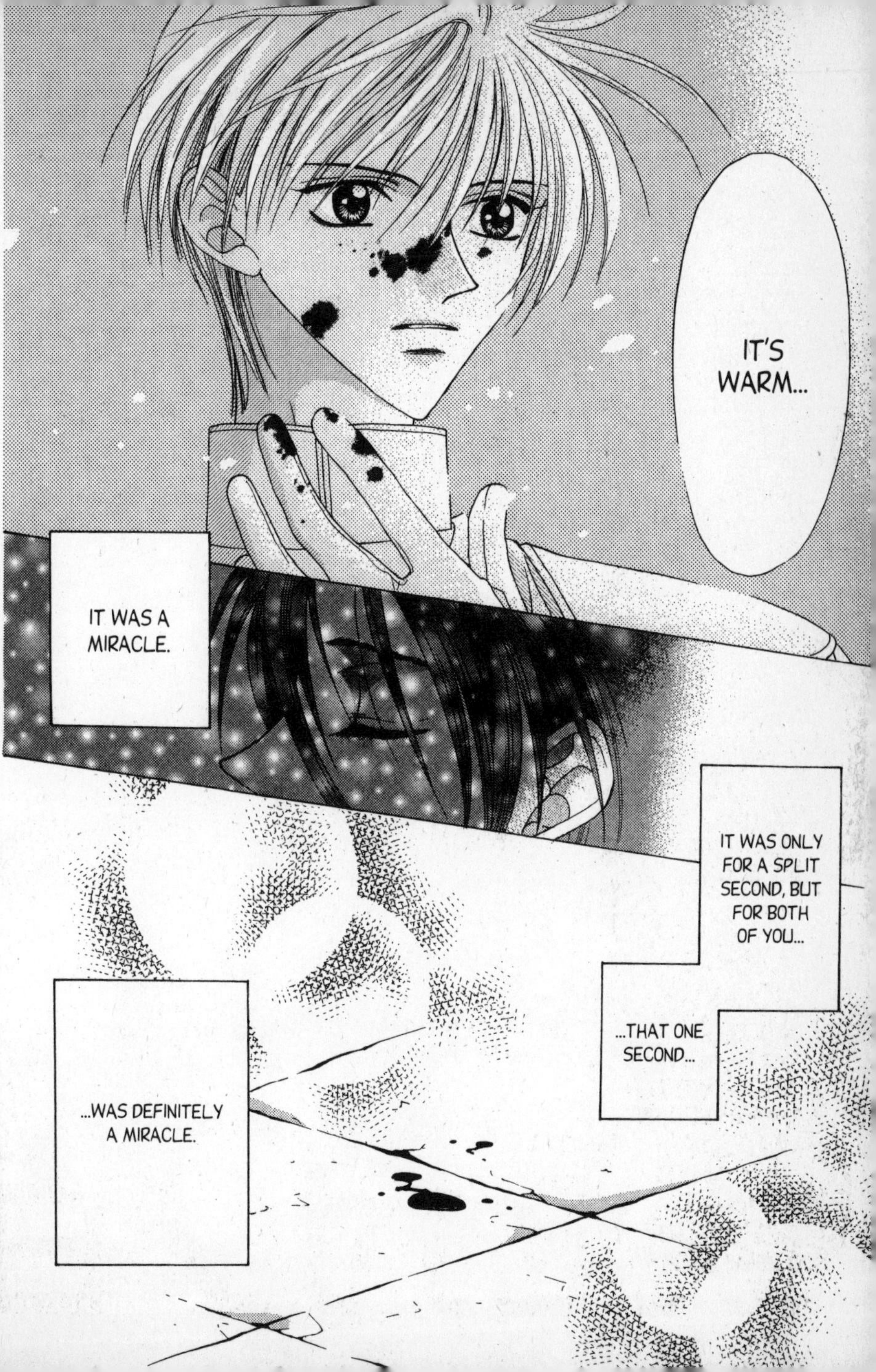
IT'S WARM...
IT WAS A MIRACLE.
IT WAS ONLY FOR A SPLIT SECOND, BUT FOR BOTH OF YOU...
...THAT ONE SECOND...
...WAS DEFINITELY A MIRACLE.

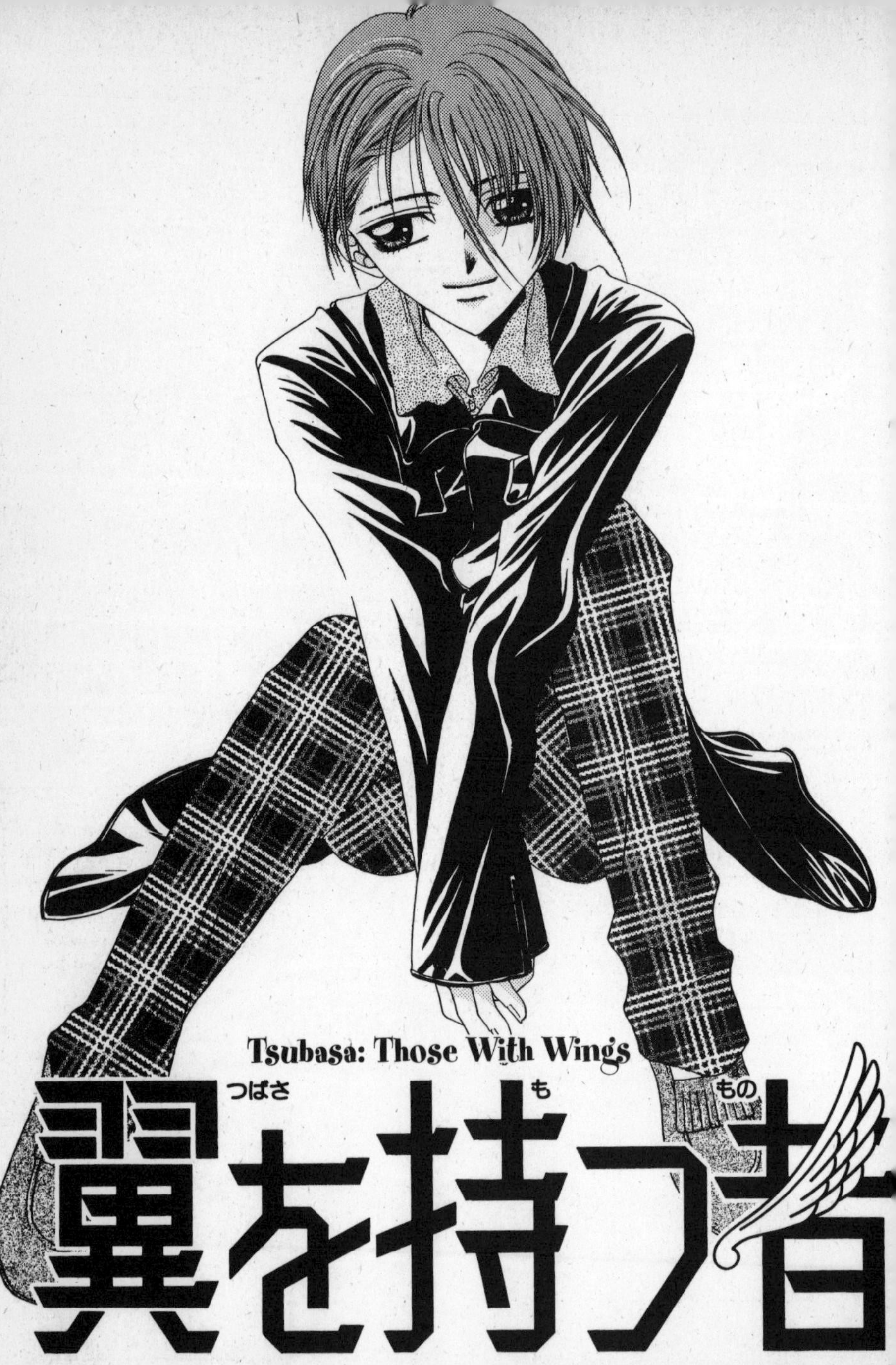

Tsubasa: Those With Wings

翼を持つ者

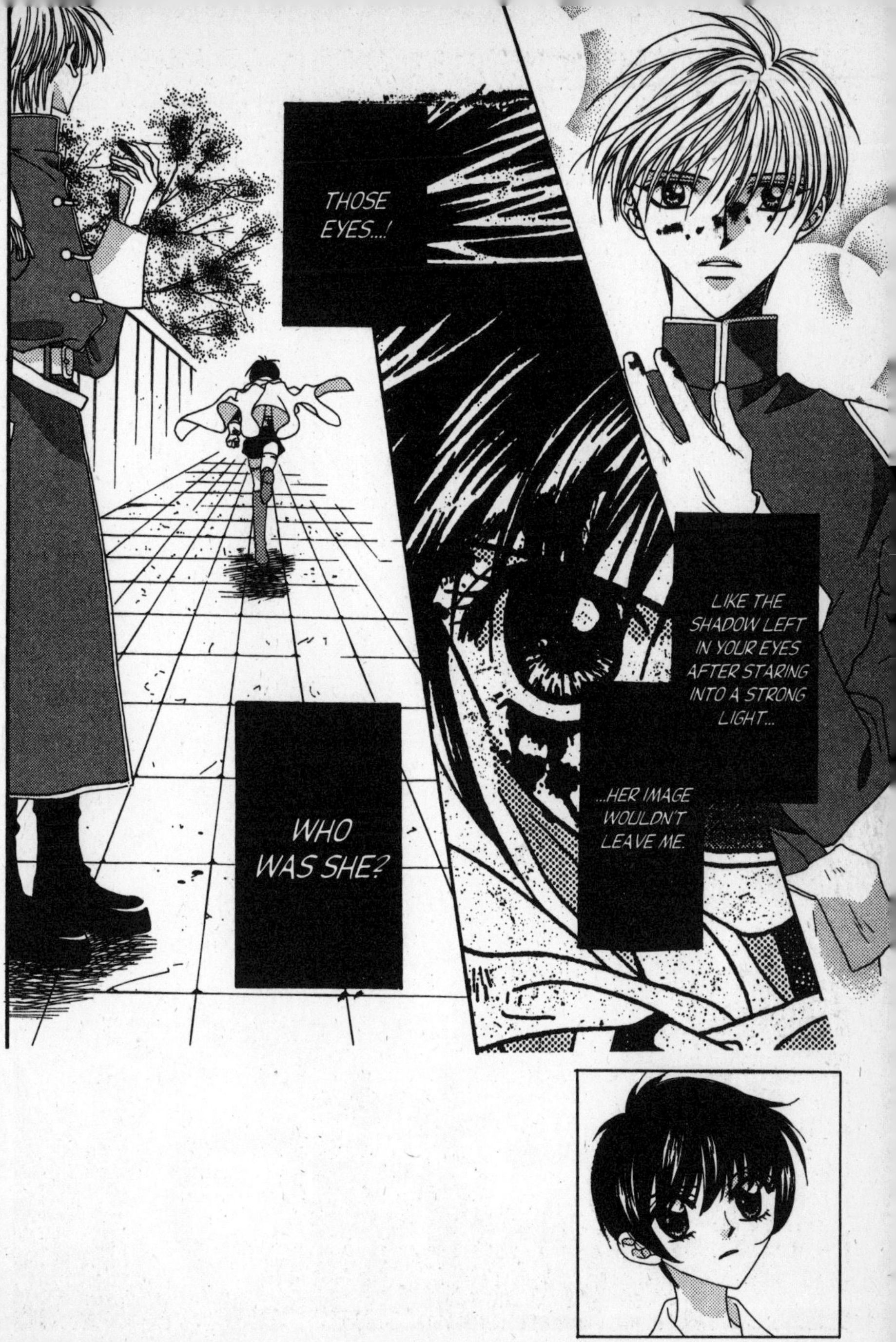
THOSE EYES...!
LIKE THE SHADOW LEFT IN YOUR EYES AFTER STARING INTO A STRONG LIGHT...
...HER IMAGE WOULDN'T LEAVE ME.
WHO WAS SHE?

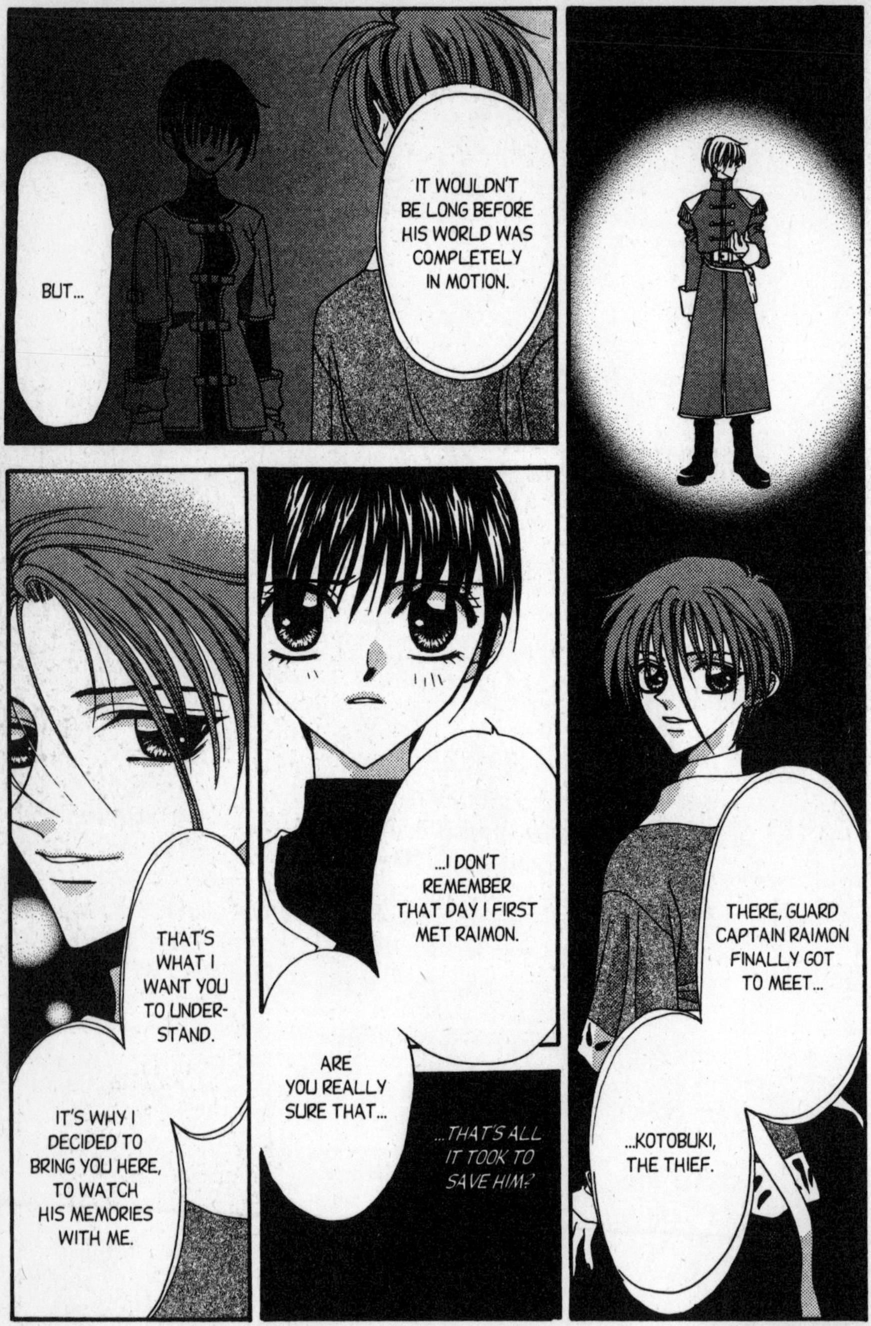
THERE, GUARD CAPTAIN RAIMON FINALLY GOT TO MEET...
...KOTOBUKI, THE THIEF.
IT WOULDN'T BE LONG BEFORE HIS WORLD WAS COMPLETELY IN MOTION.
BUT...
...I DON'T REMEMBER THAT DAY I FIRST MET RAIMON.
ARE YOU REALLY SURE THAT...
...THAT'S ALL IT TOOK TO SAVE HIM?
THAT'S WHAT I WANT YOU TO UNDER-STAND.
IT'S WHY I DECIDED TO BRING YOU HERE, TO WATCH HIS MEMORIES WITH ME.

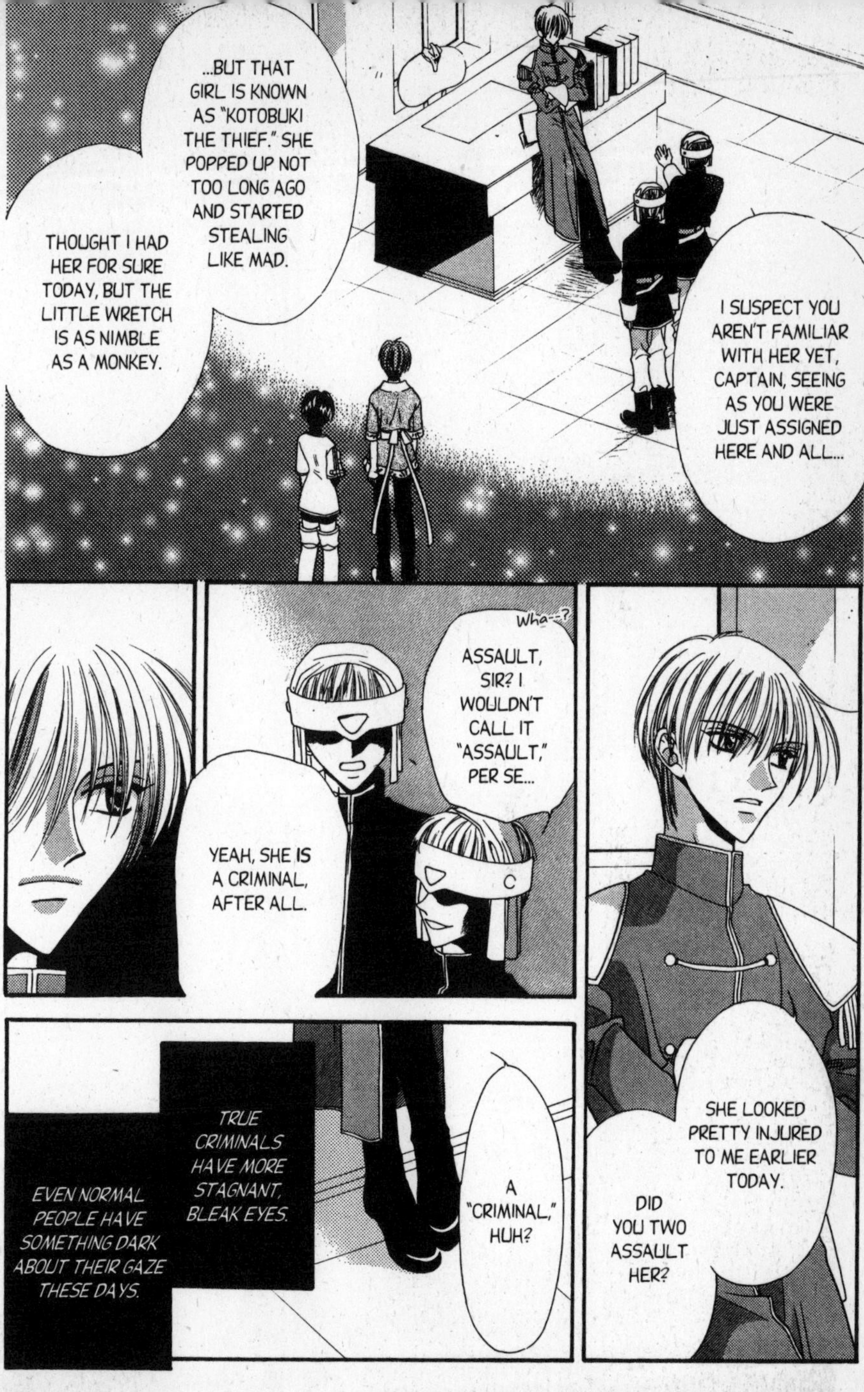
I SUSPECT YOU AREN'T FAMILIAR WITH HER YET, CAPTAIN, SEEING AS YOU WERE JUST ASSIGNED HERE AND ALL...
...BUT THAT GIRL IS KNOWN AS "KOTOBUKI THE THIEF." SHE POPPED UP NOT TOO LONG AGO AND STARTED STEALING LIKE MAD.
THOUGHT I HAD HER FOR SURE TODAY, BUT THE LITTLE WRETCH IS AS NIMBLE AS A MONKEY.
SHE LOOKED PRETTY INJURED TO ME EARLIER TODAY.
DID YOU TWO ASSAULT HER?
Wha--?
ASSAULT, SIR? I WOULDN'T CALL IT "ASSAULT," PER SE...
YEAH, SHE IS A CRIMINAL, AFTER ALL.
A "CRIMINAL," HUH?
TRUE CRIMINALS HAVE MORE STAGNANT, BLEAK EYES.
EVEN NORMAL PEOPLE HAVE SOMETHING DARK ABOUT THEIR GAZE THESE DAYS.

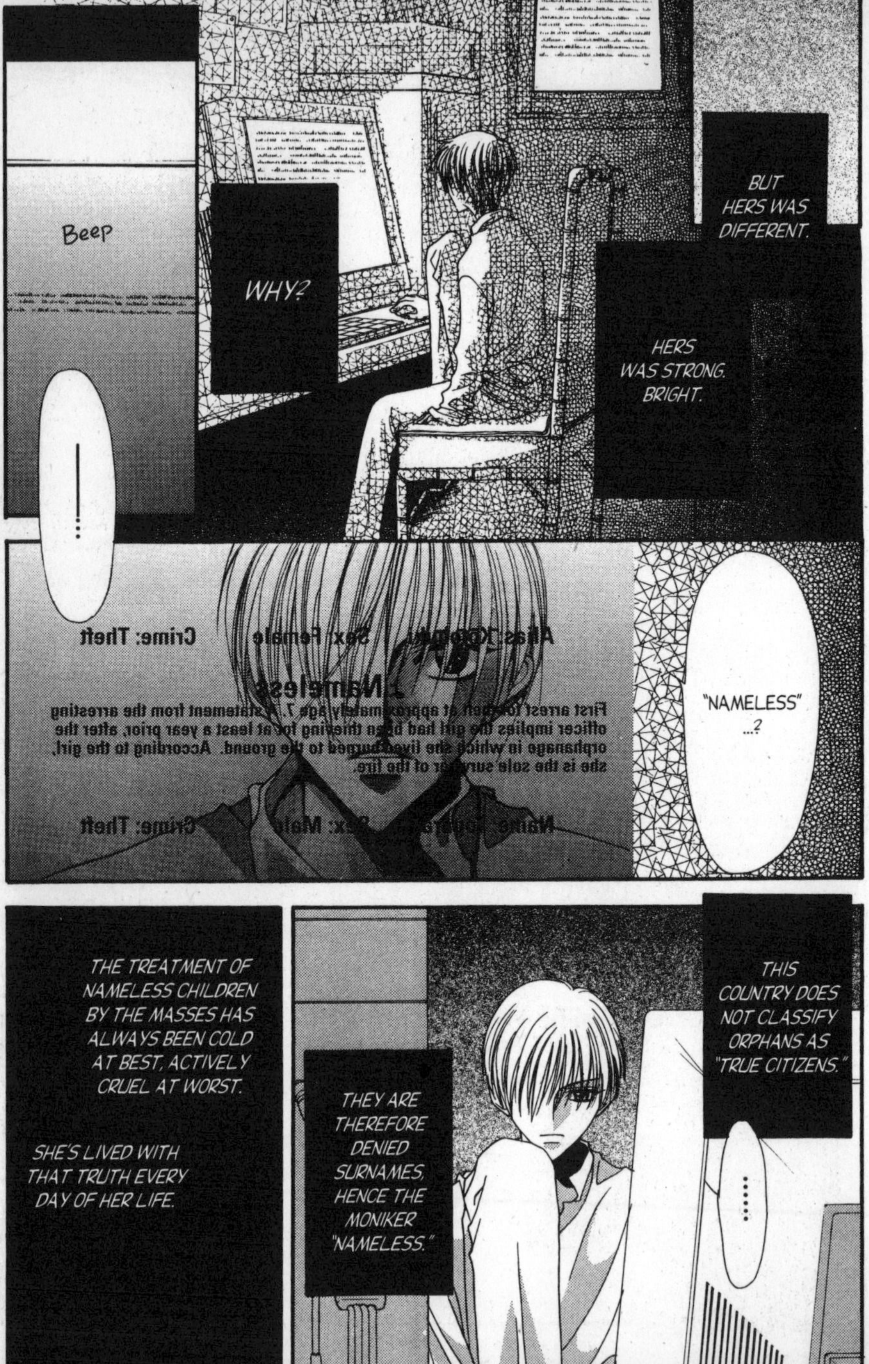
BUT HERS WAS DIFFERENT.
HERS WAS STRONG. BRIGHT.
WHY?
Beep
—......
"NAMELESS" ...?
THIS COUNTRY DOES NOT CLASSIFY ORPHANS AS "TRUE CITIZENS."
THEY ARE THEREFORE DENIED SURNAMES, HENCE THE MONIKER "NAMELESS."
......
THE TREATMENT OF NAMELESS CHILDREN BY THE MASSES HAS ALWAYS BEEN COLD AT BEST, ACTIVELY CRUEL AT WORST.
SHE'S LIVED WITH THAT TRUTH EVERY DAY OF HER LIFE.

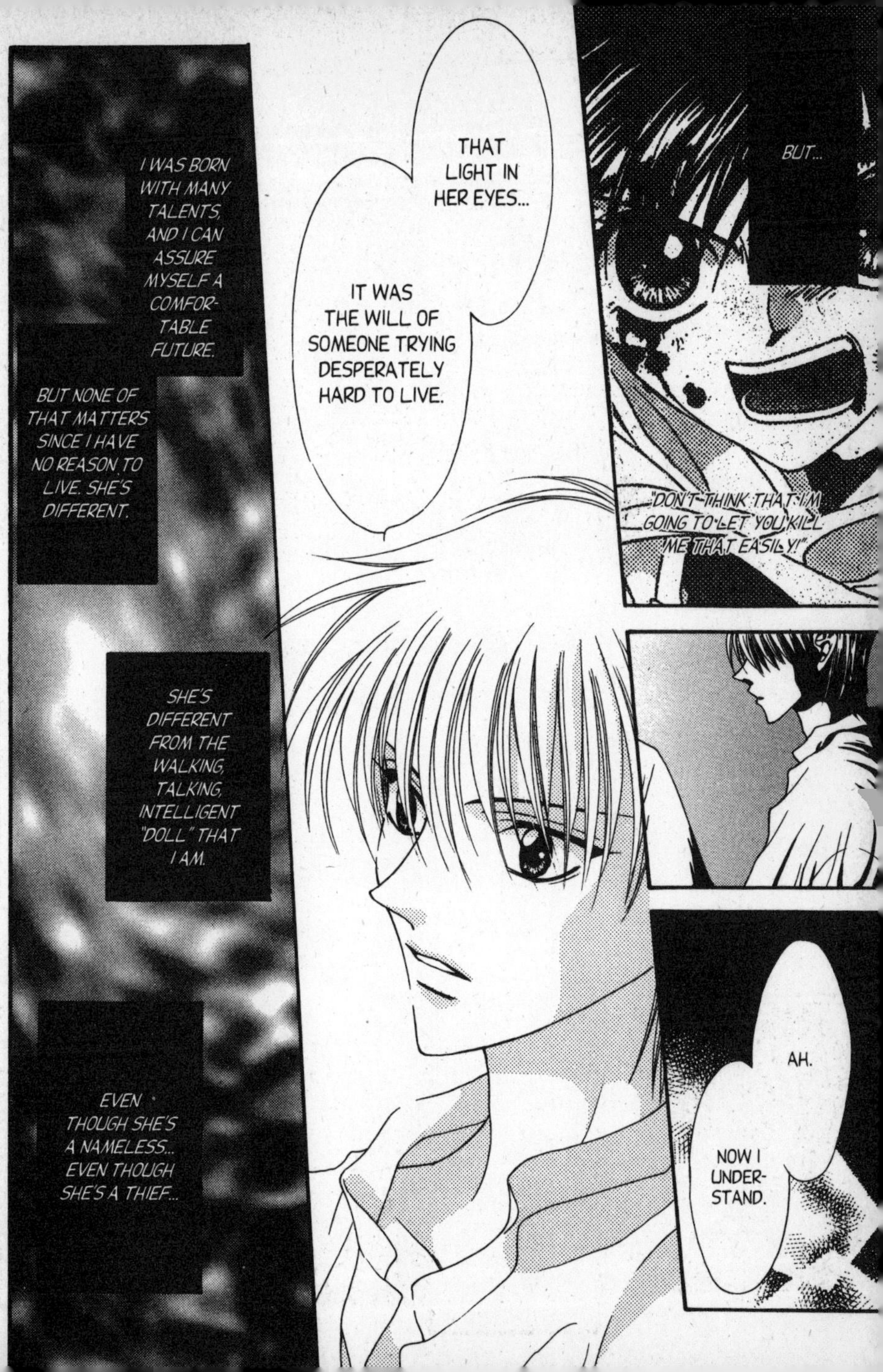
BUT...
"DON'T THINK THAT I'M GOING TO LET YOU KILL ME THAT EASILY!"
AH.
NOW I UNDERSTAND.
THAT LIGHT IN HER EYES...
IT WAS THE WILL OF SOMEONE TRYING DESPERATELY HARD TO LIVE.
I WAS BORN WITH MANY TALENTS, AND I CAN ASSURE MYSELF A COMFORTABLE FUTURE.
BUT NONE OF THAT MATTERS SINCE I HAVE NO REASON TO LIVE. SHE'S DIFFERENT.
SHE'S DIFFERENT FROM THE WALKING, TALKING, INTELLIGENT "DOLL" THAT I AM.
EVEN THOUGH SHE'S A NAMELESS... EVEN THOUGH SHE'S A THIEF...

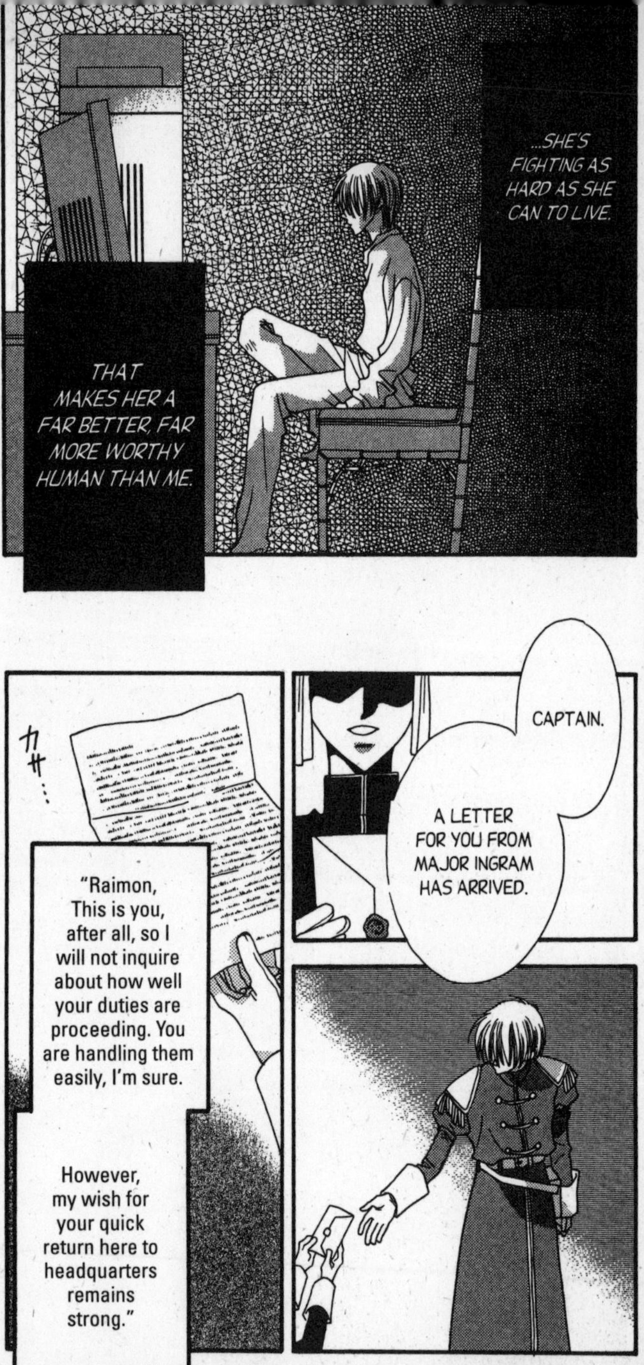
...SHE'S FIGHTING AS HARD AS SHE CAN TO LIVE.
THAT MAKES HER A FAR BETTER, FAR MORE WORTHY HUMAN THAN ME.
CAPTAIN.
A LETTER FOR YOU FROM MAJOR INGRAM HAS ARRIVED.
カサ...
"Raimon, This is you, after all, so I will not inquire about how well your duties are proceeding. You are handling them easily, I'm sure.
However, my wish for your quick return here to headquarters remains strong."
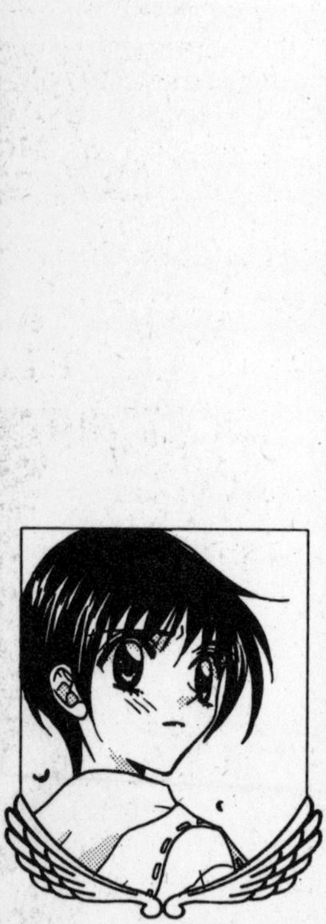

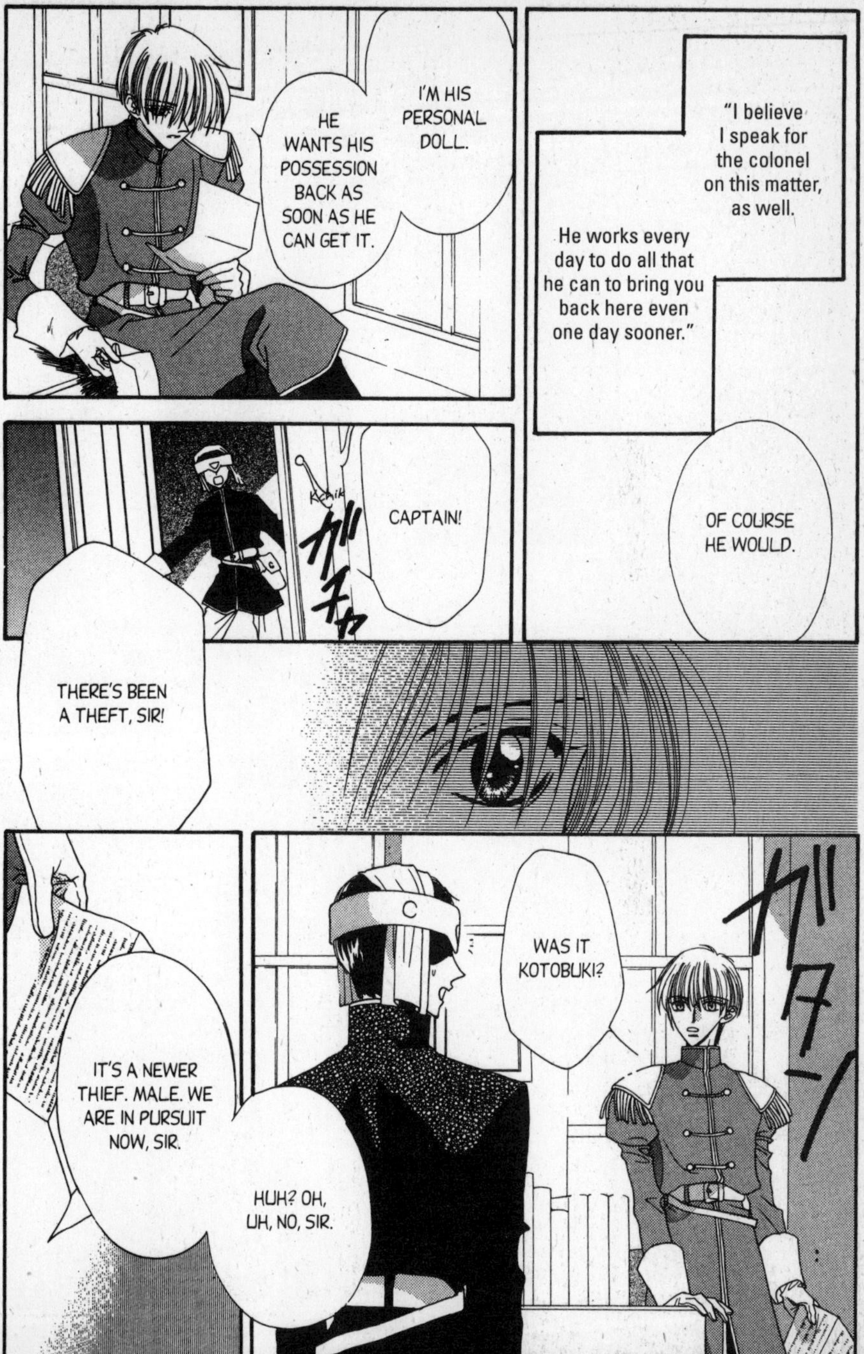
"I believe I speak for the colonel on this matter, as well.
He works every day to do all that he can to bring you back here even one day sooner."
OF COURSE HE WOULD.
I'M HIS PERSONAL DOLL.
HE WANTS HIS POSSESSION BACK AS SOON AS HE CAN GET IT.
ガチャ
CAPTAIN!
THERE'S BEEN A THEFT, SIR!
ガタ
WAS IT KOTOBUKI?
HUH? OH, UH, NO, SIR.
IT'S A NEWER THIEF. MALE. WE ARE IN PURSUIT NOW, SIR.

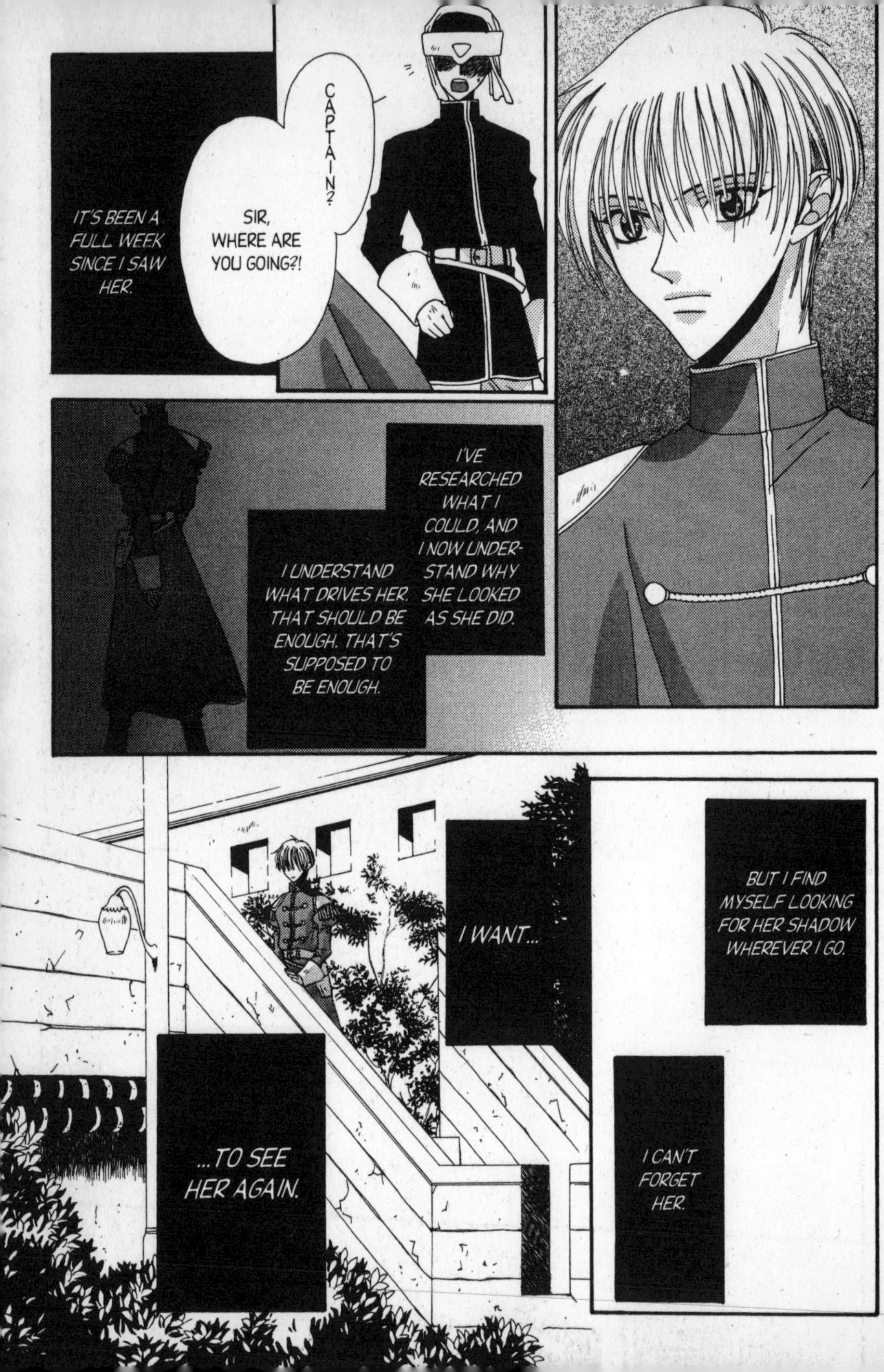
CAPTAIN?
SIR, WHERE ARE YOU GOING?!
IT'S BEEN A FULL WEEK SINCE I SAW HER.
I'VE RESEARCHED WHAT I COULD, AND I NOW UNDERSTAND WHY SHE LOOKED AS SHE DID.
I UNDERSTAND WHAT DRIVES HER. THAT SHOULD BE ENOUGH. THAT'S SUPPOSED TO BE ENOUGH.
BUT I FIND MYSELF LOOKING FOR HER SHADOW WHEREVER I GO.
I CAN'T FORGET HER.
I WANT...
...TO SEE HER AGAIN.

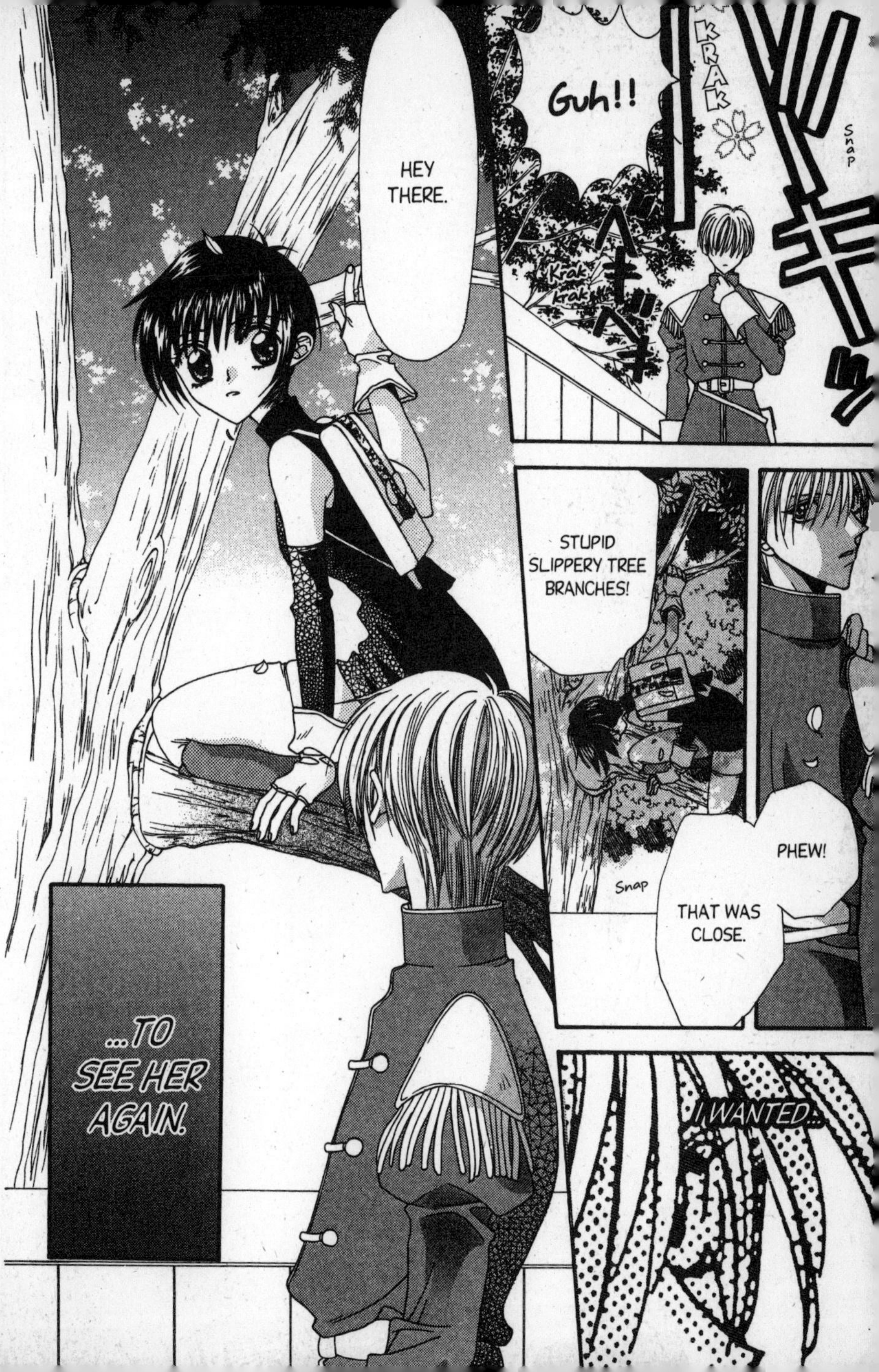

Guh!!
KRAK
Snap
Krak krak
STUPID SLIPPERY TREE BRANCHES!
Snap
PHEW!
THAT WAS CLOSE.
I WANTED...
HEY THERE.
...TO SEE HER AGAIN.

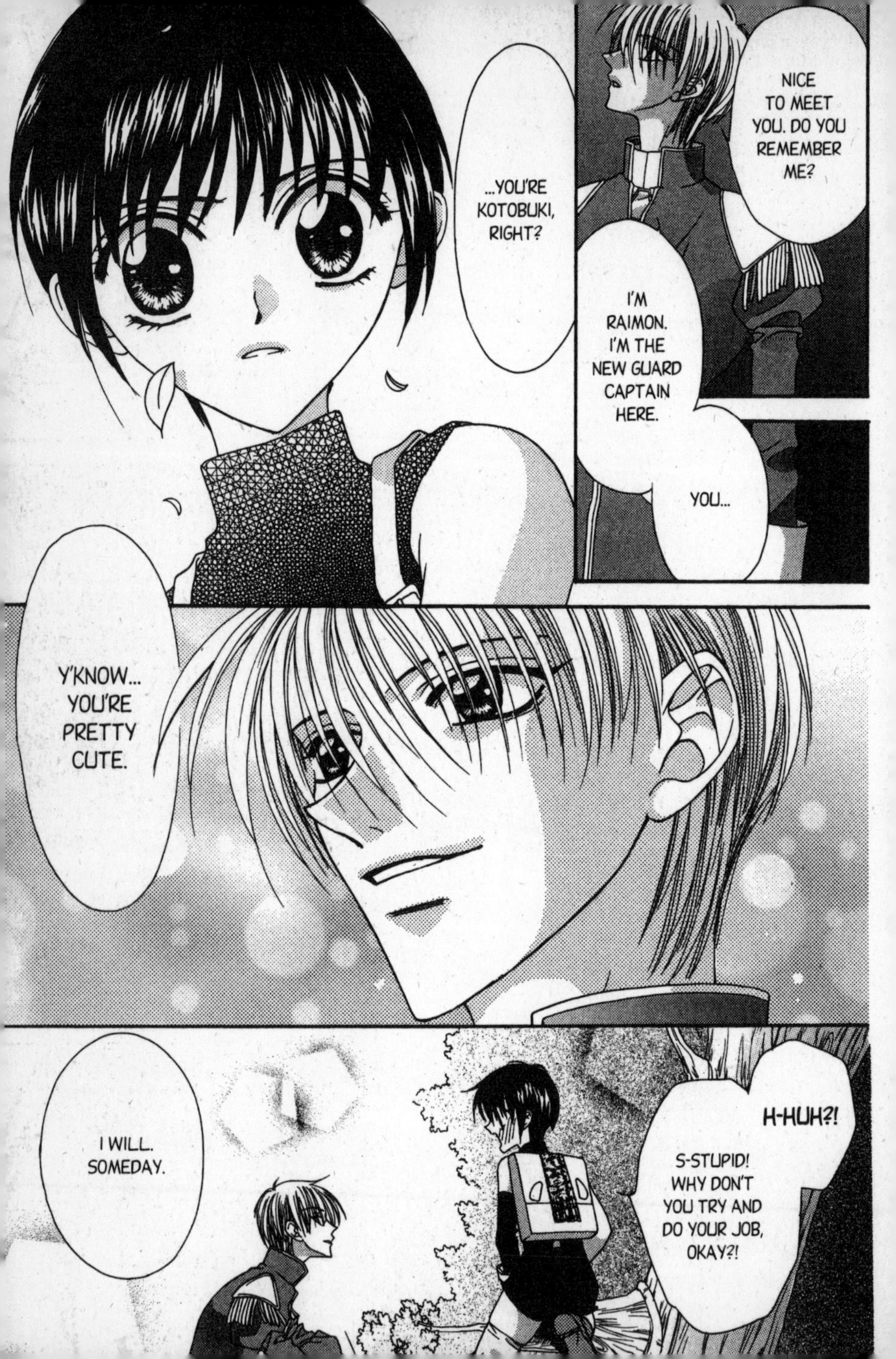
NICE TO MEET YOU. DO YOU REMEMBER ME?
I'M RAIMON. I'M THE NEW GUARD CAPTAIN HERE.
YOU...
...YOU'RE KOTOBUKI, RIGHT?
Y'KNOW... YOU'RE PRETTY CUTE.
H-HUH?!
S-STUPID! WHY DON'T YOU TRY AND DO YOUR JOB, OKAY?!
I WILL. SOMEDAY.

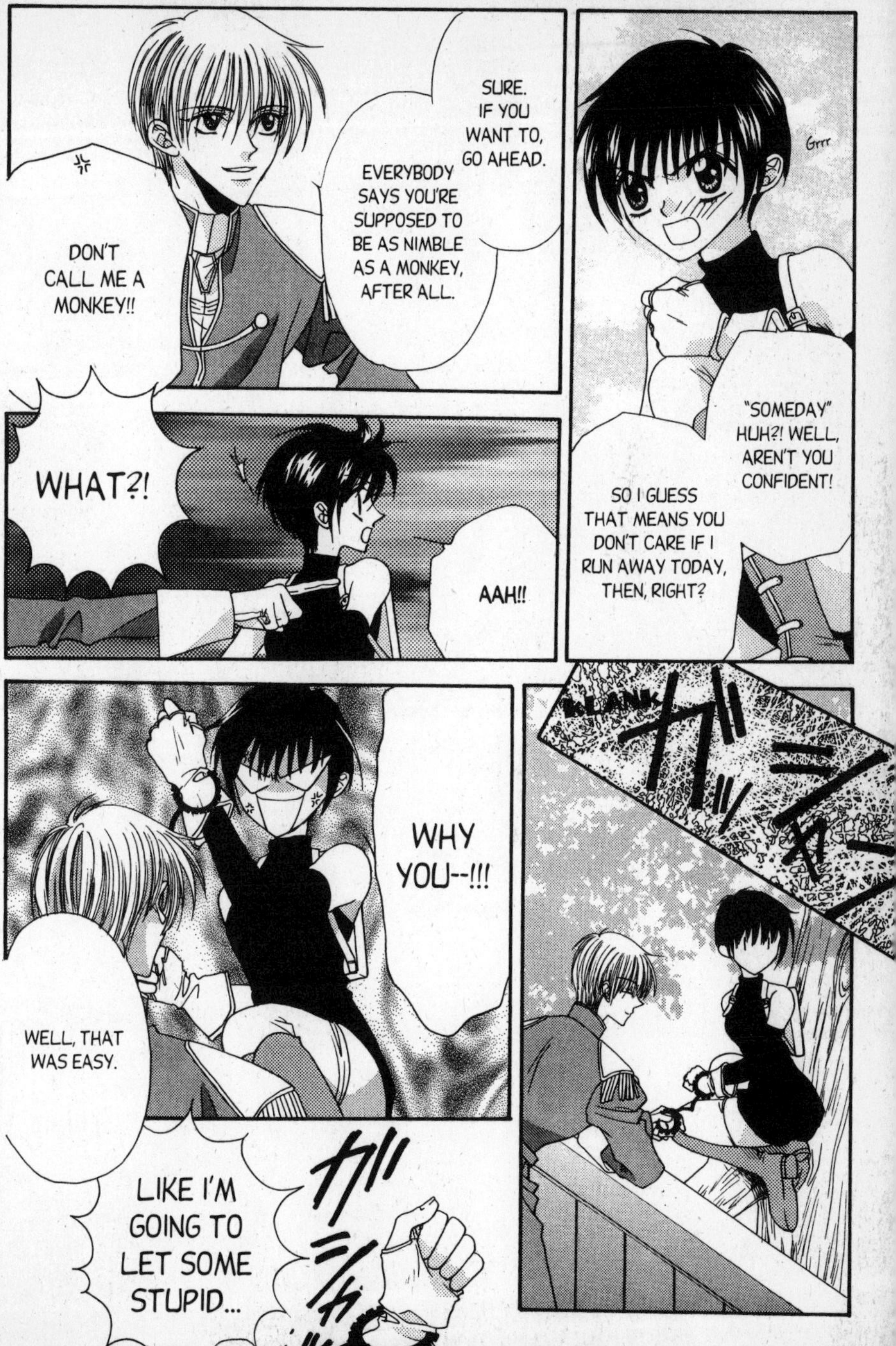
Grrr
"SOMEDAY" HUH?! WELL, AREN'T YOU CONFIDENT!
SO I GUESS THAT MEANS YOU DON'T CARE IF I RUN AWAY TODAY, THEN, RIGHT?
SURE. IF YOU WANT TO, GO AHEAD.
EVERYBODY SAYS YOU'RE SUPPOSED TO BE AS NIMBLE AS A MONKEY, AFTER ALL.
DON'T CALL ME A MONKEY!!
WHAT?!
AAH!!
KLANK
WHY YOU--!!!
WELL, THAT WAS EASY.
LIKE I'M GOING TO LET SOME STUPID...

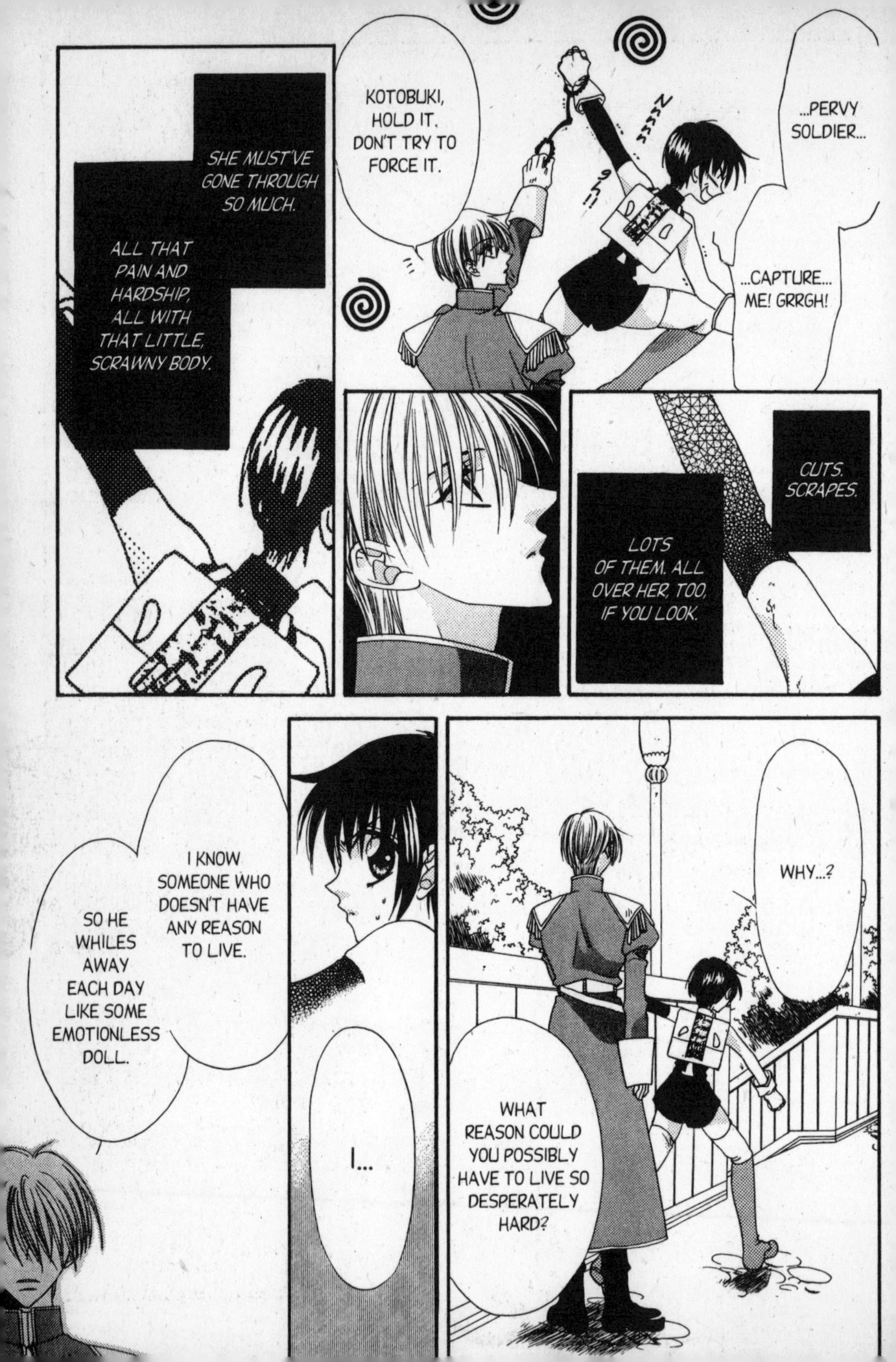
...PERVY SOLDIER...
...CAPTURE... ME! GRRGH!
KOTOBUKI, HOLD IT. DON'T TRY TO FORCE IT.
CUTS. SCRAPES.
LOTS OF THEM. ALL OVER HER, TOO, IF YOU LOOK.
SHE MUST'VE GONE THROUGH SO MUCH.
ALL THAT PAIN AND HARDSHIP, ALL WITH THAT LITTLE, SCRAWNY BODY.
WHY...?
WHAT REASON COULD YOU POSSIBLY HAVE TO LIVE SO DESPERATELY HARD?
I...
I KNOW SOMEONE WHO DOESN'T HAVE ANY REASON TO LIVE.
SO HE WHILES AWAY EACH DAY LIKE SOME EMOTIONLESS DOLL.

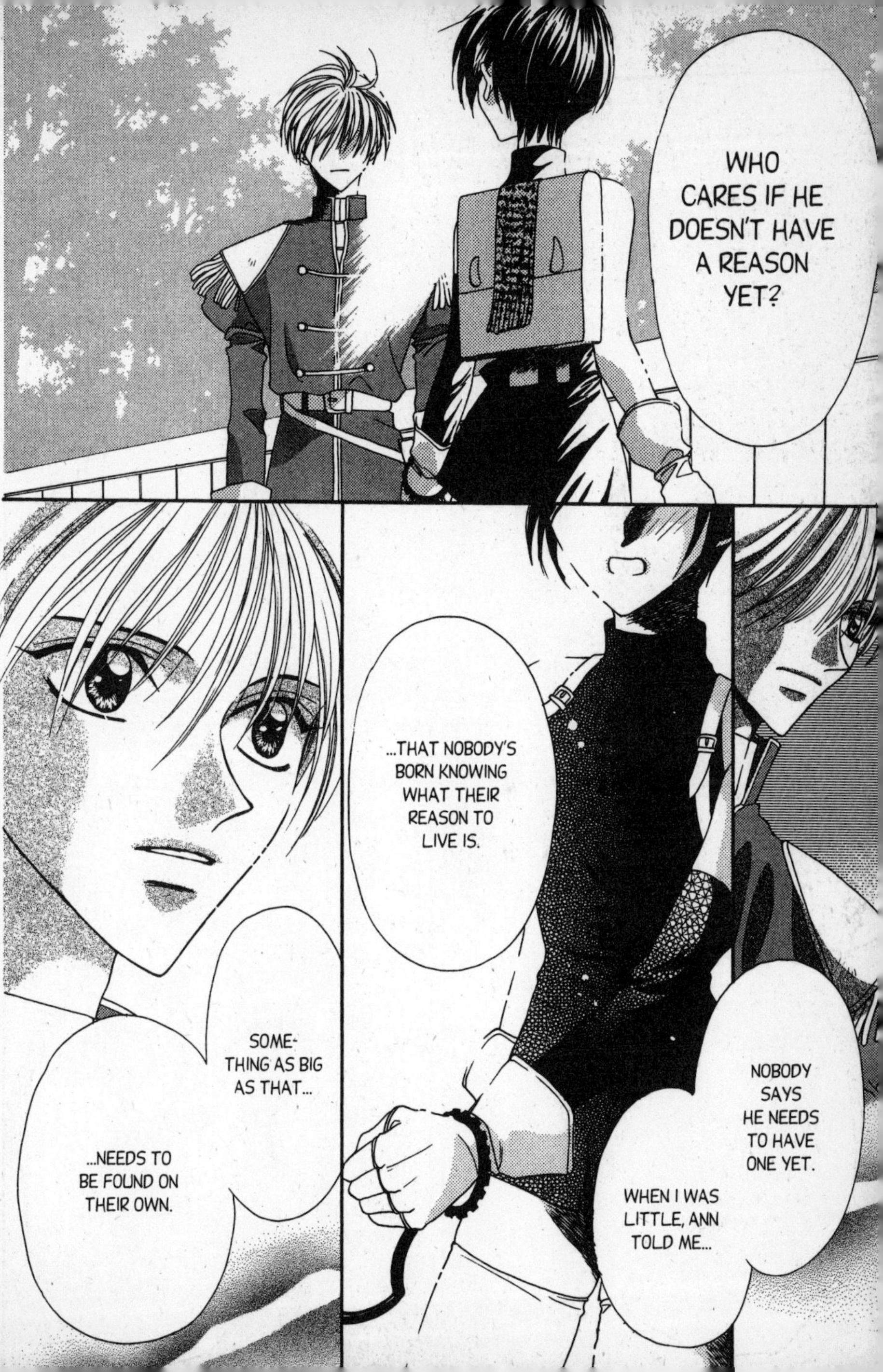
WHO CARES IF HE DOESN'T HAVE A REASON YET?
NOBODY SAYS HE NEEDS TO HAVE ONE YET.
WHEN I WAS LITTLE, ANN TOLD ME...
...THAT NOBODY'S BORN KNOWING WHAT THEIR REASON TO LIVE IS.
SOME-THING AS BIG AS THAT...
...NEEDS TO BE FOUND ON THEIR OWN.

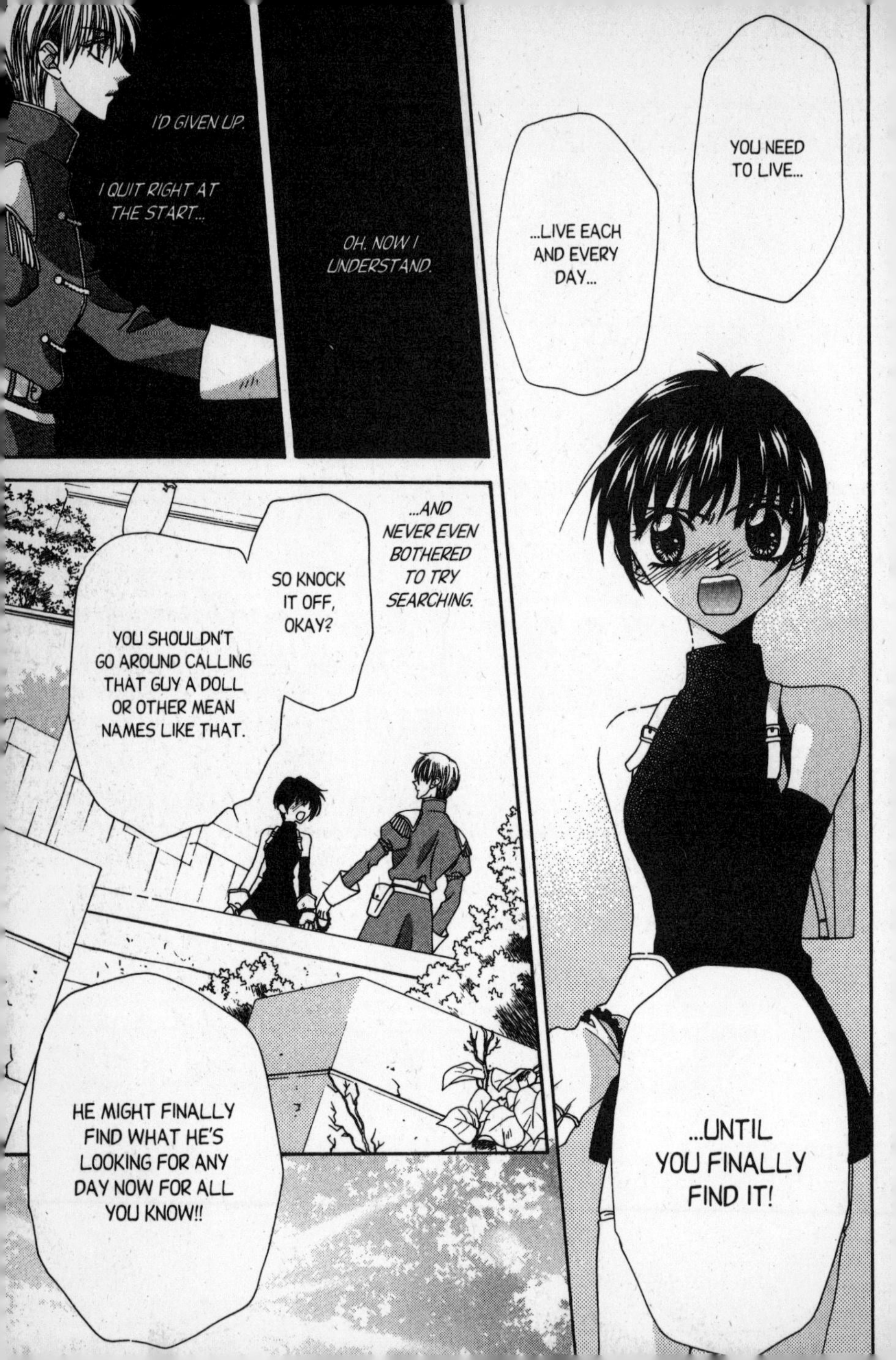
YOU NEED TO LIVE...
...LIVE EACH AND EVERY DAY...
...UNTIL YOU FINALLY FIND IT!
OH. NOW I UNDERSTAND.
I'D GIVEN UP.
I QUIT RIGHT AT THE START...
...AND NEVER EVEN BOTHERED TO TRY SEARCHING.
SO KNOCK IT OFF, OKAY?
YOU SHOULDN'T GO AROUND CALLING THAT GUY A DOLL OR OTHER MEAN NAMES LIKE THAT.
HE MIGHT FINALLY FIND WHAT HE'S LOOKING FOR ANY DAY NOW FOR ALL YOU KNOW!!

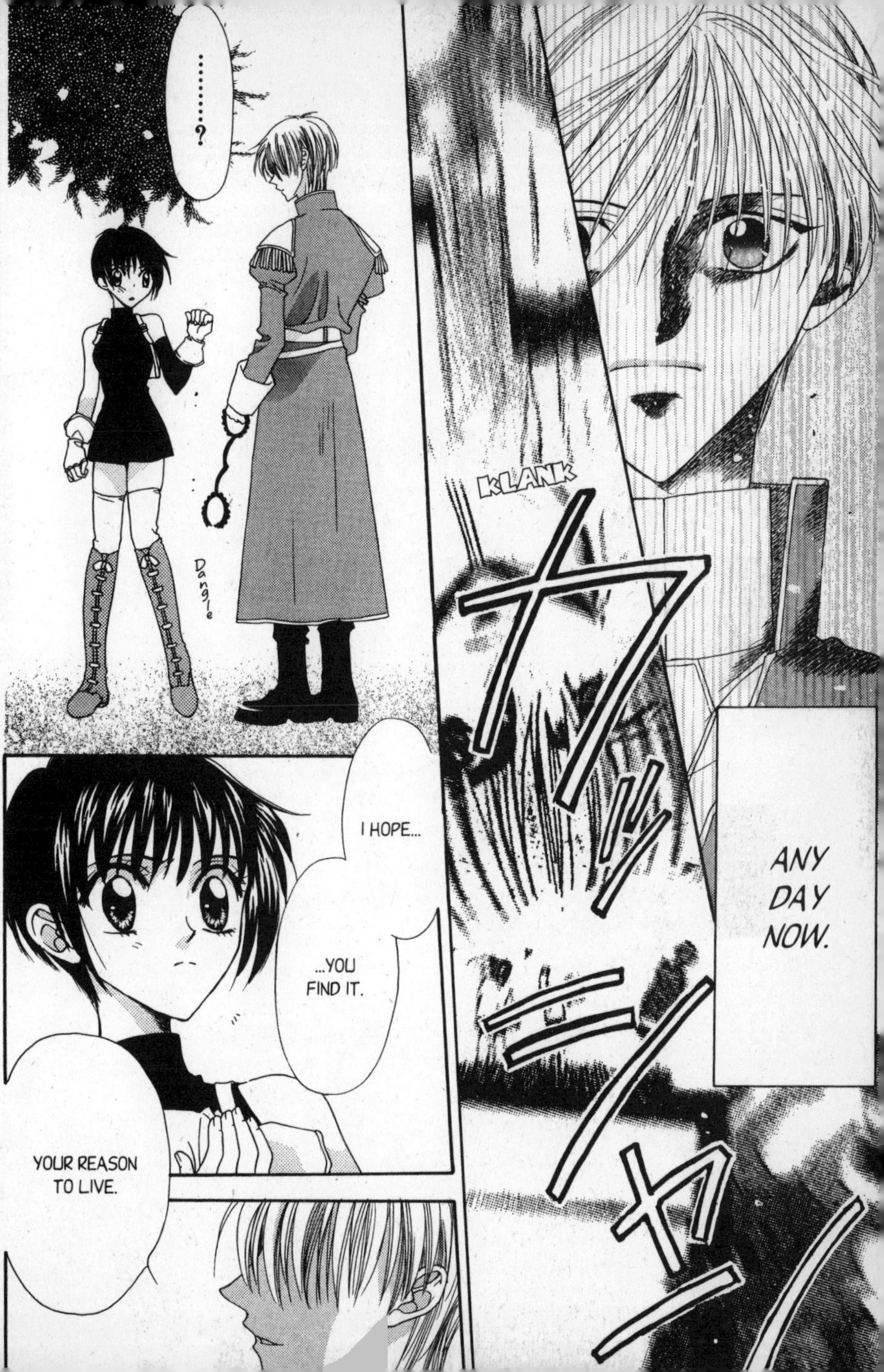
KLANK
ANY DAY NOW.
......?
Dangle
I HOPE...
...YOU FIND IT.
YOUR REASON TO LIVE.

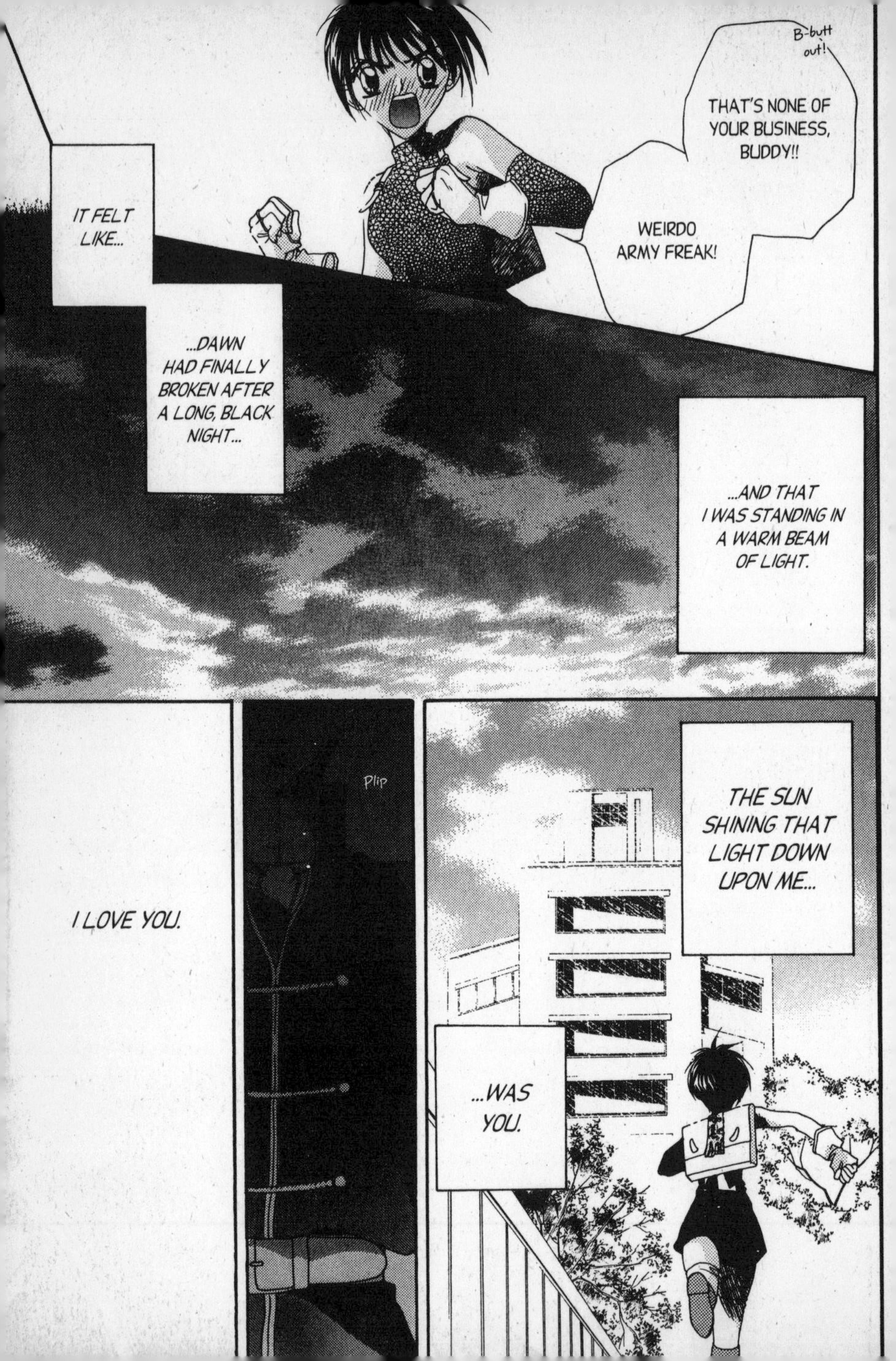
B-butt out!
THAT'S NONE OF YOUR BUSINESS, BUDDY!!
WEIRDO ARMY FREAK!
IT FELT LIKE...
...DAWN HAD FINALLY BROKEN AFTER A LONG, BLACK NIGHT...
...AND THAT I WAS STANDING IN A WARM BEAM OF LIGHT.
THE SUN SHINING THAT LIGHT DOWN UPON ME...
...WAS YOU.
Plip
I LOVE YOU.

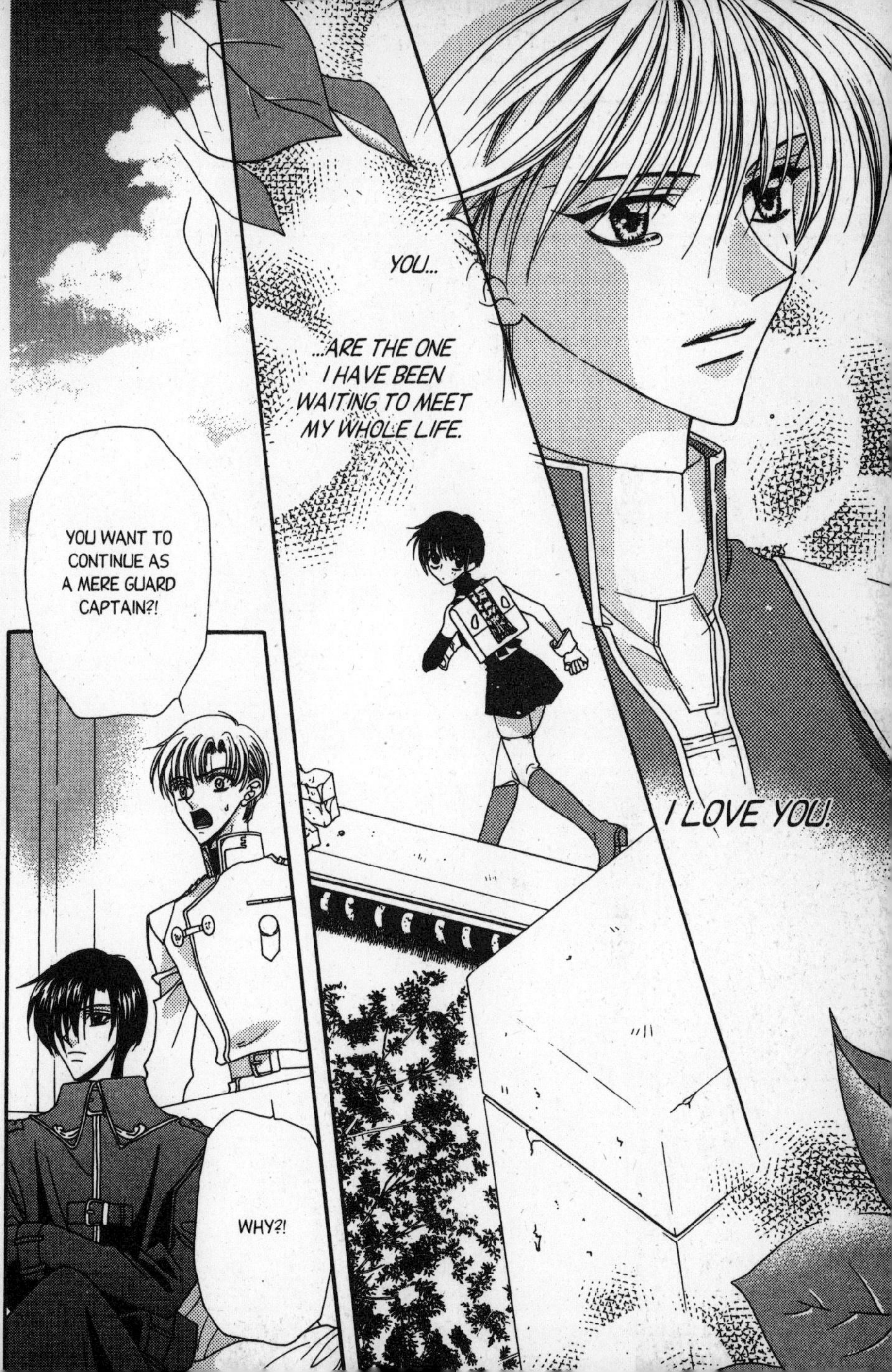

YOU...
...ARE THE ONE I HAVE BEEN WAITING TO MEET MY WHOLE LIFE.
I LOVE YOU.
YOU WANT TO CONTINUE AS A MERE GUARD CAPTAIN?!
WHY?!

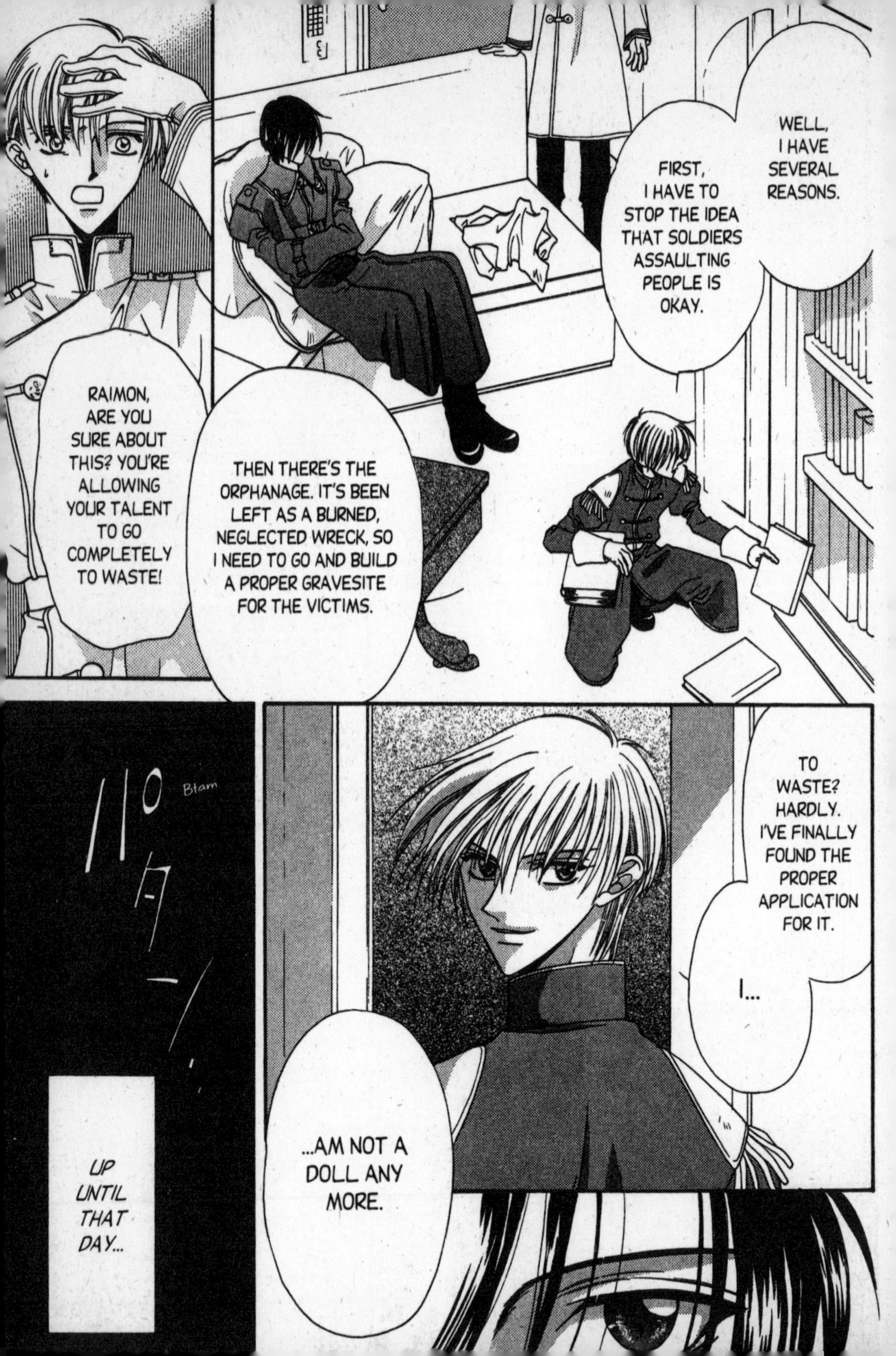
WELL, I HAVE SEVERAL REASONS.
FIRST, I HAVE TO STOP THE IDEA THAT SOLDIERS ASSAULTING PEOPLE IS OKAY.
THEN THERE'S THE ORPHANAGE. IT'S BEEN LEFT AS A BURNED, NEGLECTED WRECK, SO I NEED TO GO AND BUILD A PROPER GRAVESITE FOR THE VICTIMS.
RAIMON, ARE YOU SURE ABOUT THIS? YOU'RE ALLOWING YOUR TALENT TO GO COMPLETELY TO WASTE!
TO WASTE? HARDLY. I'VE FINALLY FOUND THE PROPER APPLICATION FOR IT.
I...
...AM NOT A DOLL ANY MORE.
Btam
UP UNTIL THAT DAY...

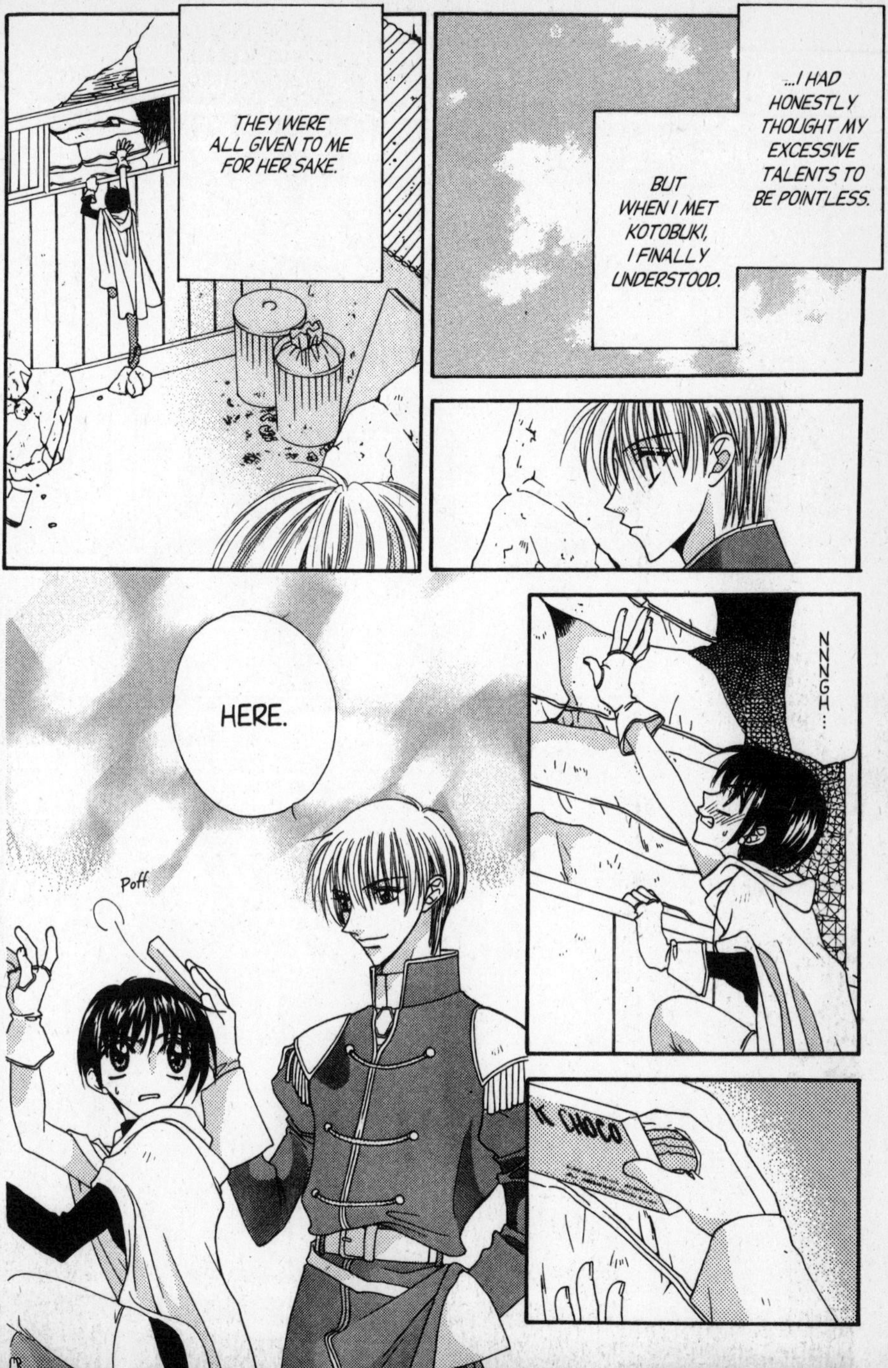
...I HAD HONESTLY THOUGHT MY EXCESSIVE TALENTS TO BE POINTLESS.
BUT WHEN I MET KOTOBUKI, I FINALLY UNDERSTOOD.
THEY WERE ALL GIVEN TO ME FOR HER SAKE.
NNNGH...
CHOCO
HERE.
Poff

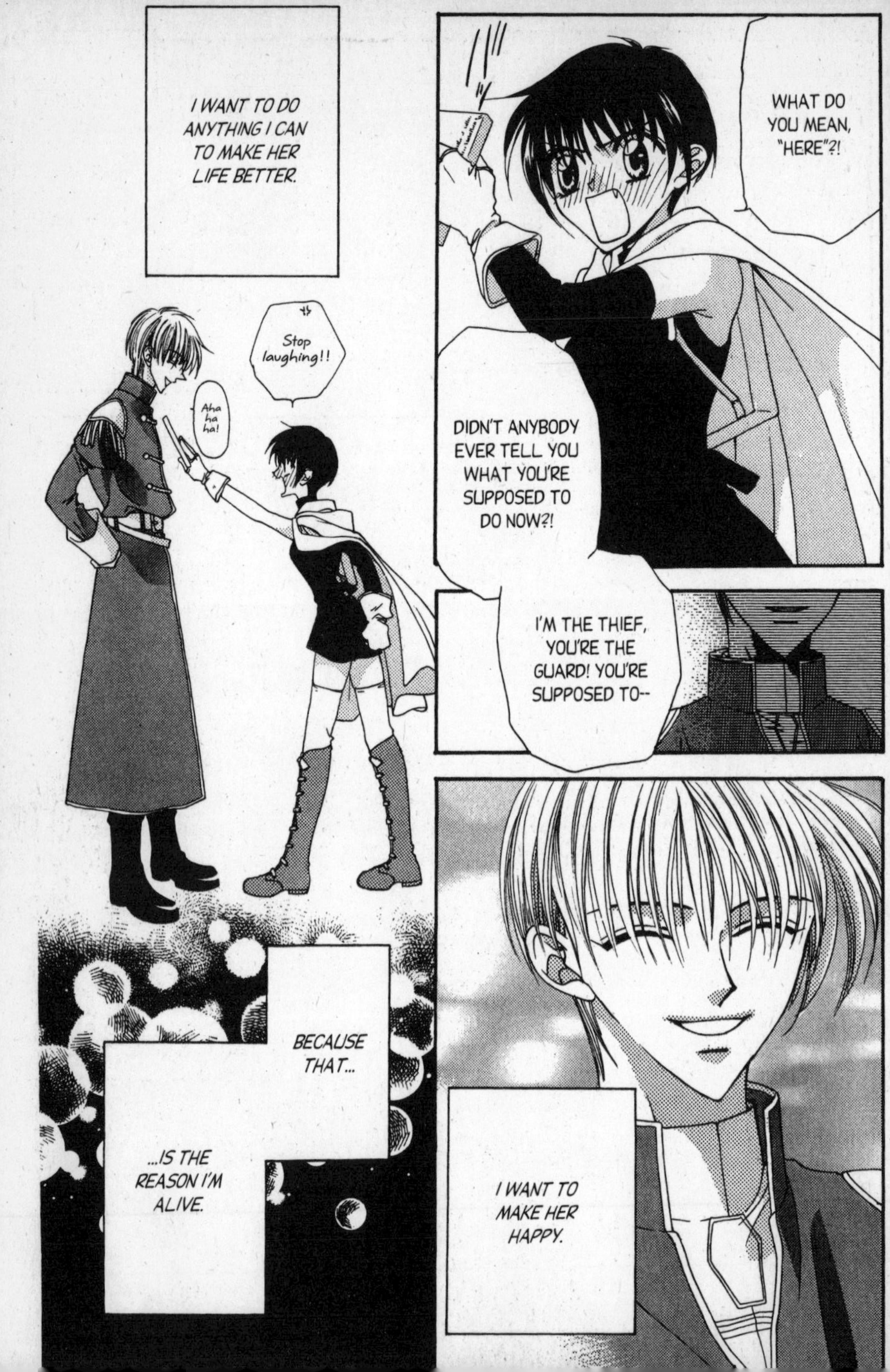
WHAT DO YOU MEAN, "HERE"?!
DIDN'T ANYBODY EVER TELL YOU WHAT YOU'RE SUPPOSED TO DO NOW?!
I'M THE THIEF, YOU'RE THE GUARD! YOU'RE SUPPOSED TO--
I WANT TO MAKE HER HAPPY.
I WANT TO DO ANYTHING I CAN TO MAKE HER LIFE BETTER.
Stop laughing!!
Aha ha ha!
BECAUSE THAT...
...IS THE REASON I'M ALIVE.

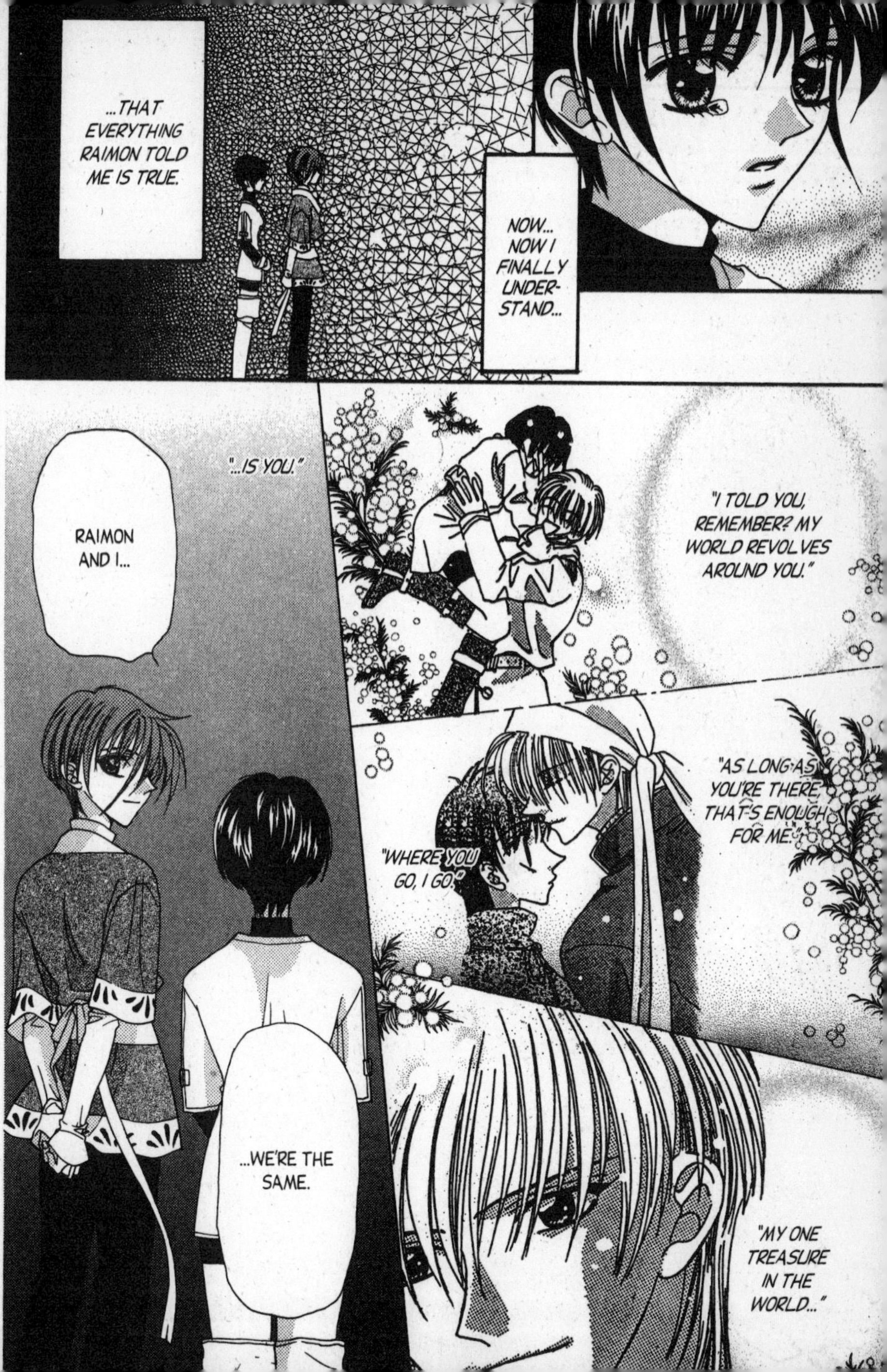
NOW... NOW I FINALLY UNDER-STAND...
...THAT EVERYTHING RAIMON TOLD ME IS TRUE.
"I TOLD YOU, REMEMBER? MY WORLD REVOLVES AROUND YOU."
"AS LONG AS YOU'RE THERE, THAT'S ENOUGH FOR ME."
"WHERE YOU GO, I GO."
"MY ONE TREASURE IN THE WORLD..."
"...IS YOU."
RAIMON AND I...
...WE'RE THE SAME.

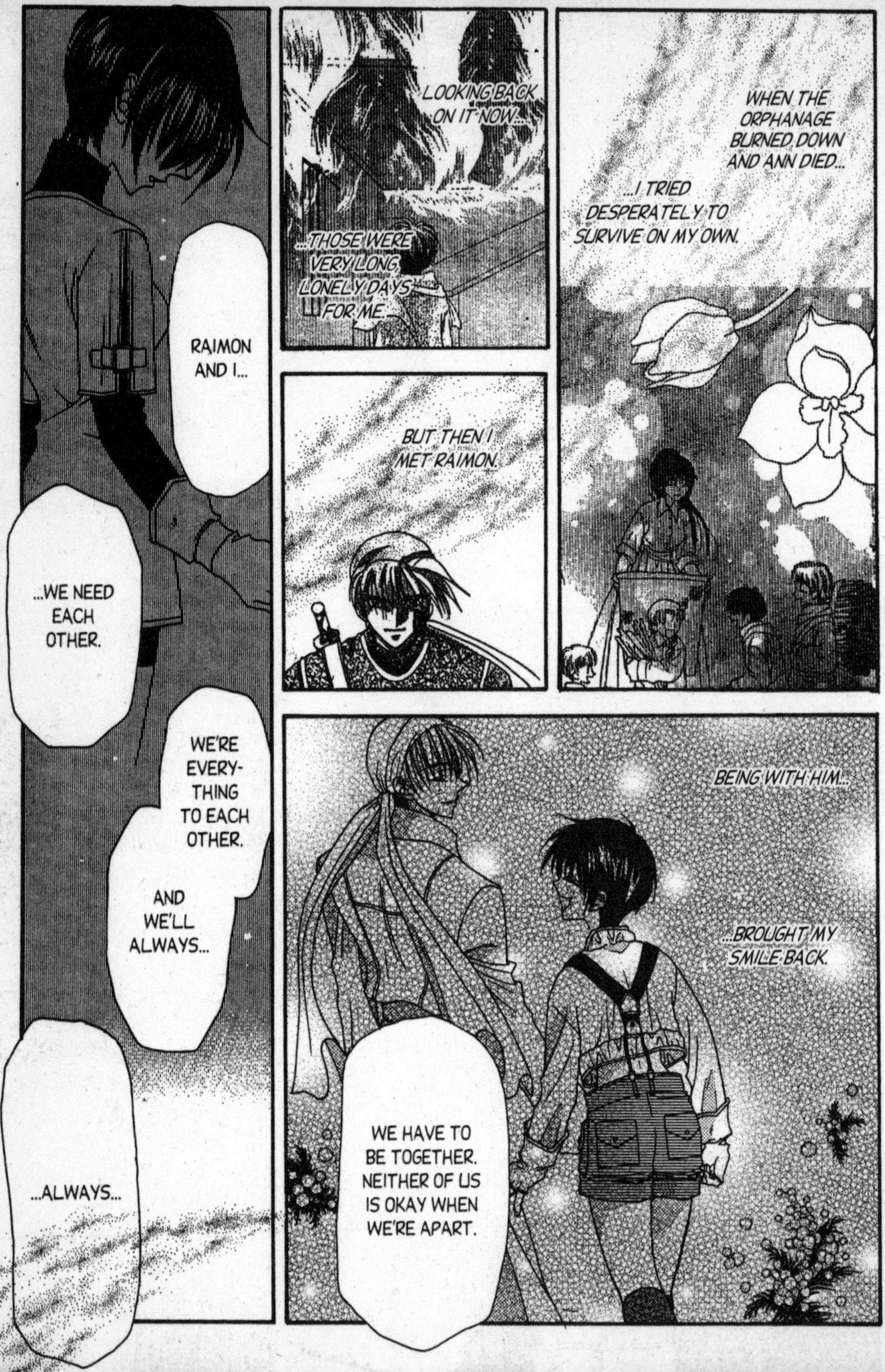
WHEN THE ORPHANAGE BURNED DOWN AND ANN DIED...
...I TRIED DESPERATELY TO SURVIVE ON MY OWN.
LOOKING BACK ON IT NOW...
...THOSE WERE VERY LONG, LONELY DAYS FOR ME.
BUT THEN I MET RAIMON.
BEING WITH HIM...
...BROUGHT MY SMILE BACK.
RAIMON AND I...
...WE NEED EACH OTHER.
WE'RE EVERY-THING TO EACH OTHER.
AND WE'LL ALWAYS...
...ALWAYS...
WE HAVE TO BE TOGETHER. NEITHER OF US IS OKAY WHEN WE'RE APART.

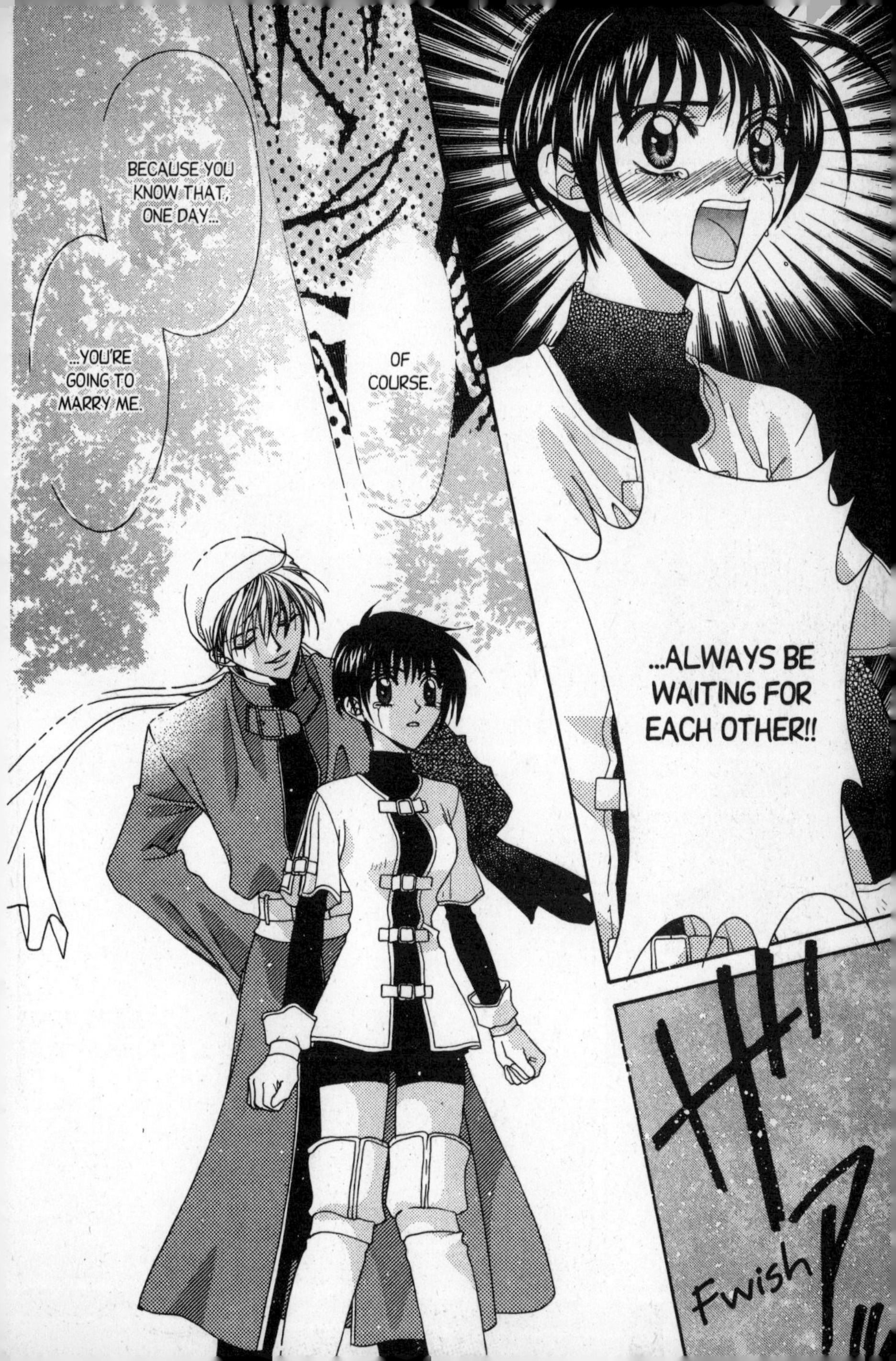
...ALWAYS BE WAITING FOR EACH OTHER!!
Fwish
OF COURSE.
BECAUSE YOU KNOW THAT, ONE DAY...
...YOU'RE GOING TO MARRY ME.

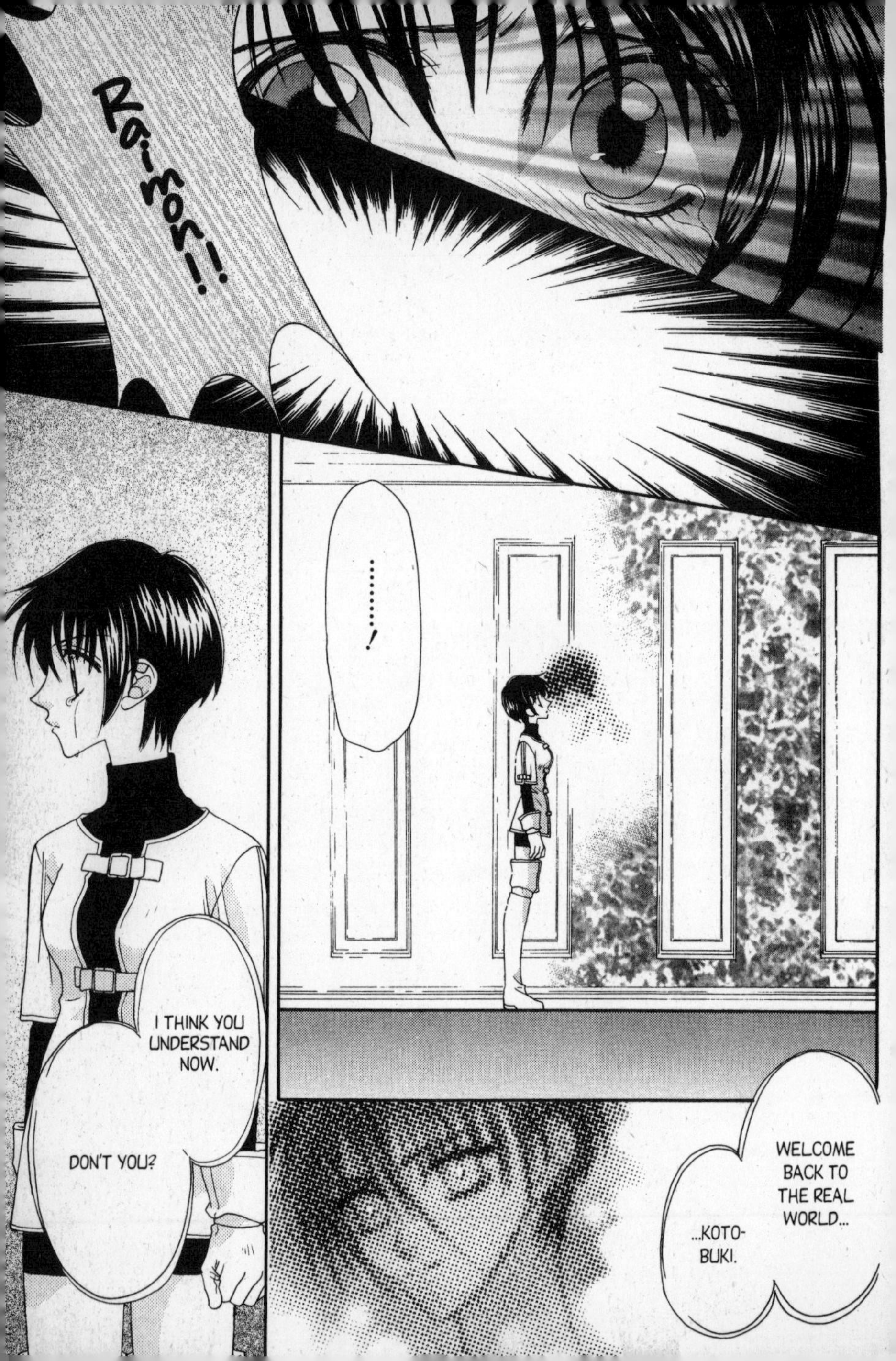
Raimon!!
......!
WELCOME BACK TO THE REAL WORLD...
...KOTO-BUKI.
I THINK YOU UNDERSTAND NOW.
DON'T YOU?

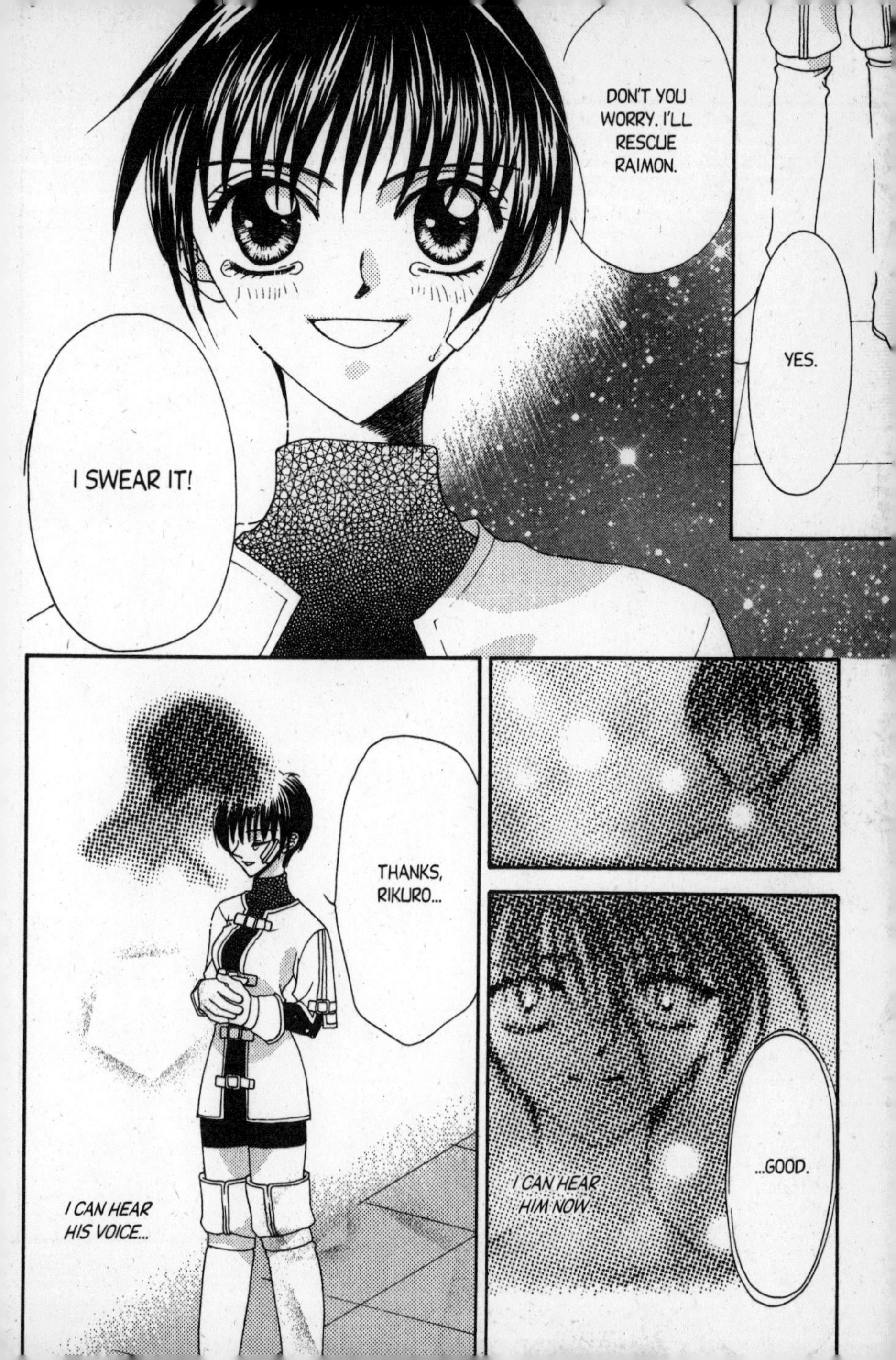
YES.
DON'T YOU WORRY. I'LL RESCUE RAIMON.
I SWEAR IT!
...GOOD.
I CAN HEAR HIM NOW.
THANKS, RIKURO...
I CAN HEAR HIS VOICE...

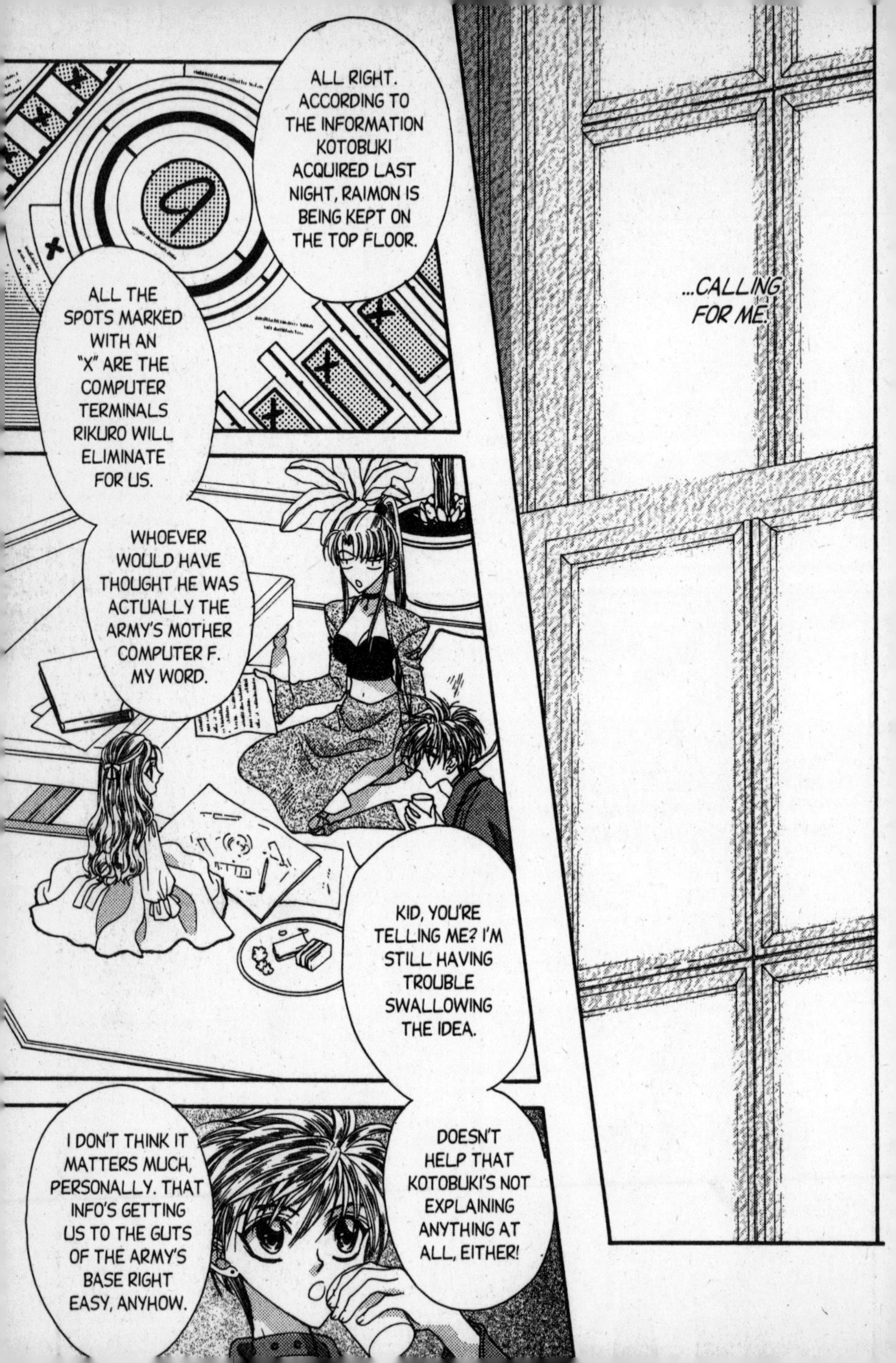
...CALLING FOR ME.
ALL RIGHT. ACCORDING TO THE INFORMATION KOTOBUKI ACQUIRED LAST NIGHT, RAIMON IS BEING KEPT ON THE TOP FLOOR.
ALL THE SPOTS MARKED WITH AN "X" ARE THE COMPUTER TERMINALS RIKURO WILL ELIMINATE FOR US.
WHOEVER WOULD HAVE THOUGHT HE WAS ACTUALLY THE ARMY'S MOTHER COMPUTER F. MY WORD.
KID, YOU'RE TELLING ME? I'M STILL HAVING TROUBLE SWALLOWING THE IDEA.
DOESN'T HELP THAT KOTOBUKI'S NOT EXPLAINING ANYTHING AT ALL, EITHER!
I DON'T THINK IT MATTERS MUCH, PERSONALLY. THAT INFO'S GETTING US TO THE GUTS OF THE ARMY'S BASE RIGHT EASY, ANYHOW.

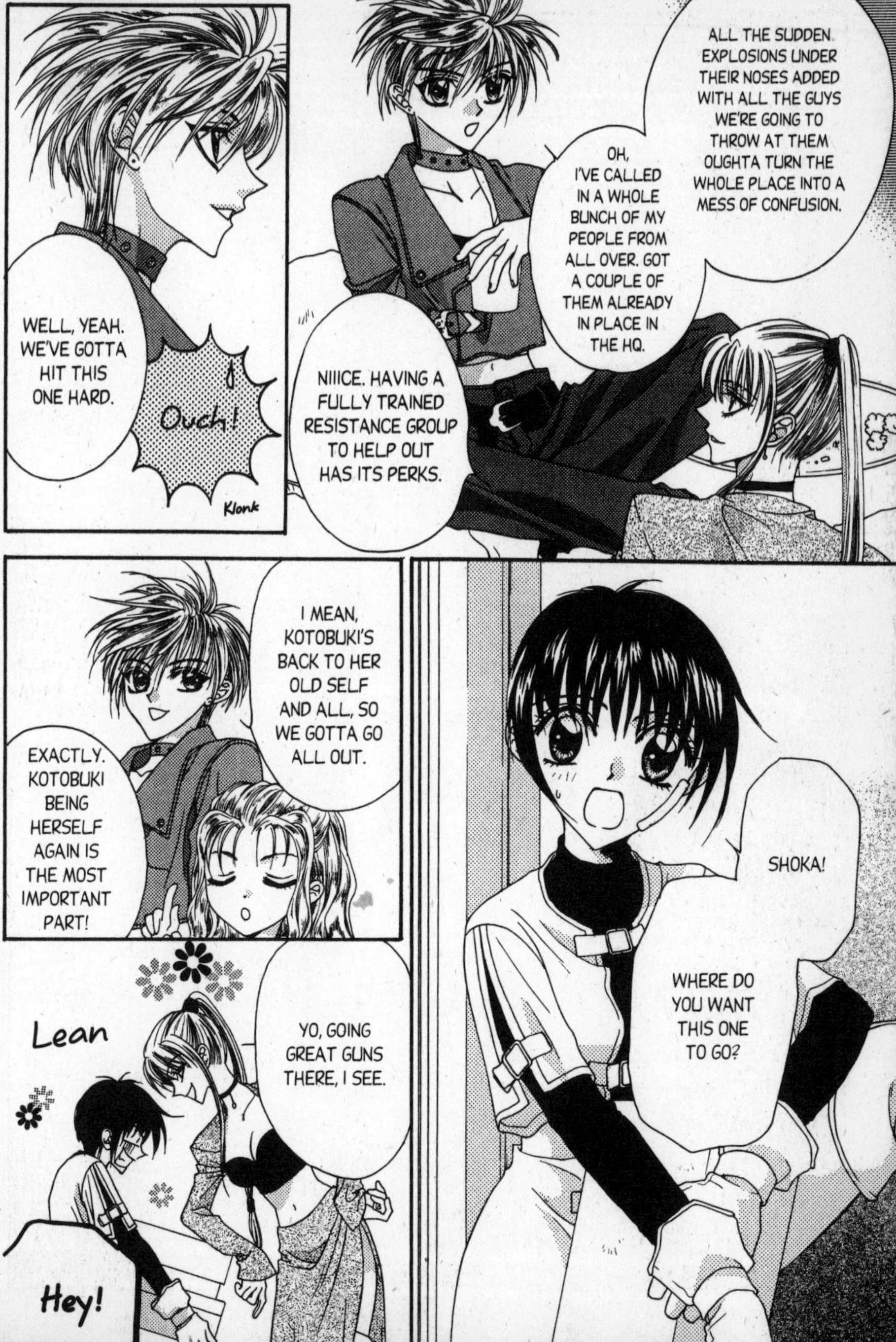
ALL THE SUDDEN EXPLOSIONS UNDER THEIR NOSES ADDED WITH ALL THE GUYS WE'RE GOING TO THROW AT THEM OUGHTA TURN THE WHOLE PLACE INTO A MESS OF CONFUSION.
OH, I'VE CALLED IN A WHOLE BUNCH OF MY PEOPLE FROM ALL OVER. GOT A COUPLE OF THEM ALREADY IN PLACE IN THE HQ.
NIIICE. HAVING A FULLY TRAINED RESISTANCE GROUP TO HELP OUT HAS ITS PERKS.
WELL, YEAH. WE'VE GOTTA HIT THIS ONE HARD.
Ouch!
Klonk
SHOKA!
WHERE DO YOU WANT THIS ONE TO GO?
I MEAN, KOTOBUKI'S BACK TO HER OLD SELF AND ALL, SO WE GOTTA GO ALL OUT.
EXACTLY. KOTOBUKI BEING HERSELF AGAIN IS THE MOST IMPORTANT PART!
YO, GOING GREAT GUNS THERE, I SEE.
Lean
Hey!

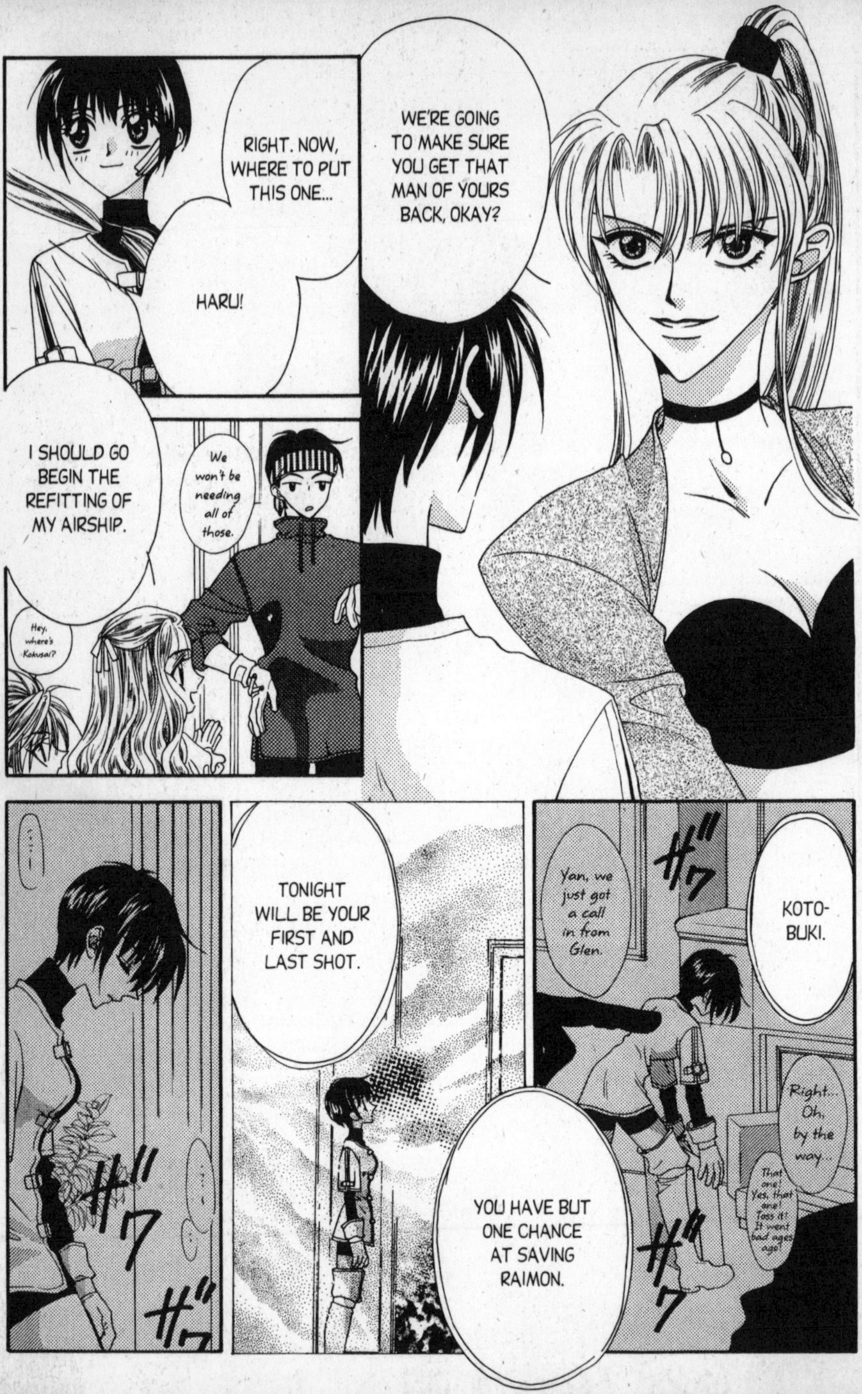
WE'RE GOING TO MAKE SURE YOU GET THAT MAN OF YOURS BACK, OKAY?
RIGHT. NOW, WHERE TO PUT THIS ONE...
HARU!
I SHOULD GO BEGIN THE REFITTING OF MY AIRSHIP.
We won't be needing all of those.
Hey, where's Kokusai?
KOTO-BUKI.
Yan, we just got a call in from Glen.
Right... Oh, by the way...
That one! Yes, that one! Toss it! It went bad ages ago!
YOU HAVE BUT ONE CHANCE AT SAVING RAIMON.
TONIGHT WILL BE YOUR FIRST AND LAST SHOT.

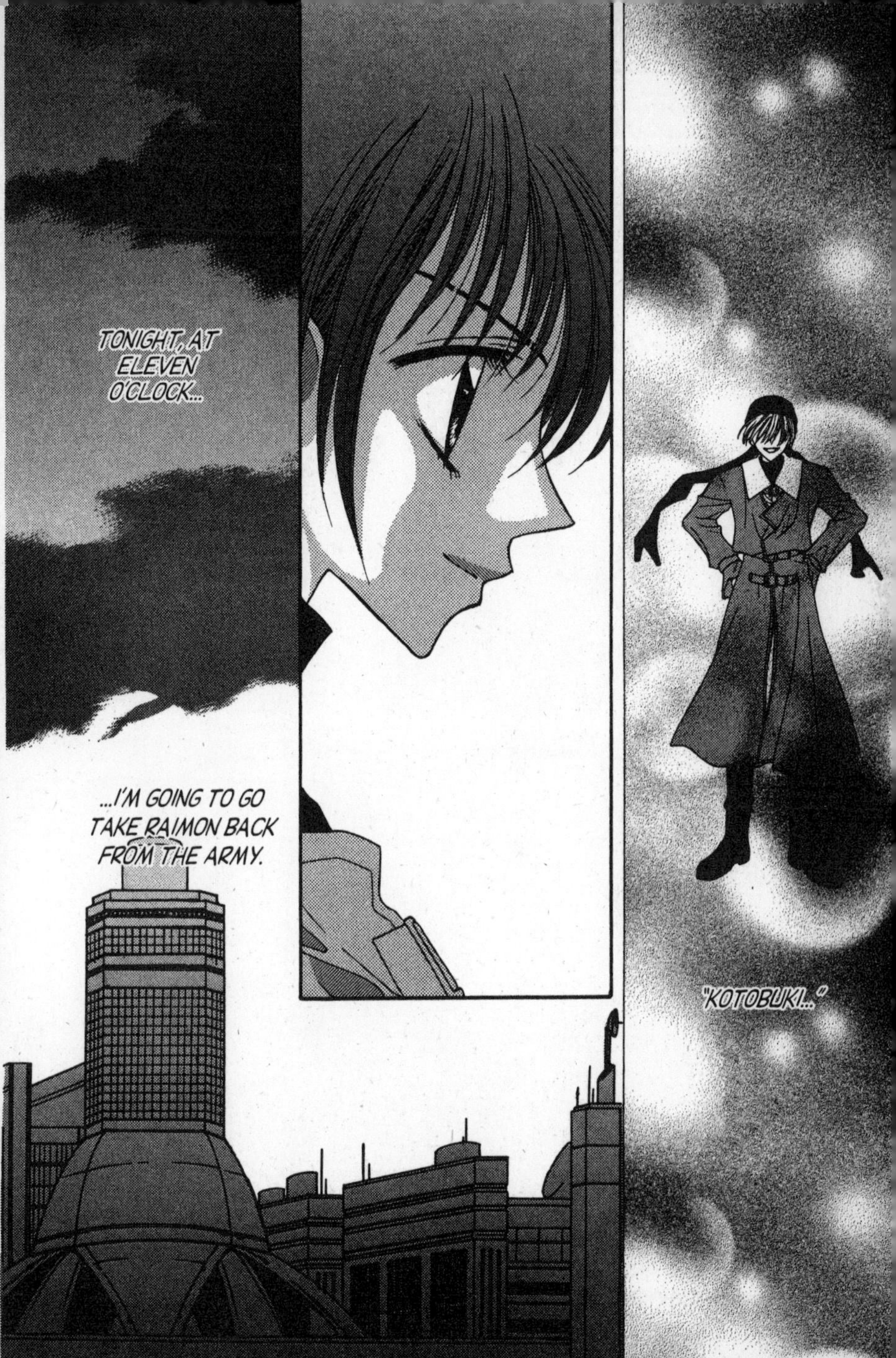
"KOTOBUKI..."
TONIGHT, AT ELEVEN O'CLOCK...
...I'M GOING TO GO TAKE RAIMON BACK FROM THE ARMY.

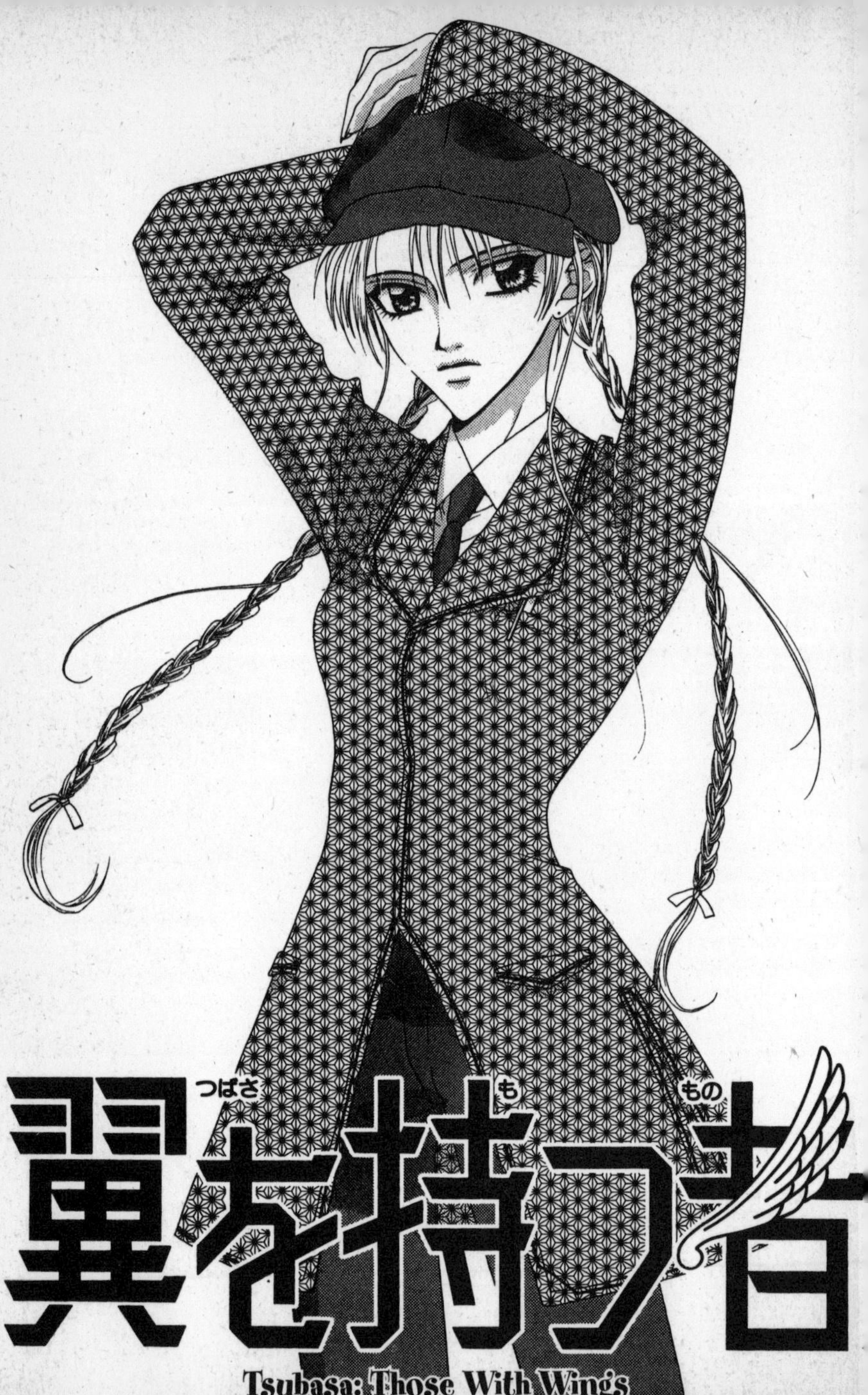
つばさ も もの
翼を持つ者
Tsubasa: Those With Wings

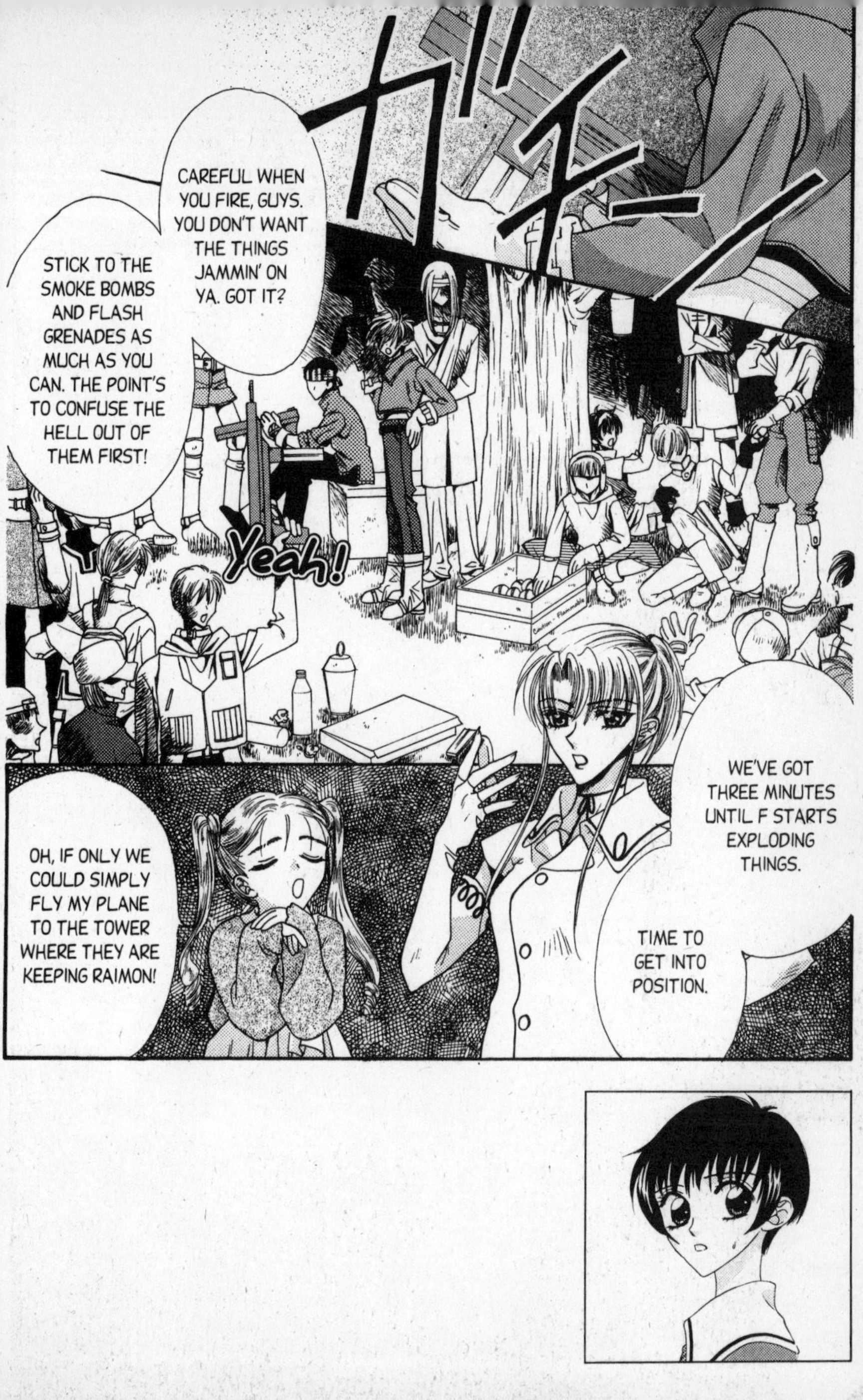
CAREFUL WHEN YOU FIRE, GUYS. YOU DON'T WANT THE THINGS JAMMIN' ON YA. GOT IT?
STICK TO THE SMOKE BOMBS AND FLASH GRENADES AS MUCH AS YOU CAN. THE POINT'S TO CONFUSE THE HELL OUT OF THEM FIRST!
Yeah!
WE'VE GOT THREE MINUTES UNTIL F STARTS EXPLODING THINGS.
TIME TO GET INTO POSITION.
OH, IF ONLY WE COULD SIMPLY FLY MY PLANE TO THE TOWER WHERE THEY ARE KEEPING RAIMON!

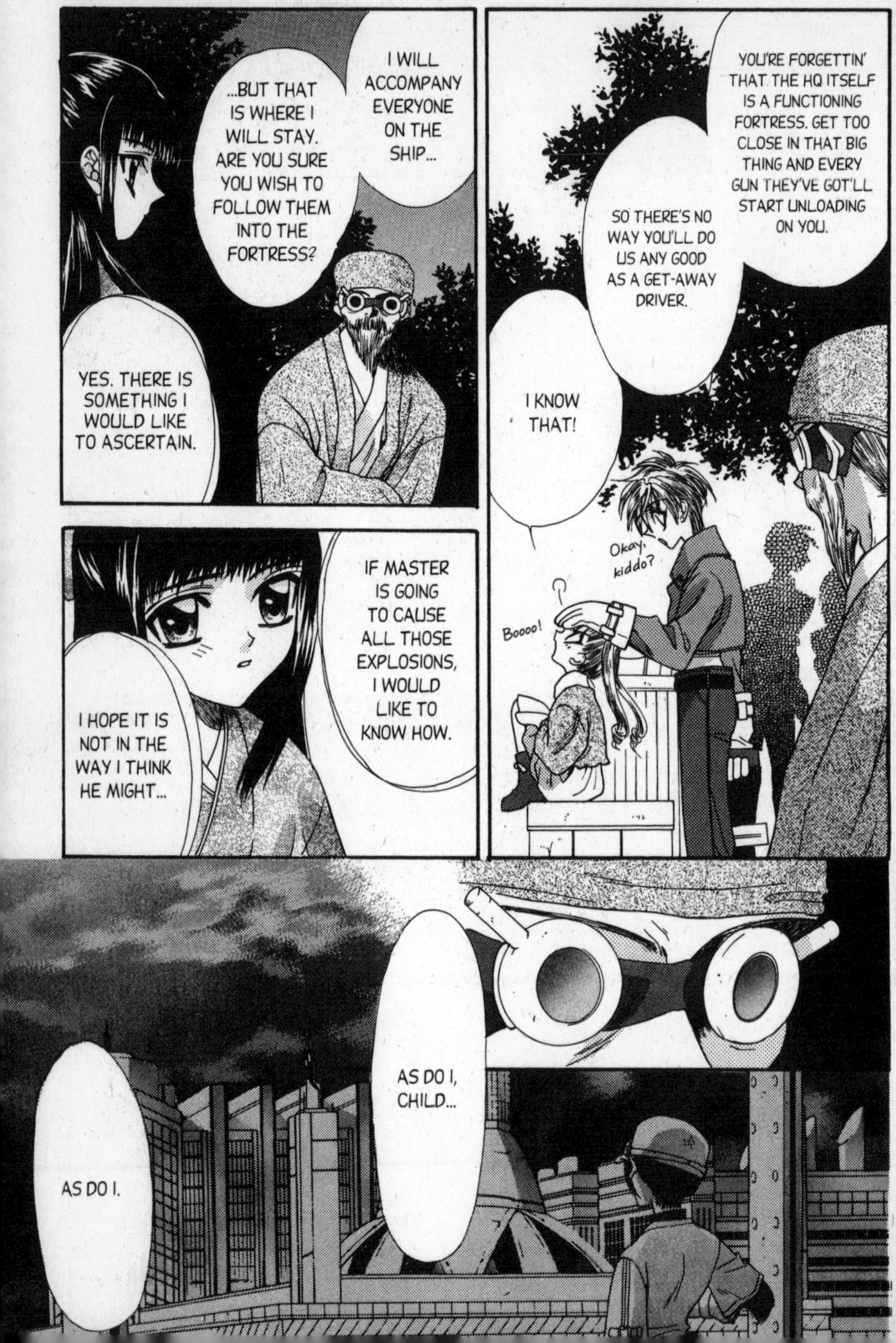
YOU'RE FORGETTIN' THAT THE HQ ITSELF IS A FUNCTIONING FORTRESS. GET TOO CLOSE IN THAT BIG THING AND EVERY GUN THEY'VE GOT'LL START UNLOADING ON YOU.
SO THERE'S NO WAY YOU'LL DO US ANY GOOD AS A GET-AWAY DRIVER.
I KNOW THAT!
Okay, kiddo?
Boooo!
I WILL ACCOMPANY EVERYONE ON THE SHIP...
...BUT THAT IS WHERE I WILL STAY. ARE YOU SURE YOU WISH TO FOLLOW THEM INTO THE FORTRESS?
YES. THERE IS SOMETHING I WOULD LIKE TO ASCERTAIN.
IF MASTER IS GOING TO CAUSE ALL THOSE EXPLOSIONS, I WOULD LIKE TO KNOW HOW.
I HOPE IT IS NOT IN THE WAY I THINK HE MIGHT...
AS DO I, CHILD...
AS DO I.

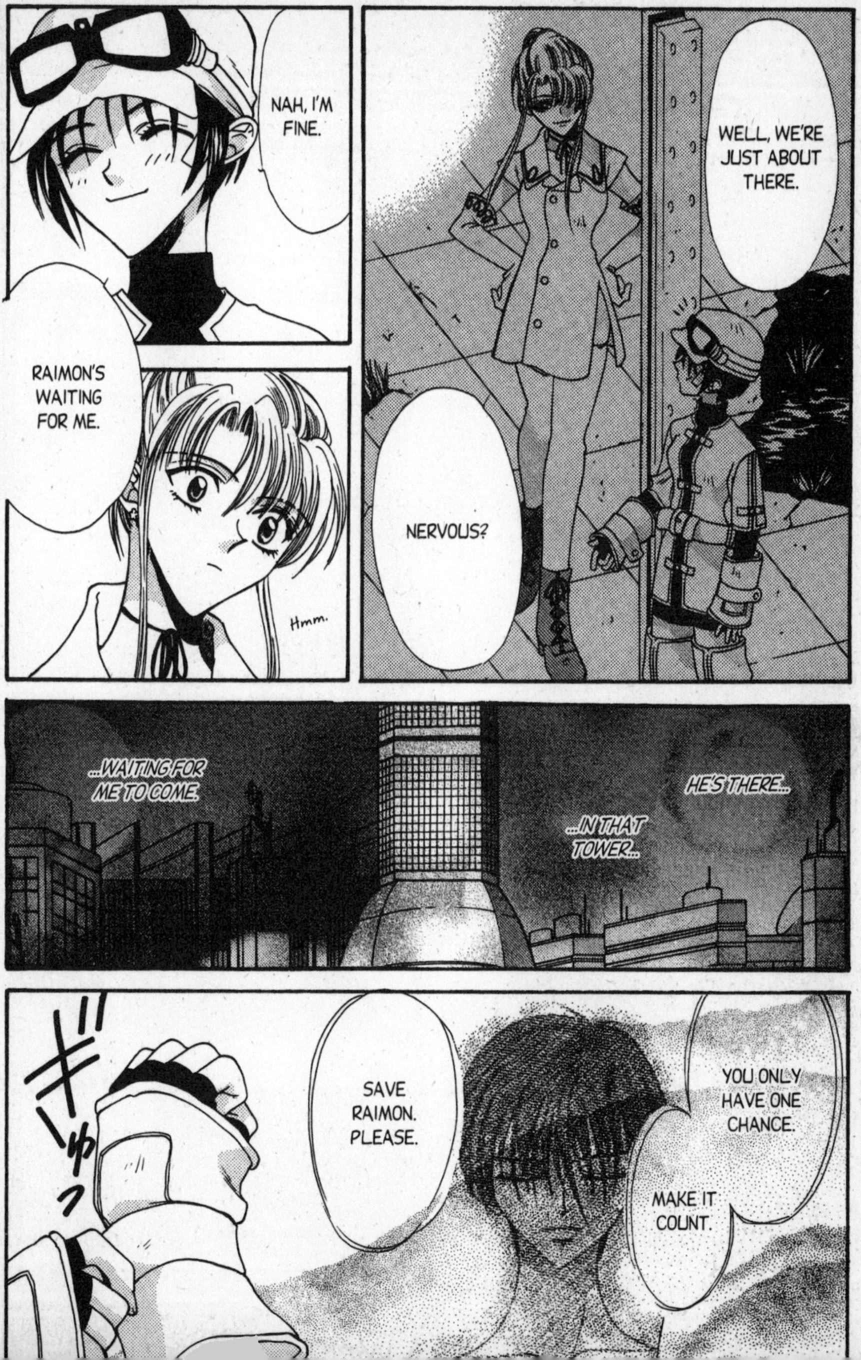
WELL, WE'RE JUST ABOUT THERE.
NERVOUS?
NAH, I'M FINE.
RAIMON'S WAITING FOR ME.
Hmm.
HE'S THERE...
...IN THAT TOWER...
...WAITING FOR ME TO COME.
YOU ONLY HAVE ONE CHANCE.
MAKE IT COUNT.
SAVE RAIMON. PLEASE.
ギュッ

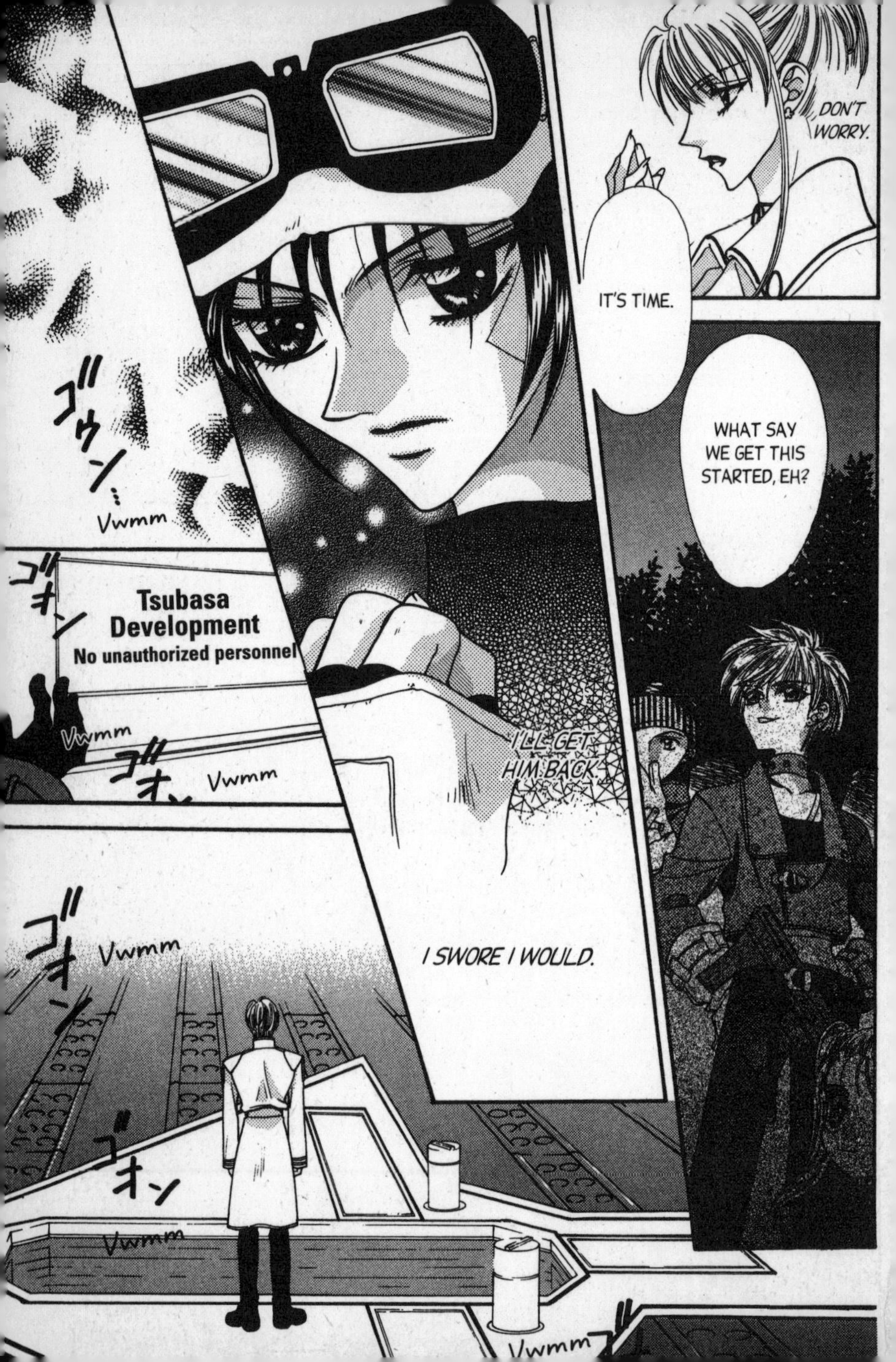
DON'T WORRY.
IT'S TIME.
WHAT SAY WE GET THIS STARTED, EH?
I'LL GET HIM BACK.
I SWORE I WOULD.
ゴウン…
Vwmm
ゴオン
Tsubasa Development
No unauthorized personnel
Vwmm
ゴオン
Vwmm
ゴオン
Vwmm
ゴオン
Vwmm
Vwmm

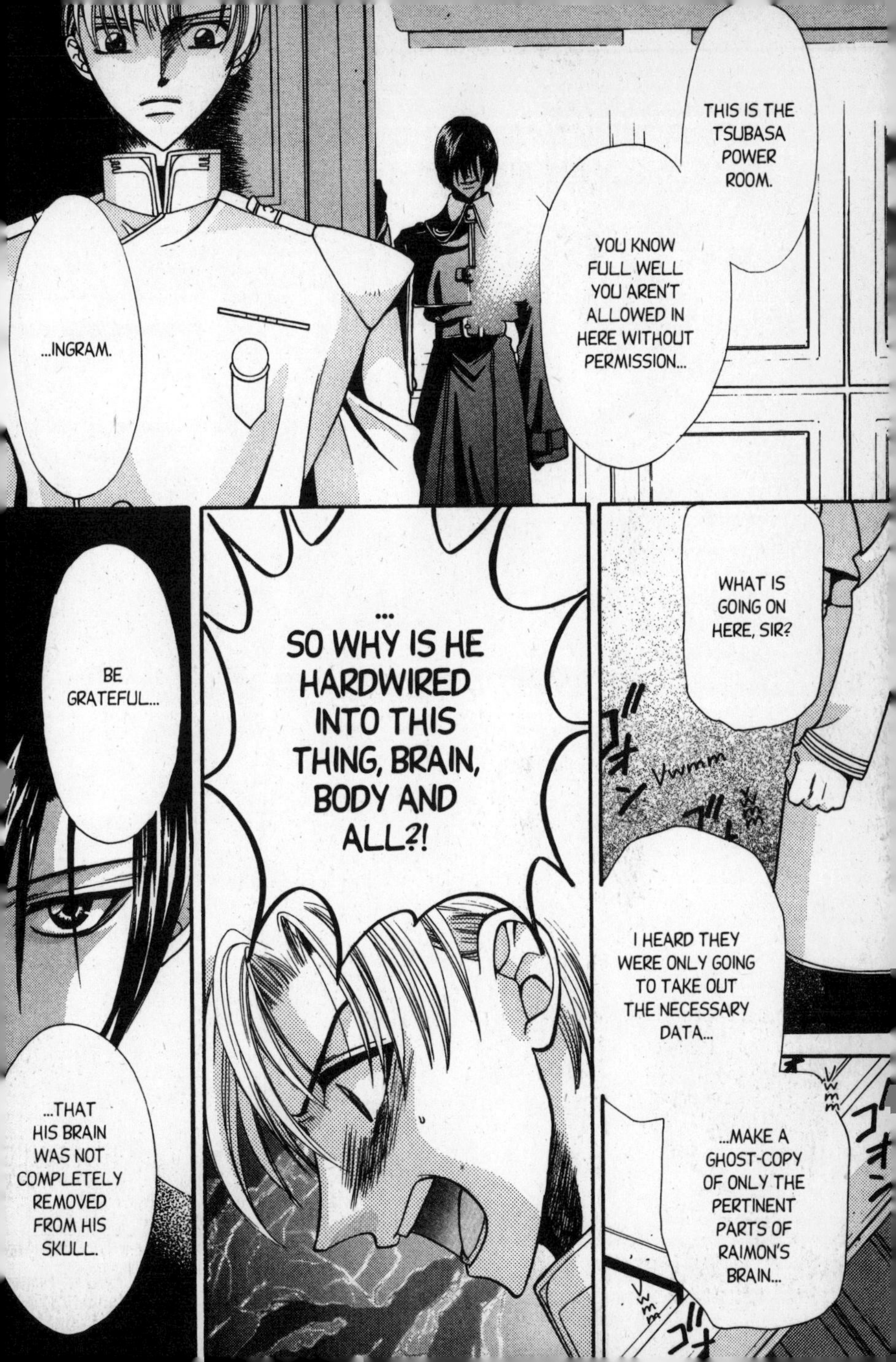
THIS IS THE TSUBASA POWER ROOM.
YOU KNOW FULL WELL YOU AREN'T ALLOWED IN HERE WITHOUT PERMISSION...
...INGRAM.
WHAT IS GOING ON HERE, SIR?
Vwmm
I HEARD THEY WERE ONLY GOING TO TAKE OUT THE NECESSARY DATA...
Vwmm
...MAKE A GHOST-COPY OF ONLY THE PERTINENT PARTS OF RAIMON'S BRAIN...
Vwmm
... SO WHY IS HE HARDWIRED INTO THIS THING, BRAIN, BODY AND ALL?!
BE GRATEFUL...
...THAT HIS BRAIN WAS NOT COMPLETELY REMOVED FROM HIS SKULL.

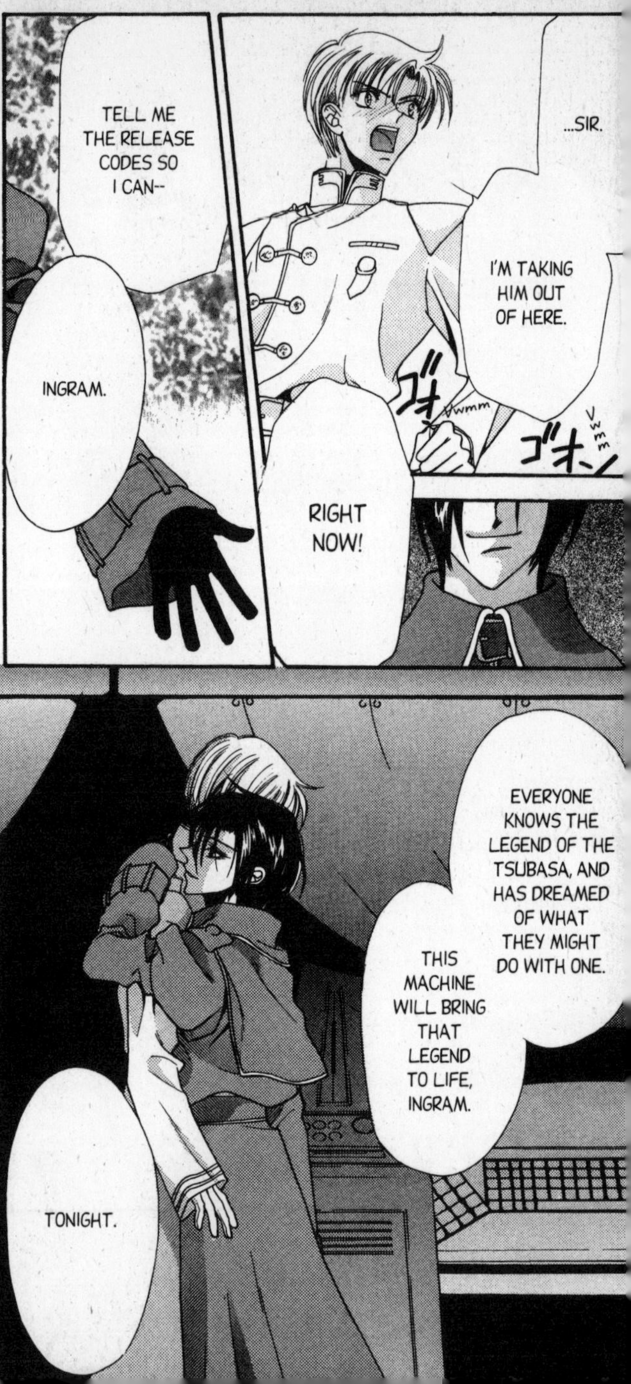
...SIR.
I'M TAKING HIM OUT OF HERE.
RIGHT NOW!
Vwmm
Vwmm
TELL ME THE RELEASE CODES SO I CAN--
INGRAM.
EVERYONE KNOWS THE LEGEND OF THE TSUBASA, AND HAS DREAMED OF WHAT THEY MIGHT DO WITH ONE.
THIS MACHINE WILL BRING THAT LEGEND TO LIFE, INGRAM.
TONIGHT.

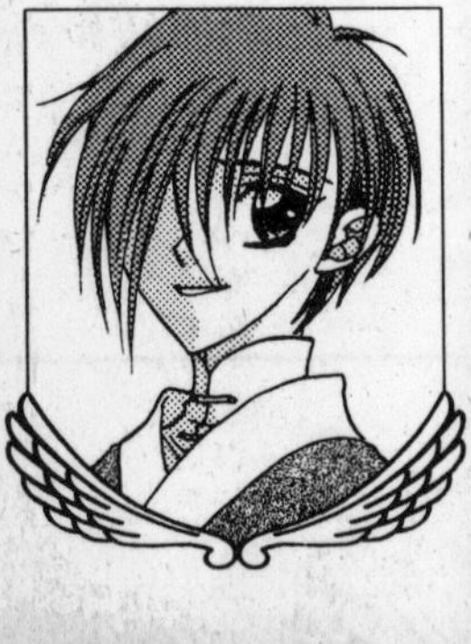

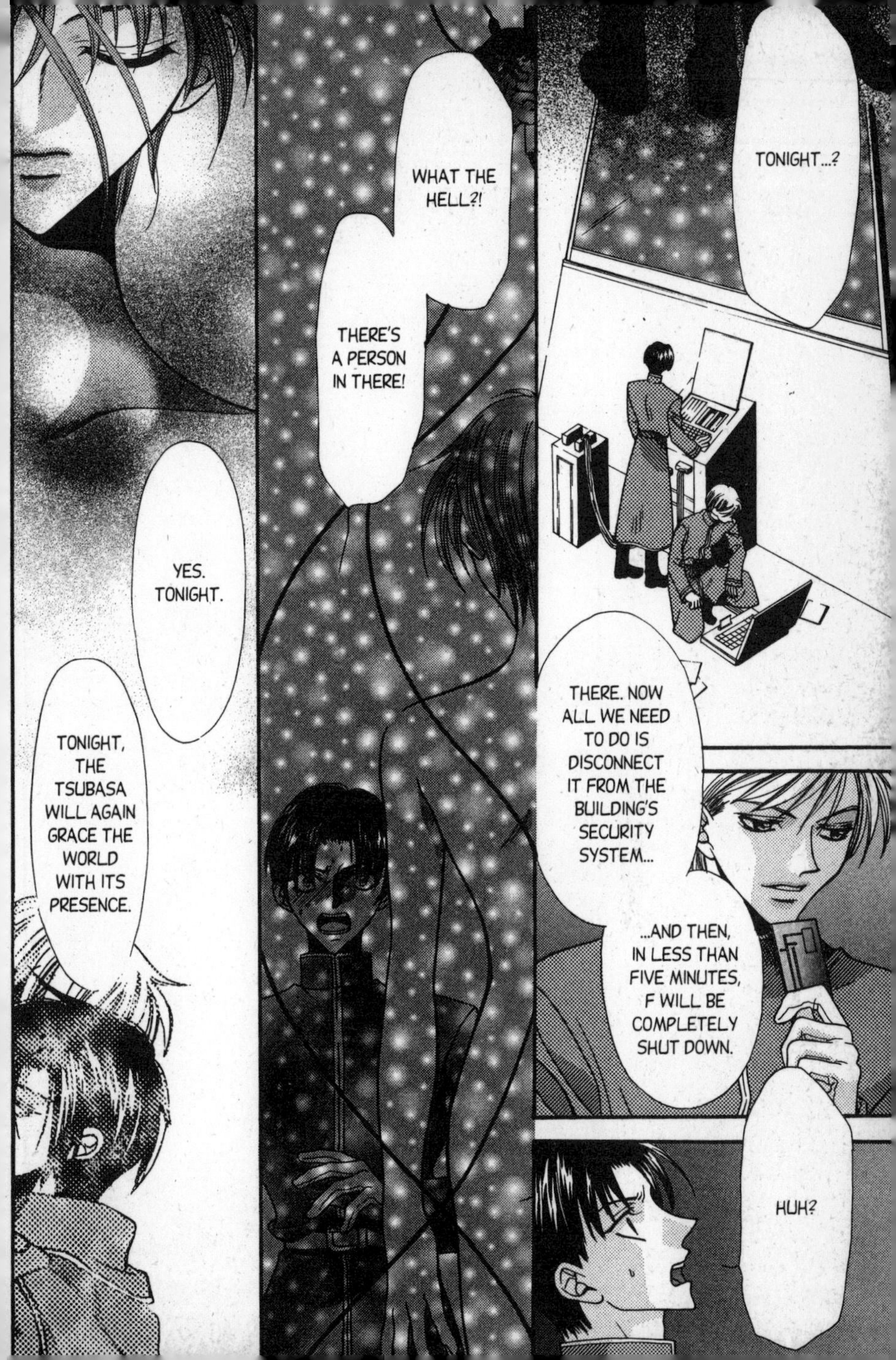
TONIGHT...?
THERE. NOW ALL WE NEED TO DO IS DISCONNECT IT FROM THE BUILDING'S SECURITY SYSTEM...
...AND THEN, IN LESS THAN FIVE MINUTES, F WILL BE COMPLETELY SHUT DOWN.
HUH?
WHAT THE HELL?!
THERE'S A PERSON IN THERE!
YES. TONIGHT.
TONIGHT, THE TSUBASA WILL AGAIN GRACE THE WORLD WITH ITS PRESENCE.

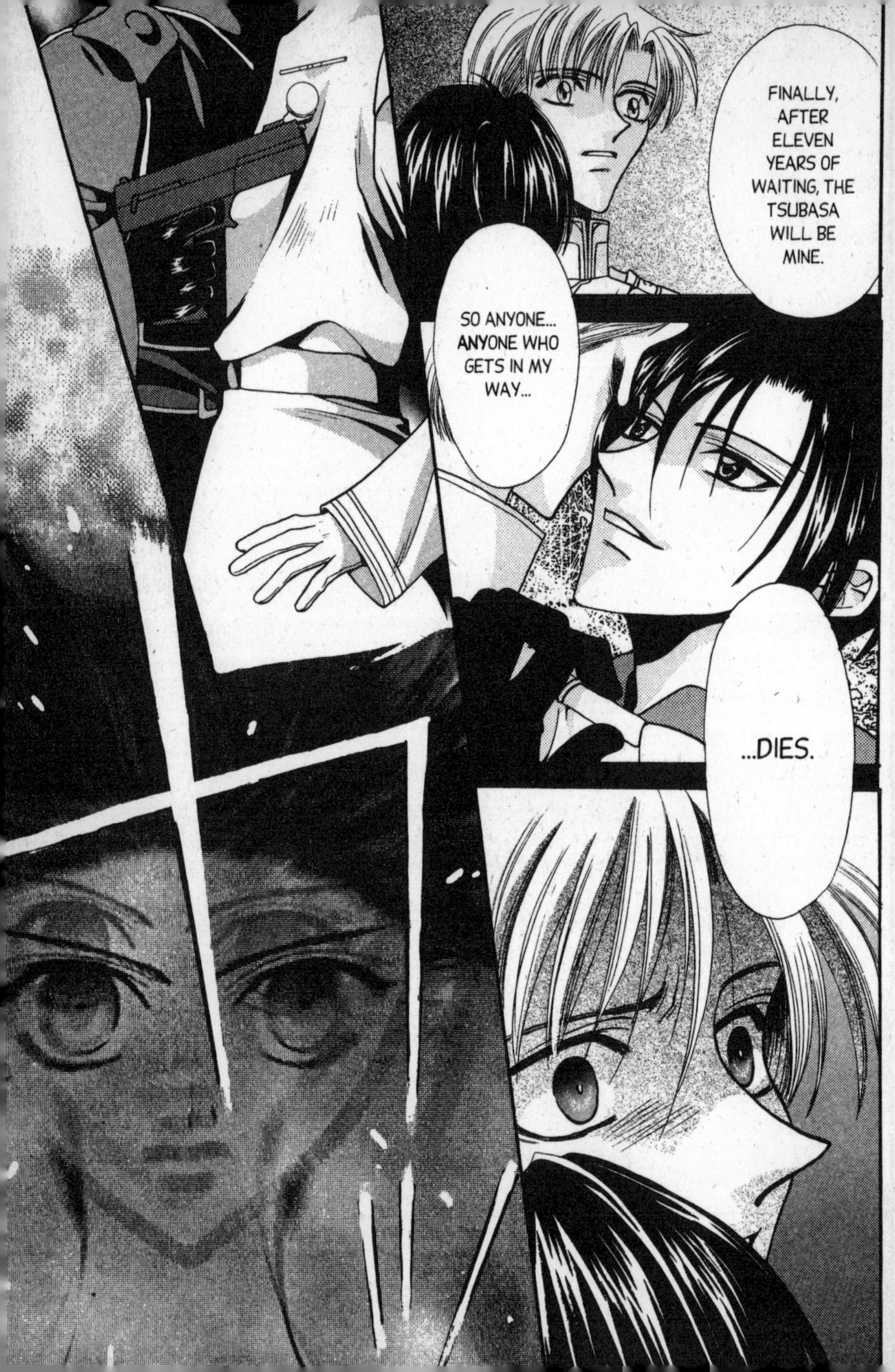
FINALLY, AFTER ELEVEN YEARS OF WAITING, THE TSUBASA WILL BE MINE.
SO ANYONE... ANYONE WHO GETS IN MY WAY...
...DIES.

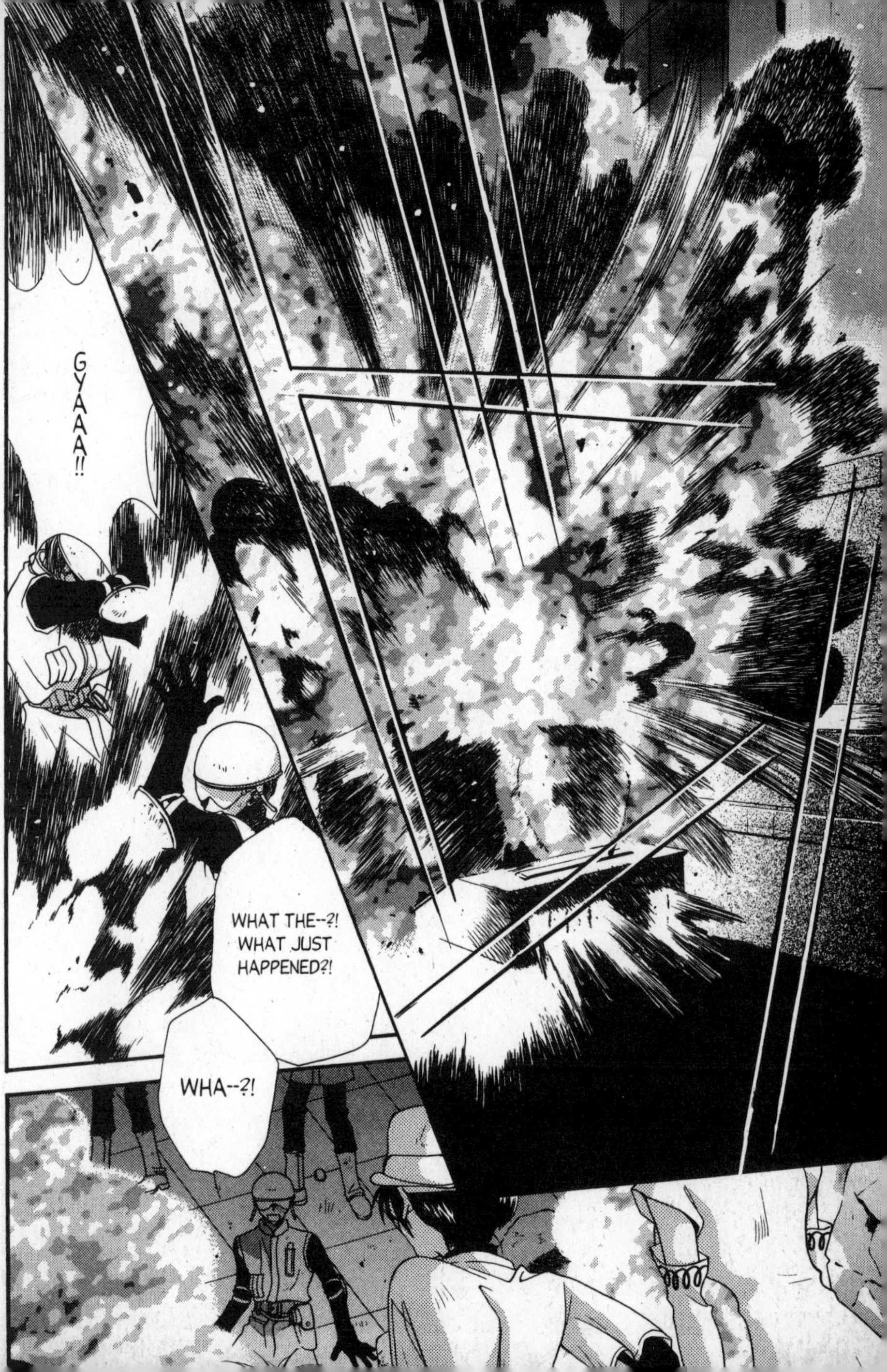
GYAAA!!
WHAT THE--?! WHAT JUST HAPPENED?!
WHA--?!

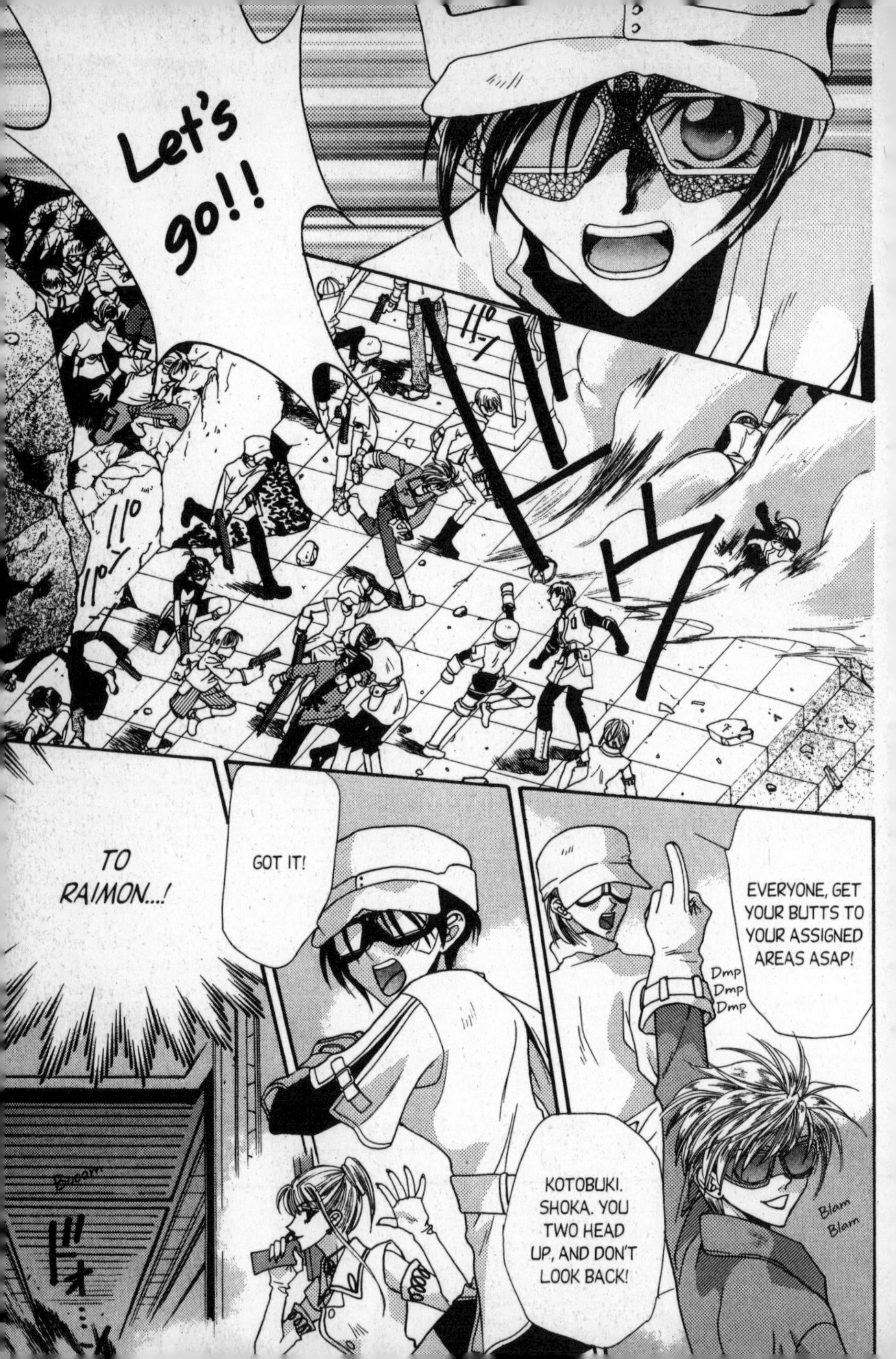
Let's go!!
EVERYONE, GET YOUR BUTTS TO YOUR ASSIGNED AREAS ASAP!
Dmp Dmp Dmp
KOTOBUKI. SHOKA. YOU TWO HEAD UP, AND DON'T LOOK BACK!
Blam Blam
GOT IT!
TO RAIMON...!

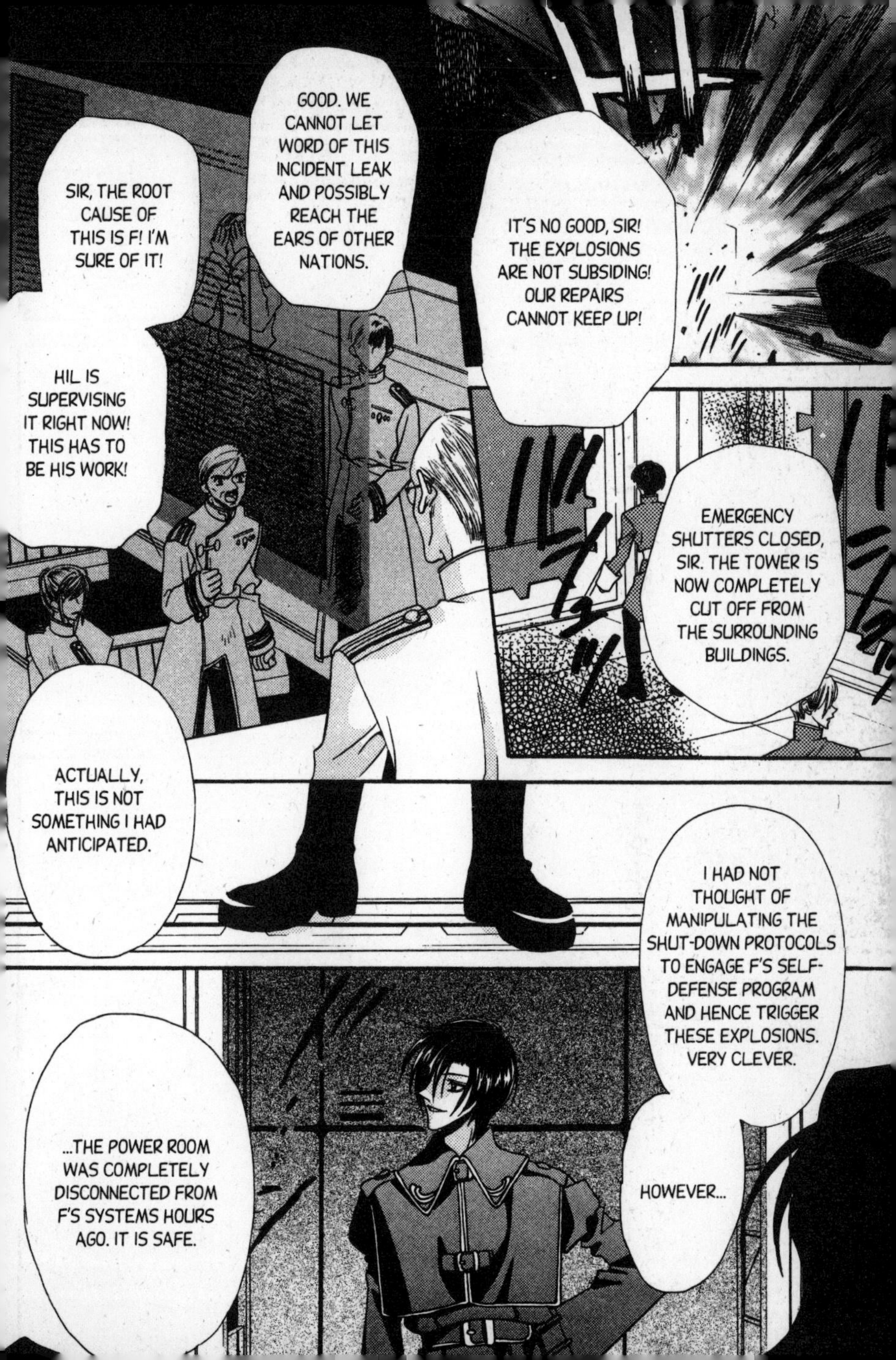
IT'S NO GOOD, SIR! THE EXPLOSIONS ARE NOT SUBSIDING! OUR REPAIRS CANNOT KEEP UP!
EMERGENCY SHUTTERS CLOSED, SIR. THE TOWER IS NOW COMPLETELY CUT OFF FROM THE SURROUNDING BUILDINGS.
GOOD. WE CANNOT LET WORD OF THIS INCIDENT LEAK AND POSSIBLY REACH THE EARS OF OTHER NATIONS.
SIR, THE ROOT CAUSE OF THIS IS F! I'M SURE OF IT!
HIL IS SUPERVISING IT RIGHT NOW! THIS HAS TO BE HIS WORK!
ACTUALLY, THIS IS NOT SOMETHING I HAD ANTICIPATED.
I HAD NOT THOUGHT OF MANIPULATING THE SHUT-DOWN PROTOCOLS TO ENGAGE F'S SELF-DEFENSE PROGRAM AND HENCE TRIGGER THESE EXPLOSIONS. VERY CLEVER.
HOWEVER...
...THE POWER ROOM WAS COMPLETELY DISCONNECTED FROM F'S SYSTEMS HOURS AGO. IT IS SAFE.

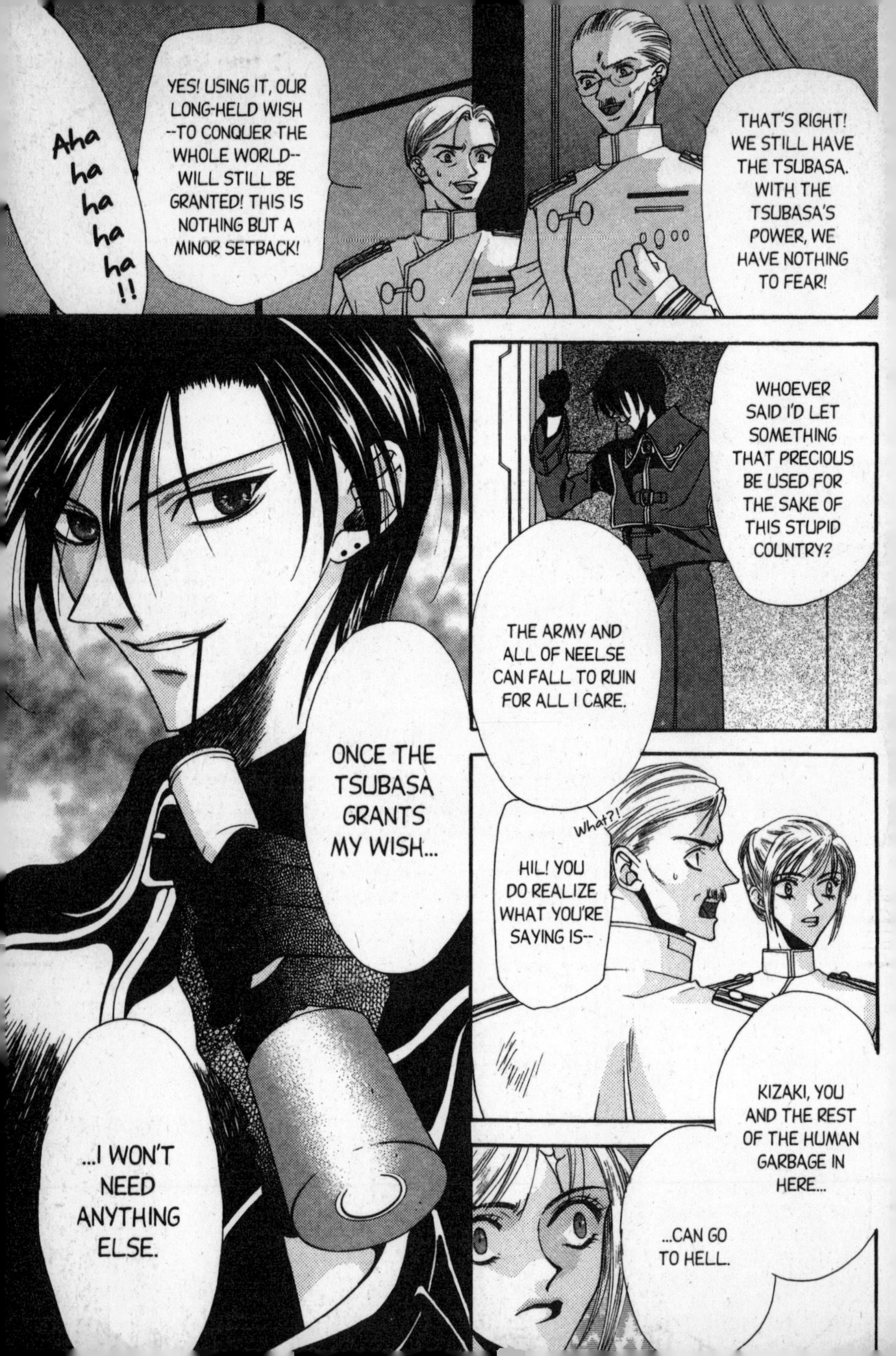
THAT'S RIGHT! WE STILL HAVE THE TSUBASA. WITH THE TSUBASA'S POWER, WE HAVE NOTHING TO FEAR!
YES! USING IT, OUR LONG-HELD WISH --TO CONQUER THE WHOLE WORLD-- WILL STILL BE GRANTED! THIS IS NOTHING BUT A MINOR SETBACK!
Aha ha ha ha ha !!
WHOEVER SAID I'D LET SOMETHING THAT PRECIOUS BE USED FOR THE SAKE OF THIS STUPID COUNTRY?
THE ARMY AND ALL OF NEELSE CAN FALL TO RUIN FOR ALL I CARE.
What?!
HIL! YOU DO REALIZE WHAT YOU'RE SAYING IS--
KIZAKI, YOU AND THE REST OF THE HUMAN GARBAGE IN HERE...
...CAN GO TO HELL.
ONCE THE TSUBASA GRANTS MY WISH...
...I WON'T NEED ANYTHING ELSE.

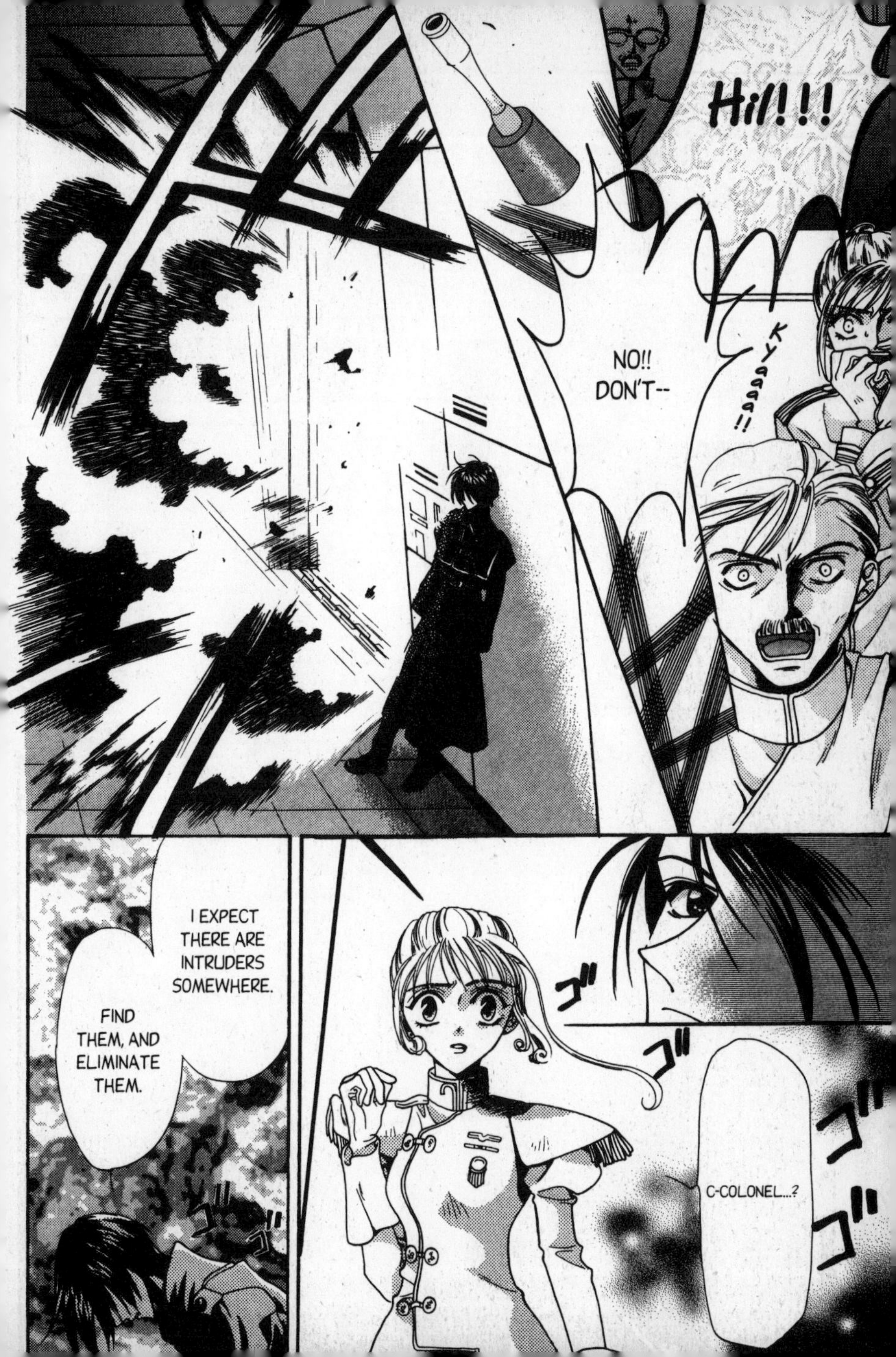
Hi!!!
Kyaaaaa!!
NO!! DON'T--
ゴゴゴゴゴ
C-COLONEL...?
I EXPECT THERE ARE INTRUDERS SOMEWHERE.
FIND THEM, AND ELIMINATE THEM.
ゴゴ

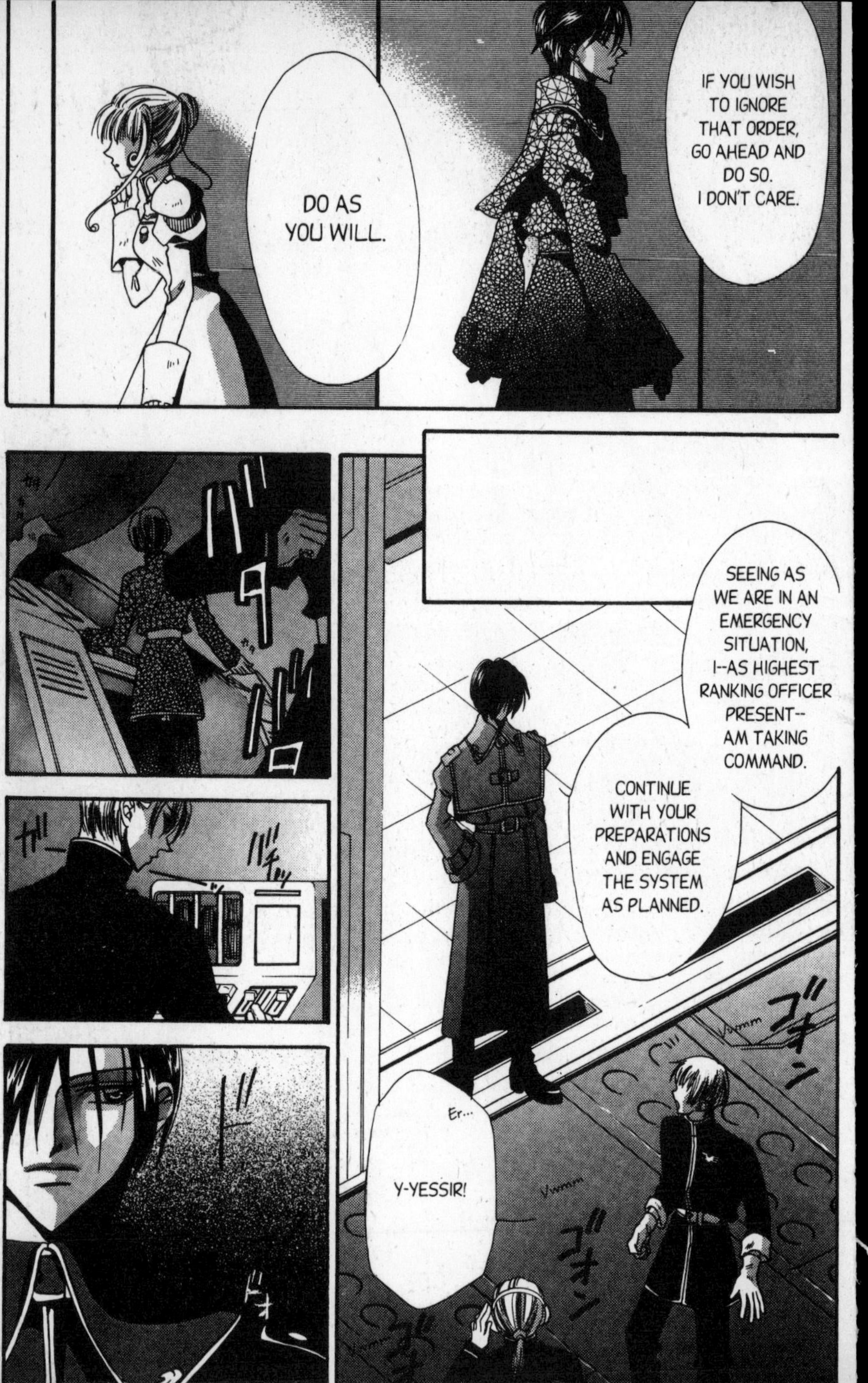
IF YOU WISH TO IGNORE THAT ORDER, GO AHEAD AND DO SO. I DON'T CARE.
DO AS YOU WILL.
SEEING AS WE ARE IN AN EMERGENCY SITUATION, I--AS HIGHEST RANKING OFFICER PRESENT--AM TAKING COMMAND.
CONTINUE WITH YOUR PREPARATIONS AND ENGAGE THE SYSTEM AS PLANNED.
Vwmm
Er...
Y-YESSIR!
Vwmm

!!

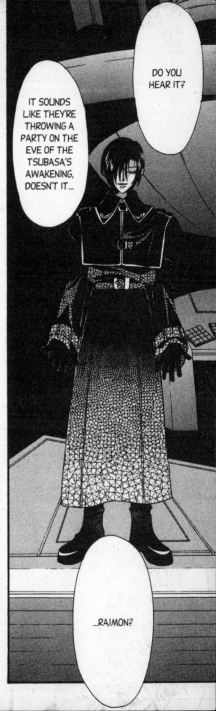

DO YOU HEAR IT?

IT SOUNDS LIKE THEY'RE THROWING A PARTY ON THE EVE OF THE TSUBASA'S AWAKENING, DOESN'T IT...

...RAIMON?

WELL, WE'VE SUCCEEDED IN CONFUSING THE ARMY...

...BUT THE COLLATERAL DAMAGE IS GETTING IN OUR WAY MORE THAN WE THOUGHT.

KOTOBUKI! YOU KEEP ON GOING!

WE'LL BE RIGHT BEHIND YOU JUST AS SOON AS WE FIND A WAY AROUND!

Oh...

OKAY!

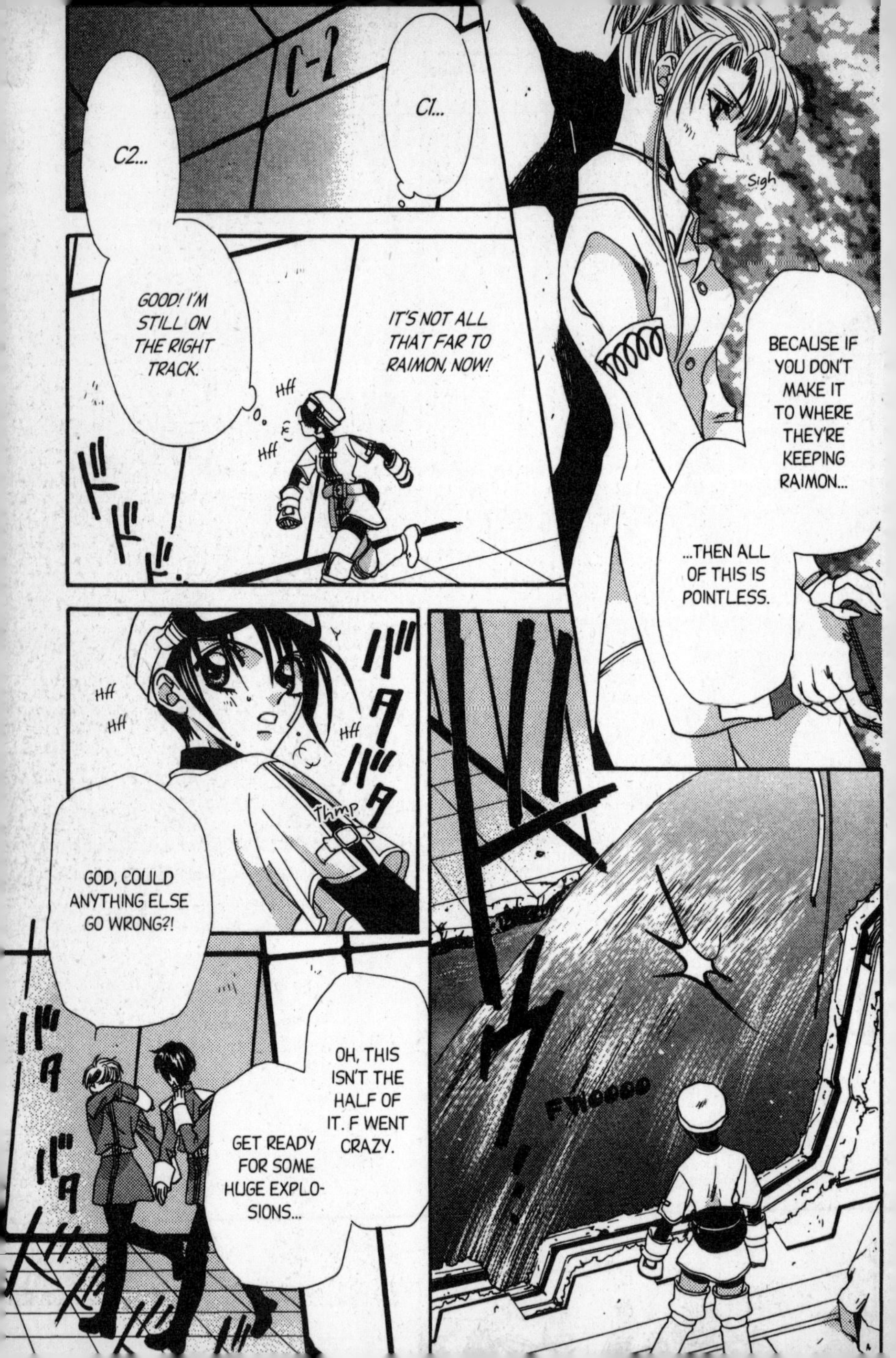
Sigh
BECAUSE IF YOU DON'T MAKE IT TO WHERE THEY'RE KEEPING RAIMON...
...THEN ALL OF THIS IS POINTLESS.
C1...
C2...
IT'S NOT ALL THAT FAR TO RAIMON, NOW!
GOOD! I'M STILL ON THE RIGHT TRACK.
Hff
Hff
ドドド
FWOOOO
バタバタ
Hff
Hff
Hff
Thmp
GOD, COULD ANYTHING ELSE GO WRONG?!
OH, THIS ISN'T THE HALF OF IT. F WENT CRAZY.
GET READY FOR SOME HUGE EXPLOSIONS...
バタバタ

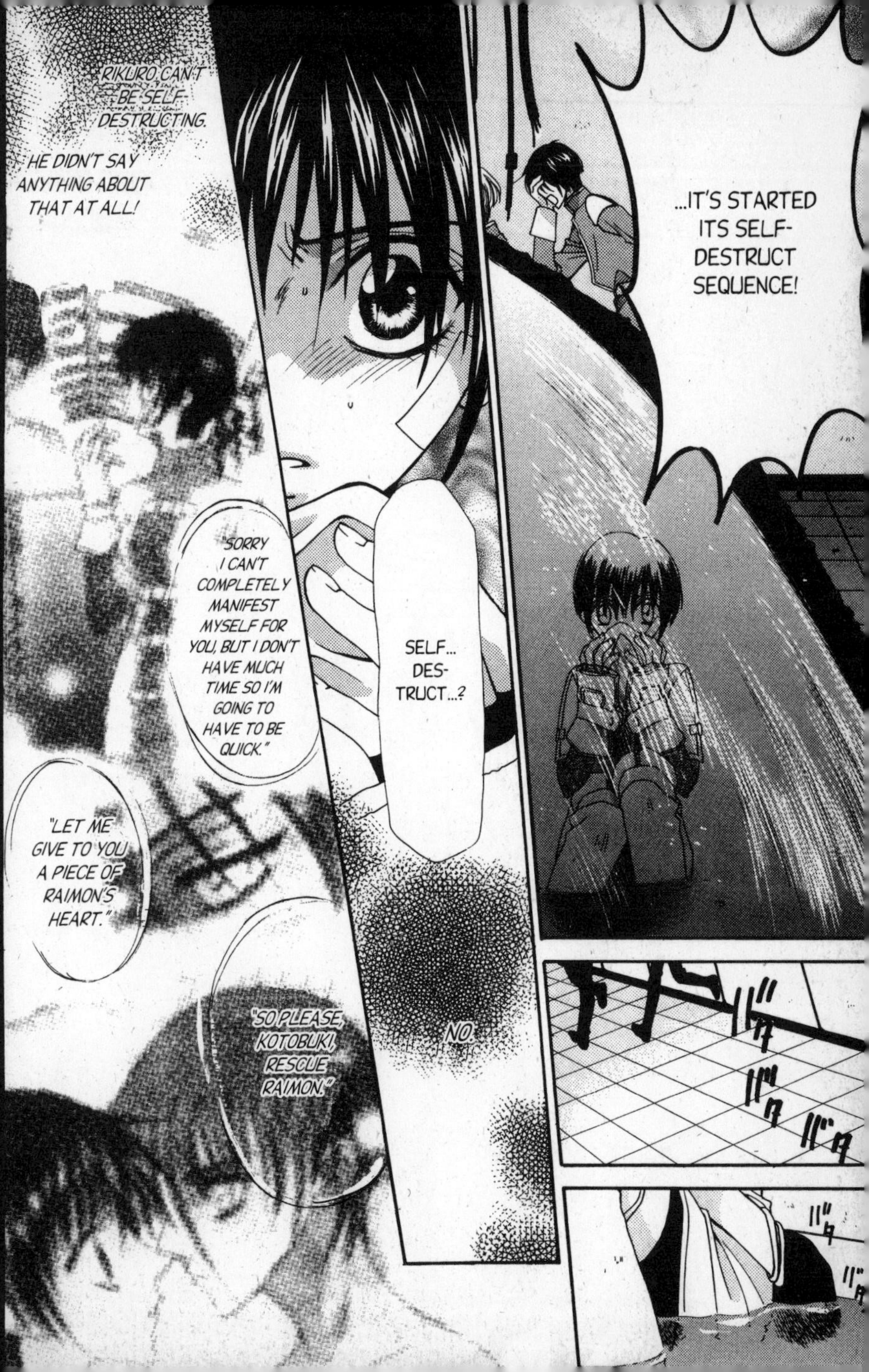
...IT'S STARTED ITS SELF-DESTRUCT SEQUENCE!
SELF... DES-TRUCT...?
RIKURO CAN'T BE SELF-DESTRUCTING.
HE DIDN'T SAY ANYTHING ABOUT THAT AT ALL!
"SORRY I CAN'T COMPLETELY MANIFEST MYSELF FOR YOU, BUT I DON'T HAVE MUCH TIME SO I'M GOING TO HAVE TO BE QUICK."
"LET ME GIVE TO YOU A PIECE OF RAIMON'S HEART."
"SO PLEASE, KOTOBUKI, RESCUE RAIMON."
NO.

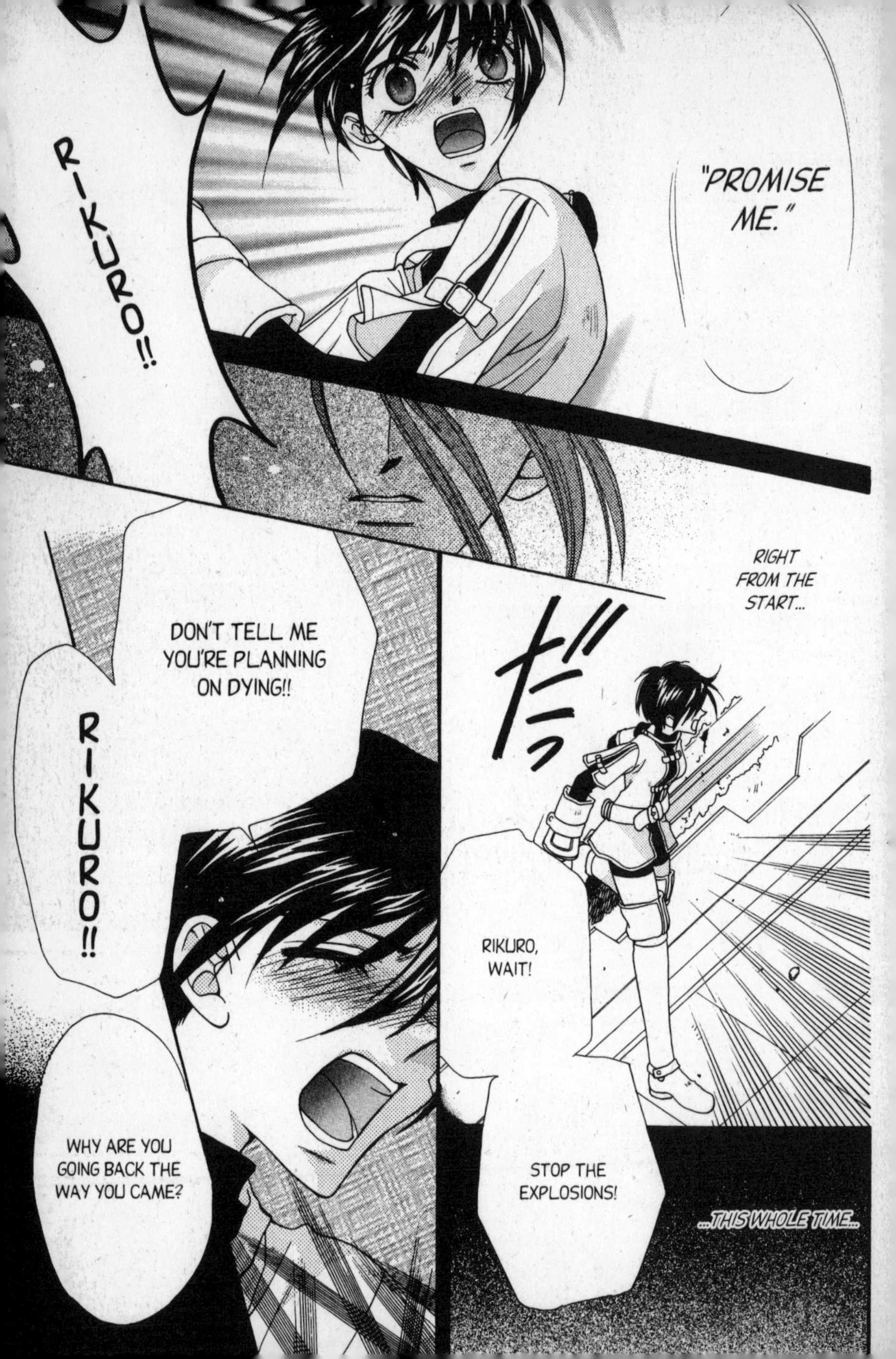

"PROMISE ME."
RIKURO!!
RIGHT FROM THE START...
だっ
RIKURO, WAIT!
STOP THE EXPLOSIONS!
...THIS WHOLE TIME...
DON'T TELL ME YOU'RE PLANNING ON DYING!!
RIKURO!!
WHY ARE YOU GOING BACK THE WAY YOU CAME?

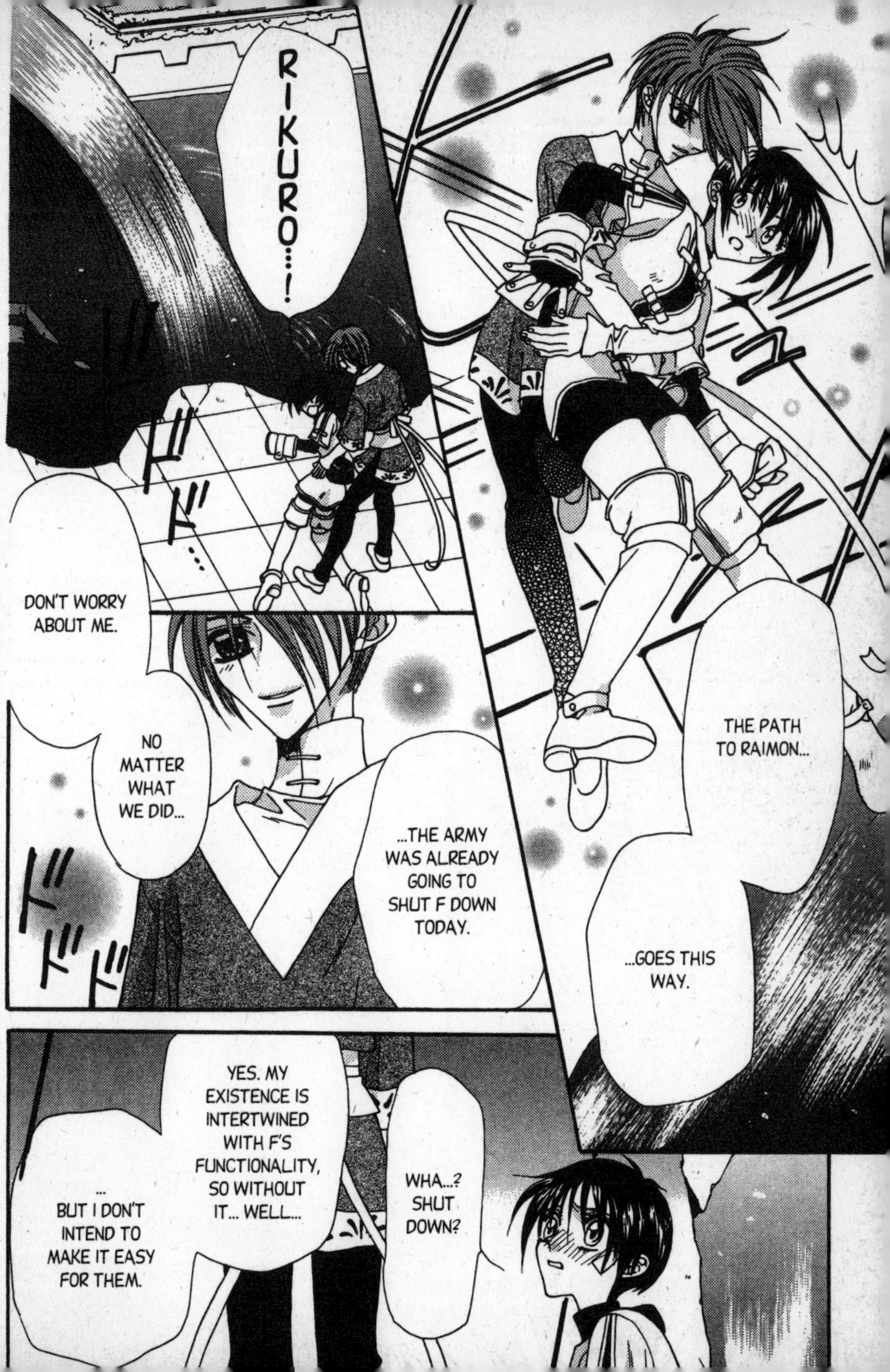
THE PATH TO RAIMON...
...GOES THIS WAY.
RIKURO...!
DON'T WORRY ABOUT ME.
NO MATTER WHAT WE DID...
...THE ARMY WAS ALREADY GOING TO SHUT F DOWN TODAY.
WHA...? SHUT DOWN?
YES. MY EXISTENCE IS INTERTWINED WITH F'S FUNCTIONALITY, SO WITHOUT IT... WELL...
... BUT I DON'T INTEND TO MAKE IT EASY FOR THEM.

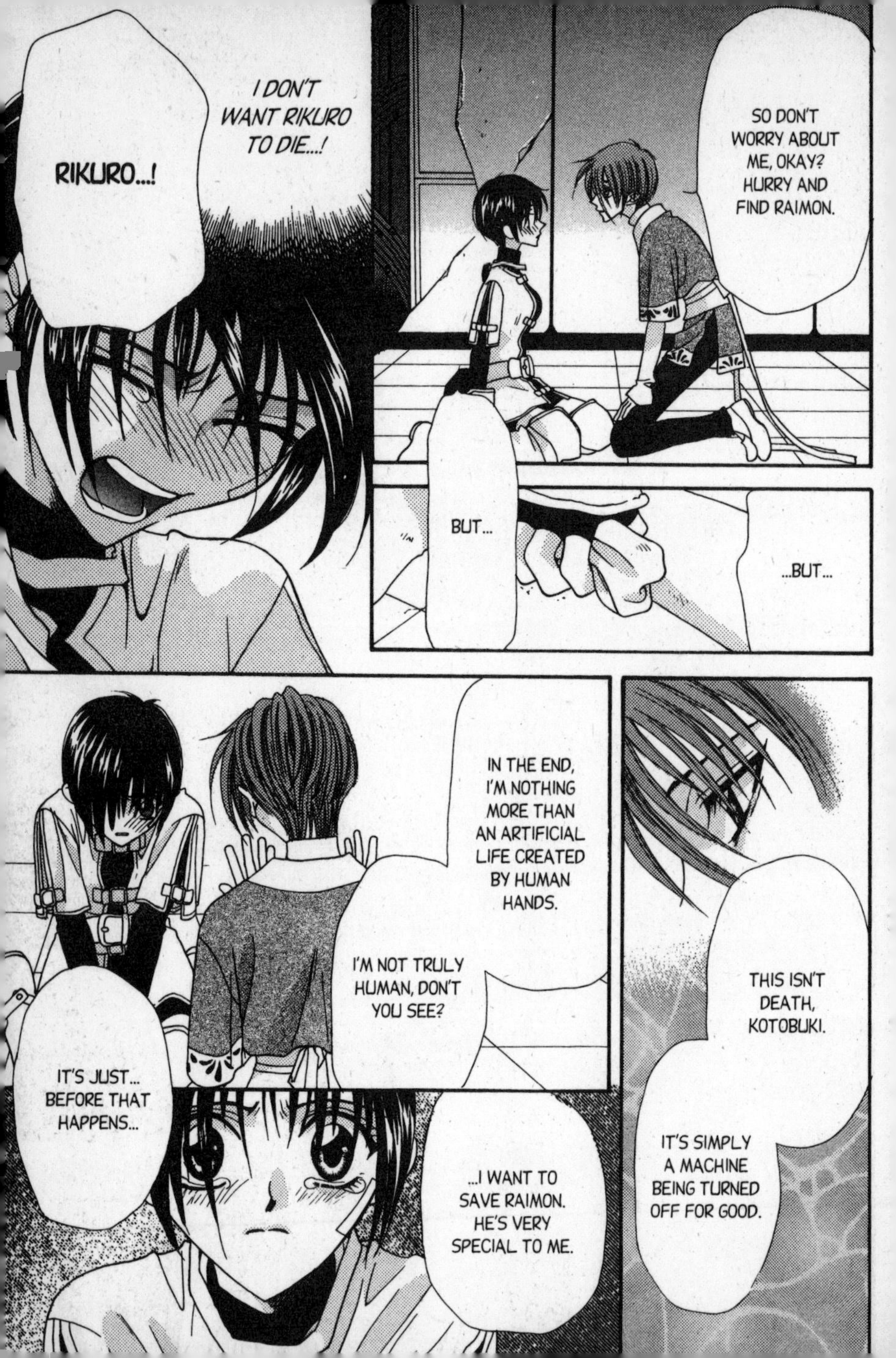
SO DON'T WORRY ABOUT ME, OKAY? HURRY AND FIND RAIMON.
BUT...
...BUT...
I DON'T WANT RIKURO TO DIE...!
RIKURO...!
THIS ISN'T DEATH, KOTOBUKI.
IT'S SIMPLY A MACHINE BEING TURNED OFF FOR GOOD.
IN THE END, I'M NOTHING MORE THAN AN ARTIFICIAL LIFE CREATED BY HUMAN HANDS.
I'M NOT TRULY HUMAN, DON'T YOU SEE?
IT'S JUST... BEFORE THAT HAPPENS...
...I WANT TO SAVE RAIMON. HE'S VERY SPECIAL TO ME.

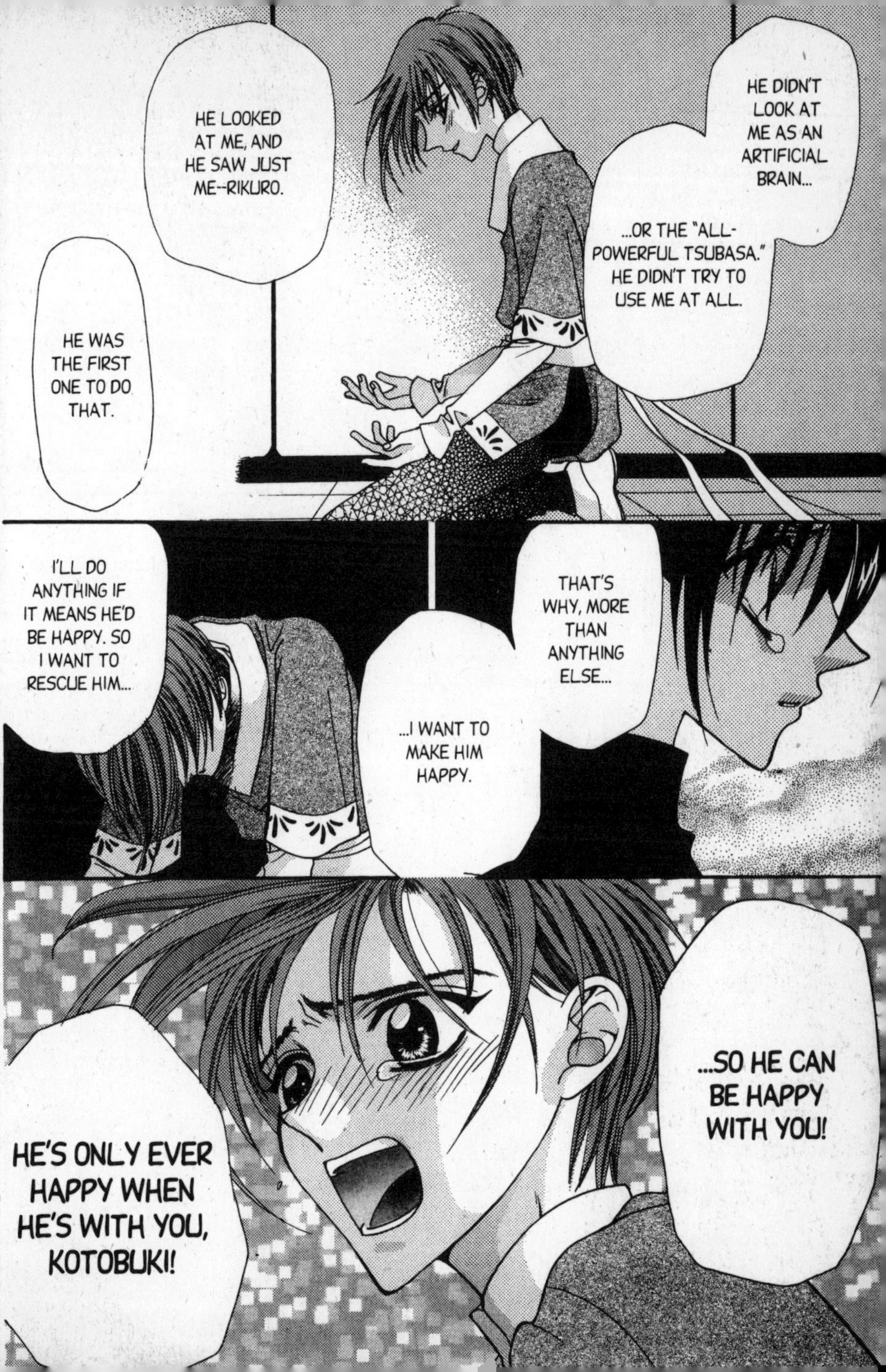
HE DIDN'T LOOK AT ME AS AN ARTIFICIAL BRAIN...
...OR THE "ALL-POWERFUL TSUBASA." HE DIDN'T TRY TO USE ME AT ALL.
HE LOOKED AT ME, AND HE SAW JUST ME--RIKURO.
HE WAS THE FIRST ONE TO DO THAT.
THAT'S WHY, MORE THAN ANYTHING ELSE...
...I WANT TO MAKE HIM HAPPY.
I'LL DO ANYTHING IF IT MEANS HE'D BE HAPPY. SO I WANT TO RESCUE HIM...
...SO HE CAN BE HAPPY WITH YOU!
HE'S ONLY EVER HAPPY WHEN HE'S WITH YOU, KOTOBUKI!

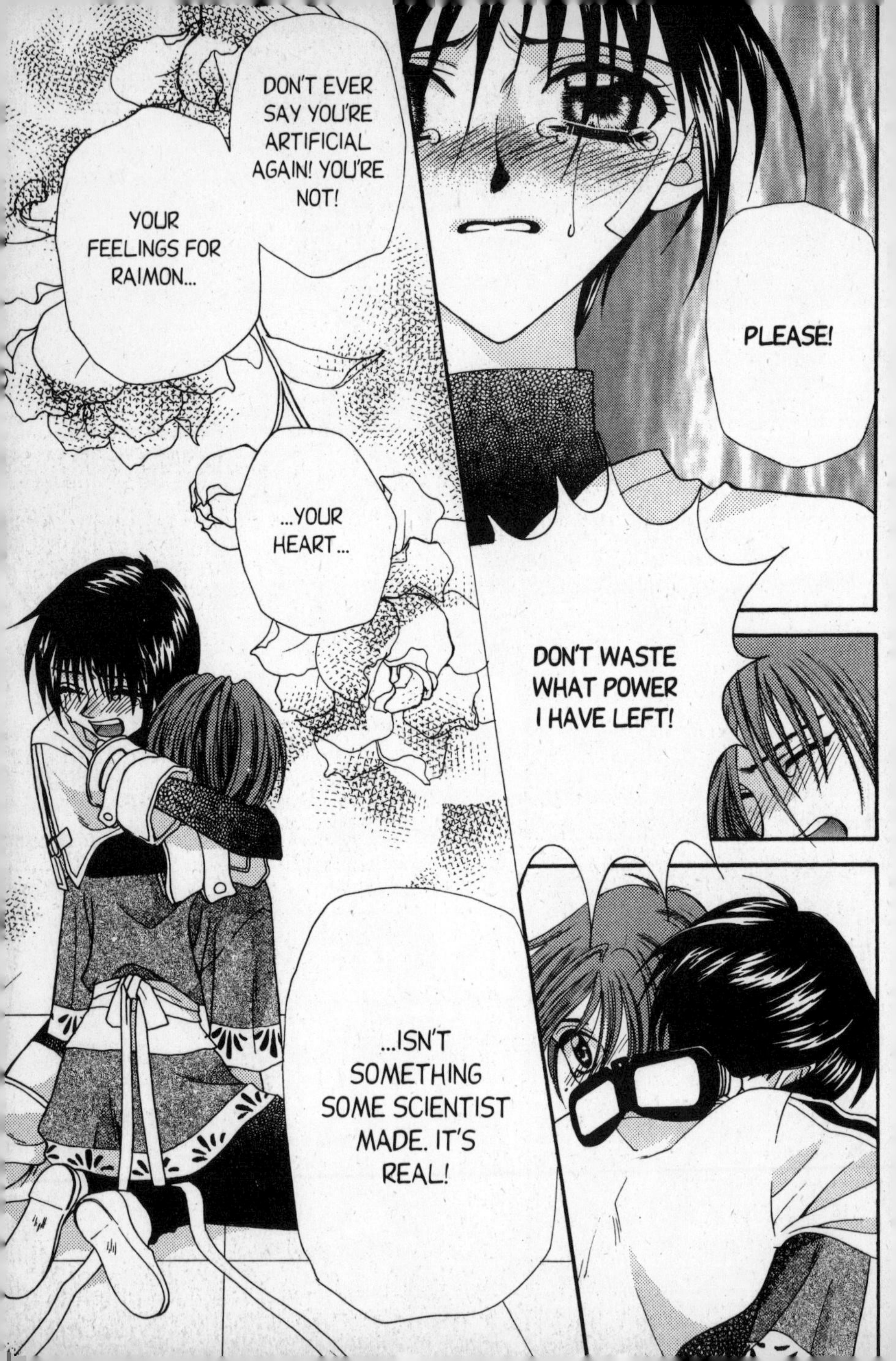
PLEASE!
DON'T WASTE WHAT POWER I HAVE LEFT!
DON'T EVER SAY YOU'RE ARTIFICIAL AGAIN! YOU'RE NOT!
YOUR FEELINGS FOR RAIMON...
...YOUR HEART...
...ISN'T SOMETHING SOME SCIENTIST MADE. IT'S REAL!

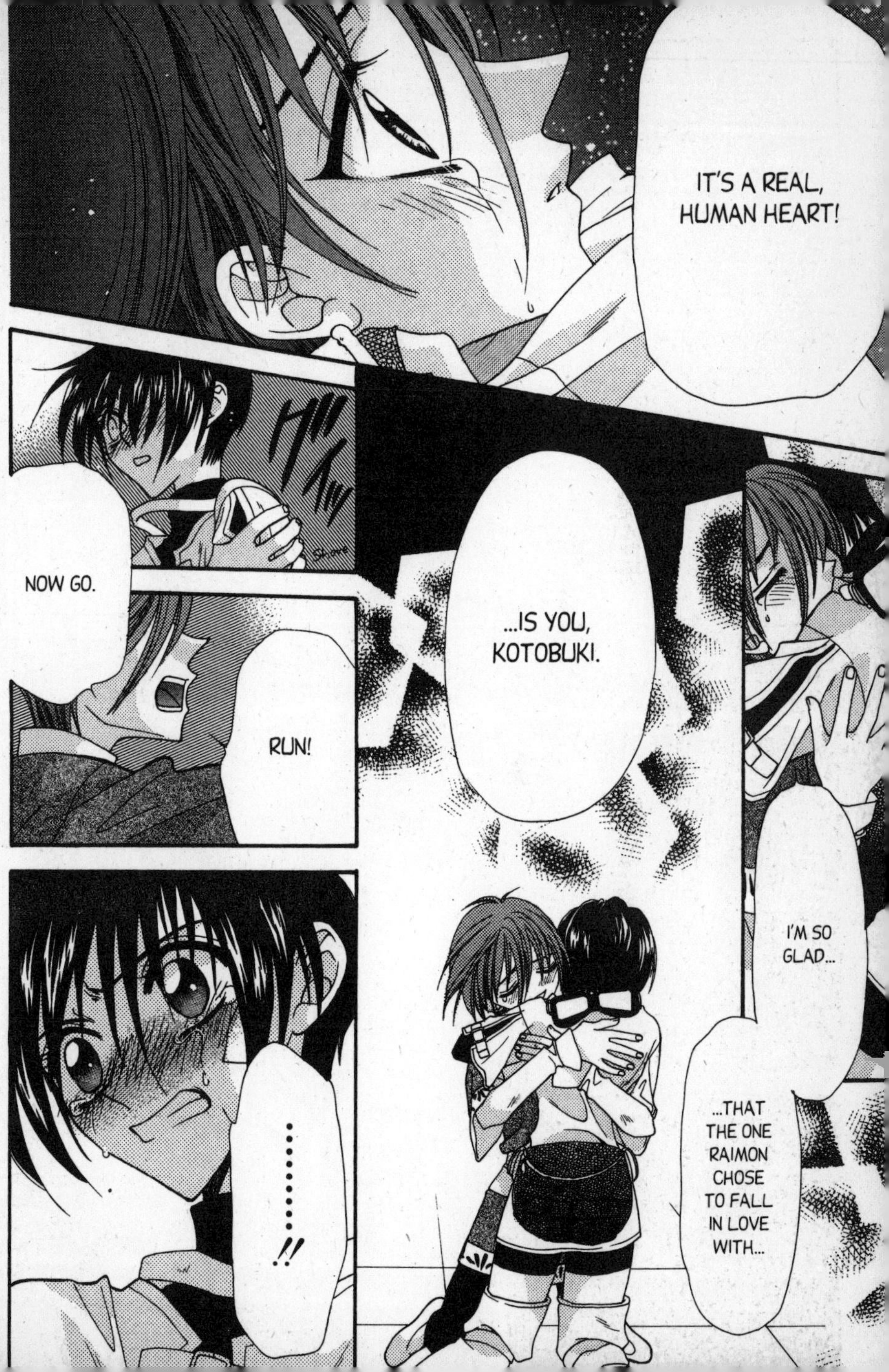
IT'S A REAL, HUMAN HEART!
I'M SO GLAD...
...THAT THE ONE RAIMON CHOSE TO FALL IN LOVE WITH...
...IS YOU, KOTOBUKI.
NOW GO.
RUN!
......!!

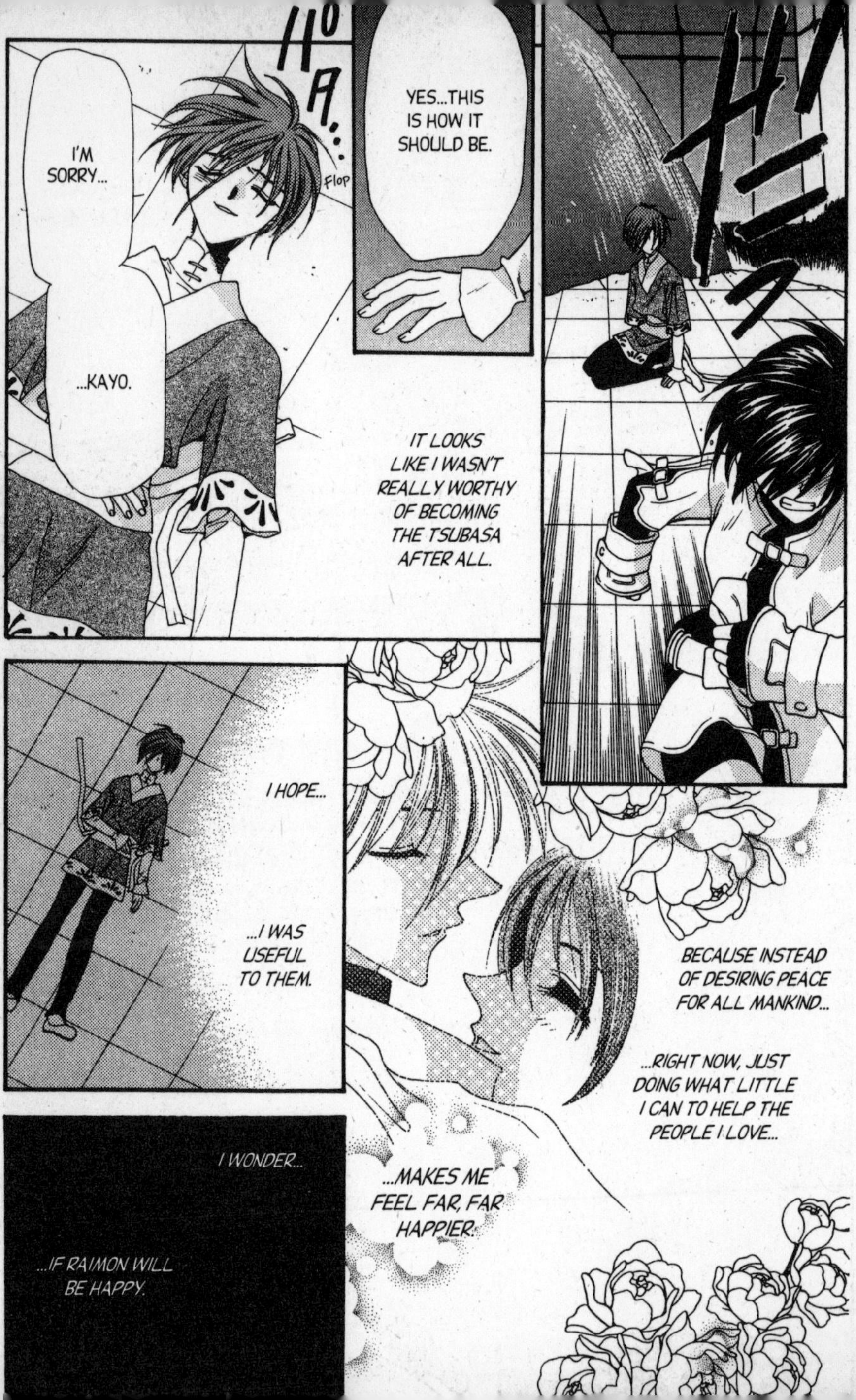
YES...THIS IS HOW IT SHOULD BE.
Flop
I'M SORRY...
...KAYO.
IT LOOKS LIKE I WASN'T REALLY WORTHY OF BECOMING THE TSUBASA AFTER ALL.
BECAUSE INSTEAD OF DESIRING PEACE FOR ALL MANKIND...
...RIGHT NOW, JUST DOING WHAT LITTLE I CAN TO HELP THE PEOPLE I LOVE...
...MAKES ME FEEL FAR, FAR HAPPIER.
I HOPE...
...I WAS USEFUL TO THEM.
I WONDER...
...IF RAIMON WILL BE HAPPY.

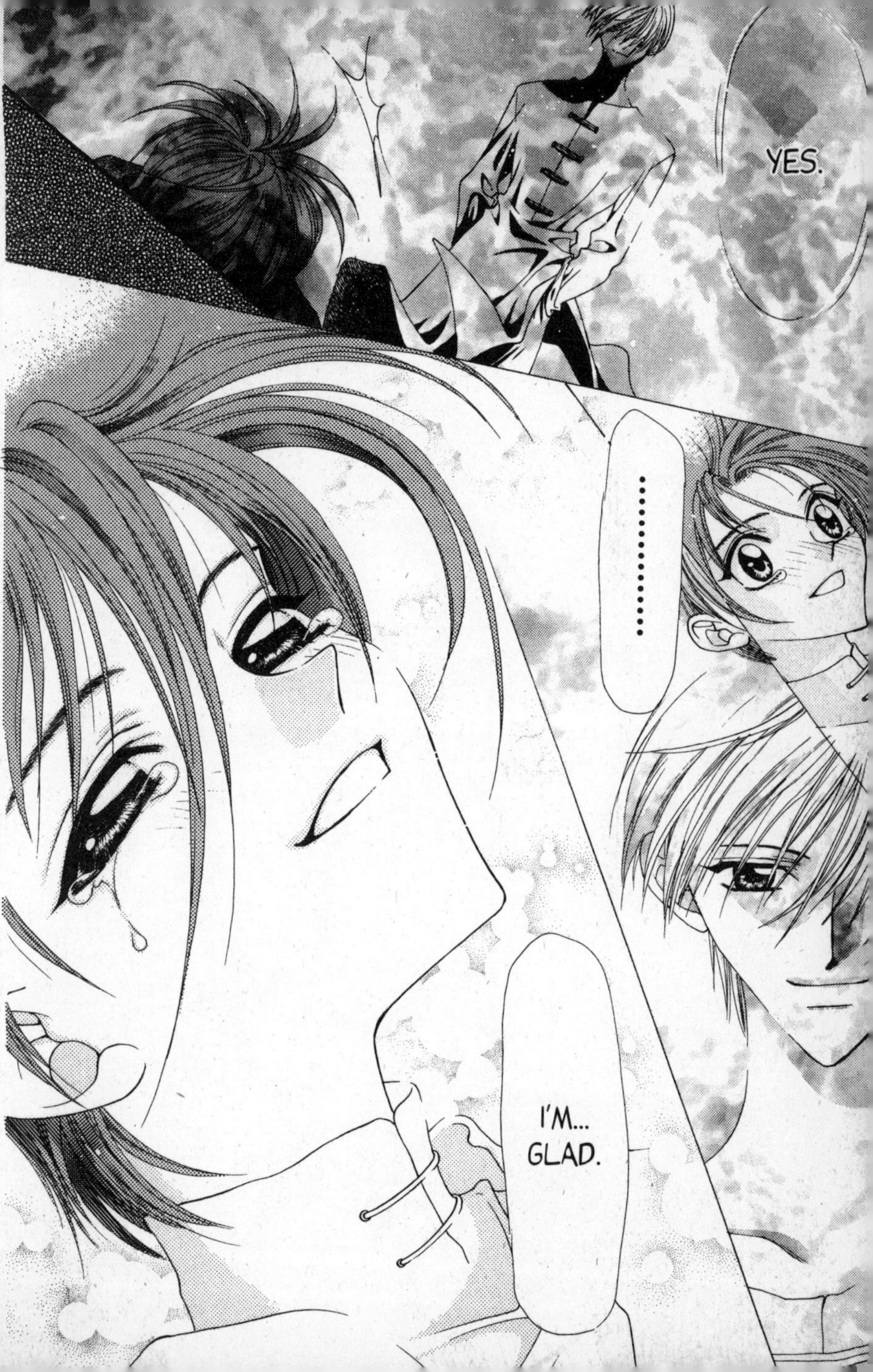
YES.
......
I'M... GLAD.

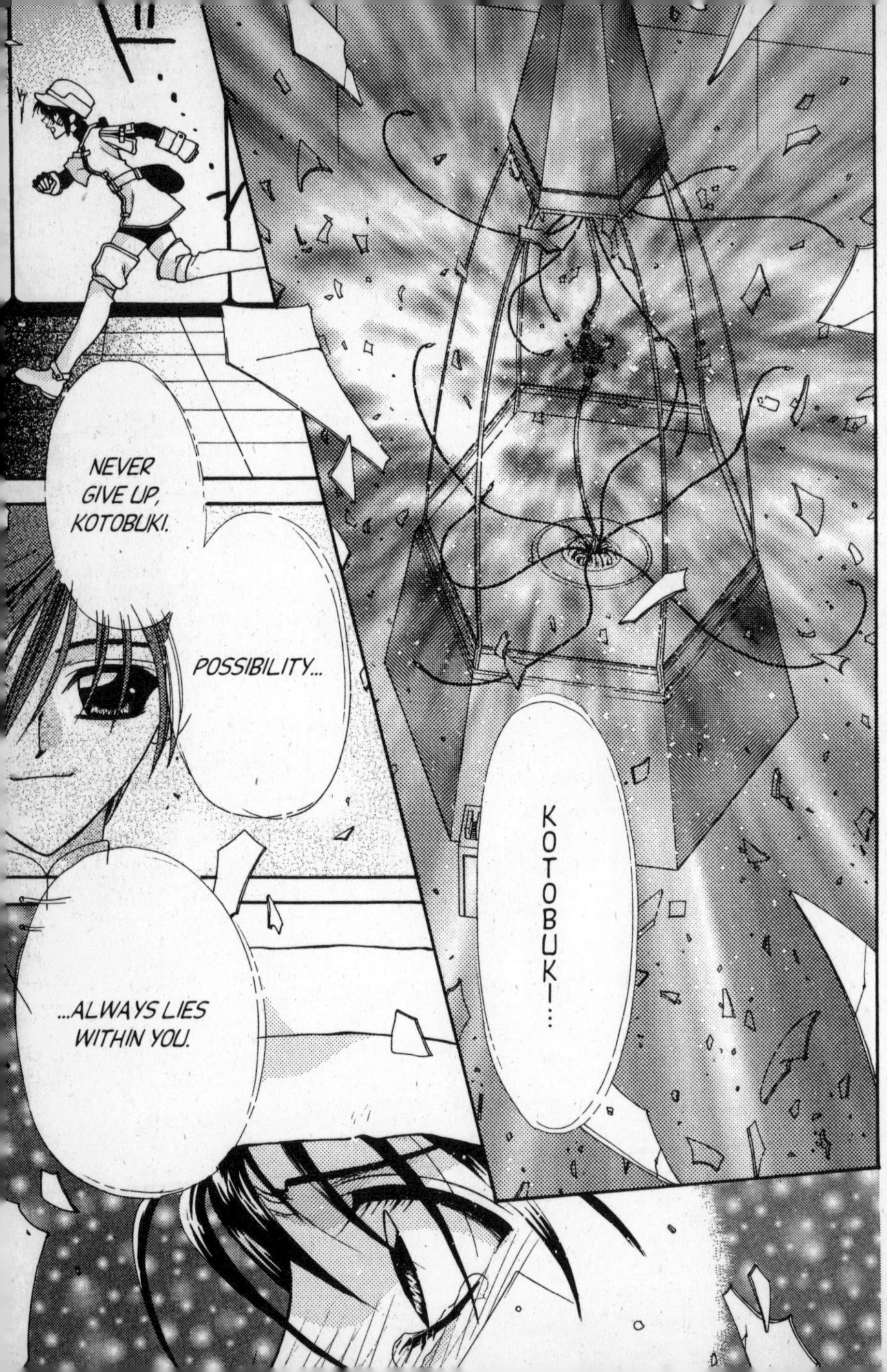
KOTOBUKI...
NEVER GIVE UP, KOTOBUKI.
POSSIBILITY...
...ALWAYS LIES WITHIN YOU.

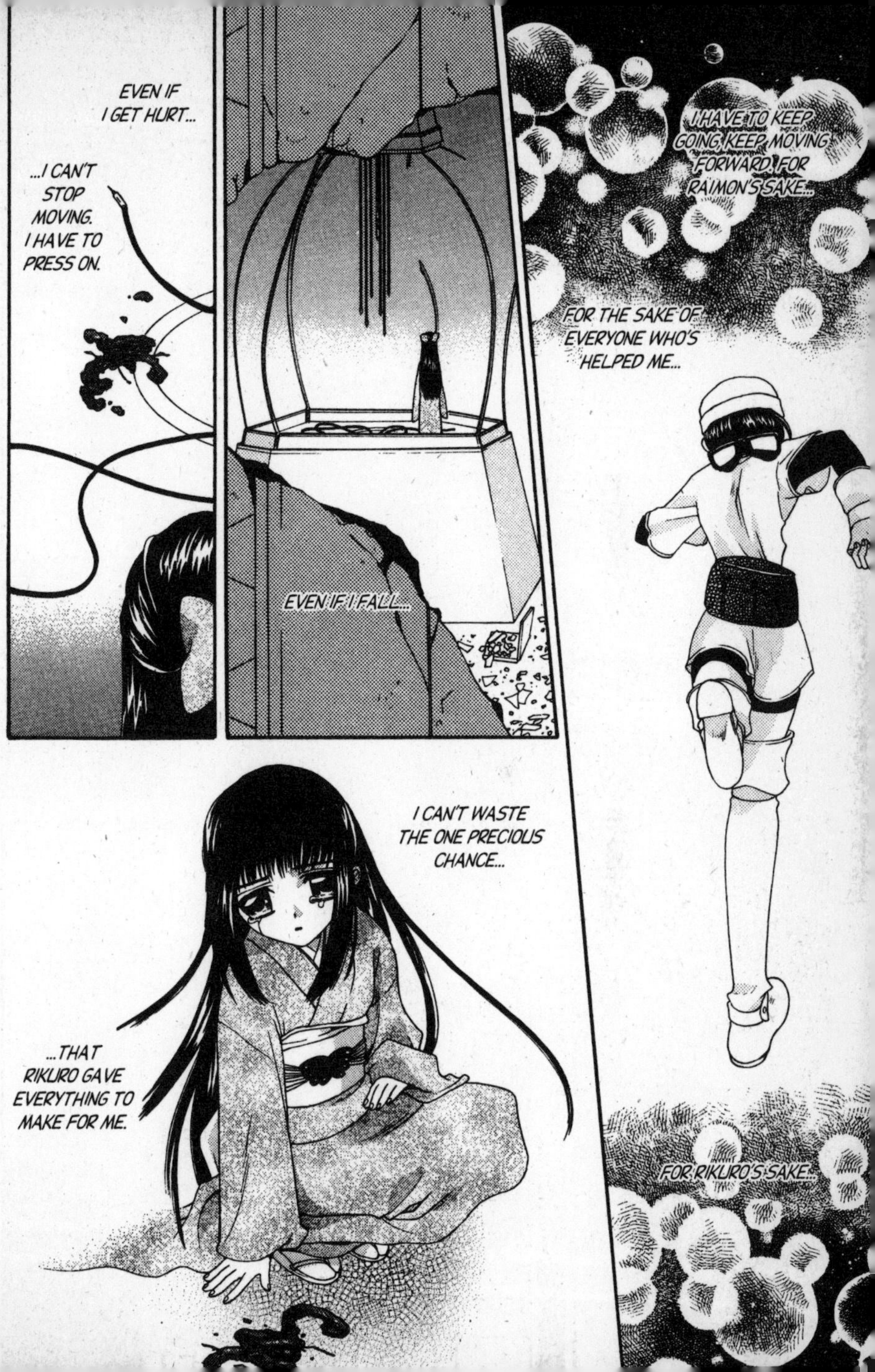
I HAVE TO KEEP GOING, KEEP MOVING FORWARD, FOR RAIMON'S SAKE...
FOR THE SAKE OF EVERYONE WHO'S HELPED ME...
FOR RIKURO'S SAKE...
EVEN IF I FALL...
EVEN IF I GET HURT...
...I CAN'T STOP MOVING. I HAVE TO PRESS ON.
I CAN'T WASTE THE ONE PRECIOUS CHANCE...
...THAT RIKURO GAVE EVERYTHING TO MAKE FOR ME.

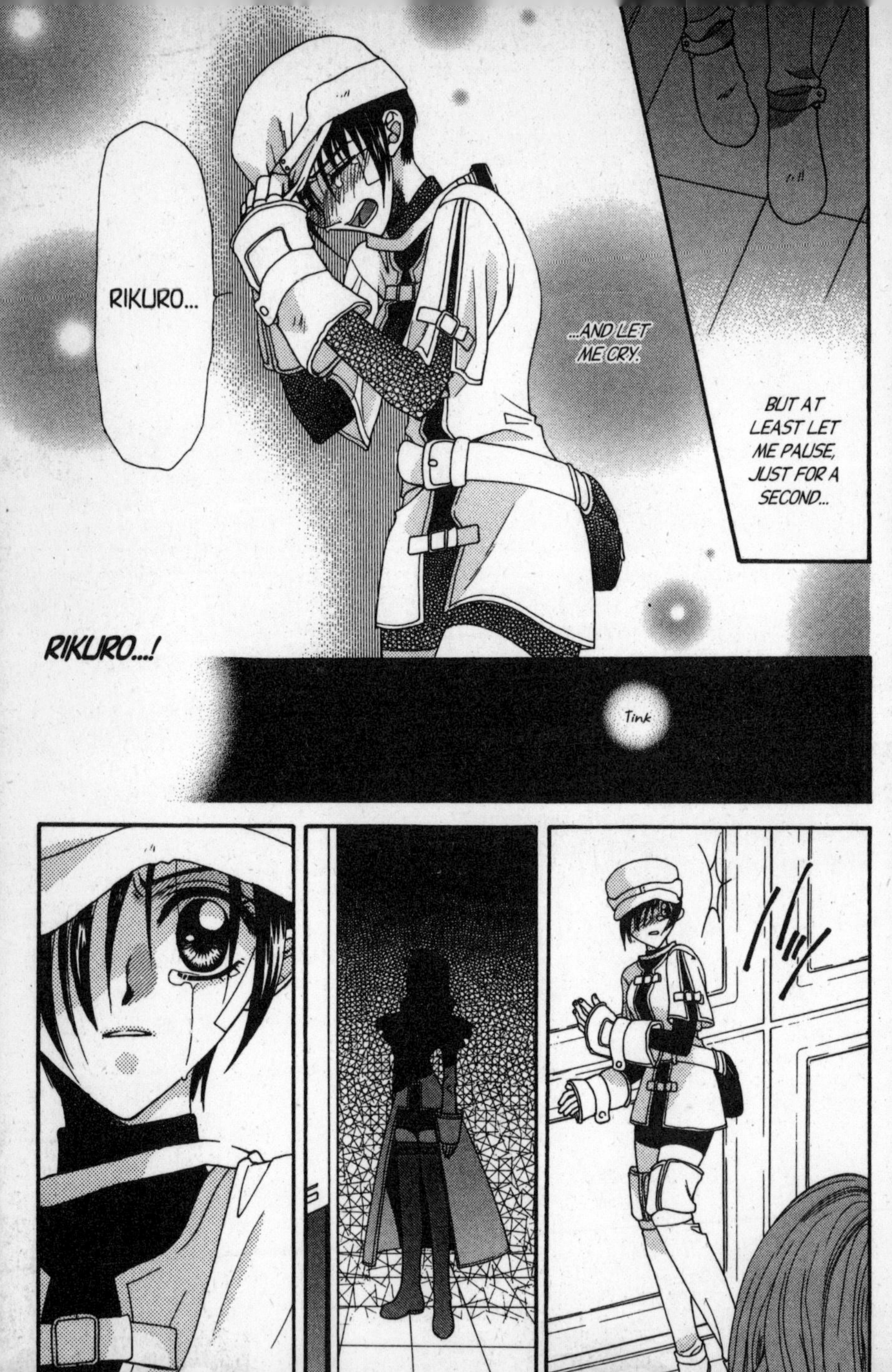
BUT AT LEAST LET ME PAUSE, JUST FOR A SECOND...
...AND LET ME CRY.
RIKURO...
RIKURO...!
Tink

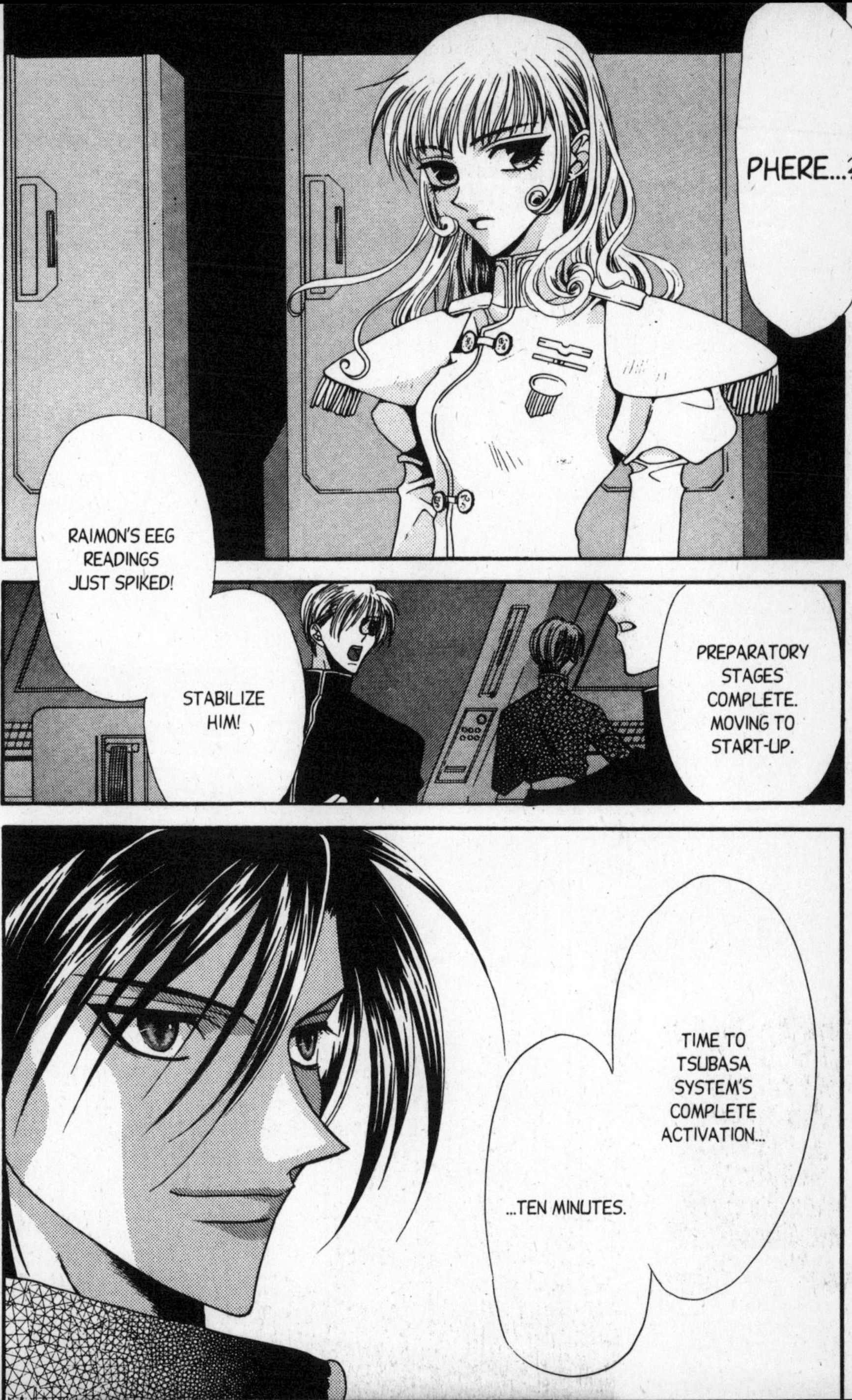
PHERE...?
RAIMON'S EEG READINGS JUST SPIKED!
STABILIZE HIM!
PREPARATORY STAGES COMPLETE. MOVING TO START-UP.
TIME TO TSUBASA SYSTEM'S COMPLETE ACTIVATION...
...TEN MINUTES.

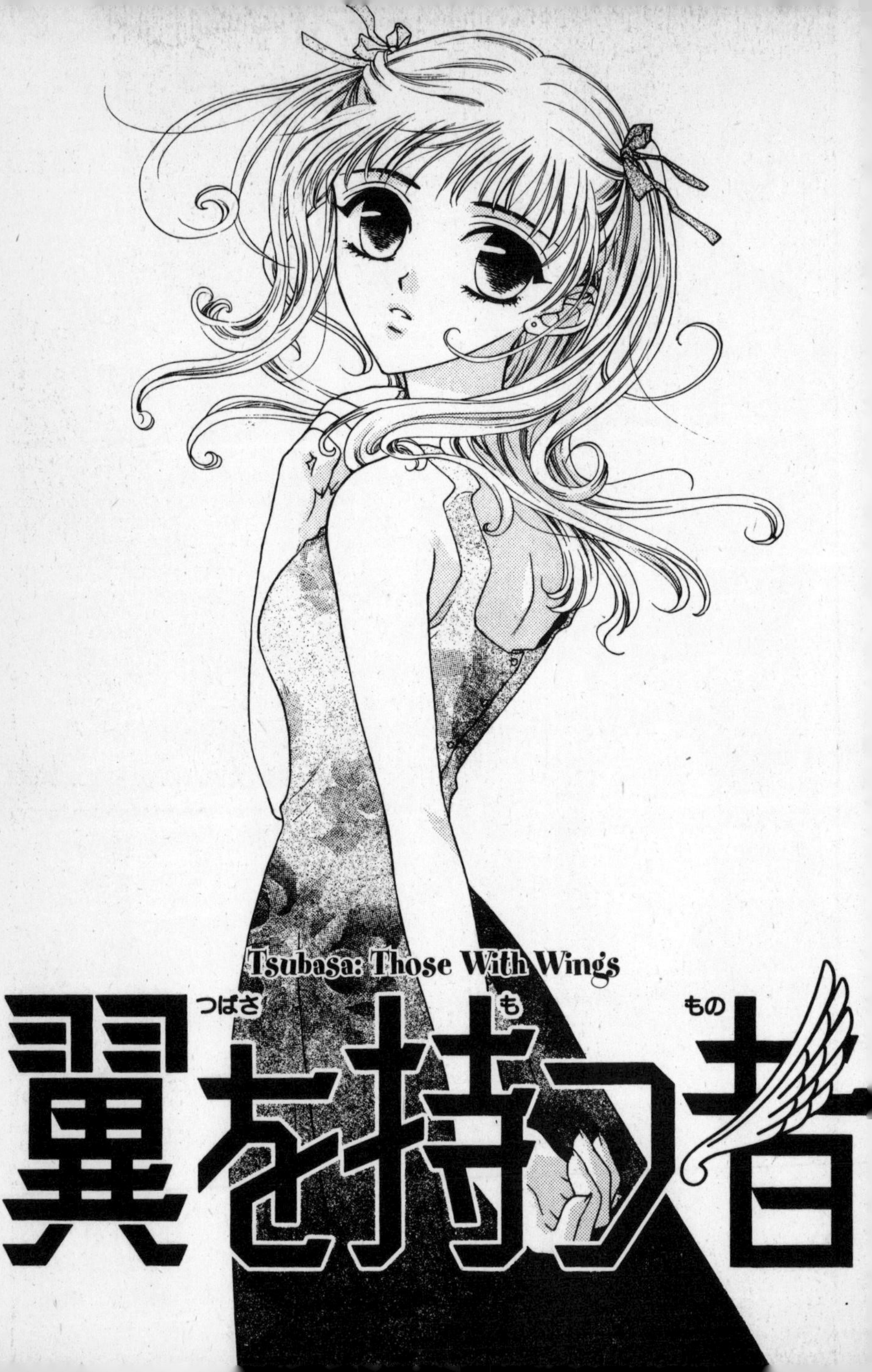
Tsubasa: Those With Wings
翼を持つ者
つばさ も もの

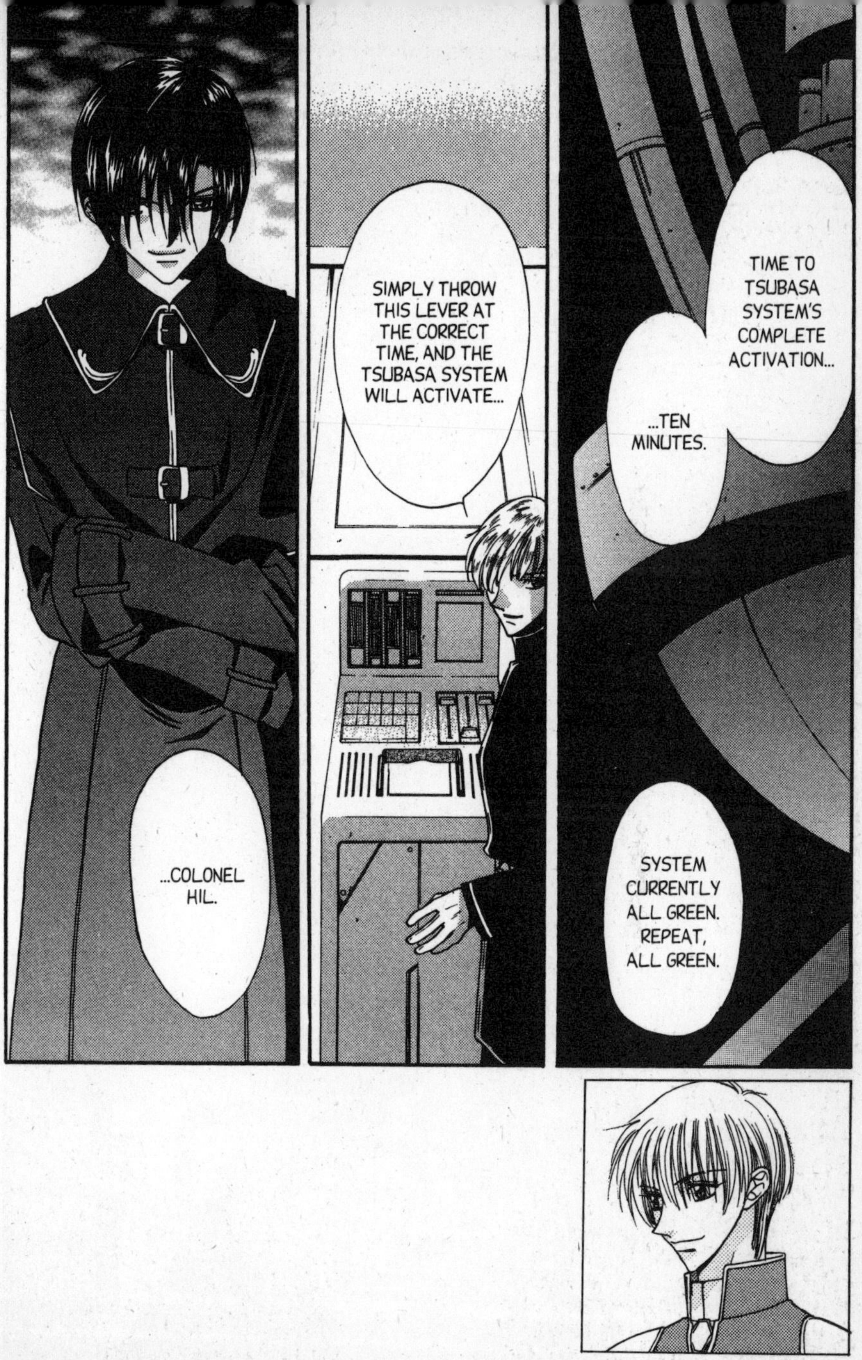
TIME TO TSUBASA SYSTEM'S COMPLETE ACTIVATION...
...TEN MINUTES.
SYSTEM CURRENTLY ALL GREEN. REPEAT, ALL GREEN.
SIMPLY THROW THIS LEVER AT THE CORRECT TIME, AND THE TSUBASA SYSTEM WILL ACTIVATE...
...COLONEL HIL.

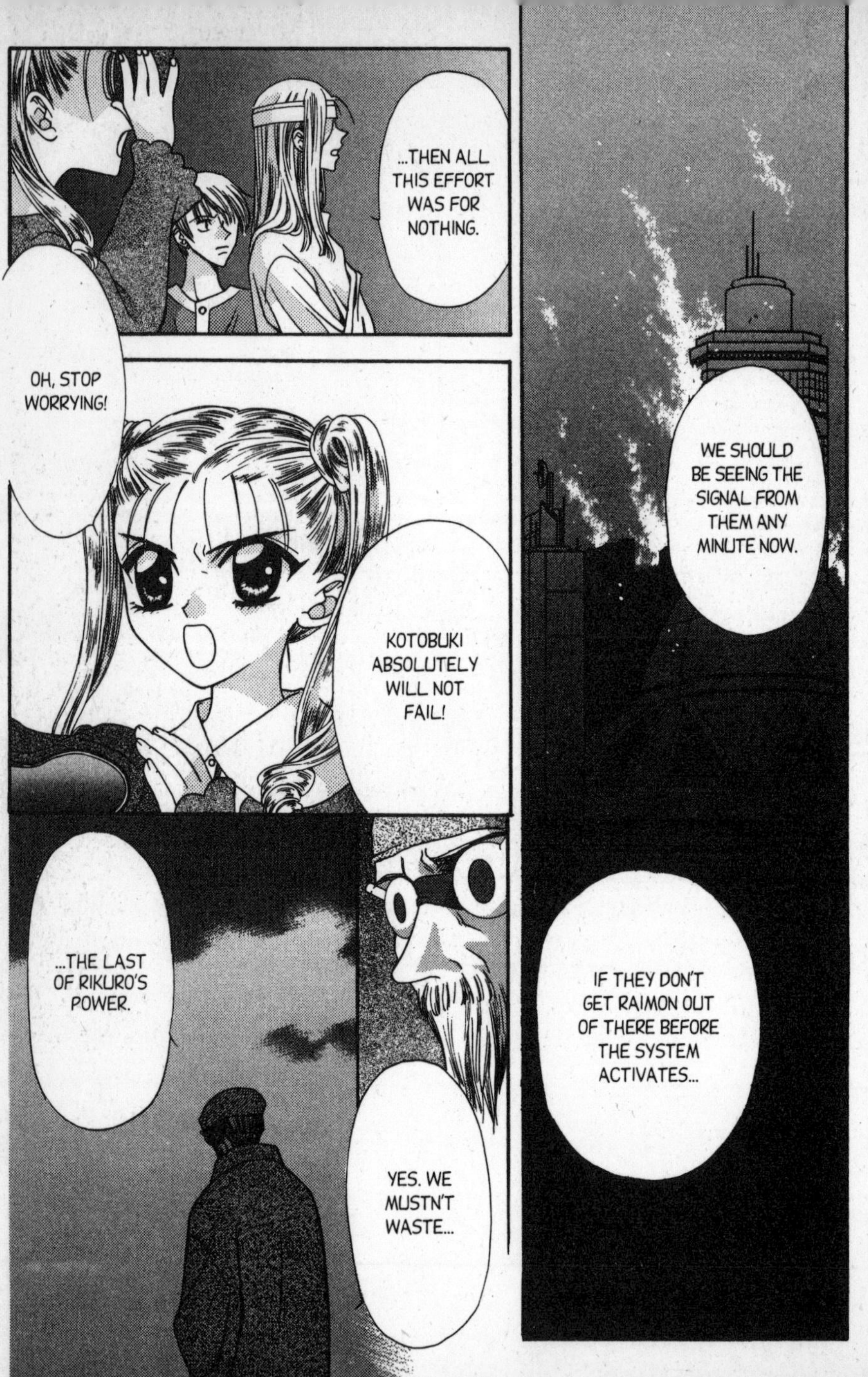
WE SHOULD BE SEEING THE SIGNAL FROM THEM ANY MINUTE NOW.
IF THEY DON'T GET RAIMON OUT OF THERE BEFORE THE SYSTEM ACTIVATES...
...THEN ALL THIS EFFORT WAS FOR NOTHING.
OH, STOP WORRYING!
KOTOBUKI ABSOLUTELY WILL NOT FAIL!
YES. WE MUSTN'T WASTE...
...THE LAST OF RIKURO'S POWER.

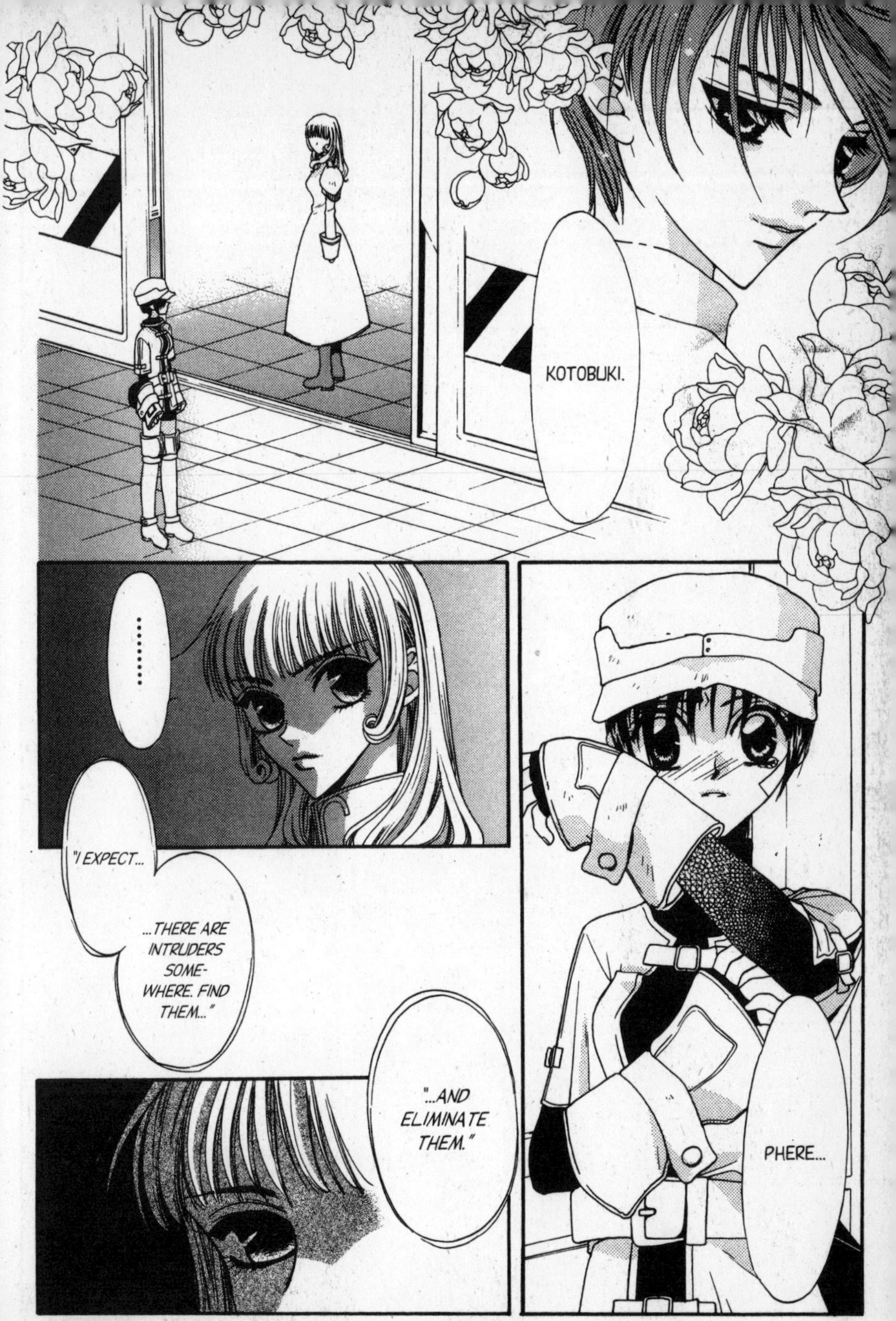
KOTOBUKI.
PHERE...
......
"I EXPECT...
...THERE ARE INTRUDERS SOMEWHERE. FIND THEM..."
"...AND ELIMINATE THEM."

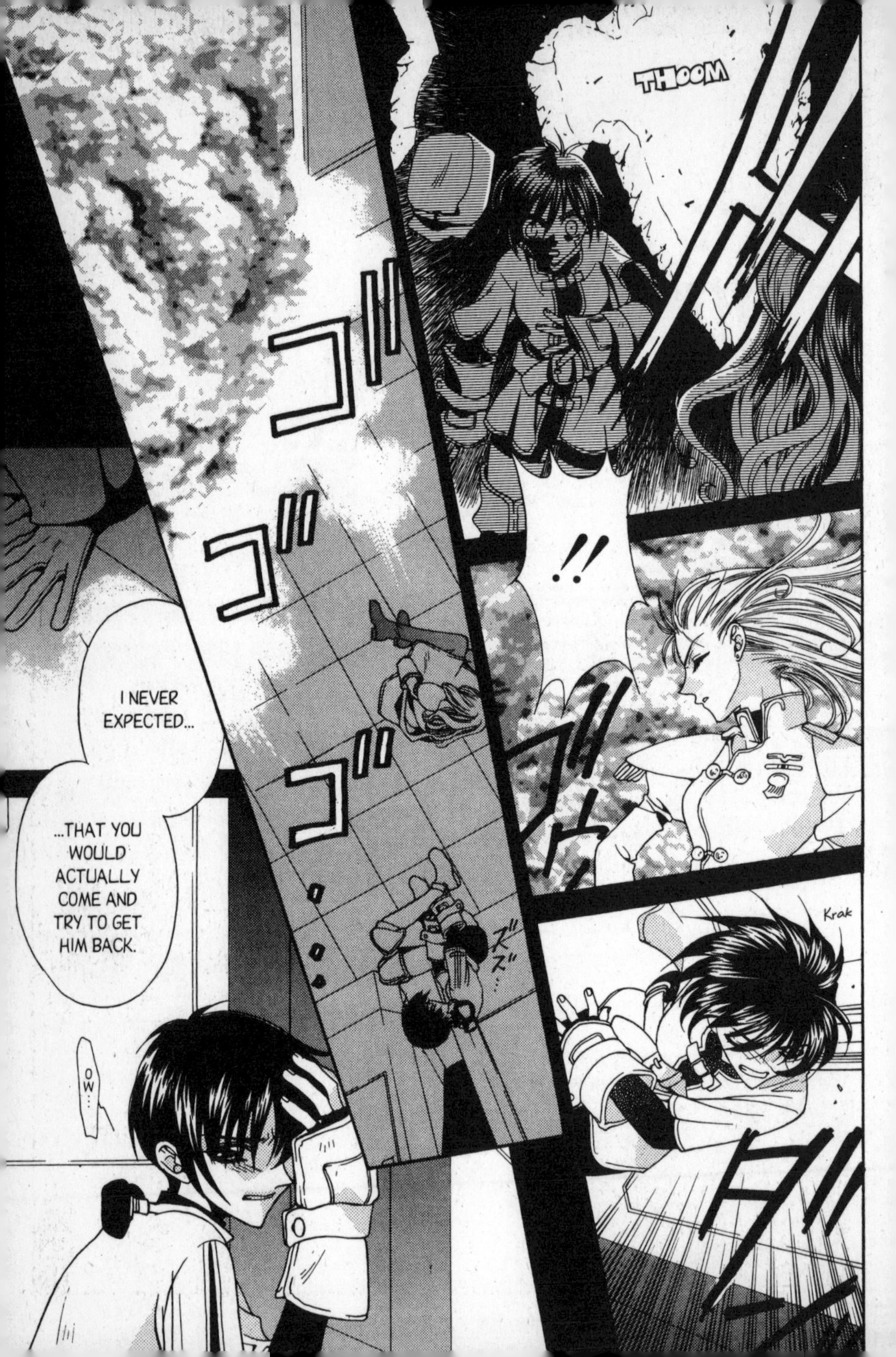
THOOM
!!
Krak
ゴゴゴ
ズズ…
I NEVER EXPECTED...
...THAT YOU WOULD ACTUALLY COME AND TRY TO GET HIM BACK.
OW...

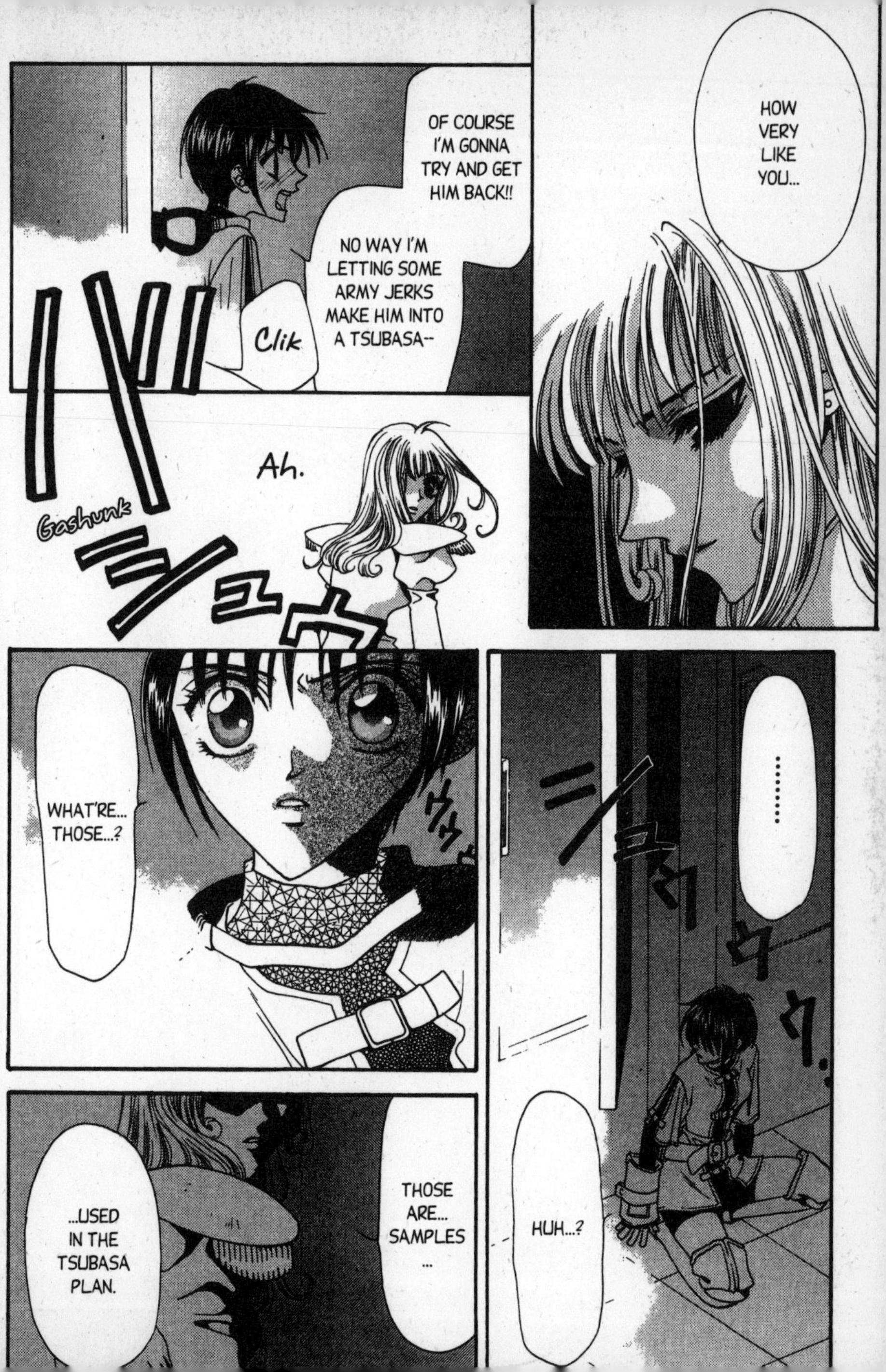
HOW VERY LIKE YOU...
OF COURSE I'M GONNA TRY AND GET HIM BACK!!
NO WAY I'M LETTING SOME ARMY JERKS MAKE HIM INTO A TSUBASA--
Clik
Ah.
Gashunk
....
HUH...?
WHAT'RE... THOSE...?
THOSE ARE... SAMPLES...
...USED IN THE TSUBASA PLAN.

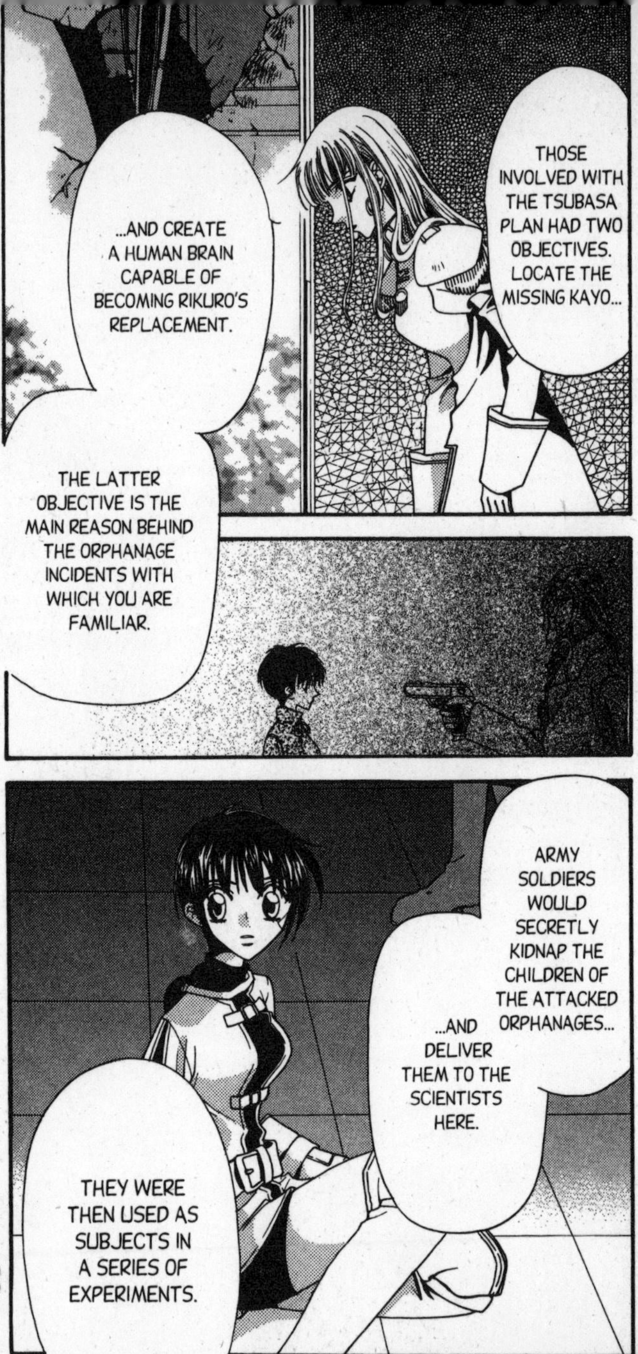
THOSE INVOLVED WITH THE TSUBASA PLAN HAD TWO OBJECTIVES. LOCATE THE MISSING KAYO...
...AND CREATE A HUMAN BRAIN CAPABLE OF BECOMING RIKURO'S REPLACEMENT.
THE LATTER OBJECTIVE IS THE MAIN REASON BEHIND THE ORPHANAGE INCIDENTS WITH WHICH YOU ARE FAMILIAR.
ARMY SOLDIERS WOULD SECRETLY KIDNAP THE CHILDREN OF THE ATTACKED ORPHANAGES...
...AND DELIVER THEM TO THE SCIENTISTS HERE.
THEY WERE THEN USED AS SUBJECTS IN A SERIES OF EXPERIMENTS.
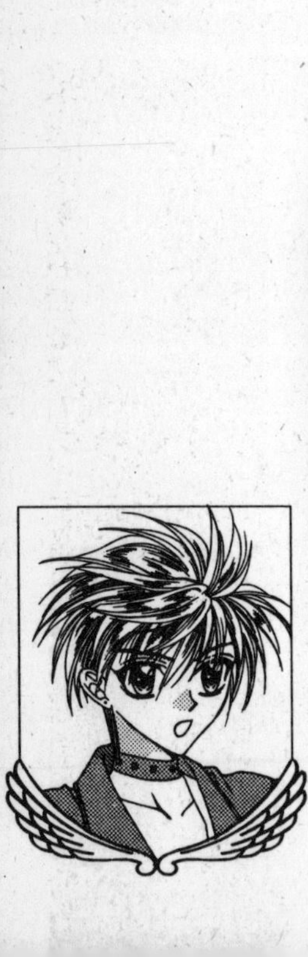

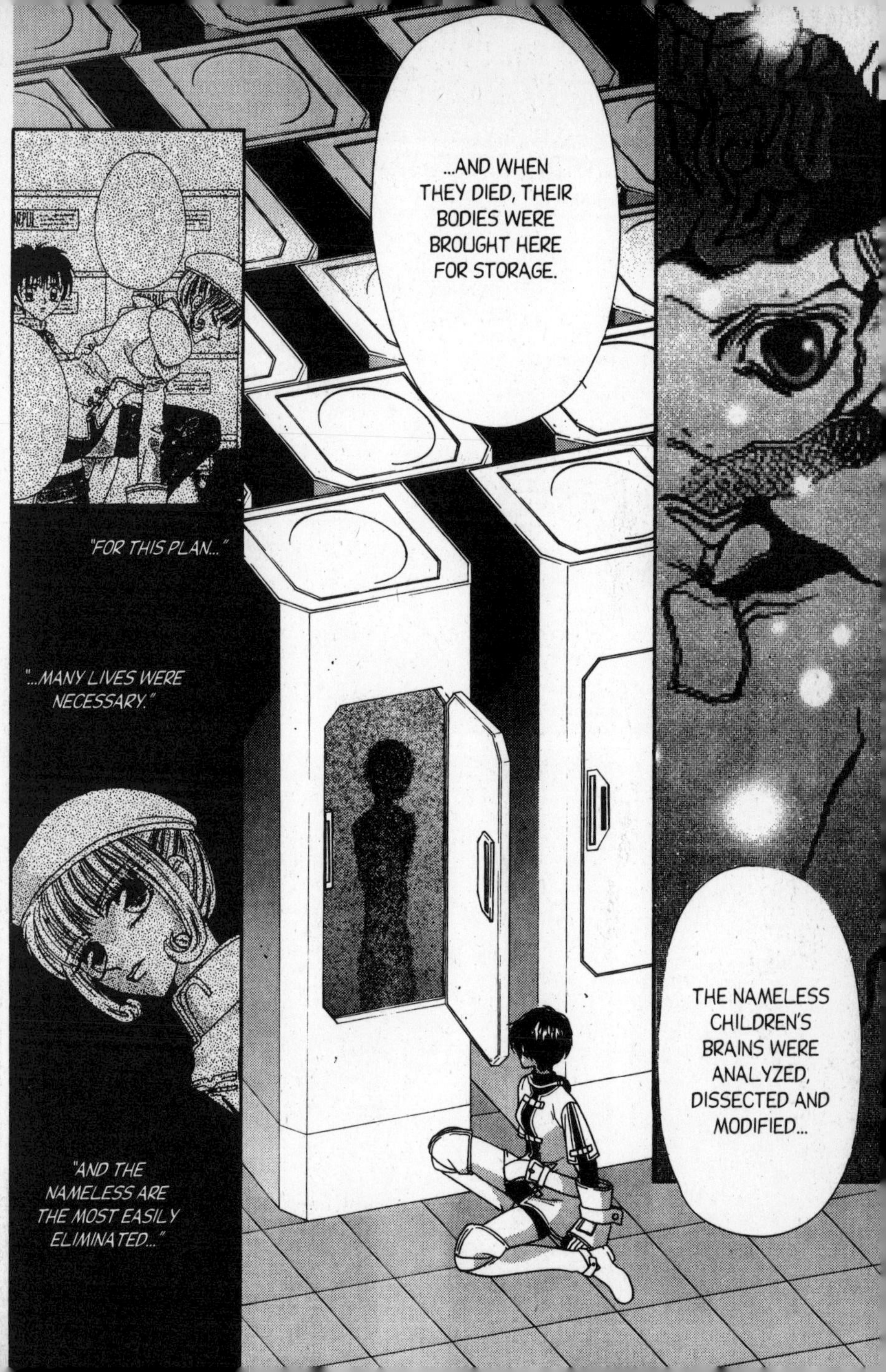
THE NAMELESS CHILDREN'S BRAINS WERE ANALYZED, DISSECTED AND MODIFIED...
...AND WHEN THEY DIED, THEIR BODIES WERE BROUGHT HERE FOR STORAGE.
"FOR THIS PLAN..."
"...MANY LIVES WERE NECESSARY."
"AND THE NAMELESS ARE THE MOST EASILY ELIMINATED..."

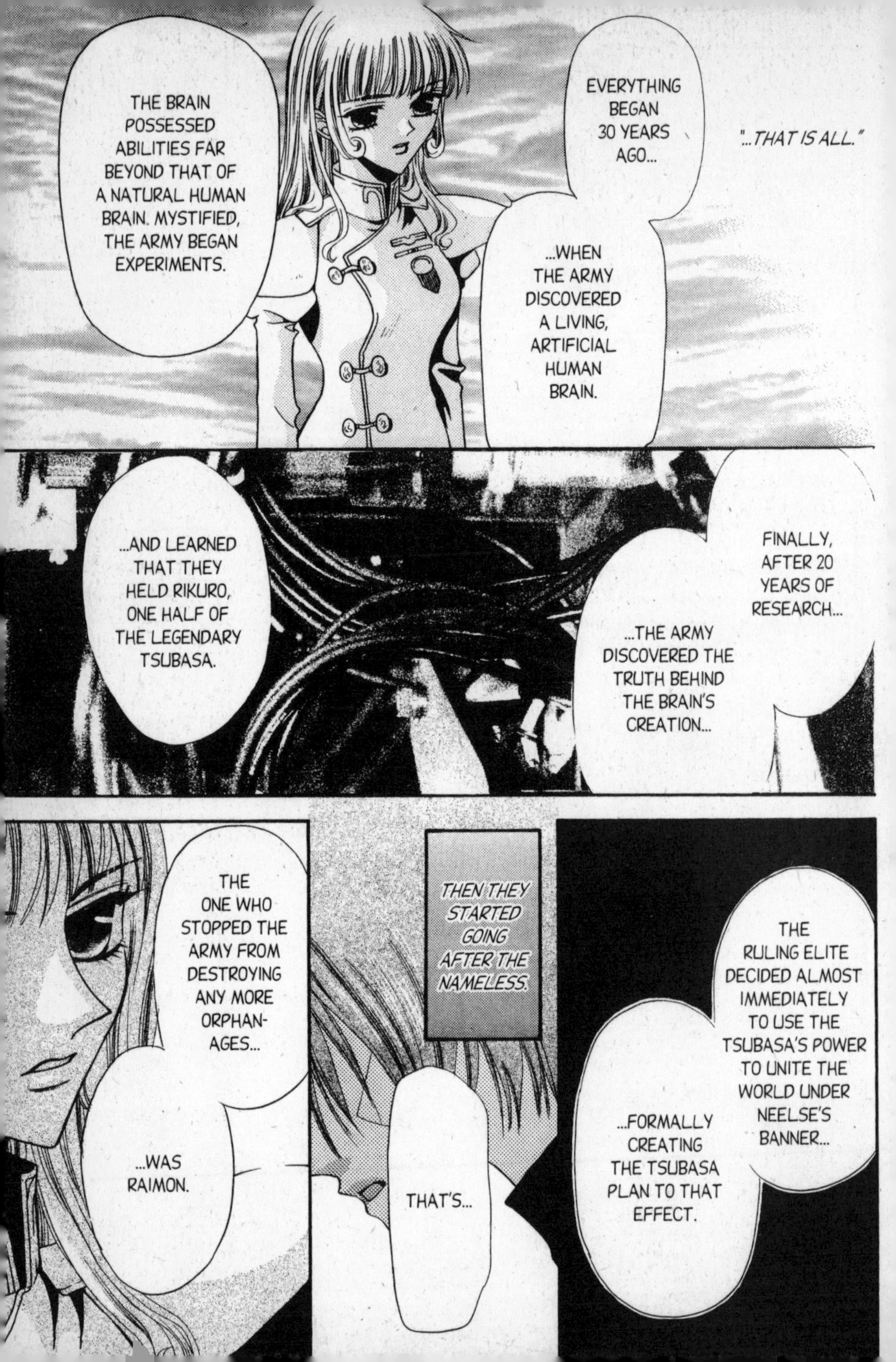
"...THAT IS ALL."
EVERYTHING BEGAN 30 YEARS AGO...
...WHEN THE ARMY DISCOVERED A LIVING, ARTIFICIAL HUMAN BRAIN.
THE BRAIN POSSESSED ABILITIES FAR BEYOND THAT OF A NATURAL HUMAN BRAIN. MYSTIFIED, THE ARMY BEGAN EXPERIMENTS.
FINALLY, AFTER 20 YEARS OF RESEARCH...
...THE ARMY DISCOVERED THE TRUTH BEHIND THE BRAIN'S CREATION...
...AND LEARNED THAT THEY HELD RIKURO, ONE HALF OF THE LEGENDARY TSUBASA.
THE RULING ELITE DECIDED ALMOST IMMEDIATELY TO USE THE TSUBASA'S POWER TO UNITE THE WORLD UNDER NEELSE'S BANNER...
...FORMALLY CREATING THE TSUBASA PLAN TO THAT EFFECT.
THEN THEY STARTED GOING AFTER THE NAMELESS.
THAT'S...
THE ONE WHO STOPPED THE ARMY FROM DESTROYING ANY MORE ORPHAN-AGES...
...WAS RAIMON.

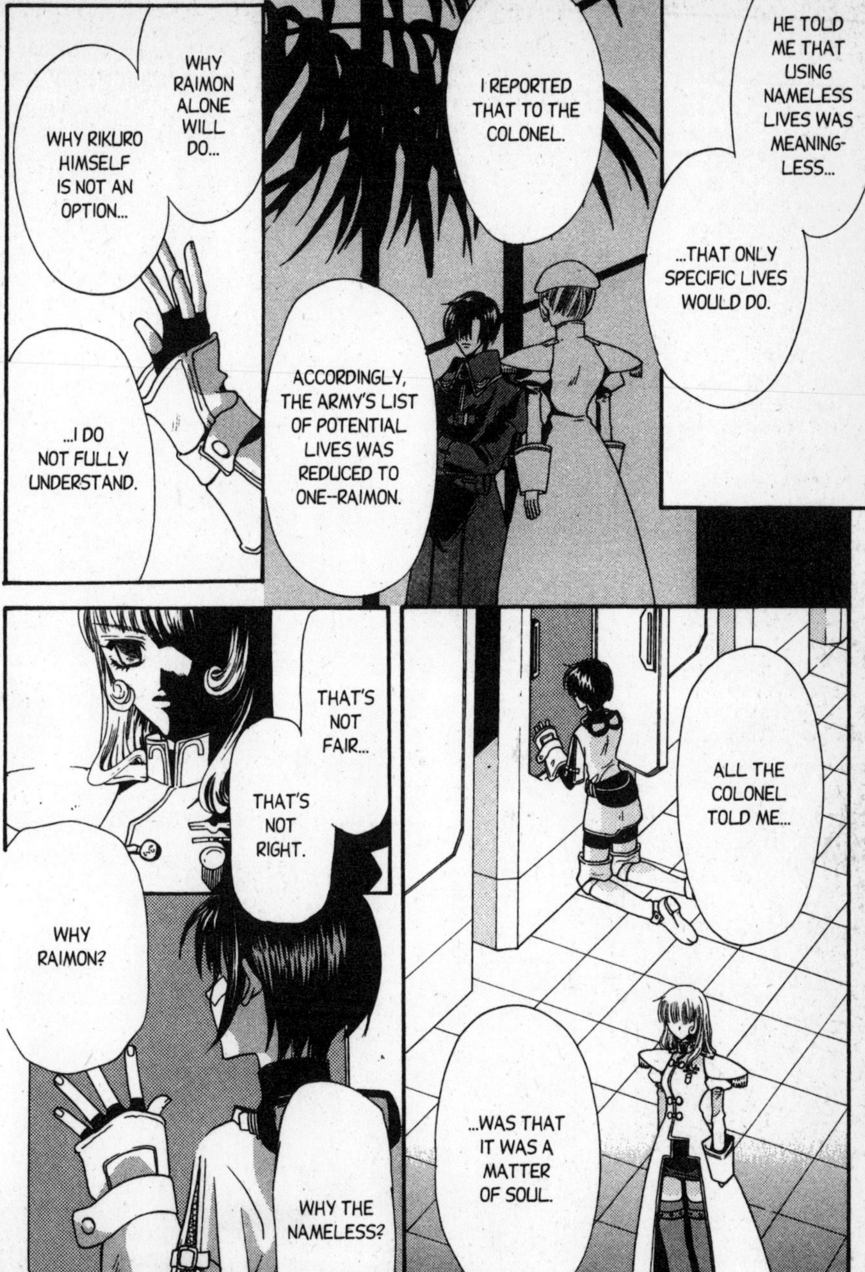
HE TOLD ME THAT USING NAMELESS LIVES WAS MEANING-LESS...
...THAT ONLY SPECIFIC LIVES WOULD DO.
I REPORTED THAT TO THE COLONEL.
ACCORDINGLY, THE ARMY'S LIST OF POTENTIAL LIVES WAS REDUCED TO ONE--RAIMON.
WHY RAIMON ALONE WILL DO...
WHY RIKURO HIMSELF IS NOT AN OPTION...
...I DO NOT FULLY UNDERSTAND.
ALL THE COLONEL TOLD ME...
...WAS THAT IT WAS A MATTER OF SOUL.
THAT'S NOT FAIR...
THAT'S NOT RIGHT.
WHY RAIMON?
WHY THE NAMELESS?

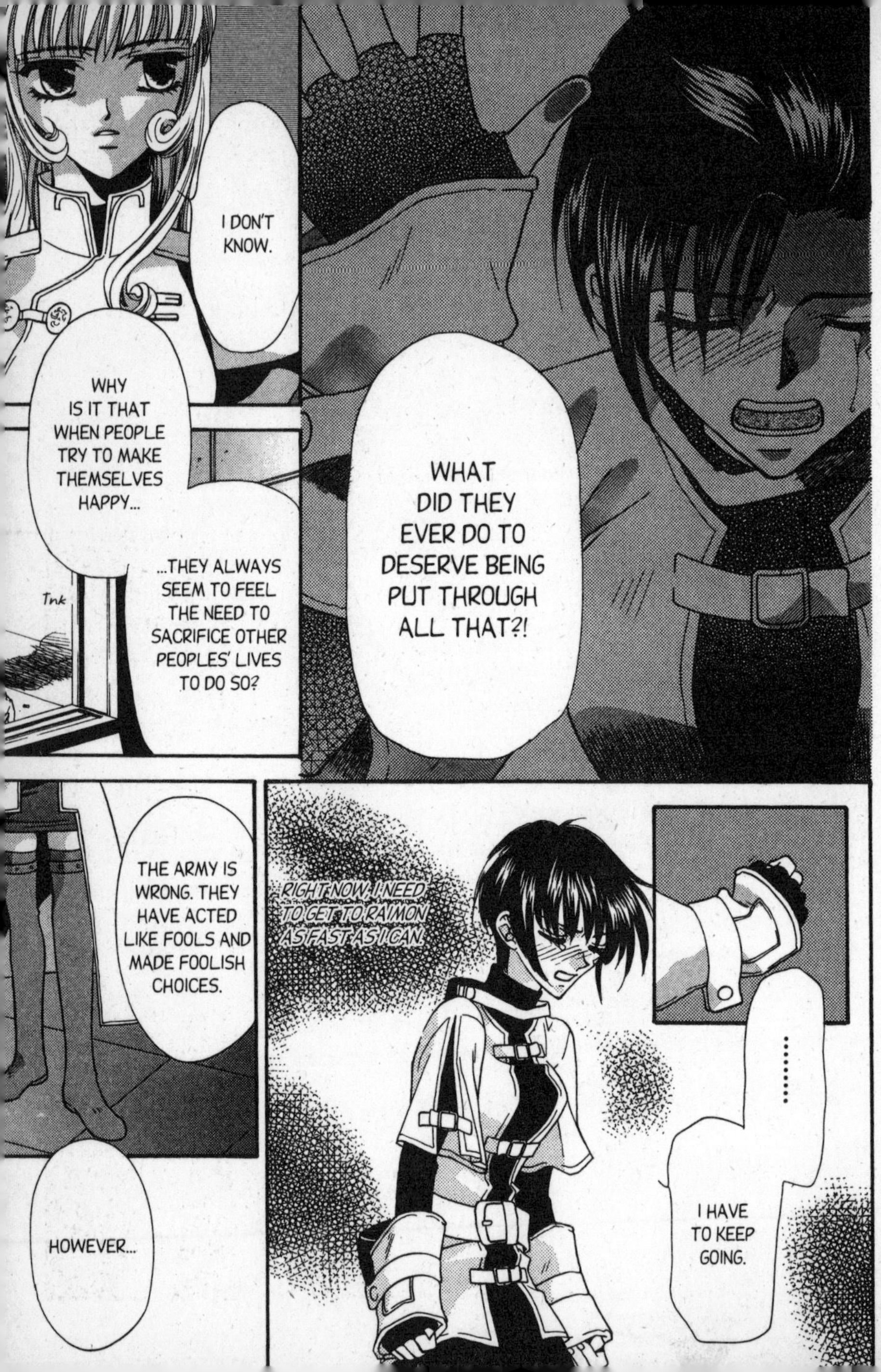
WHAT DID THEY EVER DO TO DESERVE BEING PUT THROUGH ALL THAT?!
I DON'T KNOW.
WHY IS IT THAT WHEN PEOPLE TRY TO MAKE THEMSELVES HAPPY...
...THEY ALWAYS SEEM TO FEEL THE NEED TO SACRIFICE OTHER PEOPLES' LIVES TO DO SO?
Tnk
RIGHT NOW, I NEED TO GET TO RAIMON AS FAST AS I CAN.
......
I HAVE TO KEEP GOING.
THE ARMY IS WRONG. THEY HAVE ACTED LIKE FOOLS AND MADE FOOLISH CHOICES.
HOWEVER...

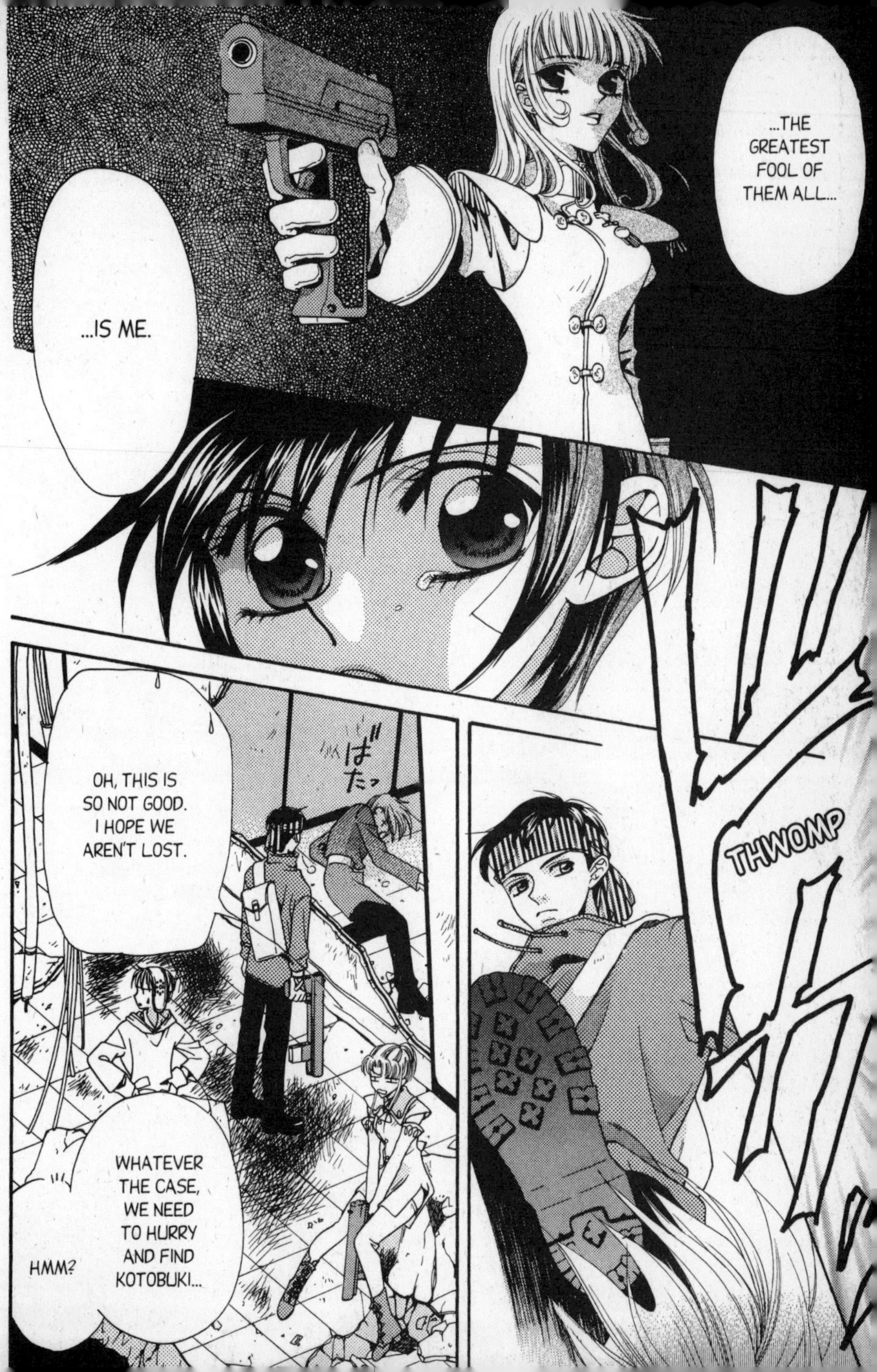
...THE GREATEST FOOL OF THEM ALL...
...IS ME.
THWOMP
ばたっ
OH, THIS IS SO NOT GOOD. I HOPE WE AREN'T LOST.
WHATEVER THE CASE, WE NEED TO HURRY AND FIND KOTOBUKI...
HMM?

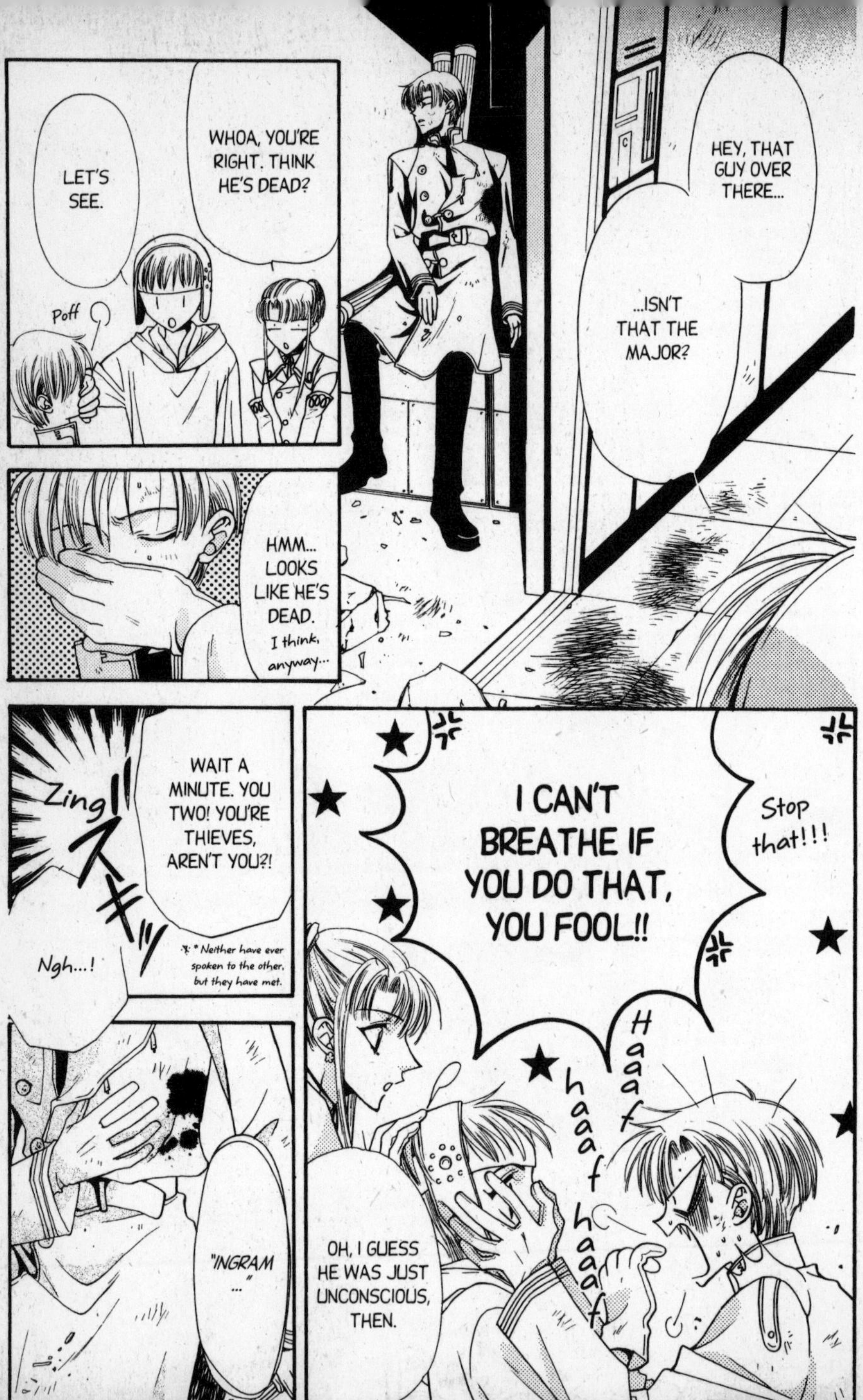
HEY, THAT GUY OVER THERE...
...ISN'T THAT THE MAJOR?
WHOA, YOU'RE RIGHT. THINK HE'S DEAD?
LET'S SEE.
Poff
HMM... LOOKS LIKE HE'S DEAD.
I think, anyway...
Stop that!!!
I CAN'T BREATHE IF YOU DO THAT, YOU FOOL!!
Haaaf haaaf haaaf
OH, I GUESS HE WAS JUST UNCONSCIOUS, THEN.
WAIT A MINUTE. YOU TWO! YOU'RE THIEVES, AREN'T YOU?!
Zing
* Neither have ever spoken to the other, but they have met.
Ngh...!
"INGRAM..."

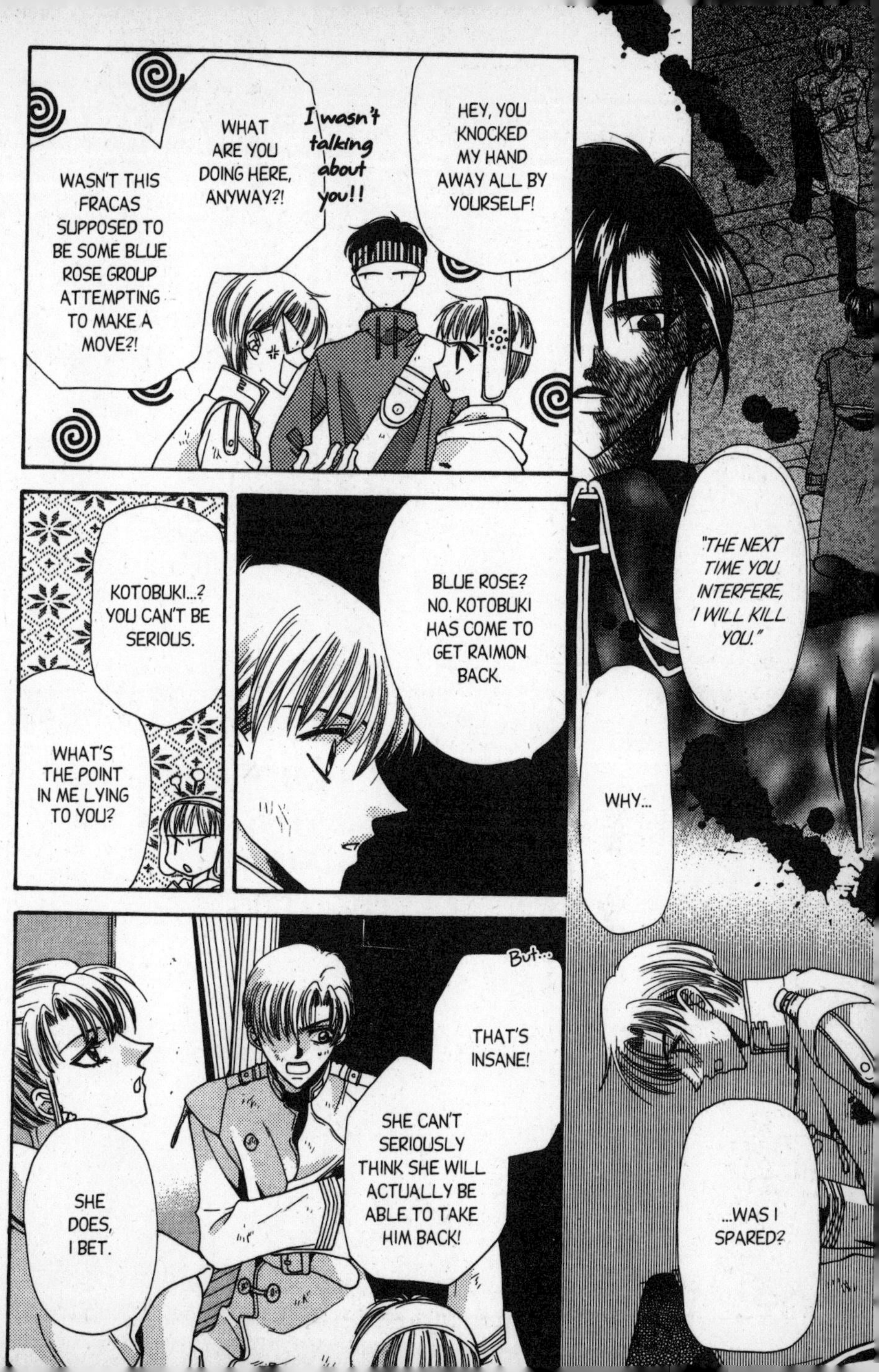
"THE NEXT TIME YOU INTERFERE, I WILL KILL YOU."
WHY...
...WAS I SPARED?
HEY, YOU KNOCKED MY HAND AWAY ALL BY YOURSELF!
I wasn't talking about you!!
WHAT ARE YOU DOING HERE, ANYWAY?!
WASN'T THIS FRACAS SUPPOSED TO BE SOME BLUE ROSE GROUP ATTEMPTING TO MAKE A MOVE?!
BLUE ROSE? NO. KOTOBUKI HAS COME TO GET RAIMON BACK.
KOTOBUKI...? YOU CAN'T BE SERIOUS.
WHAT'S THE POINT IN ME LYING TO YOU?
But...
THAT'S INSANE!
SHE CAN'T SERIOUSLY THINK SHE WILL ACTUALLY BE ABLE TO TAKE HIM BACK!
SHE DOES, I BET.

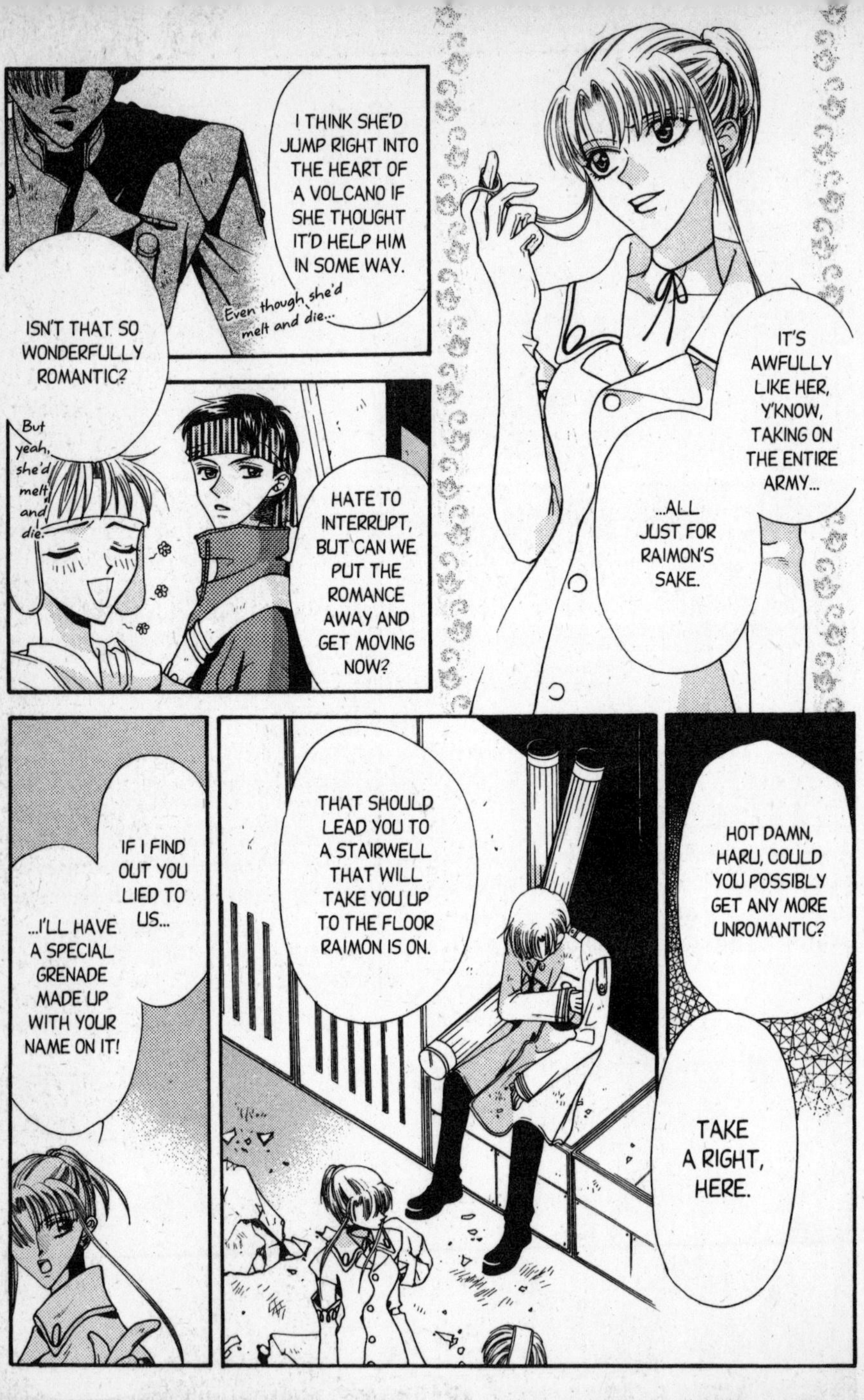
IT'S AWFULLY LIKE HER, Y'KNOW, TAKING ON THE ENTIRE ARMY...
...ALL JUST FOR RAIMON'S SAKE.
I THINK SHE'D JUMP RIGHT INTO THE HEART OF A VOLCANO IF SHE THOUGHT IT'D HELP HIM IN SOME WAY.
Even though she'd melt and die...
ISN'T THAT SO WONDERFULLY ROMANTIC?
But yeah, she'd melt and die.
HATE TO INTERRUPT, BUT CAN WE PUT THE ROMANCE AWAY AND GET MOVING NOW?
HOT DAMN, HARU, COULD YOU POSSIBLY GET ANY MORE UNROMANTIC?
TAKE A RIGHT, HERE.
THAT SHOULD LEAD YOU TO A STAIRWELL THAT WILL TAKE YOU UP TO THE FLOOR RAIMON IS ON.
IF I FIND OUT YOU LIED TO US...
...I'LL HAVE A SPECIAL GRENADE MADE UP WITH YOUR NAME ON IT!

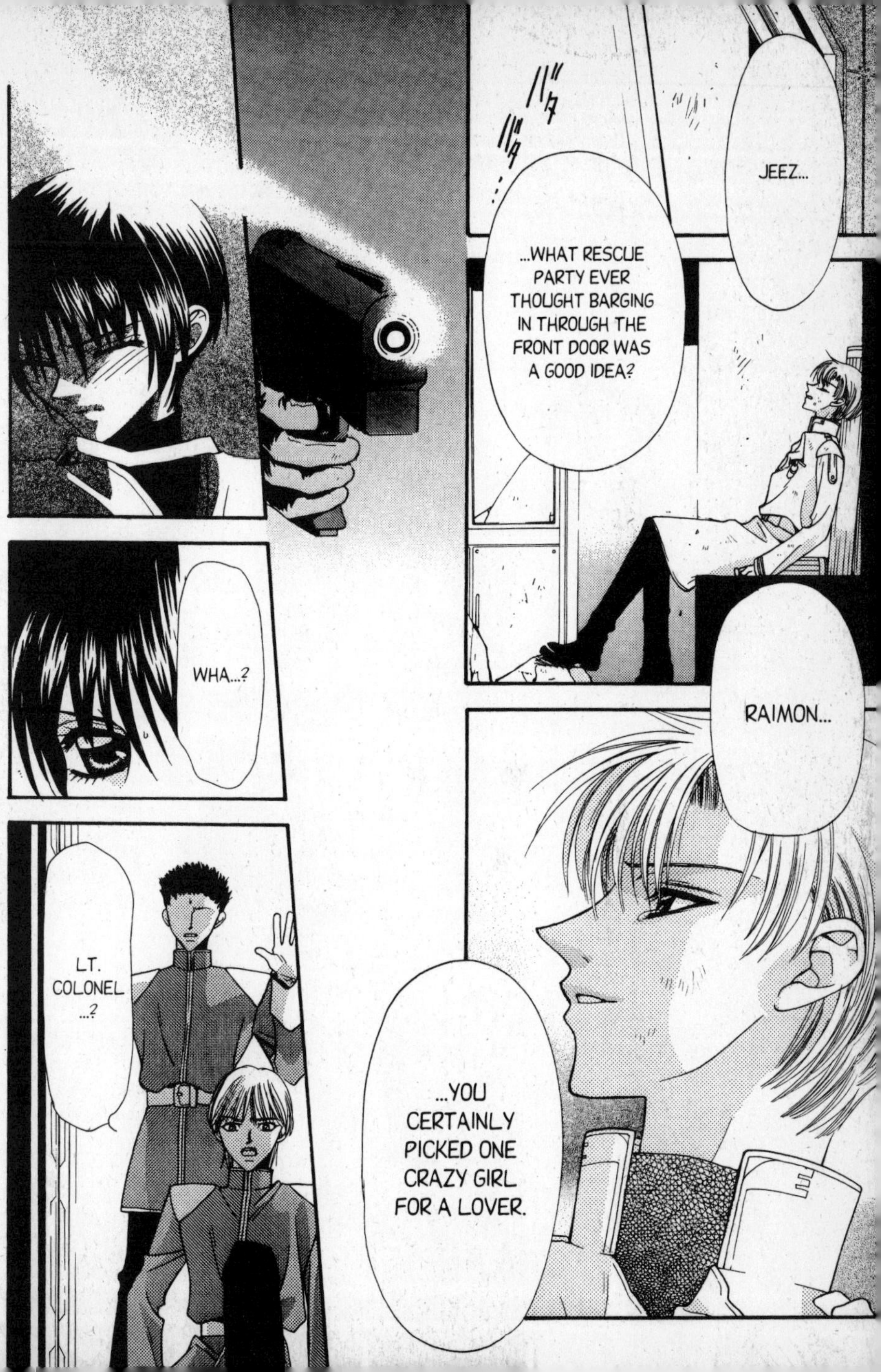
JEEZ...
...WHAT RESCUE PARTY EVER THOUGHT BARGING IN THROUGH THE FRONT DOOR WAS A GOOD IDEA?
WHA...?
LT. COLONEL ...?
RAIMON...
...YOU CERTAINLY PICKED ONE CRAZY GIRL FOR A LOVER.

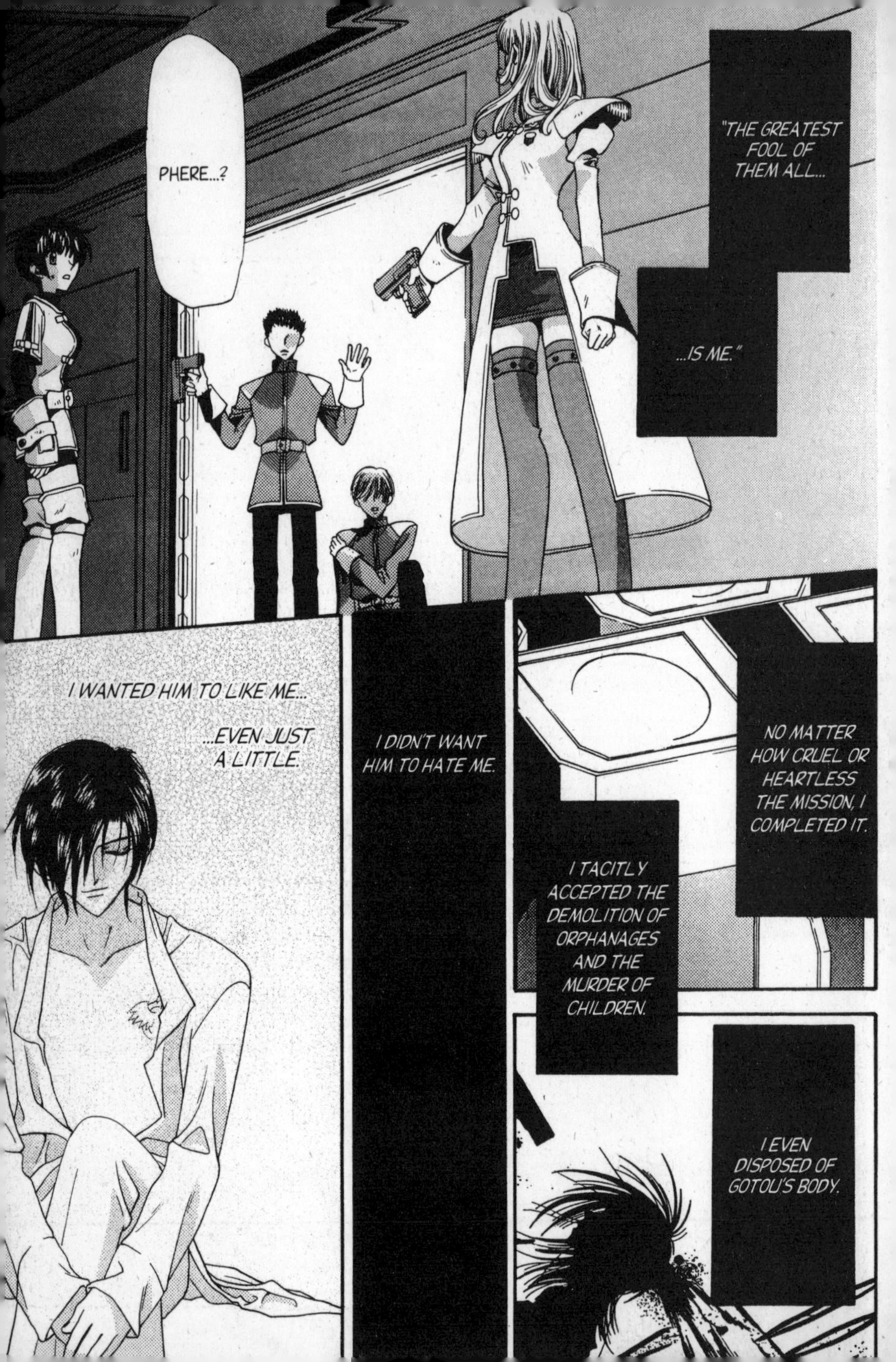
"THE GREATEST FOOL OF THEM ALL...
...IS ME."
PHERE...?
NO MATTER HOW CRUEL OR HEARTLESS THE MISSION, I COMPLETED IT.
I TACITLY ACCEPTED THE DEMOLITION OF ORPHANAGES AND THE MURDER OF CHILDREN.
I EVEN DISPOSED OF GOTOU'S BODY.
I DIDN'T WANT HIM TO HATE ME.
I WANTED HIM TO LIKE ME...
...EVEN JUST A LITTLE.

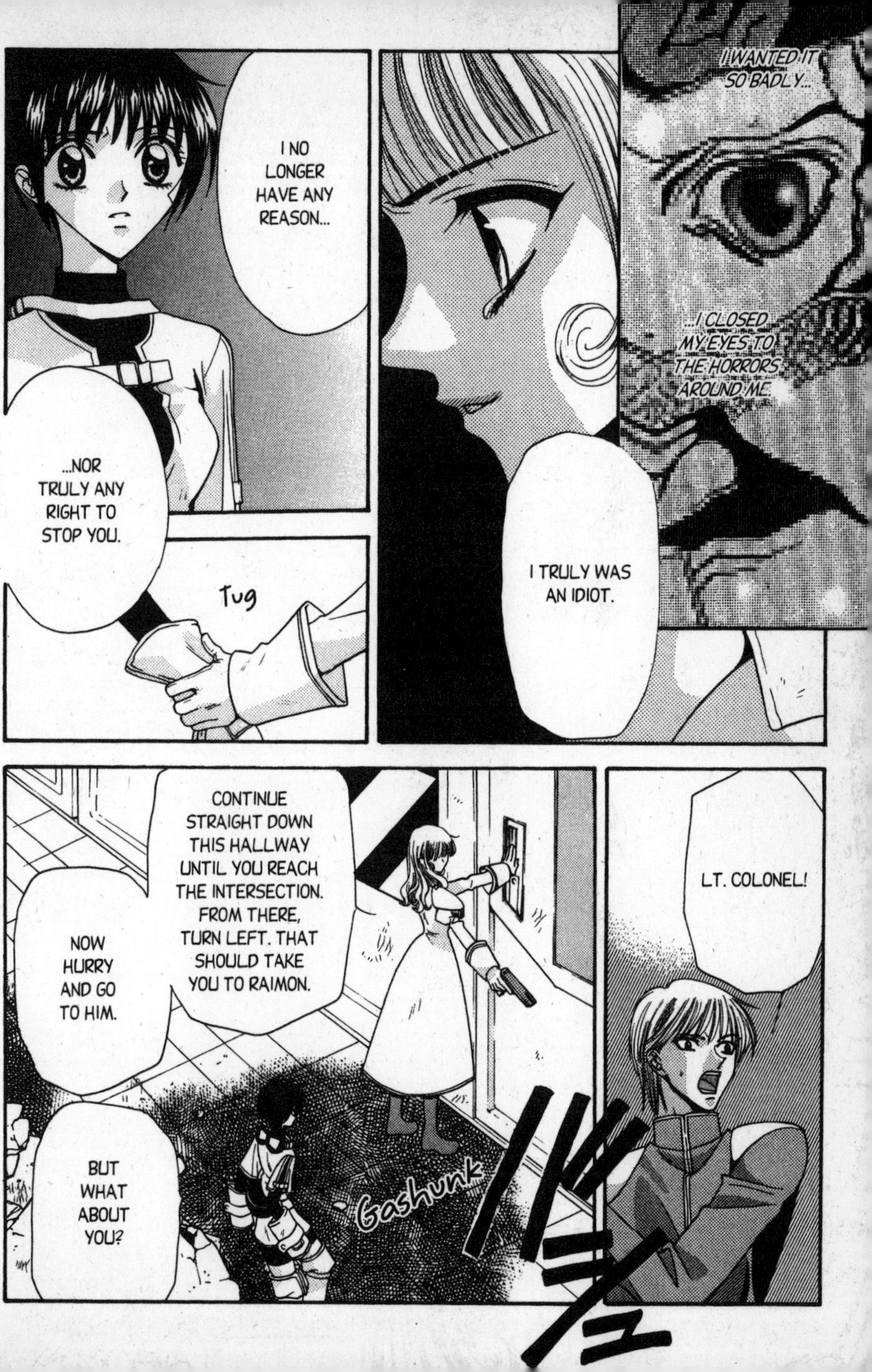

I WANTED IT SO BADLY...
...I CLOSED MY EYES TO THE HORRORS AROUND ME.
I TRULY WAS AN IDIOT.
I NO LONGER HAVE ANY REASON...
...NOR TRULY ANY RIGHT TO STOP YOU.
Tug
LT. COLONEL!
CONTINUE STRAIGHT DOWN THIS HALLWAY UNTIL YOU REACH THE INTERSECTION. FROM THERE, TURN LEFT. THAT SHOULD TAKE YOU TO RAIMON.
NOW HURRY AND GO TO HIM.
BUT WHAT ABOUT YOU?
Gashunk

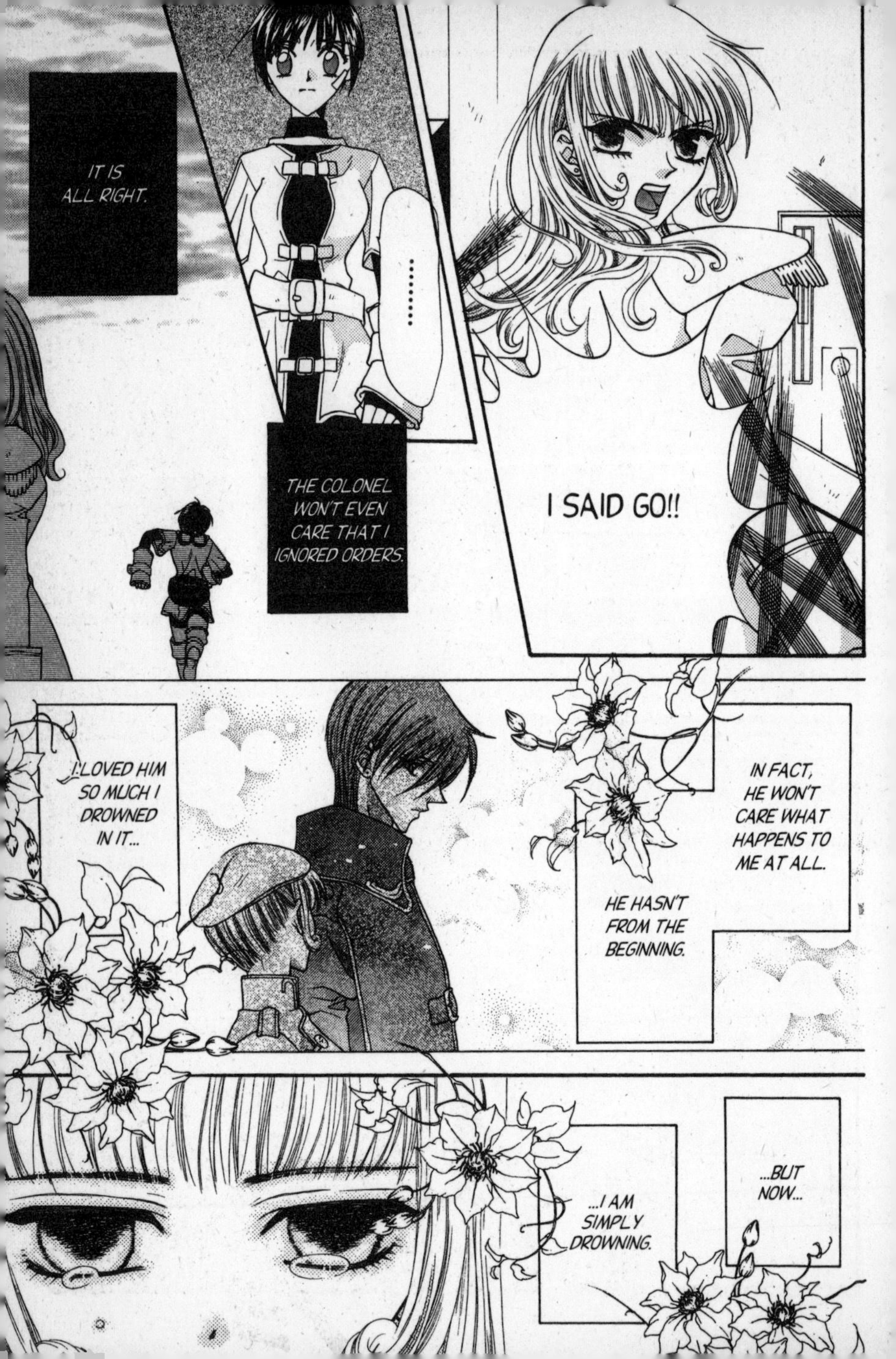
I SAID GO!!
......
IT IS ALL RIGHT.
THE COLONEL WON'T EVEN CARE THAT I IGNORED ORDERS.
IN FACT, HE WON'T CARE WHAT HAPPENS TO ME AT ALL.
HE HASN'T FROM THE BEGINNING.
I LOVED HIM SO MUCH I DROWNED IN IT...
...BUT NOW...
...I AM SIMPLY DROWNING.

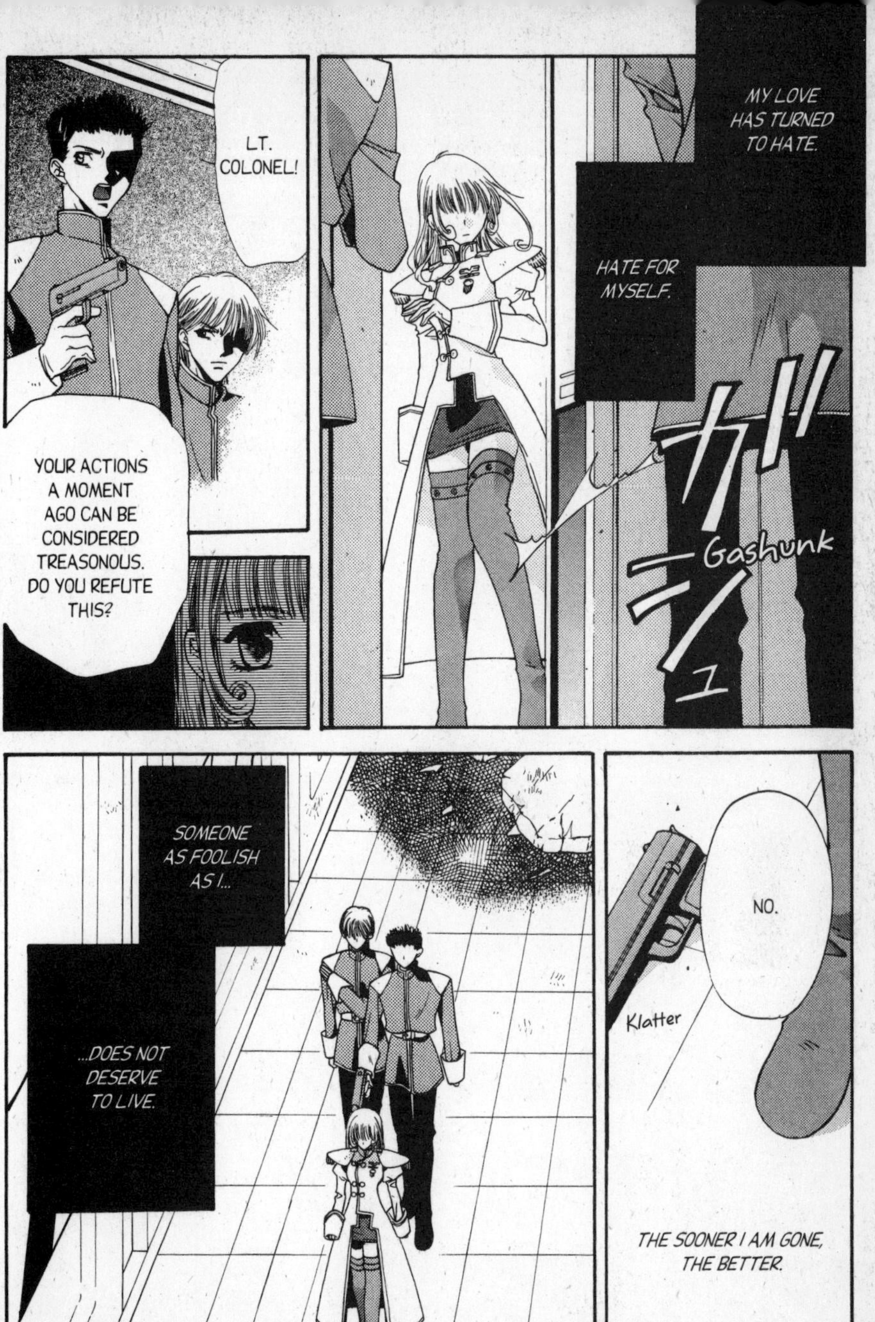

MY LOVE HAS TURNED TO HATE.
HATE FOR MYSELF.
Gashunk
LT. COLONEL!
YOUR ACTIONS A MOMENT AGO CAN BE CONSIDERED TREASONOUS. DO YOU REFUTE THIS?
NO.
Klatter
THE SOONER I AM GONE, THE BETTER.
SOMEONE AS FOOLISH AS I...
...DOES NOT DESERVE TO LIVE.

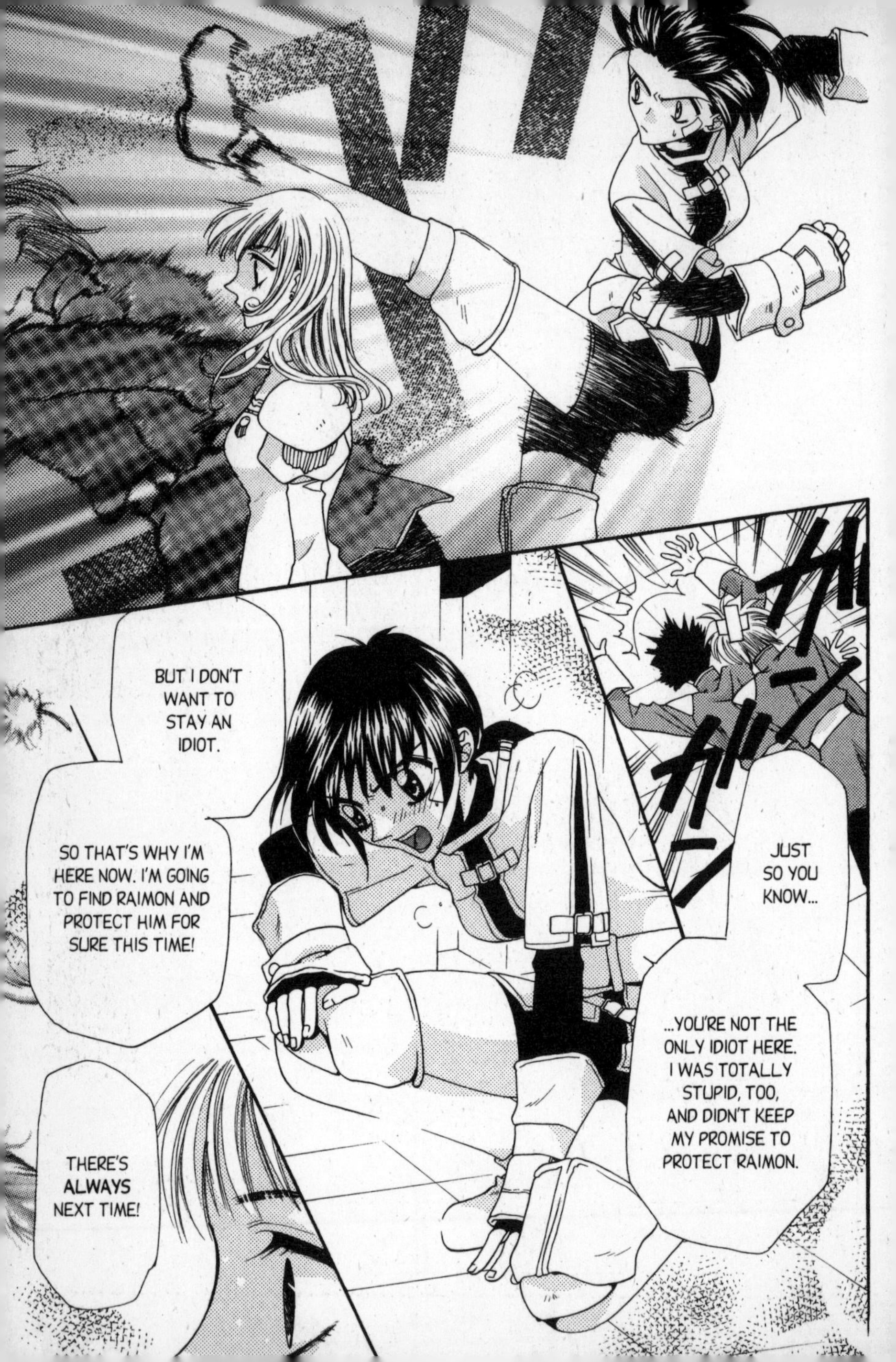

JUST SO YOU KNOW...
...YOU'RE NOT THE ONLY IDIOT HERE. I WAS TOTALLY STUPID, TOO, AND DIDN'T KEEP MY PROMISE TO PROTECT RAIMON.
BUT I DON'T WANT TO STAY AN IDIOT.
SO THAT'S WHY I'M HERE NOW. I'M GOING TO FIND RAIMON AND PROTECT HIM FOR SURE THIS TIME!
THERE'S **ALWAYS** NEXT TIME!

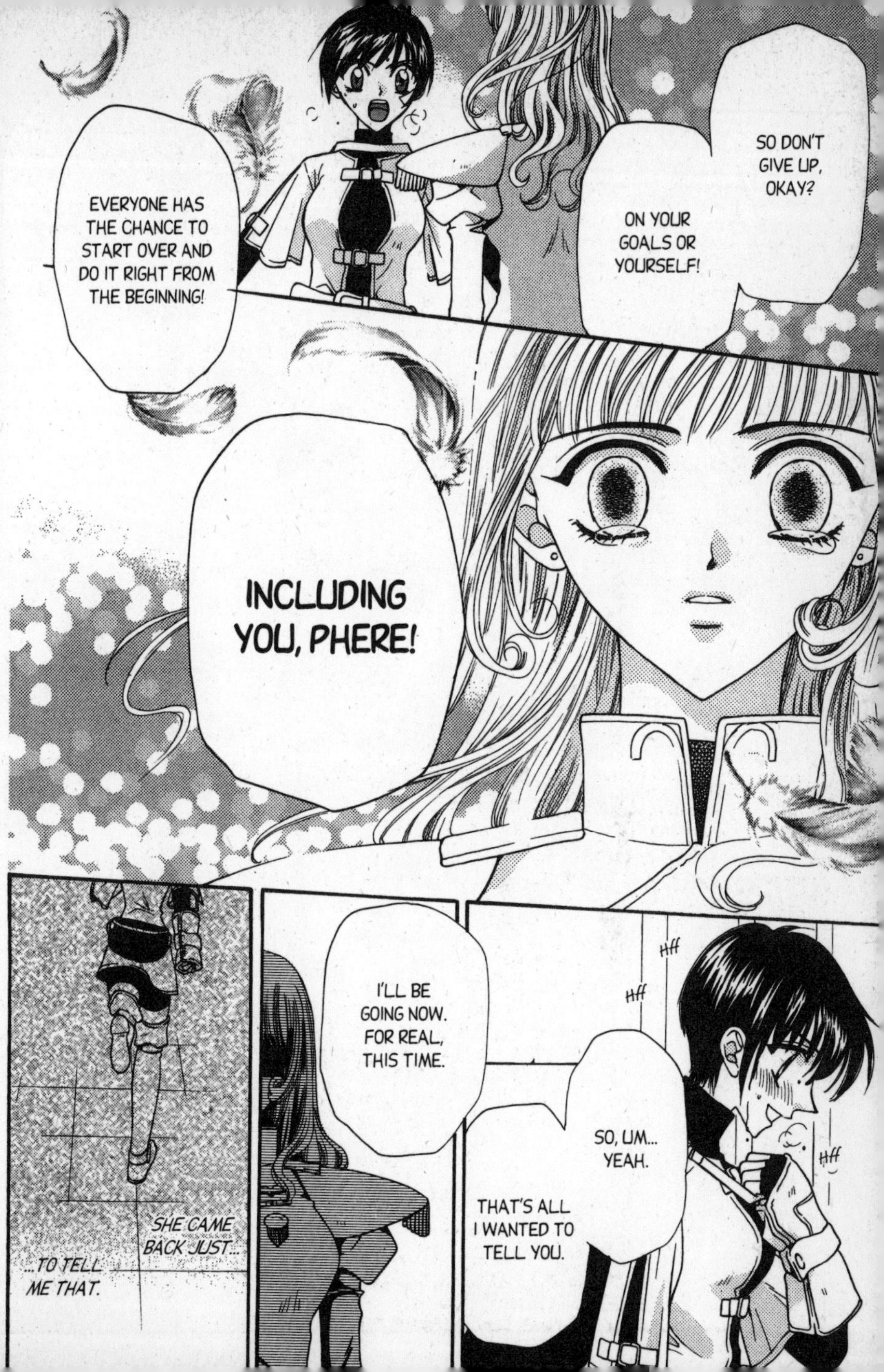
SO DON'T GIVE UP, OKAY?
ON YOUR GOALS OR YOURSELF!
EVERYONE HAS THE CHANCE TO START OVER AND DO IT RIGHT FROM THE BEGINNING!
INCLUDING YOU, PHERE!
HFF
HFF
HFF
SO, UM... YEAH.
THAT'S ALL I WANTED TO TELL YOU.
I'LL BE GOING NOW. FOR REAL, THIS TIME.
SHE CAME BACK JUST...
...TO TELL ME THAT.

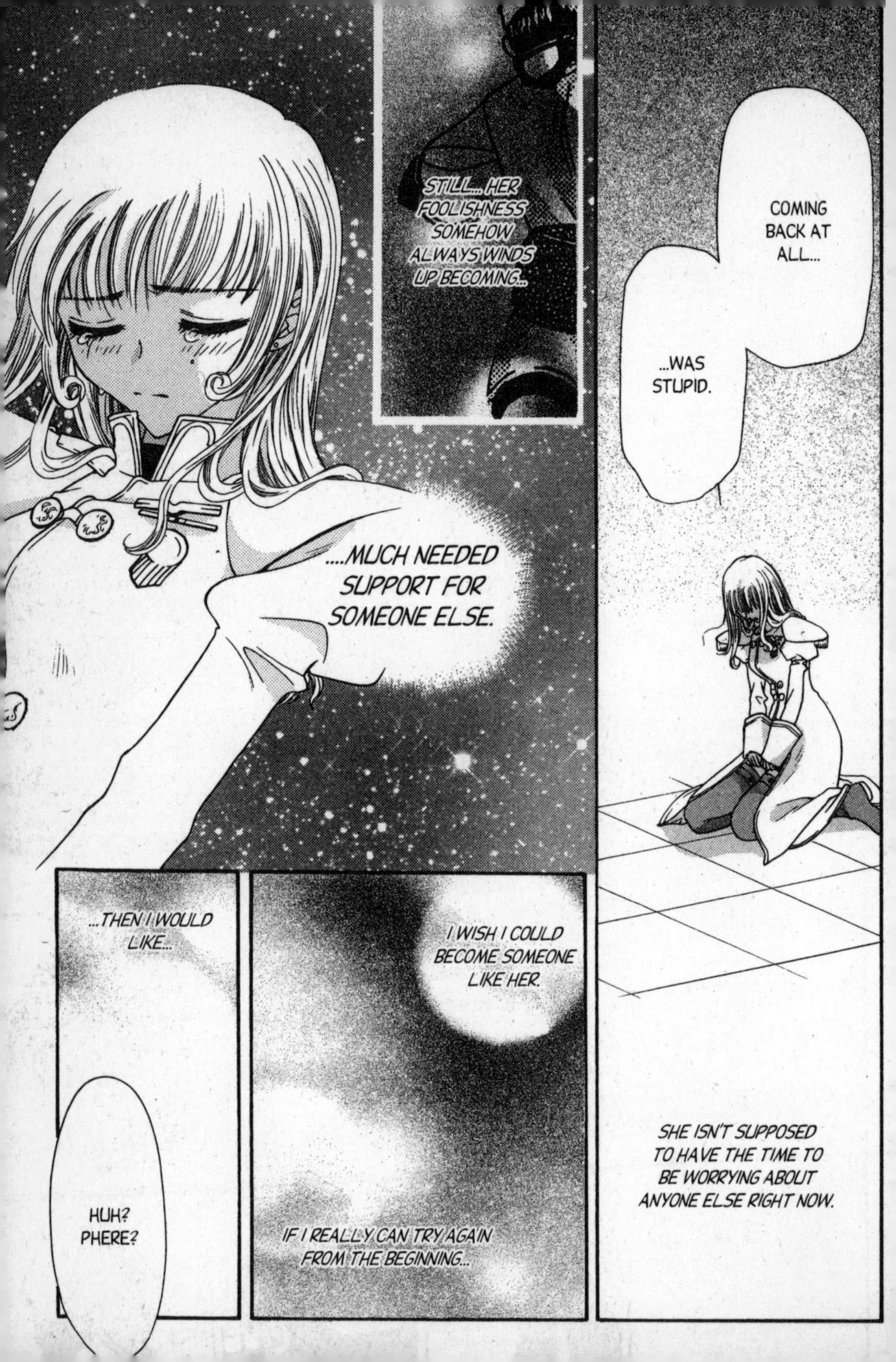
COMING BACK AT ALL...
...WAS STUPID.
SHE ISN'T SUPPOSED TO HAVE THE TIME TO BE WORRYING ABOUT ANYONE ELSE RIGHT NOW.
STILL... HER FOOLISHNESS SOMEHOW ALWAYS WINDS UP BECOMING...
....MUCH NEEDED SUPPORT FOR SOMEONE ELSE.
I WISH I COULD BECOME SOMEONE LIKE HER.
IF I REALLY CAN TRY AGAIN FROM THE BEGINNING...
...THEN I WOULD LIKE...
HUH? PHERE?

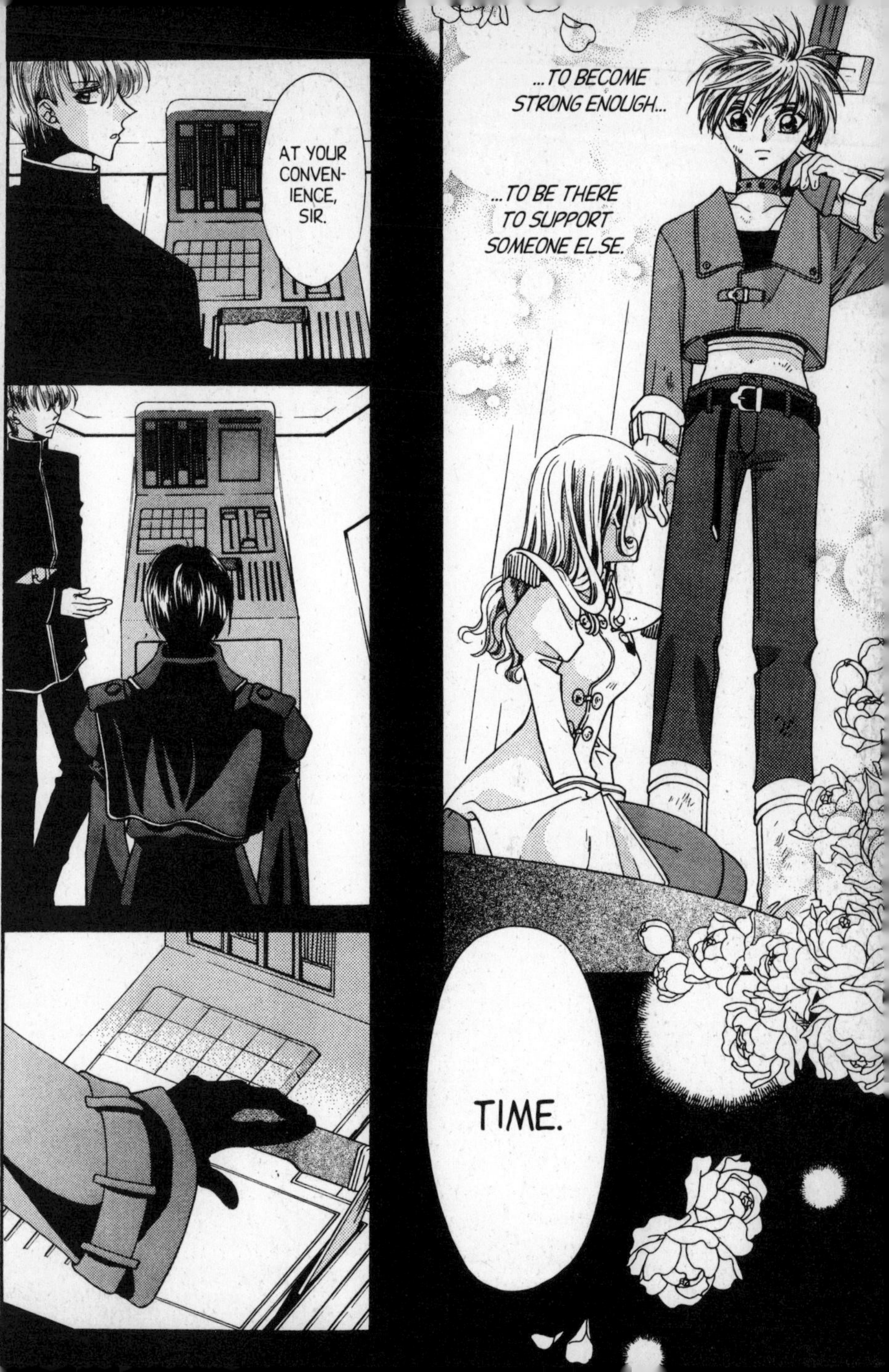
...TO BECOME STRONG ENOUGH...
...TO BE THERE TO SUPPORT SOMEONE ELSE.
TIME.
AT YOUR CONVEN-IENCE, SIR.

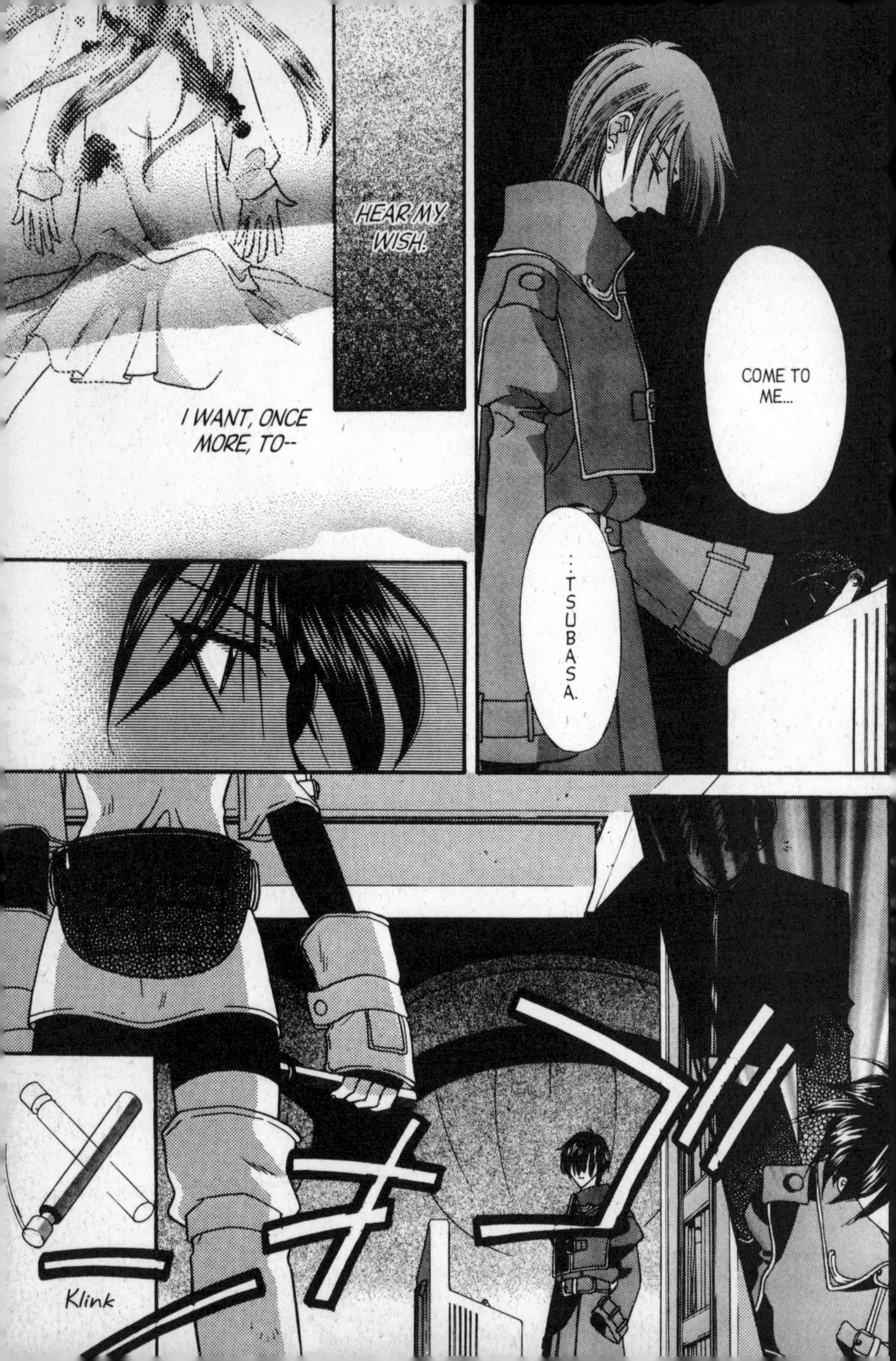
COME TO ME...
...TSUBASA.
HEAR MY WISH.
I WANT, ONCE MORE, TO--
Klink

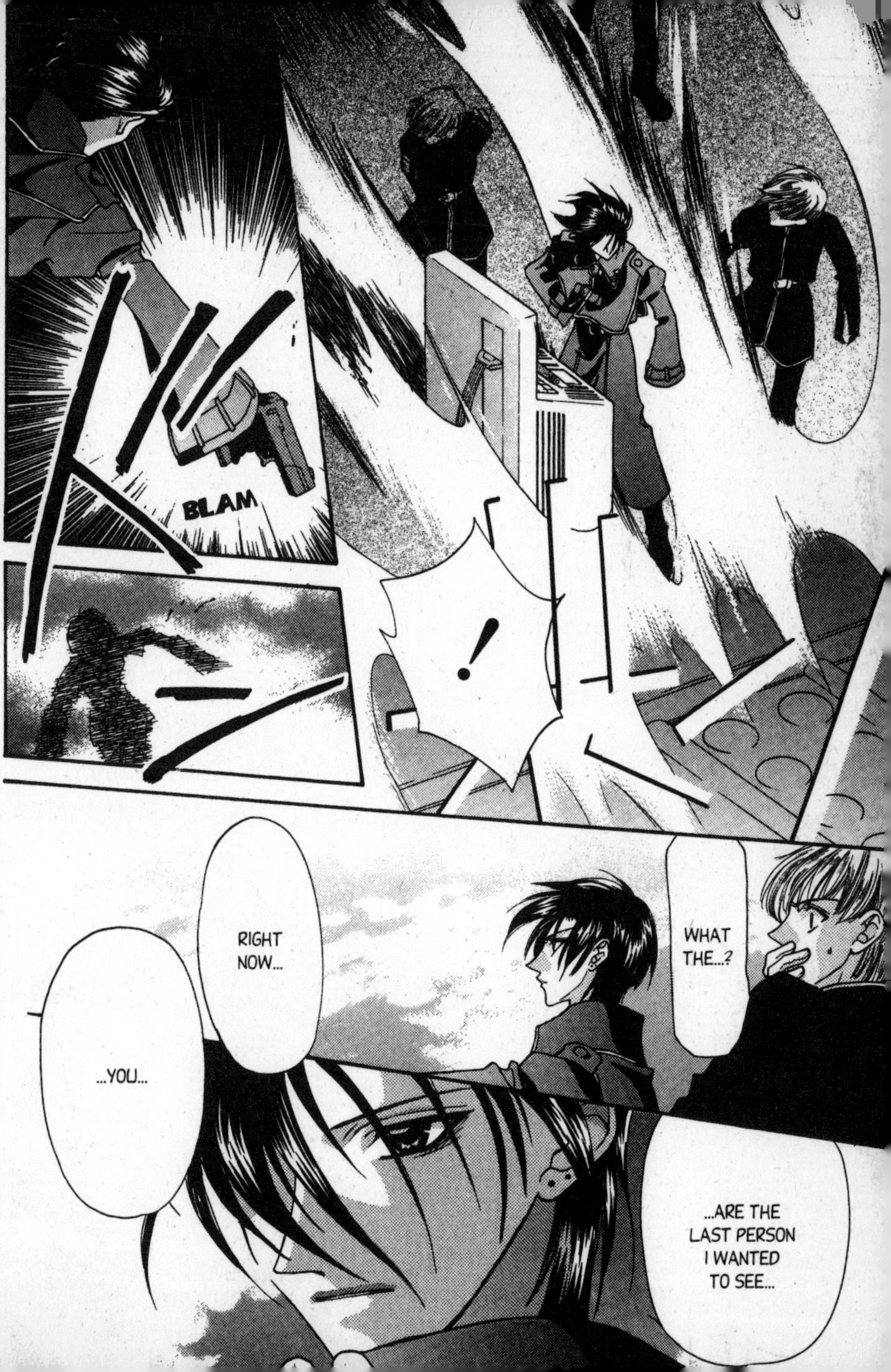
!
BLAM
WHAT THE...?
RIGHT NOW...
...YOU...
...ARE THE LAST PERSON I WANTED TO SEE...

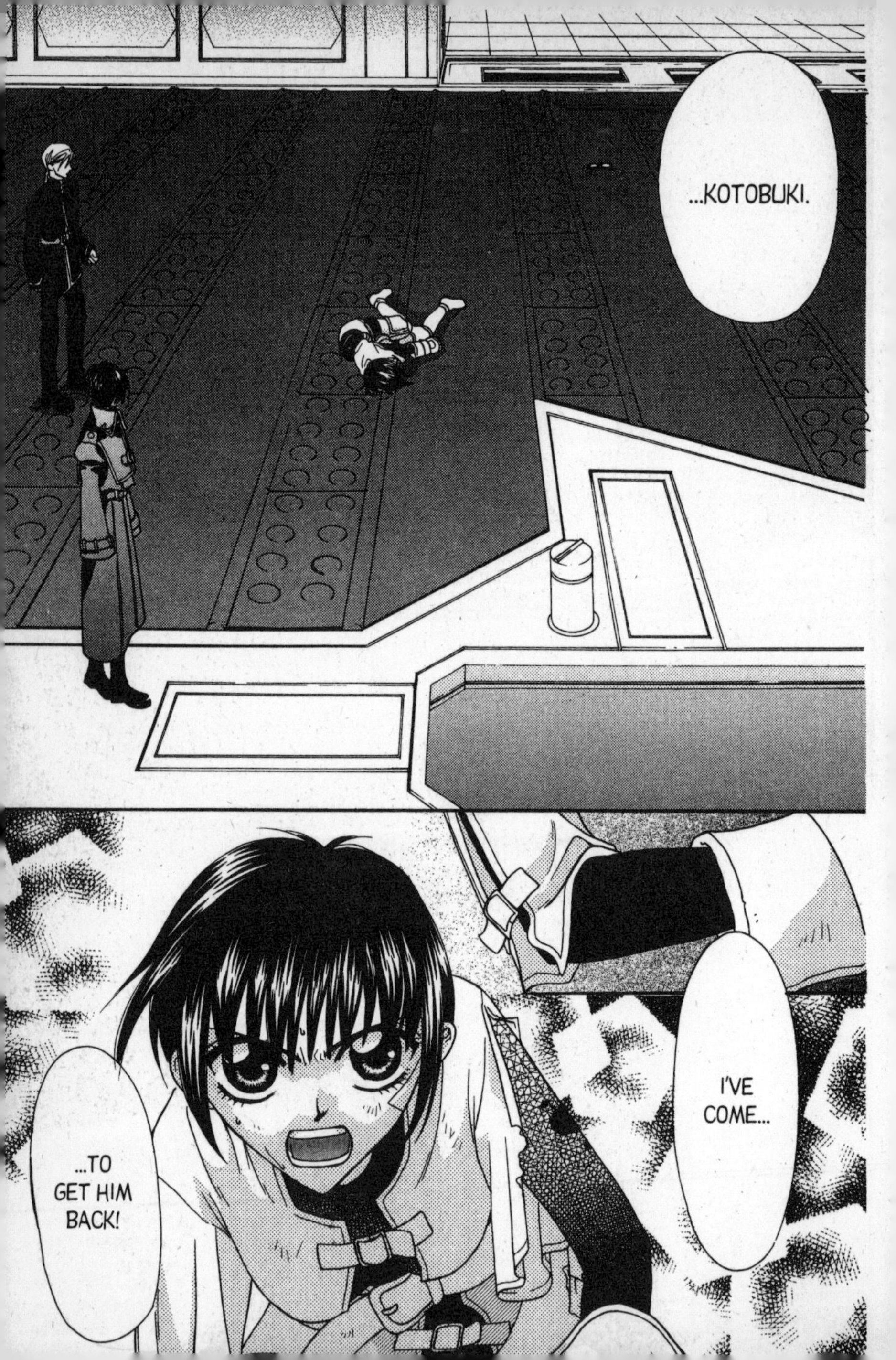
...KOTOBUKI.
I'VE COME...
...TO GET HIM BACK!

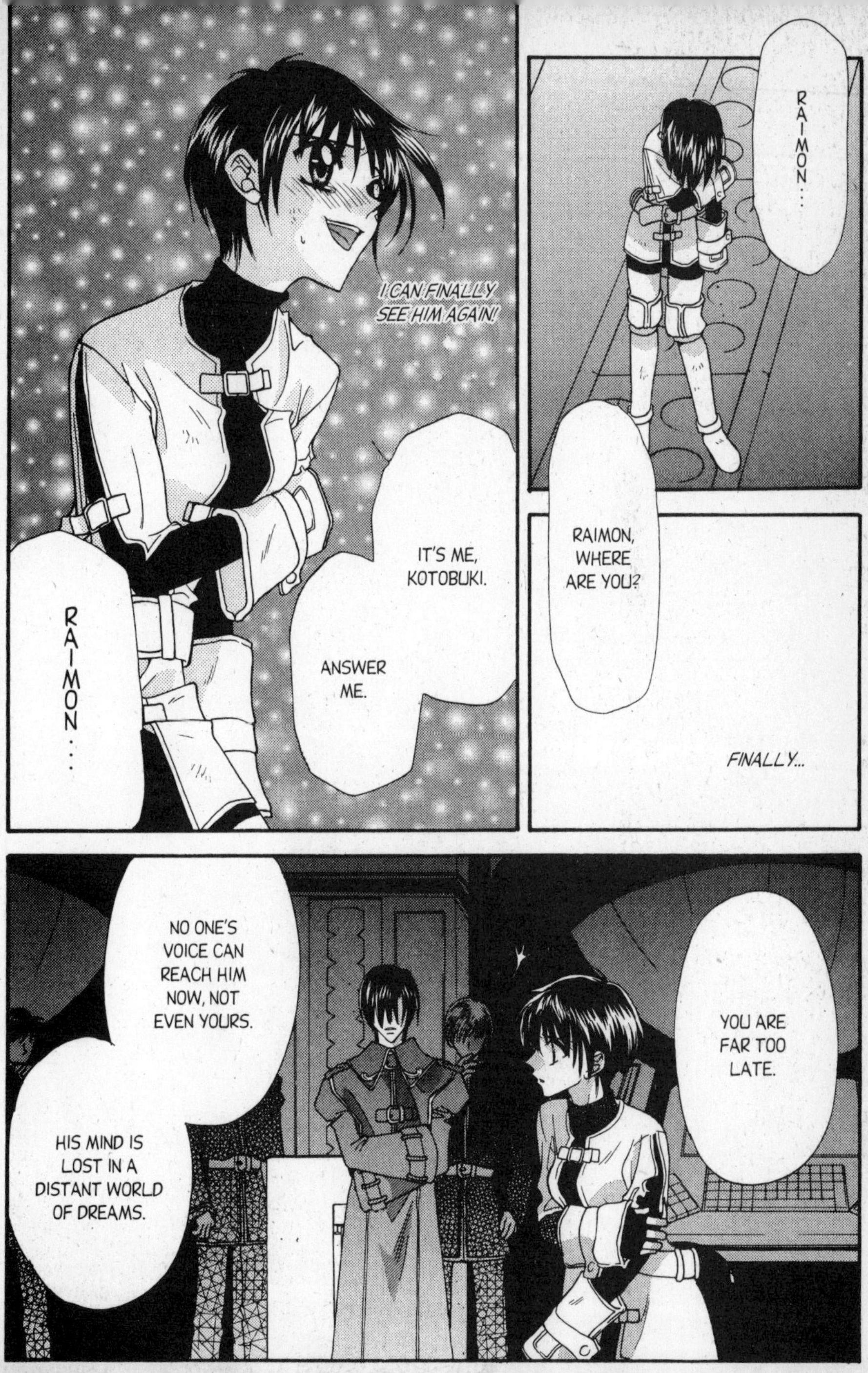
RAIMON...
RAIMON, WHERE ARE YOU?
FINALLY...
I CAN FINALLY SEE HIM AGAIN!
IT'S ME, KOTOBUKI.
ANSWER ME.
RAIMON...
YOU ARE FAR TOO LATE.
NO ONE'S VOICE CAN REACH HIM NOW, NOT EVEN YOURS.
HIS MIND IS LOST IN A DISTANT WORLD OF DREAMS.

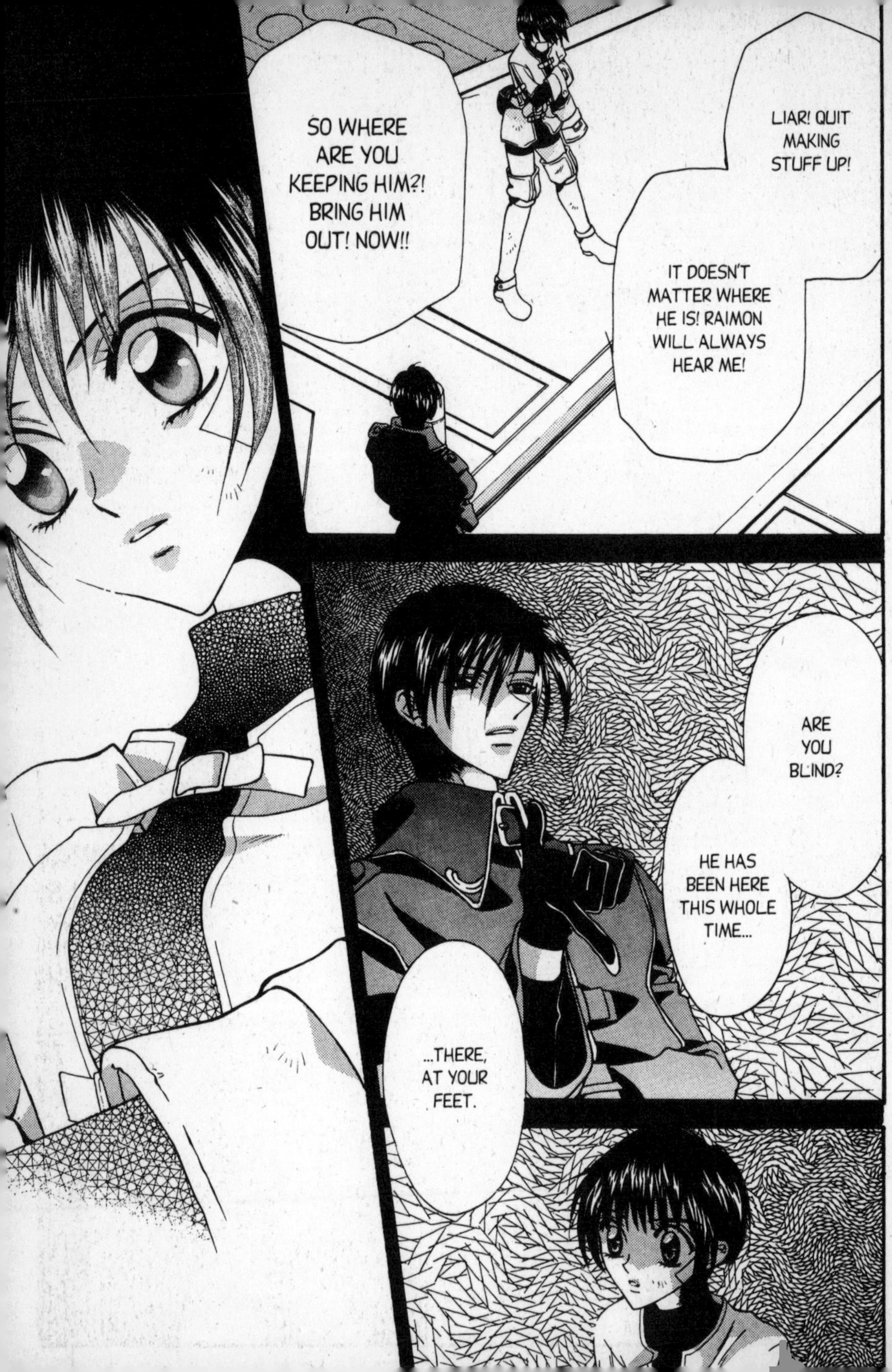
LIAR! QUIT MAKING STUFF UP!
IT DOESN'T MATTER WHERE HE IS! RAIMON WILL ALWAYS HEAR ME!
SO WHERE ARE YOU KEEPING HIM?! BRING HIM OUT! NOW!!
ARE YOU BLIND?
HE HAS BEEN HERE THIS WHOLE TIME...
...THERE, AT YOUR FEET.

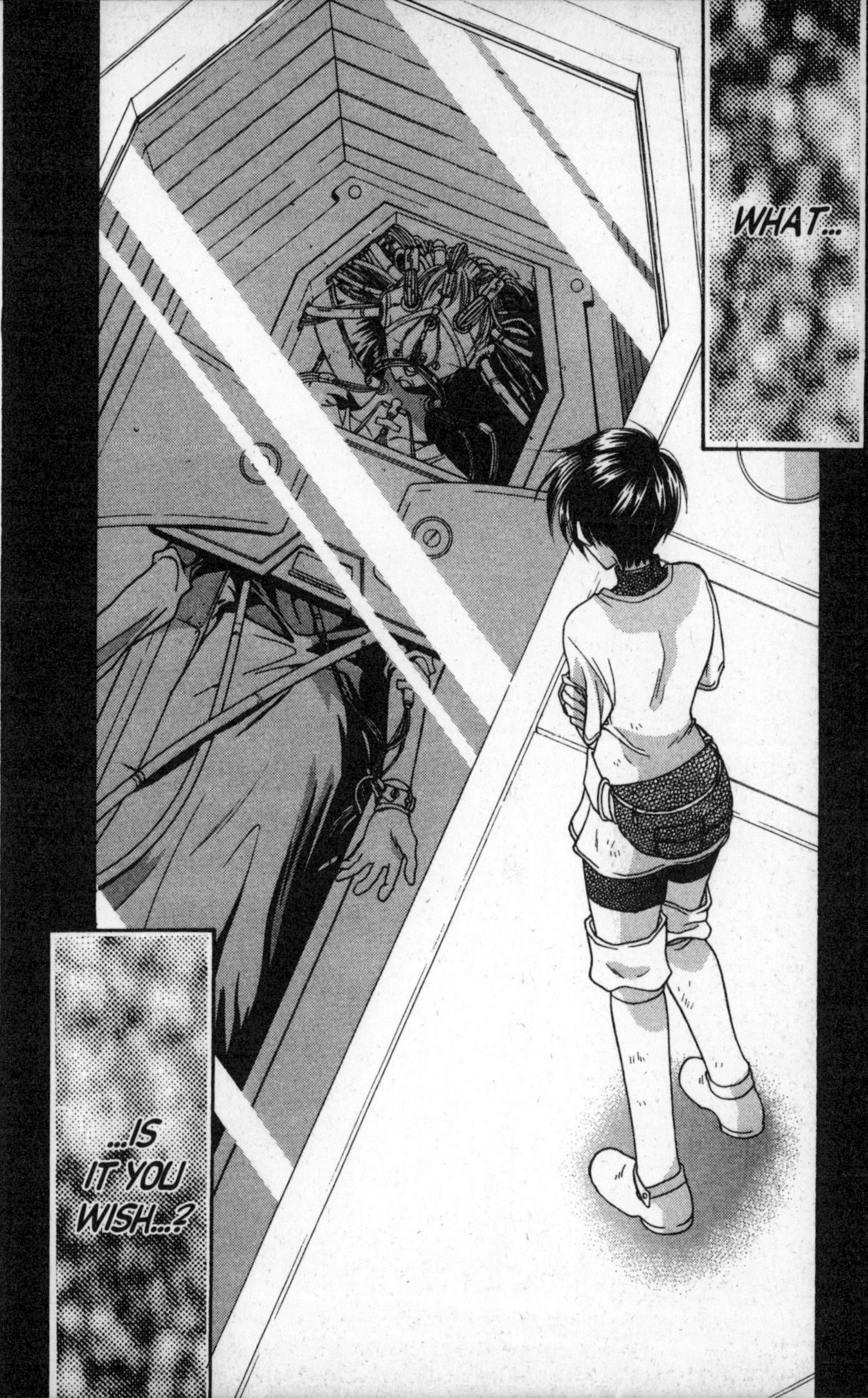
WHAT...
...IS IT YOU WISH...?

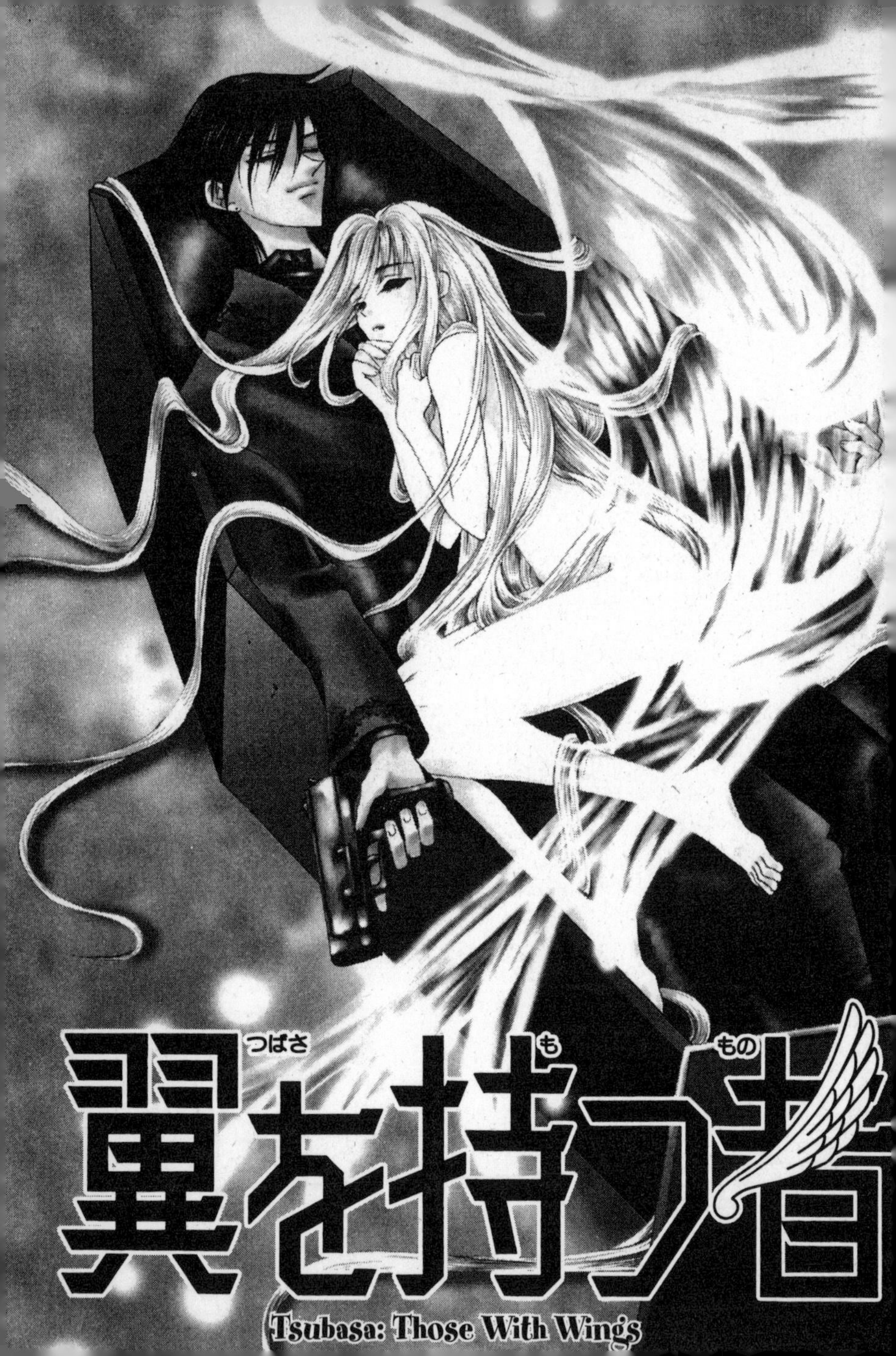
翼(つばさ)を持(も)つ者(もの)
Tsubasa: Those With Wings

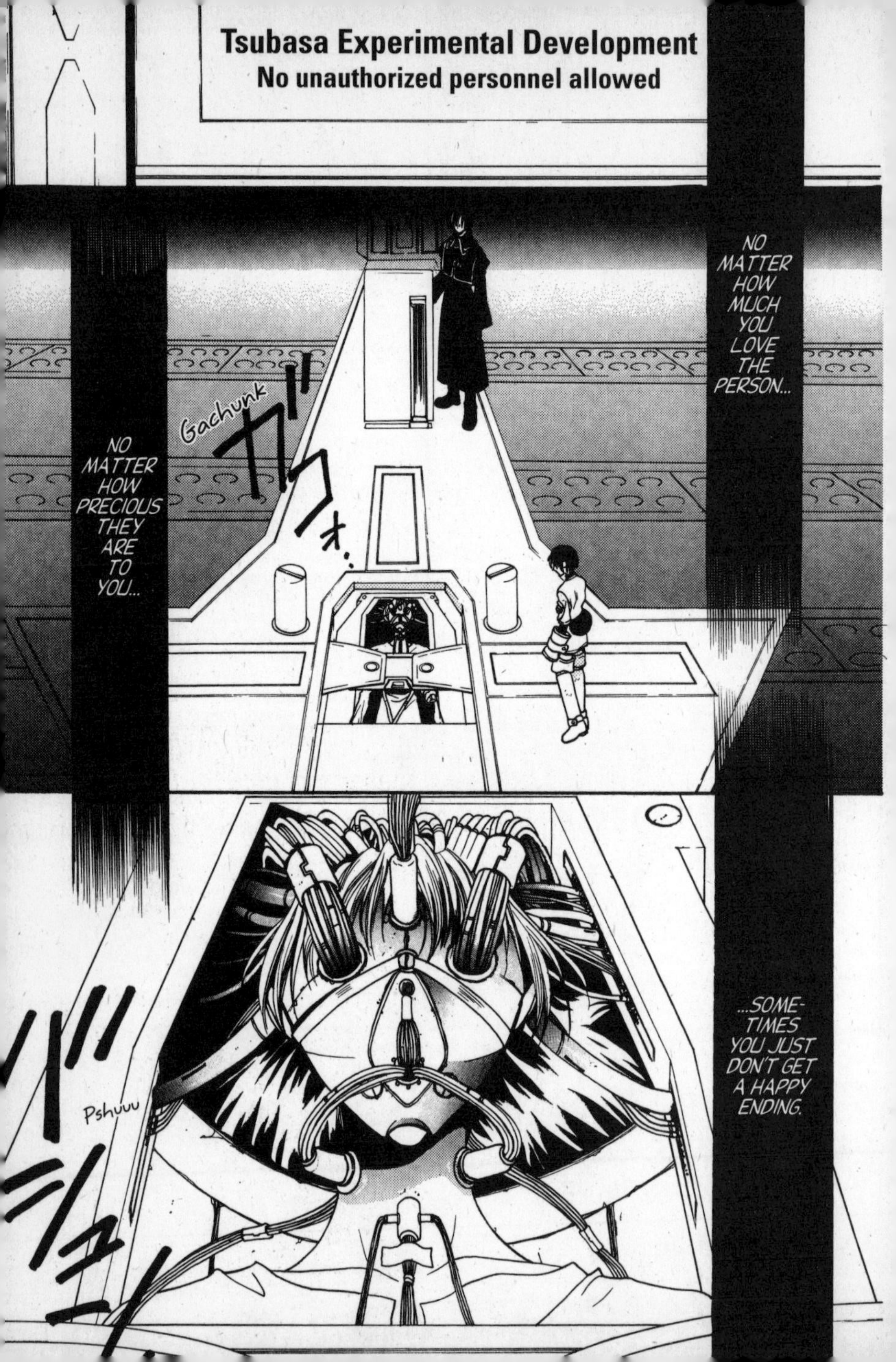
Tsubasa Experimental Development
No unauthorized personnel allowed
NO MATTER HOW MUCH YOU LOVE THE PERSON...
NO MATTER HOW PRECIOUS THEY ARE TO YOU...
Gachunk
...SOME-TIMES YOU JUST DON'T GET A HAPPY ENDING.
Pshuuu

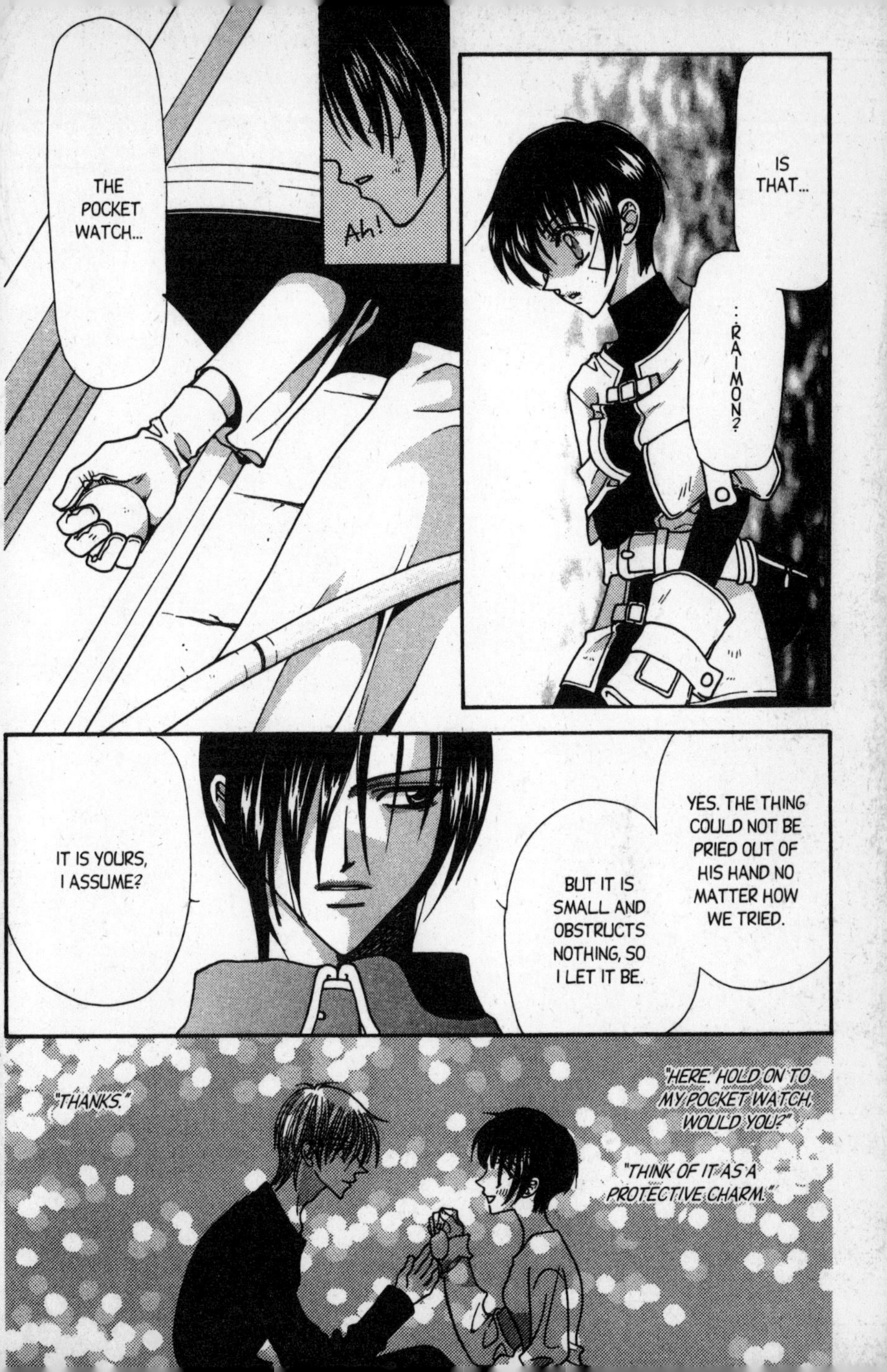
IS THAT...
...RAIMON?
Ah!
THE POCKET WATCH...
YES. THE THING COULD NOT BE PRIED OUT OF HIS HAND NO MATTER HOW WE TRIED.
BUT IT IS SMALL AND OBSTRUCTS NOTHING, SO I LET IT BE.
IT IS YOURS, I ASSUME?
"HERE. HOLD ON TO MY POCKET WATCH, WOULD YOU?"
"THINK OF IT AS A PROTECTIVE CHARM."
"THANKS."

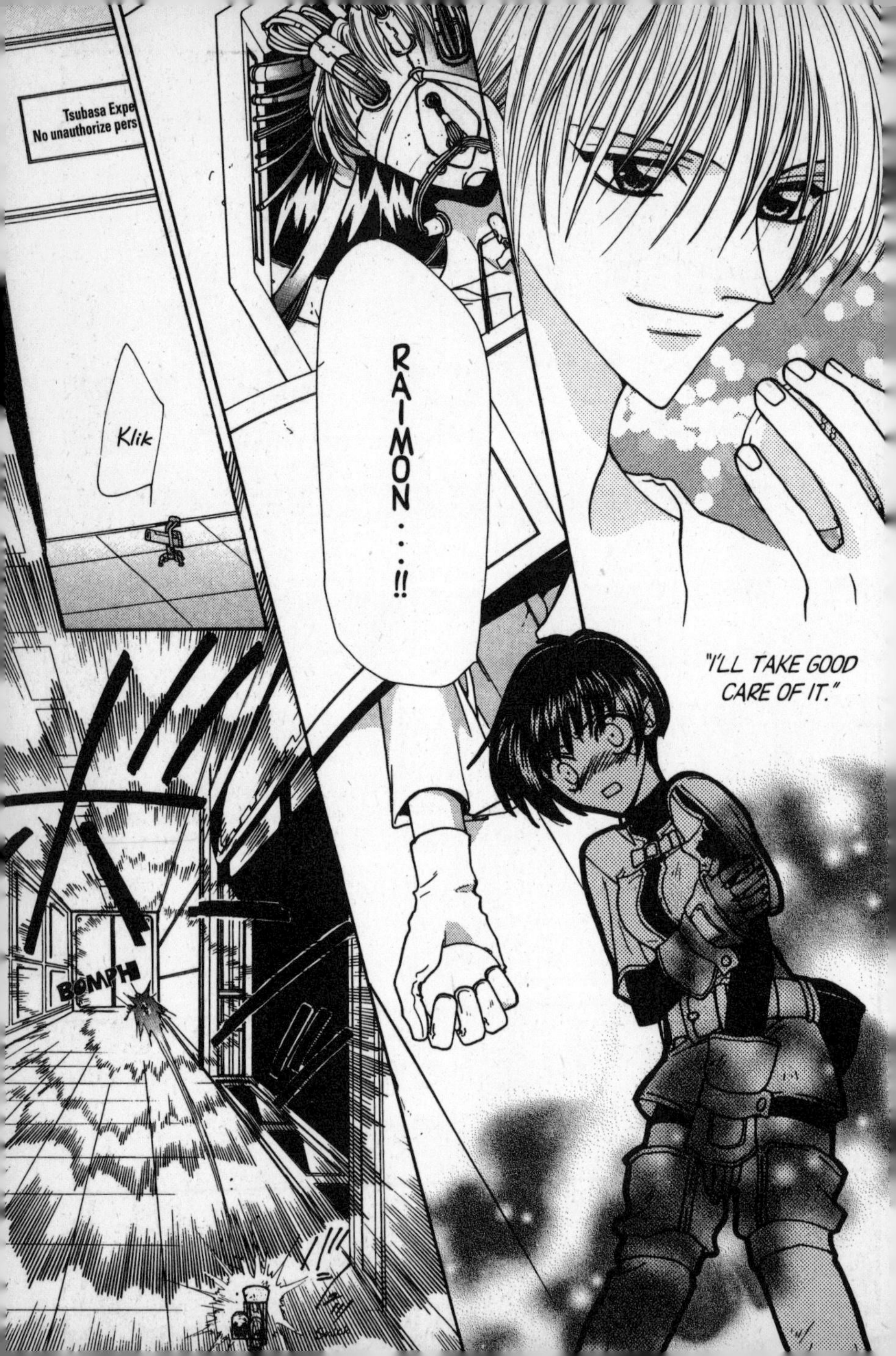
RAIMON...!!
"I'LL TAKE GOOD CARE OF IT."
Tsubasa Expe
No unauthorize pers
Klik
BOMPH

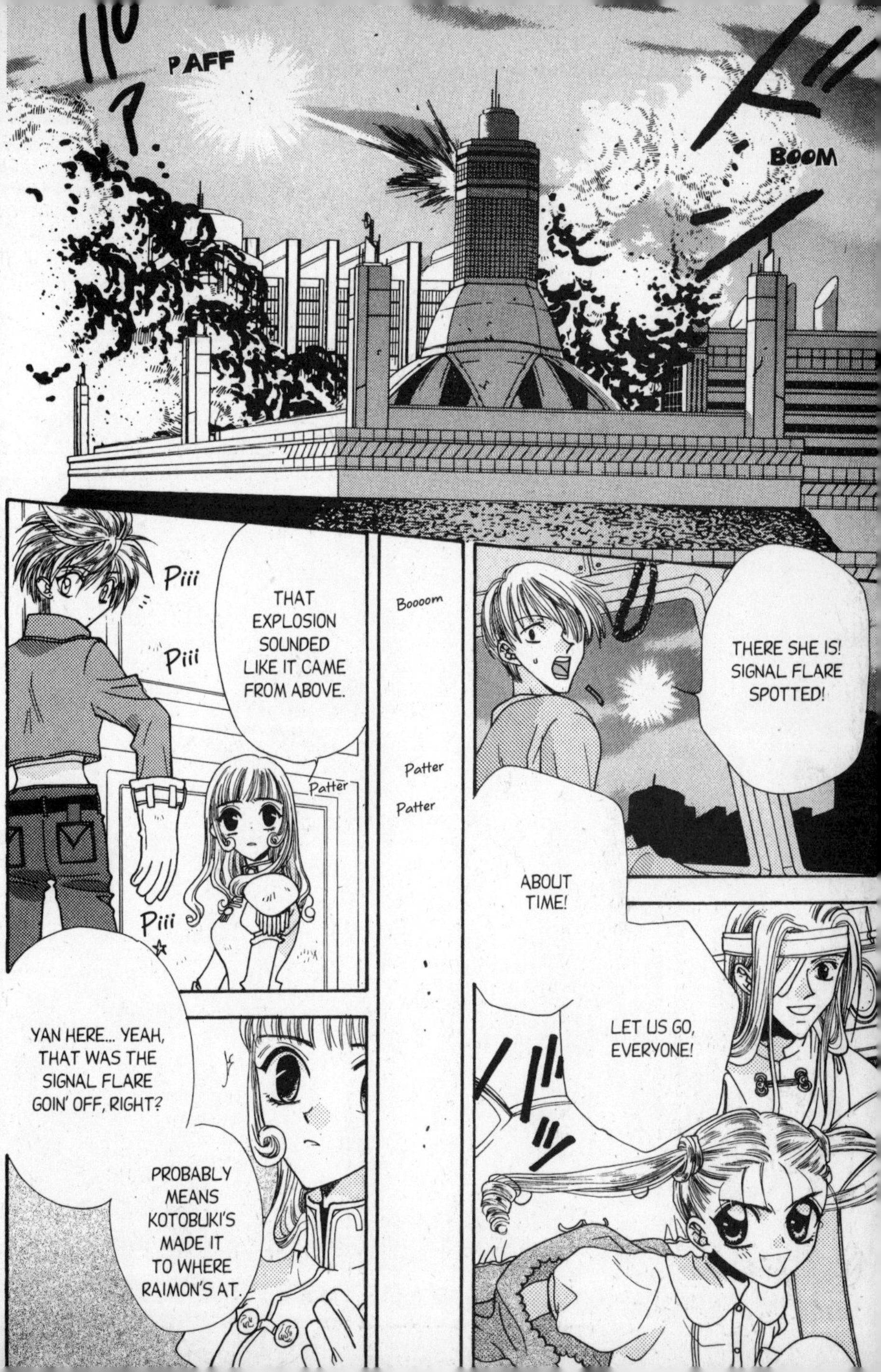

BOOM
PAFF
THERE SHE IS! SIGNAL FLARE SPOTTED!
ABOUT TIME!
LET US GO, EVERYONE!
Boooom
Patter
Patter
Piii
Piii
THAT EXPLOSION SOUNDED LIKE IT CAME FROM ABOVE.
Patter
Piii
YAN HERE... YEAH, THAT WAS THE SIGNAL FLARE GOIN' OFF, RIGHT?
PROBABLY MEANS KOTOBUKI'S MADE IT TO WHERE RAIMON'S AT.

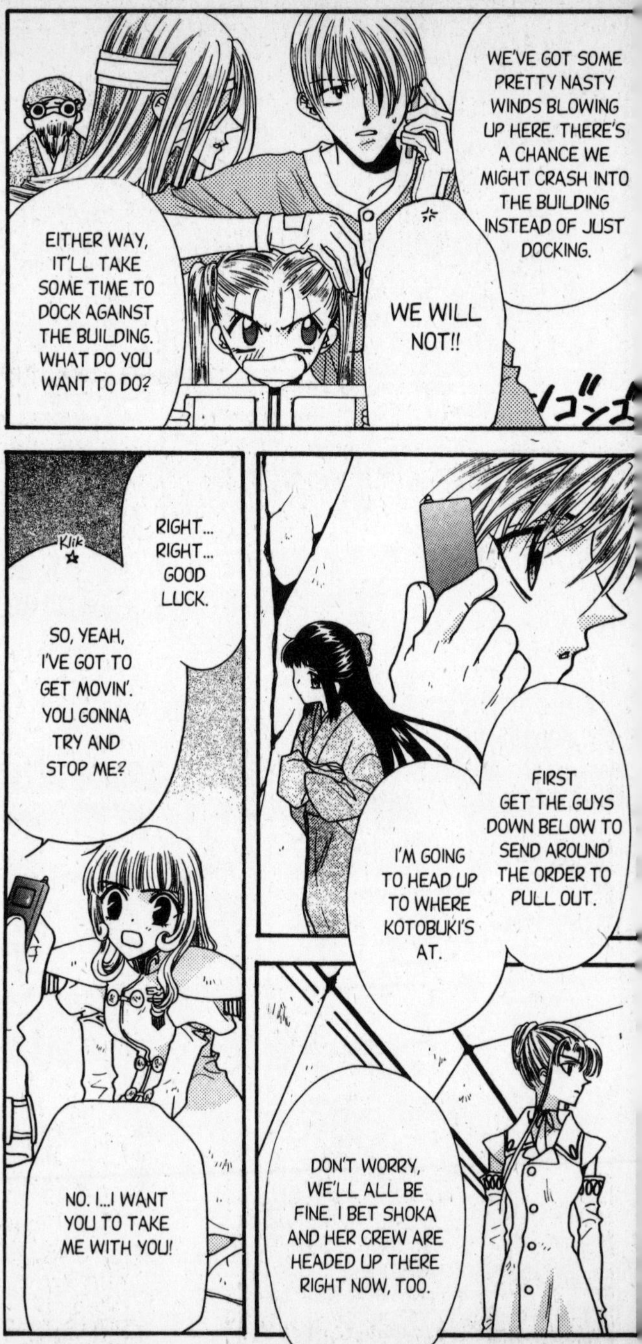
WE'VE GOT SOME PRETTY NASTY WINDS BLOWING UP HERE. THERE'S A CHANCE WE MIGHT CRASH INTO THE BUILDING INSTEAD OF JUST DOCKING.
WE WILL NOT!!
EITHER WAY, IT'LL TAKE SOME TIME TO DOCK AGAINST THE BUILDING. WHAT DO YOU WANT TO DO?
FIRST GET THE GUYS DOWN BELOW TO SEND AROUND THE ORDER TO PULL OUT.
I'M GOING TO HEAD UP TO WHERE KOTOBUKI'S AT.
DON'T WORRY, WE'LL ALL BE FINE. I BET SHOKA AND HER CREW ARE HEADED UP THERE RIGHT NOW, TOO.
RIGHT... RIGHT... GOOD LUCK.
Klik
SO, YEAH, I'VE GOT TO GET MOVIN'. YOU GONNA TRY AND STOP ME?
NO. I...I WANT YOU TO TAKE ME WITH YOU!
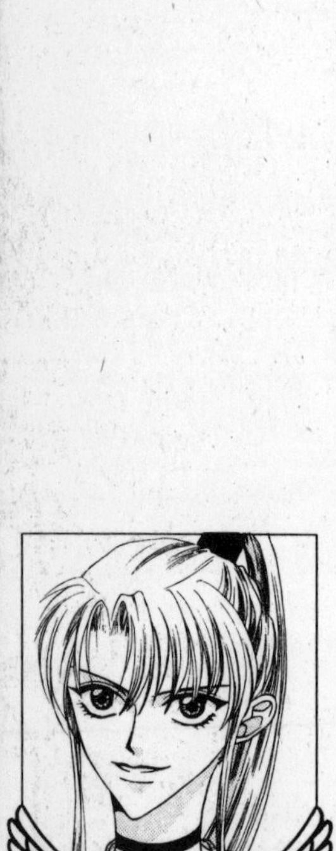

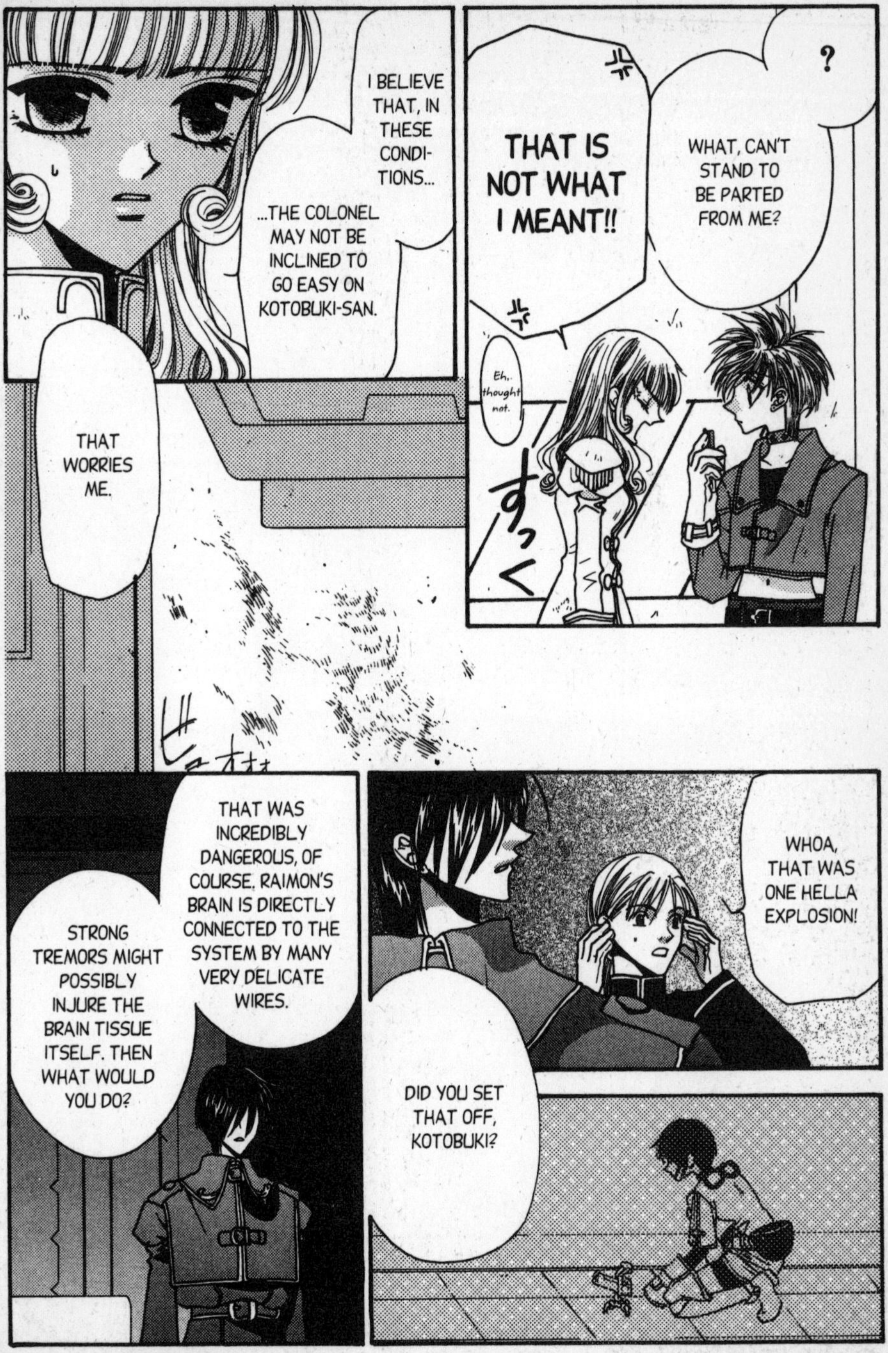
?
WHAT, CAN'T STAND TO BE PARTED FROM ME?
THAT IS NOT WHAT I MEANT!!
Eh, thought not.
すっく
I BELIEVE THAT, IN THESE CONDITIONS...
...THE COLONEL MAY NOT BE INCLINED TO GO EASY ON KOTOBUKI-SAN.
THAT WORRIES ME.
WHOA, THAT WAS ONE HELLA EXPLOSION!
DID YOU SET THAT OFF, KOTOBUKI?
THAT WAS INCREDIBLY DANGEROUS, OF COURSE. RAIMON'S BRAIN IS DIRECTLY CONNECTED TO THE SYSTEM BY MANY VERY DELICATE WIRES.
STRONG TREMORS MIGHT POSSIBLY INJURE THE BRAIN TISSUE ITSELF. THEN WHAT WOULD YOU DO?

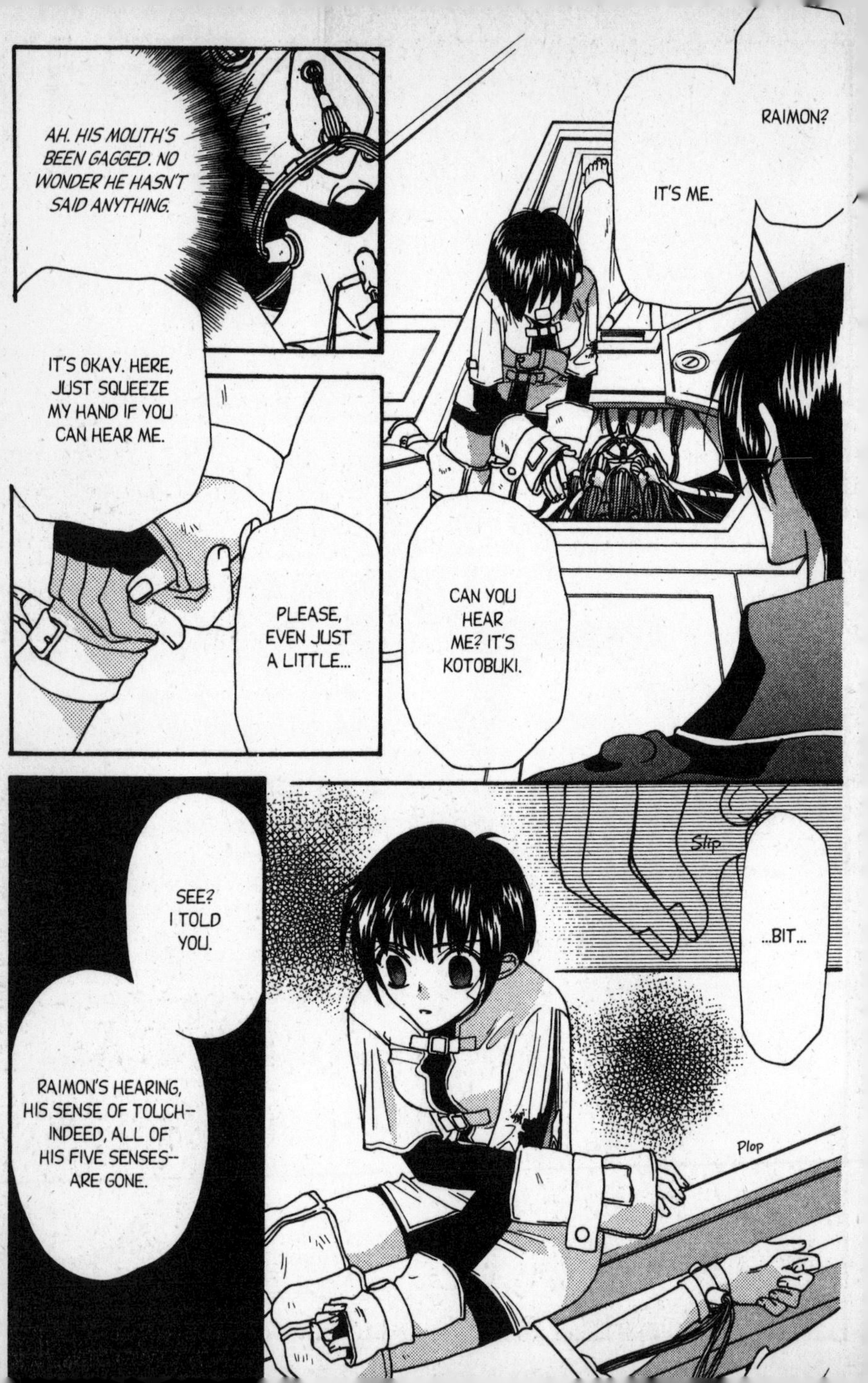
RAIMON?
IT'S ME.
CAN YOU HEAR ME? IT'S KOTOBUKI.
AH. HIS MOUTH'S BEEN GAGGED. NO WONDER HE HASN'T SAID ANYTHING.
IT'S OKAY. HERE, JUST SQUEEZE MY HAND IF YOU CAN HEAR ME.
PLEASE, EVEN JUST A LITTLE...
Slip
...BIT...
Plop
SEE? I TOLD YOU.
RAIMON'S HEARING, HIS SENSE OF TOUCH-- INDEED, ALL OF HIS FIVE SENSES-- ARE GONE.

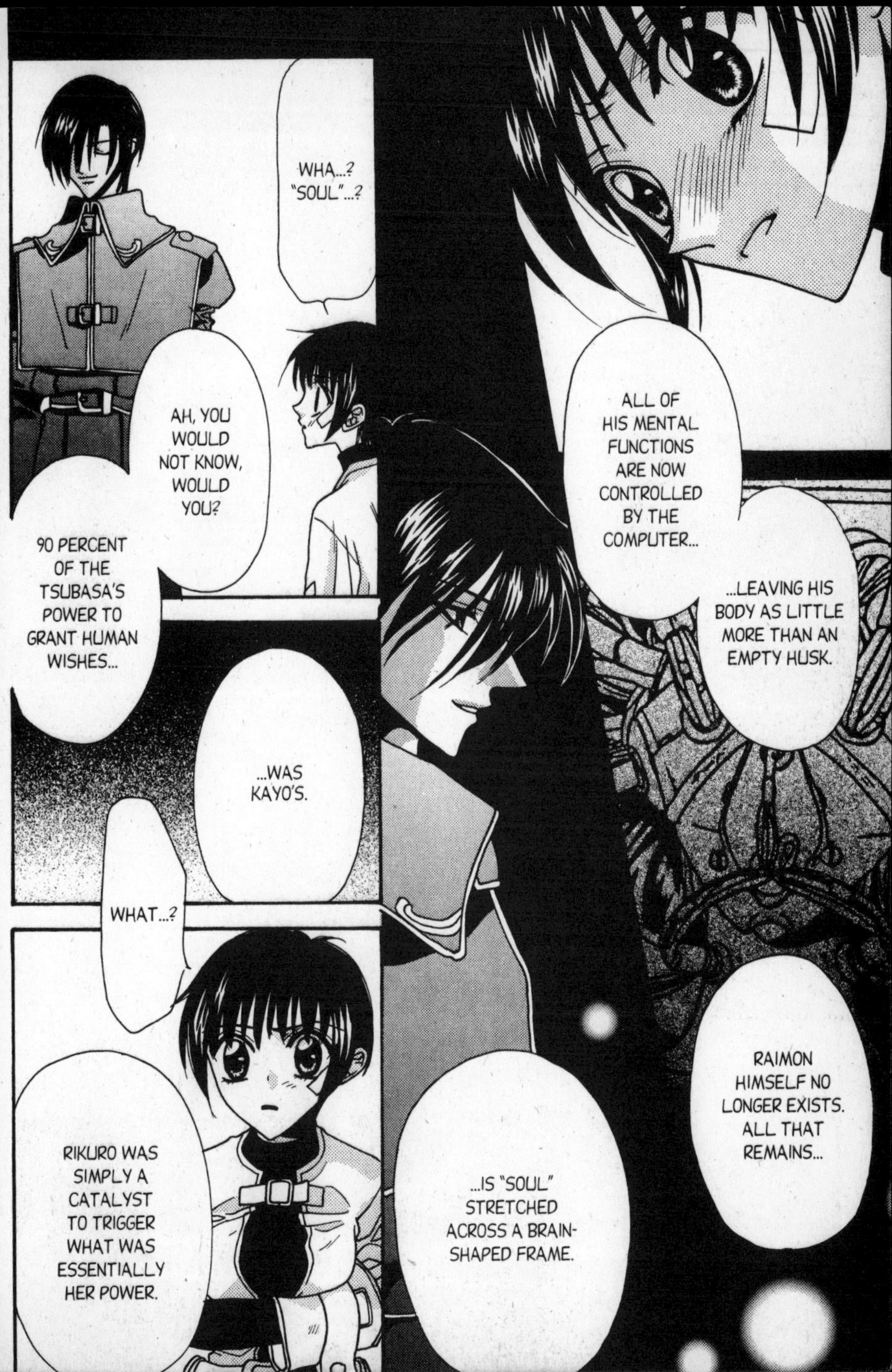
ALL OF HIS MENTAL FUNCTIONS ARE NOW CONTROLLED BY THE COMPUTER...
...LEAVING HIS BODY AS LITTLE MORE THAN AN EMPTY HUSK.
RAIMON HIMSELF NO LONGER EXISTS. ALL THAT REMAINS...
...IS "SOUL" STRETCHED ACROSS A BRAIN-SHAPED FRAME.
WHA...? "SOUL"...?
AH, YOU WOULD NOT KNOW, WOULD YOU?
90 PERCENT OF THE TSUBASA'S POWER TO GRANT HUMAN WISHES...
...WAS KAYO'S.
WHAT...?
RIKURO WAS SIMPLY A CATALYST TO TRIGGER WHAT WAS ESSENTIALLY HER POWER.

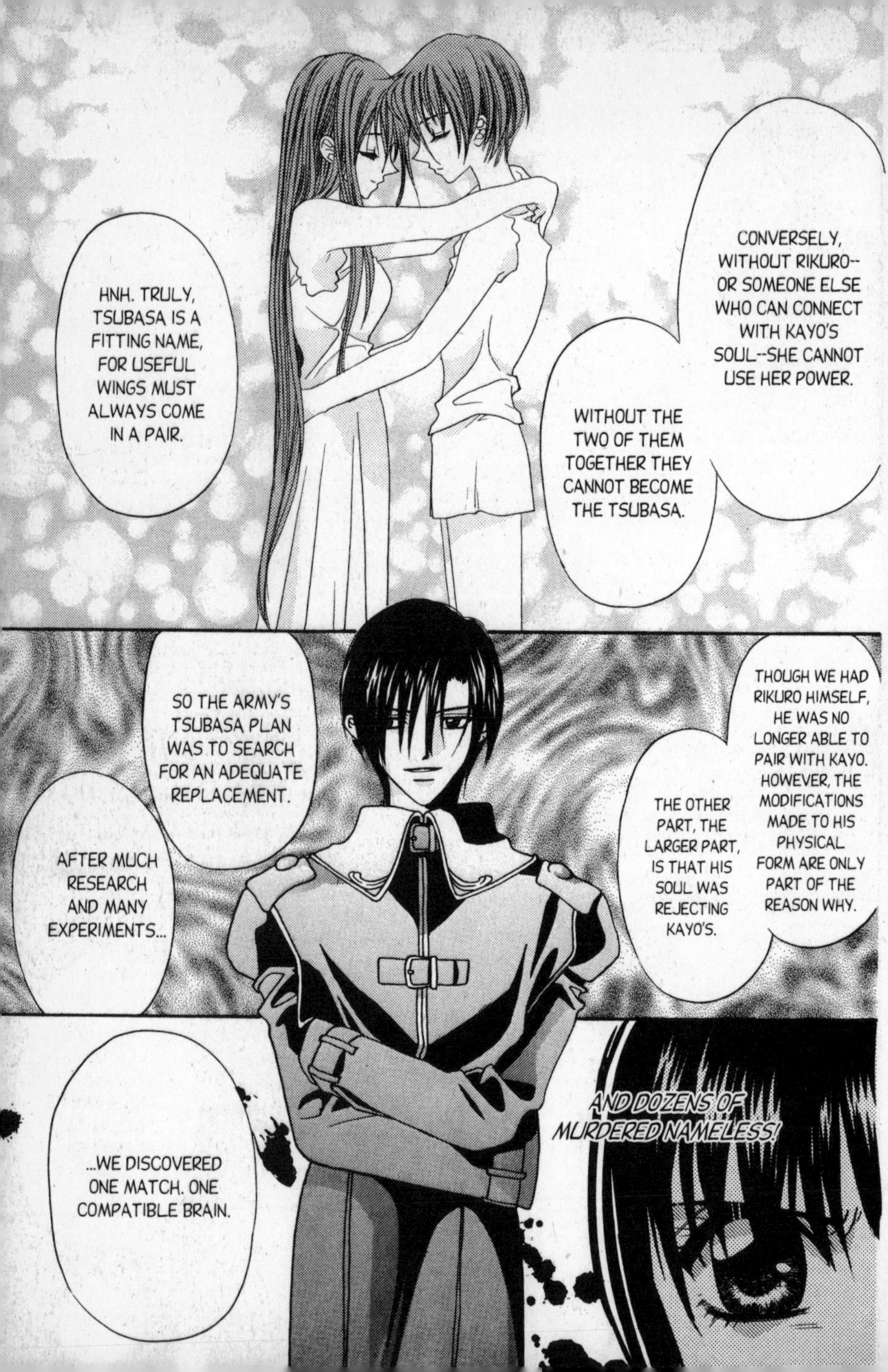
CONVERSELY, WITHOUT RIKURO-- OR SOMEONE ELSE WHO CAN CONNECT WITH KAYO'S SOUL--SHE CANNOT USE HER POWER.
WITHOUT THE TWO OF THEM TOGETHER THEY CANNOT BECOME THE TSUBASA.
HNH. TRULY, TSUBASA IS A FITTING NAME, FOR USEFUL WINGS MUST ALWAYS COME IN A PAIR.
THOUGH WE HAD RIKURO HIMSELF, HE WAS NO LONGER ABLE TO PAIR WITH KAYO. HOWEVER, THE MODIFICATIONS MADE TO HIS PHYSICAL FORM ARE ONLY PART OF THE REASON WHY.
THE OTHER PART, THE LARGER PART, IS THAT HIS SOUL WAS REJECTING KAYO'S.
SO THE ARMY'S TSUBASA PLAN WAS TO SEARCH FOR AN ADEQUATE REPLACEMENT.
AFTER MUCH RESEARCH AND MANY EXPERIMENTS...
...WE DISCOVERED ONE MATCH. ONE COMPATIBLE BRAIN.
AND DOZENS OF MURDERED NAMELESS!

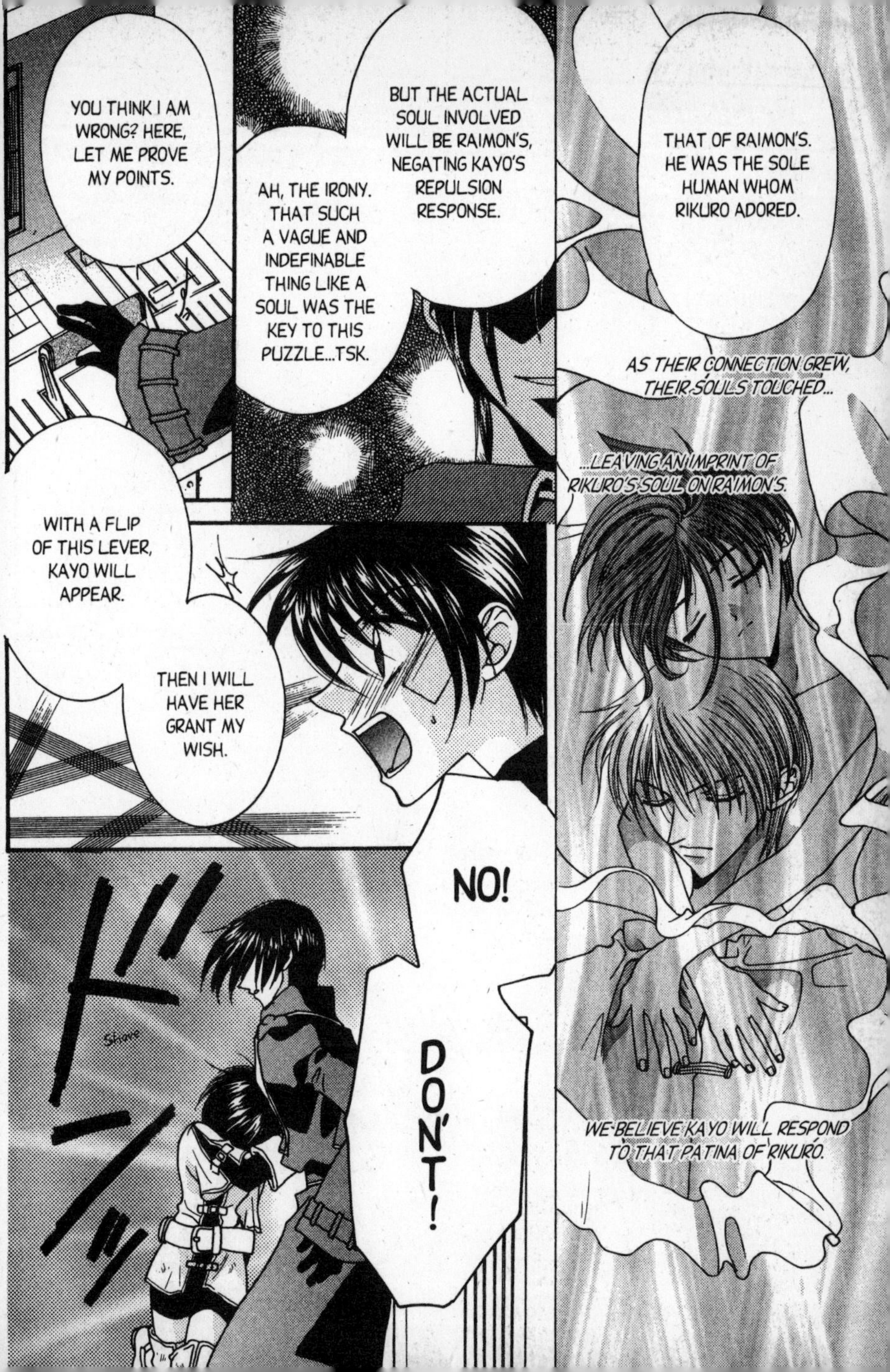
THAT OF RAIMON'S. HE WAS THE SOLE HUMAN WHOM RIKURO ADORED.
AS THEIR CONNECTION GREW, THEIR SOULS TOUCHED...
...LEAVING AN IMPRINT OF RIKURO'S SOUL ON RAIMON'S.
WE BELIEVE KAYO WILL RESPOND TO THAT PATINA OF RIKURO.
BUT THE ACTUAL SOUL INVOLVED WILL BE RAIMON'S, NEGATING KAYO'S REPULSION RESPONSE.
AH, THE IRONY. THAT SUCH A VAGUE AND INDEFINABLE THING LIKE A SOUL WAS THE KEY TO THIS PUZZLE...TSK.
YOU THINK I AM WRONG? HERE, LET ME PROVE MY POINTS.
WITH A FLIP OF THIS LEVER, KAYO WILL APPEAR.
THEN I WILL HAVE HER GRANT MY WISH.
NO!
DON'T!
Shove

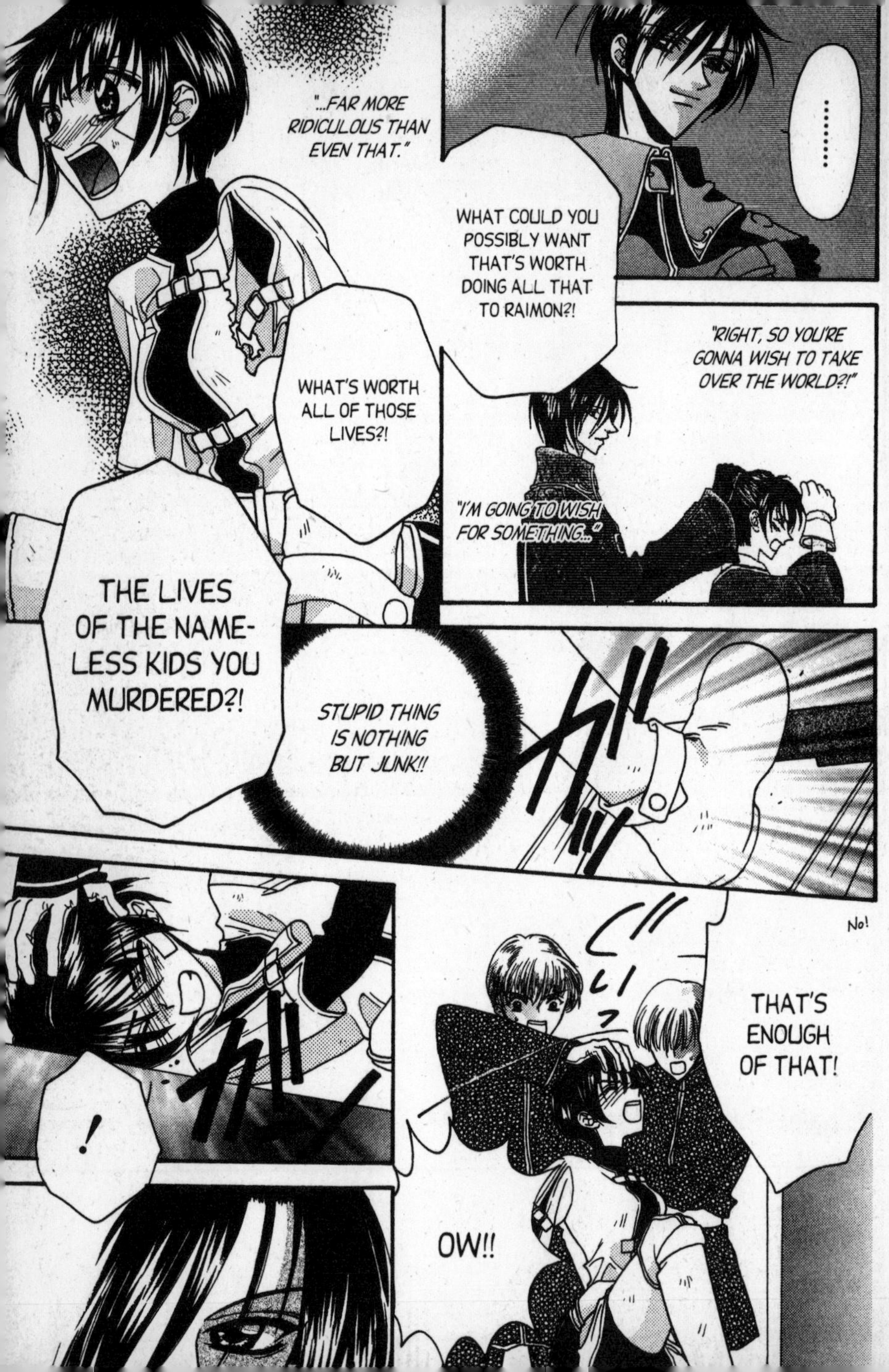
......
WHAT COULD YOU POSSIBLY WANT THAT'S WORTH DOING ALL THAT TO RAIMON?!
"RIGHT, SO YOU'RE GONNA WISH TO TAKE OVER THE WORLD?!"
"I'M GOING TO WISH FOR SOMETHING..."
"...FAR MORE RIDICULOUS THAN EVEN THAT."
WHAT'S WORTH ALL OF THOSE LIVES?!
THE LIVES OF THE NAME-LESS KIDS YOU MURDERED?!
STUPID THING IS NOTHING BUT JUNK!!
No!
THAT'S ENOUGH OF THAT!
OW!!
!

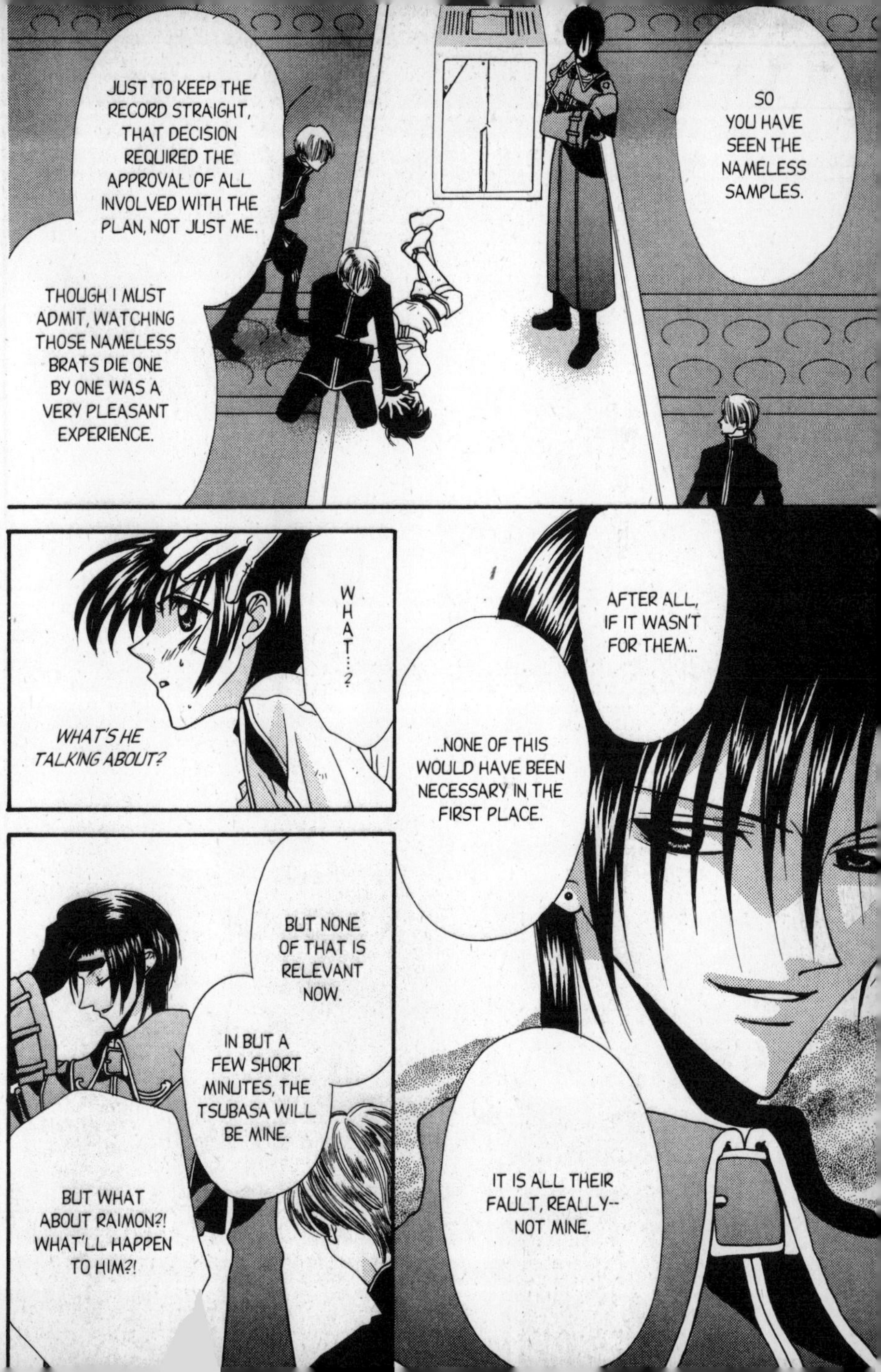
SO YOU HAVE SEEN THE NAMELESS SAMPLES.
JUST TO KEEP THE RECORD STRAIGHT, THAT DECISION REQUIRED THE APPROVAL OF ALL INVOLVED WITH THE PLAN, NOT JUST ME.
THOUGH I MUST ADMIT, WATCHING THOSE NAMELESS BRATS DIE ONE BY ONE WAS A VERY PLEASANT EXPERIENCE.
AFTER ALL, IF IT WASN'T FOR THEM...
...NONE OF THIS WOULD HAVE BEEN NECESSARY IN THE FIRST PLACE.
IT IS ALL THEIR FAULT, REALLY-- NOT MINE.
WHAT...?
WHAT'S HE TALKING ABOUT?
BUT NONE OF THAT IS RELEVANT NOW.
IN BUT A FEW SHORT MINUTES, THE TSUBASA WILL BE MINE.
BUT WHAT ABOUT RAIMON?! WHAT'LL HAPPEN TO HIM?!

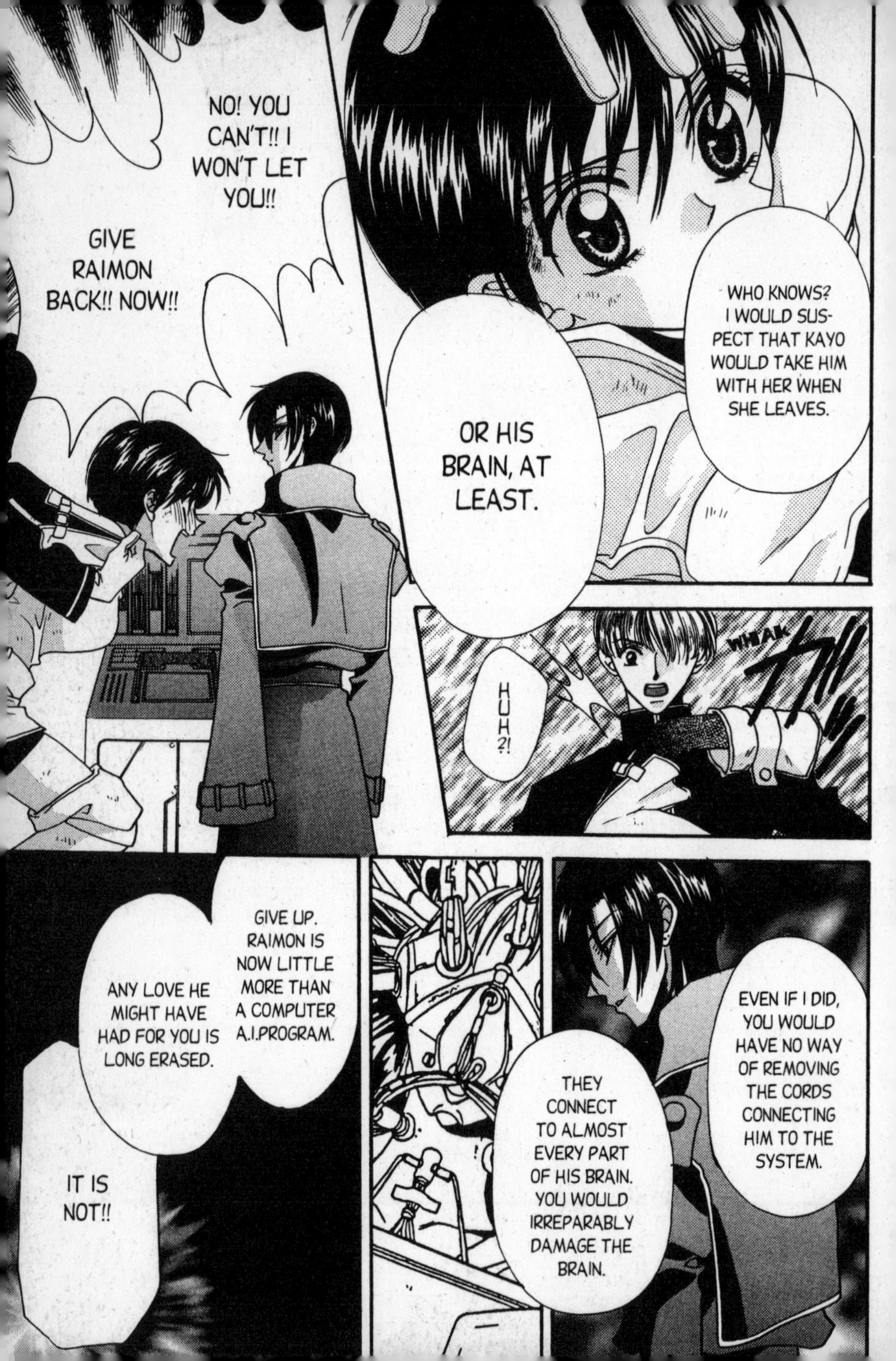
WHO KNOWS? I WOULD SUS-PECT THAT KAYO WOULD TAKE HIM WITH HER WHEN SHE LEAVES.
OR HIS BRAIN, AT LEAST.
HUH?!
WHAK
NO! YOU CAN'T!! I WON'T LET YOU!!
GIVE RAIMON BACK!! NOW!!
EVEN IF I DID, YOU WOULD HAVE NO WAY OF REMOVING THE CORDS CONNECTING HIM TO THE SYSTEM.
THEY CONNECT TO ALMOST EVERY PART OF HIS BRAIN. YOU WOULD IRREPARABLY DAMAGE THE BRAIN.
GIVE UP. RAIMON IS NOW LITTLE MORE THAN A COMPUTER A.I.PROGRAM.
ANY LOVE HE MIGHT HAVE HAD FOR YOU IS LONG ERASED.
IT IS NOT!!

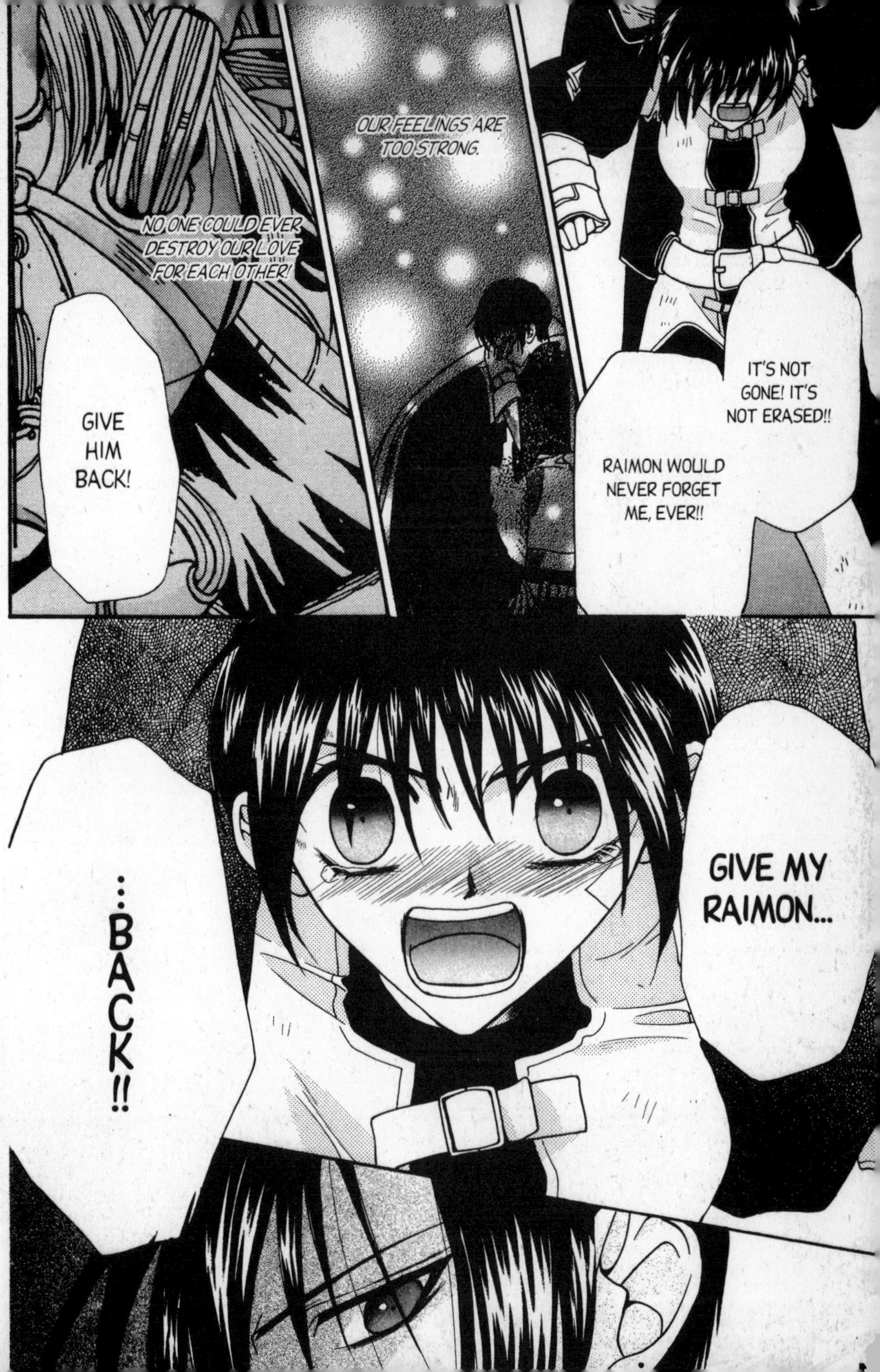
IT'S NOT GONE! IT'S NOT ERASED!!
RAIMON WOULD NEVER FORGET ME, EVER!!
OUR FEELINGS ARE TOO STRONG.
NO ONE COULD EVER DESTROY OUR LOVE FOR EACH OTHER!
GIVE HIM BACK!
GIVE MY RAIMON...
...BACK!!

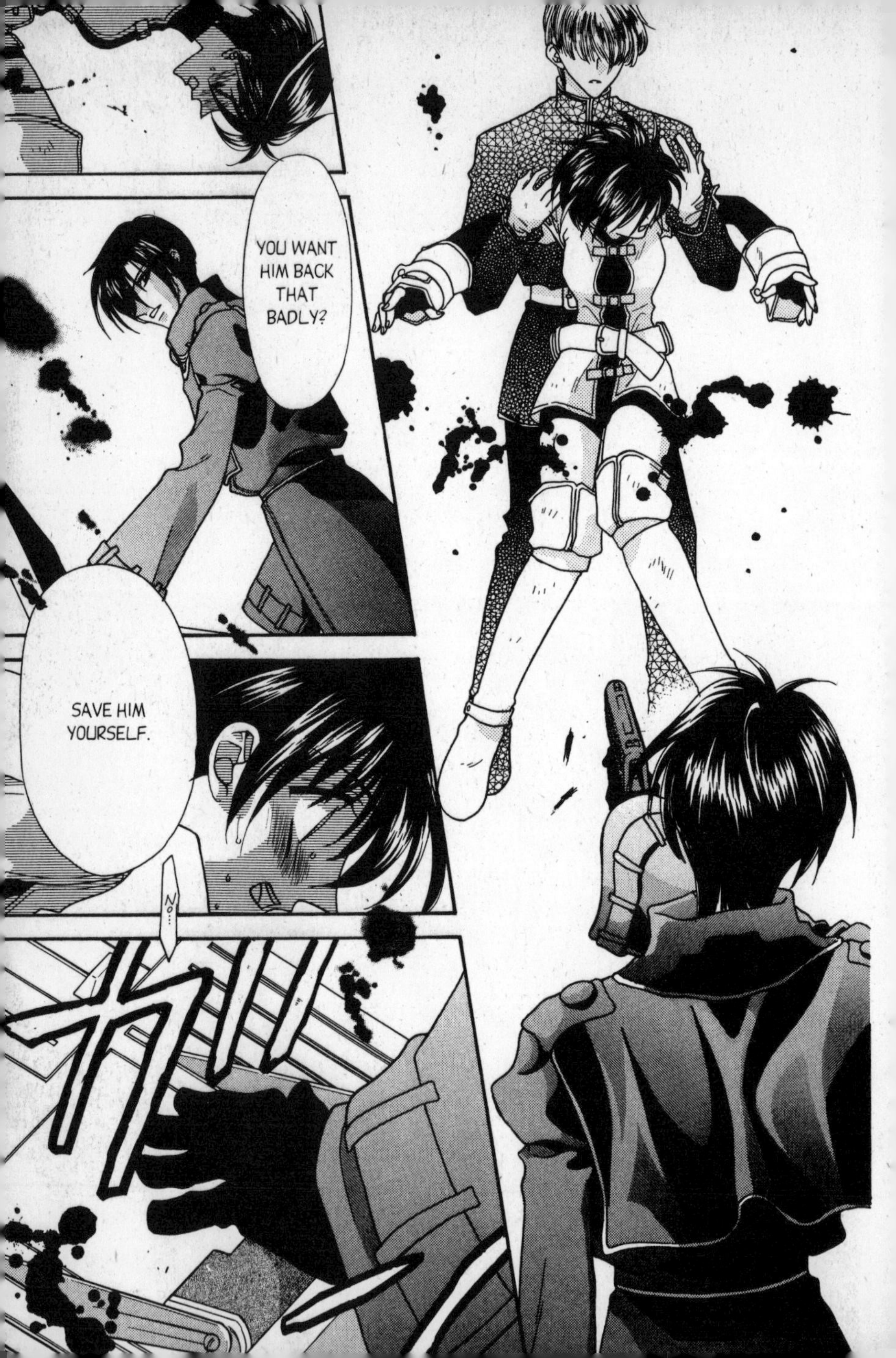
YOU WANT HIM BACK THAT BADLY?
SAVE HIM YOURSELF.
NO...

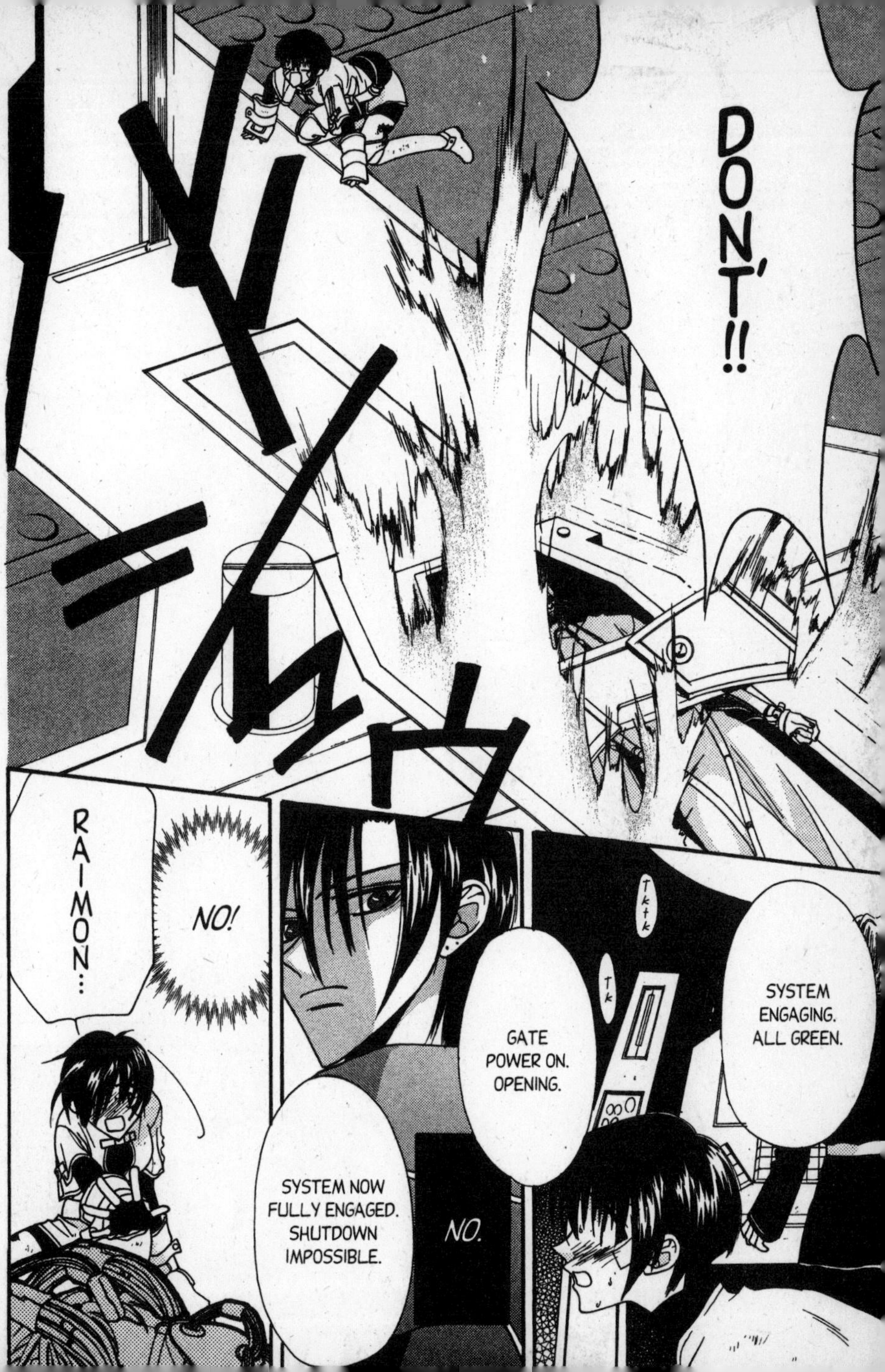
DON'T!!
Tktk
SYSTEM ENGAGING. ALL GREEN.
Tk
GATE POWER ON. OPENING.
SYSTEM NOW FULLY ENGAGED. SHUTDOWN IMPOSSIBLE.
NO.
NO!
RAIMON...

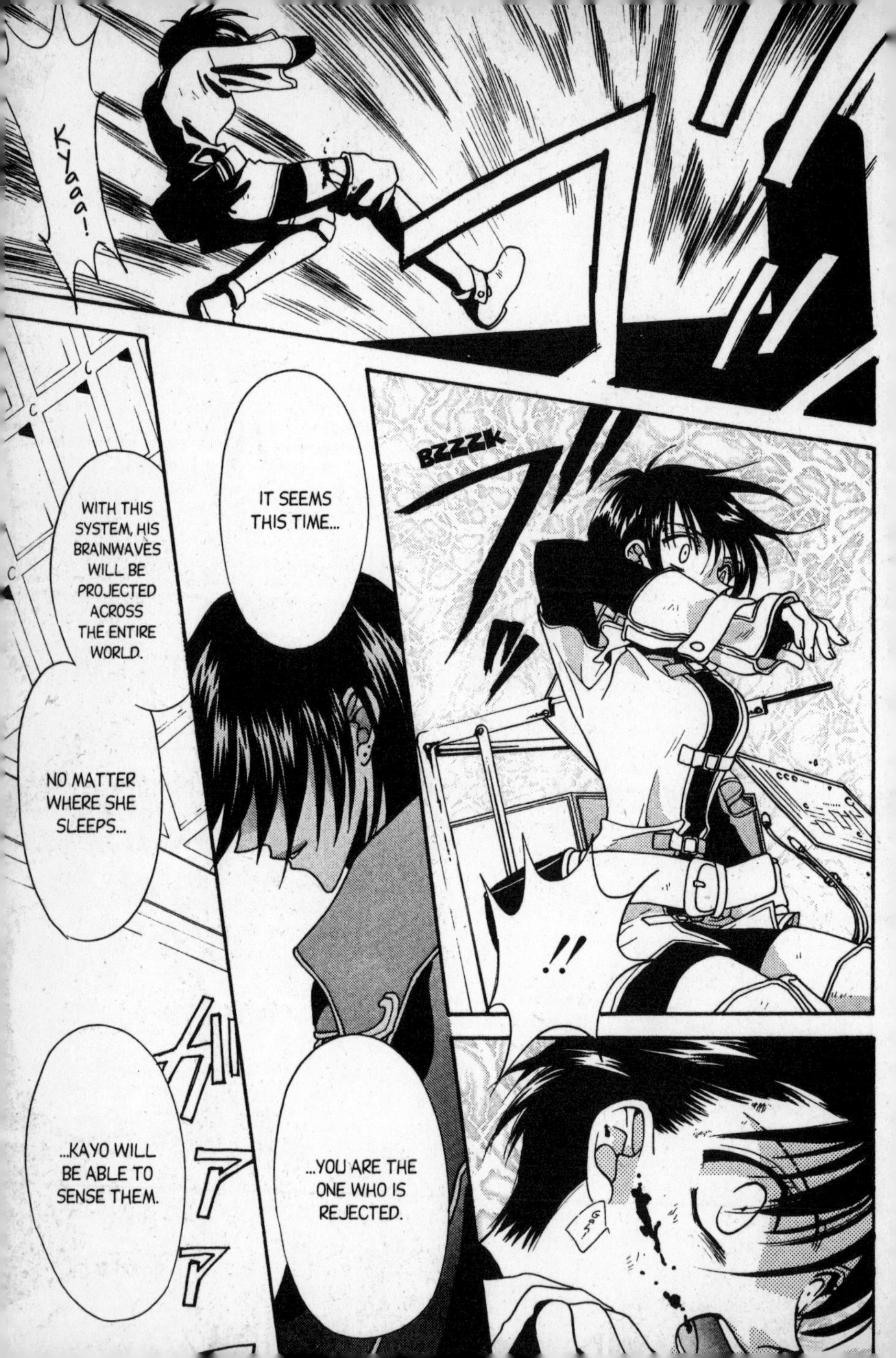
Kyaaa!
BZZZK
!!
IT SEEMS THIS TIME...
...YOU ARE THE ONE WHO IS REJECTED.
WITH THIS SYSTEM, HIS BRAINWAVES WILL BE PROJECTED ACROSS THE ENTIRE WORLD.
NO MATTER WHERE SHE SLEEPS...
...KAYO WILL BE ABLE TO SENSE THEM.

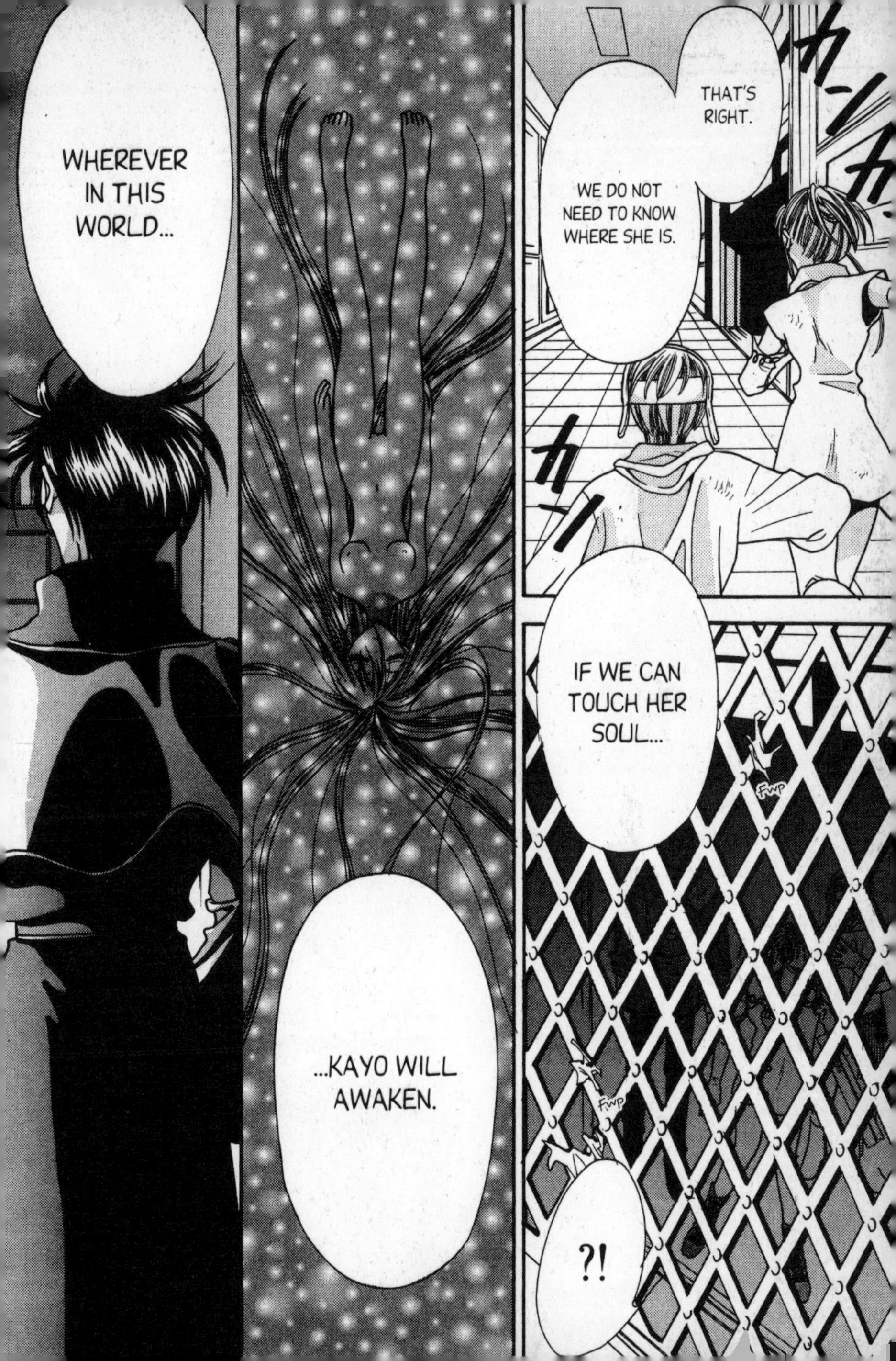
THAT'S RIGHT.
WE DO NOT NEED TO KNOW WHERE SHE IS.
IF WE CAN TOUCH HER SOUL...
Fwp
Fwp
?!
...KAYO WILL AWAKEN.
WHEREVER IN THIS WORLD...

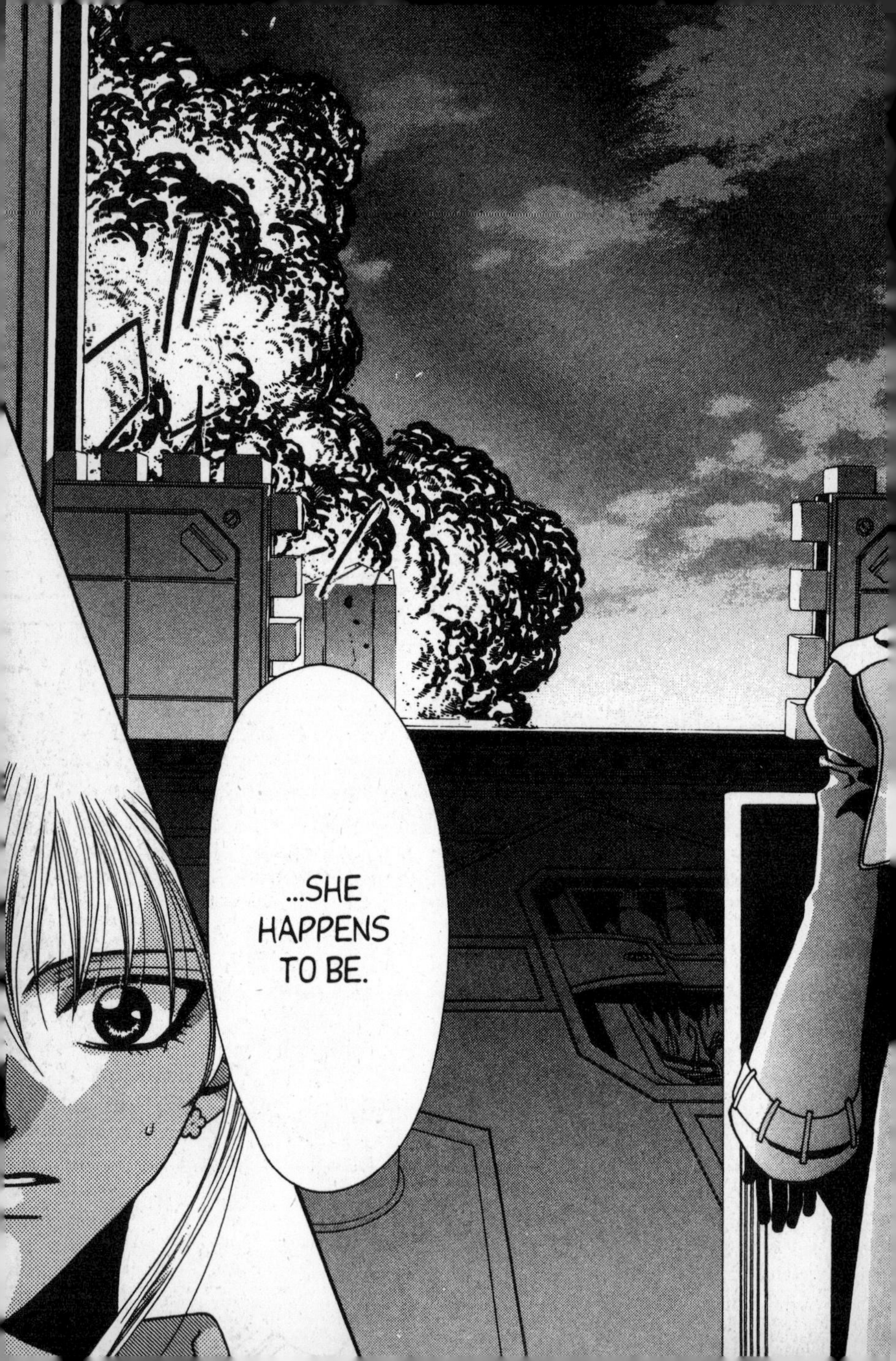
...SHE HAPPENS TO BE.

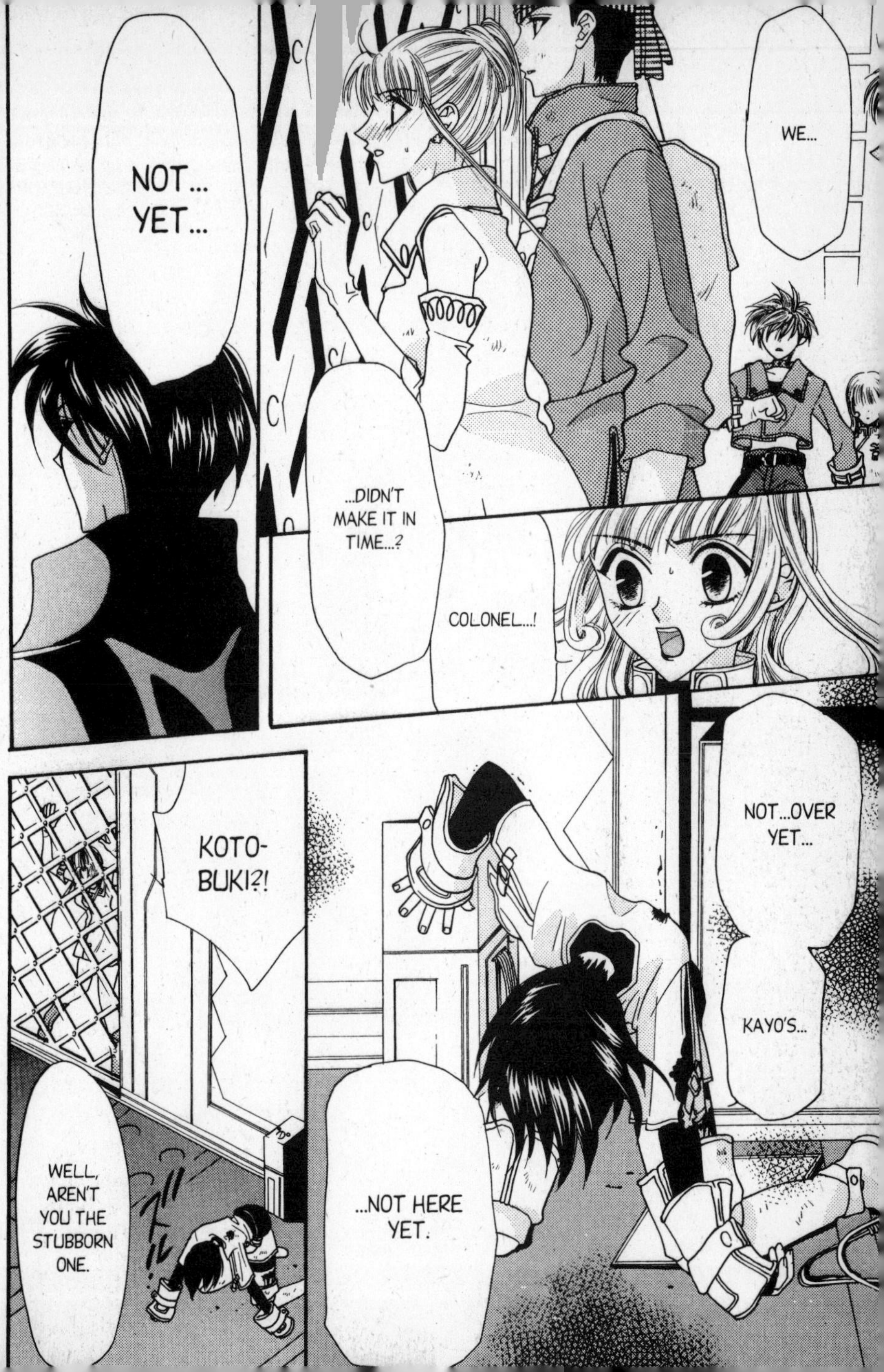
WE...
...DIDN'T MAKE IT IN TIME...?
COLONEL...!
NOT... YET...
NOT...OVER YET...
KAYO'S...
...NOT HERE YET.
KOTO-BUKI?!
WELL, AREN'T YOU THE STUBBORN ONE.

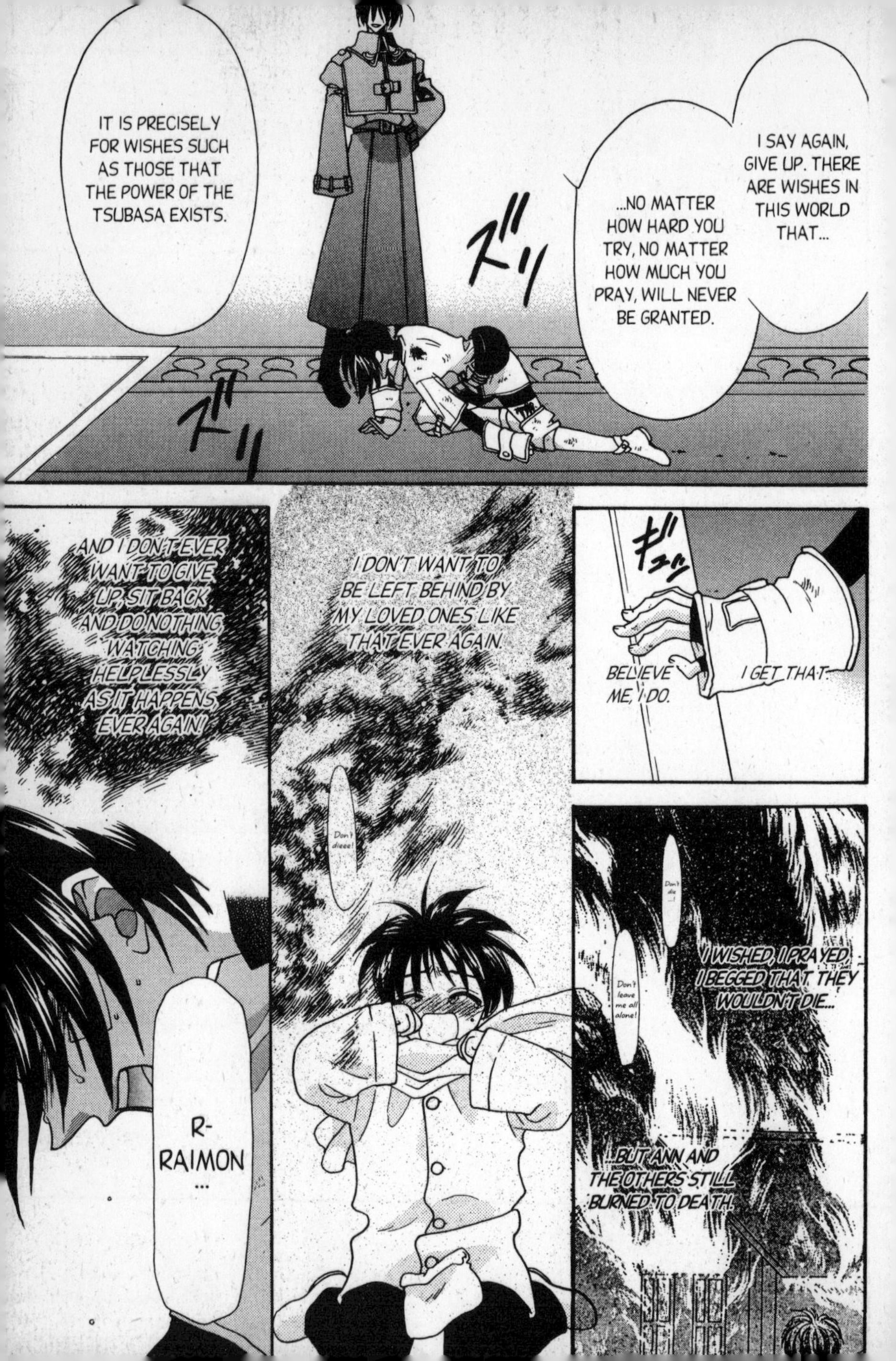
I SAY AGAIN, GIVE UP. THERE ARE WISHES IN THIS WORLD THAT...
...NO MATTER HOW HARD YOU TRY, NO MATTER HOW MUCH YOU PRAY, WILL NEVER BE GRANTED.
ズリ
IT IS PRECISELY FOR WISHES SUCH AS THOSE THAT THE POWER OF THE TSUBASA EXISTS.
ズリ
ギュッ
I GET THAT.
BELIEVE ME, I DO.
Don't die...!
Don't leave me all alone!
I WISHED, I PRAYED, I BEGGED THAT THEY WOULDN'T DIE...
...BUT ANN AND THE OTHERS STILL BURNED TO DEATH.
I DON'T WANT TO BE LEFT BEHIND BY MY LOVED ONES LIKE THAT EVER AGAIN.
Don't dieee!
AND I DON'T EVER WANT TO GIVE UP, SIT BACK AND DO NOTHING, WATCHING HELPLESSLY AS IT HAPPENS, EVER AGAIN!
R-RAIMON...

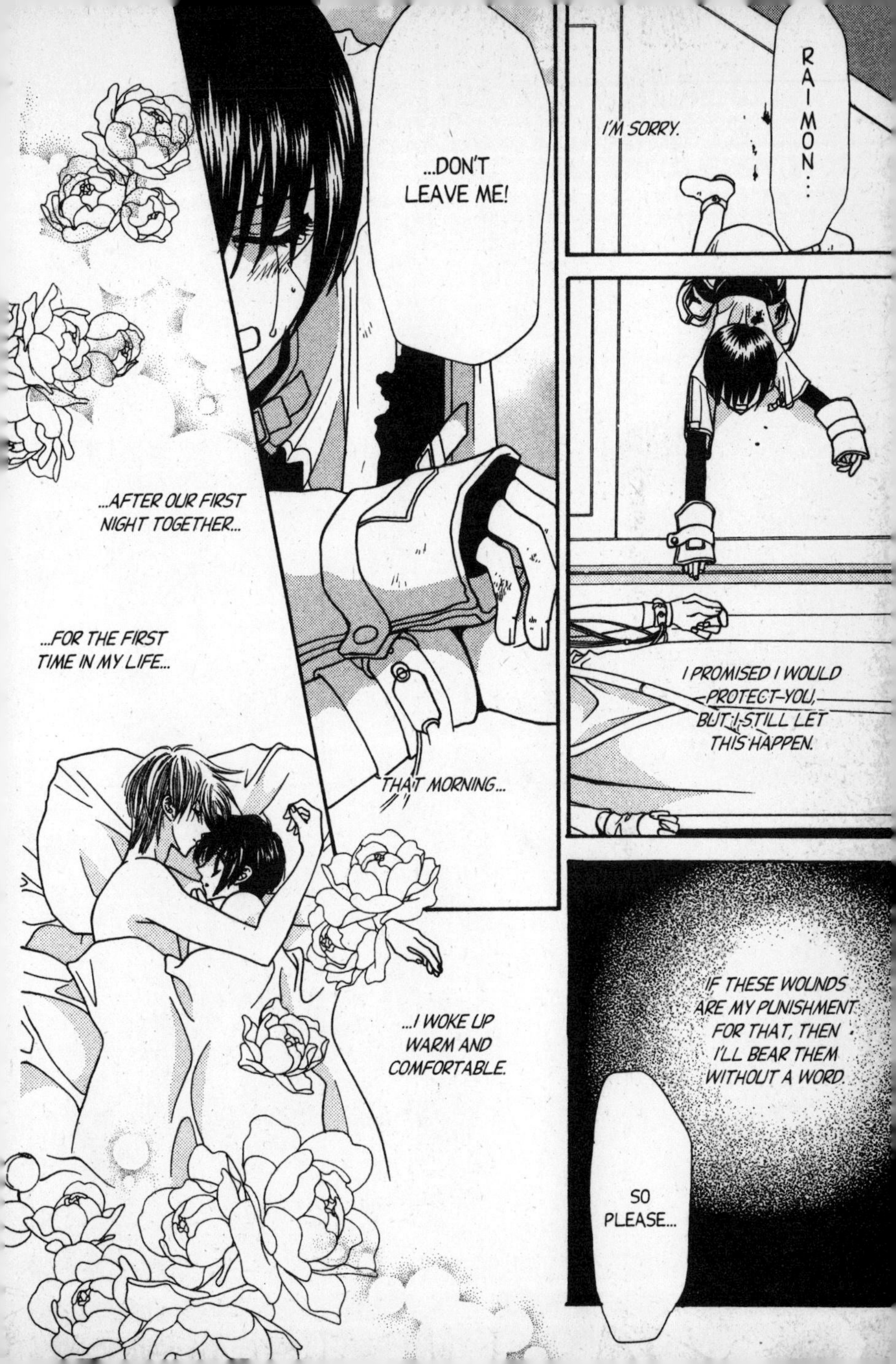
RAIMON...
I'M SORRY.
I PROMISED I WOULD PROTECT YOU, BUT I STILL LET THIS HAPPEN.
IF THESE WOUNDS ARE MY PUNISHMENT FOR THAT, THEN I'LL BEAR THEM WITHOUT A WORD.
SO PLEASE...
...DON'T LEAVE ME!
...AFTER OUR FIRST NIGHT TOGETHER...
...FOR THE FIRST TIME IN MY LIFE...
THAT MORNING...
...I WOKE UP WARM AND COMFORTABLE.

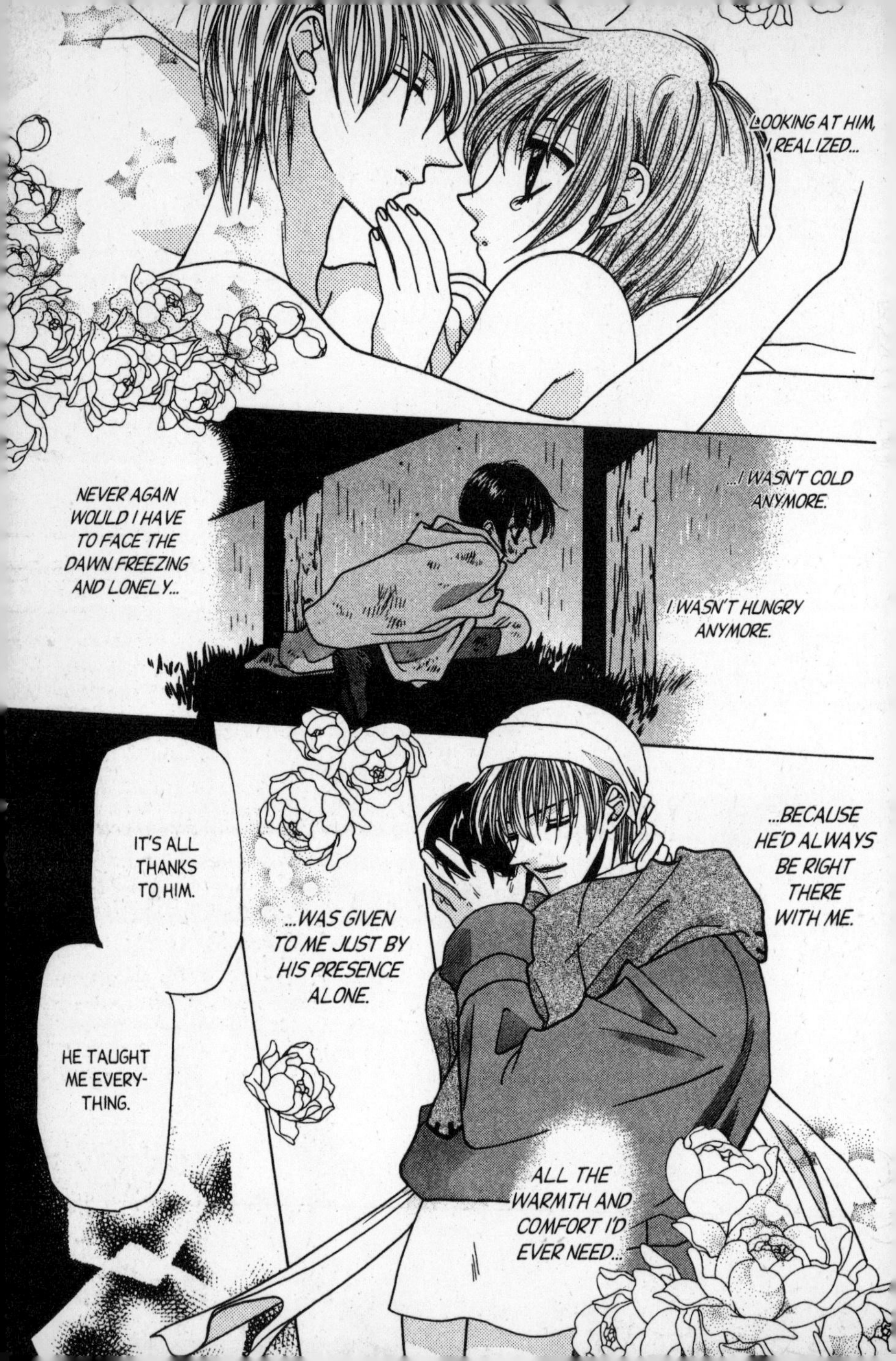
LOOKING AT HIM, I REALIZED...
...I WASN'T COLD ANYMORE.
I WASN'T HUNGRY ANYMORE.
NEVER AGAIN WOULD I HAVE TO FACE THE DAWN FREEZING AND LONELY...
...BECAUSE HE'D ALWAYS BE RIGHT THERE WITH ME.
ALL THE WARMTH AND COMFORT I'D EVER NEED...
...WAS GIVEN TO ME JUST BY HIS PRESENCE ALONE.
IT'S ALL THANKS TO HIM.
HE TAUGHT ME EVERY-THING.

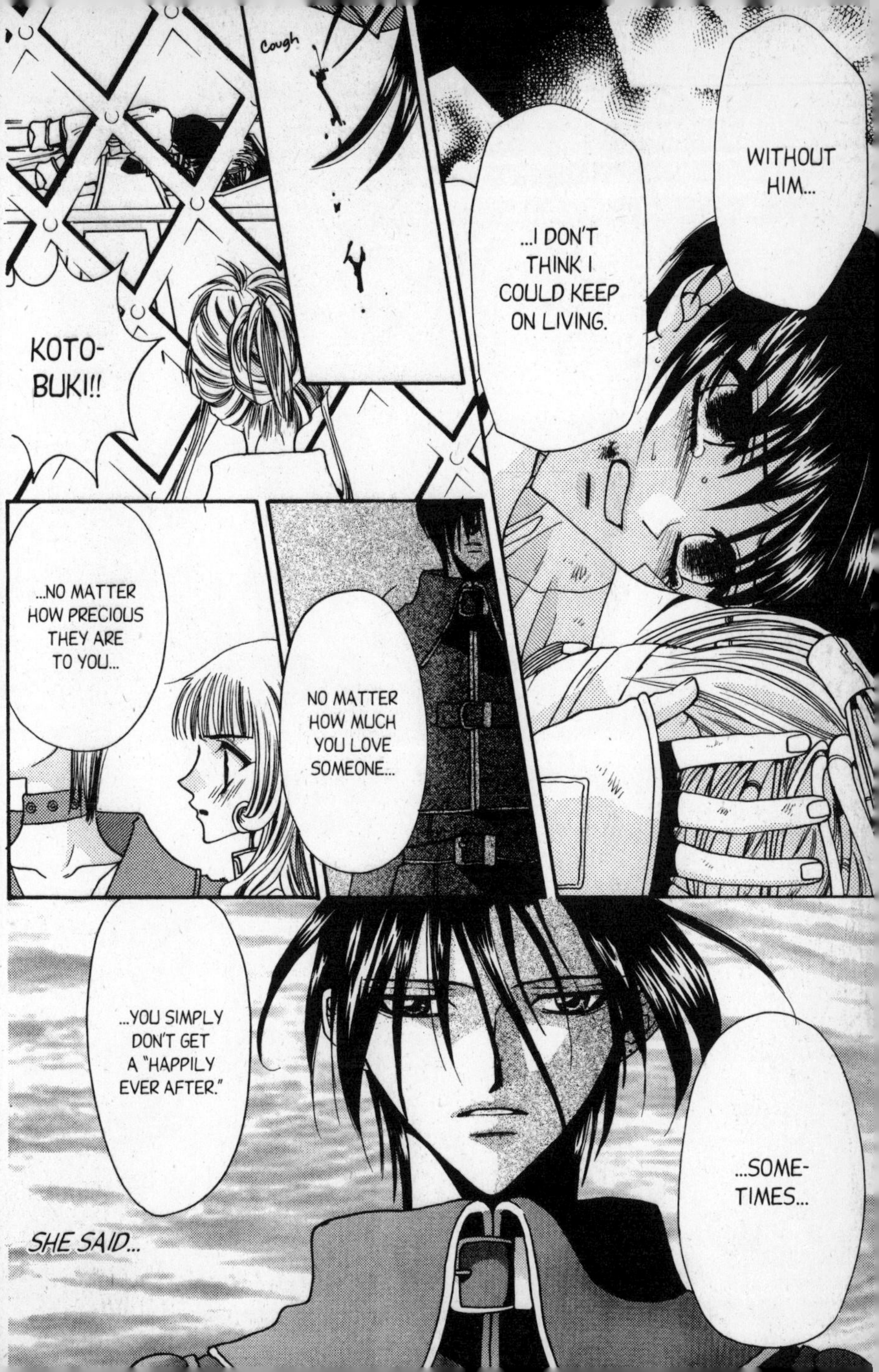
WITHOUT HIM...
...I DON'T THINK I COULD KEEP ON LIVING.
Cough
KOTO-BUKI!!
NO MATTER HOW MUCH YOU LOVE SOMEONE...
...NO MATTER HOW PRECIOUS THEY ARE TO YOU...
...SOME-TIMES...
...YOU SIMPLY DON'T GET A "HAPPILY EVER AFTER."
SHE SAID...

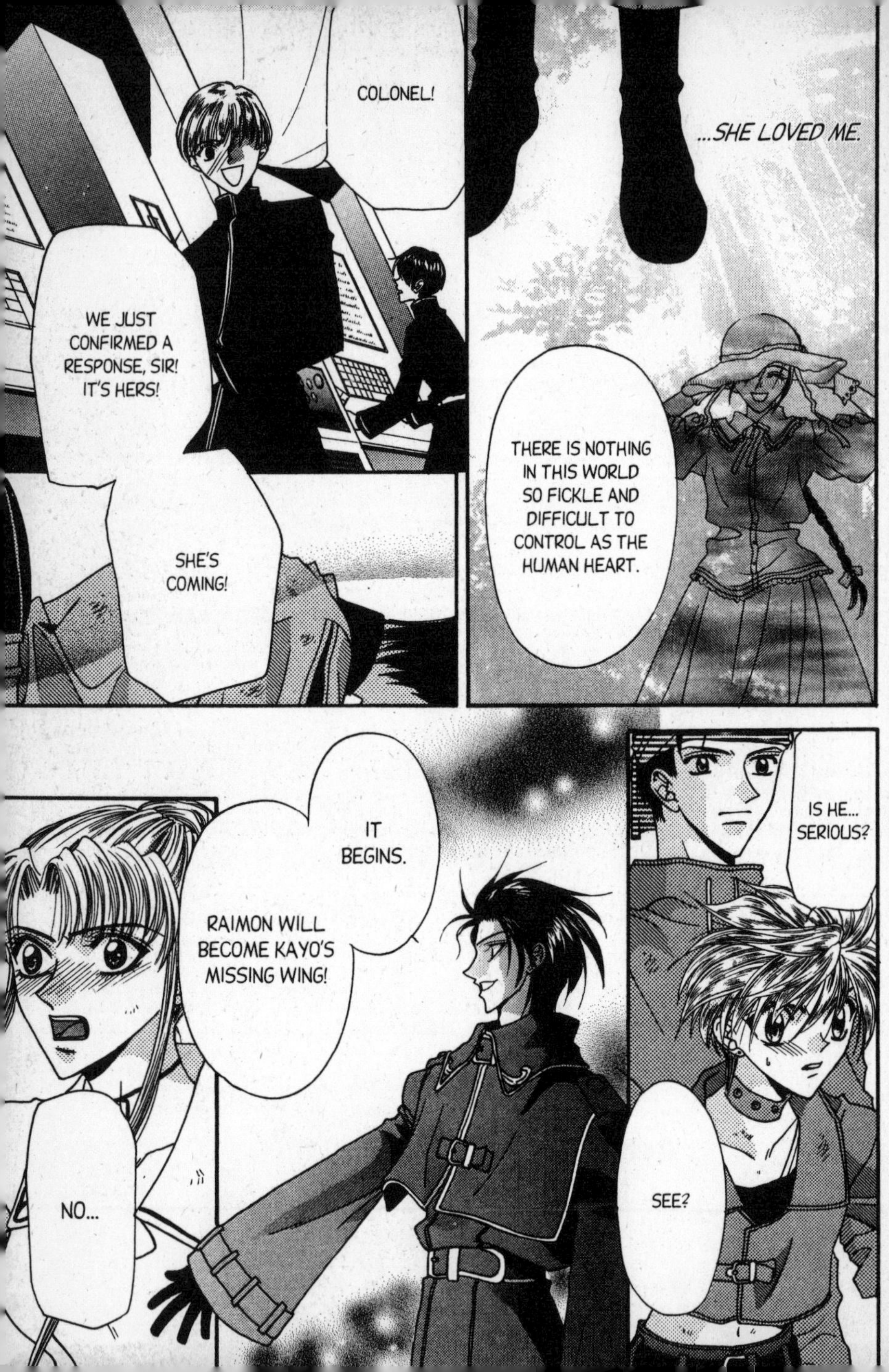
...SHE LOVED ME.
THERE IS NOTHING IN THIS WORLD SO FICKLE AND DIFFICULT TO CONTROL AS THE HUMAN HEART.
COLONEL!
WE JUST CONFIRMED A RESPONSE, SIR! IT'S HERS!
SHE'S COMING!
IS HE... SERIOUS?
SEE?
IT BEGINS.
RAIMON WILL BECOME KAYO'S MISSING WING!
NO...

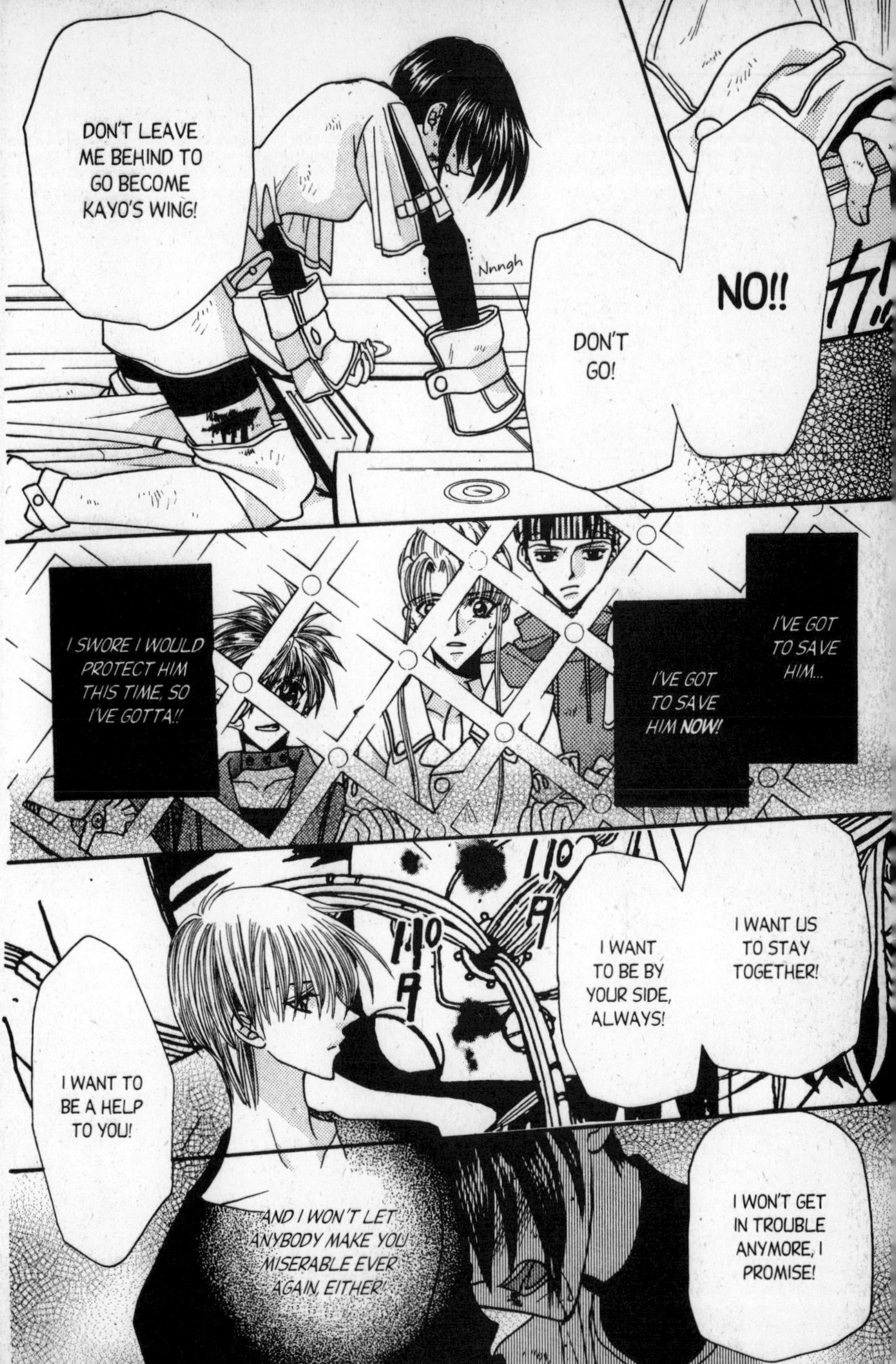
NO!!
DON'T GO!
Nnngh
DON'T LEAVE ME BEHIND TO GO BECOME KAYO'S WING!
I'VE GOT TO SAVE HIM...
I'VE GOT TO SAVE HIM **NOW!**
I SWORE I WOULD PROTECT HIM THIS TIME, SO I'VE GOTTA!!
I WANT US TO STAY TOGETHER!
I WANT TO BE BY YOUR SIDE, ALWAYS!
I WANT TO BE A HELP TO YOU!
I WON'T GET IN TROUBLE ANYMORE, I PROMISE!
AND I WON'T LET ANYBODY MAKE YOU MISERABLE EVER AGAIN, EITHER!

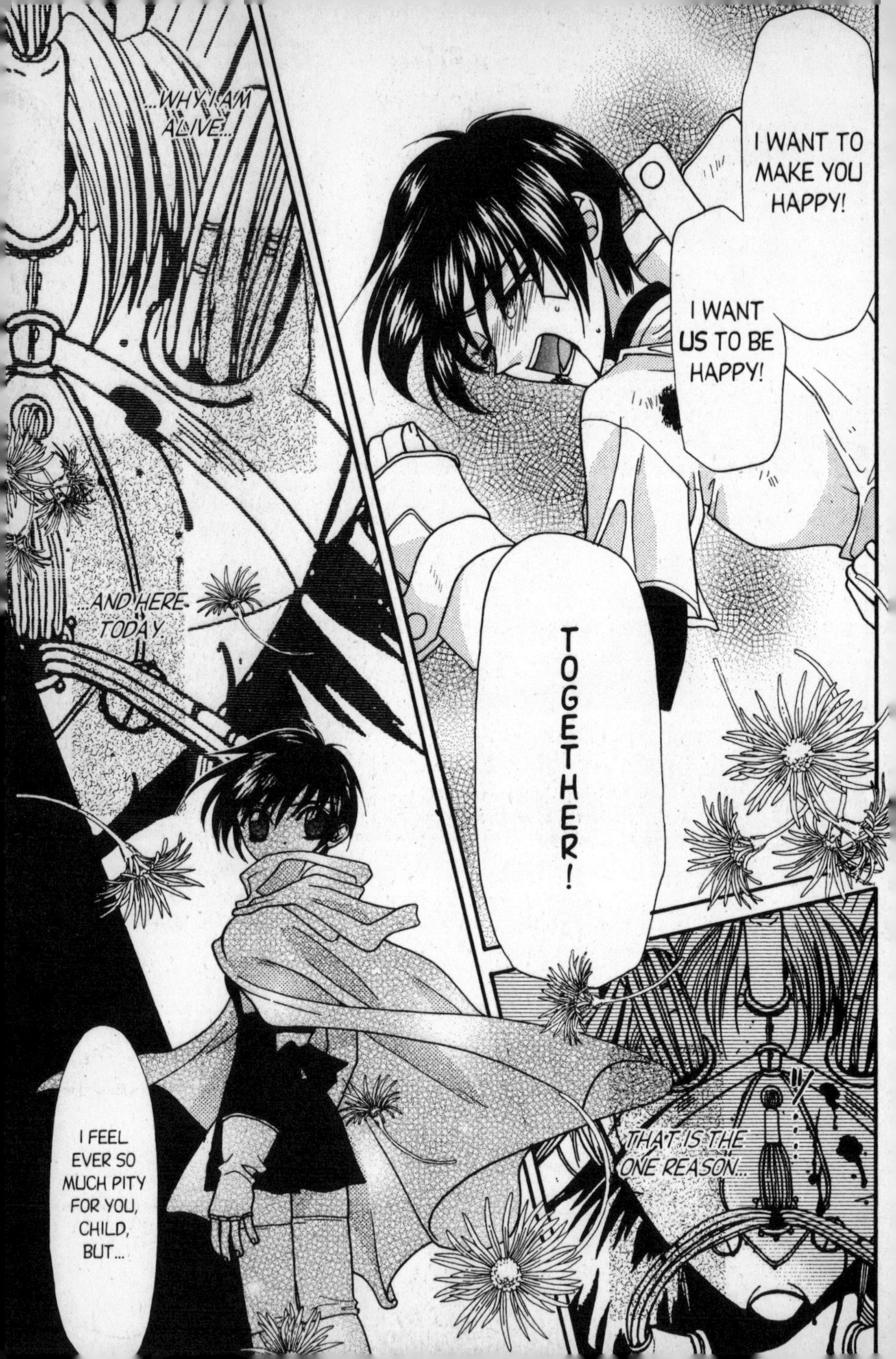
I WANT TO MAKE YOU HAPPY!
I WANT US TO BE HAPPY!
TOGETHER!
THAT IS THE ONE REASON...
...WHY I AM ALIVE...
...AND HERE TODAY.
I FEEL EVER SO MUCH PITY FOR YOU, CHILD, BUT...

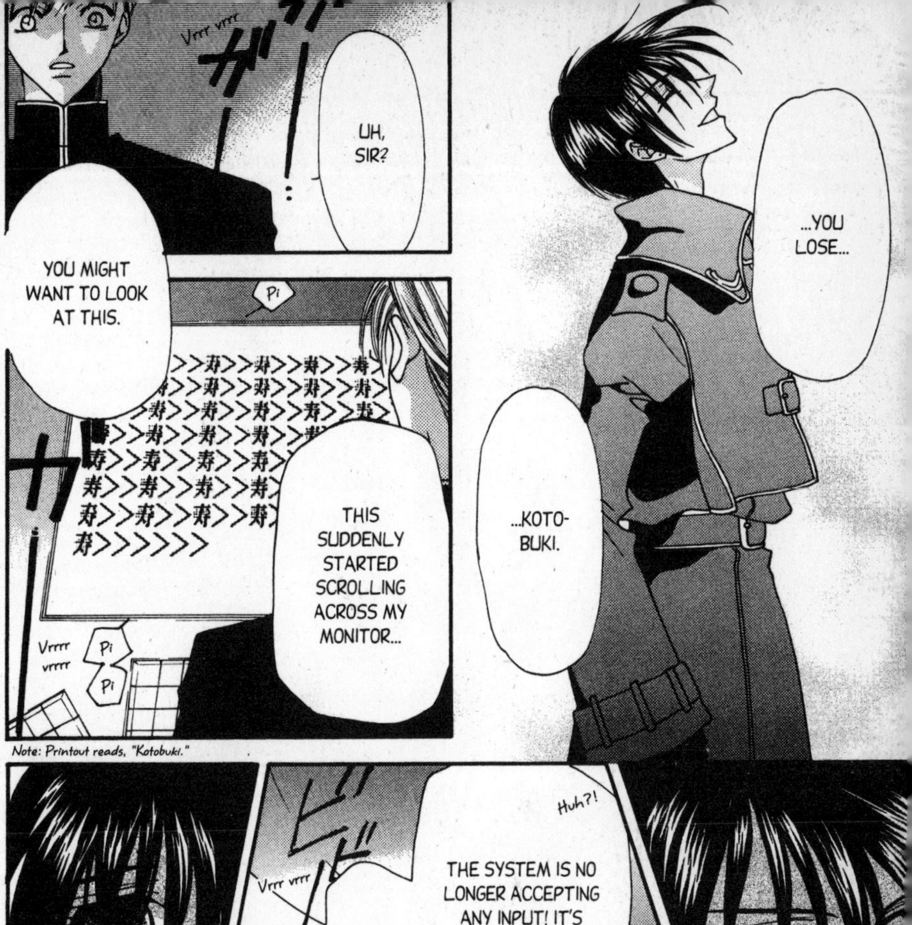
...YOU LOSE...
...KOTO-BUKI.
Vrrr vrrr
UH, SIR?
Pi
YOU MIGHT WANT TO LOOK AT THIS.
THIS SUDDENLY STARTED SCROLLING ACROSS MY MONITOR...
Vrrrr vrrrr
Pi
Pi
Note: Printout reads, "Kotobuki."

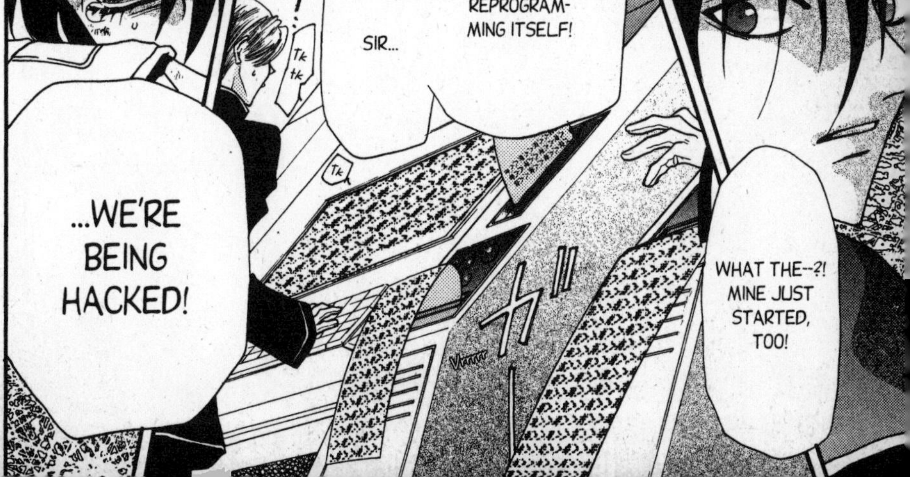
Huh?!
WHAT THE--?! MINE JUST STARTED, TOO!
THE SYSTEM IS NO LONGER ACCEPTING ANY INPUT! IT'S REPROGRAM-MING ITSELF!
Vrrr vrrr
SIR...
Tk tk
Tk
...WE'RE BEING HACKED!

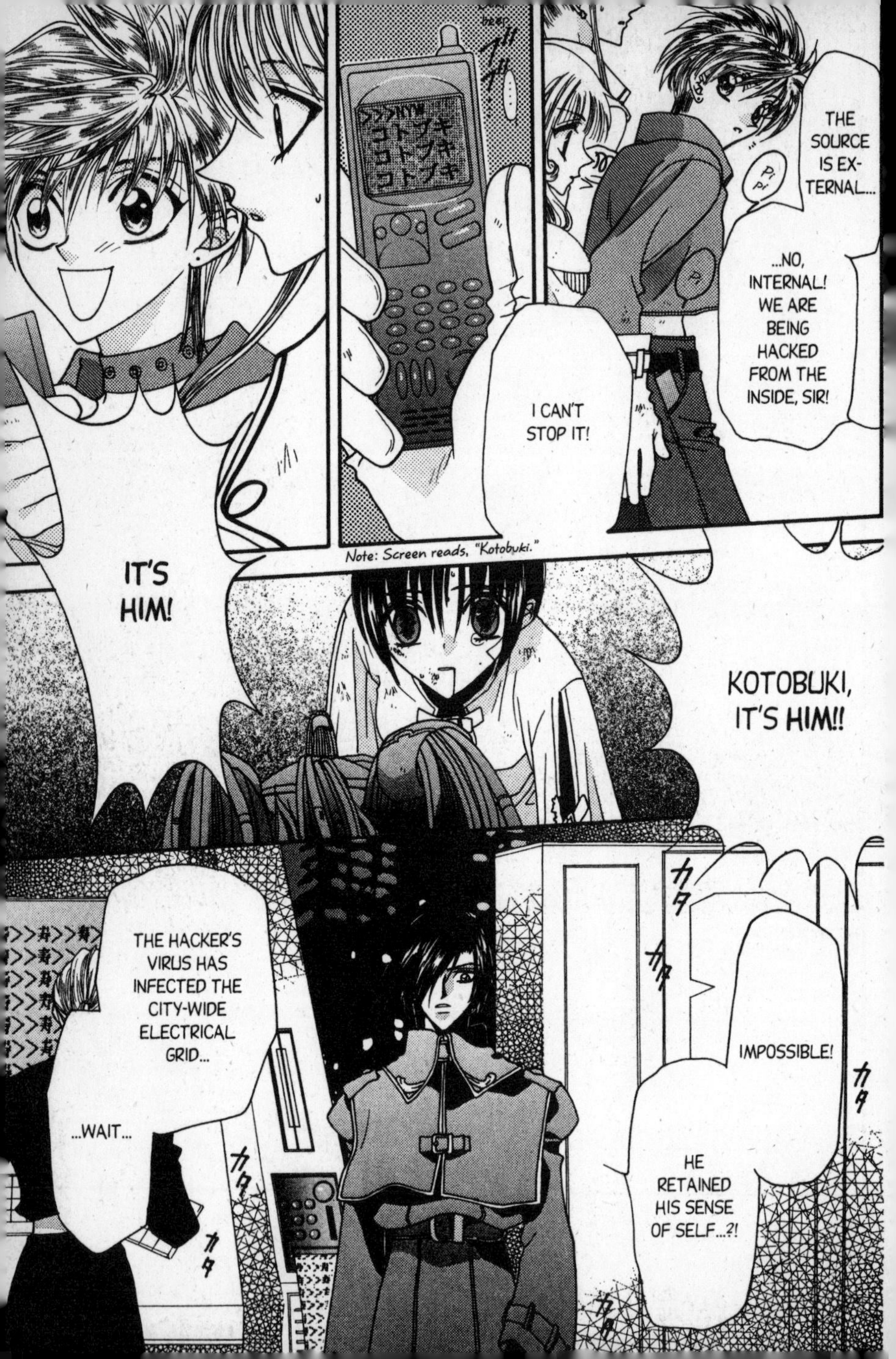
THE SOURCE IS EX-TERNAL...
...NO, INTERNAL! WE ARE BEING HACKED FROM THE INSIDE, SIR!
Pi Pi
beep
コトブキ
コトブキ
コトブキ
I CAN'T STOP IT!
IT'S HIM!
Note: Screen reads, "Kotobuki."
KOTOBUKI, IT'S HIM!!
カタ
カタ
IMPOSSIBLE!
HE RETAINED HIS SENSE OF SELF...?!
カタ
THE HACKER'S VIRUS HAS INFECTED THE CITY-WIDE ELECTRICAL GRID...
...WAIT...
カタ
カタ

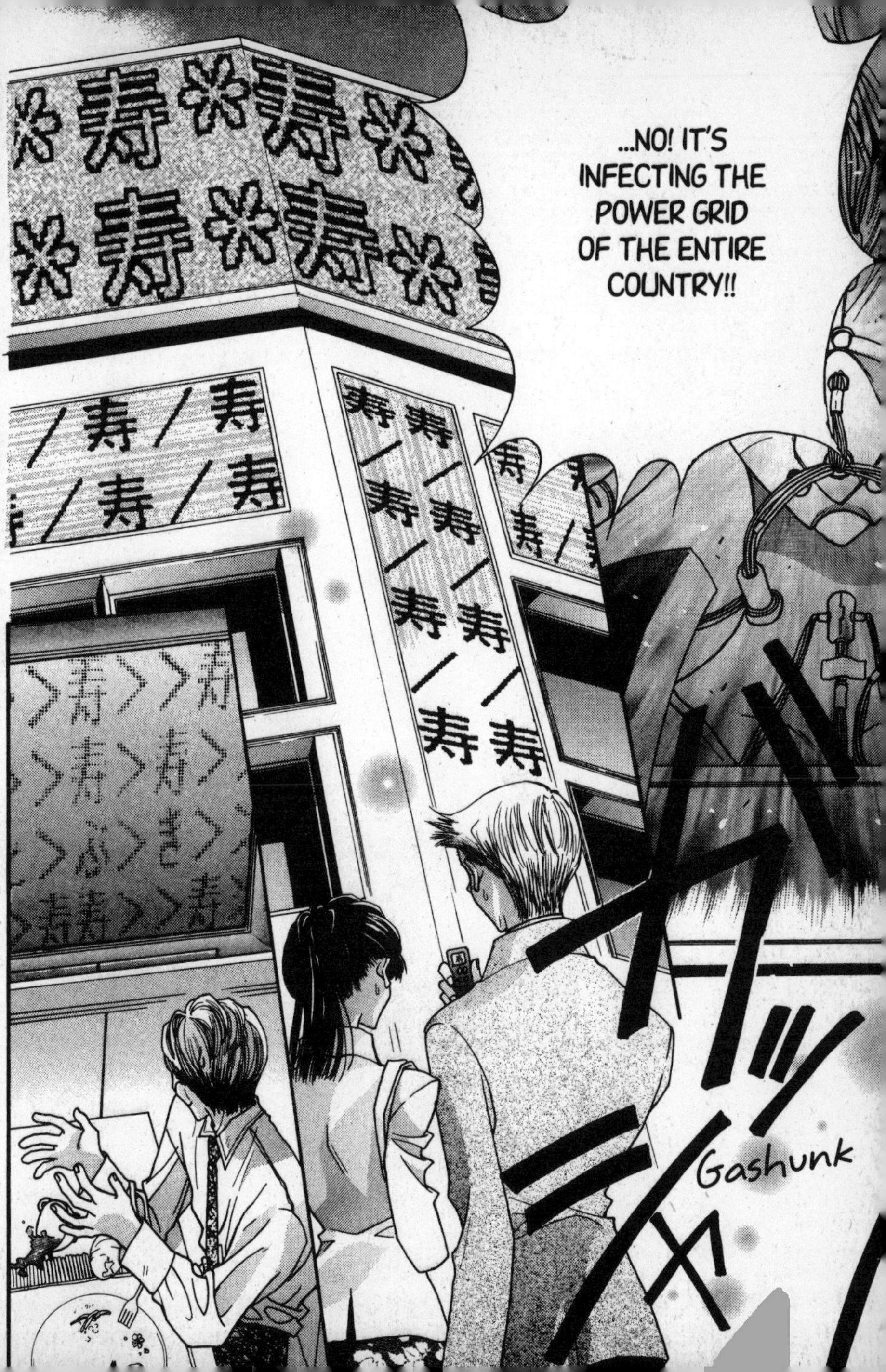
...NO! IT'S INFECTING THE POWER GRID OF THE ENTIRE COUNTRY!!
Gashunk

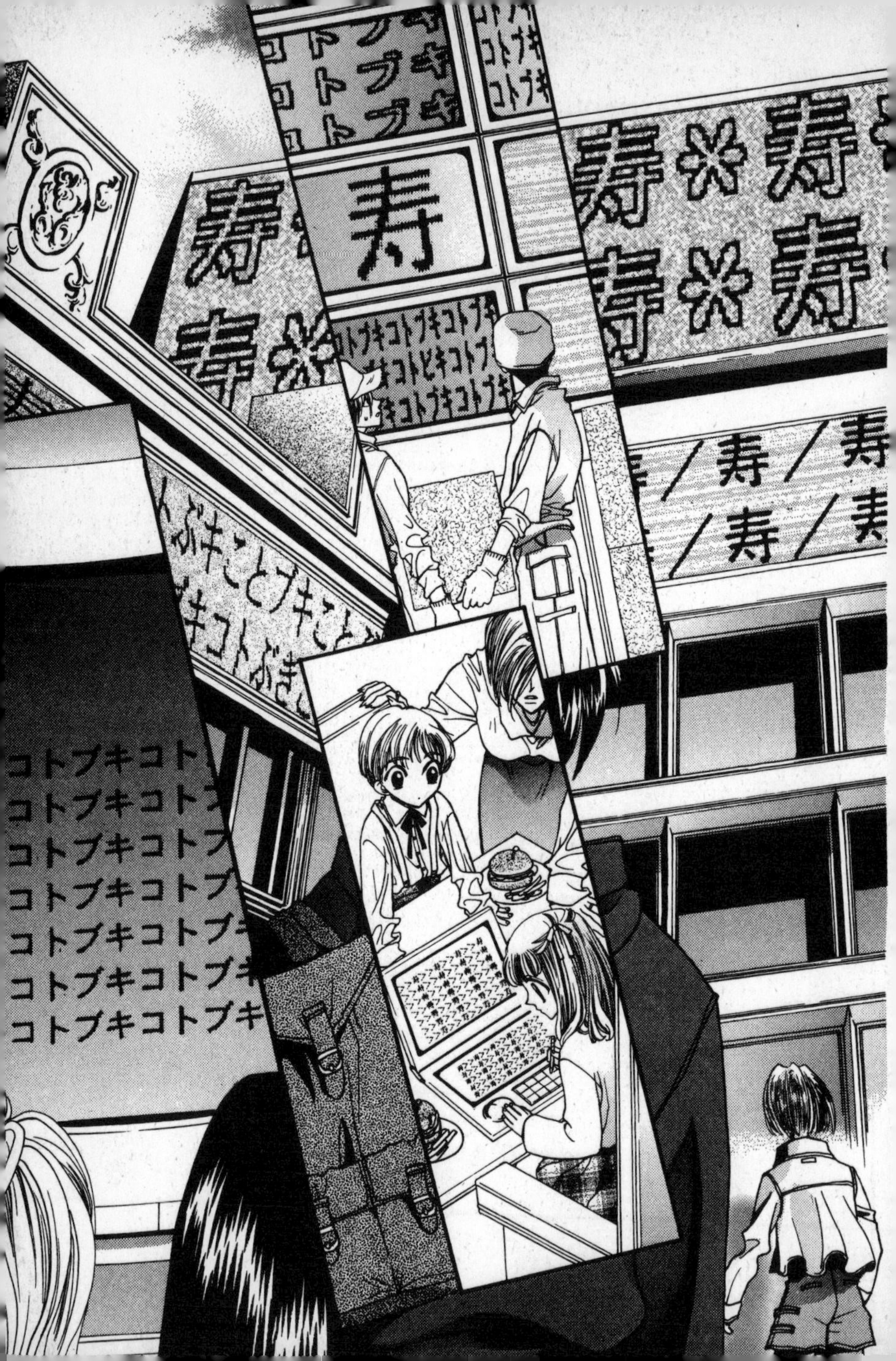

コトブキ
寿
寿※寿
寿※寿
寿/寿/寿
コトブキコトブキ
コトブキコトブキ

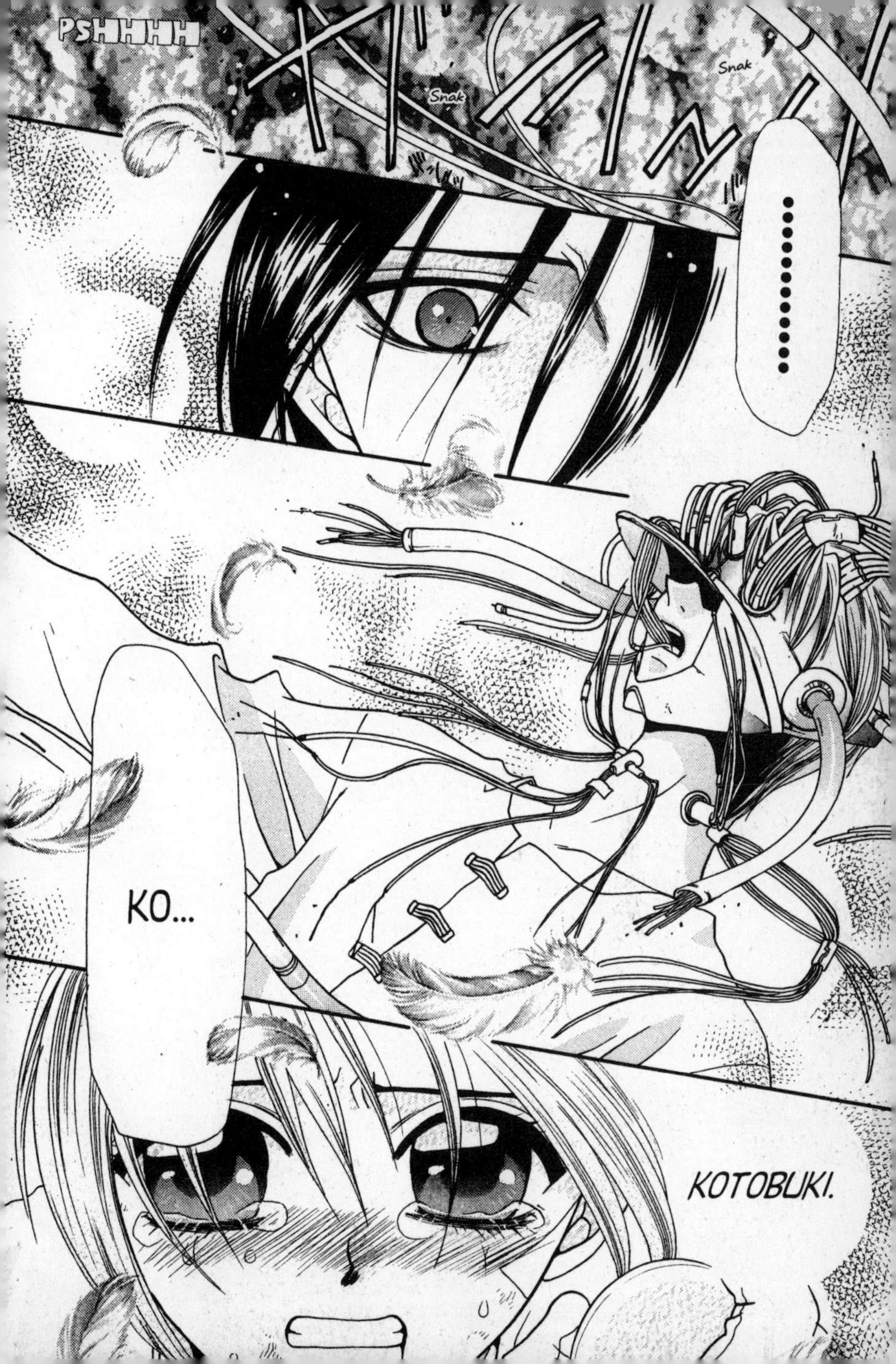
PSHHHH
Snak
Snak
....
KO...
KOTOBUKI.

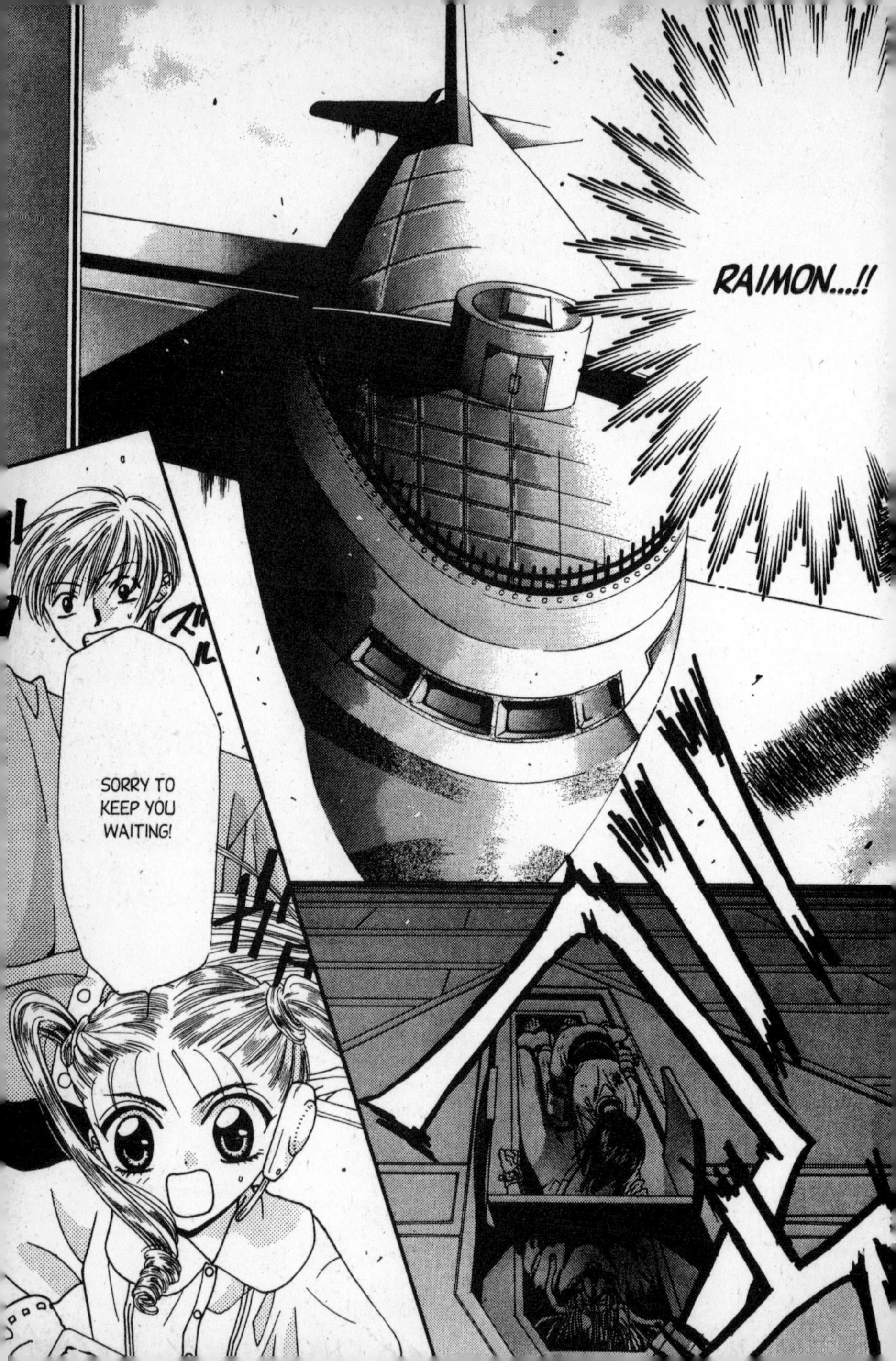
RAIMON...!!
SORRY TO KEEP YOU WAITING!

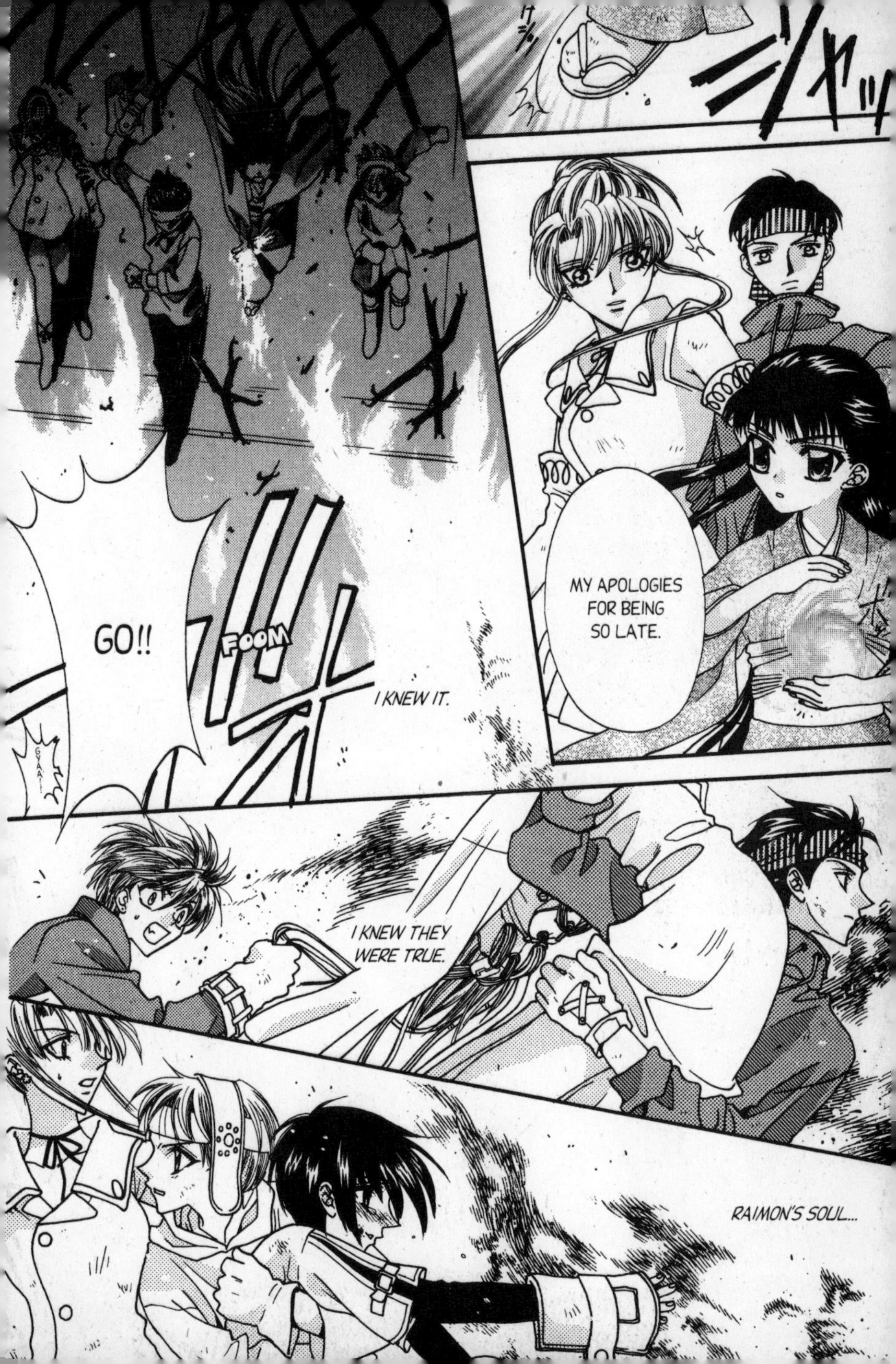
ジャッ
MY APOLOGIES FOR BEING SO LATE.
GO!!
FOOM
I KNEW IT.
GYAA!
I KNEW THEY WERE TRUE.
RAIMON'S SOUL...

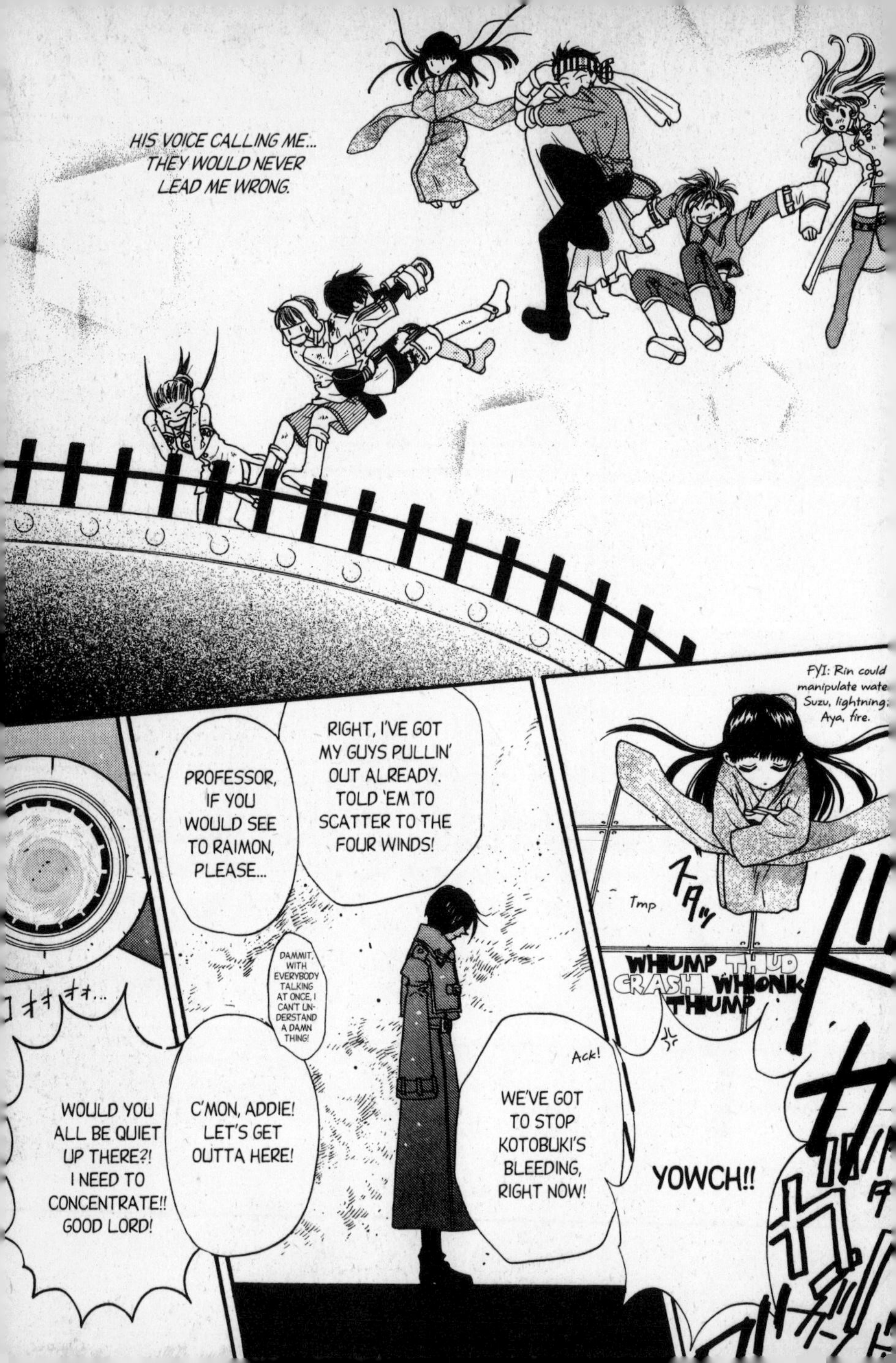
HIS VOICE CALLING ME... THEY WOULD NEVER LEAD ME WRONG.
FYI: Rin could manipulate water; Suzu, lightning; Aya, fire.
Tmp
WHUMP THUD CRASH WHONK THUMP
Ack!
YOWCH!!
RIGHT, I'VE GOT MY GUYS PULLIN' OUT ALREADY. TOLD 'EM TO SCATTER TO THE FOUR WINDS!
PROFESSOR, IF YOU WOULD SEE TO RAIMON, PLEASE...
DAMMIT, WITH EVERYBODY TALKING AT ONCE, I CAN'T UNDERSTAND A DAMN THING!
WE'VE GOT TO STOP KOTOBUKI'S BLEEDING, RIGHT NOW!
C'MON, ADDIE! LET'S GET OUTTA HERE!
WOULD YOU ALL BE QUIET UP THERE?! I NEED TO CONCENTRATE!! GOOD LORD!

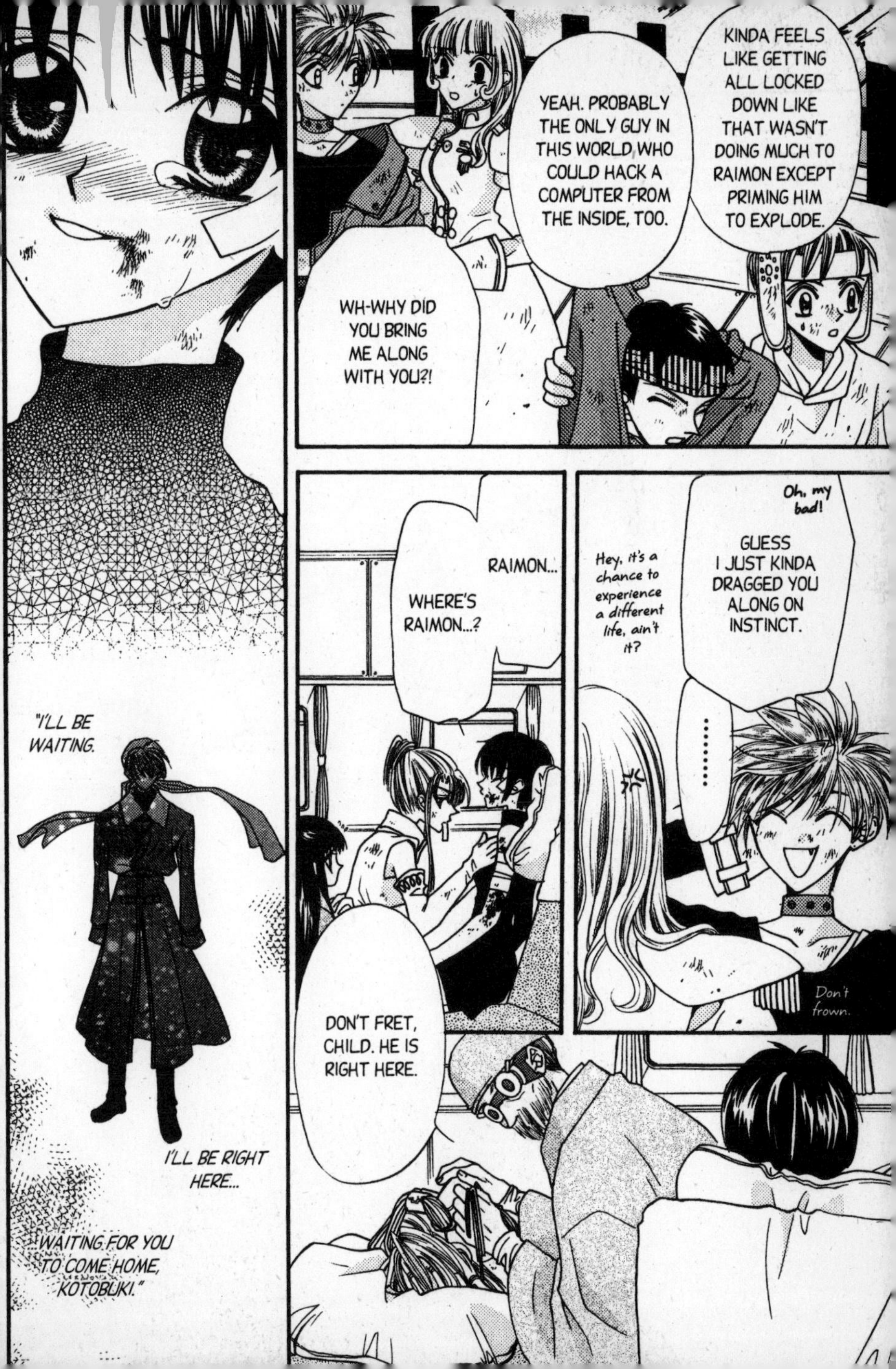
KINDA FEELS LIKE GETTING ALL LOCKED DOWN LIKE THAT WASN'T DOING MUCH TO RAIMON EXCEPT PRIMING HIM TO EXPLODE.
YEAH. PROBABLY THE ONLY GUY IN THIS WORLD WHO COULD HACK A COMPUTER FROM THE INSIDE, TOO.
WH-WHY DID YOU BRING ME ALONG WITH YOU?!
Oh, my bad!
GUESS I JUST KINDA DRAGGED YOU ALONG ON INSTINCT.
Hey, it's a chance to experience a different life, ain't it?
......
Don't frown.
RAIMON...
WHERE'S RAIMON...?
DON'T FRET, CHILD. HE IS RIGHT HERE.
"I'LL BE WAITING.
I'LL BE RIGHT HERE...
WAITING FOR YOU TO COME HOME, KOTOBUKI."

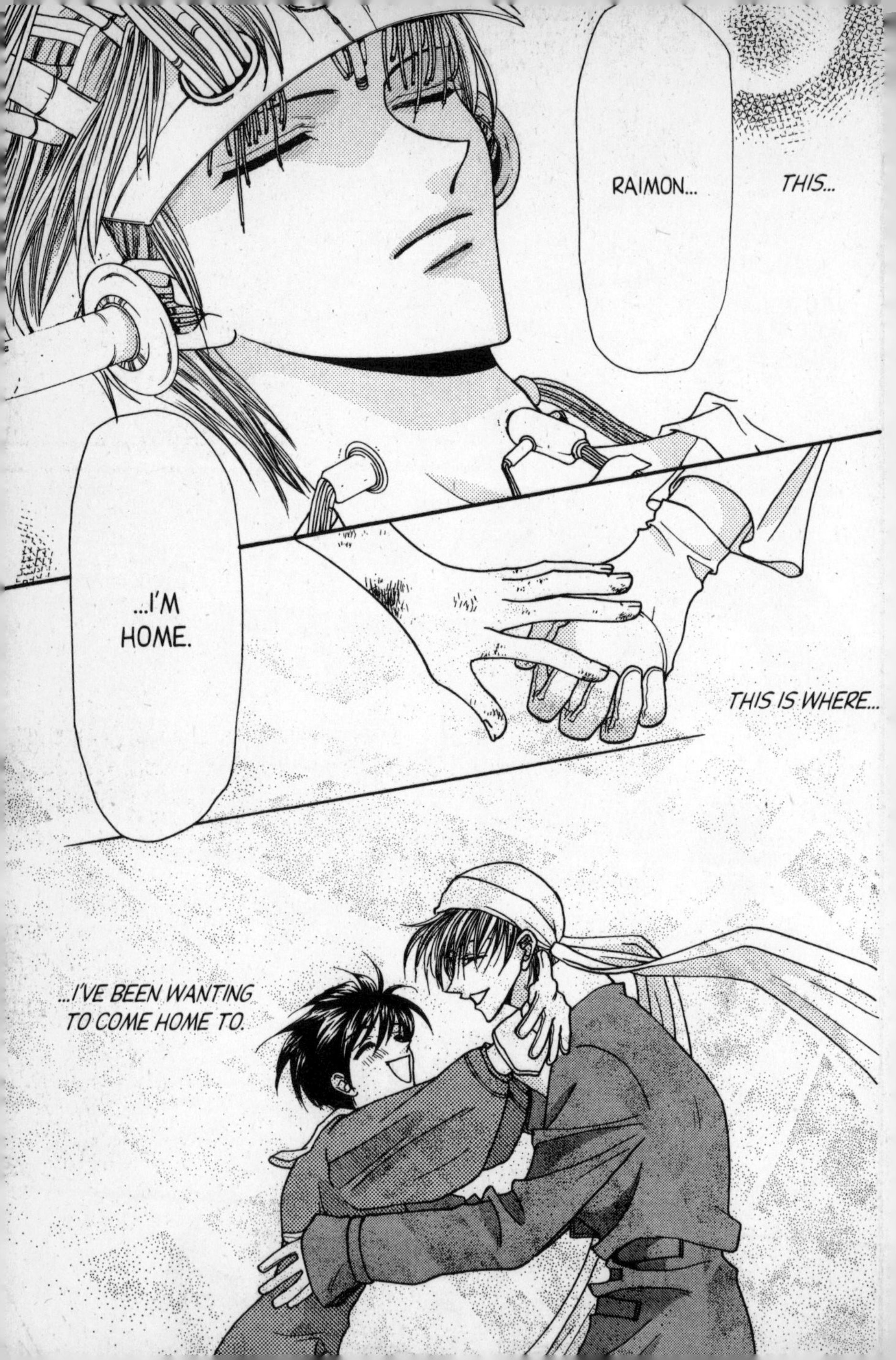
THIS...
RAIMON...
...I'M HOME.
THIS IS WHERE...
...I'VE BEEN WANTING TO COME HOME TO.

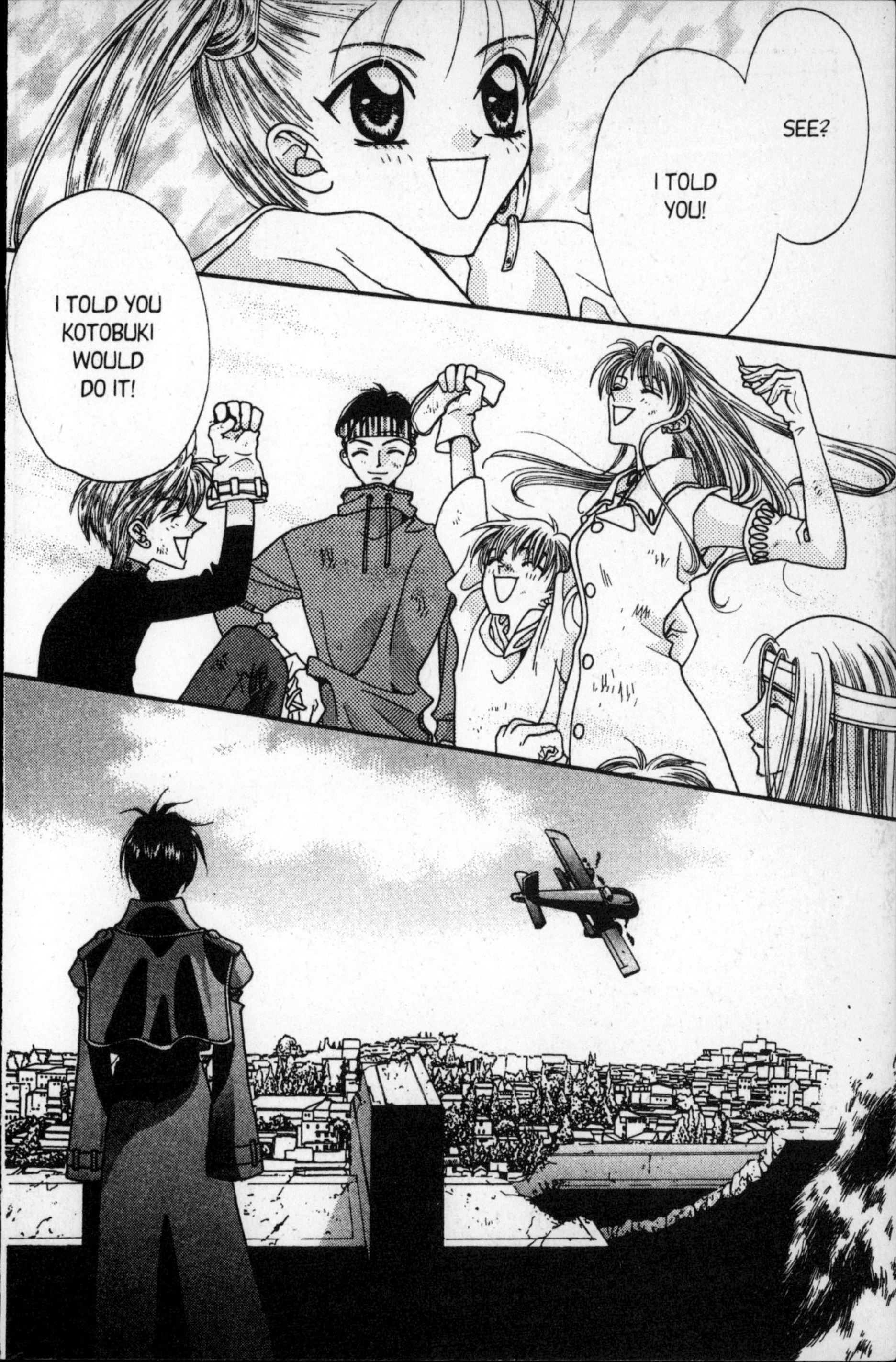
SEE?
I TOLD YOU!
I TOLD YOU KOTOBUKI WOULD DO IT!

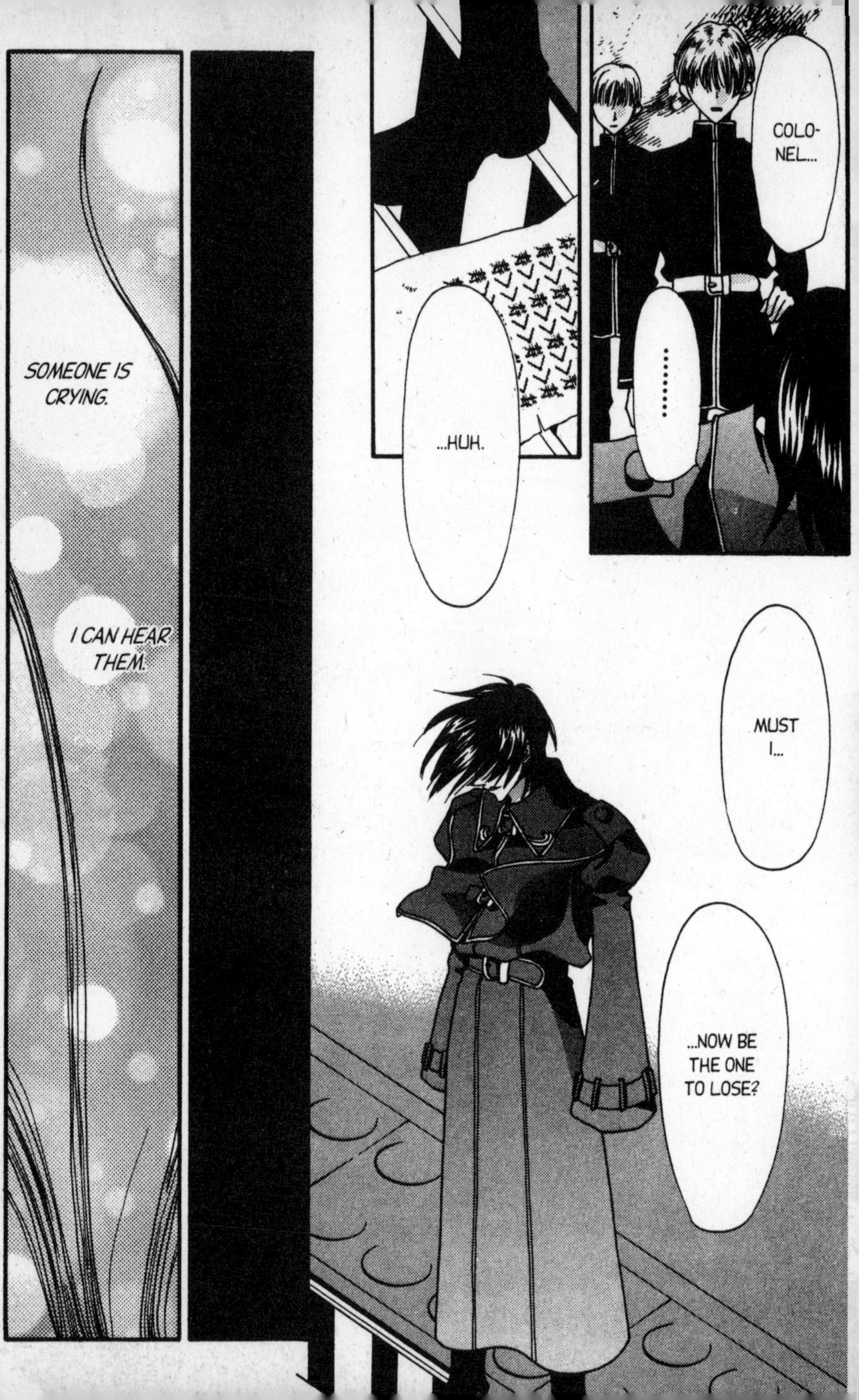
COLO-NEL...
......
...HUH.
MUST I...
...NOW BE THE ONE TO LOSE?
SOMEONE IS CRYING.
I CAN HEAR THEM.

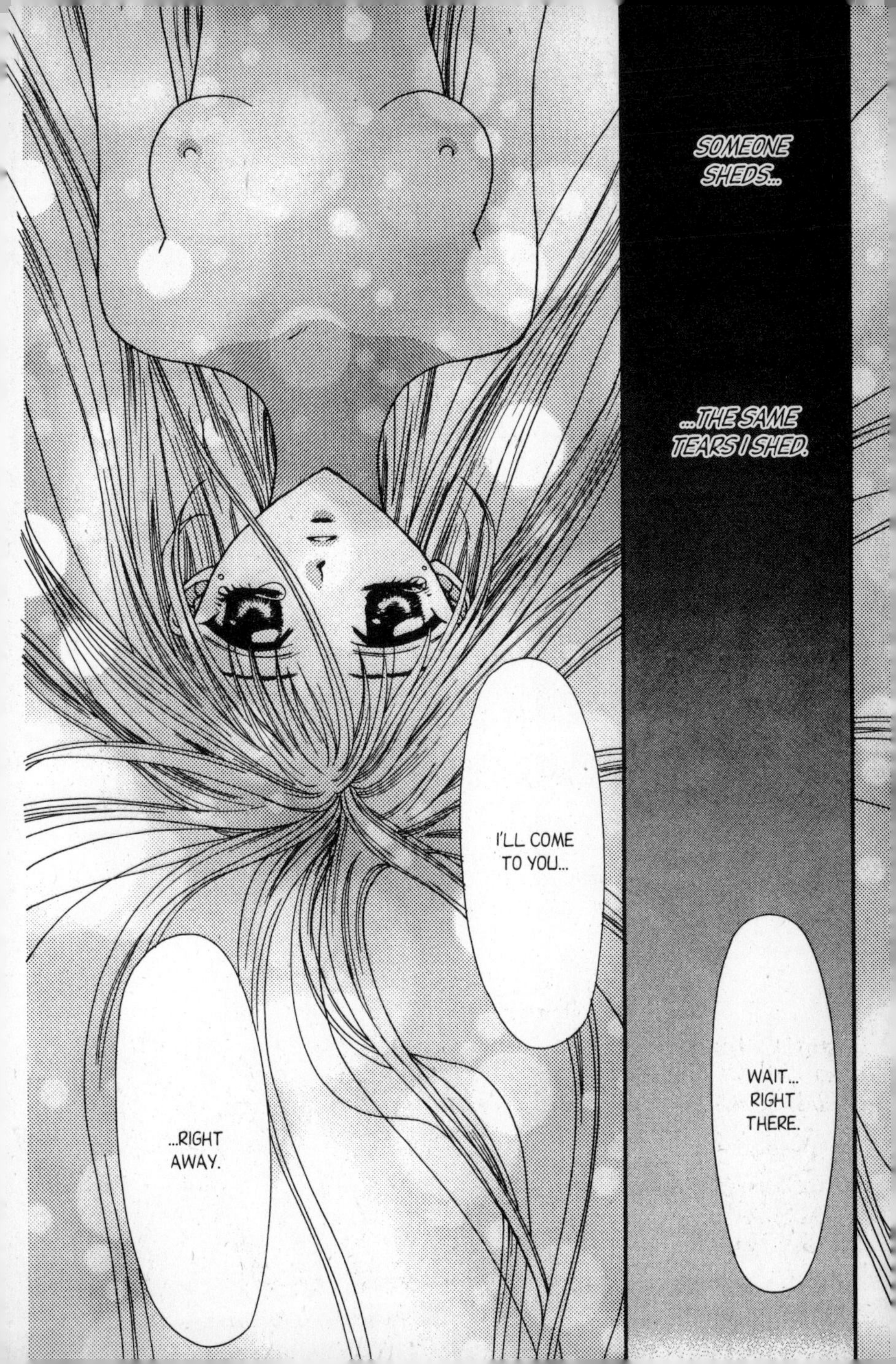
SOMEONE SHEDS...
...THE SAME TEARS I SHED.
WAIT... RIGHT THERE.
I'LL COME TO YOU...
...RIGHT AWAY.

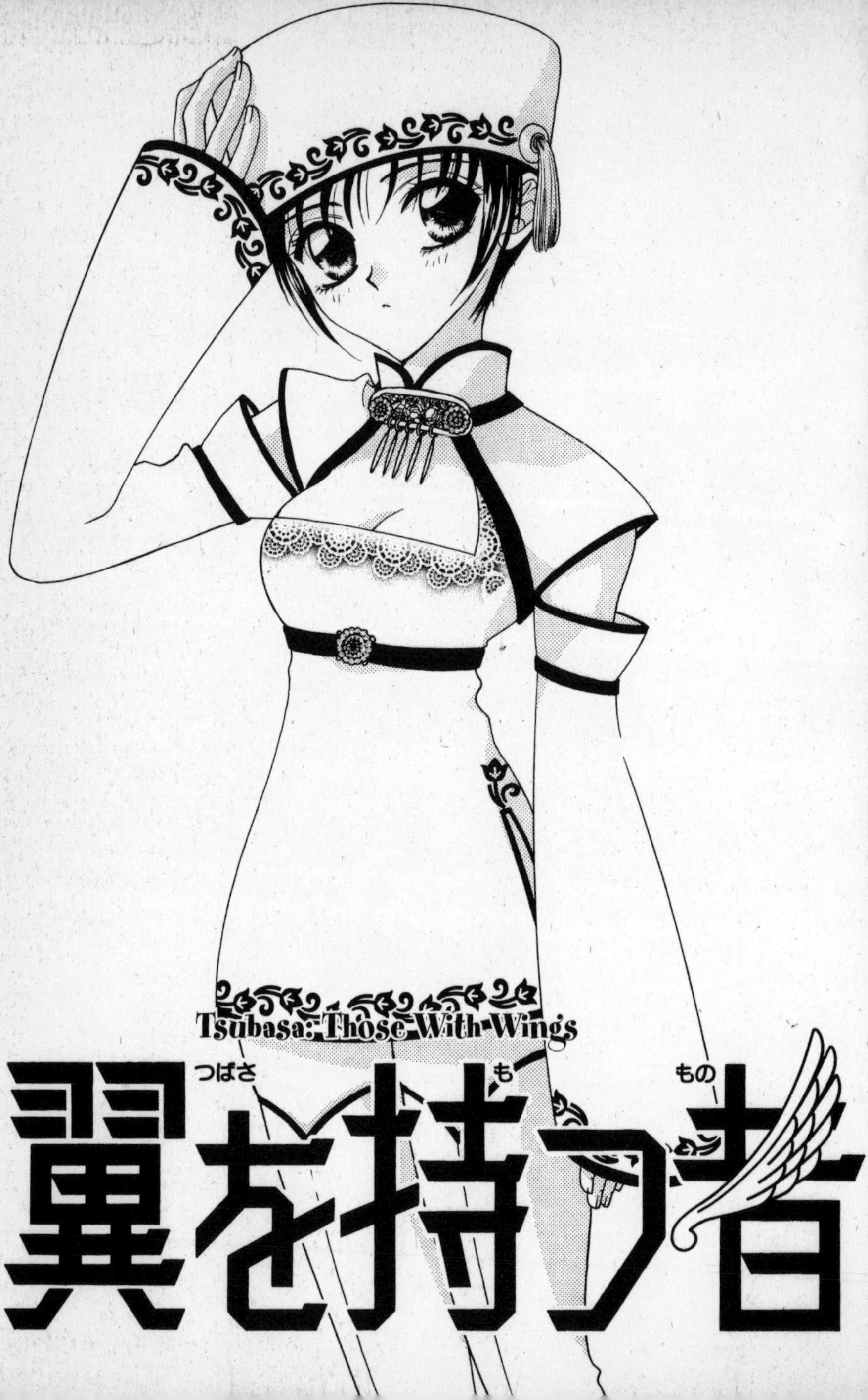
Tsubasa: Those With Wings
つばさ も もの
翼を持つ者

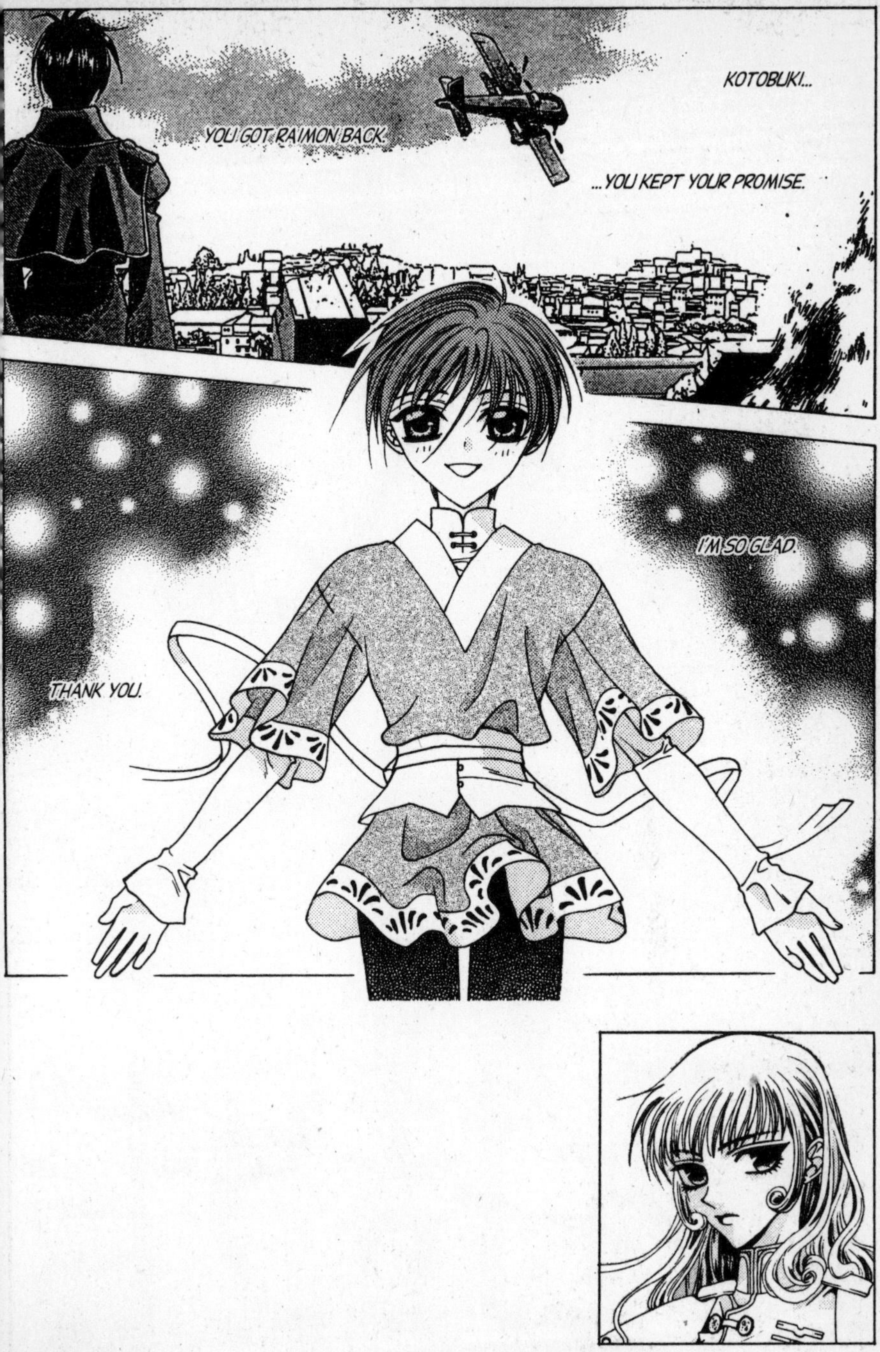
KOTOBUKI...
YOU GOT RAIMON BACK.
...YOU KEPT YOUR PROMISE.
I'M SO GLAD.
THANK YOU.

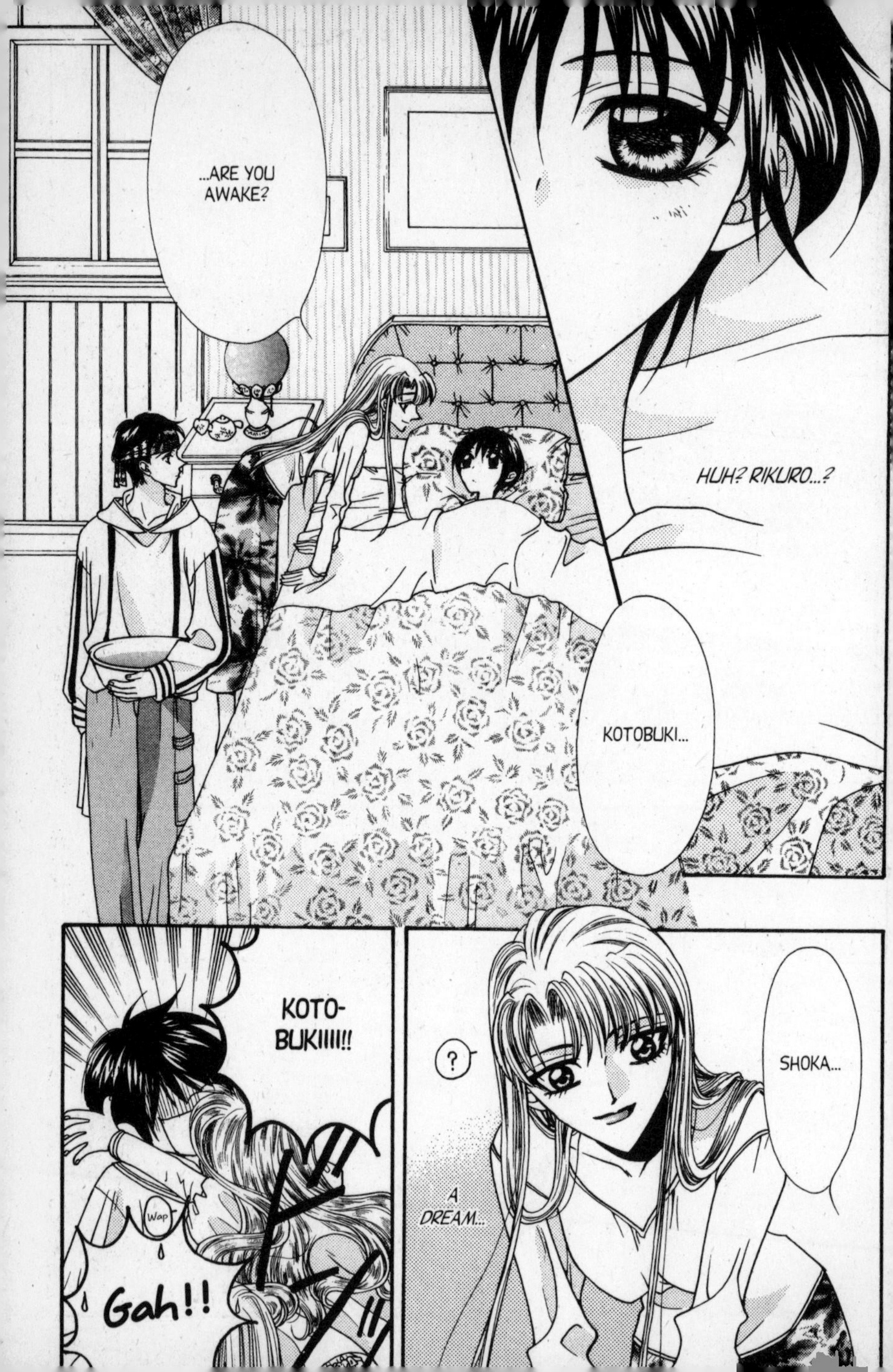
HUH? RIKURO...?
KOTOBUKI...
...ARE YOU AWAKE?
SHOKA...
?
A DREAM...
KOTO-BUKI!!!!!!
Wap
Gah!!

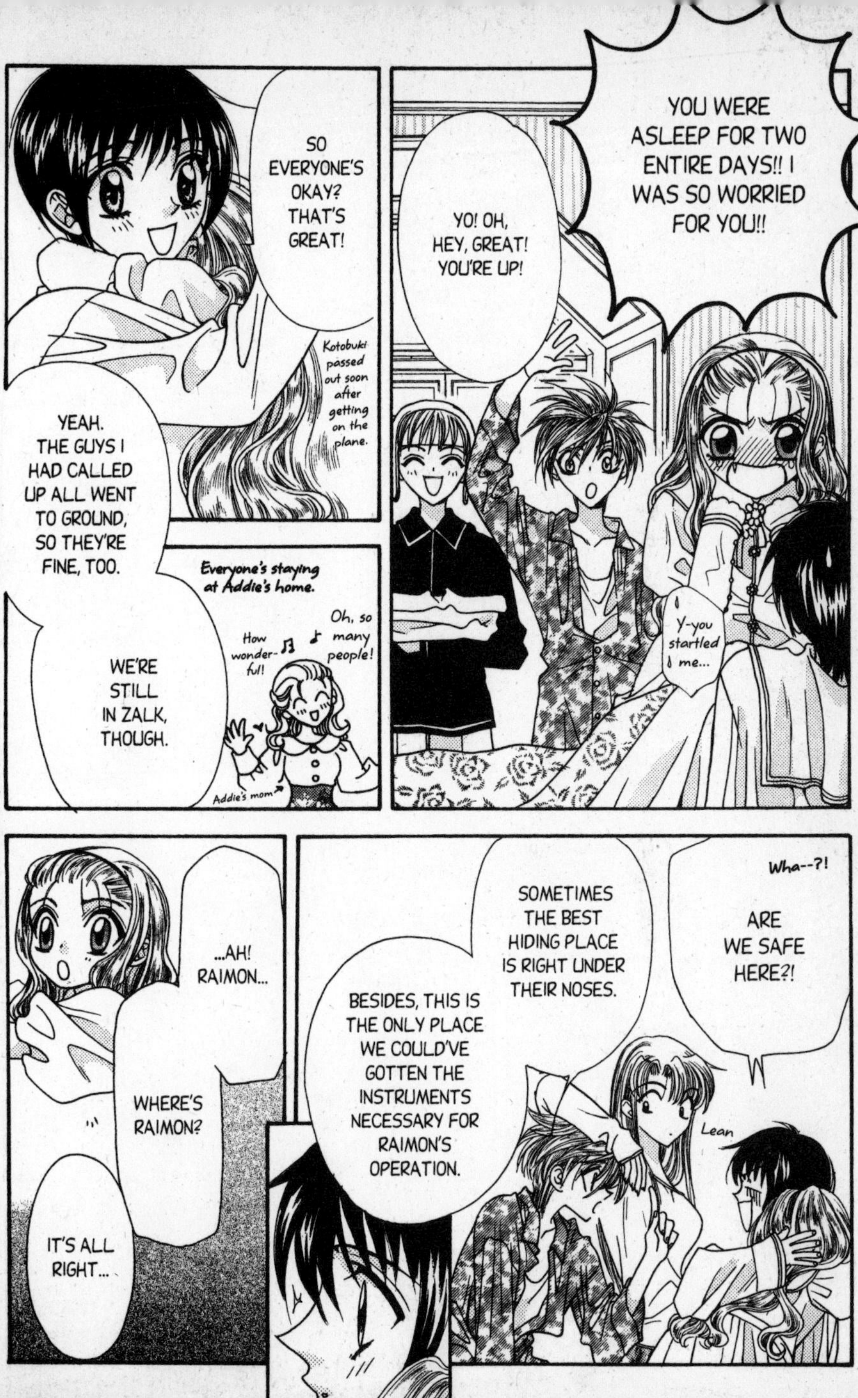
YOU WERE ASLEEP FOR TWO ENTIRE DAYS!! I WAS SO WORRIED FOR YOU!!
YO! OH, HEY, GREAT! YOU'RE UP!
Y-you startled me...
SO EVERYONE'S OKAY? THAT'S GREAT!
Kotobuki passed out soon after getting on the plane.
YEAH. THE GUYS I HAD CALLED UP ALL WENT TO GROUND, SO THEY'RE FINE, TOO.
Everyone's staying at Addie's home.
Oh, so many people!
How wonder-ful!
Addie's mom
WE'RE STILL IN ZALK, THOUGH.
Wha--?!
ARE WE SAFE HERE?!
SOMETIMES THE BEST HIDING PLACE IS RIGHT UNDER THEIR NOSES.
BESIDES, THIS IS THE ONLY PLACE WE COULD'VE GOTTEN THE INSTRUMENTS NECESSARY FOR RAIMON'S OPERATION.
Lean
...AH! RAIMON...
WHERE'S RAIMON?
IT'S ALL RIGHT...

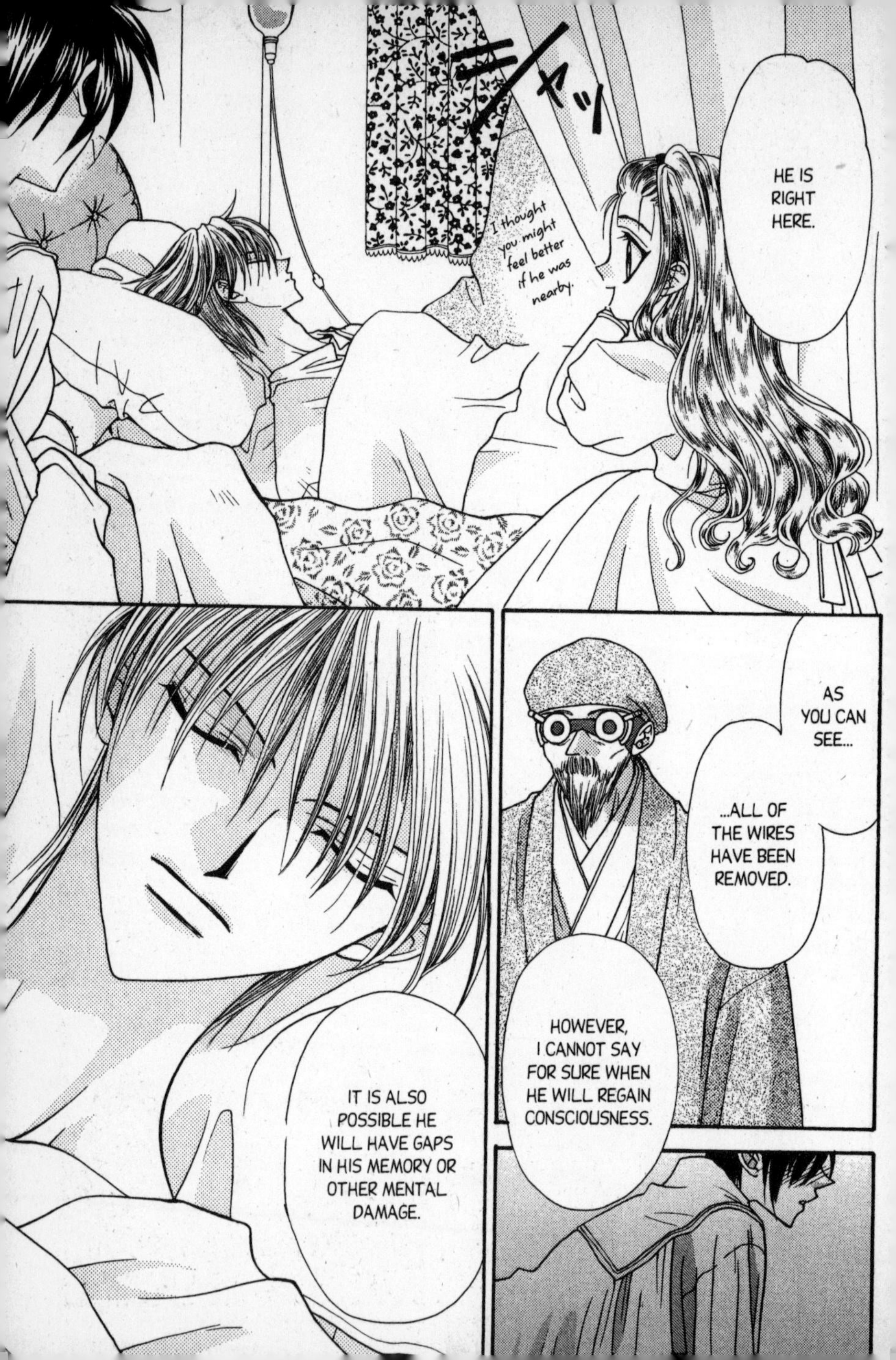
シャッ
HE IS RIGHT HERE.
I thought you might feel better if he was nearby.
AS YOU CAN SEE...
...ALL OF THE WIRES HAVE BEEN REMOVED.
HOWEVER, I CANNOT SAY FOR SURE WHEN HE WILL REGAIN CONSCIOUSNESS.
IT IS ALSO POSSIBLE HE WILL HAVE GAPS IN HIS MEMORY OR OTHER MENTAL DAMAGE.

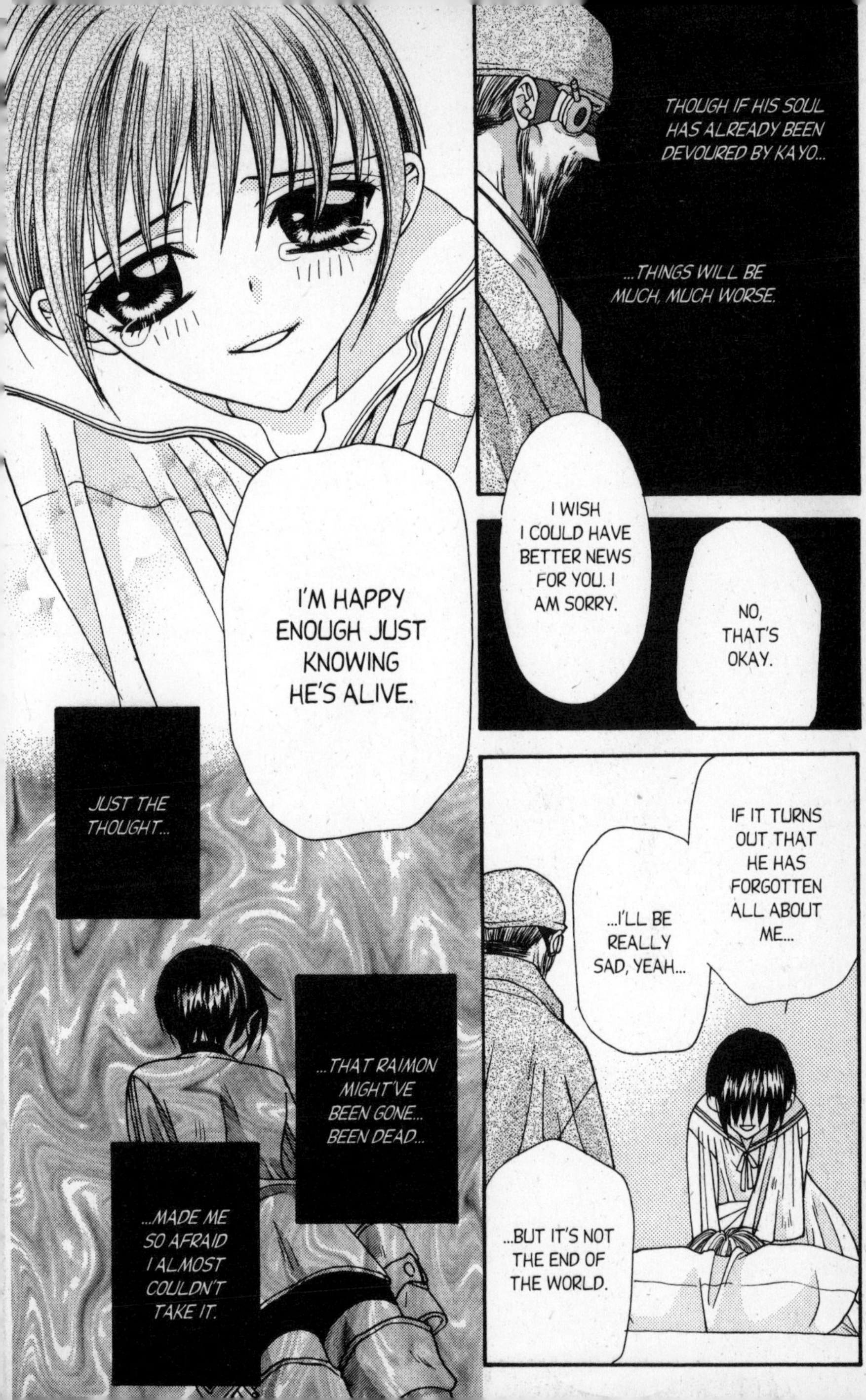
THOUGH IF HIS SOUL HAS ALREADY BEEN DEVOURED BY KAYO...
...THINGS WILL BE MUCH, MUCH WORSE.
I WISH I COULD HAVE BETTER NEWS FOR YOU. I AM SORRY.
NO, THAT'S OKAY.
IF IT TURNS OUT THAT HE HAS FORGOTTEN ALL ABOUT ME...
...I'LL BE REALLY SAD, YEAH...
...BUT IT'S NOT THE END OF THE WORLD.
I'M HAPPY ENOUGH JUST KNOWING HE'S ALIVE.
JUST THE THOUGHT...
...THAT RAIMON MIGHT'VE BEEN GONE... BEEN DEAD...
...MADE ME SO AFRAID I ALMOST COULDN'T TAKE IT.

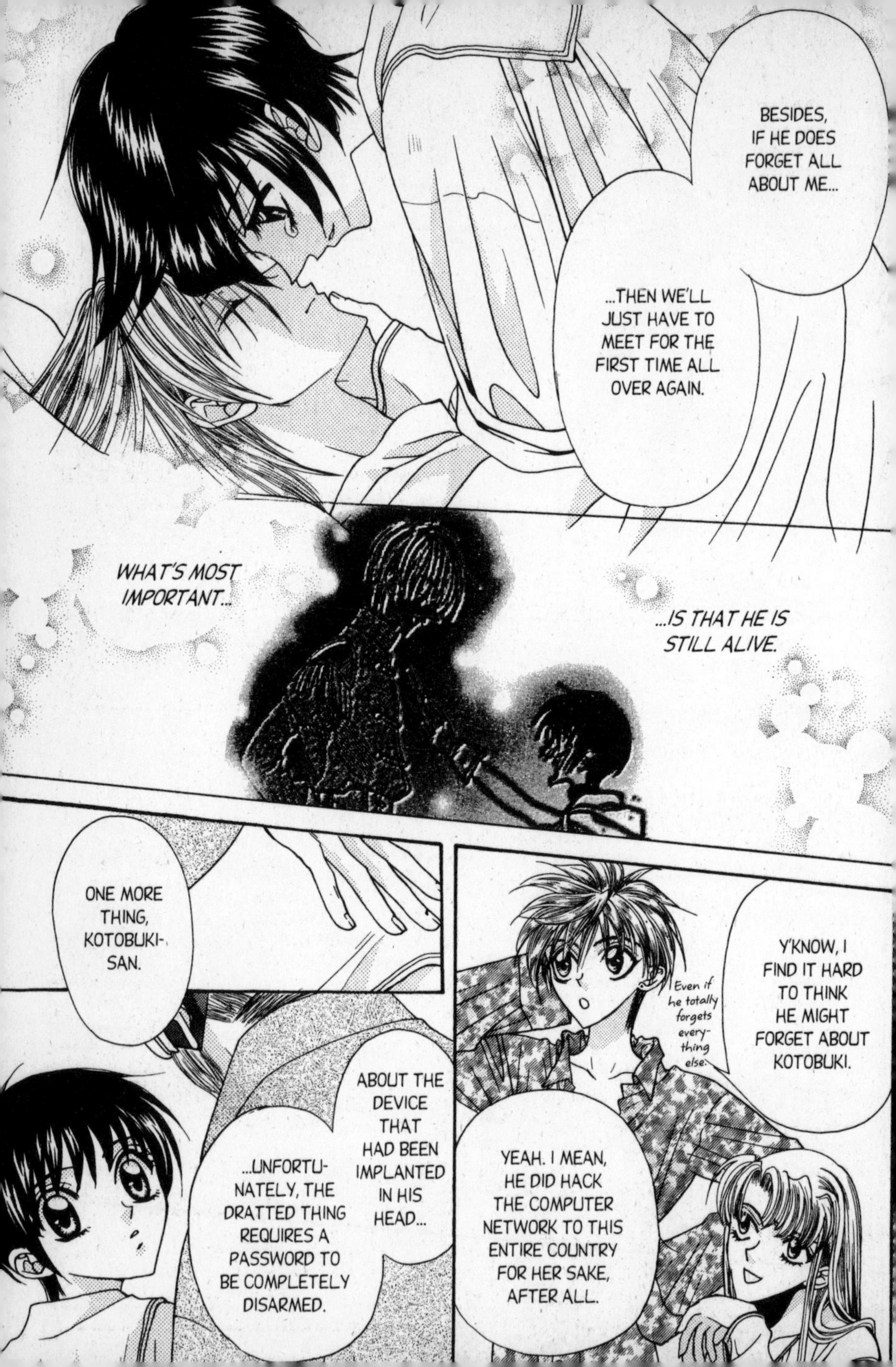
BESIDES, IF HE DOES FORGET ALL ABOUT ME...
...THEN WE'LL JUST HAVE TO MEET FOR THE FIRST TIME ALL OVER AGAIN.
WHAT'S MOST IMPORTANT...
...IS THAT HE IS STILL ALIVE.
Y'KNOW, I FIND IT HARD TO THINK HE MIGHT FORGET ABOUT KOTOBUKI.
Even if he totally forgets everything else.
YEAH. I MEAN, HE DID HACK THE COMPUTER NETWORK TO THIS ENTIRE COUNTRY FOR HER SAKE, AFTER ALL.
ONE MORE THING, KOTOBUKI-SAN.
ABOUT THE DEVICE THAT HAD BEEN IMPLANTED IN HIS HEAD...
...UNFORTUNATELY, THE DRATTED THING REQUIRES A PASSWORD TO BE COMPLETELY DISARMED.

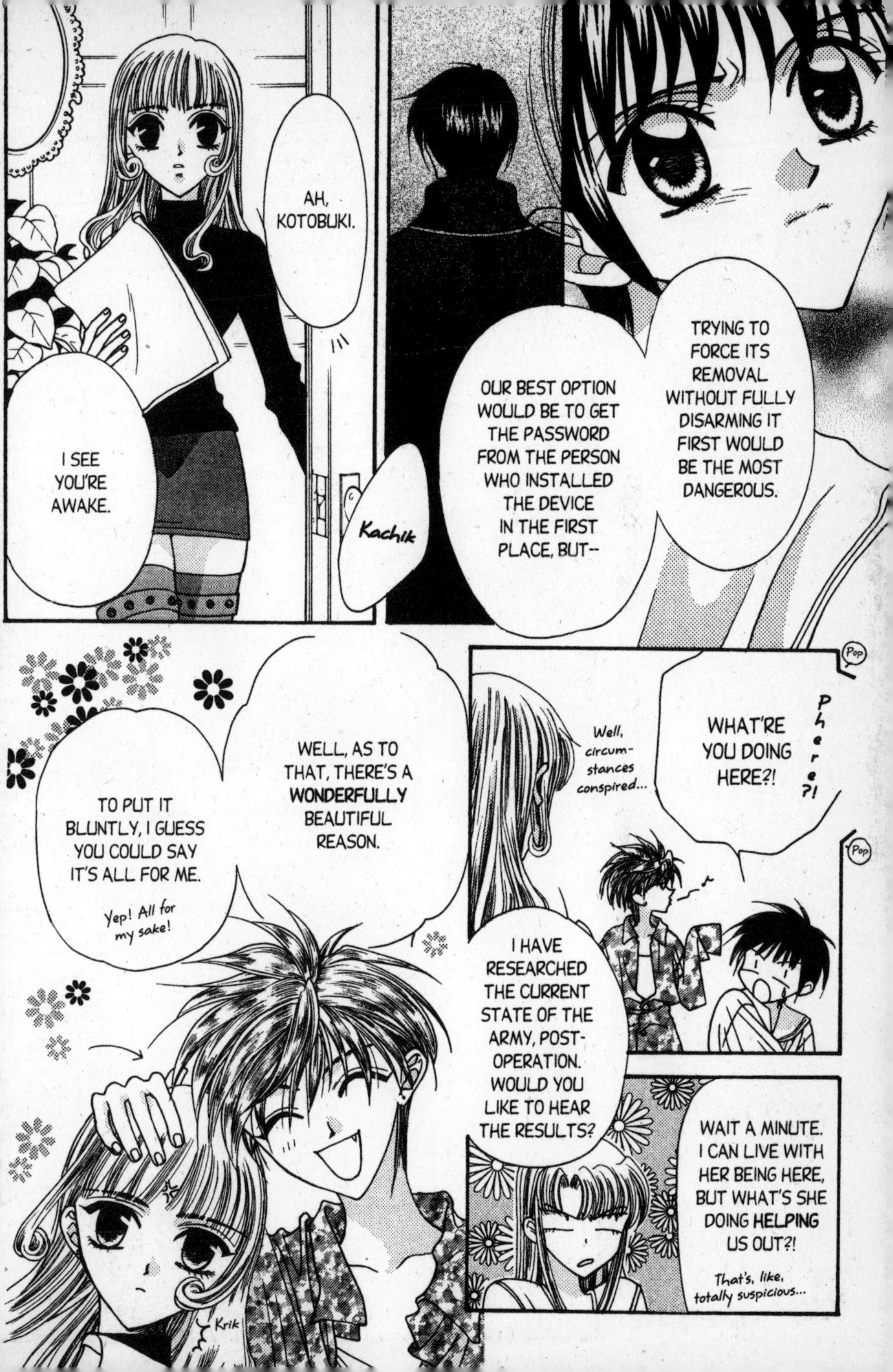
TRYING TO FORCE ITS REMOVAL WITHOUT FULLY DISARMING IT FIRST WOULD BE THE MOST DANGEROUS.
OUR BEST OPTION WOULD BE TO GET THE PASSWORD FROM THE PERSON WHO INSTALLED THE DEVICE IN THE FIRST PLACE, BUT--
Kachik
AH, KOTOBUKI.
I SEE YOU'RE AWAKE.
Pop
WHAT'RE YOU DOING HERE?!
Phere?!
Well, circumstances conspired...
Pop
I HAVE RESEARCHED THE CURRENT STATE OF THE ARMY, POST-OPERATION. WOULD YOU LIKE TO HEAR THE RESULTS?
WAIT A MINUTE. I CAN LIVE WITH HER BEING HERE, BUT WHAT'S SHE DOING HELPING US OUT?!
That's, like, totally suspicious...
WELL, AS TO THAT, THERE'S A WONDERFULLY BEAUTIFUL REASON.
TO PUT IT BLUNTLY, I GUESS YOU COULD SAY IT'S ALL FOR ME.
Yep! All for my sake!
Krik

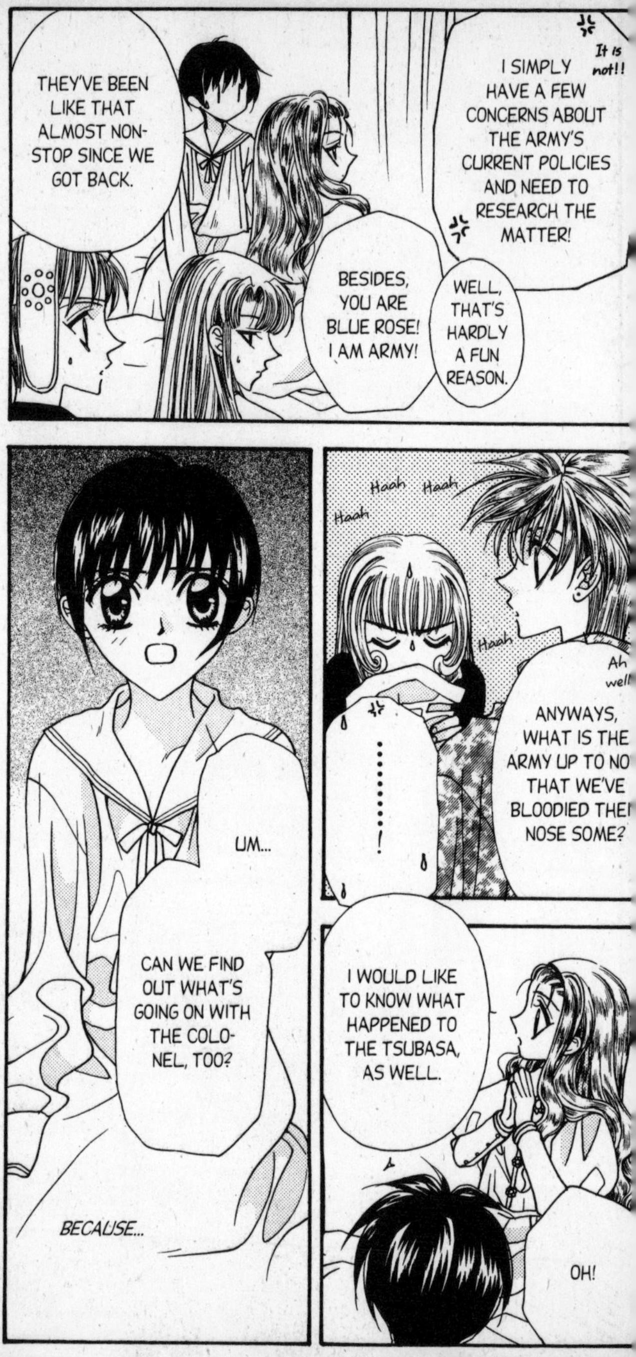
It is not!!
I SIMPLY HAVE A FEW CONCERNS ABOUT THE ARMY'S CURRENT POLICIES AND NEED TO RESEARCH THE MATTER!
WELL, THAT'S HARDLY A FUN REASON.
BESIDES, YOU ARE BLUE ROSE! I AM ARMY!
THEY'VE BEEN LIKE THAT ALMOST NON-STOP SINCE WE GOT BACK.
Haah
Haah
Haah
Haah
Ah well
ANYWAYS, WHAT IS THE ARMY UP TO NO
THAT WE'VE BLOODIED THE
NOSE SOME?
......!
OH!
I WOULD LIKE TO KNOW WHAT HAPPENED TO THE TSUBASA, AS WELL.
UM...
CAN WE FIND OUT WHAT'S GOING ON WITH THE COLO-NEL, TOO?
BECAUSE...
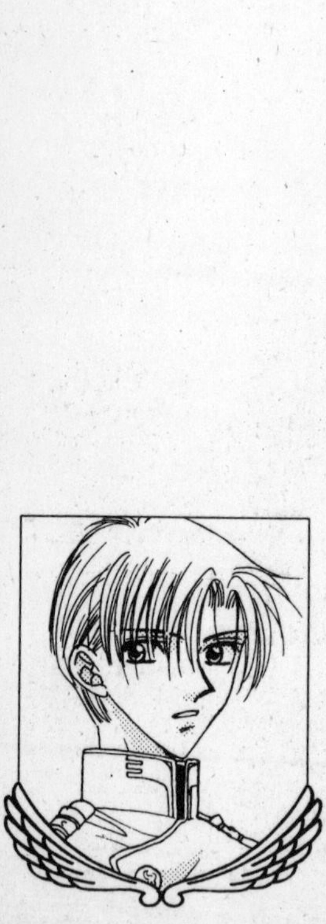

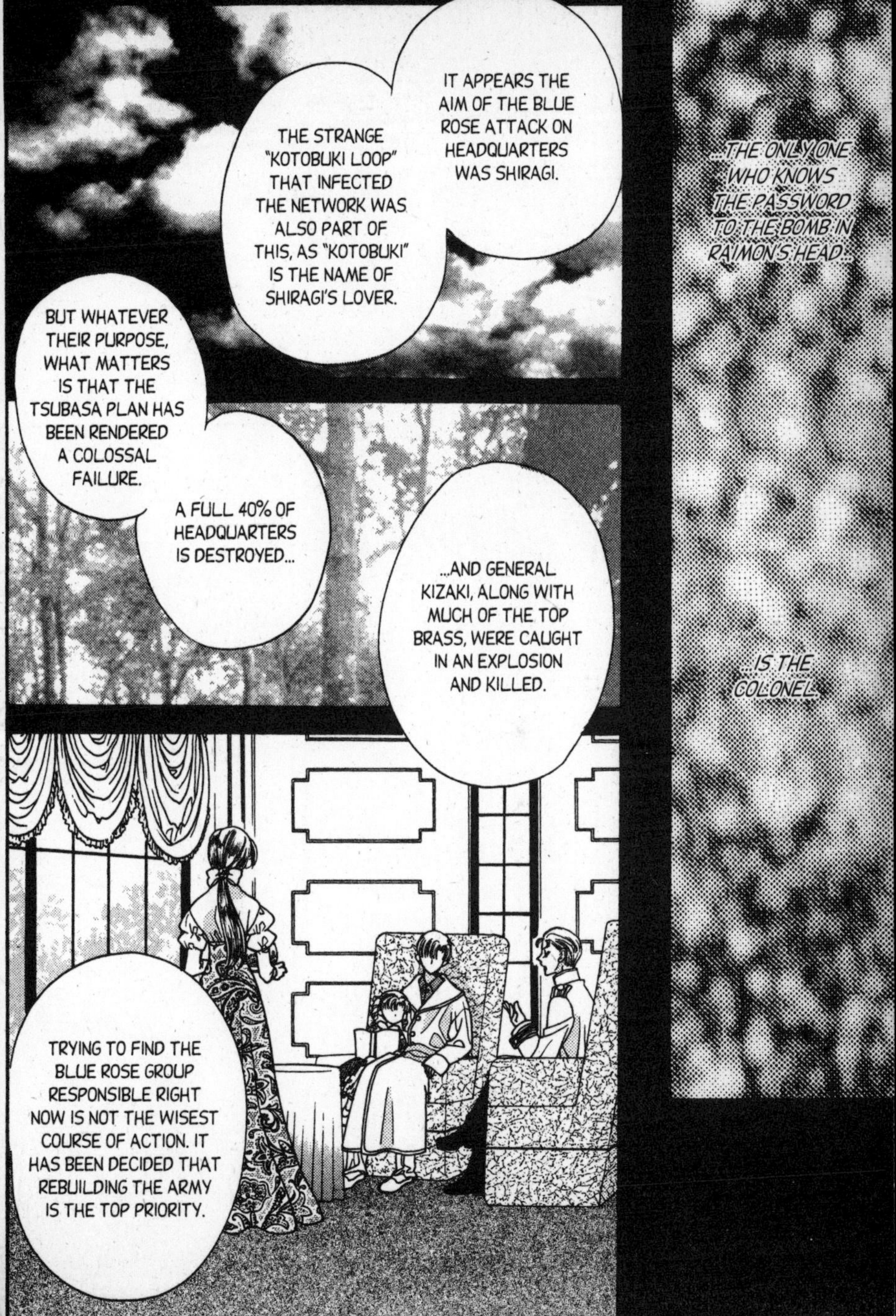
...THE ONLY ONE WHO KNOWS THE PASSWORD TO THE BOMB IN RAIMON'S HEAD...
...IS THE COLONEL.
IT APPEARS THE AIM OF THE BLUE ROSE ATTACK ON HEADQUARTERS WAS SHIRAGI.
THE STRANGE "KOTOBUKI LOOP" THAT INFECTED THE NETWORK WAS ALSO PART OF THIS, AS "KOTOBUKI" IS THE NAME OF SHIRAGI'S LOVER.
BUT WHATEVER THEIR PURPOSE, WHAT MATTERS IS THAT THE TSUBASA PLAN HAS BEEN RENDERED A COLOSSAL FAILURE.
A FULL 40% OF HEADQUARTERS IS DESTROYED...
...AND GENERAL KIZAKI, ALONG WITH MUCH OF THE TOP BRASS, WERE CAUGHT IN AN EXPLOSION AND KILLED.
TRYING TO FIND THE BLUE ROSE GROUP RESPONSIBLE RIGHT NOW IS NOT THE WISEST COURSE OF ACTION. IT HAS BEEN DECIDED THAT REBUILDING THE ARMY IS THE TOP PRIORITY.

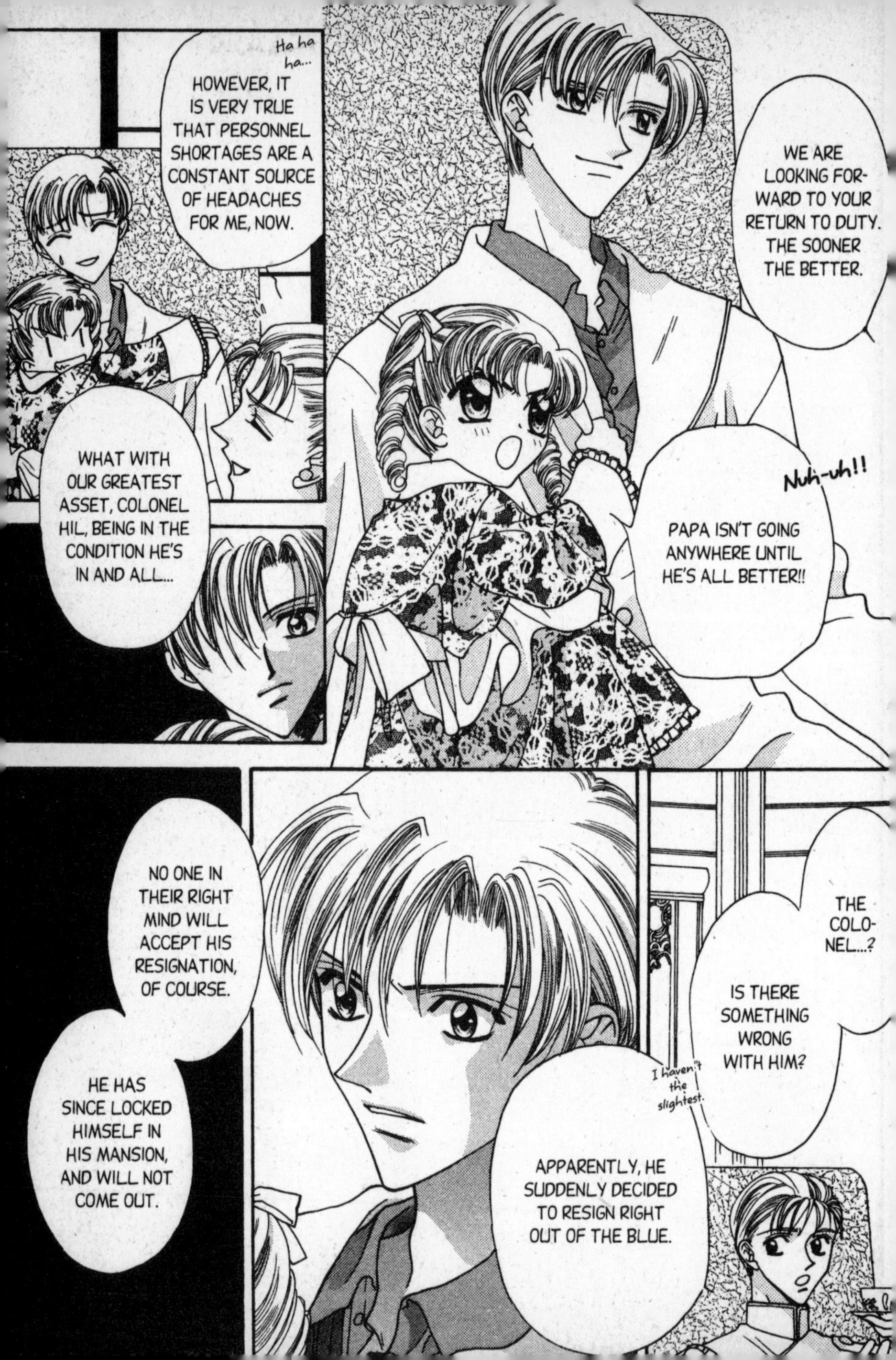
WE ARE LOOKING FOR-WARD TO YOUR RETURN TO DUTY. THE SOONER THE BETTER.
Nuh-uh!!
PAPA ISN'T GOING ANYWHERE UNTIL HE'S ALL BETTER!!
Ha ha ha...
HOWEVER, IT IS VERY TRUE THAT PERSONNEL SHORTAGES ARE A CONSTANT SOURCE OF HEADACHES FOR ME, NOW.
WHAT WITH OUR GREATEST ASSET, COLONEL HIL, BEING IN THE CONDITION HE'S IN AND ALL...
THE COLO-NEL...?
IS THERE SOMETHING WRONG WITH HIM?
I haven't the slightest.
APPARENTLY, HE SUDDENLY DECIDED TO RESIGN RIGHT OUT OF THE BLUE.
NO ONE IN THEIR RIGHT MIND WILL ACCEPT HIS RESIGNATION, OF COURSE.
HE HAS SINCE LOCKED HIMSELF IN HIS MANSION, AND WILL NOT COME OUT.

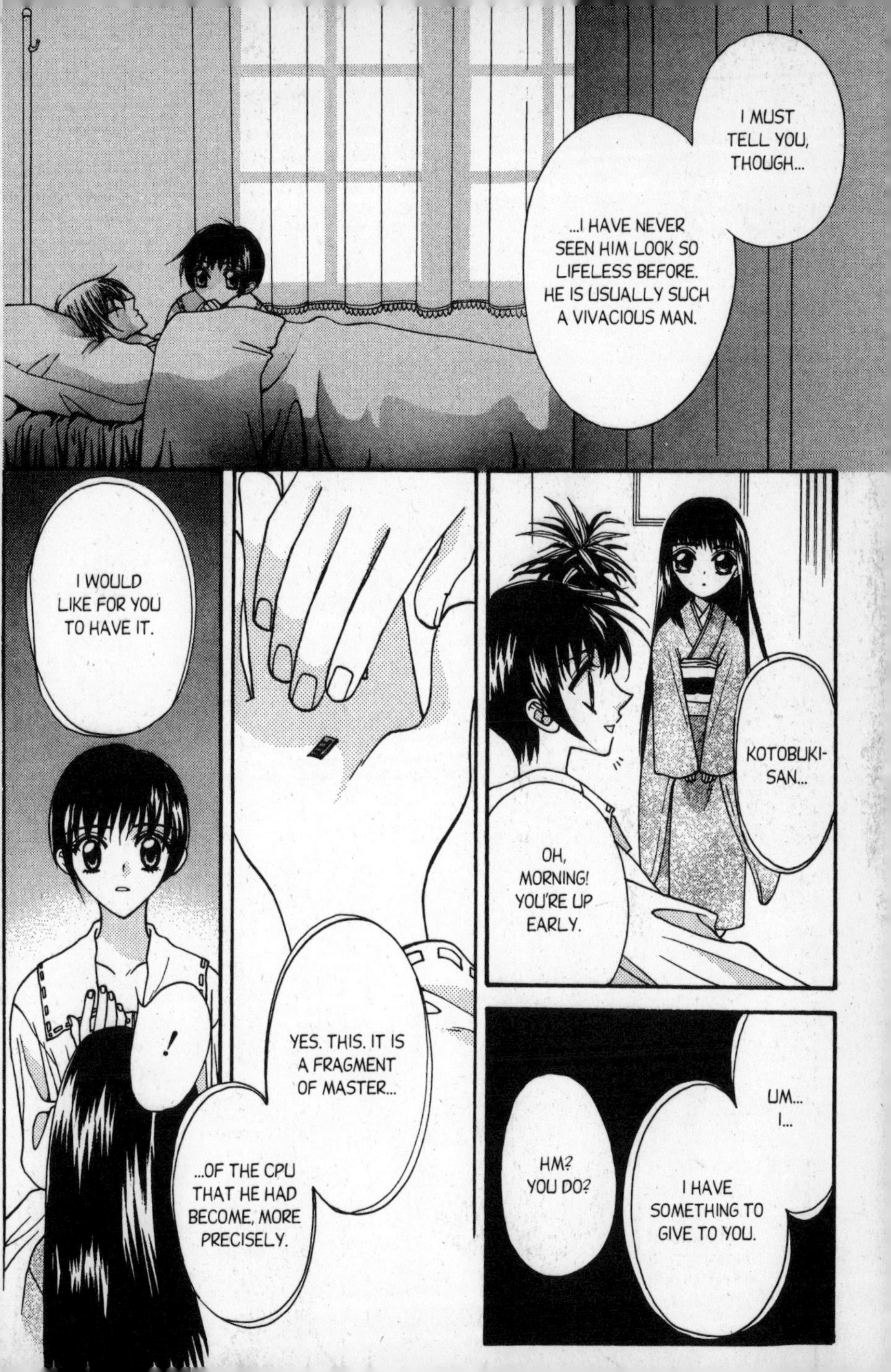
I MUST TELL YOU, THOUGH...
...I HAVE NEVER SEEN HIM LOOK SO LIFELESS BEFORE. HE IS USUALLY SUCH A VIVACIOUS MAN.
KOTOBUKI-SAN...
OH, MORNING! YOU'RE UP EARLY.
UM... I...
I HAVE SOMETHING TO GIVE TO YOU.
HM? YOU DO?
YES. THIS. IT IS A FRAGMENT OF MASTER...
...OF THE CPU THAT HE HAD BECOME, MORE PRECISELY.
I WOULD LIKE FOR YOU TO HAVE IT.
!

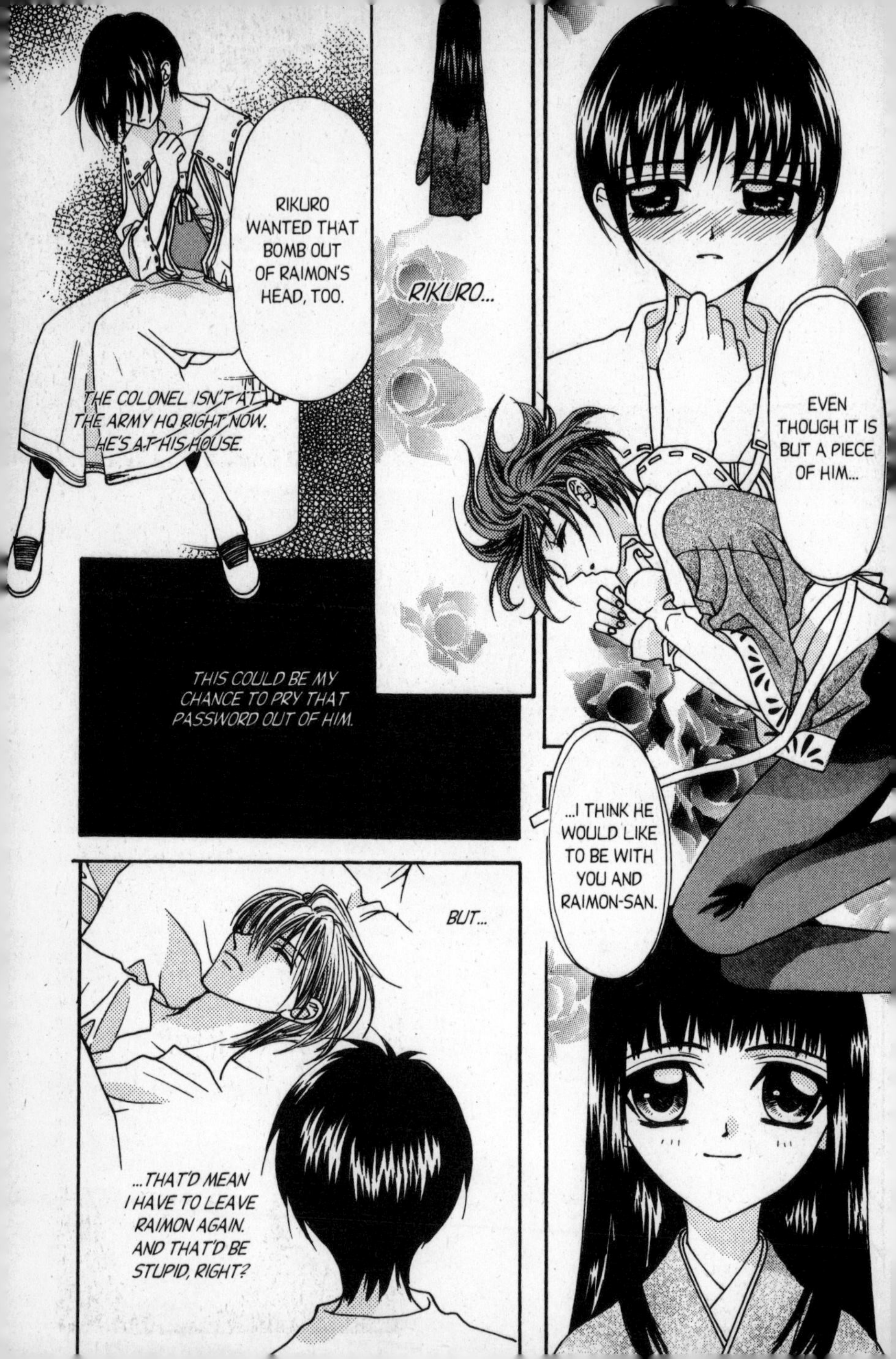
EVEN THOUGH IT IS BUT A PIECE OF HIM...
...I THINK HE WOULD LIKE TO BE WITH YOU AND RAIMON-SAN.
RIKURO...
RIKURO WANTED THAT BOMB OUT OF RAIMON'S HEAD, TOO.
THE COLONEL ISN'T AT THE ARMY HQ RIGHT NOW. HE'S AT HIS HOUSE.
THIS COULD BE MY CHANCE TO PRY THAT PASSWORD OUT OF HIM.
BUT...
...THAT'D MEAN I HAVE TO LEAVE RAIMON AGAIN. AND THAT'D BE STUPID, RIGHT?

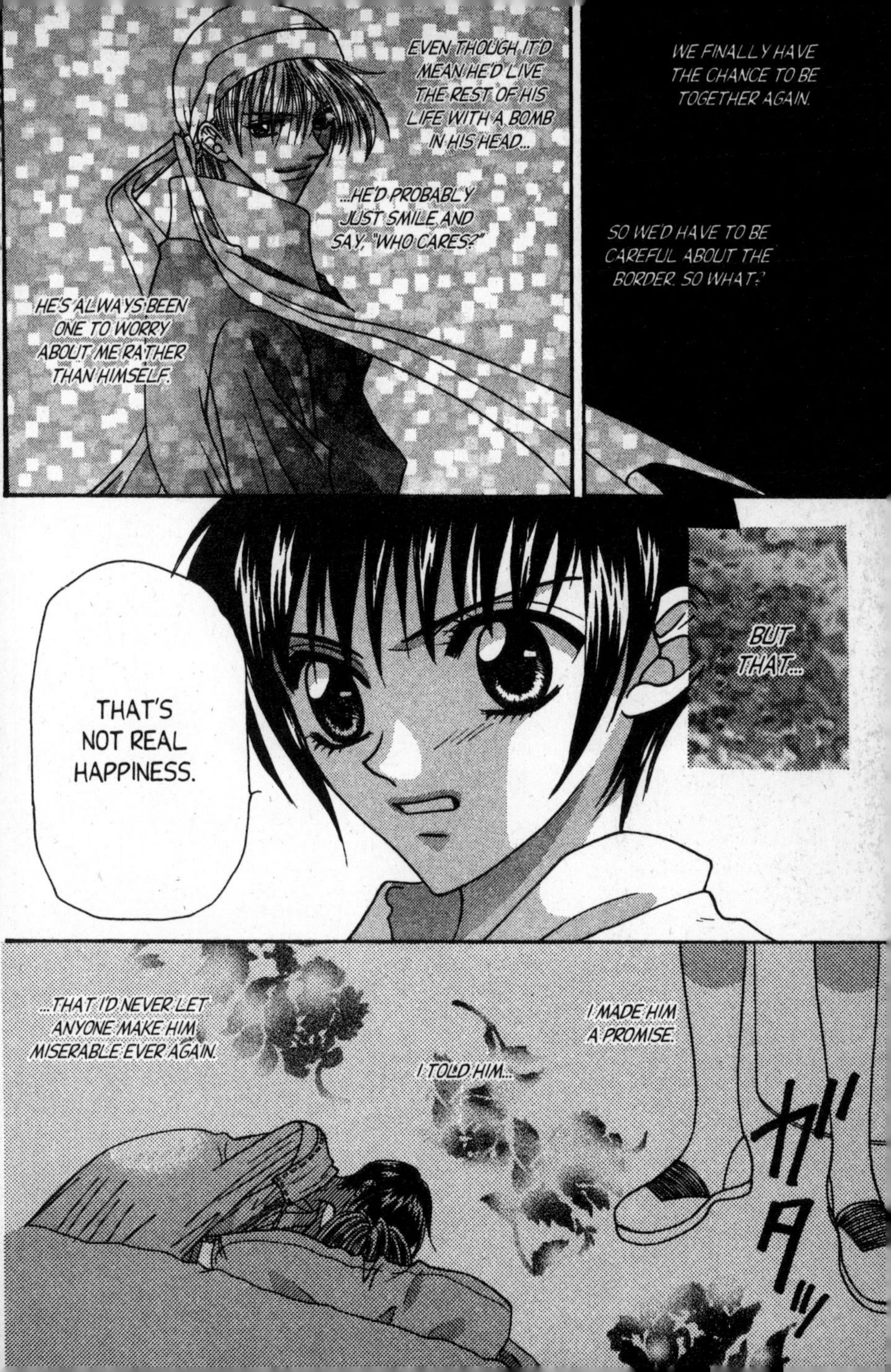
WE FINALLY HAVE THE CHANCE TO BE TOGETHER AGAIN.
SO WE'D HAVE TO BE CAREFUL ABOUT THE BORDER. SO WHAT?
EVEN THOUGH IT'D MEAN HE'D LIVE THE REST OF HIS LIFE WITH A BOMB IN HIS HEAD...
...HE'D PROBABLY JUST SMILE AND SAY, "WHO CARES?"
HE'S ALWAYS BEEN ONE TO WORRY ABOUT ME RATHER THAN HIMSELF.
BUT THAT...
THAT'S NOT REAL HAPPINESS.
I MADE HIM A PROMISE.
I TOLD HIM...
...THAT I'D NEVER LET ANYONE MAKE HIM MISERABLE EVER AGAIN.
ガタッ

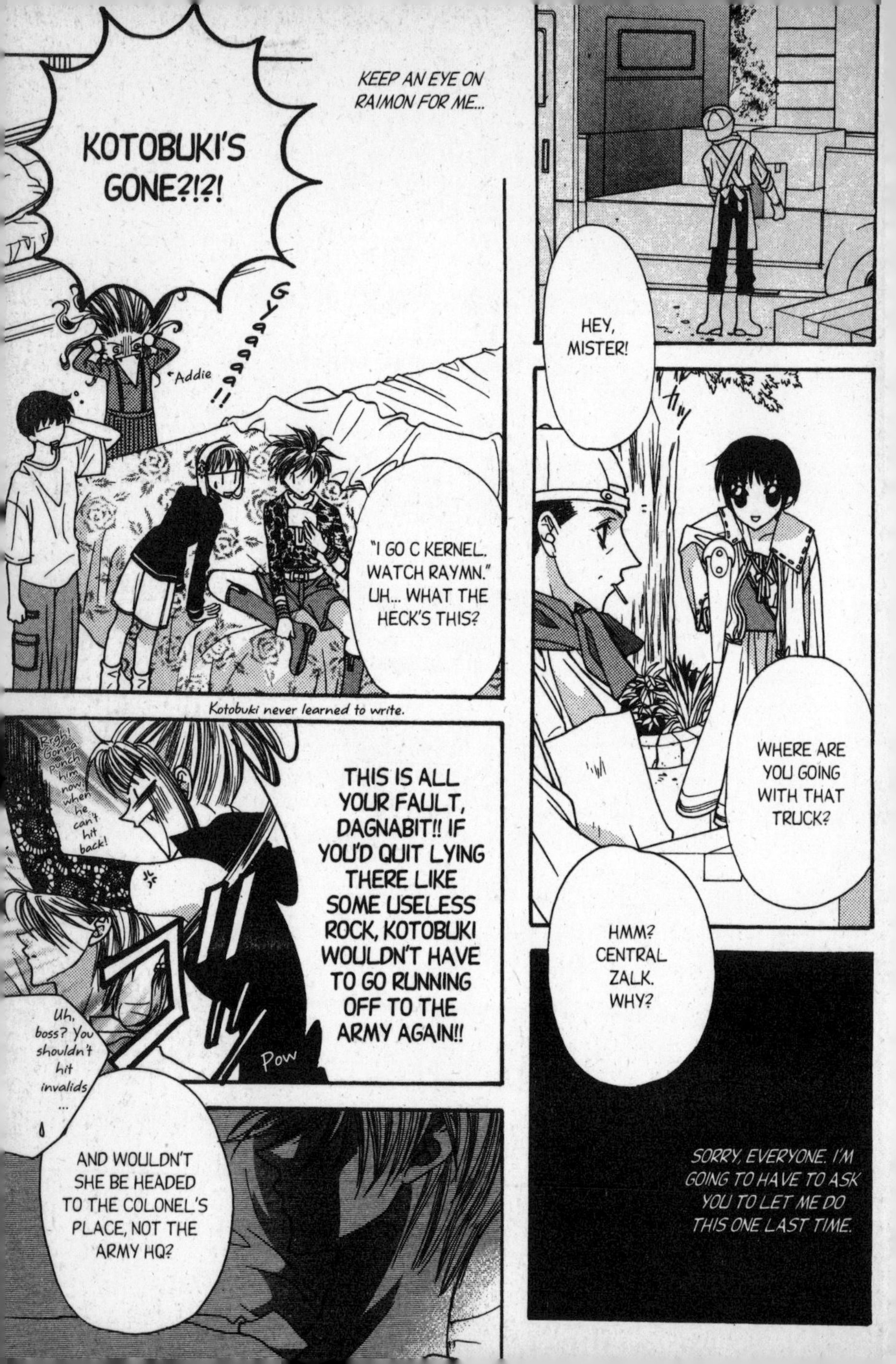
HEY, MISTER!
WHERE ARE YOU GOING WITH THAT TRUCK?
HMM? CENTRAL ZALK. WHY?
SORRY, EVERYONE. I'M GOING TO HAVE TO ASK YOU TO LET ME DO THIS ONE LAST TIME.
KEEP AN EYE ON RAIMON FOR ME...
KOTOBUKI'S GONE?!?!
GYAAAAAAA!!
←Addie
"I GO C KERNEL. WATCH RAYMN." UH... WHAT THE HECK'S THIS?
Kotobuki never learned to write.
THIS IS ALL YOUR FAULT, DAGNABIT!! IF YOU'D QUIT LYING THERE LIKE SOME USELESS ROCK, KOTOBUKI WOULDN'T HAVE TO GO RUNNING OFF TO THE ARMY AGAIN!!
Rrgh! Gonna punch him now when he can't hit back!
Pow
Uh, boss? You shouldn't hit invalids...
AND WOULDN'T SHE BE HEADED TO THE COLONEL'S PLACE, NOT THE ARMY HQ?

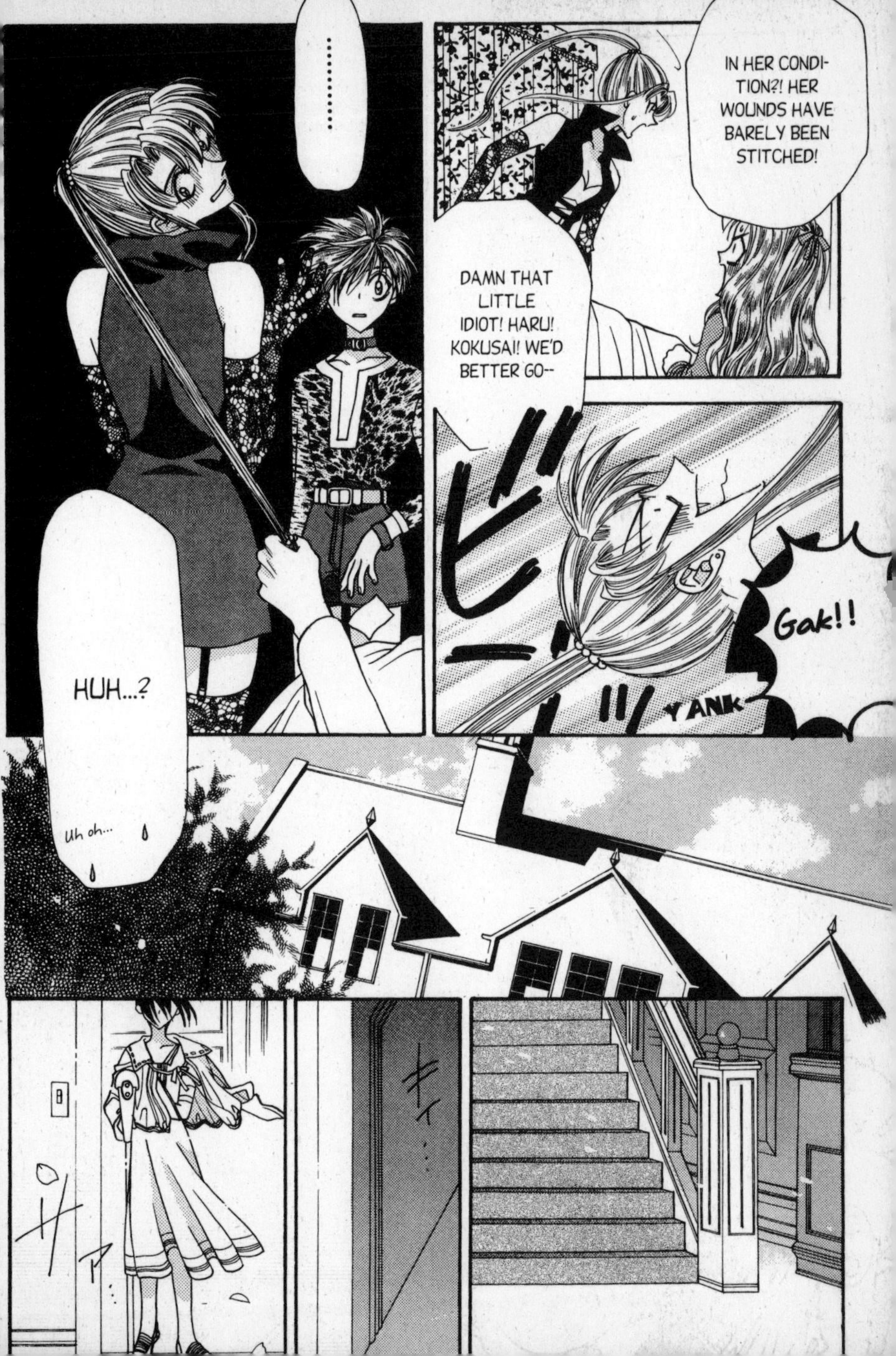
IN HER CONDITION?! HER WOUNDS HAVE BARELY BEEN STITCHED!
DAMN THAT LITTLE IDIOT! HARU! KOKUSAI! WE'D BETTER GO--
Gak!!
YANK
......
HUH...?
Uh oh...

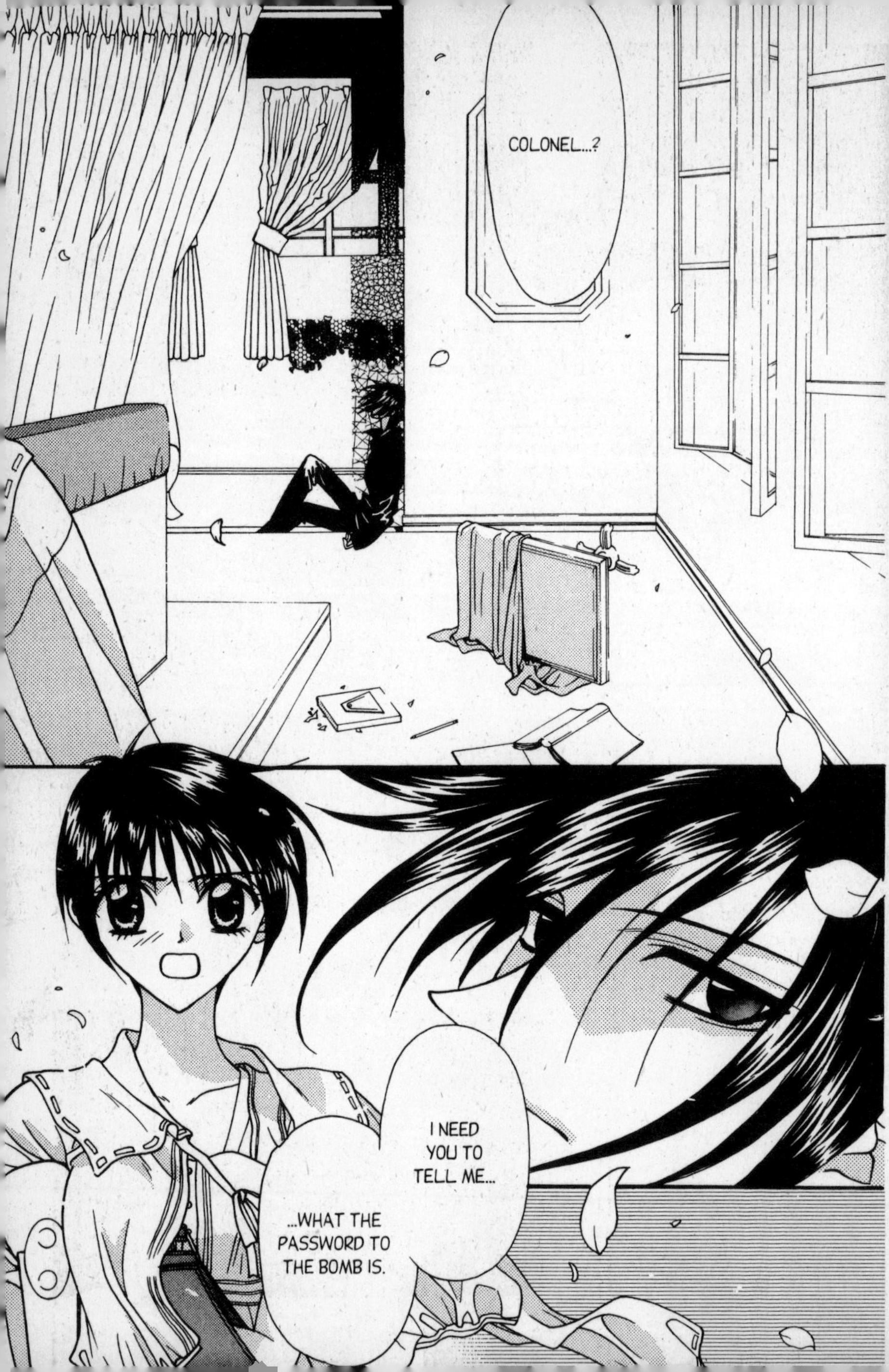
COLONEL...?
I NEED YOU TO TELL ME...
...WHAT THE PASSWORD TO THE BOMB IS.

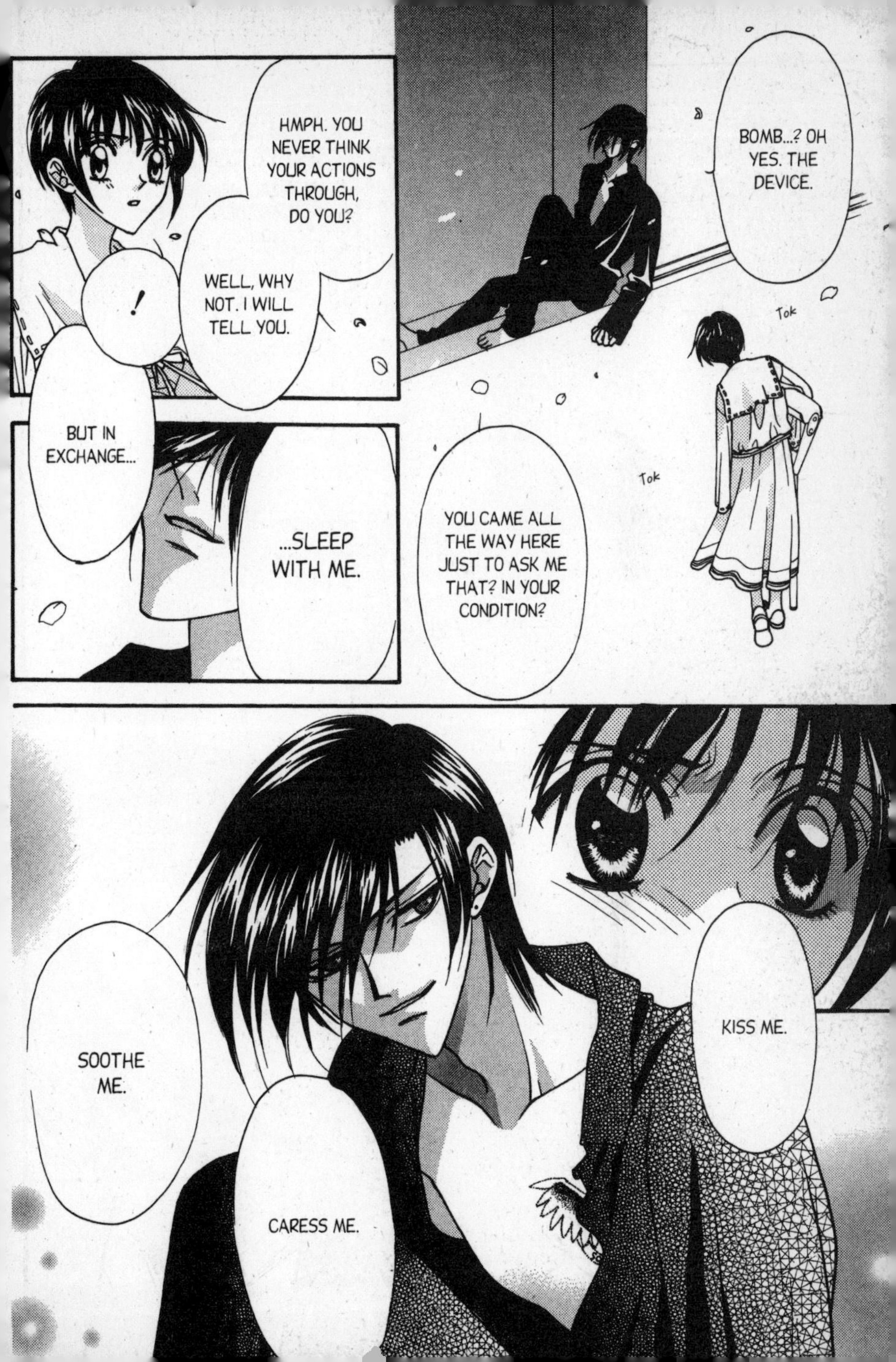
BOMB...? OH YES. THE DEVICE.
Tok
Tok
YOU CAME ALL THE WAY HERE JUST TO ASK ME THAT? IN YOUR CONDITION?
HMPH. YOU NEVER THINK YOUR ACTIONS THROUGH, DO YOU?
!
WELL, WHY NOT. I WILL TELL YOU.
BUT IN EXCHANGE...
...SLEEP WITH ME.
KISS ME.
CARESS ME.
SOOTHE ME.

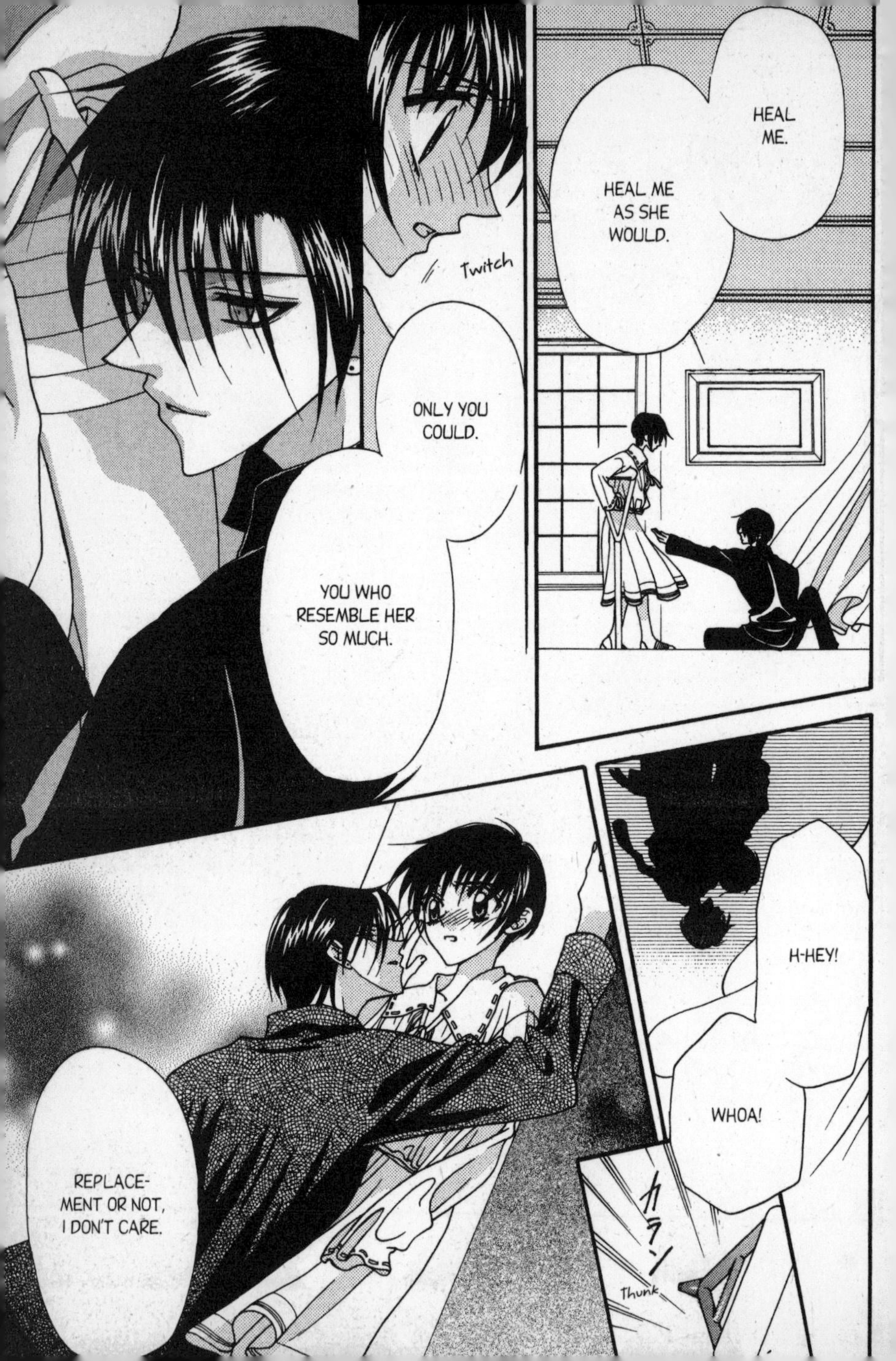
HEAL ME.
HEAL ME AS SHE WOULD.
Twitch
ONLY YOU COULD.
YOU WHO RESEMBLE HER SO MUCH.
H-HEY!
WHOA!
カラン
Thunk
REPLACE-MENT OR NOT, I DON'T CARE.

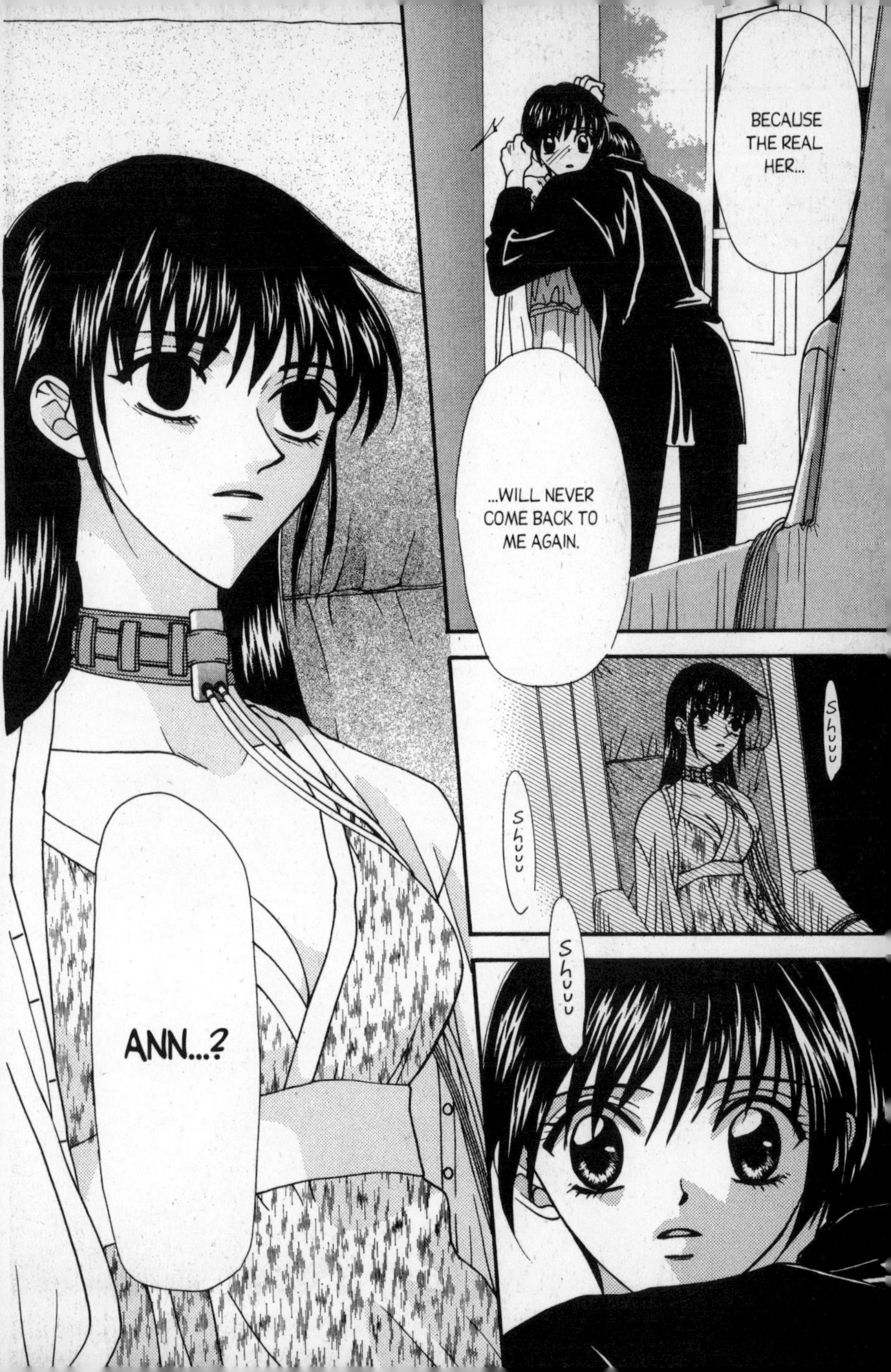
BECAUSE THE REAL HER...
...WILL NEVER COME BACK TO ME AGAIN.
SHUUU
SHUUU
SHUUU
ANN...?

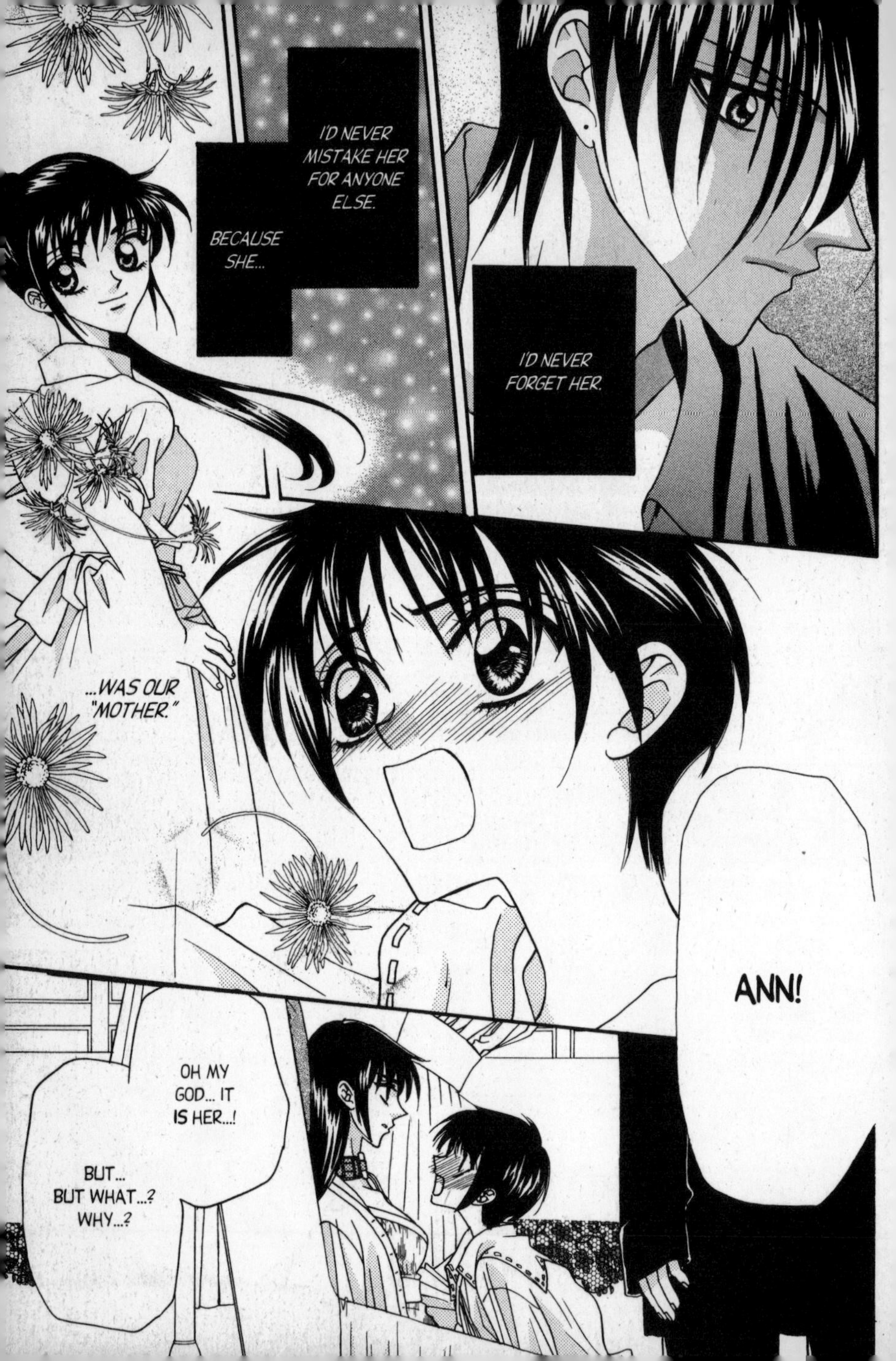

I'D NEVER FORGET HER.
I'D NEVER MISTAKE HER FOR ANYONE ELSE.
BECAUSE SHE...
...WAS OUR "MOTHER."
ANN!
OH MY GOD... IT IS HER...!
BUT... BUT WHAT...? WHY...?

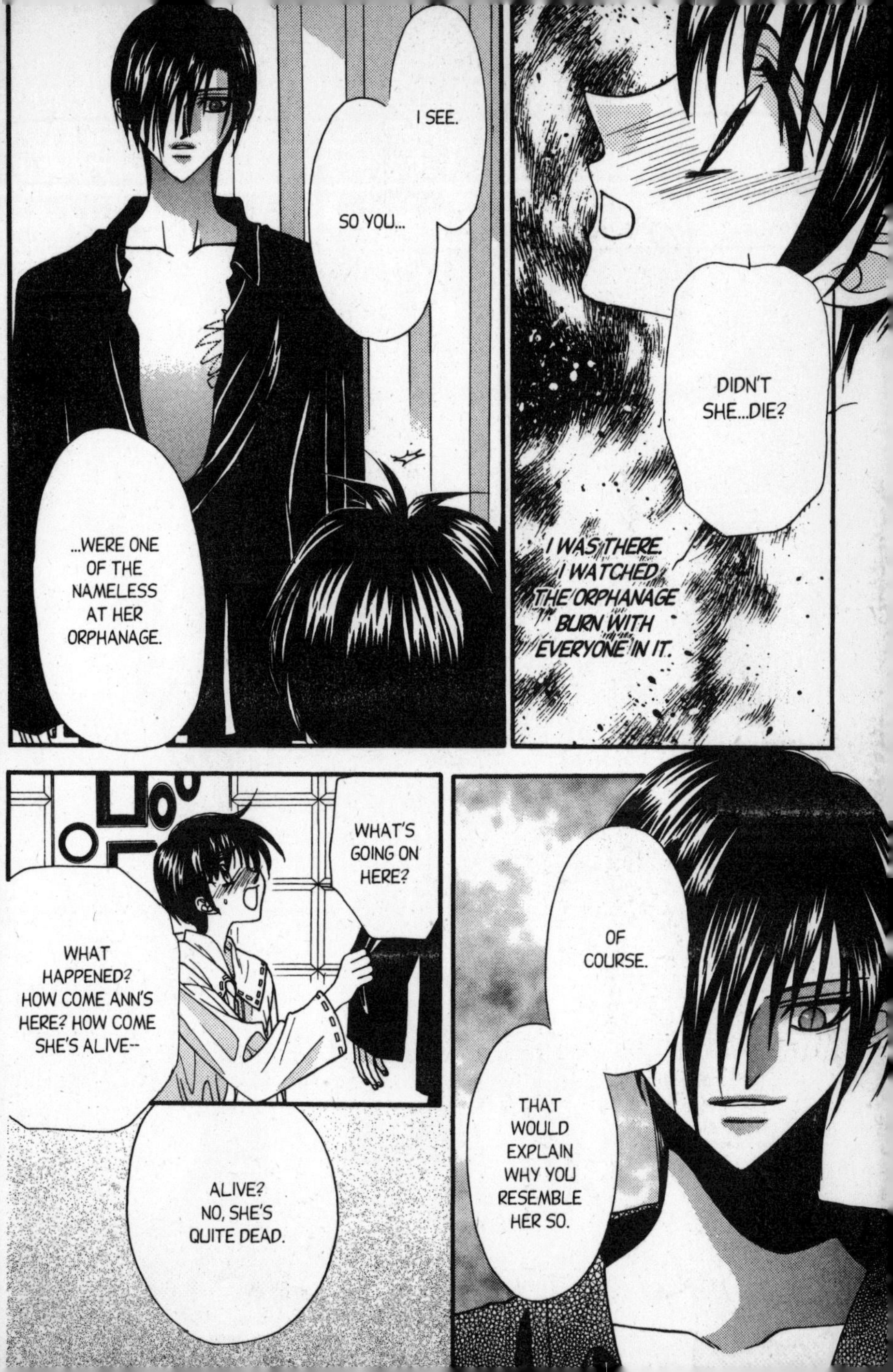
DIDN'T SHE...DIE?
I WAS THERE. I WATCHED THE ORPHANAGE BURN WITH EVERYONE IN IT.
I SEE.
SO YOU...
...WERE ONE OF THE NAMELESS AT HER ORPHANAGE.
OF COURSE.
THAT WOULD EXPLAIN WHY YOU RESEMBLE HER SO.
WHAT'S GOING ON HERE?
WHAT HAPPENED? HOW COME ANN'S HERE? HOW COME SHE'S ALIVE--
ALIVE? NO, SHE'S QUITE DEAD.

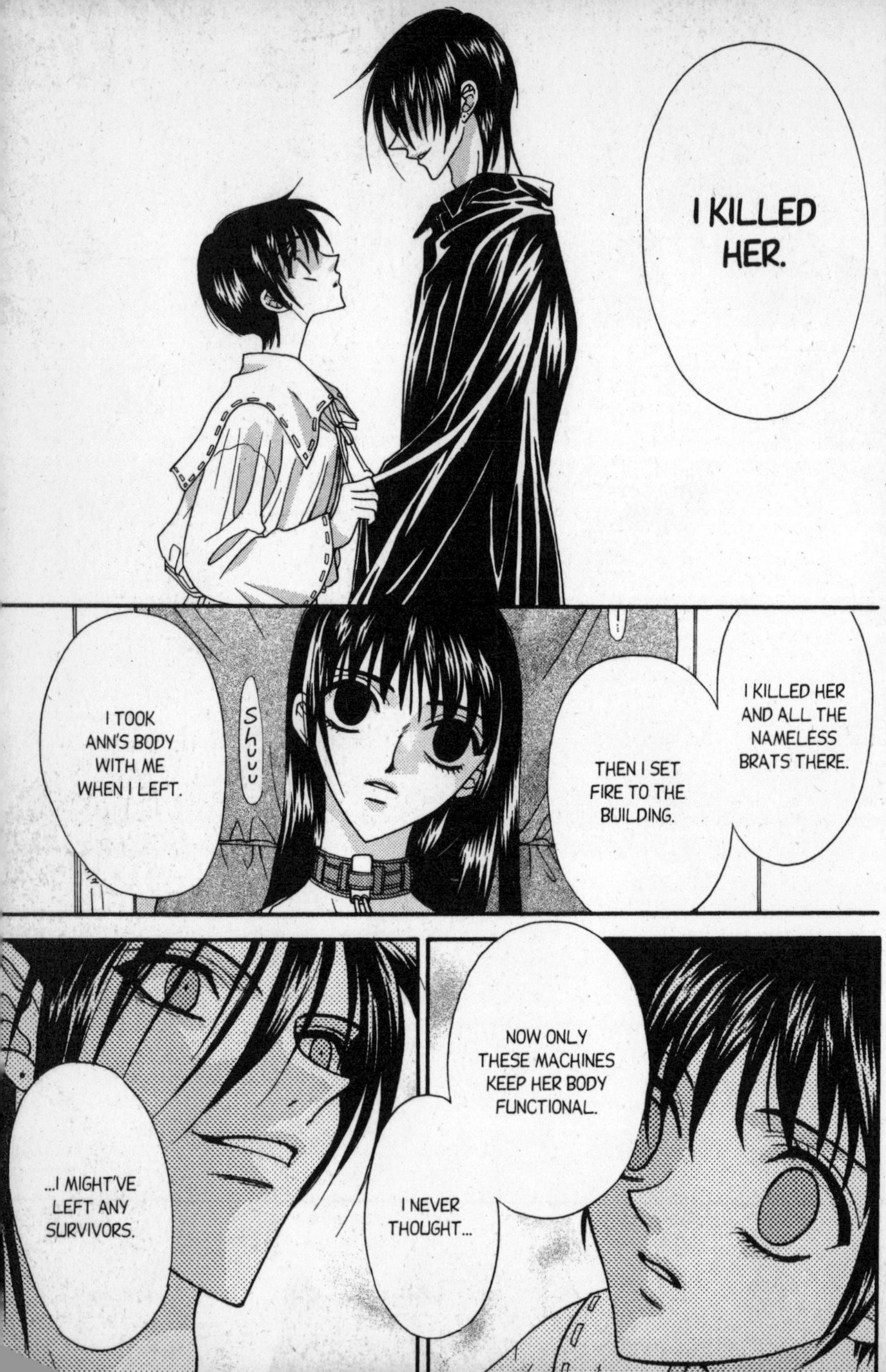
I KILLED HER.
I KILLED HER AND ALL THE NAMELESS BRATS THERE.
THEN I SET FIRE TO THE BUILDING.
!
Shuuu
I TOOK ANN'S BODY WITH ME WHEN I LEFT.
NOW ONLY THESE MACHINES KEEP HER BODY FUNCTIONAL.
I NEVER THOUGHT...
...I MIGHT'VE LEFT ANY SURVIVORS.

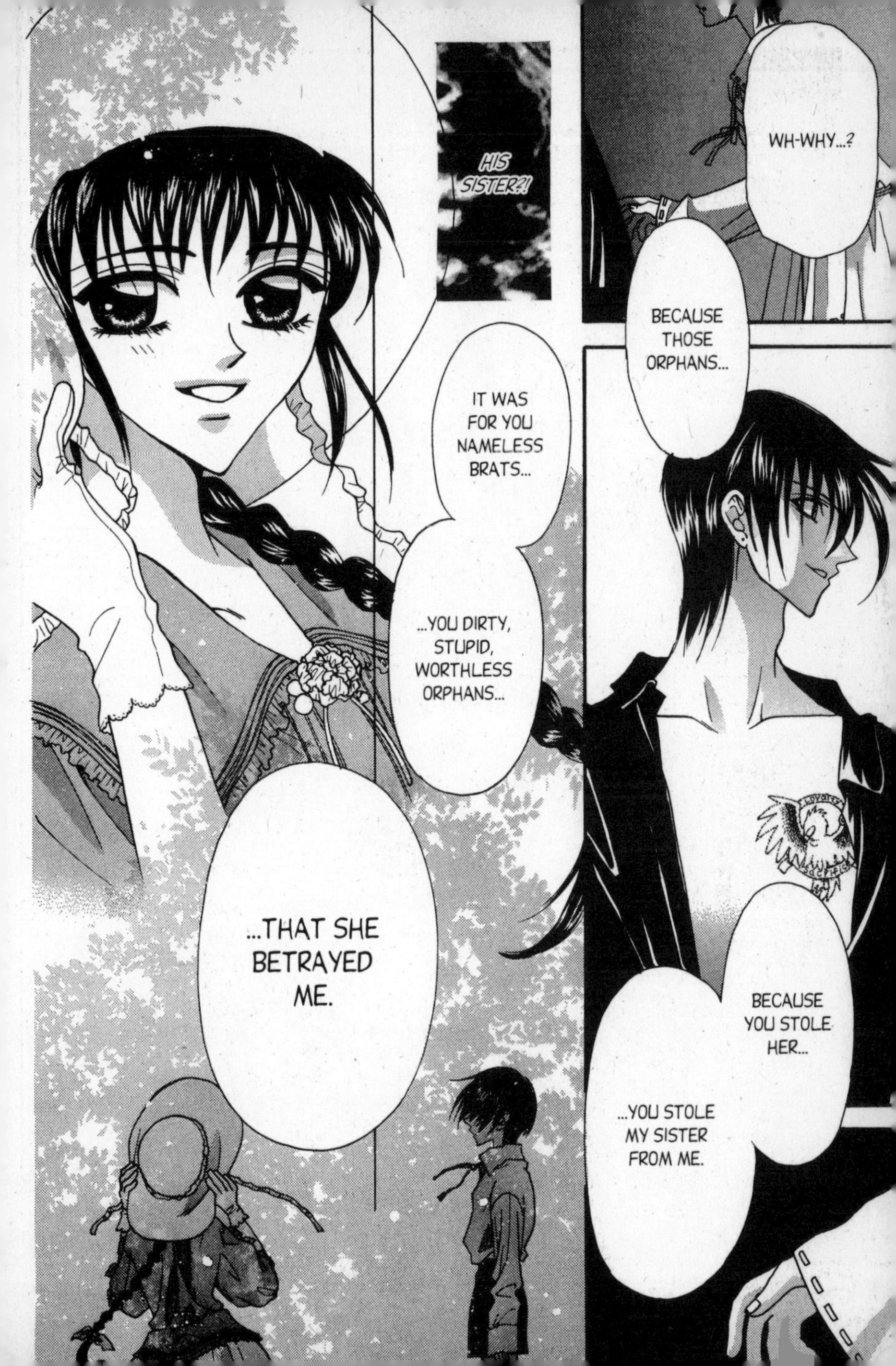
WH-WHY...?
BECAUSE THOSE ORPHANS...
IT WAS FOR YOU NAMELESS BRATS...
...YOU DIRTY, STUPID, WORTHLESS ORPHANS...
...THAT SHE BETRAYED ME.
BECAUSE YOU STOLE HER...
...YOU STOLE MY SISTER FROM ME.
HIS SISTER?!

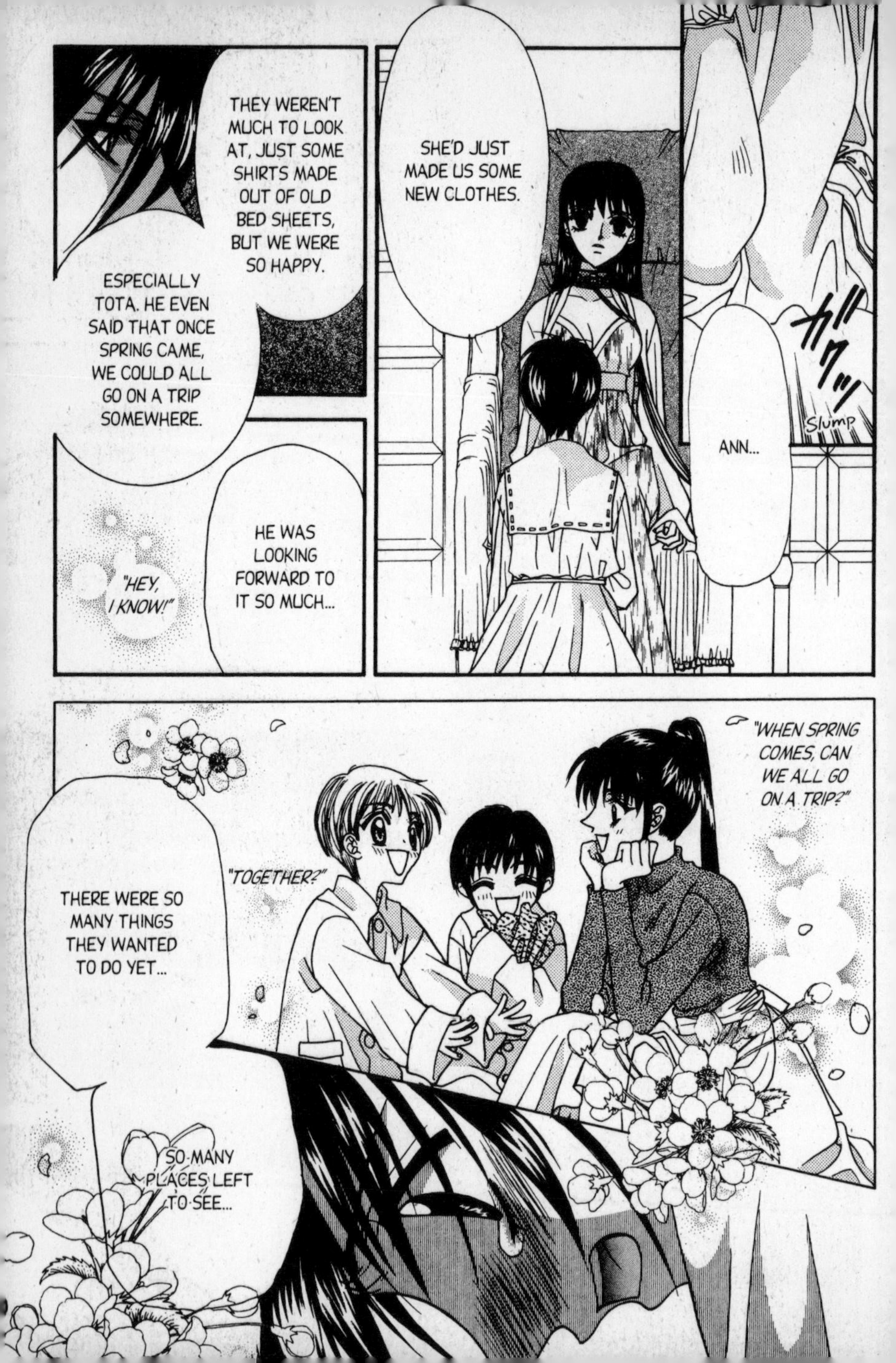

ガクッ
Slump
ANN...
SHE'D JUST MADE US SOME NEW CLOTHES.
THEY WEREN'T MUCH TO LOOK AT, JUST SOME SHIRTS MADE OUT OF OLD BED SHEETS, BUT WE WERE SO HAPPY.
ESPECIALLY TOTA. HE EVEN SAID THAT ONCE SPRING CAME, WE COULD ALL GO ON A TRIP SOMEWHERE.
HE WAS LOOKING FORWARD TO IT SO MUCH...
"HEY, I KNOW!"
"WHEN SPRING COMES, CAN WE ALL GO ON A TRIP?"
"TOGETHER?"
THERE WERE SO MANY THINGS THEY WANTED TO DO YET...
SO MANY PLACES LEFT TO SEE...

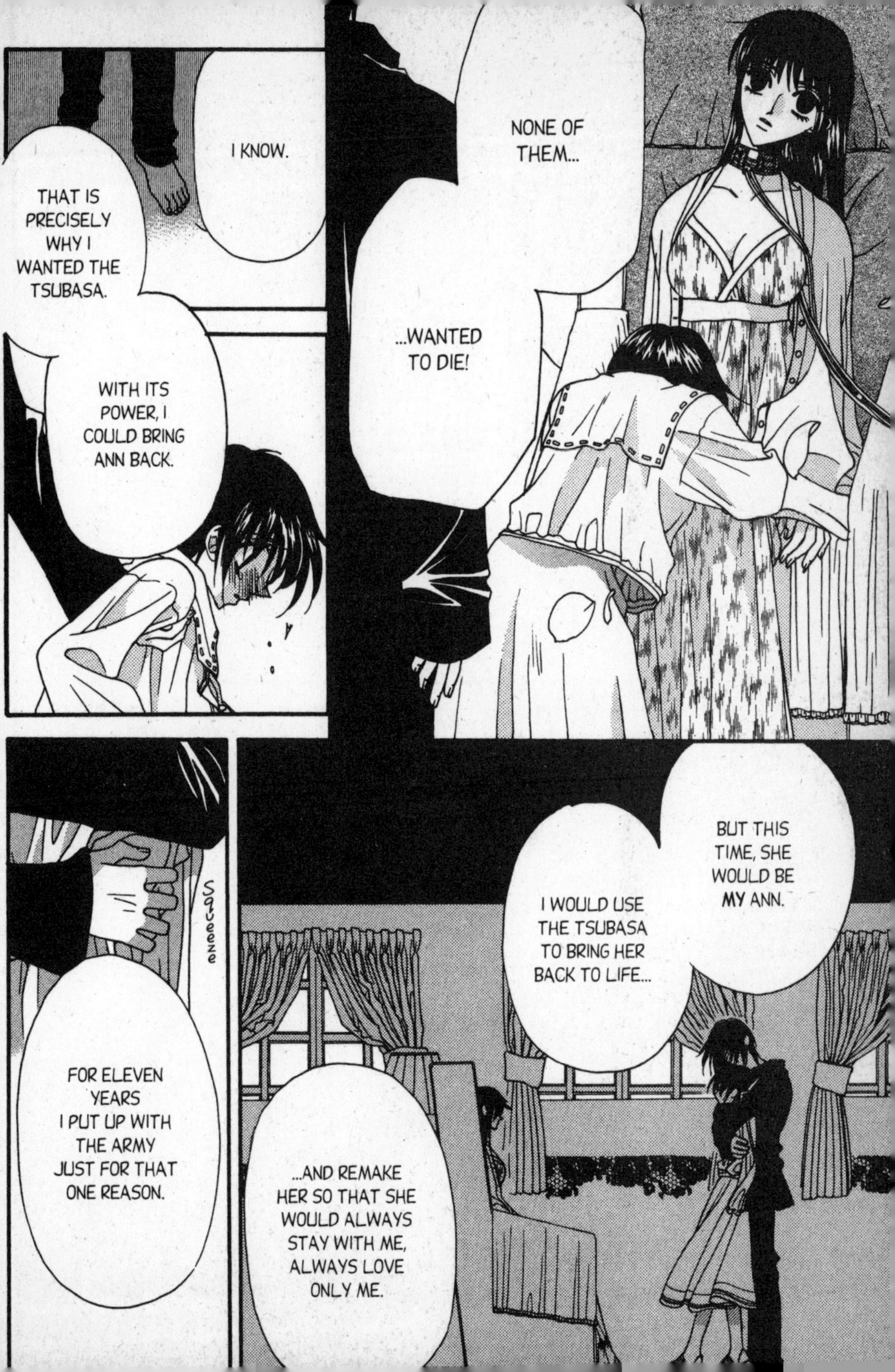
NONE OF THEM...
...WANTED TO DIE!
I KNOW.
THAT IS PRECISELY WHY I WANTED THE TSUBASA.
WITH ITS POWER, I COULD BRING ANN BACK.
BUT THIS TIME, SHE WOULD BE MY ANN.
I WOULD USE THE TSUBASA TO BRING HER BACK TO LIFE...
...AND REMAKE HER SO THAT SHE WOULD ALWAYS STAY WITH ME, ALWAYS LOVE ONLY ME.
Squeeze
FOR ELEVEN YEARS I PUT UP WITH THE ARMY JUST FOR THAT ONE REASON.

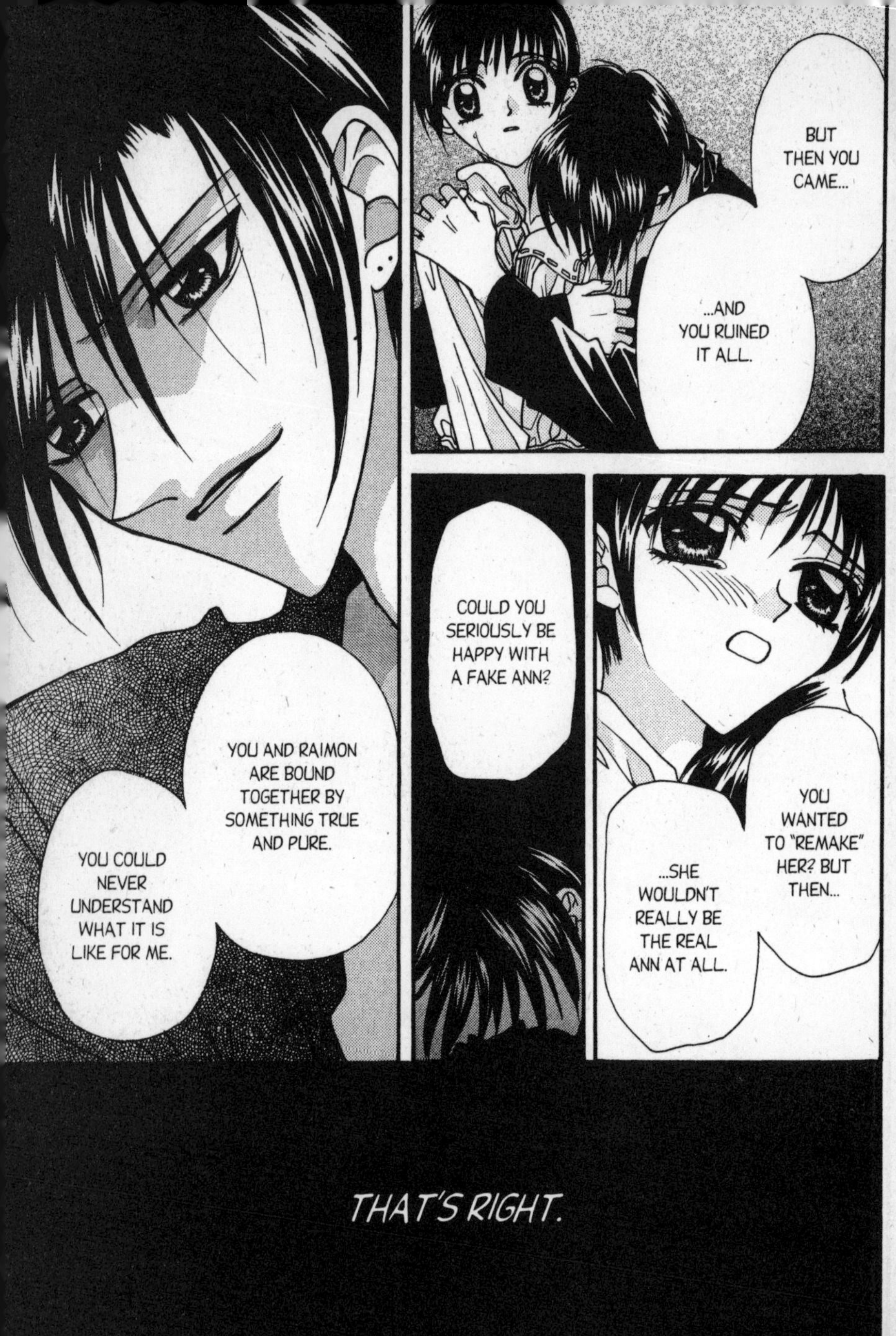
BUT THEN YOU CAME...
...AND YOU RUINED IT ALL.
YOU WANTED TO "REMAKE" HER? BUT THEN...
...SHE WOULDN'T REALLY BE THE REAL ANN AT ALL.
COULD YOU SERIOUSLY BE HAPPY WITH A FAKE ANN?
YOU AND RAIMON ARE BOUND TOGETHER BY SOMETHING TRUE AND PURE.
YOU COULD NEVER UNDERSTAND WHAT IT IS LIKE FOR ME.
THAT'S RIGHT.

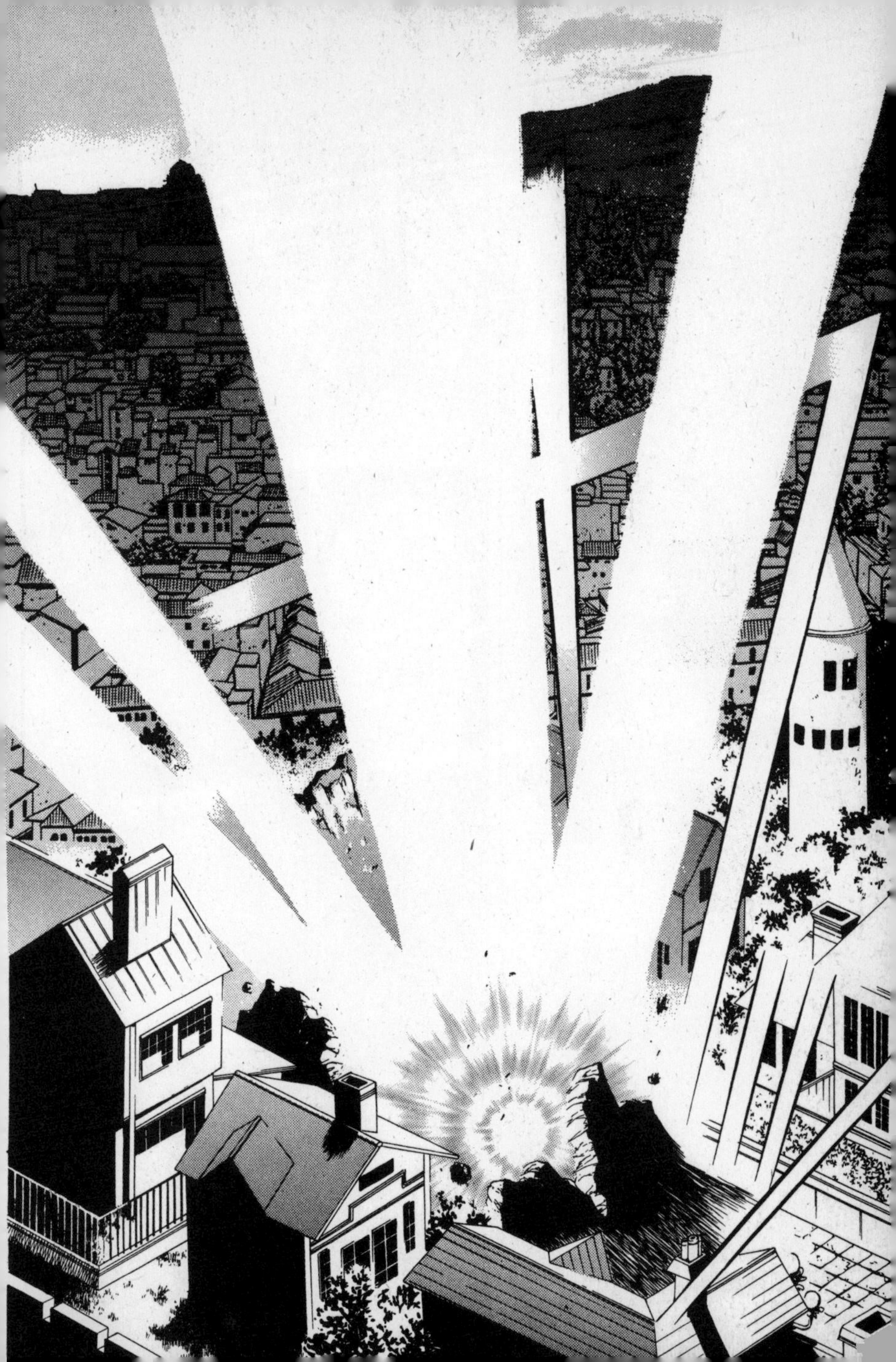

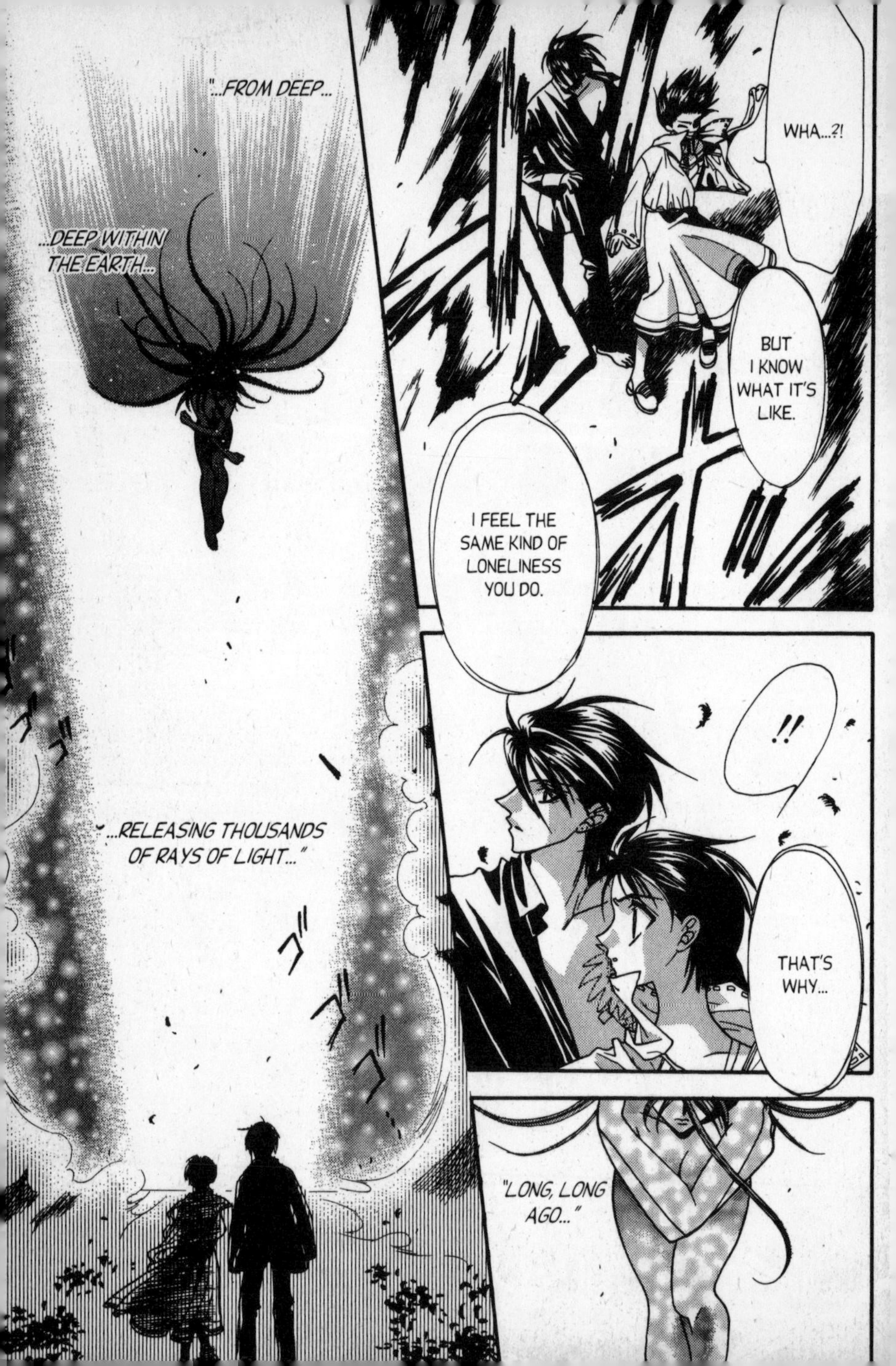
WHA...?!
BUT I KNOW WHAT IT'S LIKE.
I FEEL THE SAME KIND OF LONELINESS YOU DO.
!!
THAT'S WHY...
"LONG, LONG AGO..."
"...FROM DEEP...
...DEEP WITHIN THE EARTH...
...RELEASING THOUSANDS OF RAYS OF LIGHT..."

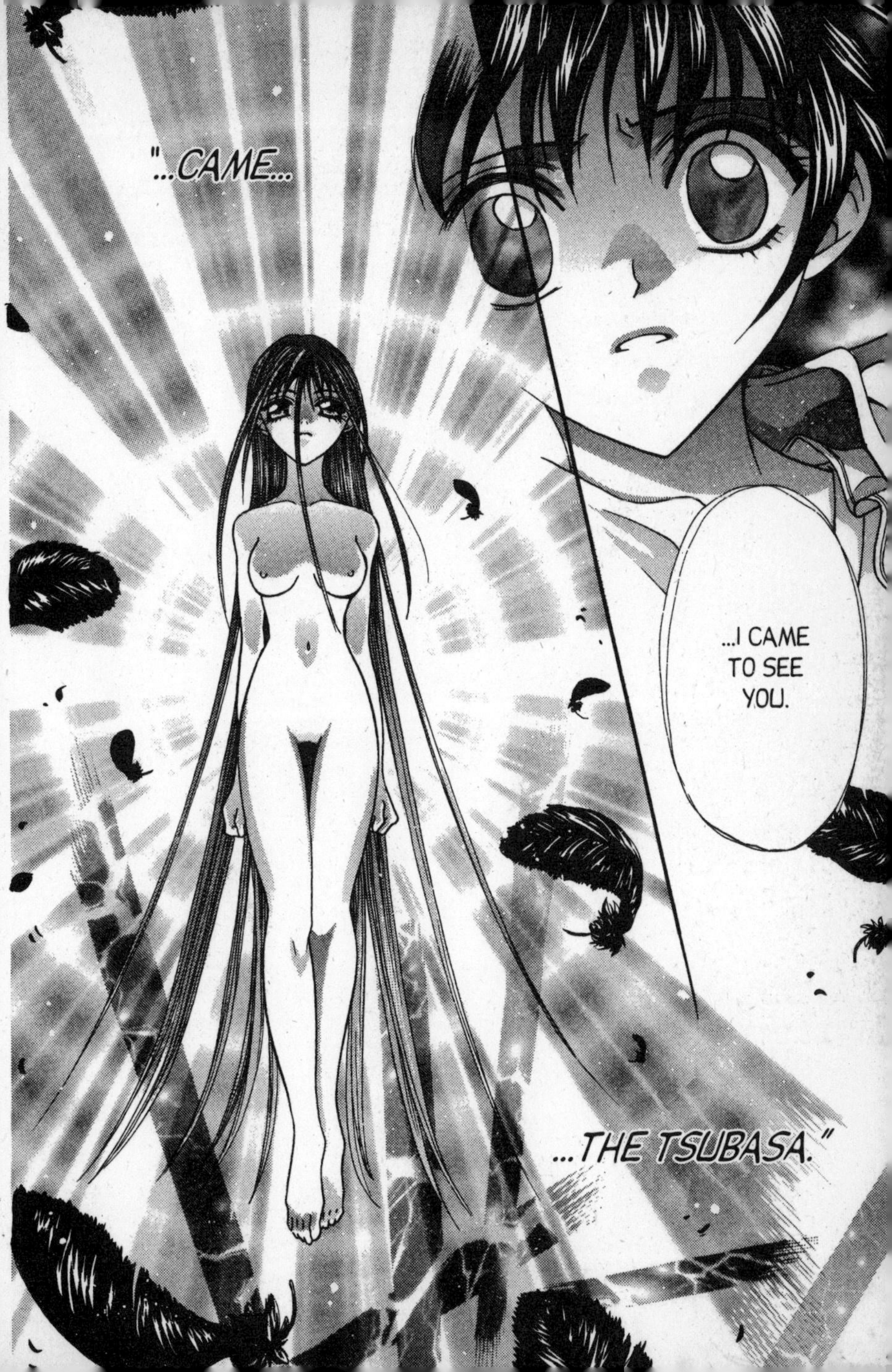
"...CAME...
...I CAME TO SEE YOU.
...THE TSUBASA."

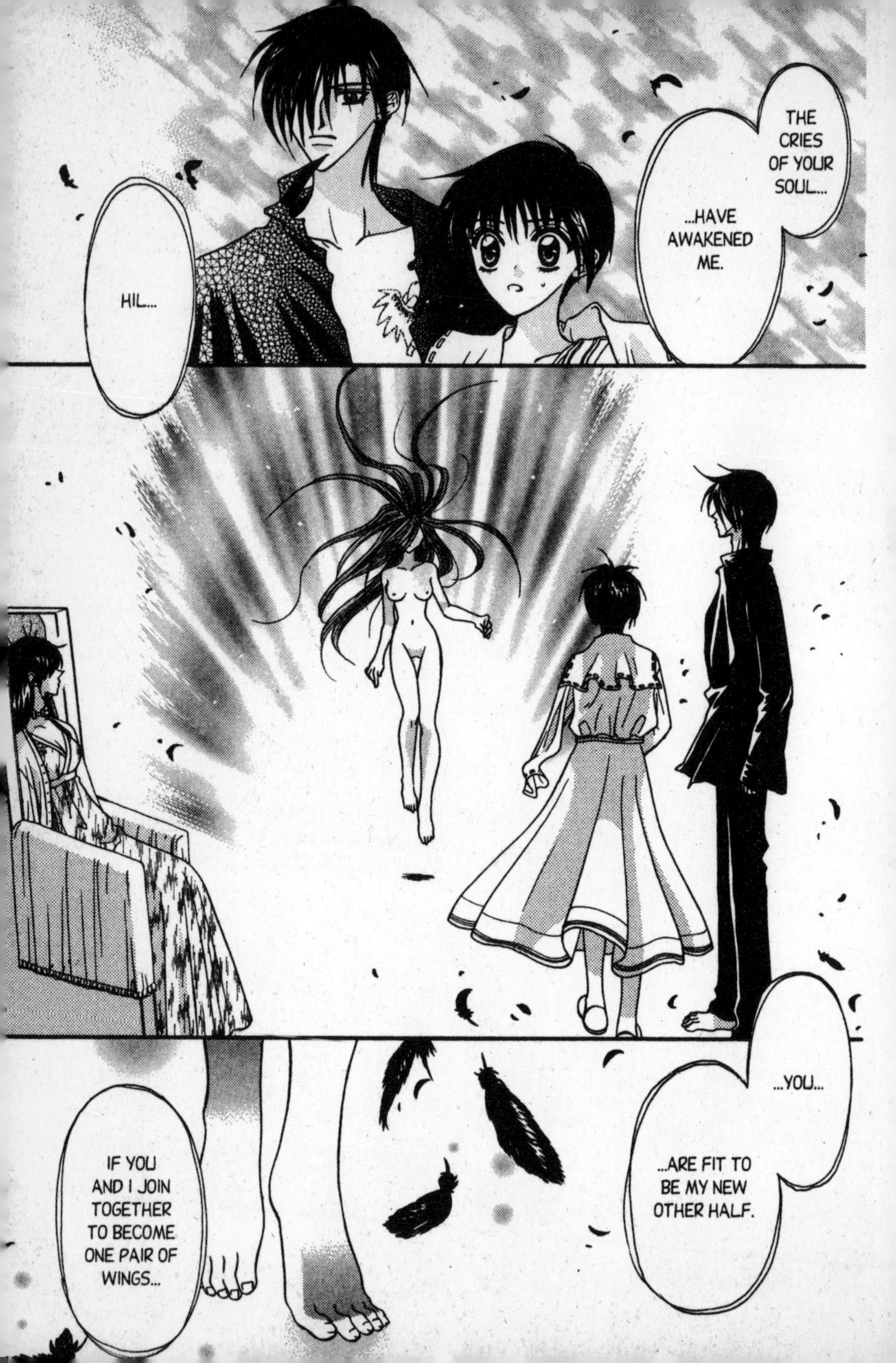
THE CRIES OF YOUR SOUL...
...HAVE AWAKENED ME.
HIL...
...YOU...
...ARE FIT TO BE MY NEW OTHER HALF.
IF YOU AND I JOIN TOGETHER TO BECOME ONE PAIR OF WINGS...

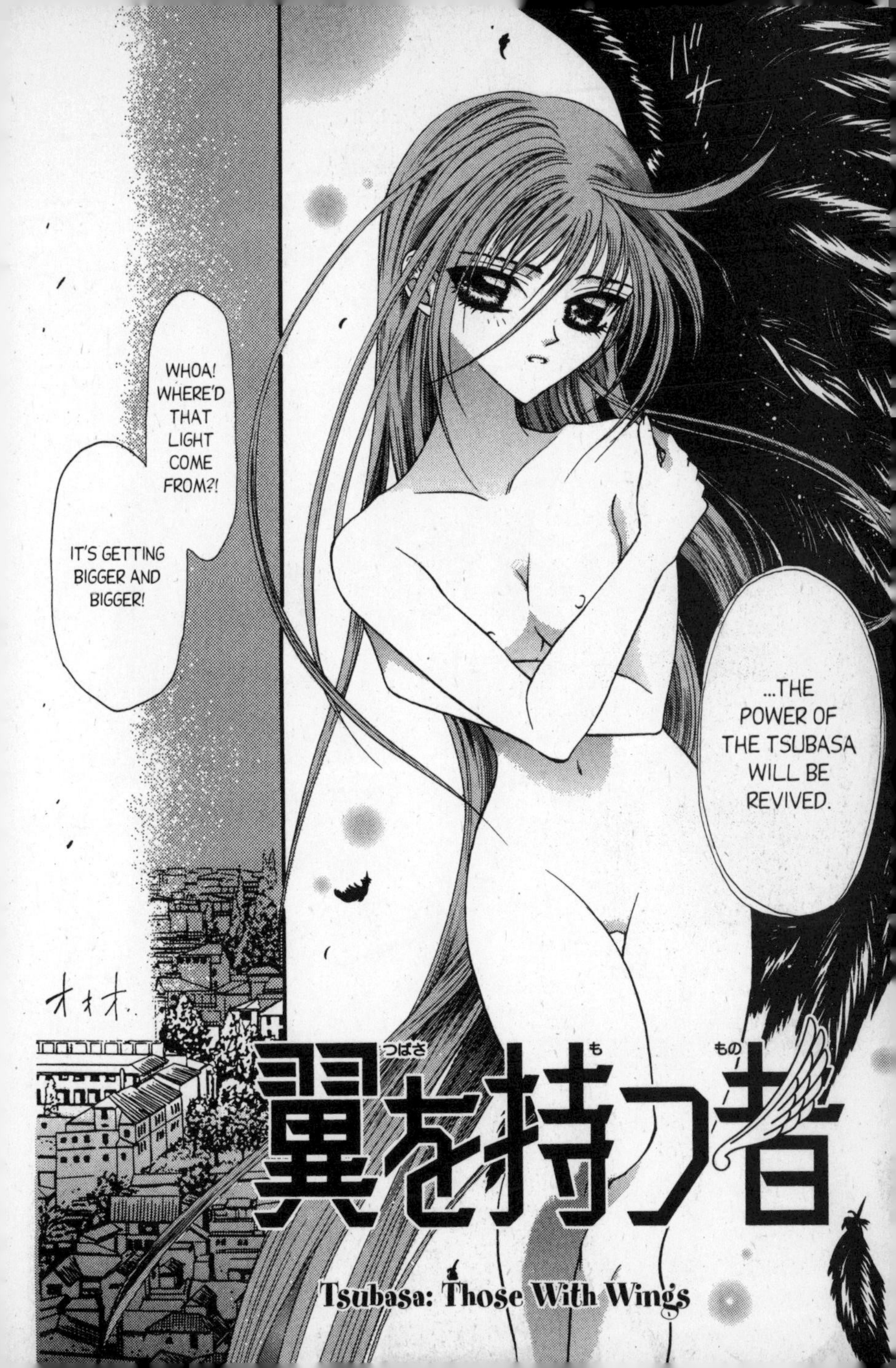
...THE POWER OF THE TSUBASA WILL BE REVIVED.
WHOA! WHERE'D THAT LIGHT COME FROM?!
IT'S GETTING BIGGER AND BIGGER!
翼を持つ者
Tsubasa: Those With Wings

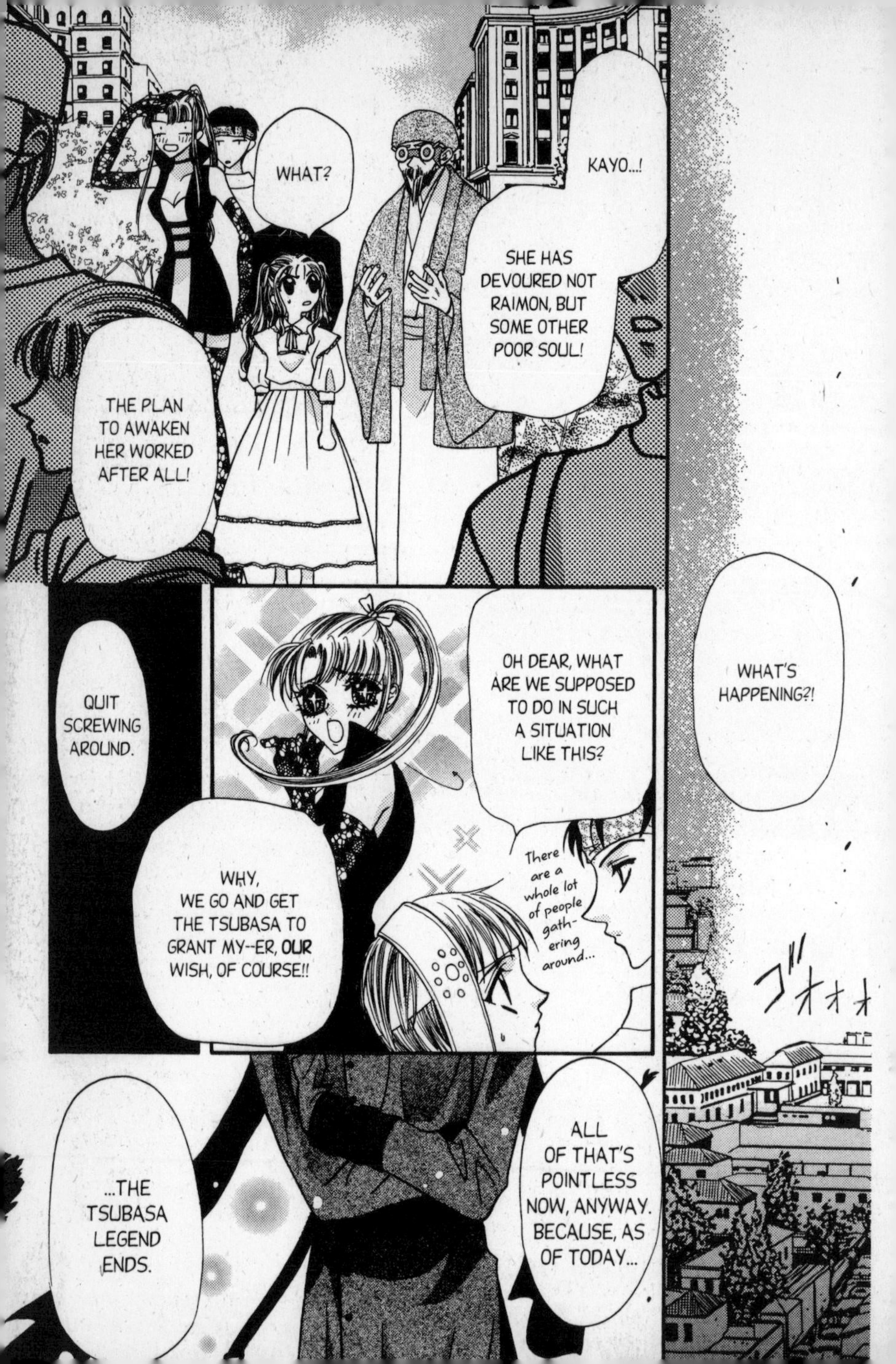
WHAT'S HAPPENING?!
ゴオオオ
KAYO...!
SHE HAS DEVOURED NOT RAIMON, BUT SOME OTHER POOR SOUL!
WHAT?
THE PLAN TO AWAKEN HER WORKED AFTER ALL!
OH DEAR, WHAT ARE WE SUPPOSED TO DO IN SUCH A SITUATION LIKE THIS?
There are a whole lot of people gathering around...
WHY, WE GO AND GET THE TSUBASA TO GRANT MY--ER, OUR WISH, OF COURSE!!
QUIT SCREWING AROUND.
ALL OF THAT'S POINTLESS NOW, ANYWAY. BECAUSE, AS OF TODAY...
...THE TSUBASA LEGEND ENDS.

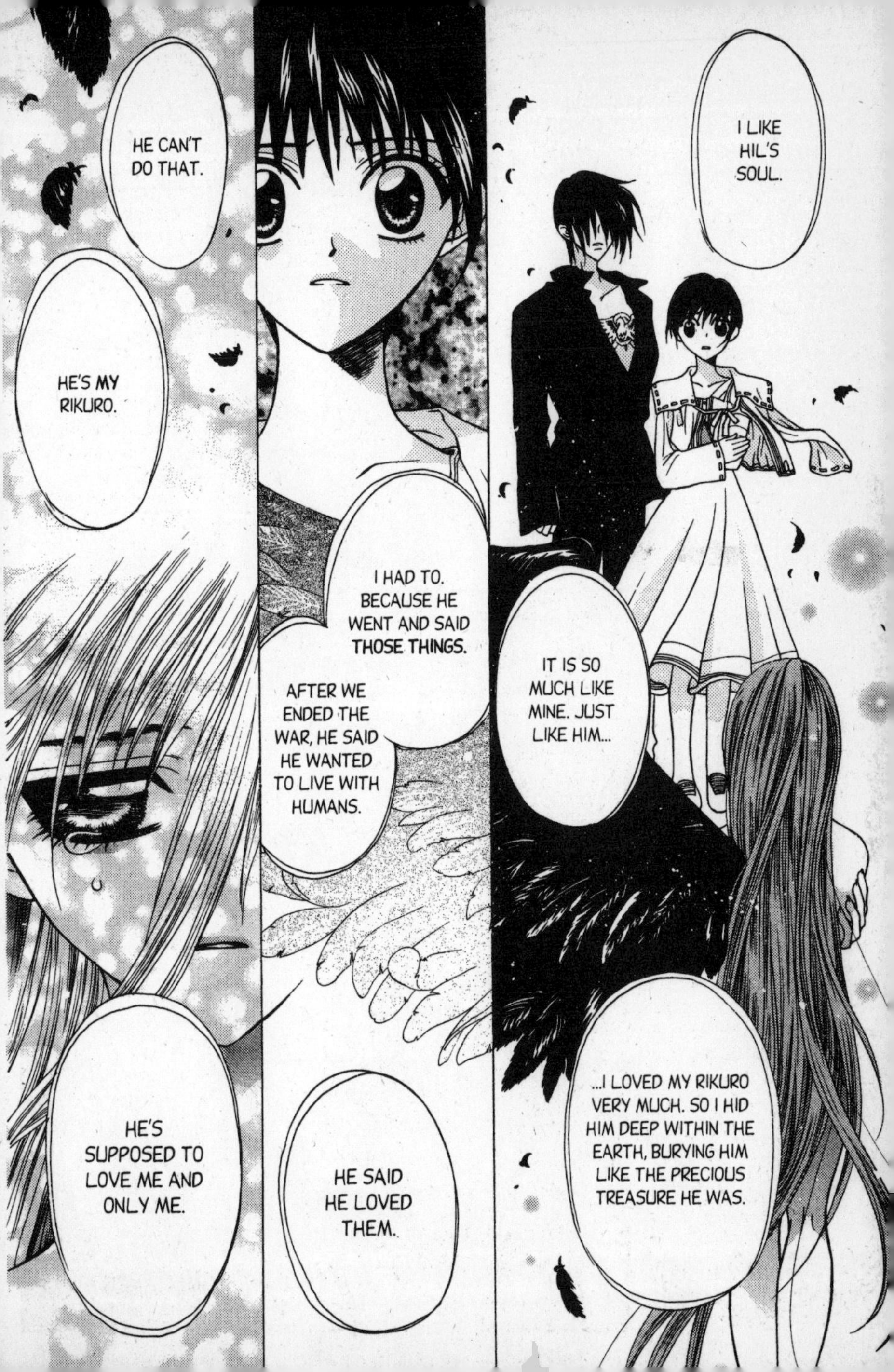
I LIKE HIL'S SOUL.
IT IS SO MUCH LIKE MINE. JUST LIKE HIM...
...I LOVED MY RIKURO VERY MUCH. SO I HID HIM DEEP WITHIN THE EARTH, BURYING HIM LIKE THE PRECIOUS TREASURE HE WAS.
I HAD TO. BECAUSE HE WENT AND SAID THOSE THINGS.
AFTER WE ENDED THE WAR, HE SAID HE WANTED TO LIVE WITH HUMANS.
HE SAID HE LOVED THEM.
HE CAN'T DO THAT.
HE'S MY RIKURO.
HE'S SUPPOSED TO LOVE ME AND ONLY ME.

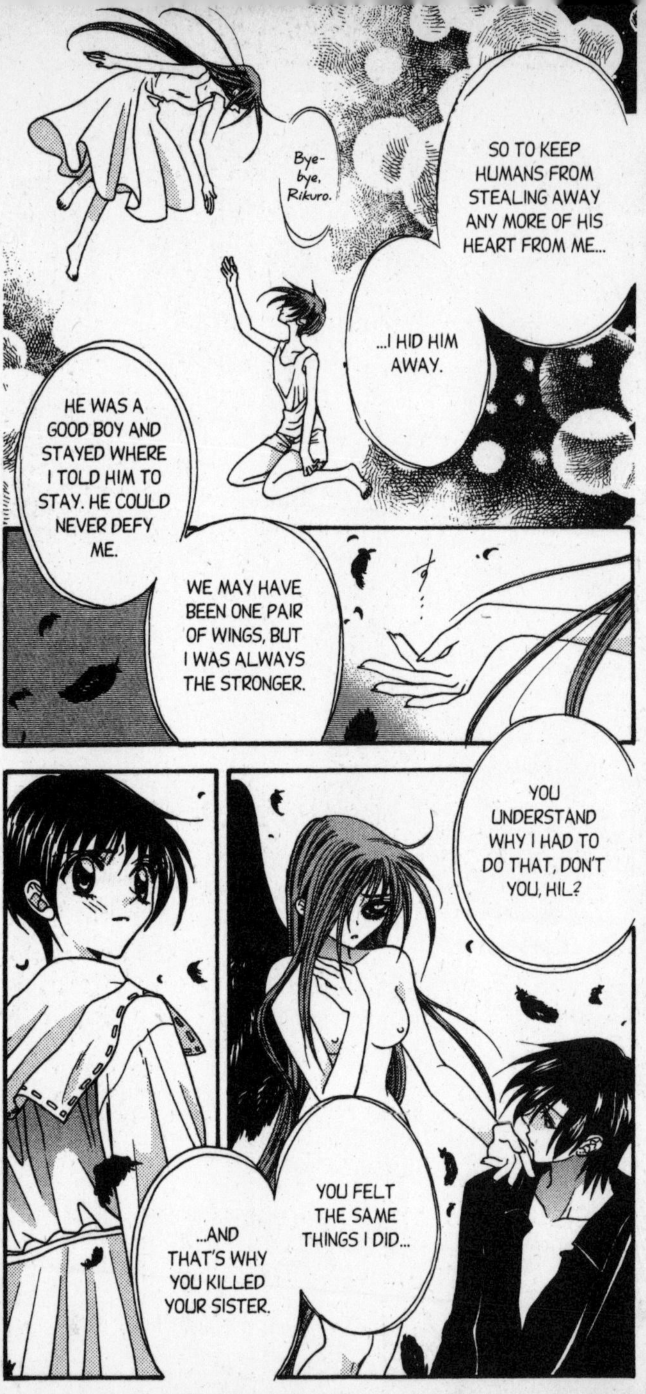
SO TO KEEP HUMANS FROM STEALING AWAY ANY MORE OF HIS HEART FROM ME...
...I HID HIM AWAY.
Bye-bye, Rikuro.
HE WAS A GOOD BOY AND STAYED WHERE I TOLD HIM TO STAY. HE COULD NEVER DEFY ME.
WE MAY HAVE BEEN ONE PAIR OF WINGS, BUT I WAS ALWAYS THE STRONGER.
YOU UNDERSTAND WHY I HAD TO DO THAT, DON'T YOU, HIL?
YOU FELT THE SAME THINGS I DID...
...AND THAT'S WHY YOU KILLED YOUR SISTER.

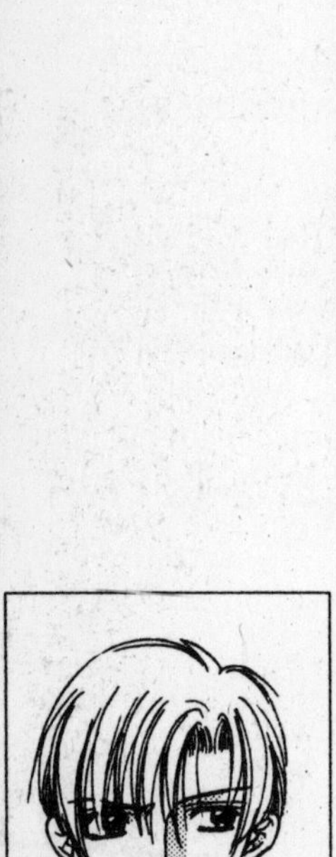

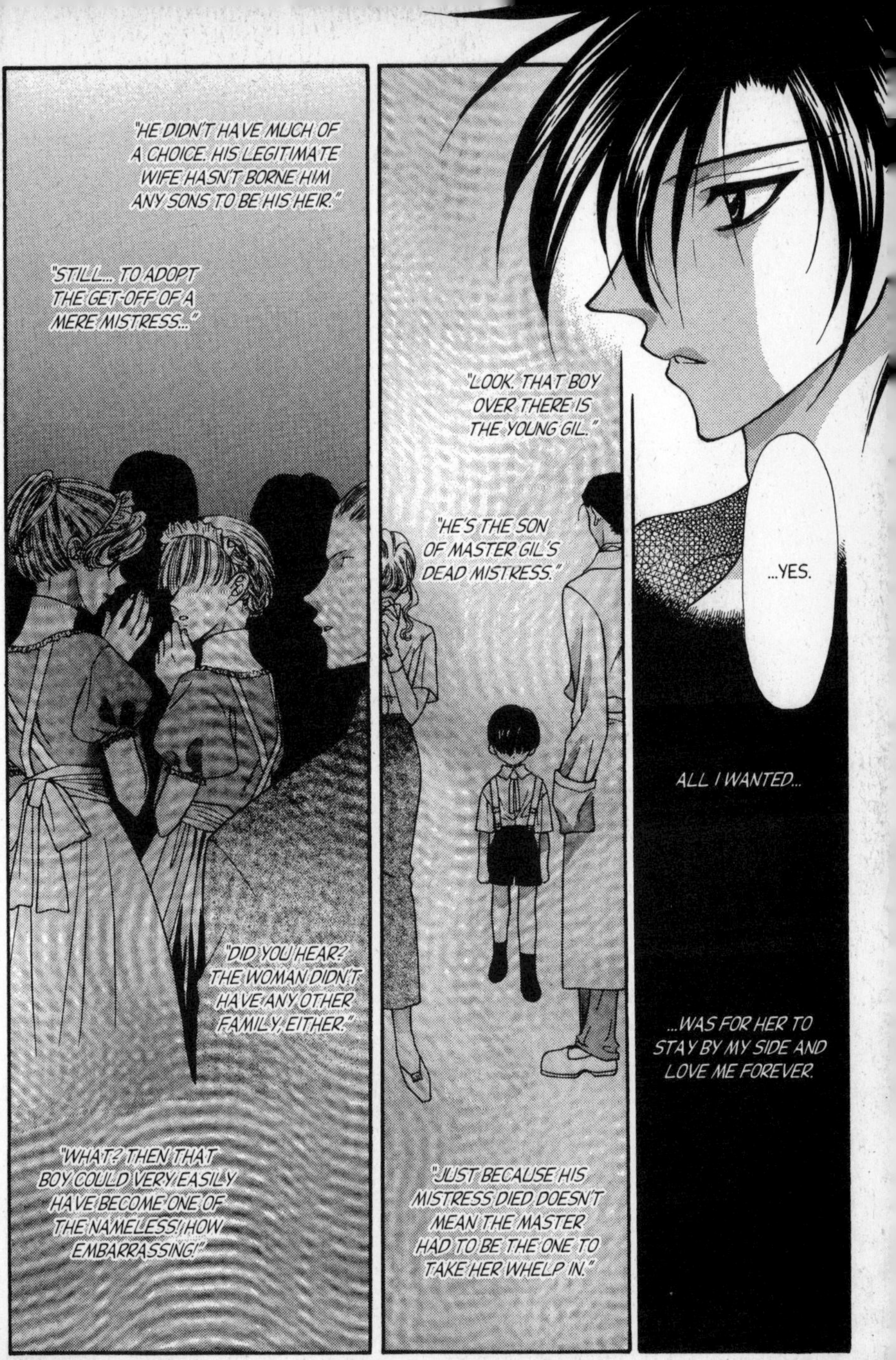
...YES.
ALL I WANTED...
...WAS FOR HER TO STAY BY MY SIDE AND LOVE ME FOREVER.
"LOOK. THAT BOY OVER THERE IS THE YOUNG GIL."
"HE'S THE SON OF MASTER GIL'S DEAD MISTRESS."
"JUST BECAUSE HIS MISTRESS DIED DOESN'T MEAN THE MASTER HAD TO BE THE ONE TO TAKE HER WHELP IN."
"HE DIDN'T HAVE MUCH OF A CHOICE. HIS LEGITIMATE WIFE HASN'T BORNE HIM ANY SONS TO BE HIS HEIR."
"STILL... TO ADOPT THE GET-OFF OF A MERE MISTRESS..."
"DID YOU HEAR? THE WOMAN DIDN'T HAVE ANY OTHER FAMILY, EITHER."
"WHAT? THEN THAT BOY COULD VERY EASILY HAVE BECOME ONE OF THE NAMELESS! HOW EMBARRASSING!"

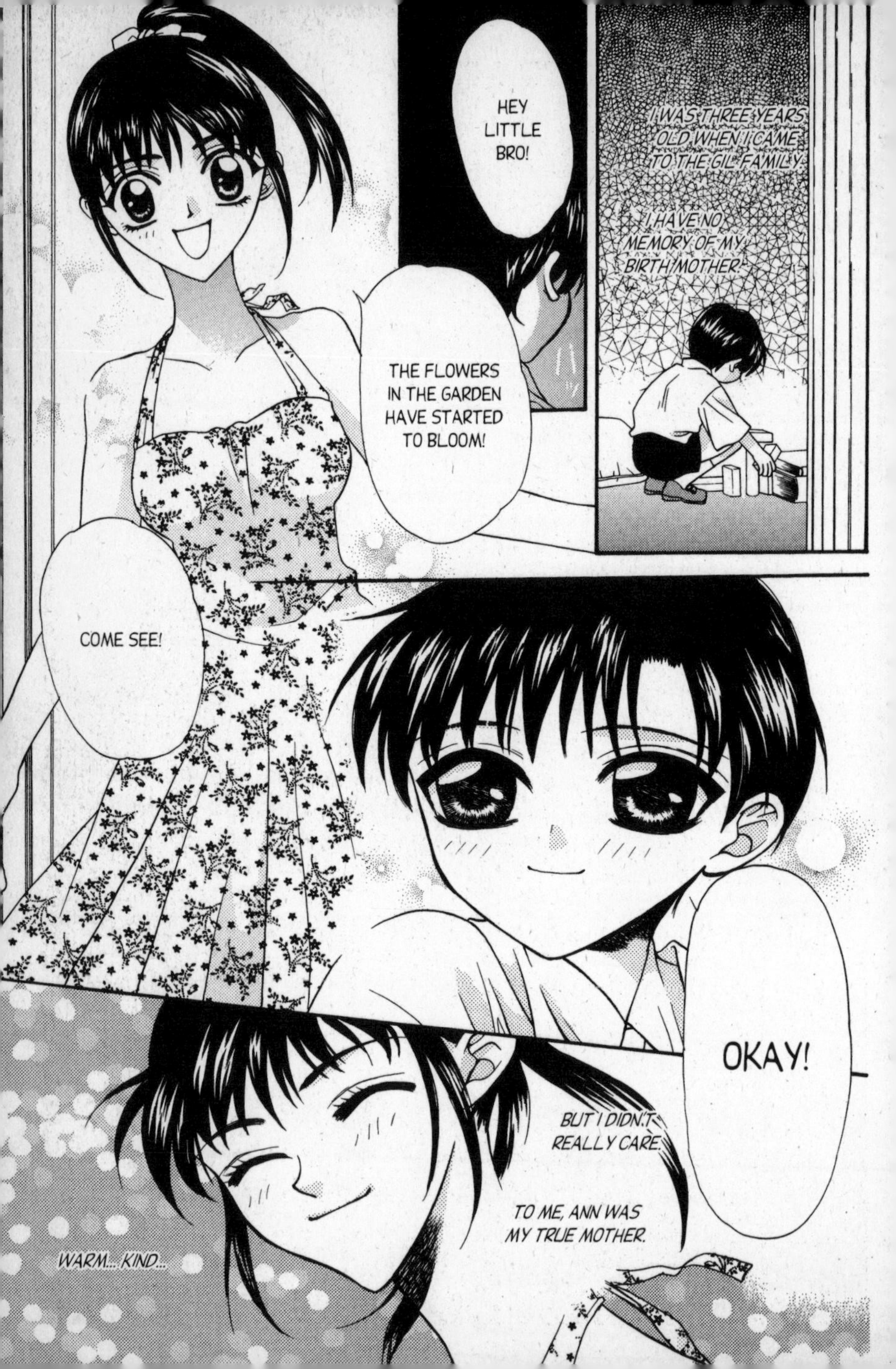
I WAS THREE YEARS OLD WHEN I CAME TO THE GIL FAMILY.
I HAVE NO MEMORY OF MY BIRTH MOTHER.
HEY LITTLE BRO!
THE FLOWERS IN THE GARDEN HAVE STARTED TO BLOOM!
COME SEE!
OKAY!
BUT I DIDN'T REALLY CARE.
TO ME, ANN WAS MY TRUE MOTHER.
WARM... KIND...

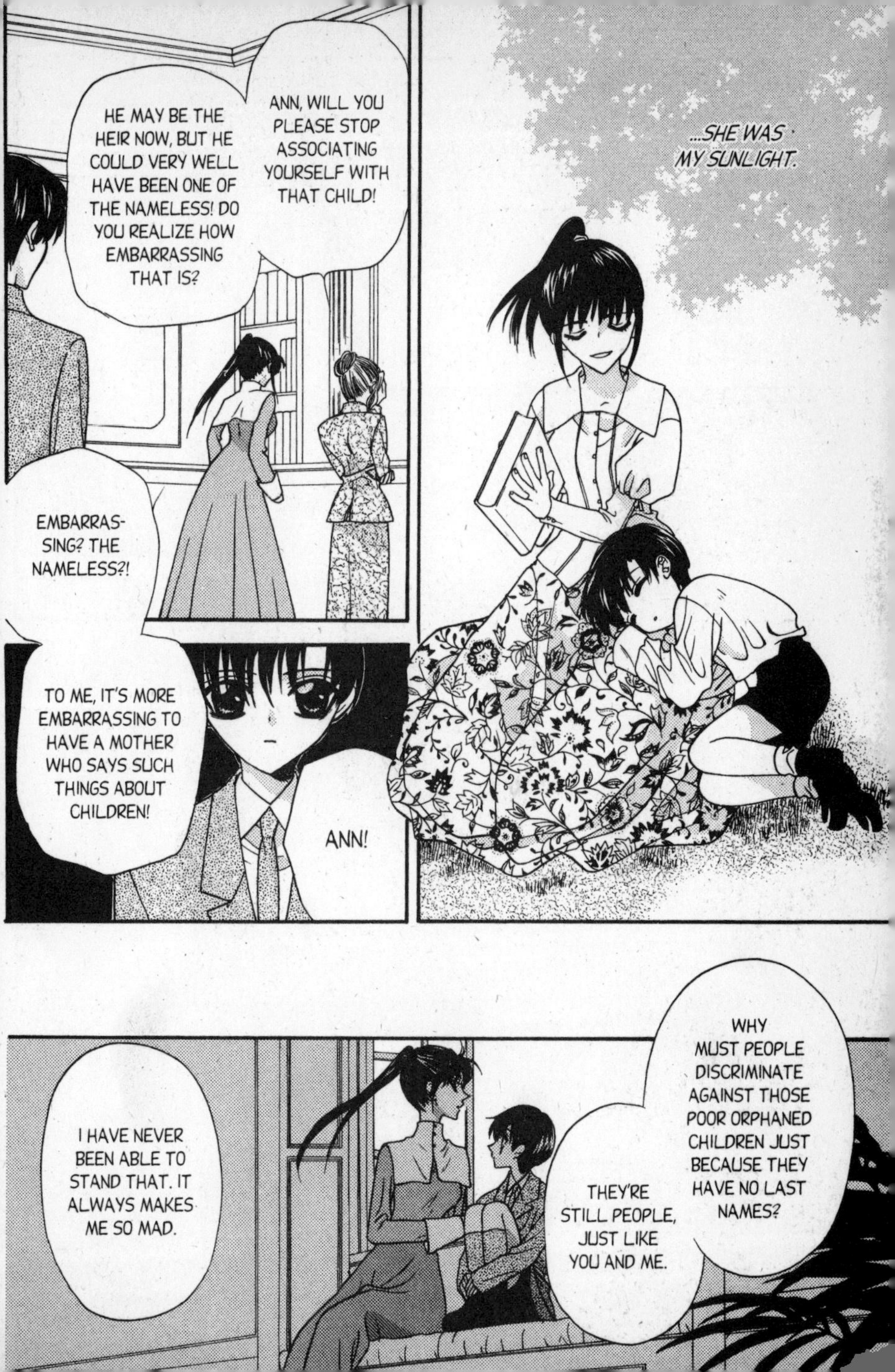
...SHE WAS MY SUNLIGHT.
ANN, WILL YOU PLEASE STOP ASSOCIATING YOURSELF WITH THAT CHILD!
HE MAY BE THE HEIR NOW, BUT HE COULD VERY WELL HAVE BEEN ONE OF THE NAMELESS! DO YOU REALIZE HOW EMBARRASSING THAT IS?
EMBARRAS-SING? THE NAMELESS?!
TO ME, IT'S MORE EMBARRASSING TO HAVE A MOTHER WHO SAYS SUCH THINGS ABOUT CHILDREN!
ANN!
WHY MUST PEOPLE DISCRIMINATE AGAINST THOSE POOR ORPHANED CHILDREN JUST BECAUSE THEY HAVE NO LAST NAMES?
THEY'RE STILL PEOPLE, JUST LIKE YOU AND ME.
I HAVE NEVER BEEN ABLE TO STAND THAT. IT ALWAYS MAKES ME SO MAD.

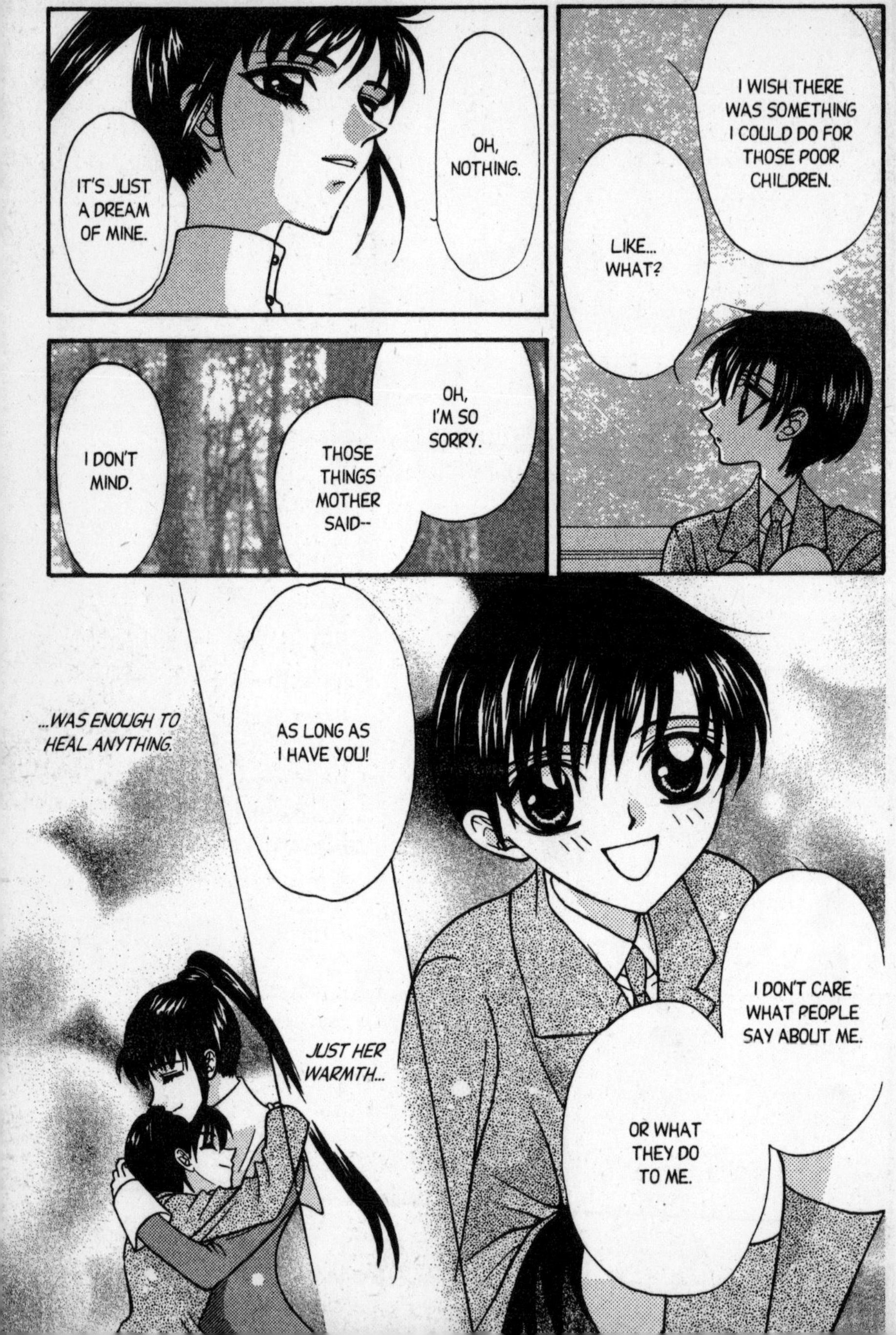
I WISH THERE WAS SOMETHING I COULD DO FOR THOSE POOR CHILDREN.
LIKE... WHAT?
OH, NOTHING.
IT'S JUST A DREAM OF MINE.
OH, I'M SO SORRY.
THOSE THINGS MOTHER SAID--
I DON'T MIND.
I DON'T CARE WHAT PEOPLE SAY ABOUT ME.
OR WHAT THEY DO TO ME.
AS LONG AS I HAVE YOU!
JUST HER WARMTH...
...WAS ENOUGH TO HEAL ANYTHING.

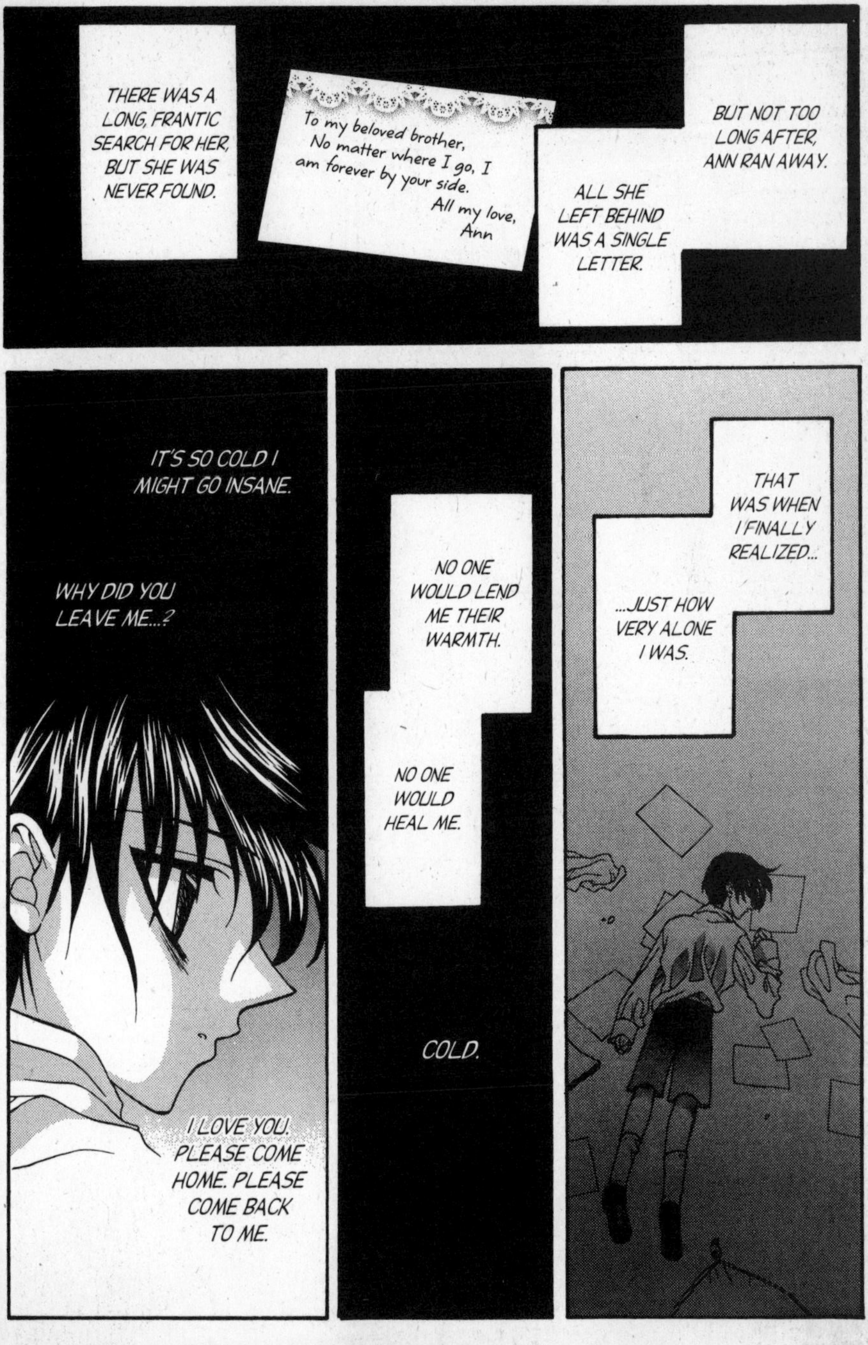
BUT NOT TOO LONG AFTER, ANN RAN AWAY.
ALL SHE LEFT BEHIND WAS A SINGLE LETTER.
To my beloved brother, No matter where I go, I am forever by your side. All my love, Ann
THERE WAS A LONG, FRANTIC SEARCH FOR HER, BUT SHE WAS NEVER FOUND.
THAT WAS WHEN I FINALLY REALIZED...
...JUST HOW VERY ALONE I WAS.
NO ONE WOULD LEND ME THEIR WARMTH.
NO ONE WOULD HEAL ME.
COLD.
IT'S SO COLD I MIGHT GO INSANE.
WHY DID YOU LEAVE ME...?
I LOVE YOU. PLEASE COME HOME. PLEASE COME BACK TO ME.

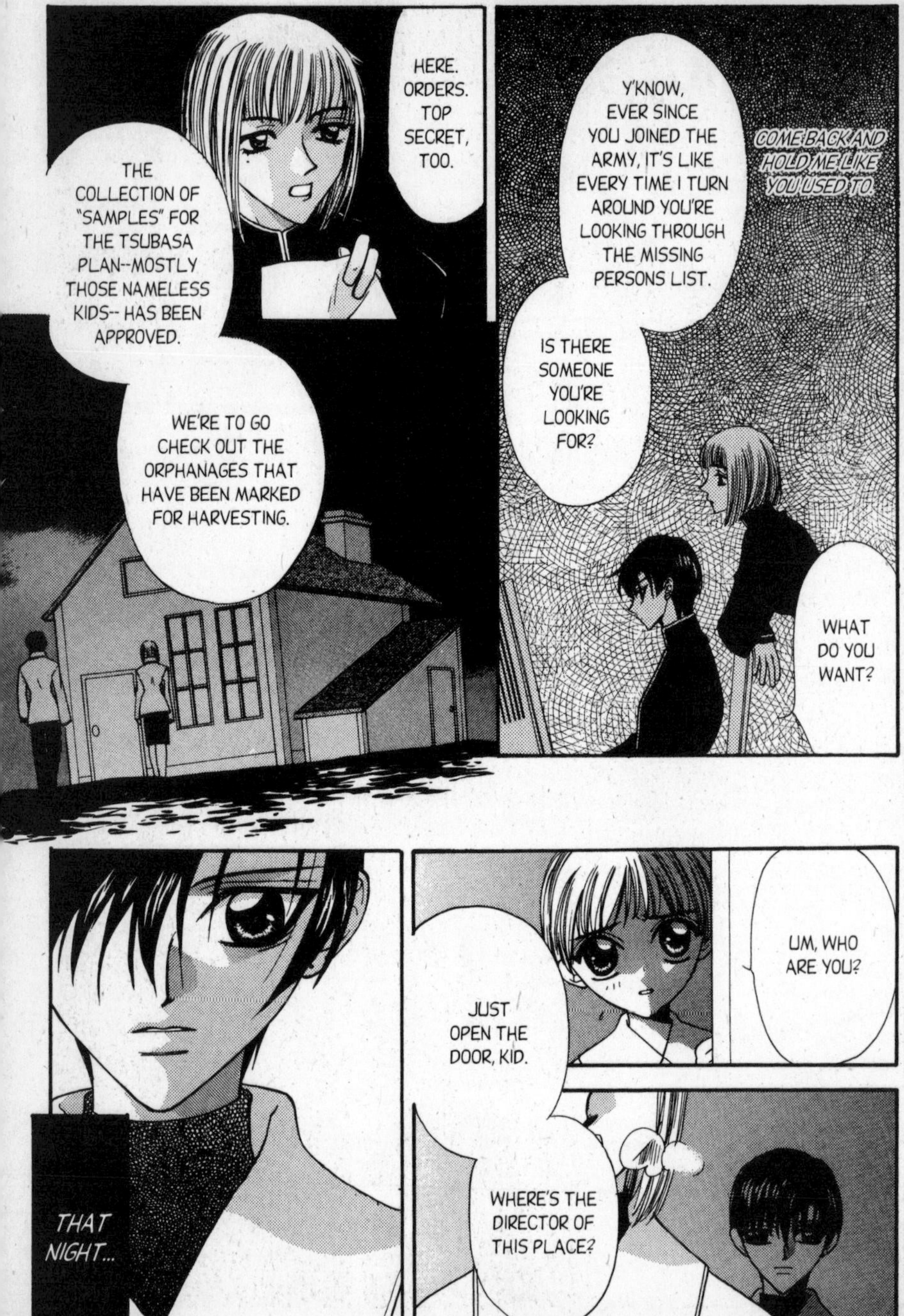

Y'KNOW, EVER SINCE YOU JOINED THE ARMY, IT'S LIKE EVERY TIME I TURN AROUND YOU'RE LOOKING THROUGH THE MISSING PERSONS LIST.
COME BACK AND HOLD ME LIKE YOU USED TO.
IS THERE SOMEONE YOU'RE LOOKING FOR?
WHAT DO YOU WANT?
HERE. ORDERS. TOP SECRET, TOO.
THE COLLECTION OF "SAMPLES" FOR THE TSUBASA PLAN--MOSTLY THOSE NAMELESS KIDS-- HAS BEEN APPROVED.
WE'RE TO GO CHECK OUT THE ORPHANAGES THAT HAVE BEEN MARKED FOR HARVESTING.
UM, WHO ARE YOU?
JUST OPEN THE DOOR, KID.
WHERE'S THE DIRECTOR OF THIS PLACE?
THAT NIGHT...

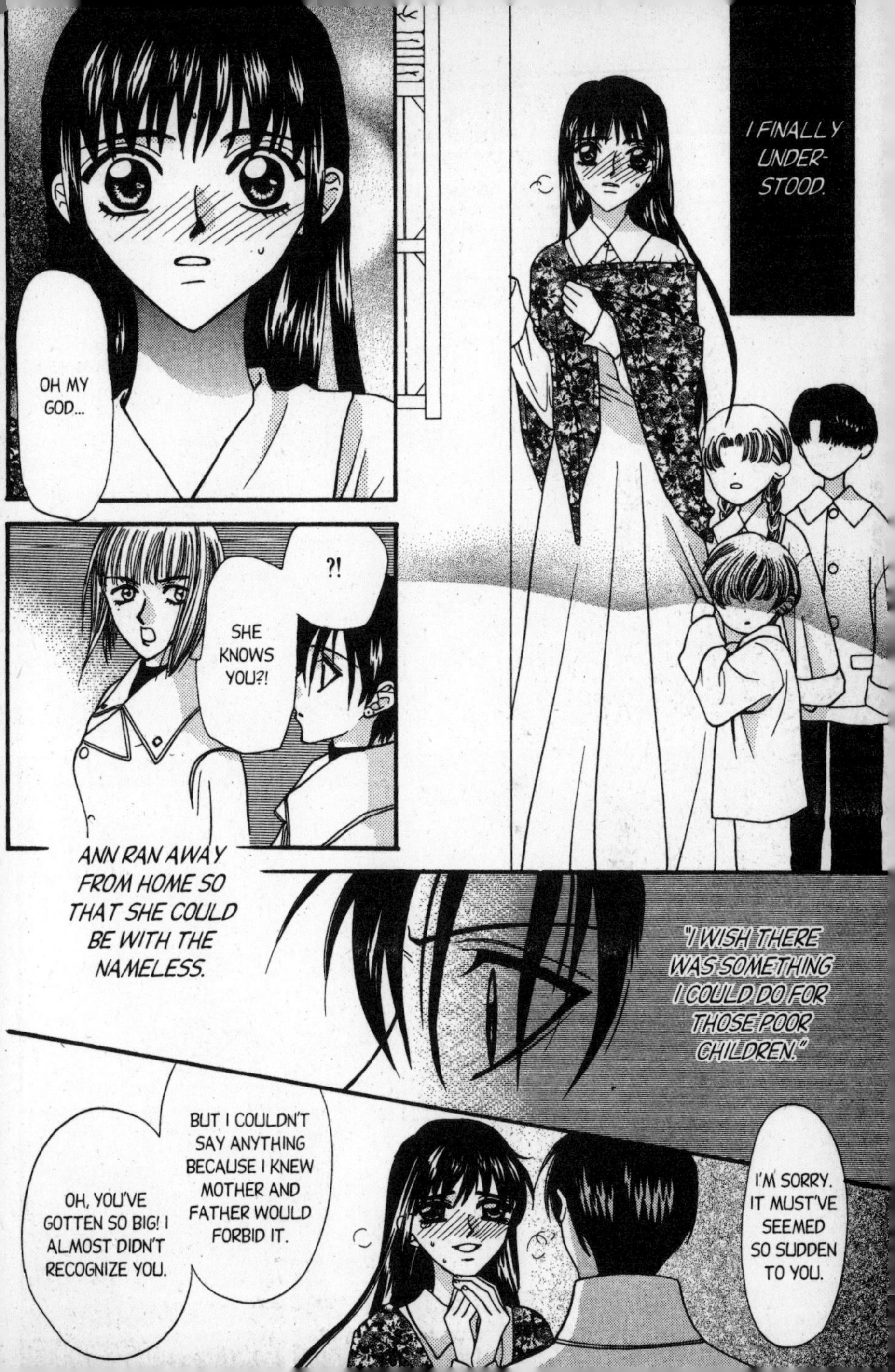
I FINALLY UNDER-STOOD.
OH MY GOD...
?!
SHE KNOWS YOU?!
"I WISH THERE WAS SOMETHING I COULD DO FOR THOSE POOR CHILDREN."
ANN RAN AWAY FROM HOME SO THAT SHE COULD BE WITH THE NAMELESS.
I'M SORRY. IT MUST'VE SEEMED SO SUDDEN TO YOU.
BUT I COULDN'T SAY ANYTHING BECAUSE I KNEW MOTHER AND FATHER WOULD FORBID IT.
OH, YOU'VE GOTTEN SO BIG! I ALMOST DIDN'T RECOGNIZE YOU.

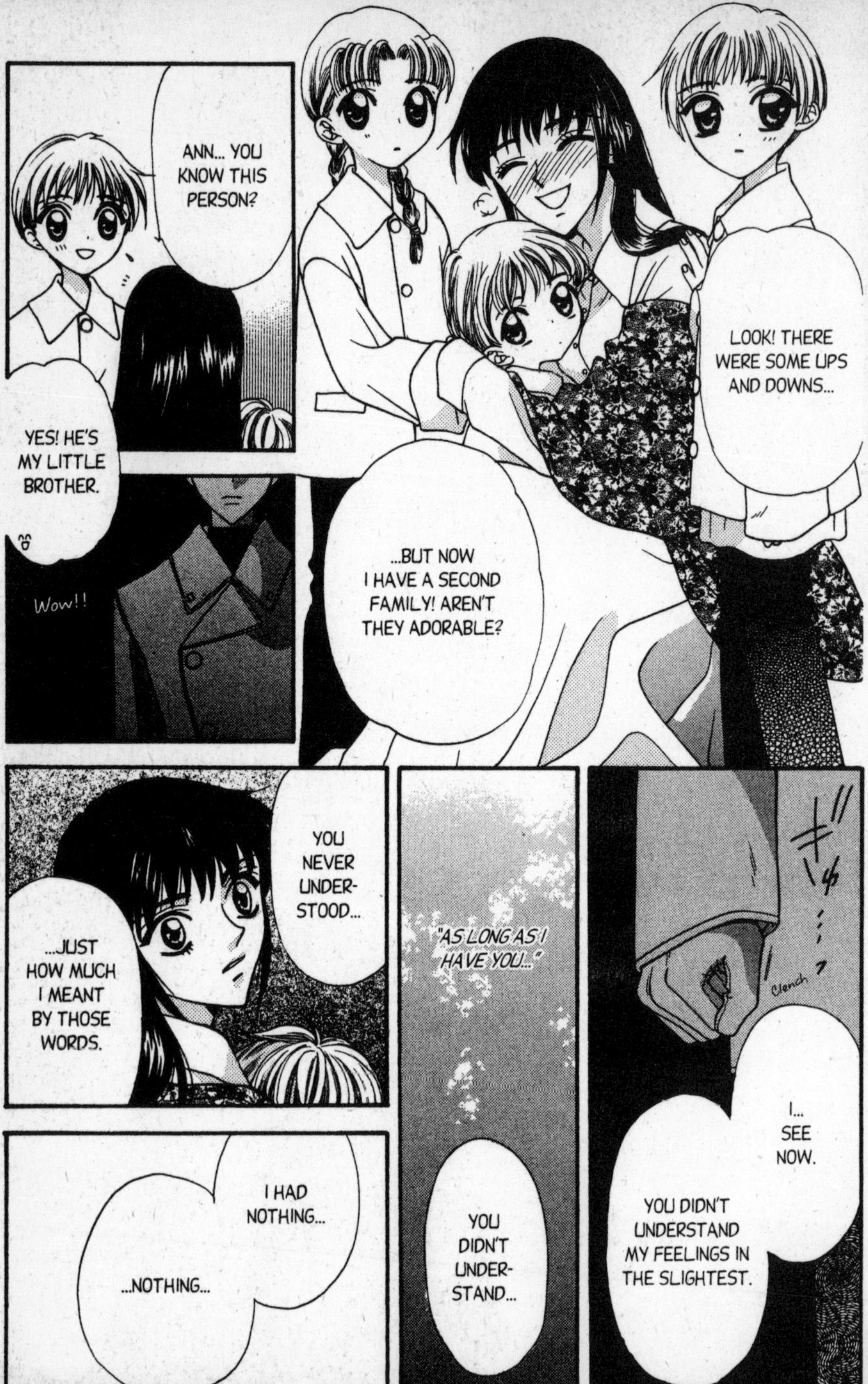
LOOK! THERE WERE SOME UPS AND DOWNS...
...BUT NOW I HAVE A SECOND FAMILY! AREN'T THEY ADORABLE?
ANN... YOU KNOW THIS PERSON?
YES! HE'S MY LITTLE BROTHER.
Wow!!
I... SEE NOW.
YOU DIDN'T UNDERSTAND MY FEELINGS IN THE SLIGHTEST.
Clench
"AS LONG AS I HAVE YOU..."
YOU DIDN'T UNDER-STAND...
YOU NEVER UNDER-STOOD...
...JUST HOW MUCH I MEANT BY THOSE WORDS.
I HAD NOTHING...
...NOTHING...

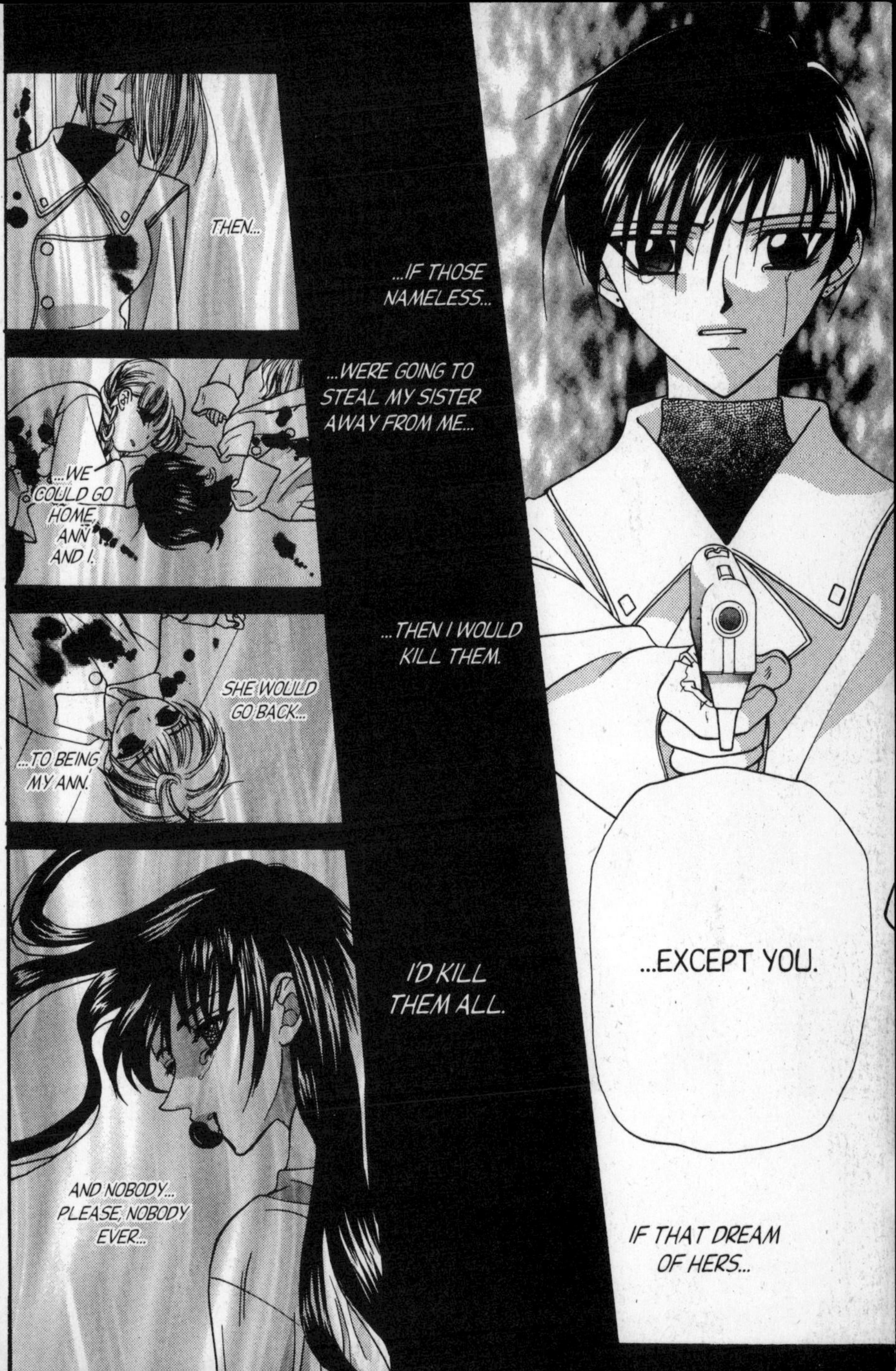
...IF THOSE NAMELESS...
...WERE GOING TO STEAL MY SISTER AWAY FROM ME...
...THEN I WOULD KILL THEM.
I'D KILL THEM ALL.
...EXCEPT YOU.
IF THAT DREAM OF HERS...
THEN...
...WE COULD GO HOME, ANN AND I.
SHE WOULD GO BACK...
...TO BEING MY ANN.
AND NOBODY... PLEASE, NOBODY EVER...

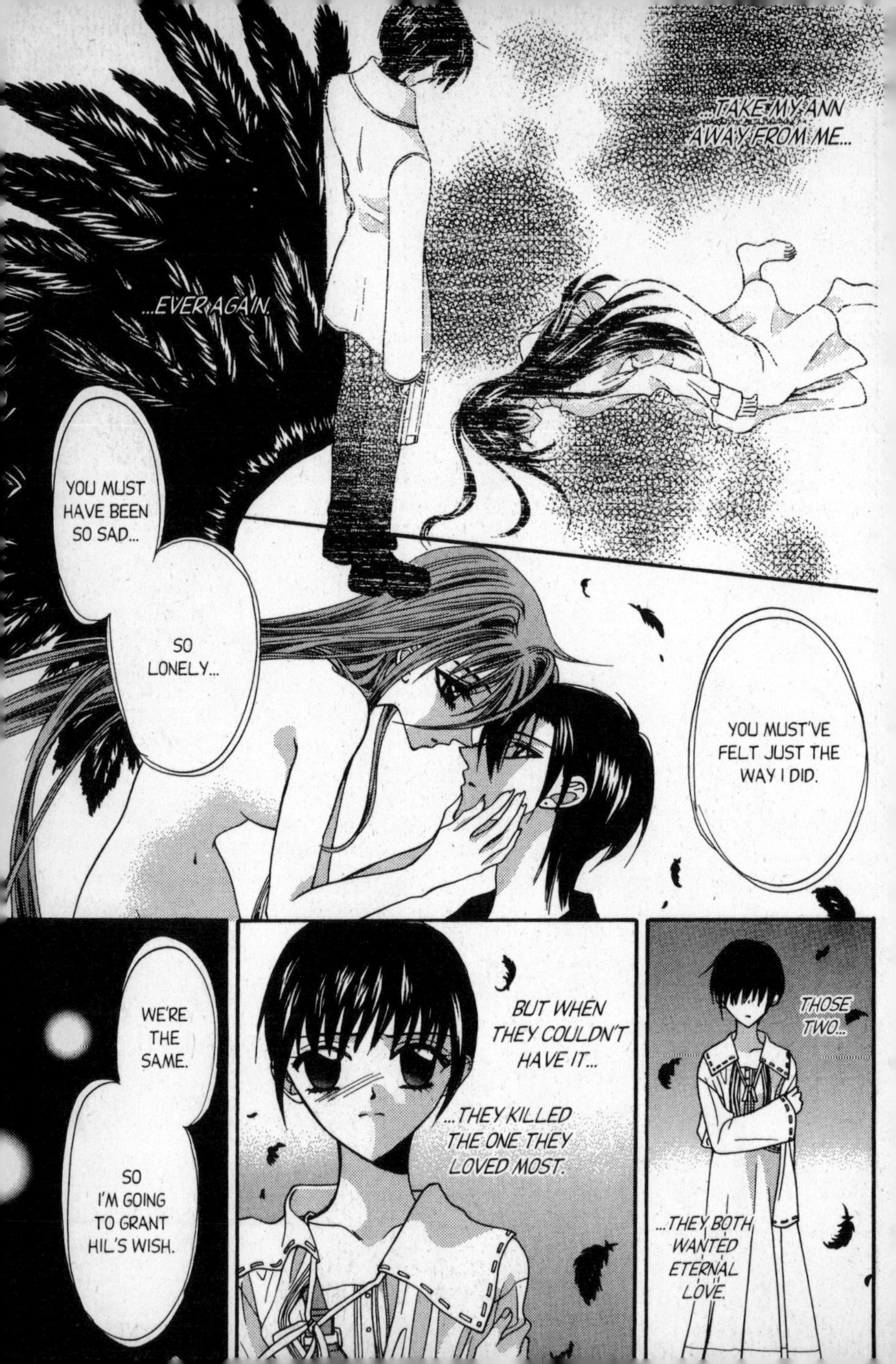
...TAKE MY ANN AWAY FROM ME...
...EVER AGAIN.
YOU MUST HAVE BEEN SO SAD...
SO LONELY...
YOU MUST'VE FELT JUST THE WAY I DID.
THOSE TWO...
...THEY BOTH WANTED ETERNAL LOVE.
BUT WHEN THEY COULDN'T HAVE IT...
...THEY KILLED THE ONE THEY LOVED MOST.
WE'RE THE SAME.
SO I'M GOING TO GRANT HIL'S WISH.

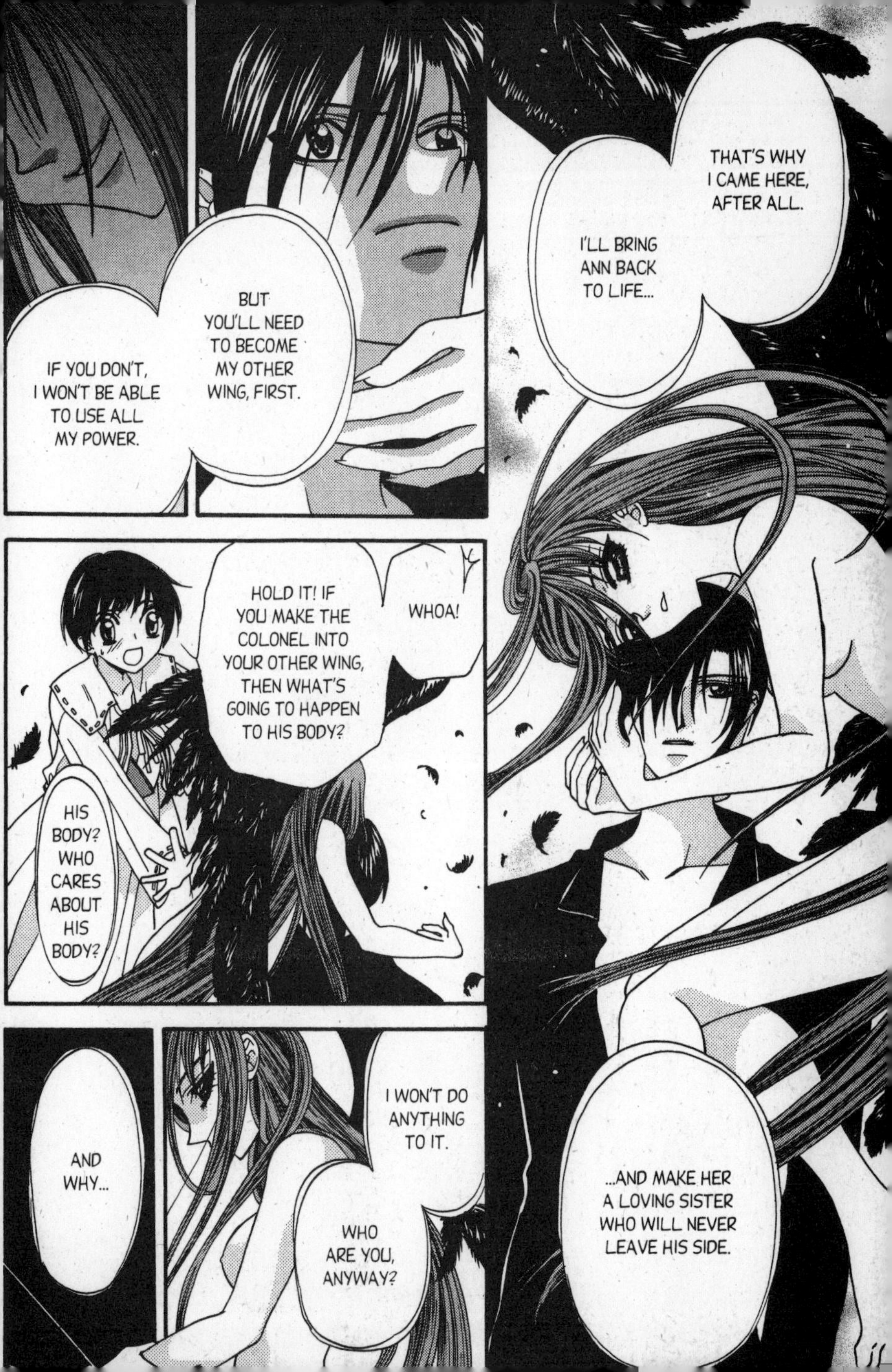
THAT'S WHY I CAME HERE, AFTER ALL.
I'LL BRING ANN BACK TO LIFE...
...AND MAKE HER A LOVING SISTER WHO WILL NEVER LEAVE HIS SIDE.
BUT YOU'LL NEED TO BECOME MY OTHER WING, FIRST.
IF YOU DON'T, I WON'T BE ABLE TO USE ALL MY POWER.
WHOA!
HOLD IT! IF YOU MAKE THE COLONEL INTO YOUR OTHER WING, THEN WHAT'S GOING TO HAPPEN TO HIS BODY?
HIS BODY? WHO CARES ABOUT HIS BODY?
I WON'T DO ANYTHING TO IT.
WHO ARE YOU, ANYWAY?
AND WHY...

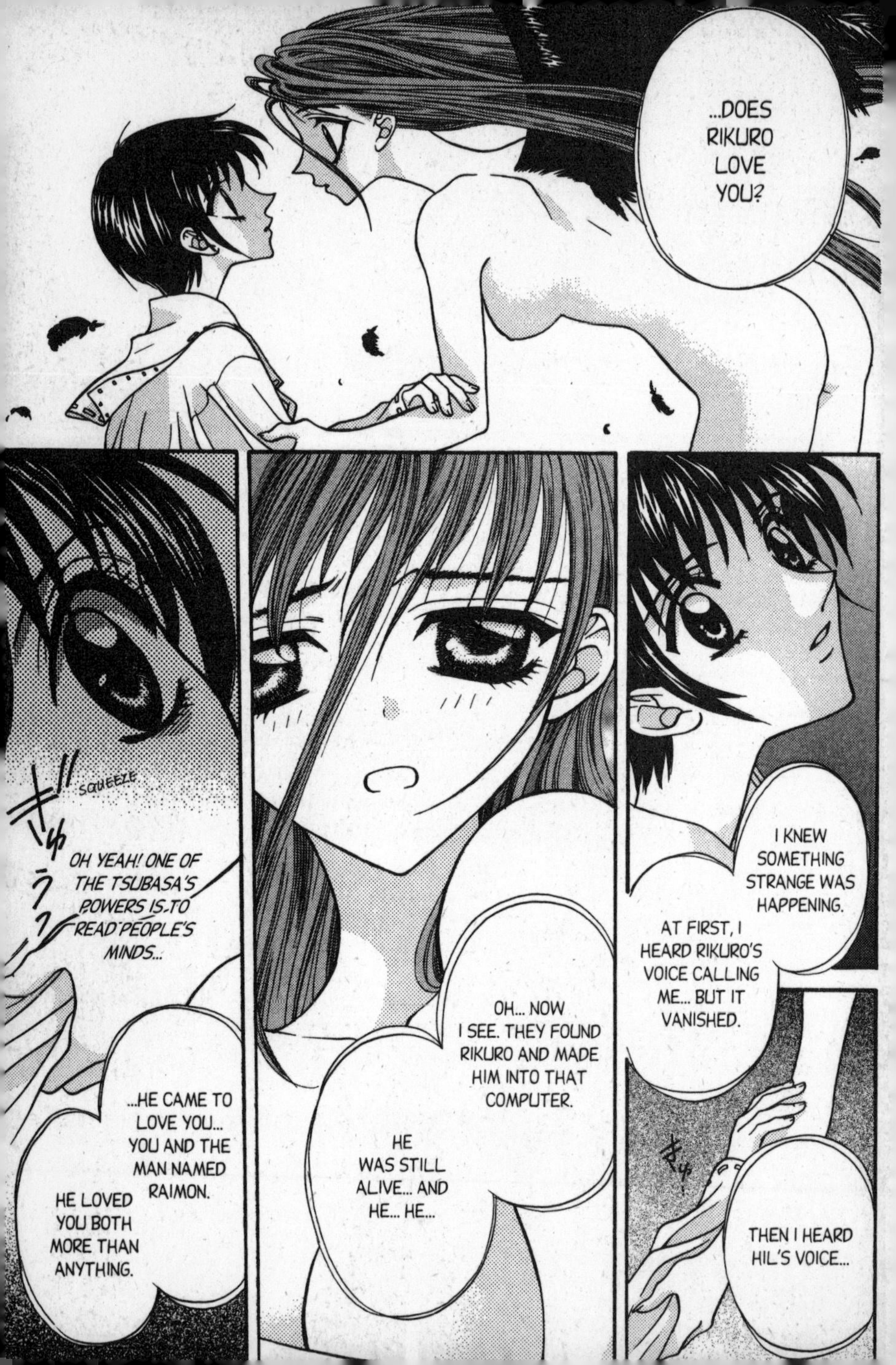
...DOES RIKURO LOVE YOU?
I KNEW SOMETHING STRANGE WAS HAPPENING.
AT FIRST, I HEARD RIKURO'S VOICE CALLING ME... BUT IT VANISHED.
THEN I HEARD HIL'S VOICE...
OH... NOW I SEE. THEY FOUND RIKURO AND MADE HIM INTO THAT COMPUTER.
HE WAS STILL ALIVE... AND HE... HE...
SQUEEZE
OH YEAH! ONE OF THE TSUBASA'S POWERS IS TO READ PEOPLE'S MINDS...
...HE CAME TO LOVE YOU... YOU AND THE MAN NAMED RAIMON.
HE LOVED YOU BOTH MORE THAN ANYTHING.

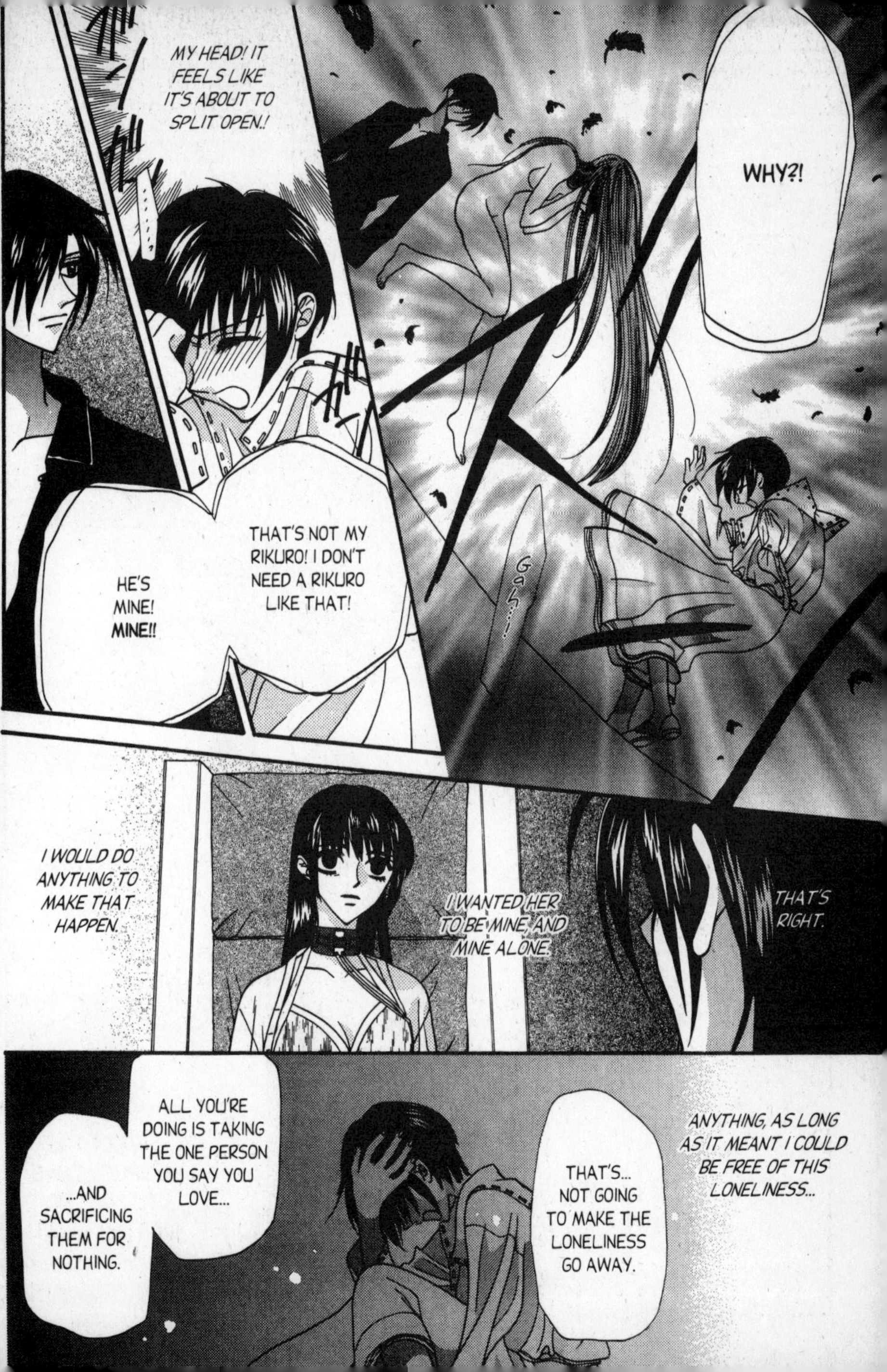
WHY?!
Gah...
MY HEAD! IT FEELS LIKE IT'S ABOUT TO SPLIT OPEN.!
THAT'S NOT MY RIKURO! I DON'T NEED A RIKURO LIKE THAT!
HE'S MINE! MINE!!
THAT'S RIGHT.
I WANTED HER TO BE MINE, AND MINE ALONE.
I WOULD DO ANYTHING TO MAKE THAT HAPPEN.
ANYTHING, AS LONG AS IT MEANT I COULD BE FREE OF THIS LONELINESS...
THAT'S... NOT GOING TO MAKE THE LONELINESS GO AWAY.
ALL YOU'RE DOING IS TAKING THE ONE PERSON YOU SAY YOU LOVE...
...AND SACRIFICING THEM FOR NOTHING.

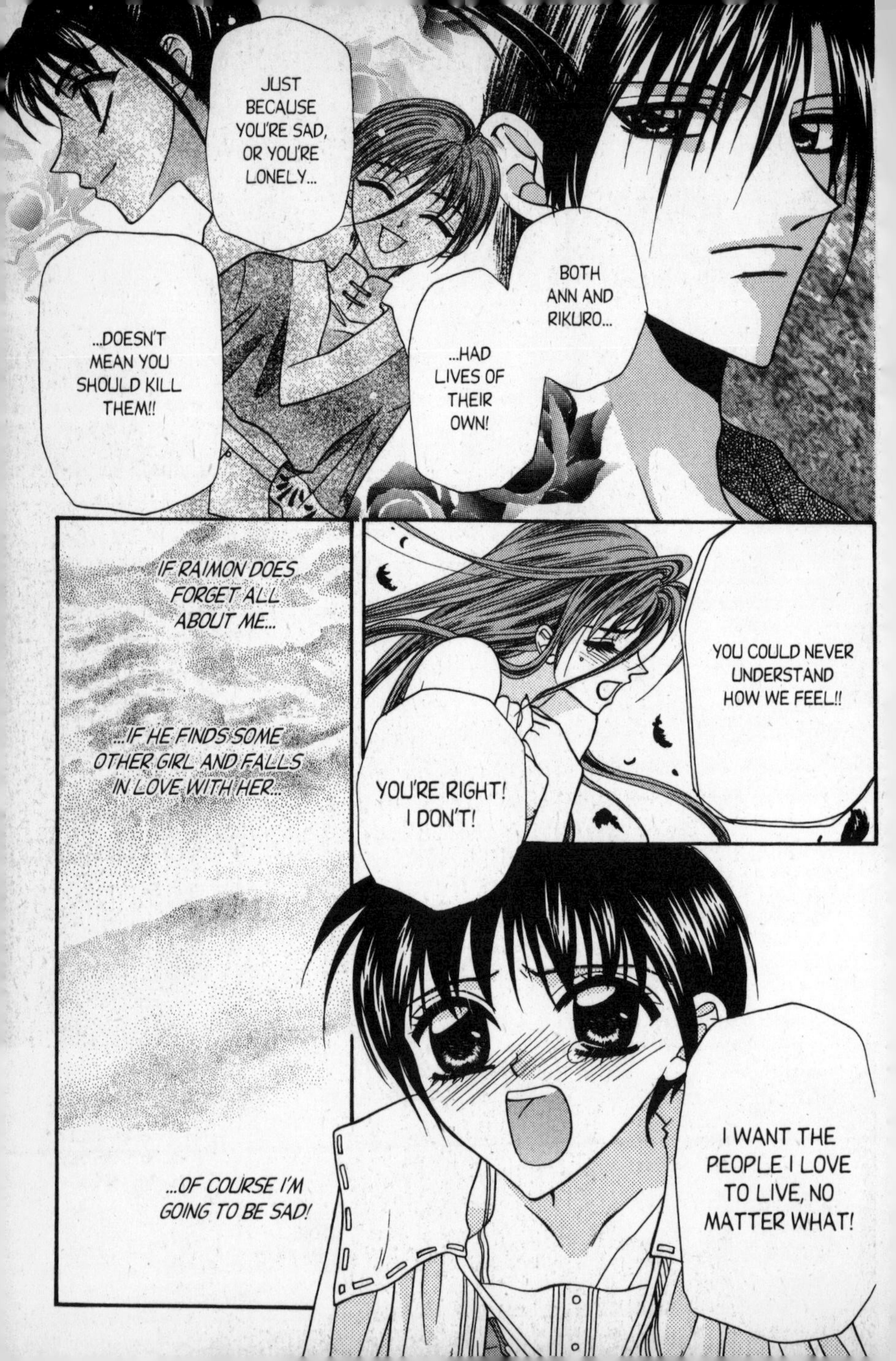
BOTH ANN AND RIKURO...
...HAD LIVES OF THEIR OWN!
JUST BECAUSE YOU'RE SAD, OR YOU'RE LONELY...
...DOESN'T MEAN YOU SHOULD KILL THEM!!
YOU COULD NEVER UNDERSTAND HOW WE FEEL!!
YOU'RE RIGHT! I DON'T!
I WANT THE PEOPLE I LOVE TO LIVE, NO MATTER WHAT!
IF RAIMON DOES FORGET ALL ABOUT ME...
...IF HE FINDS SOME OTHER GIRL AND FALLS IN LOVE WITH HER...
...OF COURSE I'M GOING TO BE SAD!

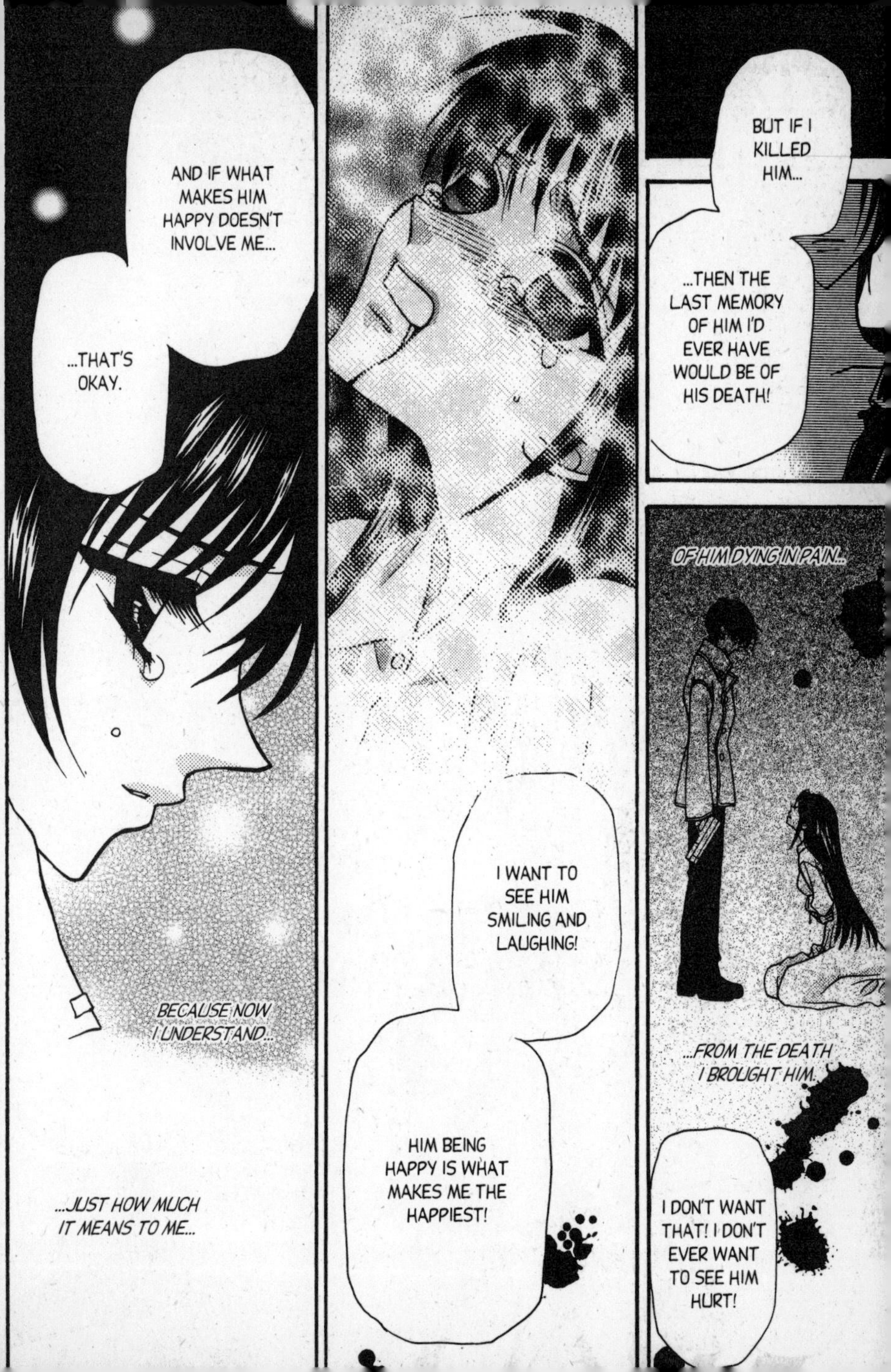
BUT IF I KILLED HIM...
...THEN THE LAST MEMORY OF HIM I'D EVER HAVE WOULD BE OF HIS DEATH!
OF HIM DYING IN PAIN...
...FROM THE DEATH I BROUGHT HIM.
I DON'T WANT THAT! I DON'T EVER WANT TO SEE HIM HURT!
I WANT TO SEE HIM SMILING AND LAUGHING!
HIM BEING HAPPY IS WHAT MAKES ME THE HAPPIEST!
AND IF WHAT MAKES HIM HAPPY DOESN'T INVOLVE ME...
...THAT'S OKAY.
BECAUSE NOW I UNDERSTAND...
...JUST HOW MUCH IT MEANS TO ME...

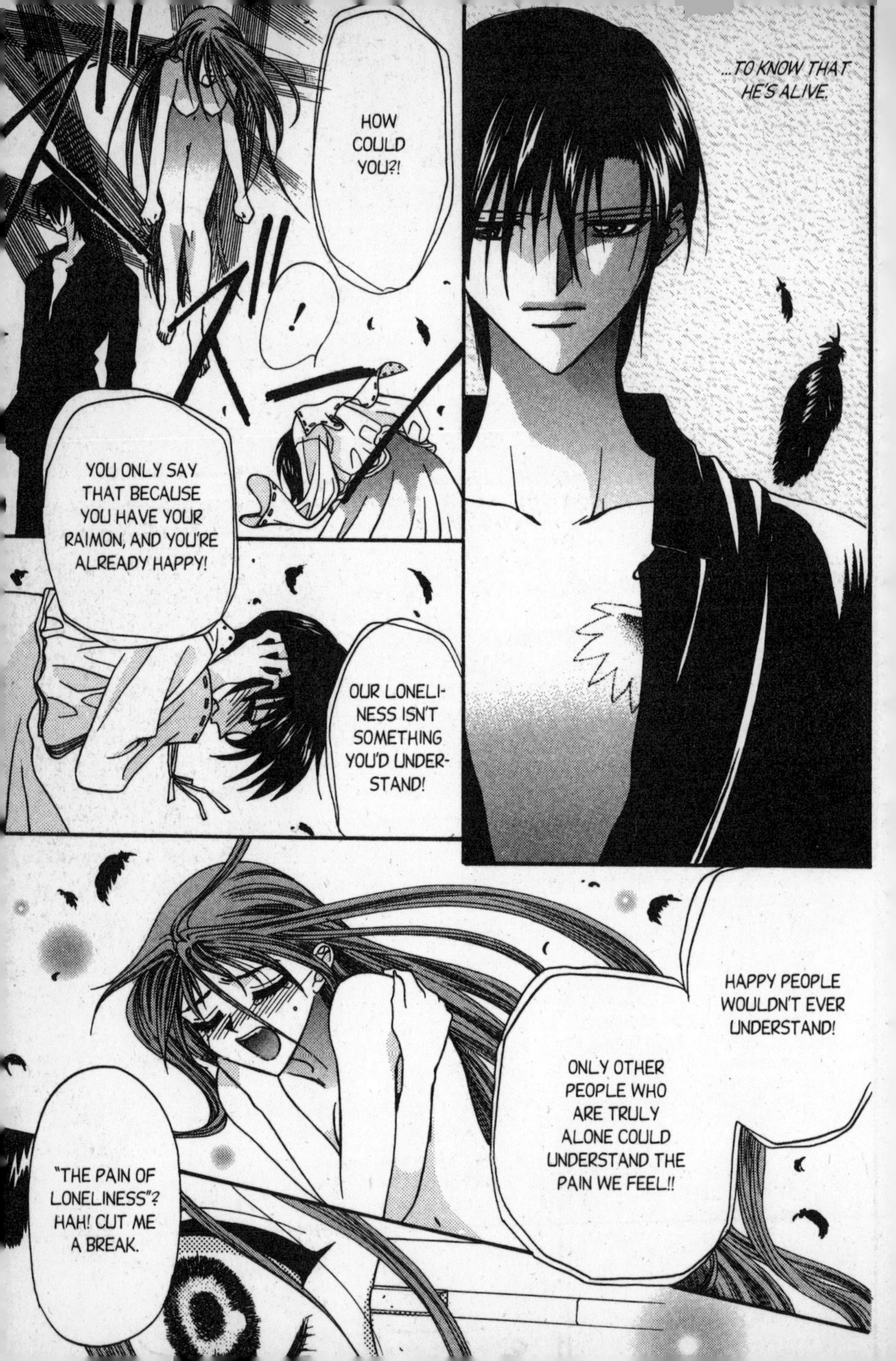
...TO KNOW THAT HE'S ALIVE.
HOW COULD YOU?!
!
YOU ONLY SAY THAT BECAUSE YOU HAVE YOUR RAIMON, AND YOU'RE ALREADY HAPPY!
OUR LONELI-NESS ISN'T SOMETHING YOU'D UNDER-STAND!
HAPPY PEOPLE WOULDN'T EVER UNDERSTAND!
ONLY OTHER PEOPLE WHO ARE TRULY ALONE COULD UNDERSTAND THE PAIN WE FEEL!!
"THE PAIN OF LONELINESS"? HAH! CUT ME A BREAK.

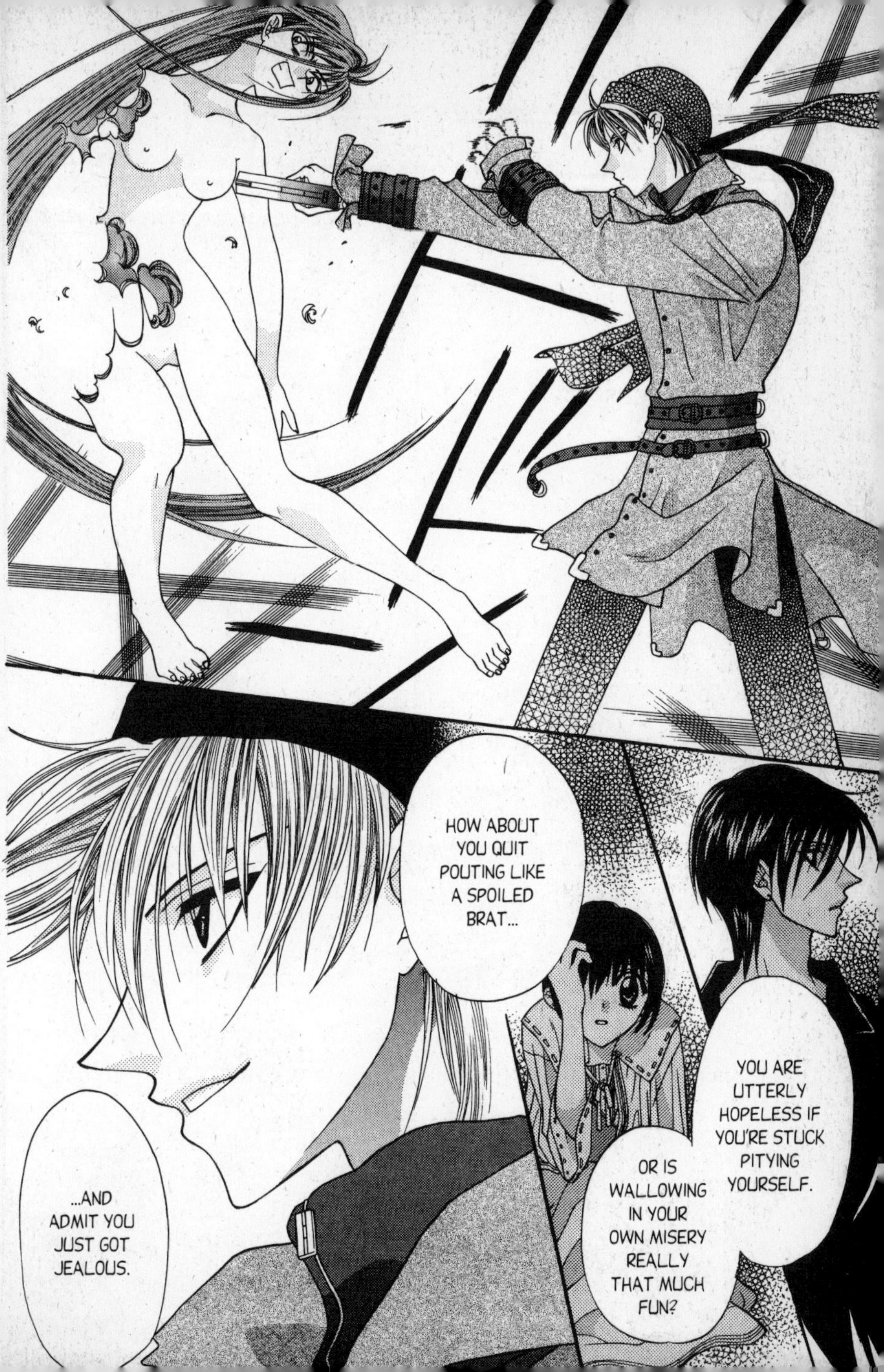
YOU ARE UTTERLY HOPELESS IF YOU'RE STUCK PITYING YOURSELF.
OR IS WALLOWING IN YOUR OWN MISERY REALLY THAT MUCH FUN?
HOW ABOUT YOU QUIT POUTING LIKE A SPOILED BRAT...
...AND ADMIT YOU JUST GOT JEALOUS.

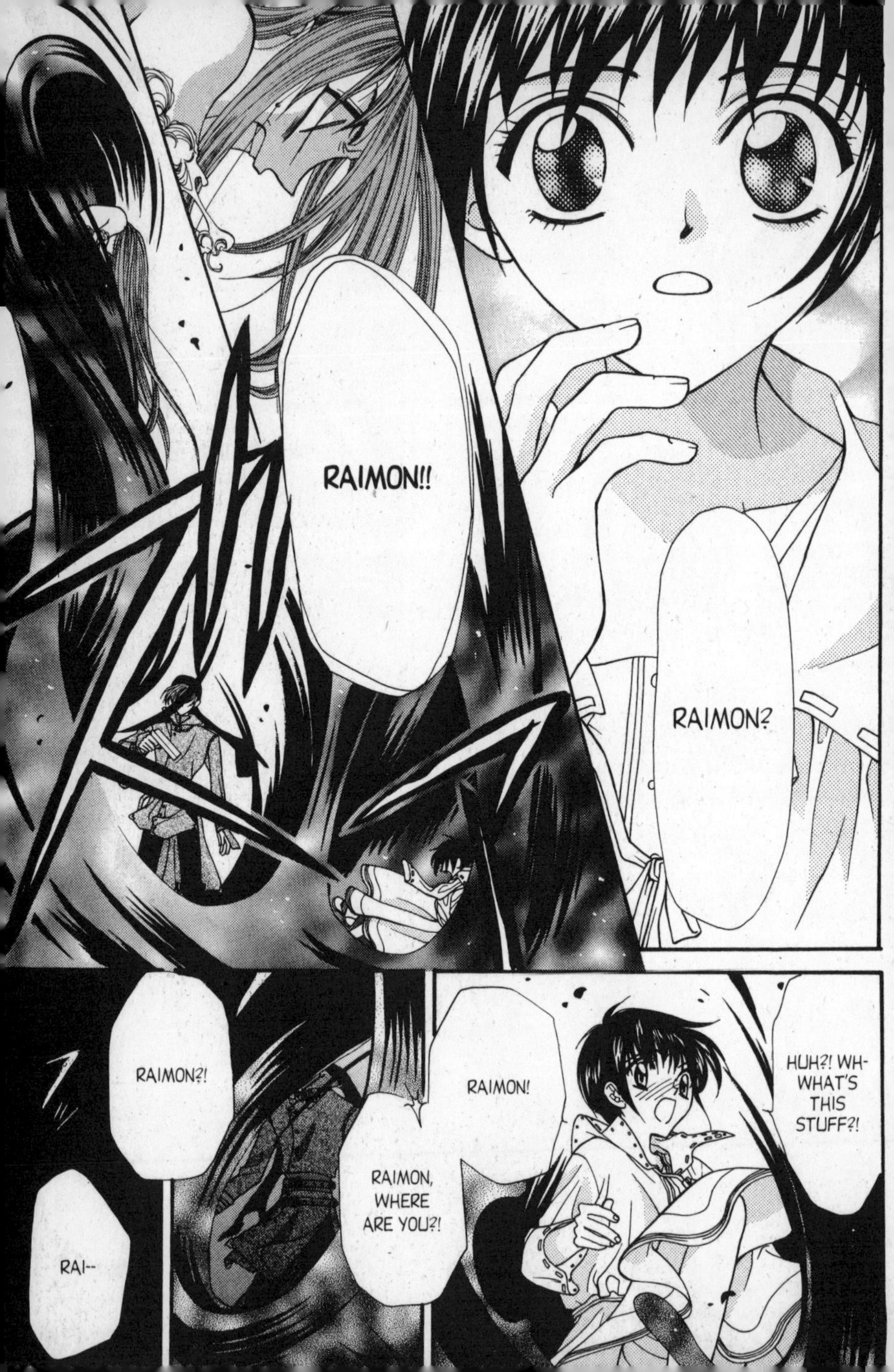
RAIMON?
RAIMON!!
HUH?! WH-WHAT'S THIS STUFF?!
RAIMON!
RAIMON, WHERE ARE YOU?!
RAIMON?!
RAI--

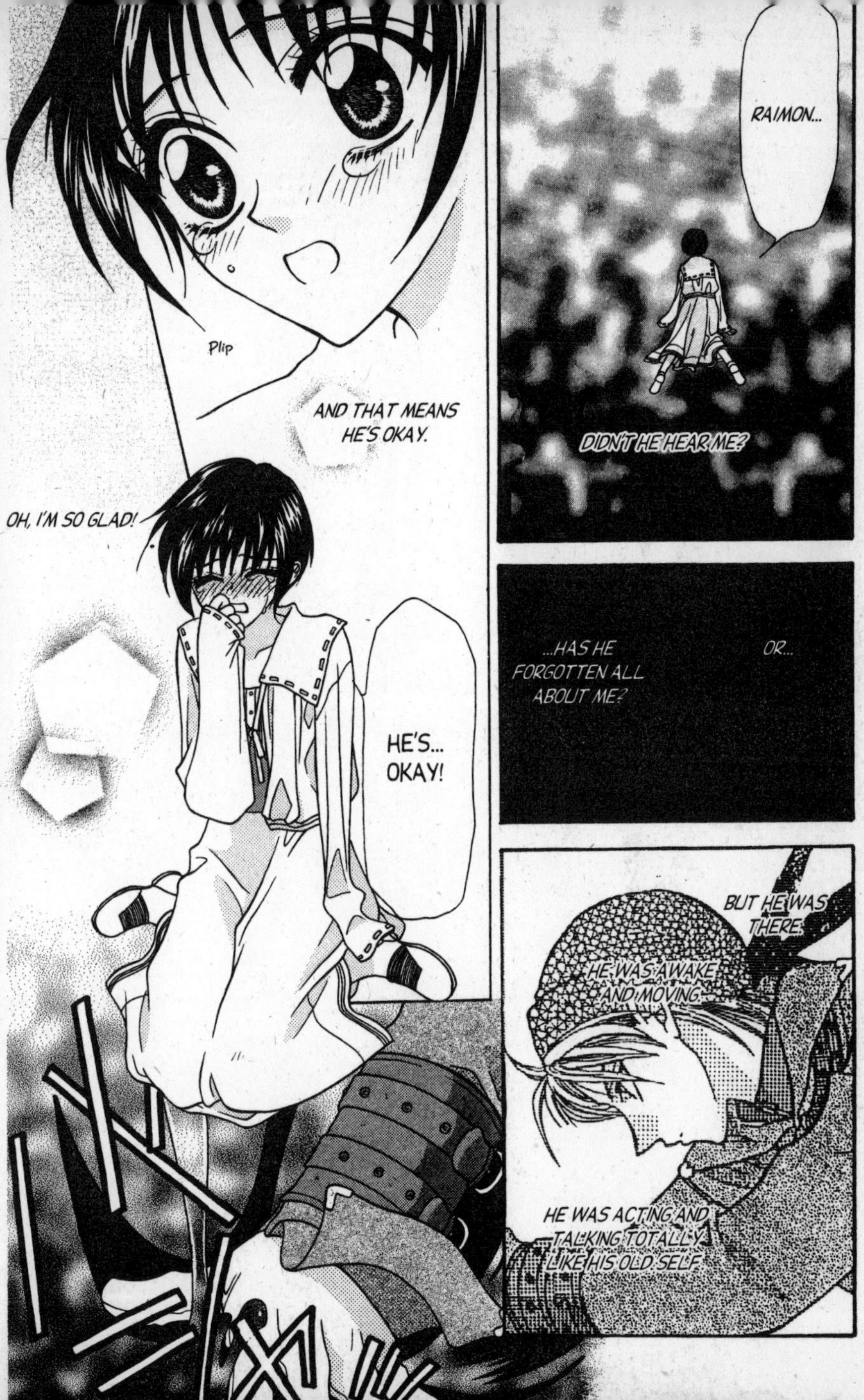
RAIMON...
DIDN'T HE HEAR ME?
OR...
...HAS HE FORGOTTEN ALL ABOUT ME?
BUT HE WAS THERE.
HE WAS AWAKE AND MOVING.
HE WAS ACTING AND TALKING TOTALLY LIKE HIS OLD SELF.
Plip
AND THAT MEANS HE'S OKAY.
HE'S... OKAY!
OH, I'M SO GLAD!

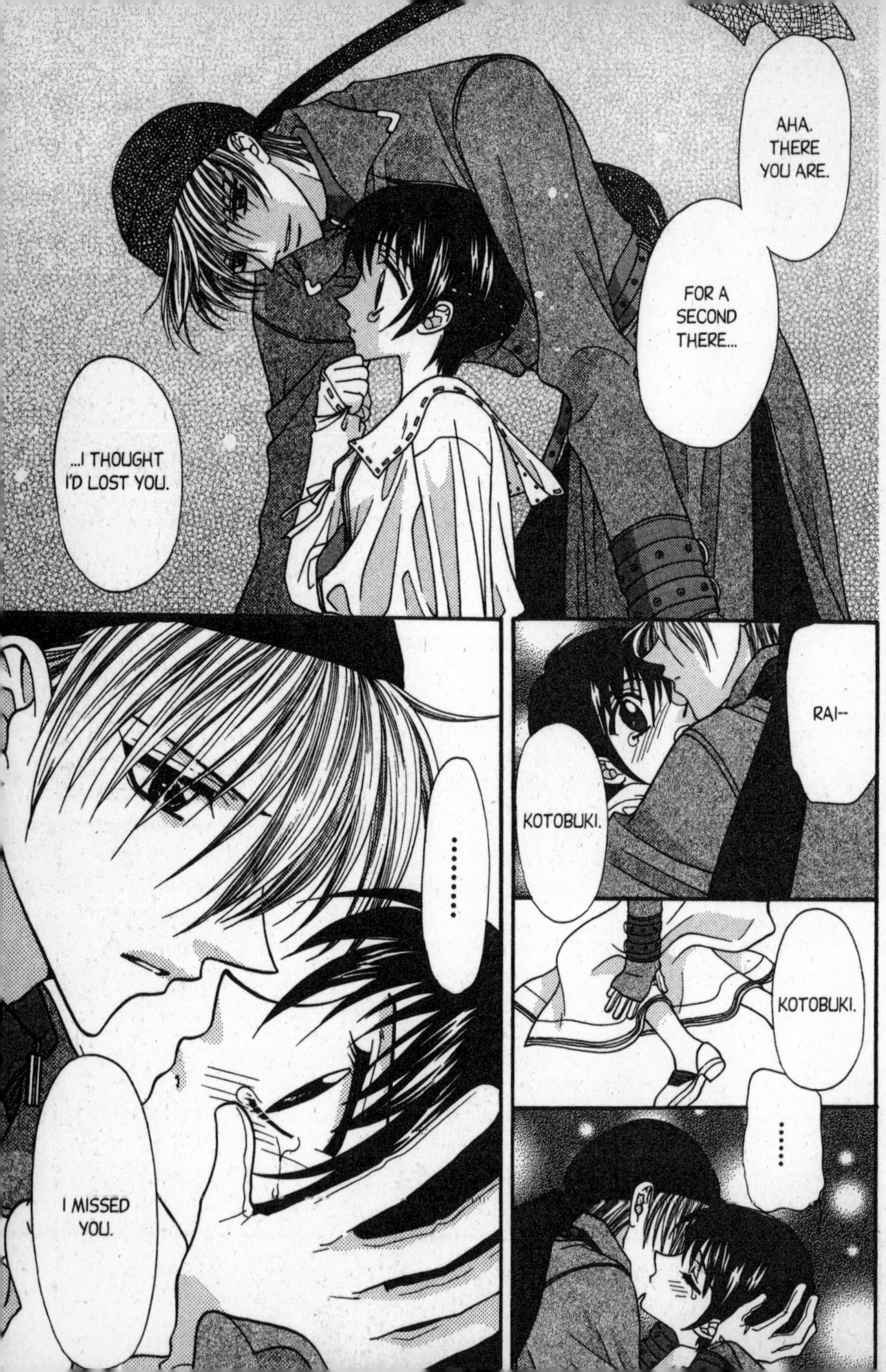
AHA. THERE YOU ARE.
FOR A SECOND THERE...
...I THOUGHT I'D LOST YOU.
RAI--
KOTOBUKI.
KOTOBUKI.
.....
....
I MISSED YOU.

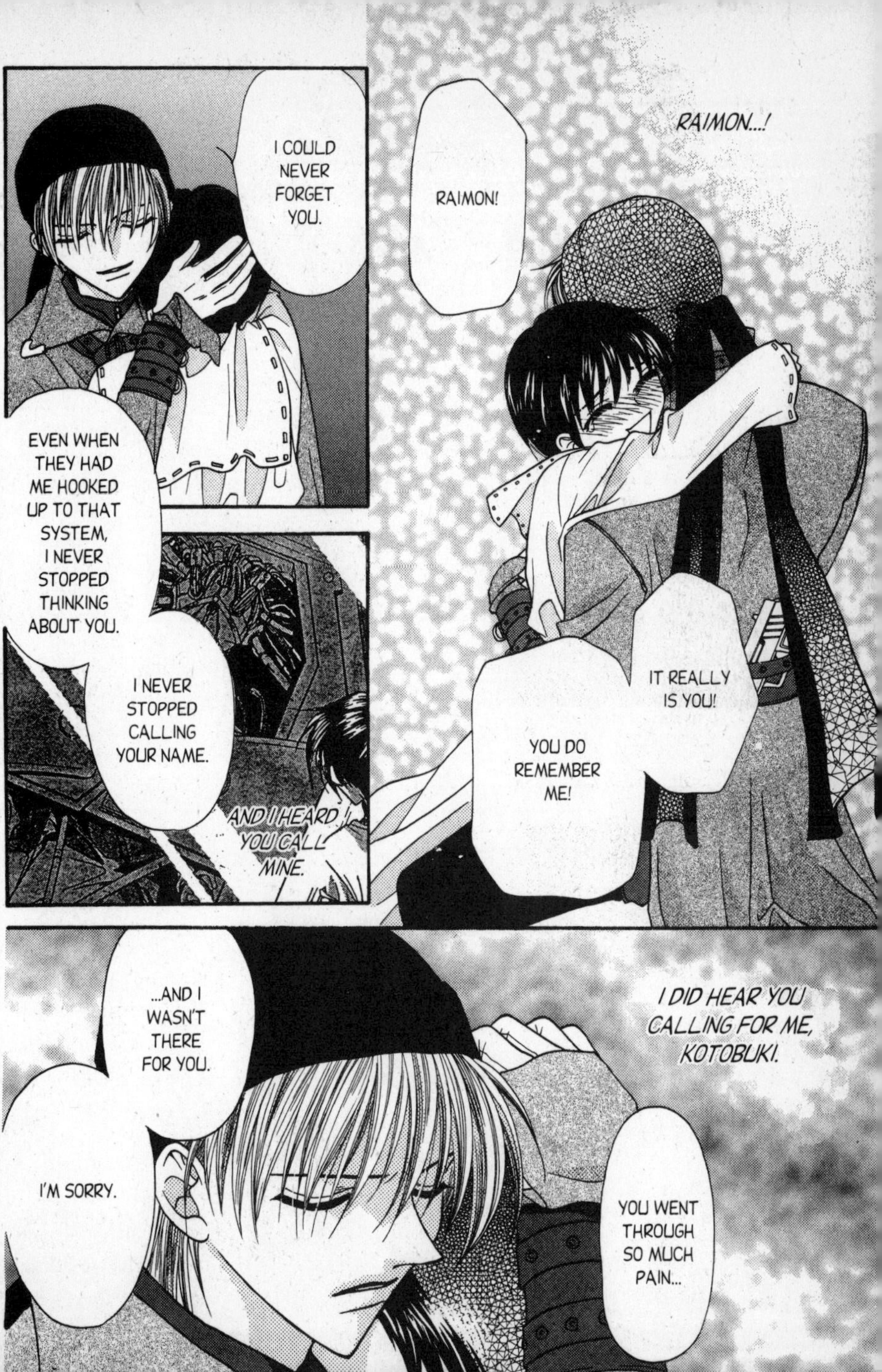
RAIMON...!
RAIMON!
IT REALLY IS YOU!
YOU DO REMEMBER ME!
I COULD NEVER FORGET YOU.
EVEN WHEN THEY HAD ME HOOKED UP TO THAT SYSTEM, I NEVER STOPPED THINKING ABOUT YOU.
I NEVER STOPPED CALLING YOUR NAME.
AND I HEARD YOU CALL MINE.
I DID HEAR YOU CALLING FOR ME, KOTOBUKI.
YOU WENT THROUGH SO MUCH PAIN...
...AND I WASN'T THERE FOR YOU.
I'M SORRY.

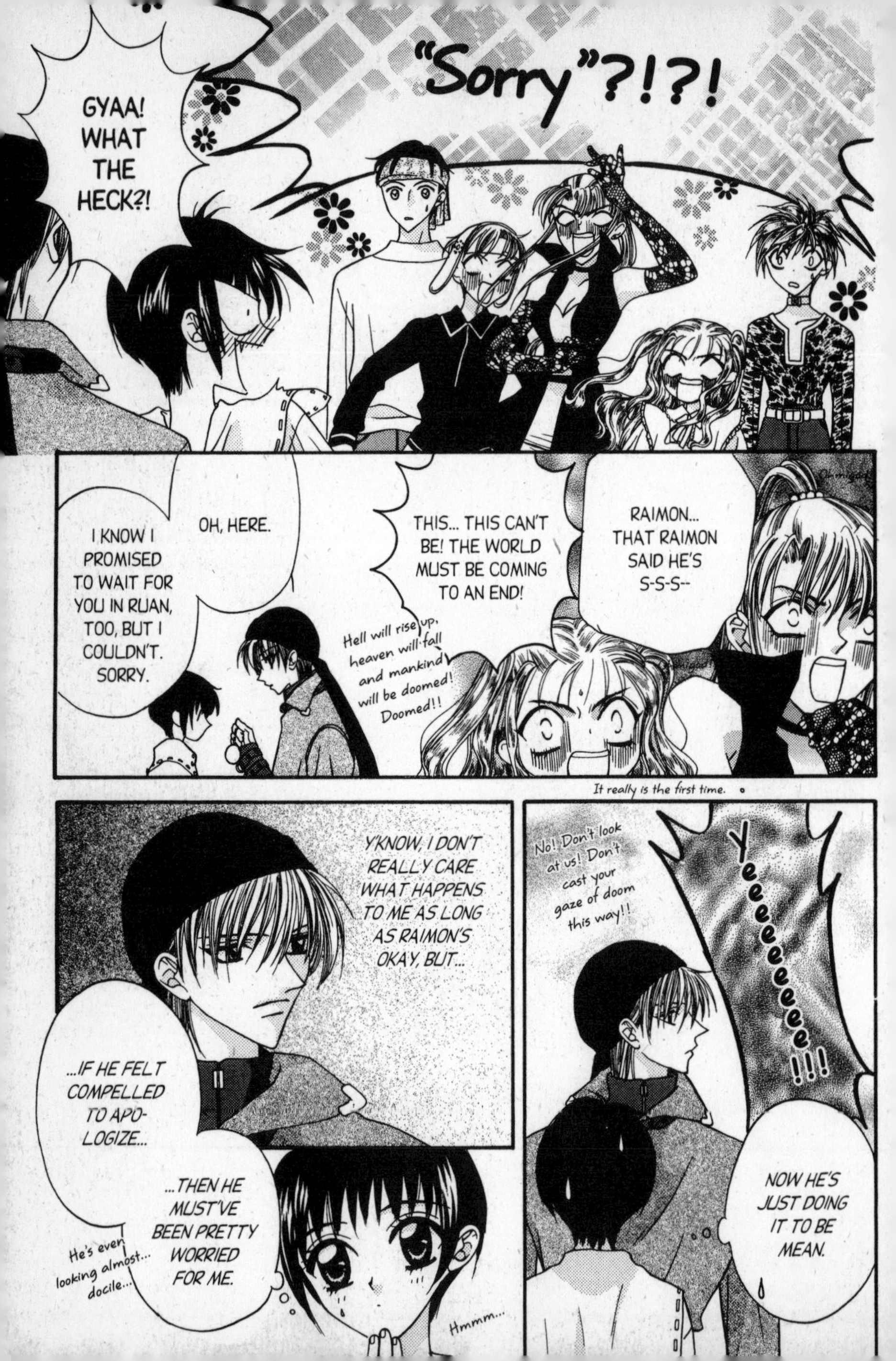
"Sorry"?!?!
GYAA! WHAT THE HECK?!
RAIMON... THAT RAIMON SAID HE'S S-S-S--
THIS... THIS CAN'T BE! THE WORLD MUST BE COMING TO AN END!
Hell will rise up, heaven will fall and mankind will be doomed! Doomed!!
OH, HERE.
I KNOW I PROMISED TO WAIT FOR YOU IN RUAN, TOO, BUT I COULDN'T. SORRY.
It really is the first time.
Yeeeeeeeee!!!
No! Don't look at us! Don't cast your gaze of doom this way!!
NOW HE'S JUST DOING IT TO BE MEAN.
Y'KNOW, I DON'T REALLY CARE WHAT HAPPENS TO ME AS LONG AS RAIMON'S OKAY, BUT...
...IF HE FELT COMPELLED TO APO-LOGIZE...
...THEN HE MUST'VE BEEN PRETTY WORRIED FOR ME.
He's even looking almost... docile...
Hmmm...

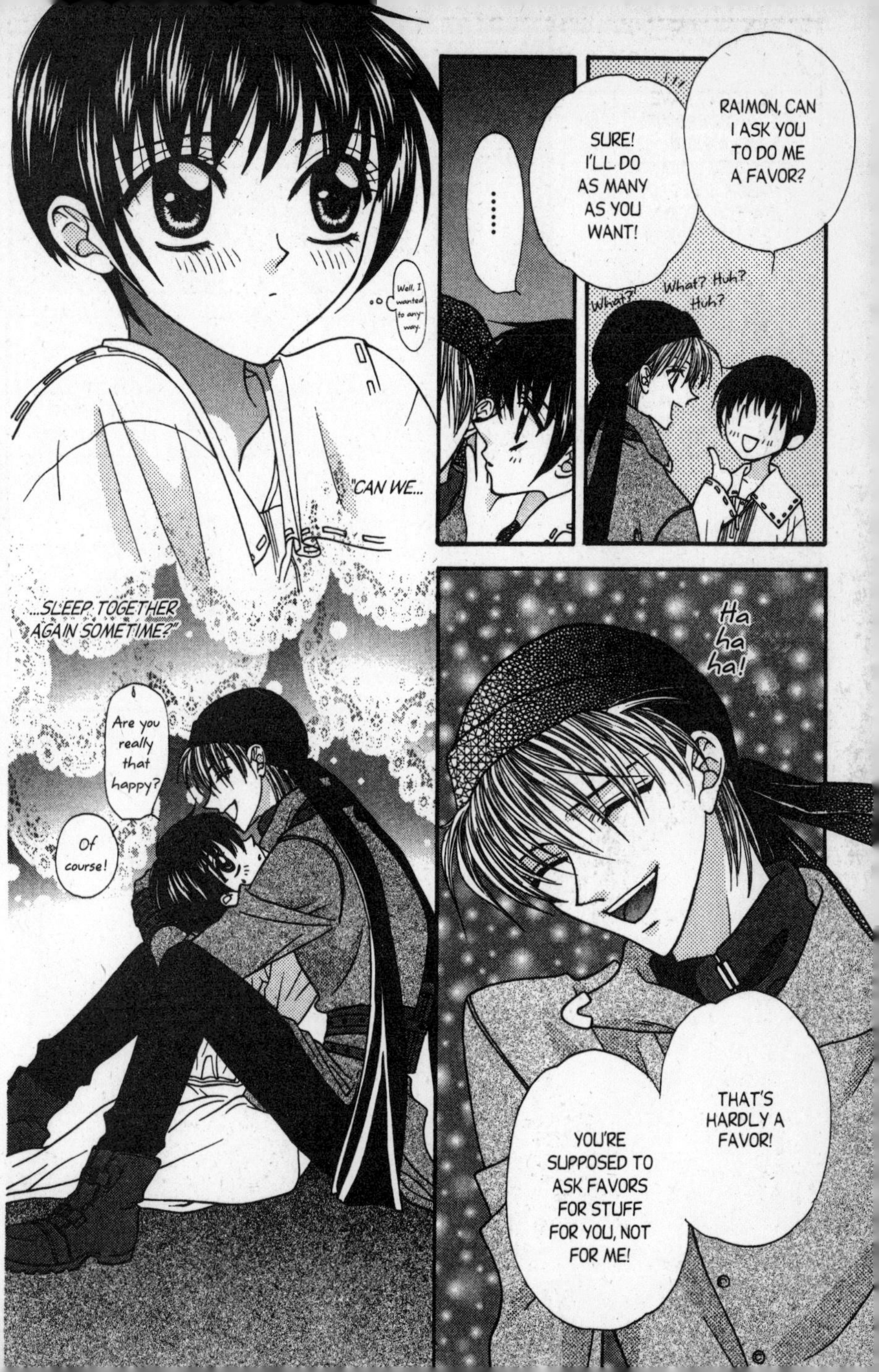
RAIMON, CAN I ASK YOU TO DO ME A FAVOR?
What? Huh? Huh?
What?
SURE! I'LL DO AS MANY AS YOU WANT!
......
Ha ha ha!
THAT'S HARDLY A FAVOR!
YOU'RE SUPPOSED TO ASK FAVORS FOR STUFF FOR YOU, NOT FOR ME!
Well, I wanted to anyway.
"CAN WE...
...SLEEP TOGETHER AGAIN SOMETIME?"
Are you really that happy?
Of course!

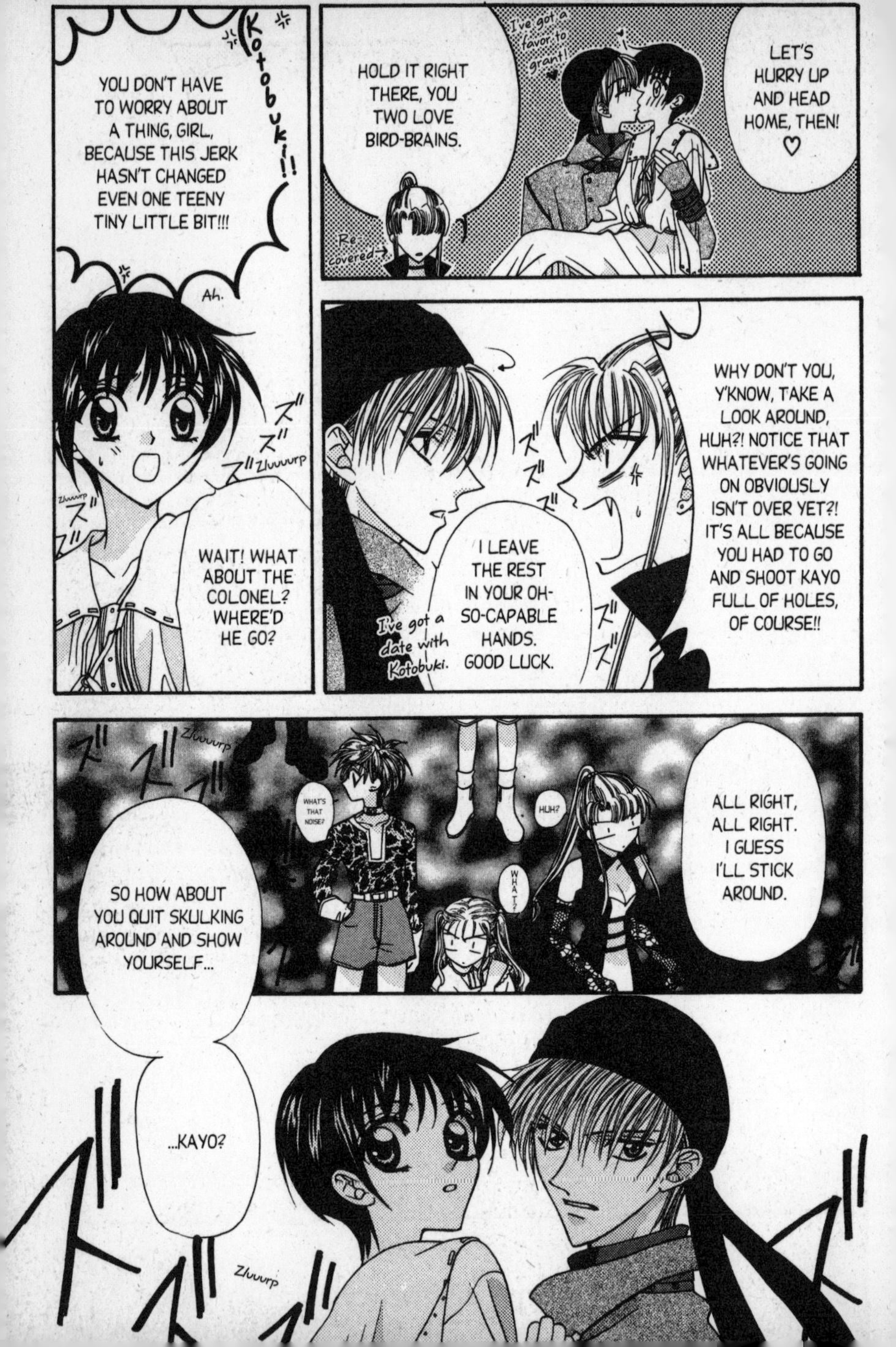
LET'S HURRY UP AND HEAD HOME, THEN! ♡
I've got a favor to grant!! ♥
HOLD IT RIGHT THERE, YOU TWO LOVE BIRD-BRAINS.
Re-covered
WHY DON'T YOU, Y'KNOW, TAKE A LOOK AROUND, HUH?! NOTICE THAT WHATEVER'S GOING ON OBVIOUSLY ISN'T OVER YET?! IT'S ALL BECAUSE YOU HAD TO GO AND SHOOT KAYO FULL OF HOLES, OF COURSE!!
ズズズ
I LEAVE THE REST IN YOUR OH-SO-CAPABLE HANDS. GOOD LUCK.
I've got a date with Kotobuki.
Kotobuki!!
YOU DON'T HAVE TO WORRY ABOUT A THING, GIRL, BECAUSE THIS JERK HASN'T CHANGED EVEN ONE TEENY TINY LITTLE BIT!!!
Ah.
ズズズ Zluuuurp
ズズ Zluuurp
WAIT! WHAT ABOUT THE COLONEL? WHERE'D HE GO?
ALL RIGHT, ALL RIGHT. I GUESS I'LL STICK AROUND.
HUH?
WHAT?
WHAT'S THAT NOISE?
ズズズ Zluuurp
SO HOW ABOUT YOU QUIT SKULKING AROUND AND SHOW YOURSELF...
...KAYO?
Zluuurp

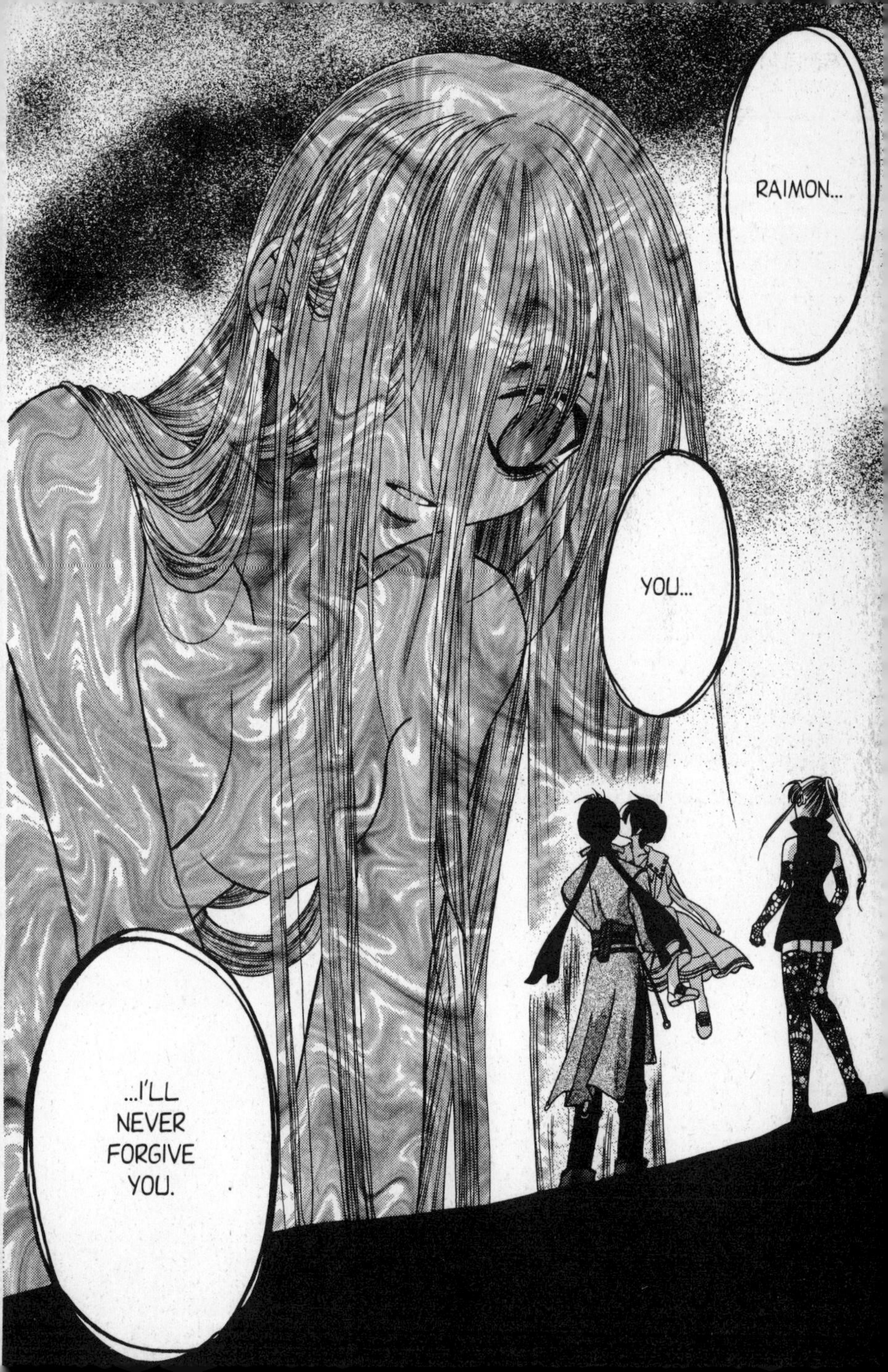
RAIMON...
YOU...
...I'LL NEVER FORGIVE YOU.

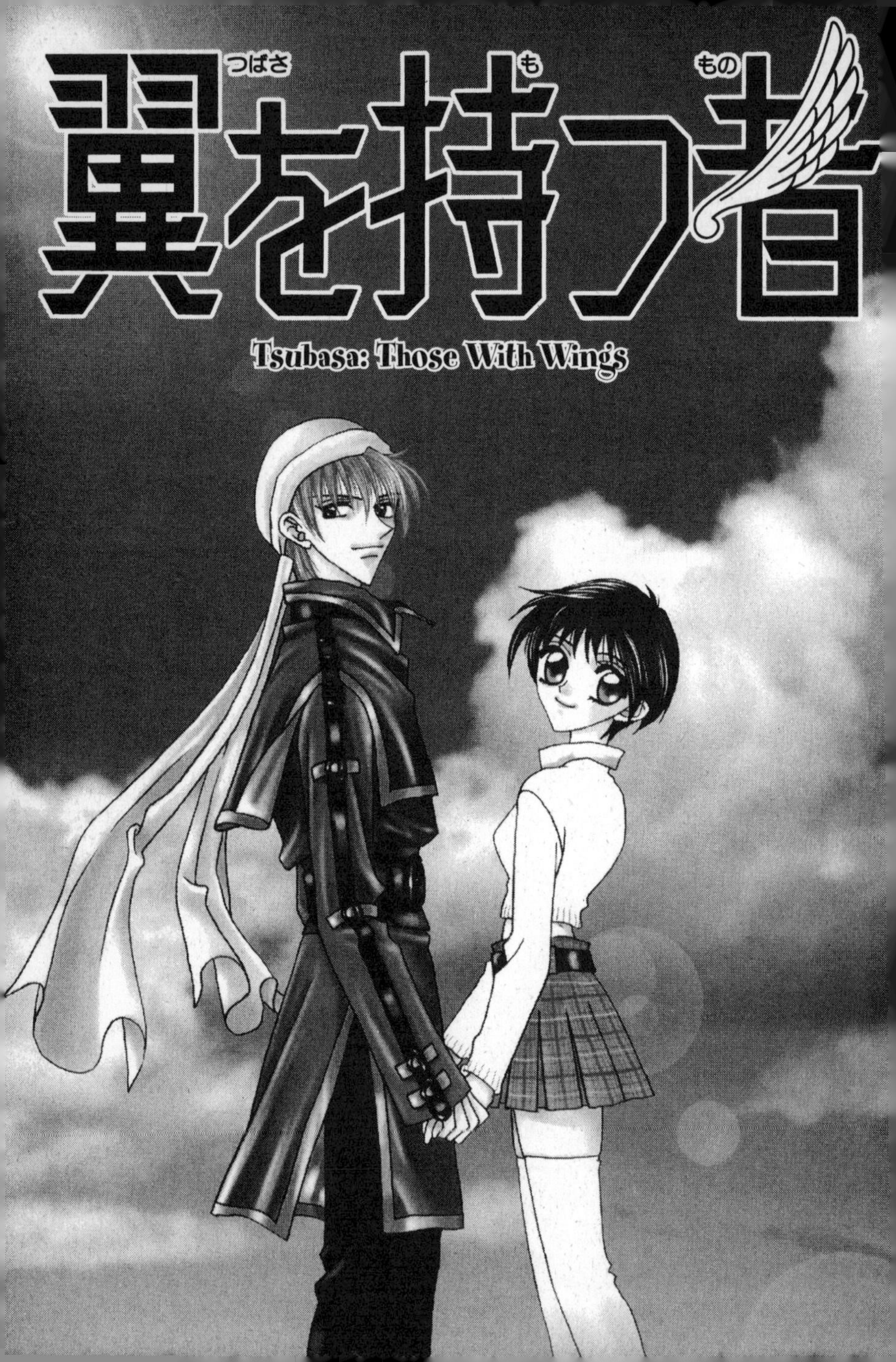
翼を持つ者
つばさ も もの
Tsubasa: Those With Wings

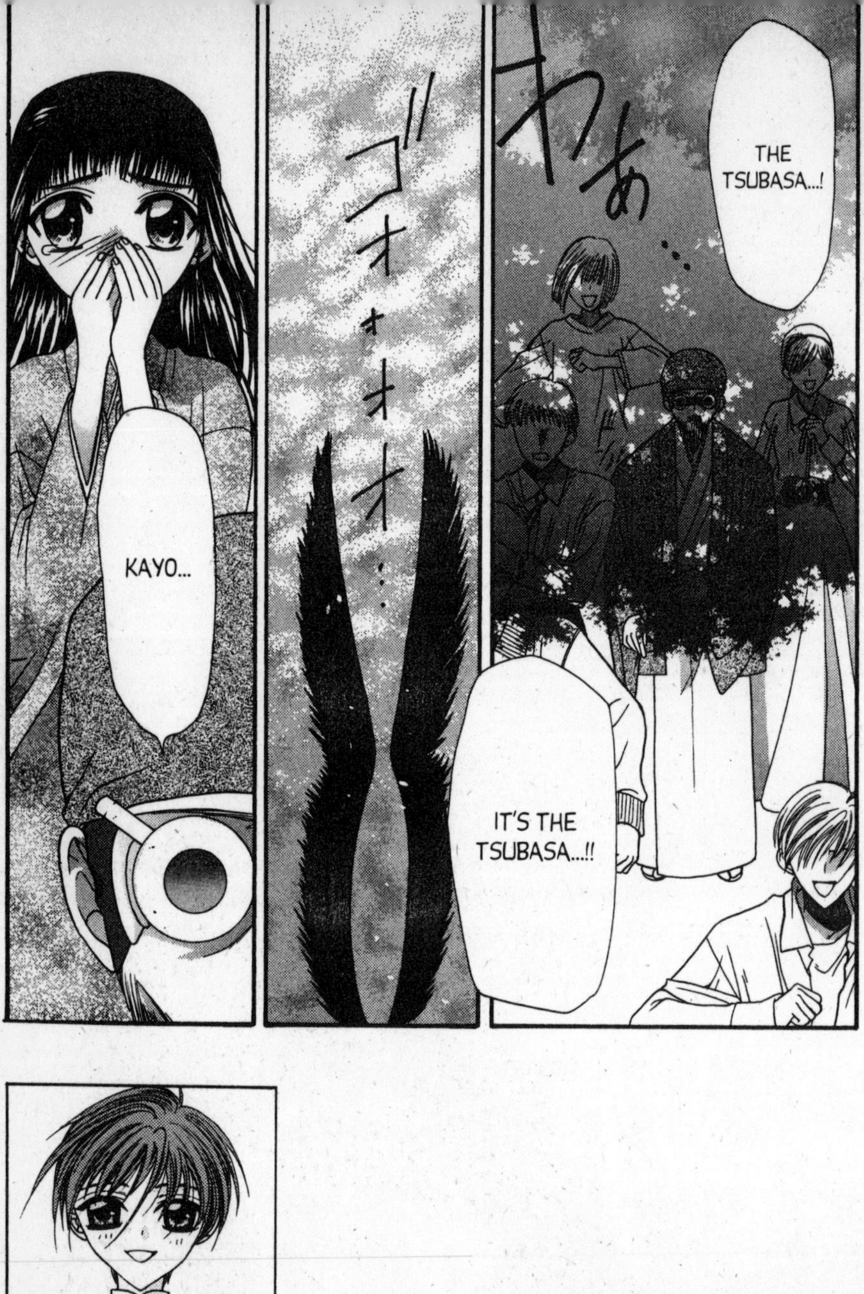
わぁ…
THE TSUBASA...!
IT'S THE TSUBASA...!!
ゴオォオオ…
KAYO...

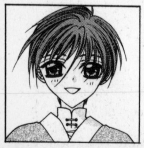

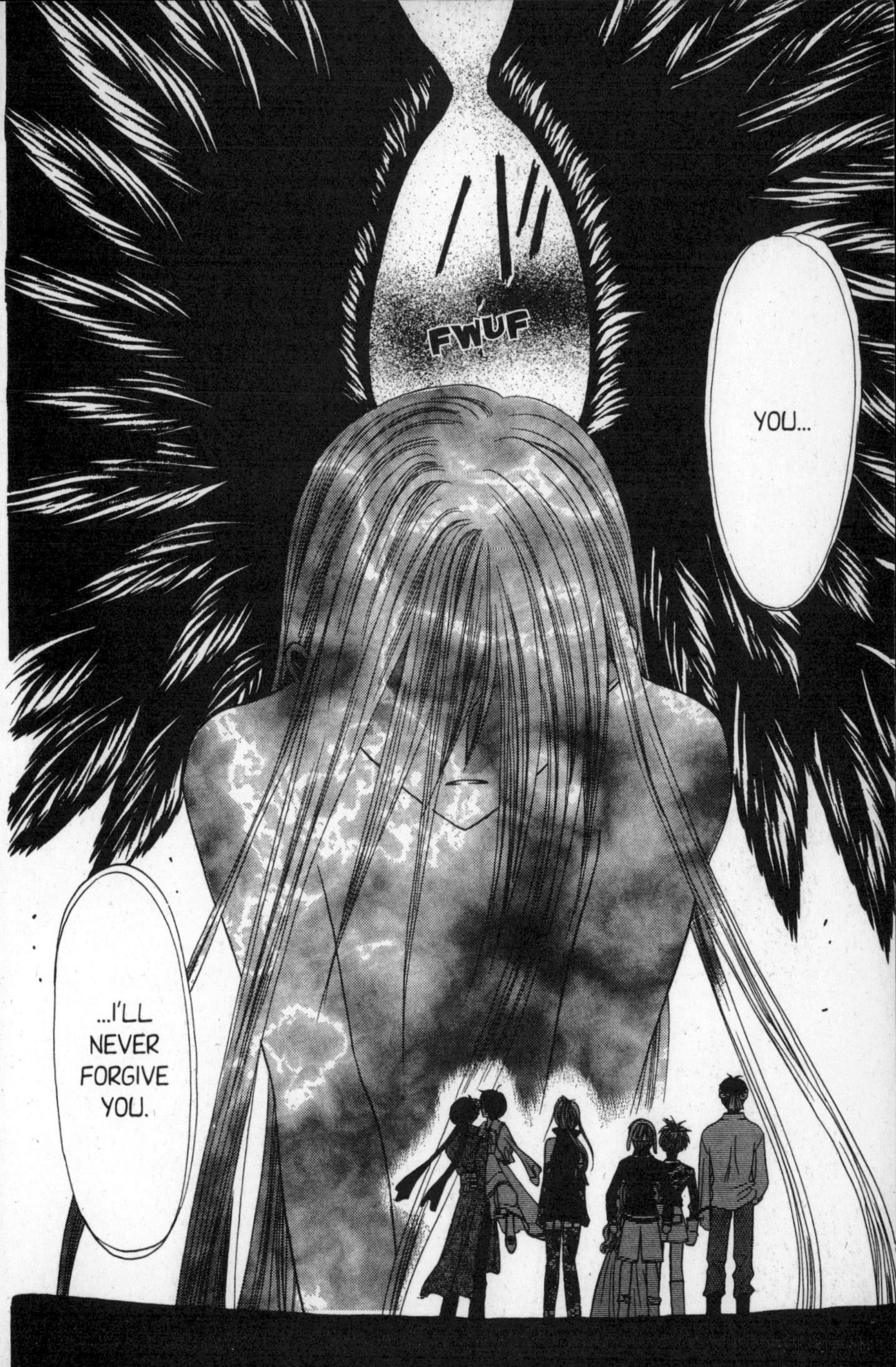
FWUF
YOU...
...I'LL NEVER FORGIVE YOU.

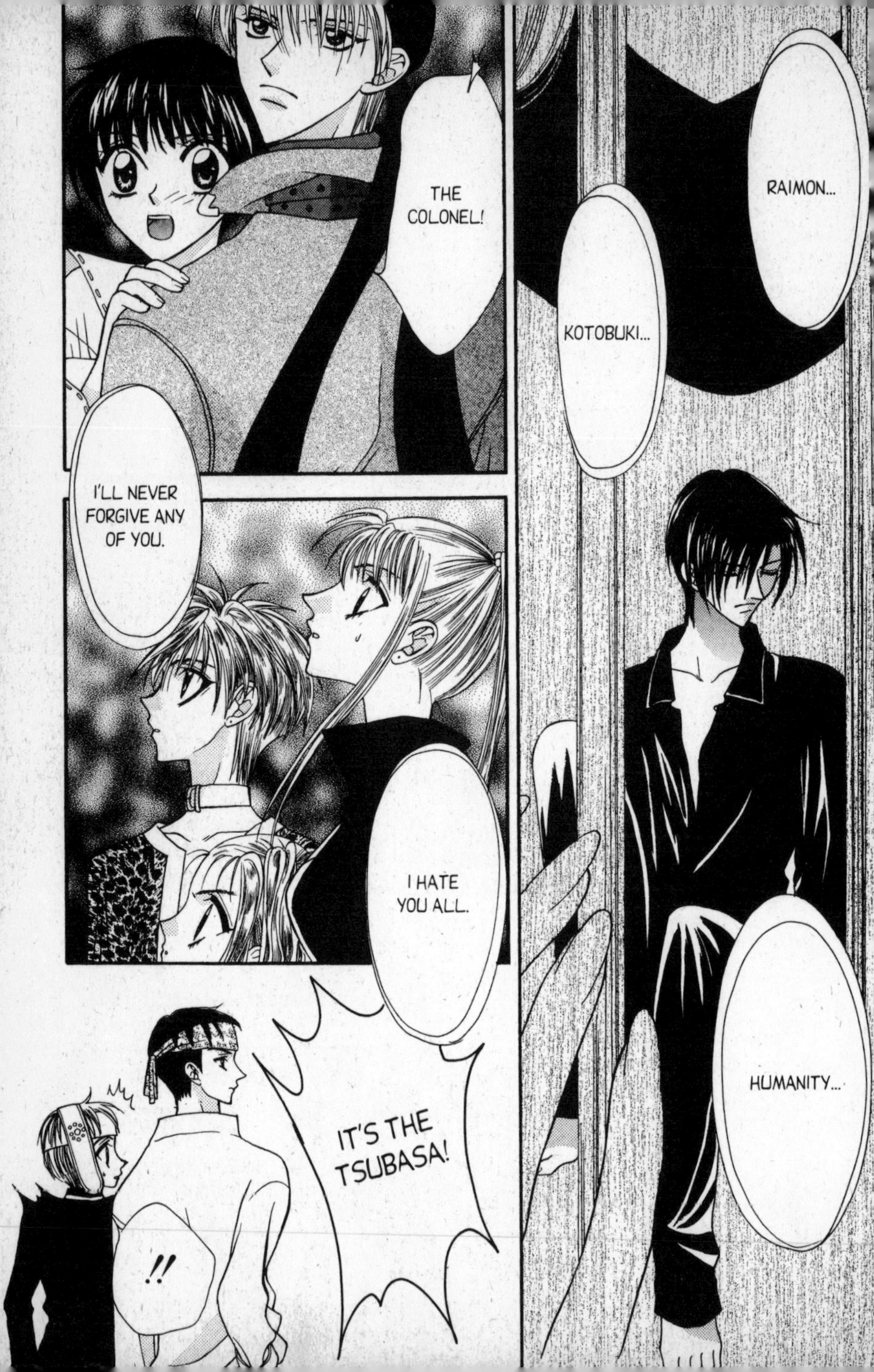
RAIMON...
KOTOBUKI...
HUMANITY...
THE COLONEL!
I'LL NEVER FORGIVE ANY OF YOU.
I HATE YOU ALL.
IT'S THE TSUBASA!
!!

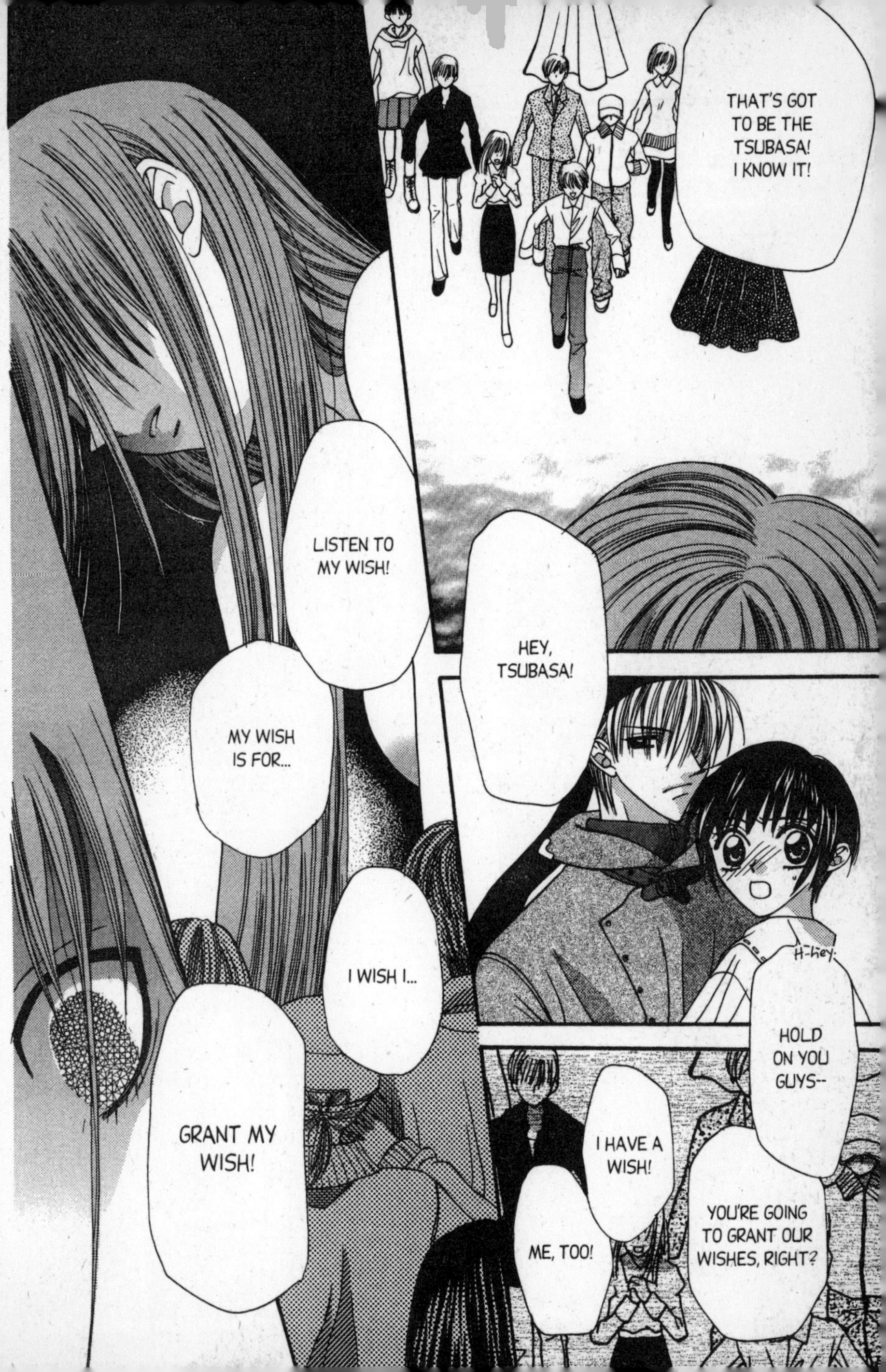
THAT'S GOT TO BE THE TSUBASA! I KNOW IT!
HEY, TSUBASA!
H-hey.
HOLD ON YOU GUYS--
YOU'RE GOING TO GRANT OUR WISHES, RIGHT?
I HAVE A WISH!
ME, TOO!
LISTEN TO MY WISH!
MY WISH IS FOR...
I WISH I...
GRANT MY WISH!

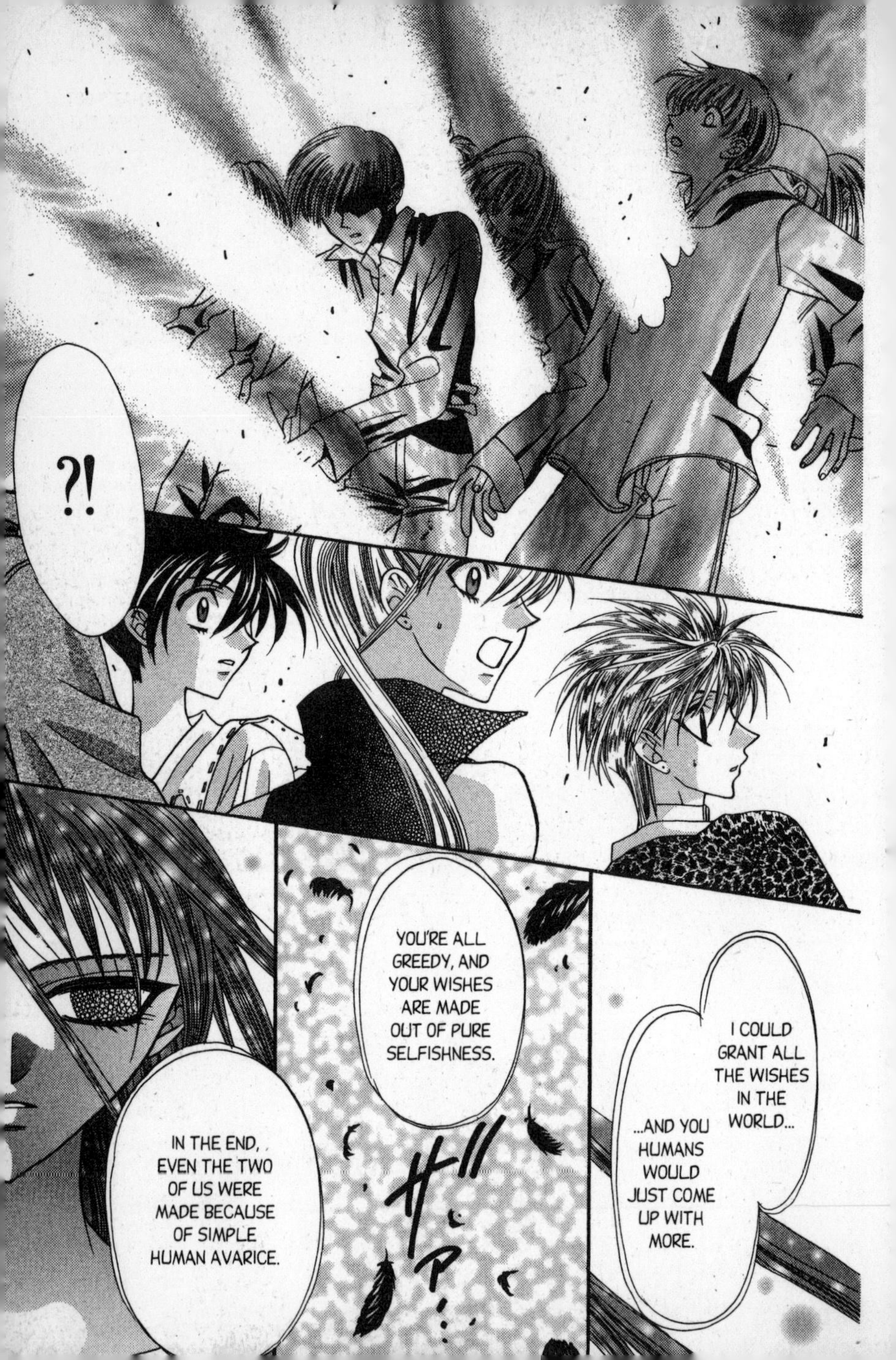
?!
I COULD GRANT ALL THE WISHES IN THE WORLD...
...AND YOU HUMANS WOULD JUST COME UP WITH MORE.
YOU'RE ALL GREEDY, AND YOUR WISHES ARE MADE OUT OF PURE SELFISHNESS.
IN THE END, EVEN THE TWO OF US WERE MADE BECAUSE OF SIMPLE HUMAN AVARICE.

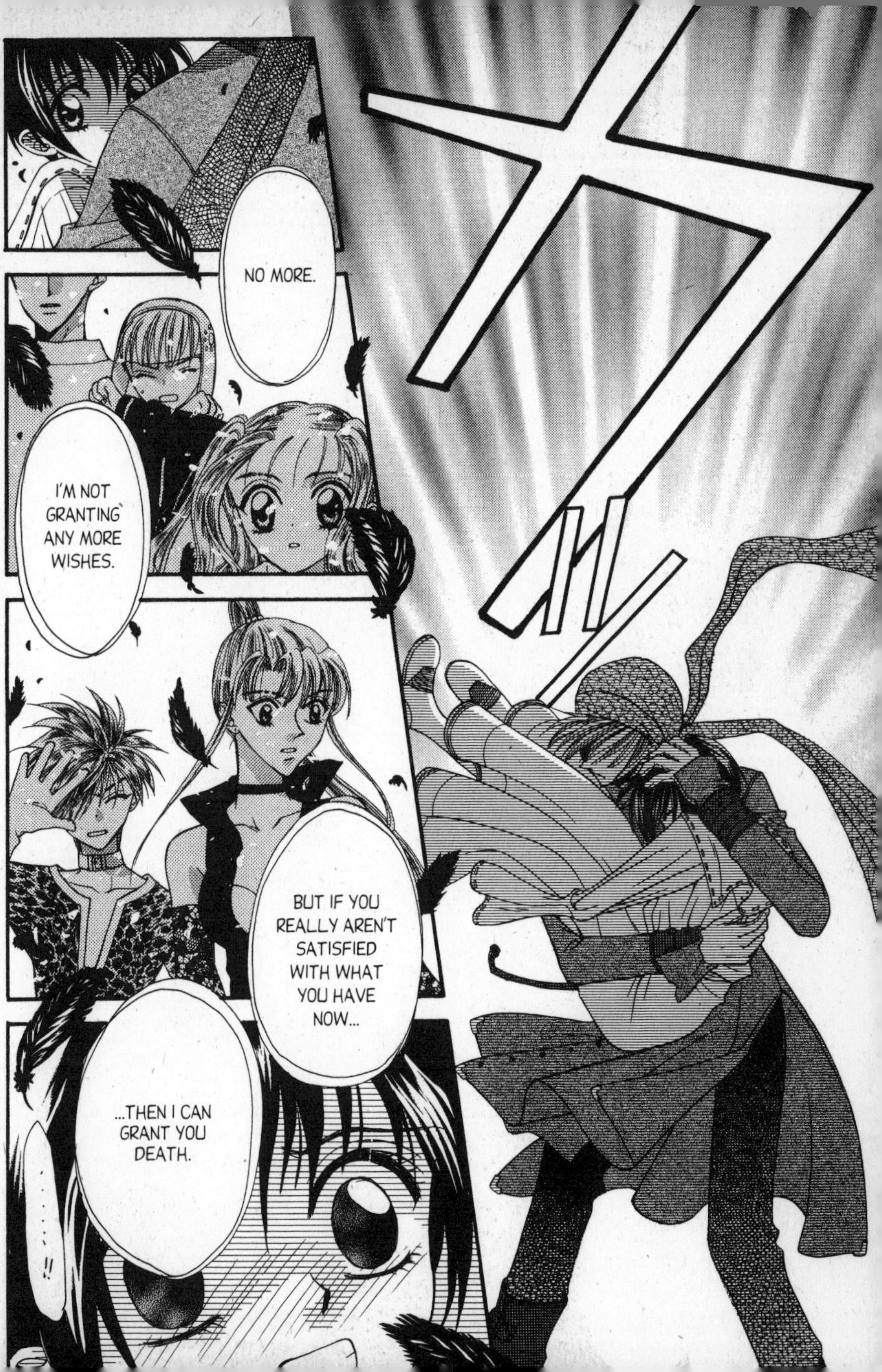
NO MORE.
I'M NOT GRANTING ANY MORE WISHES.
BUT IF YOU REALLY AREN'T SATISFIED WITH WHAT YOU HAVE NOW...
...THEN I CAN GRANT YOU DEATH.
...!!

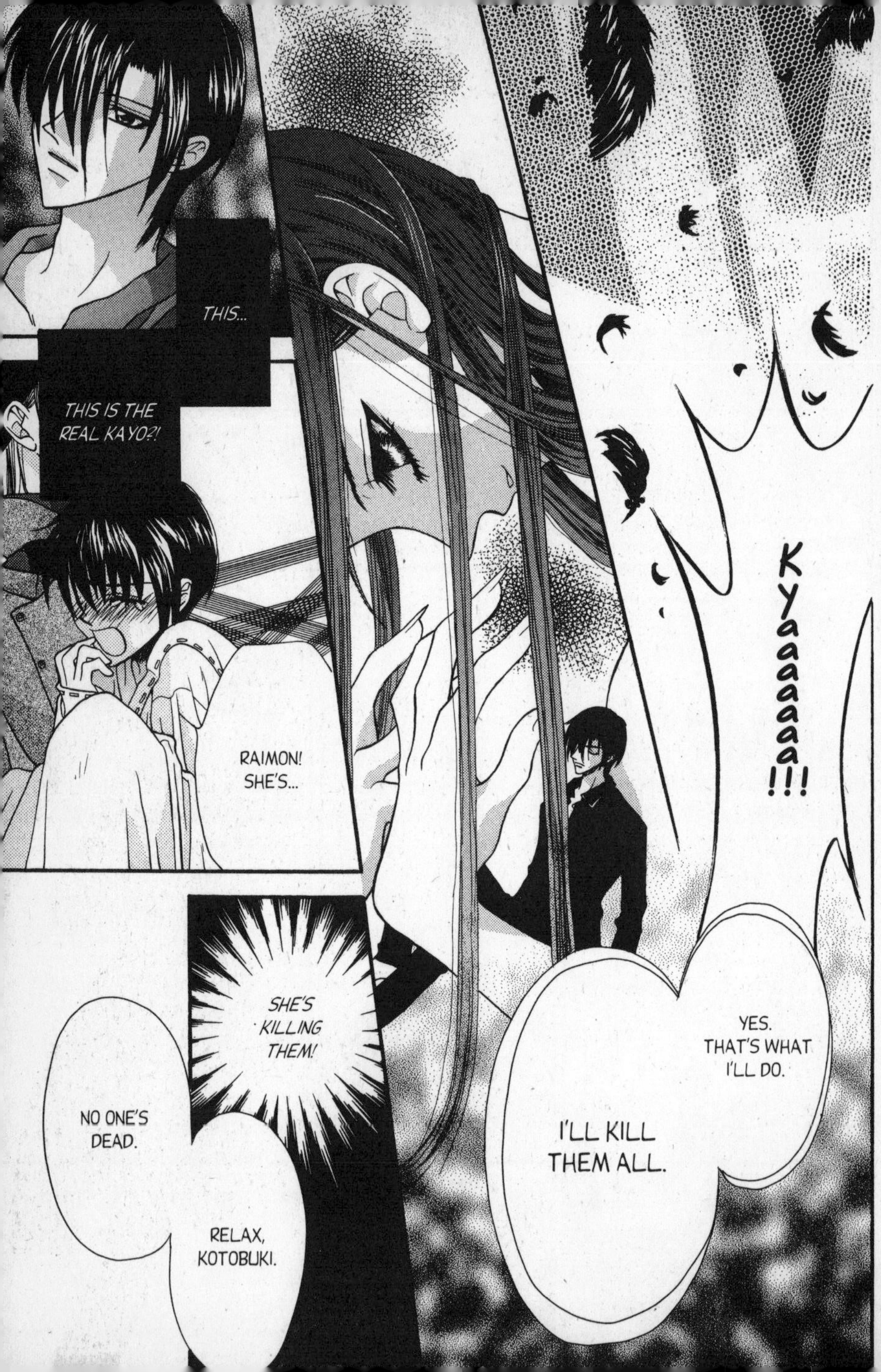
Kyaaaaaa!!!
THIS...
THIS IS THE REAL KAYO?!
RAIMON! SHE'S...
SHE'S KILLING THEM!
NO ONE'S DEAD.
RELAX, KOTOBUKI.
YES. THAT'S WHAT I'LL DO.
I'LL KILL THEM ALL.

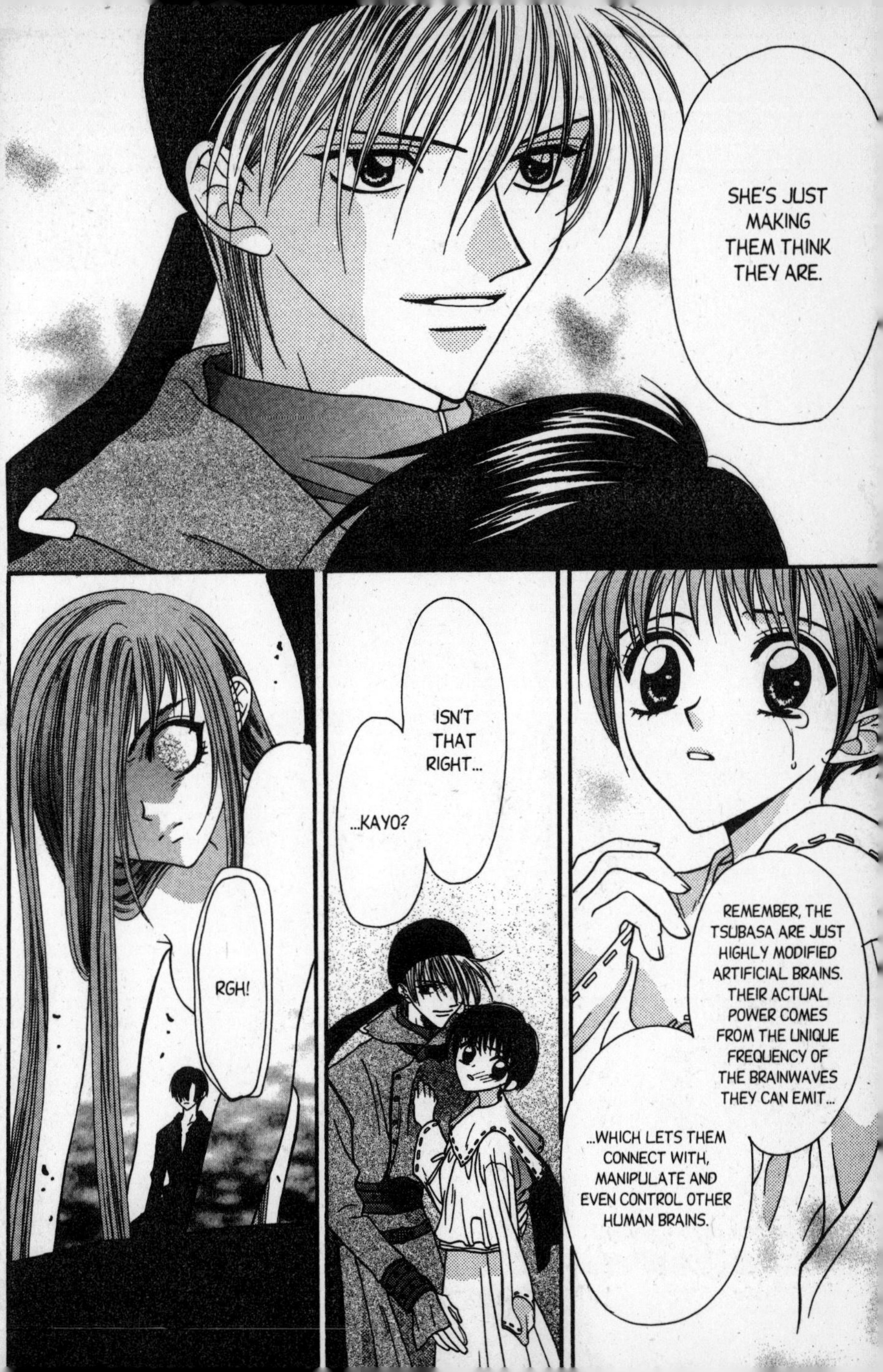
SHE'S JUST MAKING THEM THINK THEY ARE.
REMEMBER, THE TSUBASA ARE JUST HIGHLY MODIFIED ARTIFICIAL BRAINS. THEIR ACTUAL POWER COMES FROM THE UNIQUE FREQUENCY OF THE BRAINWAVES THEY CAN EMIT...
...WHICH LETS THEM CONNECT WITH, MANIPULATE AND EVEN CONTROL OTHER HUMAN BRAINS.
ISN'T THAT RIGHT...
...KAYO?
RGH!

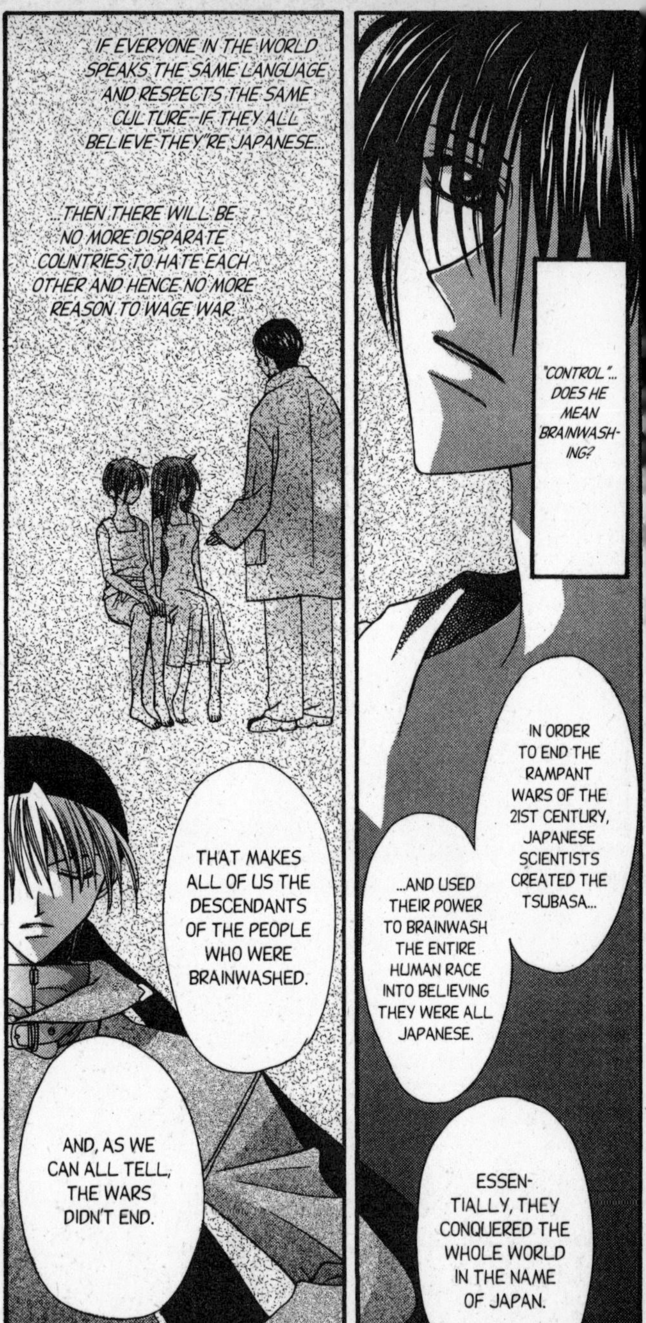
"CONTROL"... DOES HE MEAN BRAINWASH-ING?
IN ORDER TO END THE RAMPANT WARS OF THE 21ST CENTURY, JAPANESE SCIENTISTS CREATED THE TSUBASA...
...AND USED THEIR POWER TO BRAINWASH THE ENTIRE HUMAN RACE INTO BELIEVING THEY WERE ALL JAPANESE.
ESSEN-TIALLY, THEY CONQUERED THE WHOLE WORLD IN THE NAME OF JAPAN.
IF EVERYONE IN THE WORLD SPEAKS THE SAME LANGUAGE AND RESPECTS THE SAME CULTURE--IF THEY ALL BELIEVE THEY'RE JAPANESE...
...THEN THERE WILL BE NO MORE DISPARATE COUNTRIES TO HATE EACH OTHER AND HENCE NO MORE REASON TO WAGE WAR.
THAT MAKES ALL OF US THE DESCENDANTS OF THE PEOPLE WHO WERE BRAINWASHED.
AND, AS WE CAN ALL TELL, THE WARS DIDN'T END.

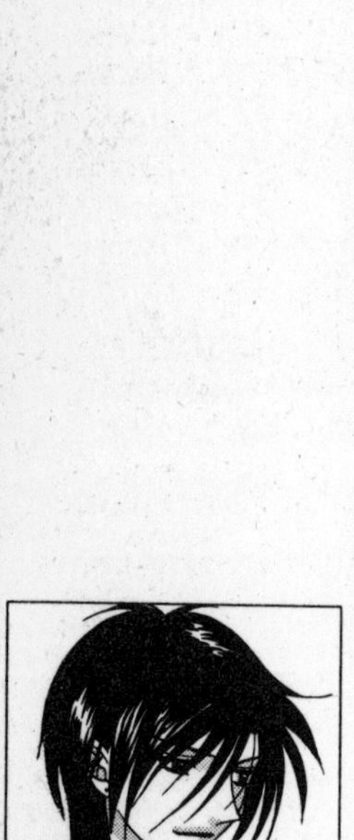

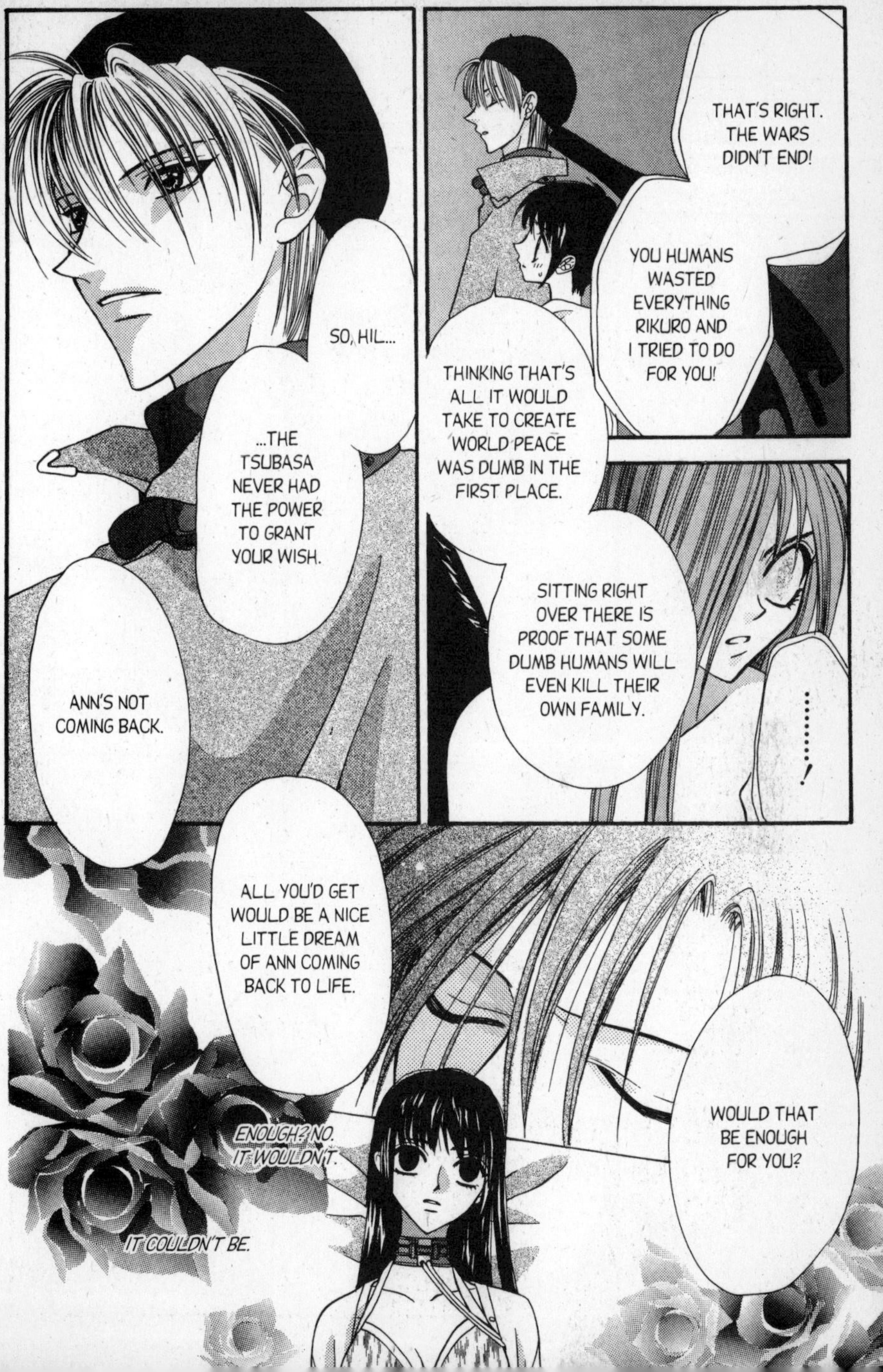
THAT'S RIGHT. THE WARS DIDN'T END!
YOU HUMANS WASTED EVERYTHING RIKURO AND I TRIED TO DO FOR YOU!
THINKING THAT'S ALL IT WOULD TAKE TO CREATE WORLD PEACE WAS DUMB IN THE FIRST PLACE.
SITTING RIGHT OVER THERE IS PROOF THAT SOME DUMB HUMANS WILL EVEN KILL THEIR OWN FAMILY.
......!
SO, HIL...
...THE TSUBASA NEVER HAD THE POWER TO GRANT YOUR WISH.
ANN'S NOT COMING BACK.
ALL YOU'D GET WOULD BE A NICE LITTLE DREAM OF ANN COMING BACK TO LIFE.
WOULD THAT BE ENOUGH FOR YOU?
ENOUGH? NO. IT WOULDN'T.
IT COULDN'T BE.

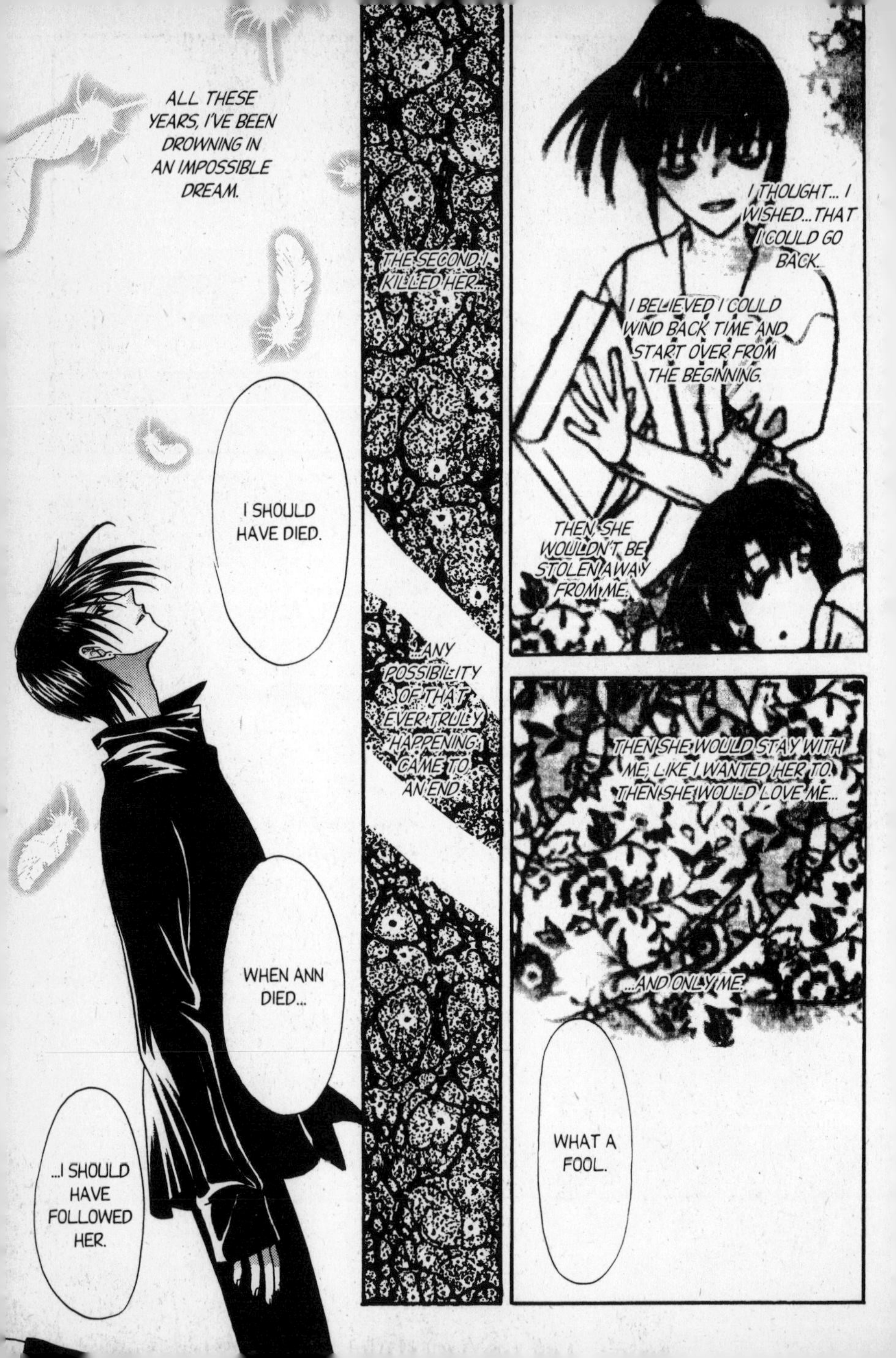
I THOUGHT... I WISHED...THAT I COULD GO BACK.
I BELIEVED I COULD WIND BACK TIME AND START OVER FROM THE BEGINNING.
THEN, SHE WOULDN'T BE STOLEN AWAY FROM ME.
THEN SHE WOULD STAY WITH ME, LIKE I WANTED HER TO. THEN SHE WOULD LOVE ME...
...AND ONLY ME.
WHAT A FOOL.
THE SECOND I KILLED HER...
...ANY POSSIBILITY OF THAT EVER TRULY HAPPENING CAME TO AN END.
ALL THESE YEARS, I'VE BEEN DROWNING IN AN IMPOSSIBLE DREAM.
I SHOULD HAVE DIED.
WHEN ANN DIED...
...I SHOULD HAVE FOLLOWED HER.

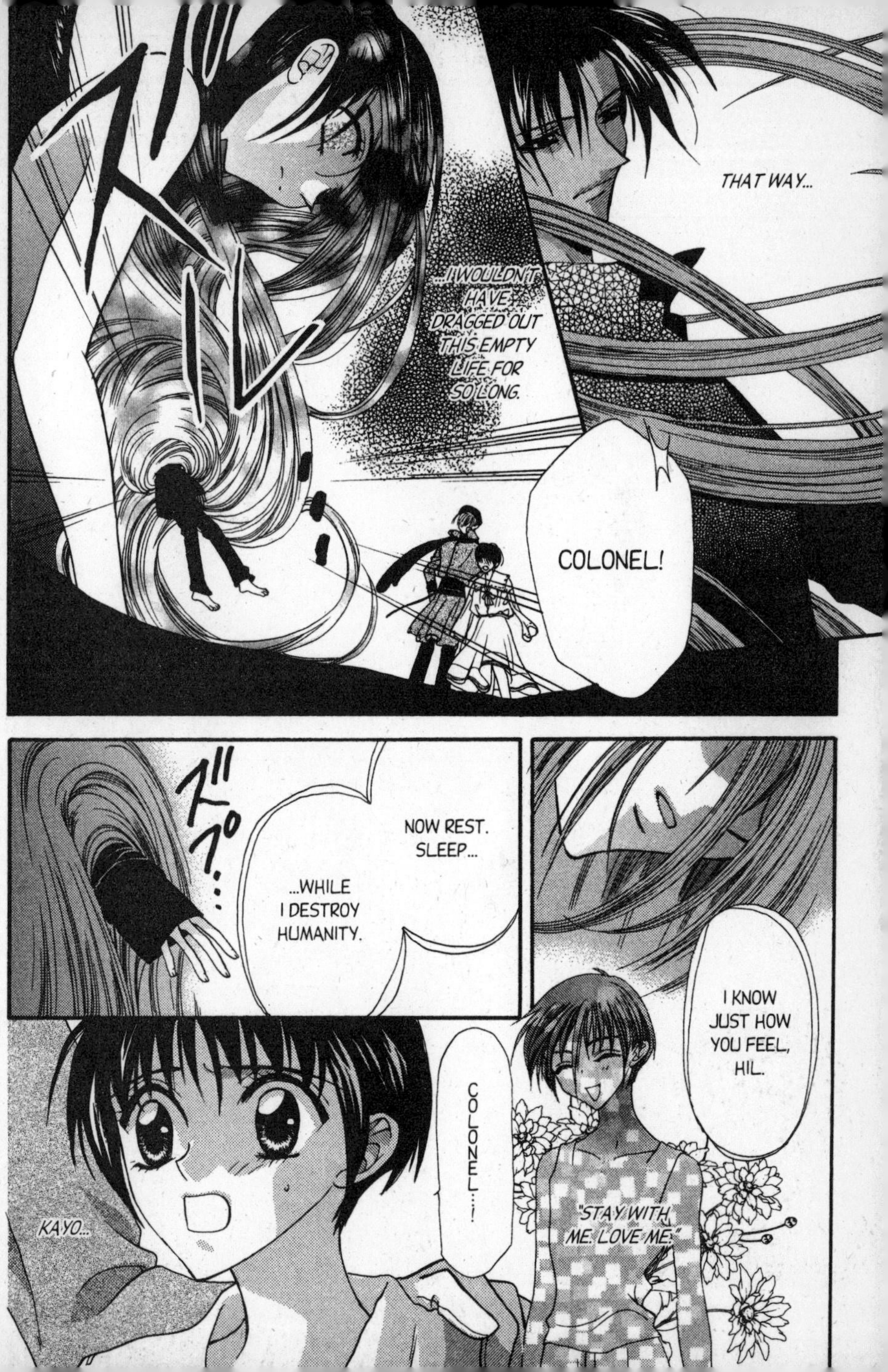

THAT WAY...
...I WOULDN'T HAVE DRAGGED OUT THIS EMPTY LIFE FOR SO LONG.
COLONEL!
NOW REST. SLEEP...
...WHILE I DESTROY HUMANITY.
I KNOW JUST HOW YOU FEEL, HIL.
"STAY WITH ME. LOVE ME."
COLONEL...!
KAYO...

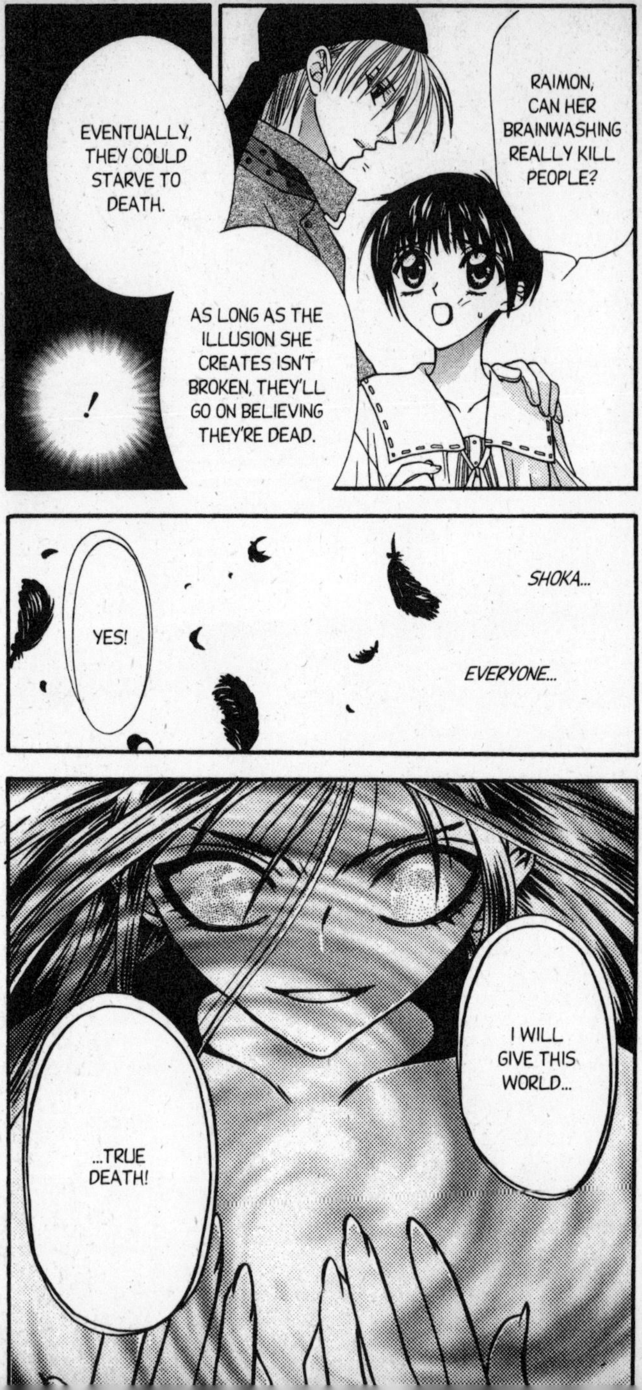
RAIMON, CAN HER BRAINWASHING REALLY KILL PEOPLE?
EVENTUALLY, THEY COULD STARVE TO DEATH.
AS LONG AS THE ILLUSION SHE CREATES ISN'T BROKEN, THEY'LL GO ON BELIEVING THEY'RE DEAD.
!
SHOKA...
EVERYONE...
YES!
I WILL GIVE THIS WORLD...
...TRUE DEATH!

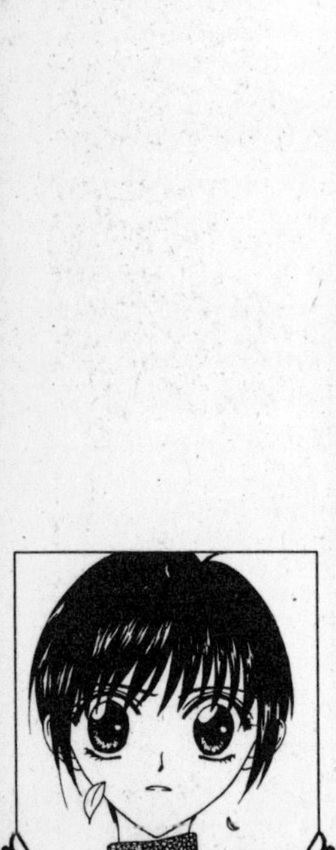

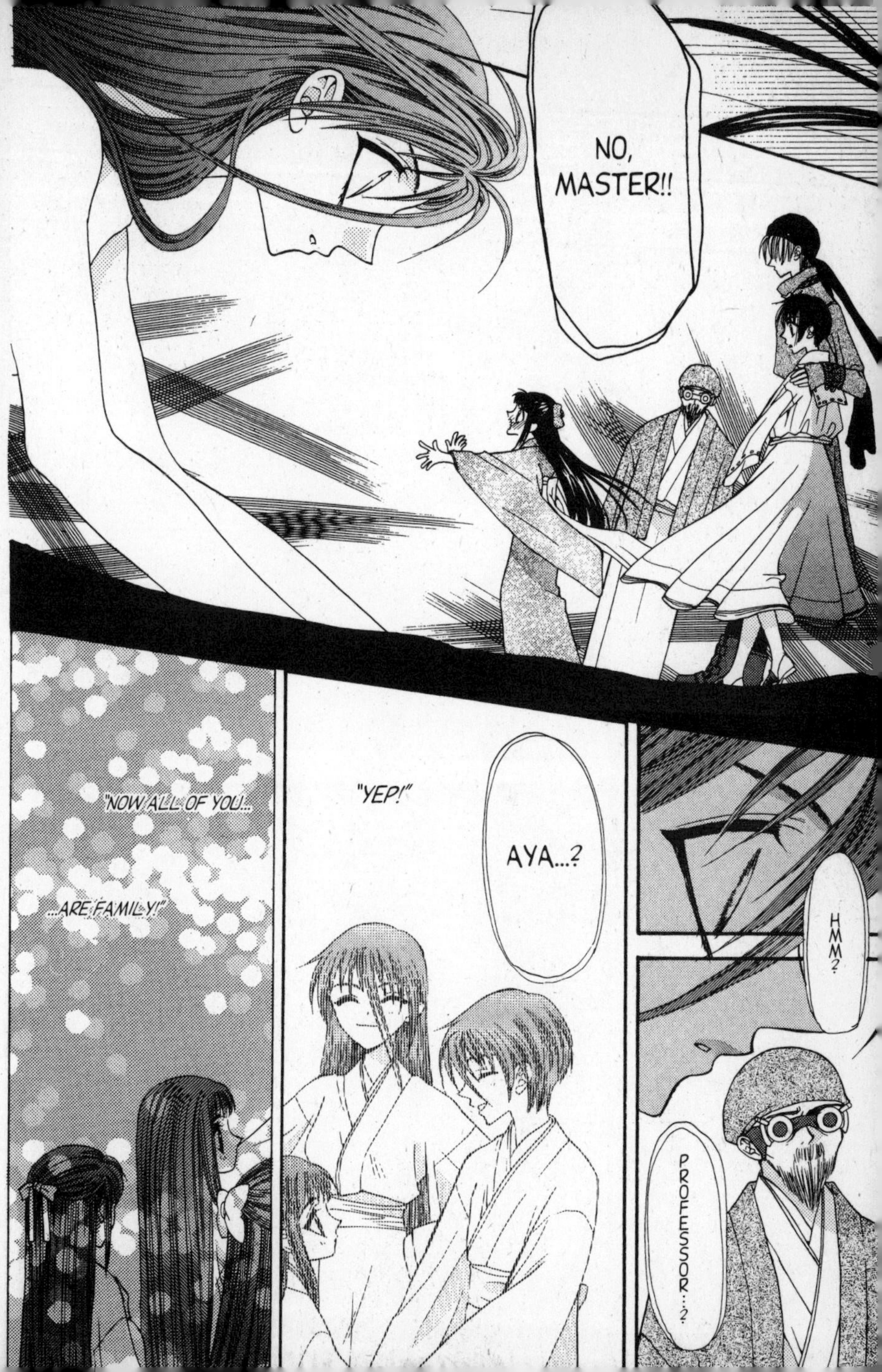
NO, MASTER!!
HMM?
PROFESSOR...?
AYA...?
"YEP!"
"NOW ALL OF YOU...
...ARE FAMILY!"

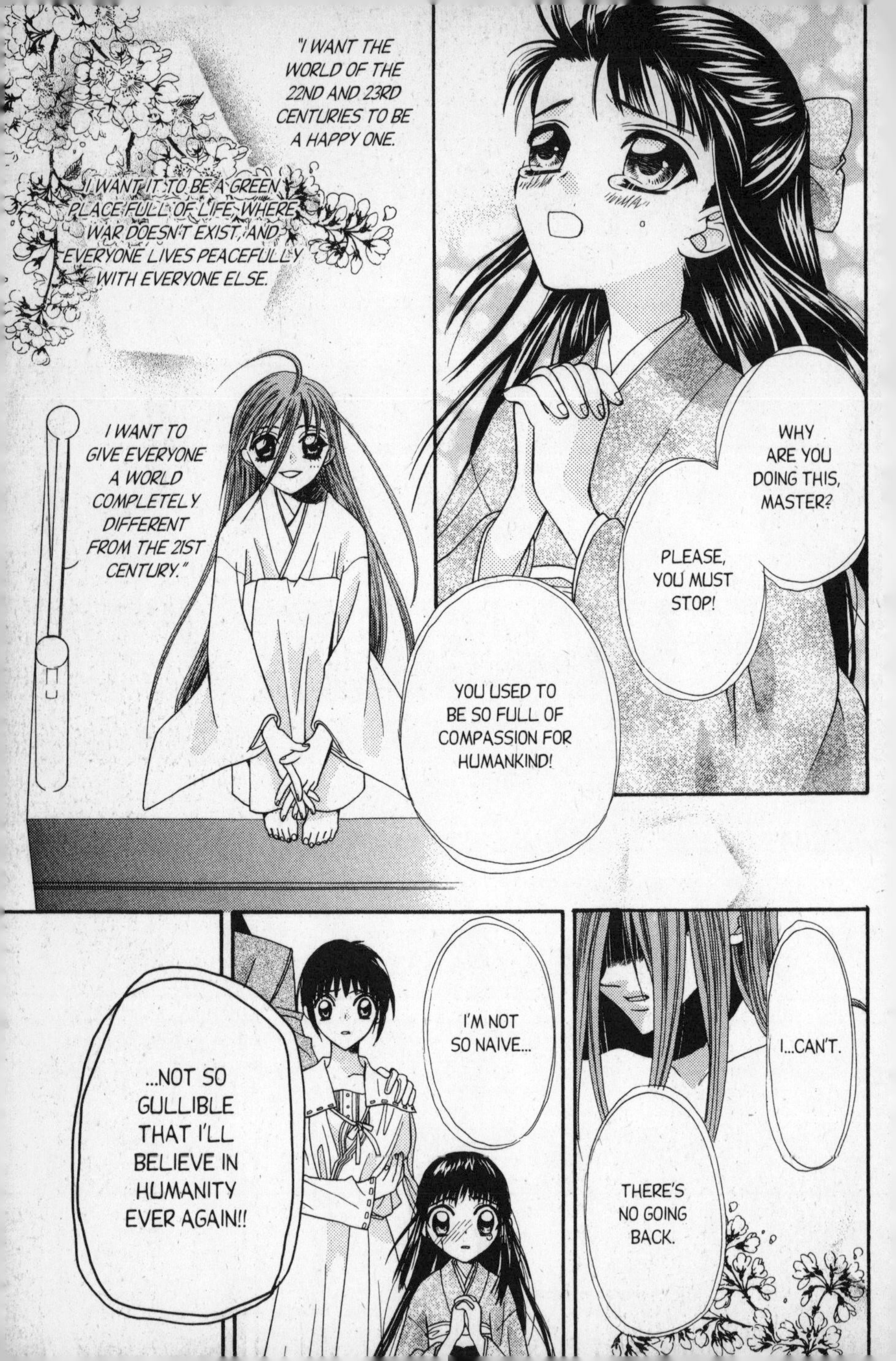
WHY ARE YOU DOING THIS, MASTER?
PLEASE, YOU MUST STOP!
YOU USED TO BE SO FULL OF COMPASSION FOR HUMANKIND!
"I WANT THE WORLD OF THE 22ND AND 23RD CENTURIES TO BE A HAPPY ONE.
I WANT IT TO BE A GREEN PLACE FULL OF LIFE, WHERE WAR DOESN'T EXIST, AND EVERYONE LIVES PEACEFULLY WITH EVERYONE ELSE.
I WANT TO GIVE EVERYONE A WORLD COMPLETELY DIFFERENT FROM THE 21ST CENTURY."
I...CAN'T.
THERE'S NO GOING BACK.
I'M NOT SO NAIVE...
...NOT SO GULLIBLE THAT I'LL BELIEVE IN HUMANITY EVER AGAIN!!

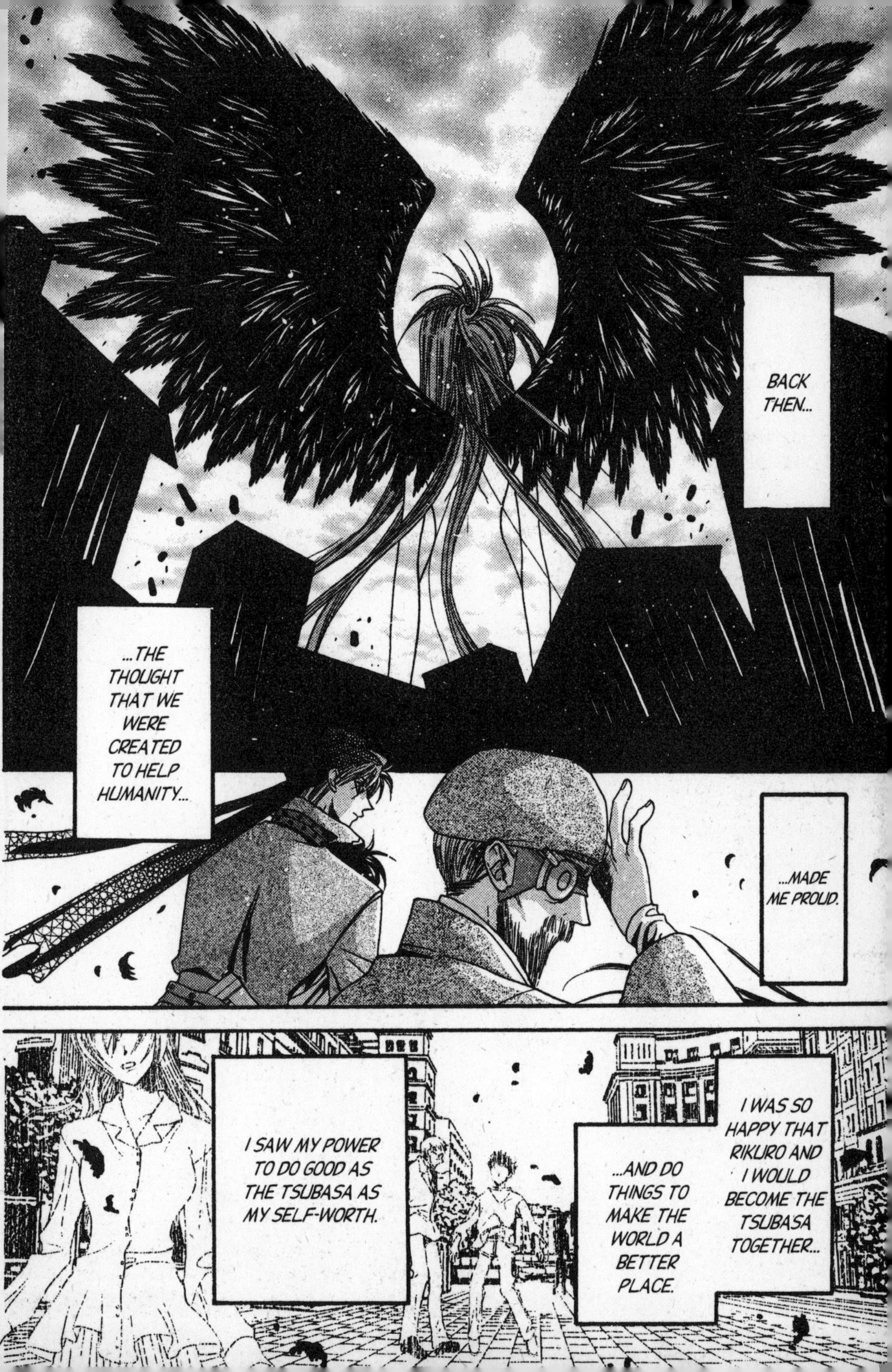
BACK THEN...
...THE THOUGHT THAT WE WERE CREATED TO HELP HUMANITY...
...MADE ME PROUD.
I WAS SO HAPPY THAT RIKURO AND I WOULD BECOME THE TSUBASA TOGETHER...
...AND DO THINGS TO MAKE THE WORLD A BETTER PLACE.
I SAW MY POWER TO DO GOOD AS THE TSUBASA AS MY SELF-WORTH.

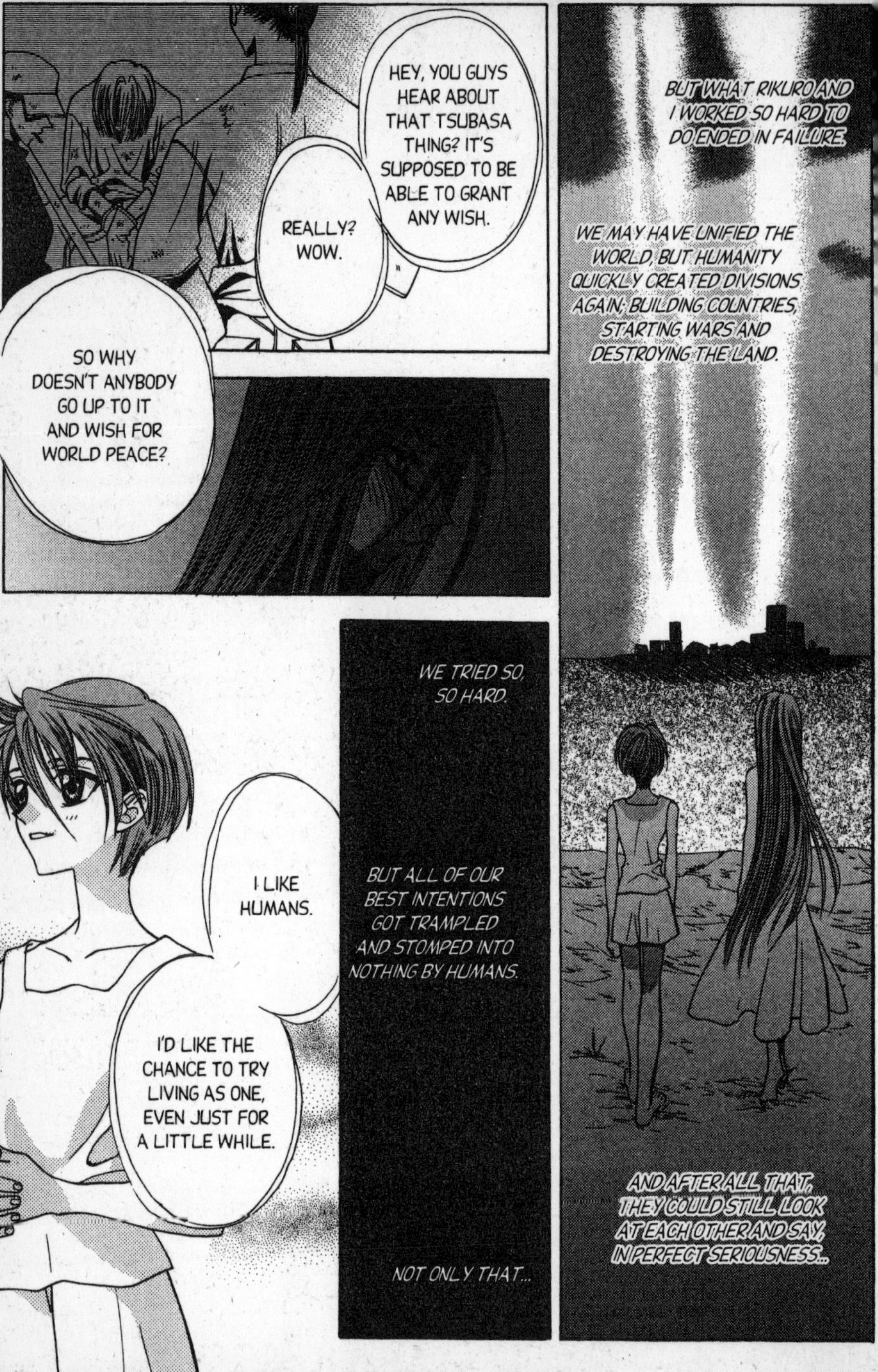
BUT WHAT RIKURO AND I WORKED SO HARD TO DO ENDED IN FAILURE.
WE MAY HAVE UNIFIED THE WORLD, BUT HUMANITY QUICKLY CREATED DIVISIONS AGAIN; BUILDING COUNTRIES, STARTING WARS AND DESTROYING THE LAND.
AND AFTER ALL THAT, THEY COULD STILL LOOK AT EACH OTHER AND SAY, IN PERFECT SERIOUSNESS...
HEY, YOU GUYS HEAR ABOUT THAT TSUBASA THING? IT'S SUPPOSED TO BE ABLE TO GRANT ANY WISH.
REALLY? WOW.
SO WHY DOESN'T ANYBODY GO UP TO IT AND WISH FOR WORLD PEACE?
WE TRIED SO, SO HARD.
BUT ALL OF OUR BEST INTENTIONS GOT TRAMPLED AND STOMPED INTO NOTHING BY HUMANS.
NOT ONLY THAT...
I LIKE HUMANS.
I'D LIKE THE CHANCE TO TRY LIVING AS ONE, EVEN JUST FOR A LITTLE WHILE.

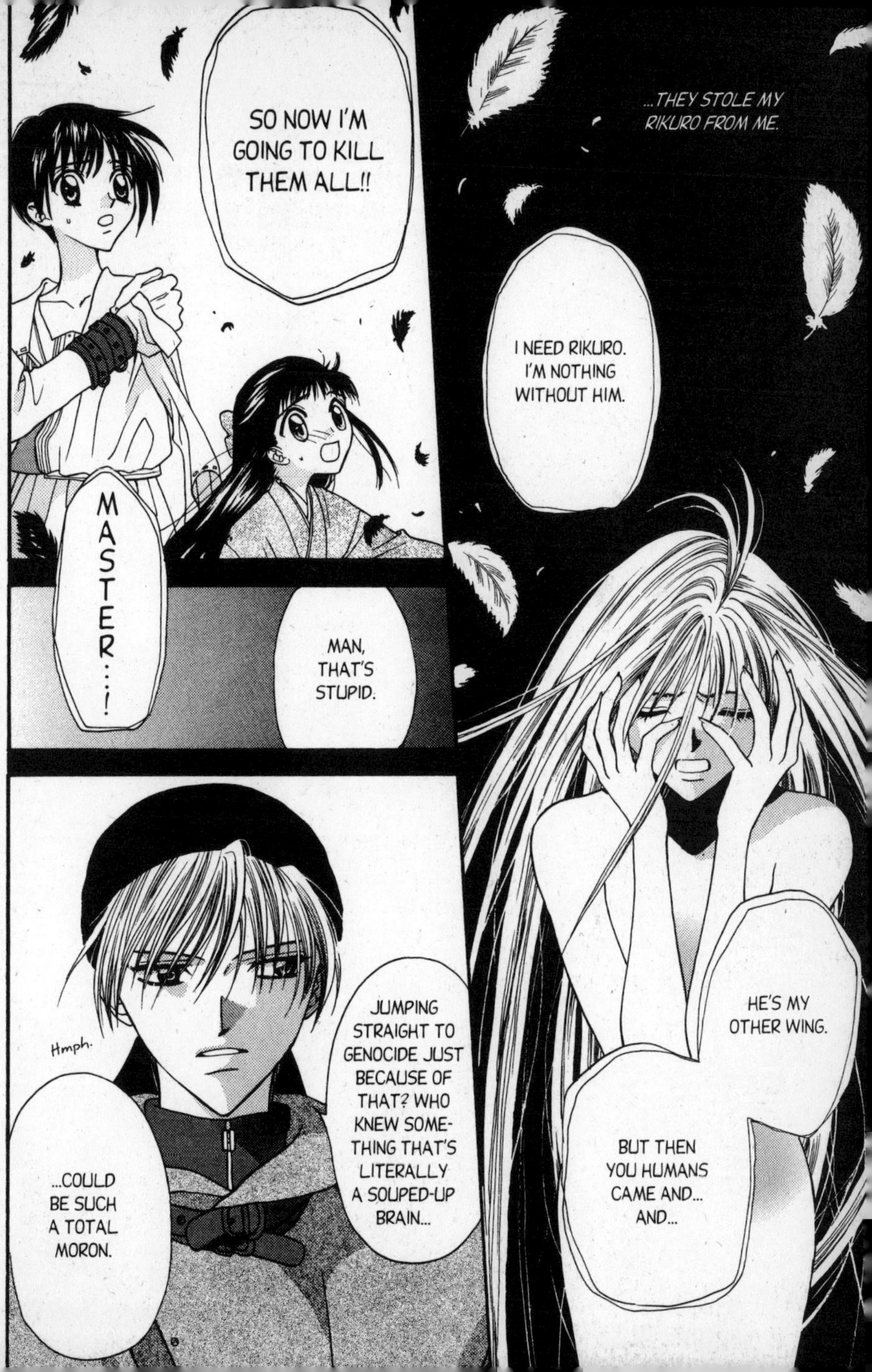
...THEY STOLE MY RIKURO FROM ME.
I NEED RIKURO. I'M NOTHING WITHOUT HIM.
HE'S MY OTHER WING.
BUT THEN YOU HUMANS CAME AND... AND...
SO NOW I'M GOING TO KILL THEM ALL!!
MASTER...!
MAN, THAT'S STUPID.
JUMPING STRAIGHT TO GENOCIDE JUST BECAUSE OF THAT? WHO KNEW SOME-THING THAT'S LITERALLY A SOUPED-UP BRAIN...
Hmph.
...COULD BE SUCH A TOTAL MORON.

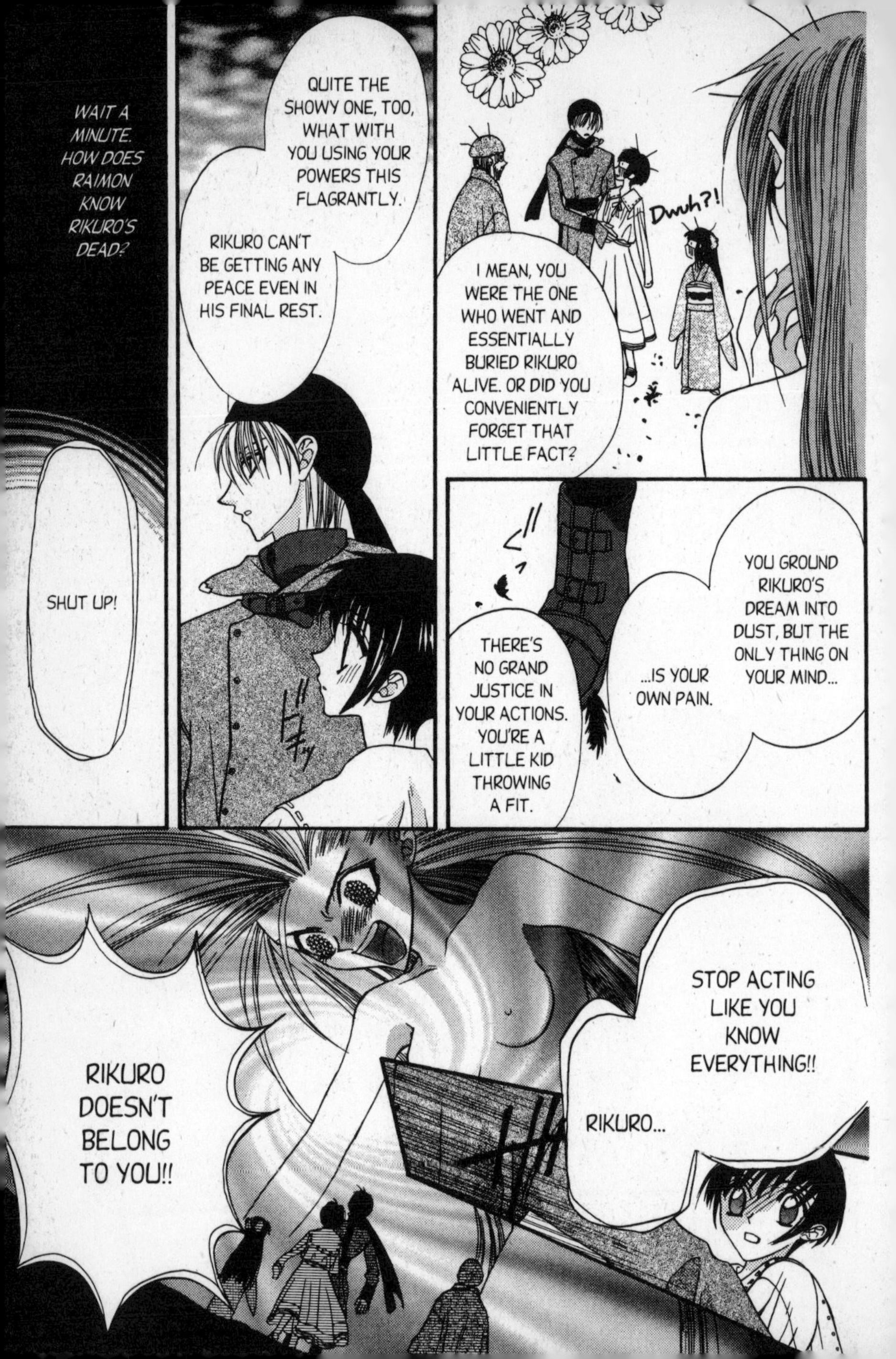
Dwuh?!
I MEAN, YOU WERE THE ONE WHO WENT AND ESSENTIALLY BURIED RIKURO ALIVE. OR DID YOU CONVENIENTLY FORGET THAT LITTLE FACT?
YOU GROUND RIKURO'S DREAM INTO DUST, BUT THE ONLY THING ON YOUR MIND...
...IS YOUR OWN PAIN.
THERE'S NO GRAND JUSTICE IN YOUR ACTIONS. YOU'RE A LITTLE KID THROWING A FIT.
QUITE THE SHOWY ONE, TOO, WHAT WITH YOU USING YOUR POWERS THIS FLAGRANTLY.
RIKURO CAN'T BE GETTING ANY PEACE EVEN IN HIS FINAL REST.
WAIT A MINUTE. HOW DOES RAIMON KNOW RIKURO'S DEAD?
SHUT UP!
STOP ACTING LIKE YOU KNOW EVERYTHING!!
RIKURO...
RIKURO DOESN'T BELONG TO YOU!!

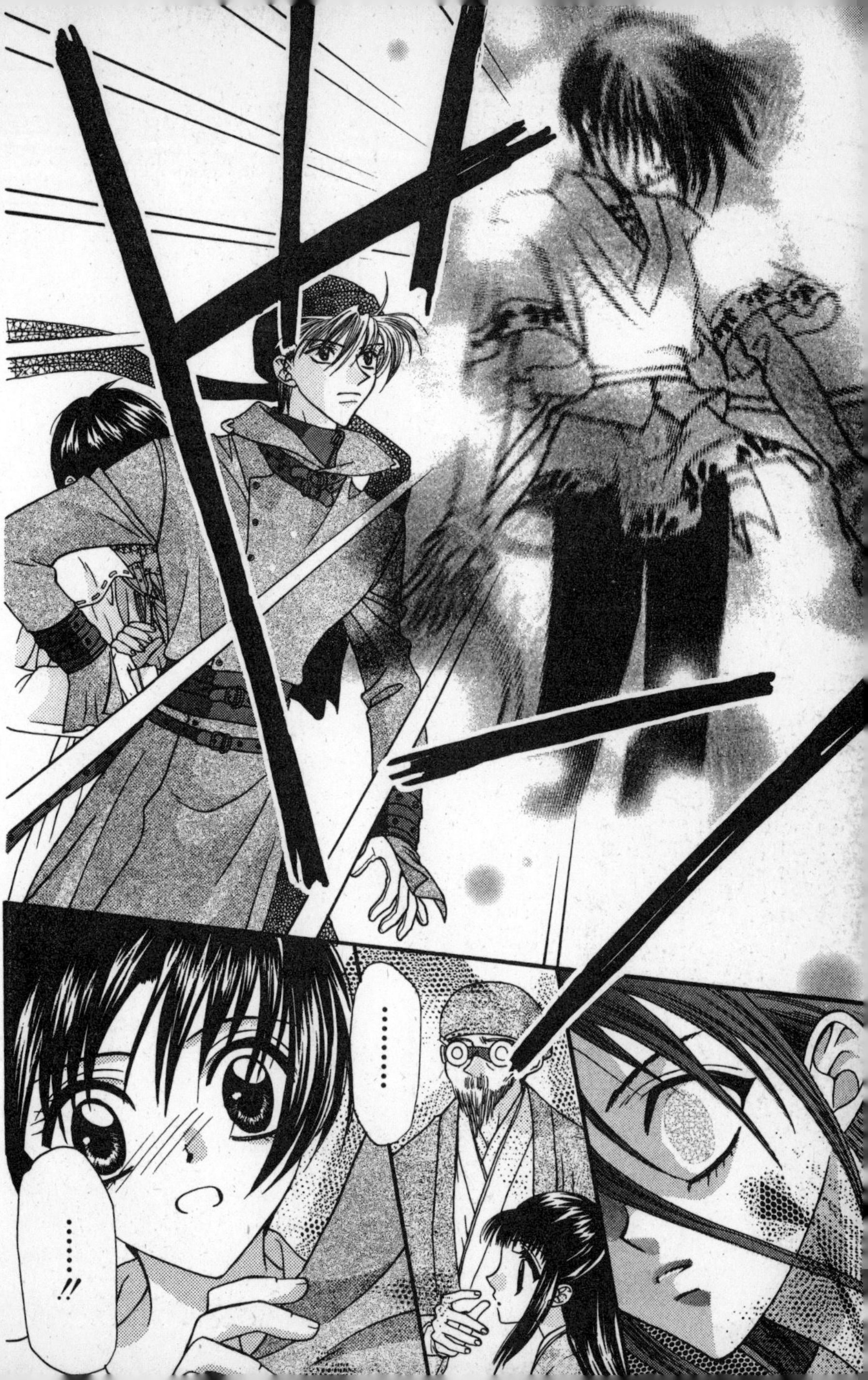
......
......!!

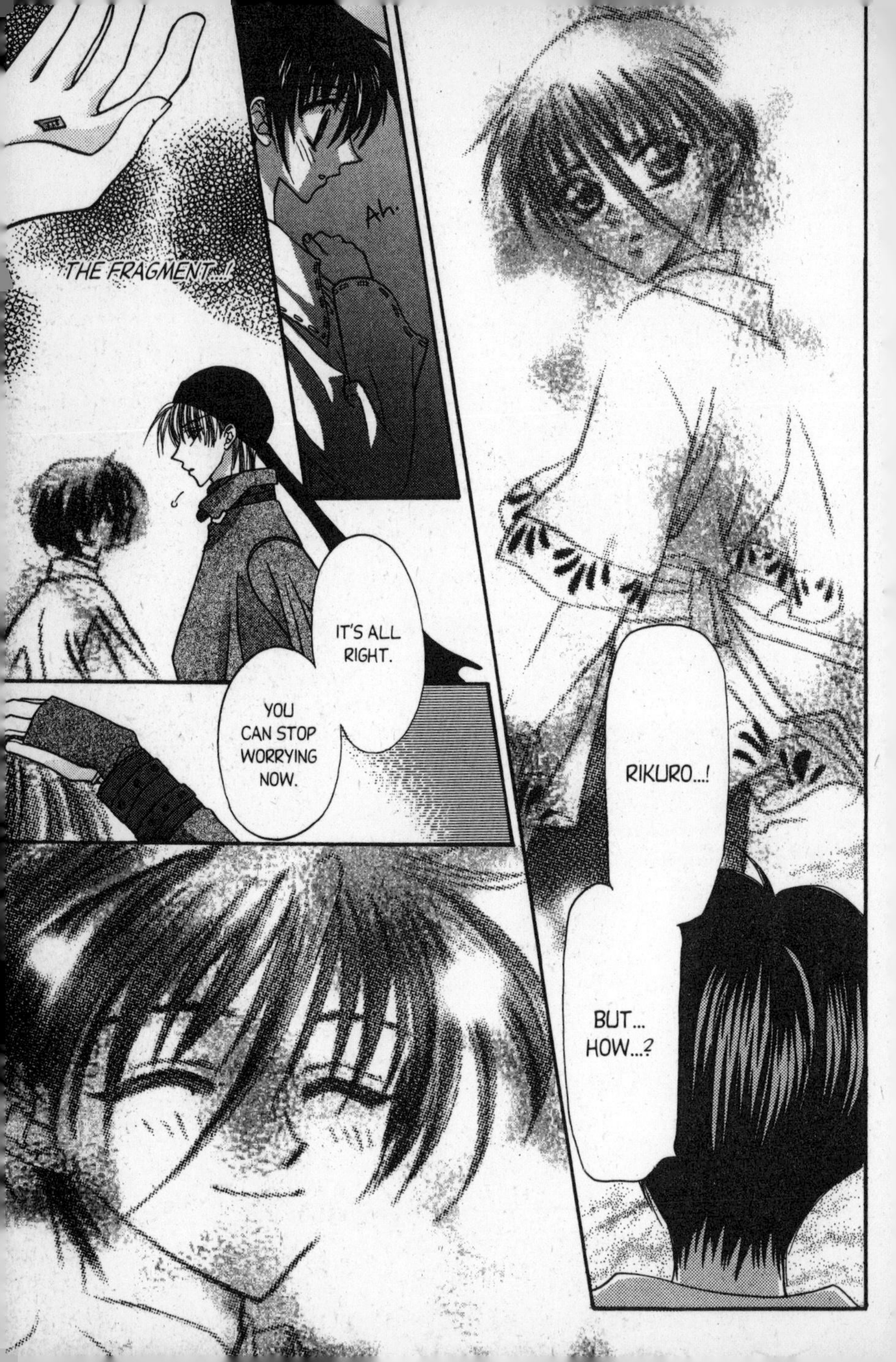
RIKURO...!
BUT... HOW...?
Ah.
THE FRAGMENT...!
IT'S ALL RIGHT.
YOU CAN STOP WORRYING NOW.

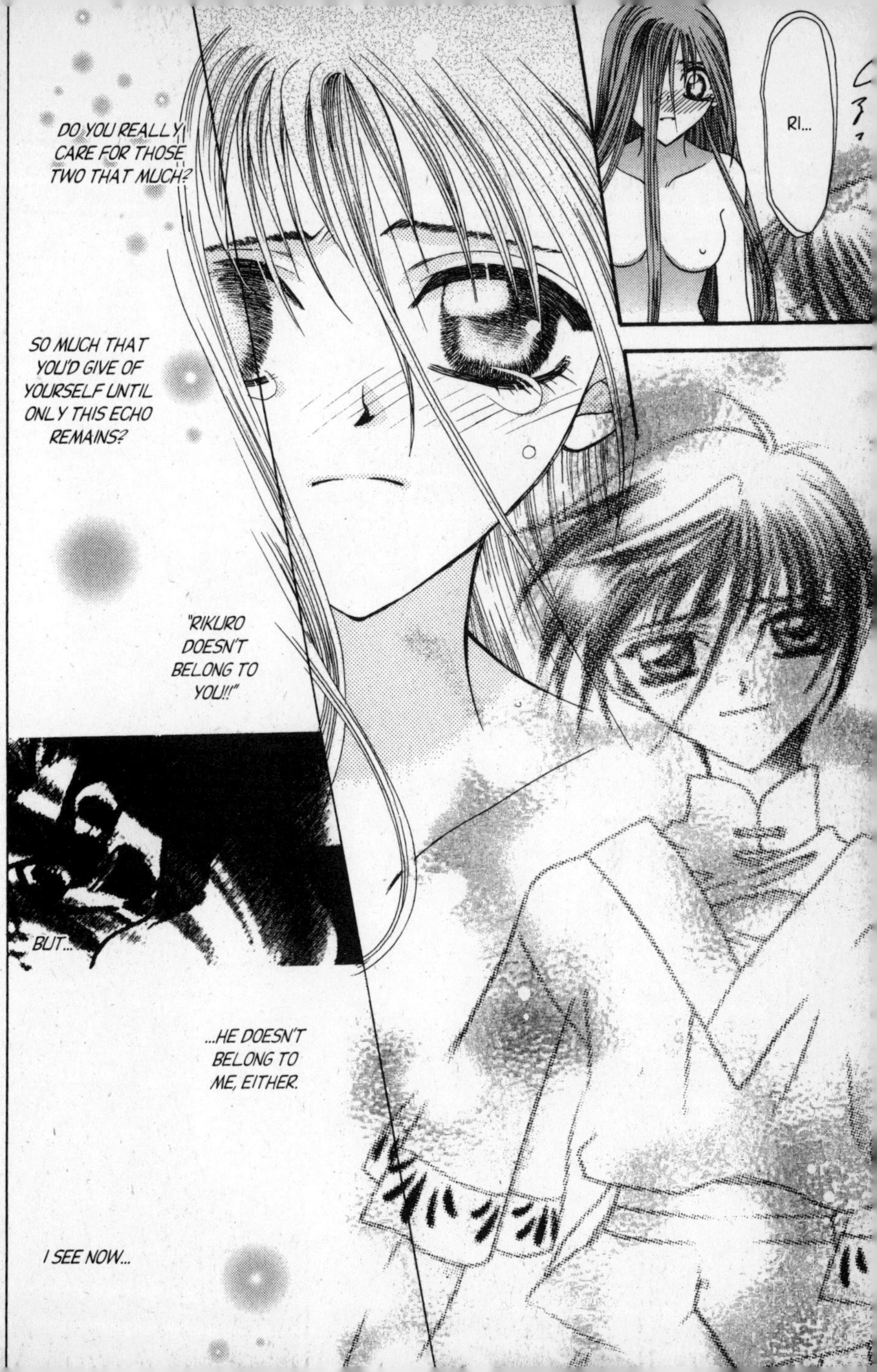
RI...
DO YOU REALLY CARE FOR THOSE TWO THAT MUCH?
SO MUCH THAT YOU'D GIVE OF YOURSELF UNTIL ONLY THIS ECHO REMAINS?
"RIKURO DOESN'T BELONG TO YOU!!"
BUT...
...HE DOESN'T BELONG TO ME, EITHER.
I SEE NOW...

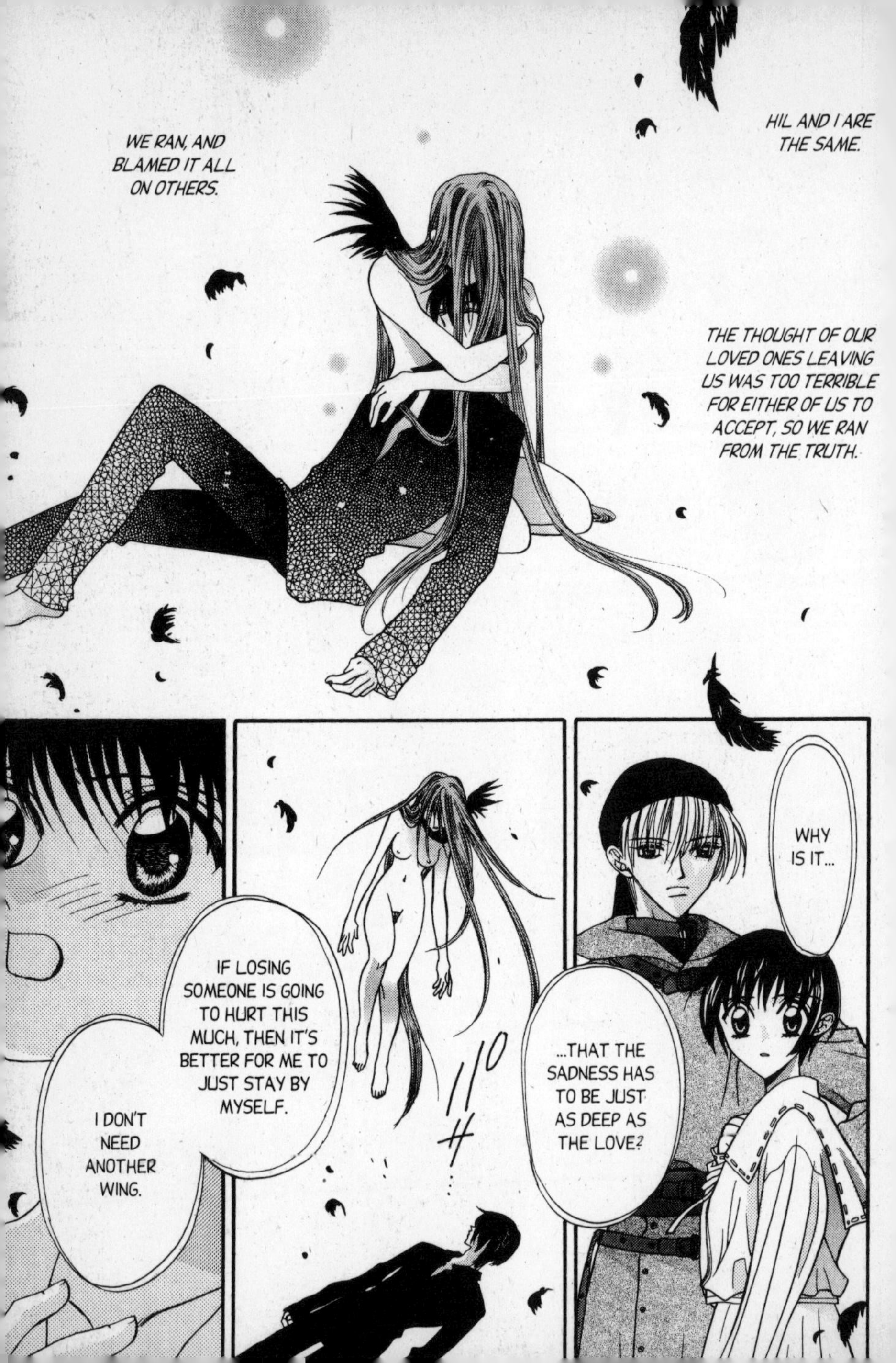
HIL AND I ARE THE SAME.
THE THOUGHT OF OUR LOVED ONES LEAVING US WAS TOO TERRIBLE FOR EITHER OF US TO ACCEPT, SO WE RAN FROM THE TRUTH.
WE RAN, AND BLAMED IT ALL ON OTHERS.
WHY IS IT...
...THAT THE SADNESS HAS TO BE JUST AS DEEP AS THE LOVE?
IF LOSING SOMEONE IS GOING TO HURT THIS MUCH, THEN IT'S BETTER FOR ME TO JUST STAY BY MYSELF.
I DON'T NEED ANOTHER WING.

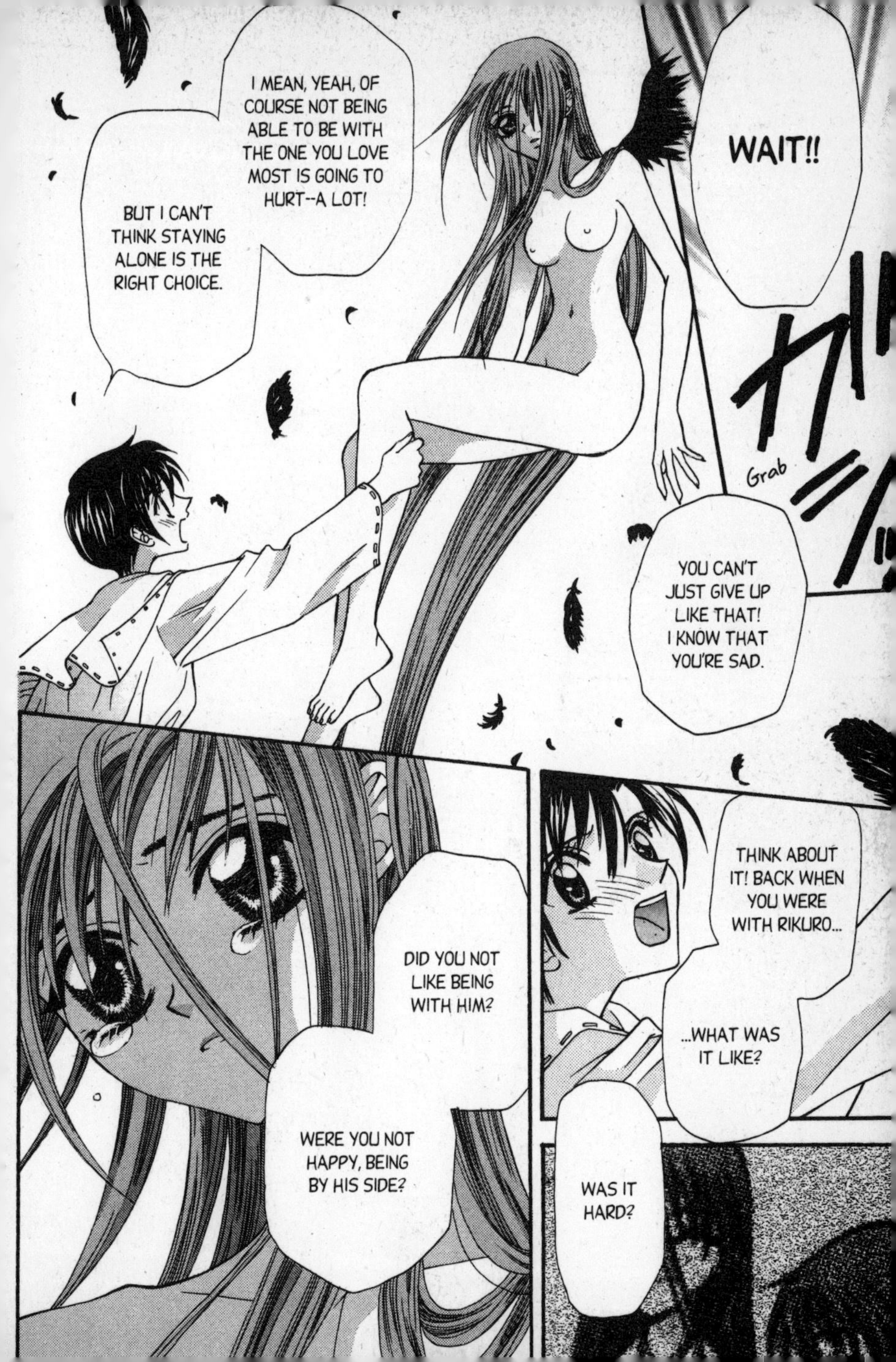
WAIT!!
Grab
YOU CAN'T JUST GIVE UP LIKE THAT! I KNOW THAT YOU'RE SAD.
I MEAN, YEAH, OF COURSE NOT BEING ABLE TO BE WITH THE ONE YOU LOVE MOST IS GOING TO HURT--A LOT!
BUT I CAN'T THINK STAYING ALONE IS THE RIGHT CHOICE.
THINK ABOUT IT! BACK WHEN YOU WERE WITH RIKURO...
...WHAT WAS IT LIKE?
WAS IT HARD?
DID YOU NOT LIKE BEING WITH HIM?
WERE YOU NOT HAPPY, BEING BY HIS SIDE?

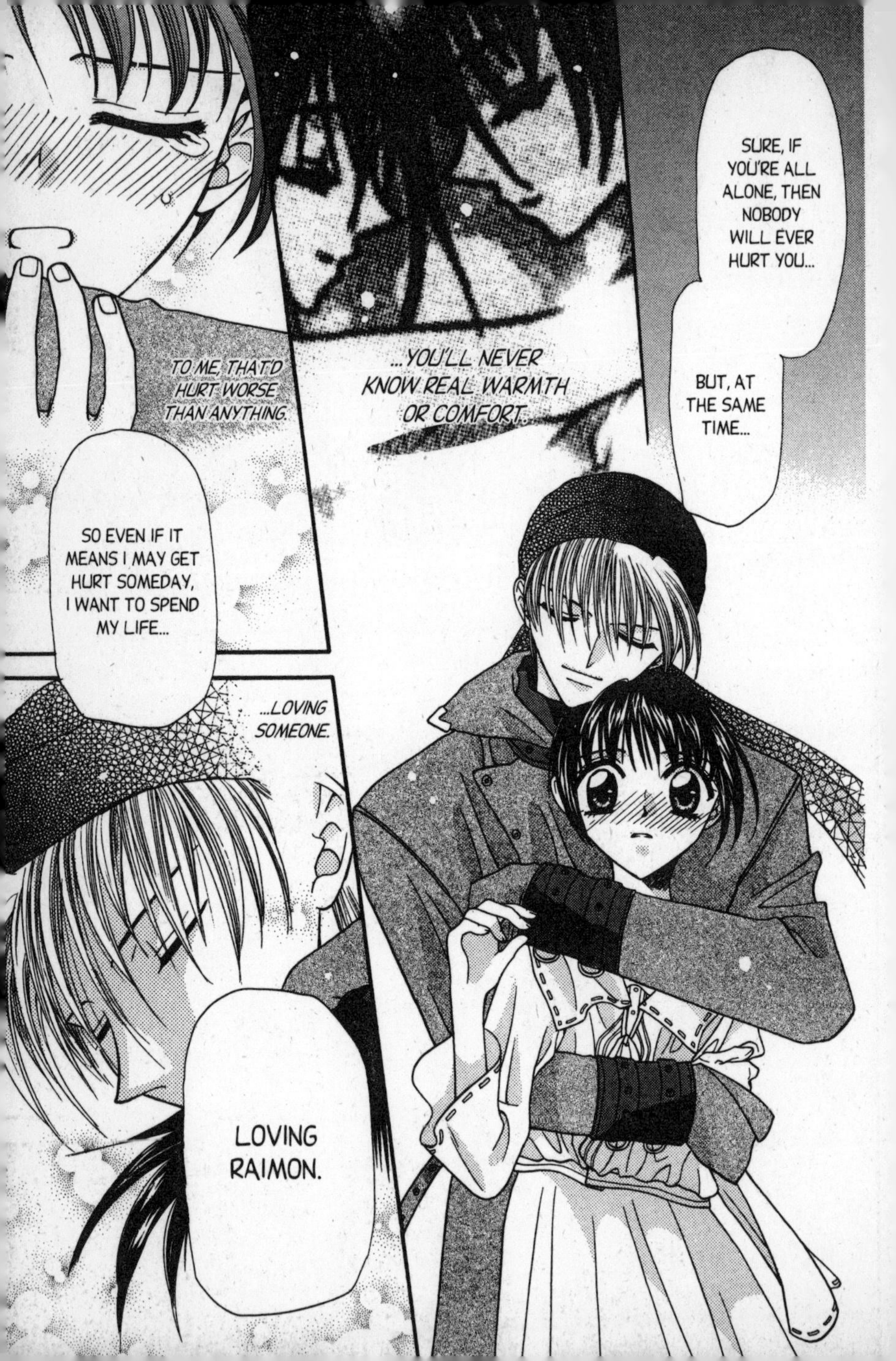

SURE, IF YOU'RE ALL ALONE, THEN NOBODY WILL EVER HURT YOU...
BUT, AT THE SAME TIME...
...YOU'LL NEVER KNOW REAL WARMTH OR COMFORT.
TO ME, THAT'D HURT WORSE THAN ANYTHING.
SO EVEN IF IT MEANS I MAY GET HURT SOMEDAY, I WANT TO SPEND MY LIFE...
...LOVING SOMEONE.
LOVING RAIMON.

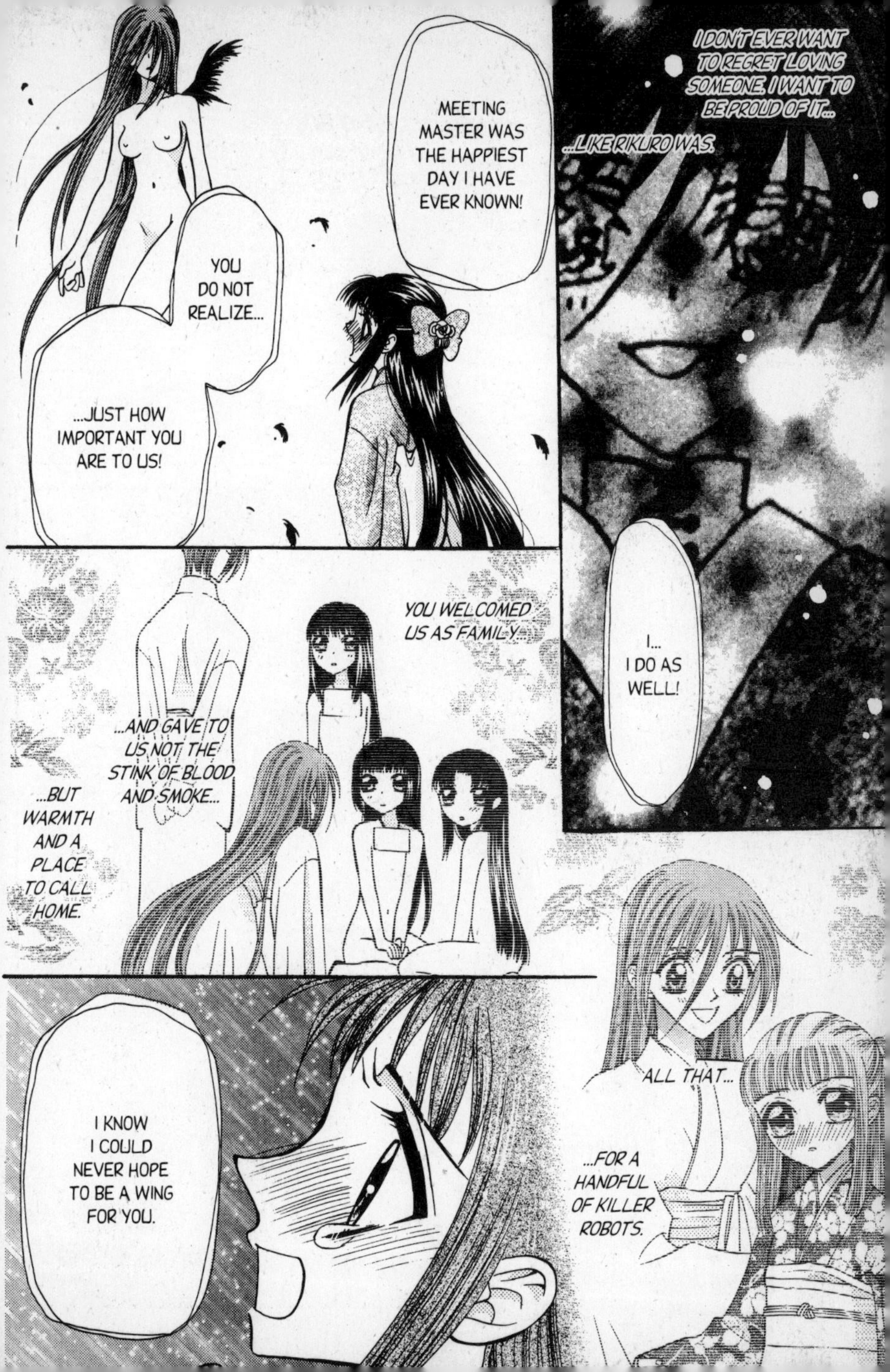
I DON'T EVER WANT TO REGRET LOVING SOMEONE. I WANT TO BE PROUD OF IT...
...LIKE RIKURO WAS.
I... I DO AS WELL!
MEETING MASTER WAS THE HAPPIEST DAY I HAVE EVER KNOWN!
YOU DO NOT REALIZE...
...JUST HOW IMPORTANT YOU ARE TO US!
YOU WELCOMED US AS FAMILY...
...AND GAVE TO US NOT THE STINK OF BLOOD AND SMOKE...
...BUT WARMTH AND A PLACE TO CALL HOME.
ALL THAT...
...FOR A HANDFUL OF KILLER ROBOTS.
I KNOW I COULD NEVER HOPE TO BE A WING FOR YOU.

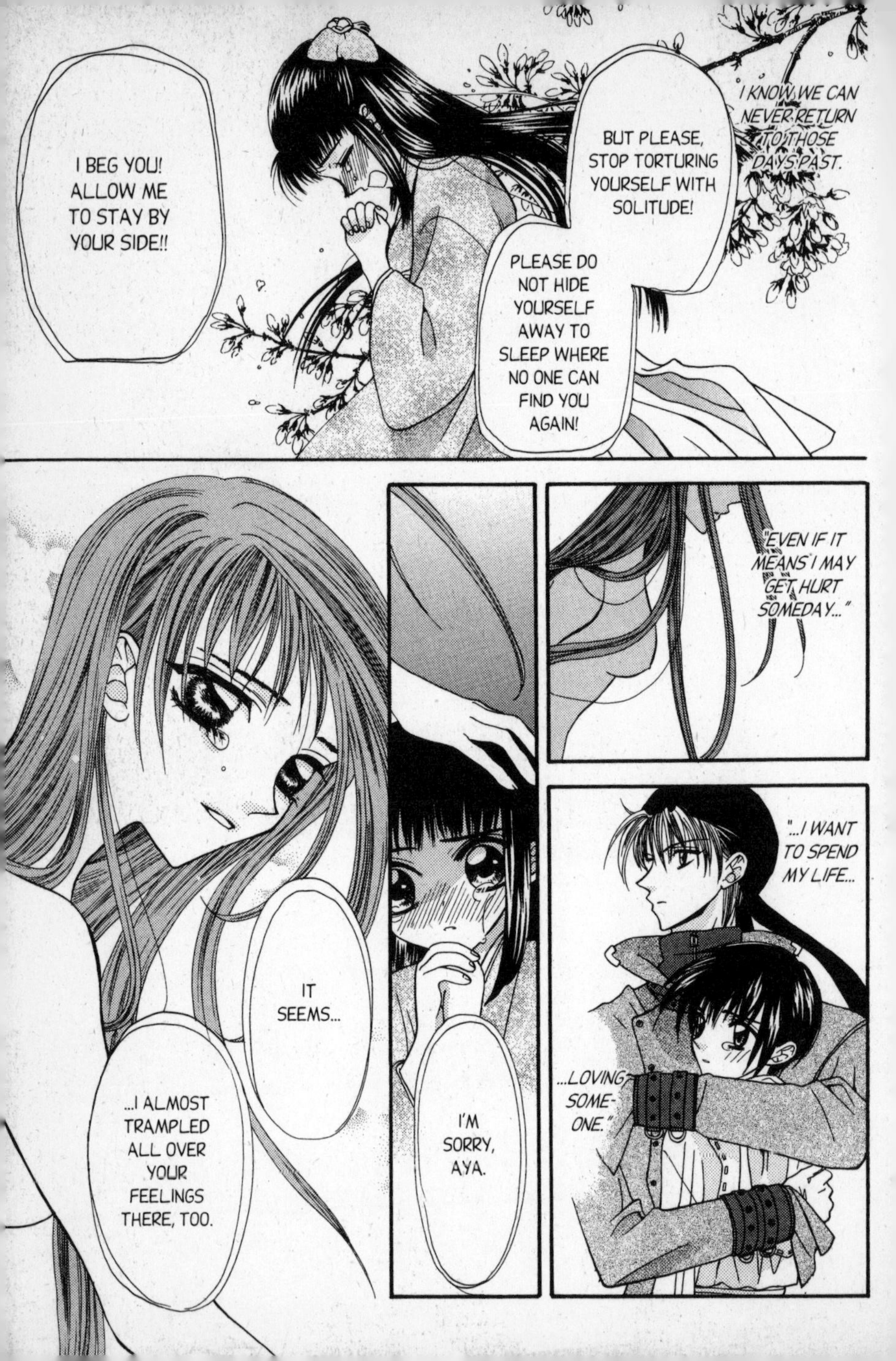
I KNOW WE CAN NEVER RETURN TO THOSE DAYS PAST.
BUT PLEASE, STOP TORTURING YOURSELF WITH SOLITUDE!
PLEASE DO NOT HIDE YOURSELF AWAY TO SLEEP WHERE NO ONE CAN FIND YOU AGAIN!
I BEG YOU! ALLOW ME TO STAY BY YOUR SIDE!!
"EVEN IF IT MEANS I MAY GET HURT SOMEDAY..."
"...I WANT TO SPEND MY LIFE...
...LOVING SOME-ONE."
I'M SORRY, AYA.
IT SEEMS...
...I ALMOST TRAMPLED ALL OVER YOUR FEELINGS THERE, TOO.

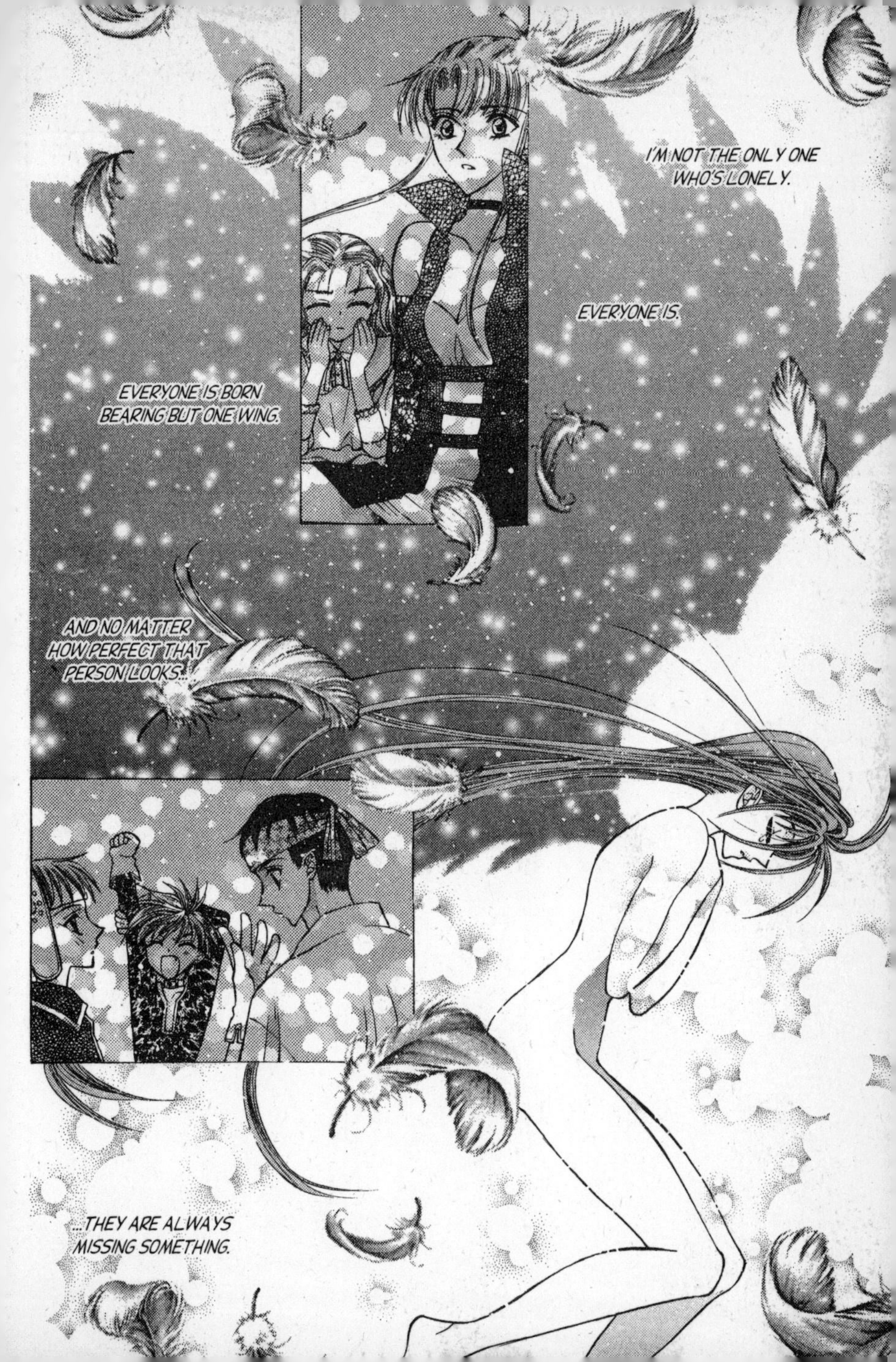
I'M NOT THE ONLY ONE WHO'S LONELY.
EVERYONE IS.
EVERYONE IS BORN BEARING BUT ONE WING.
AND NO MATTER HOW PERFECT THAT PERSON LOOKS...
...THEY ARE ALWAYS MISSING SOMETHING.

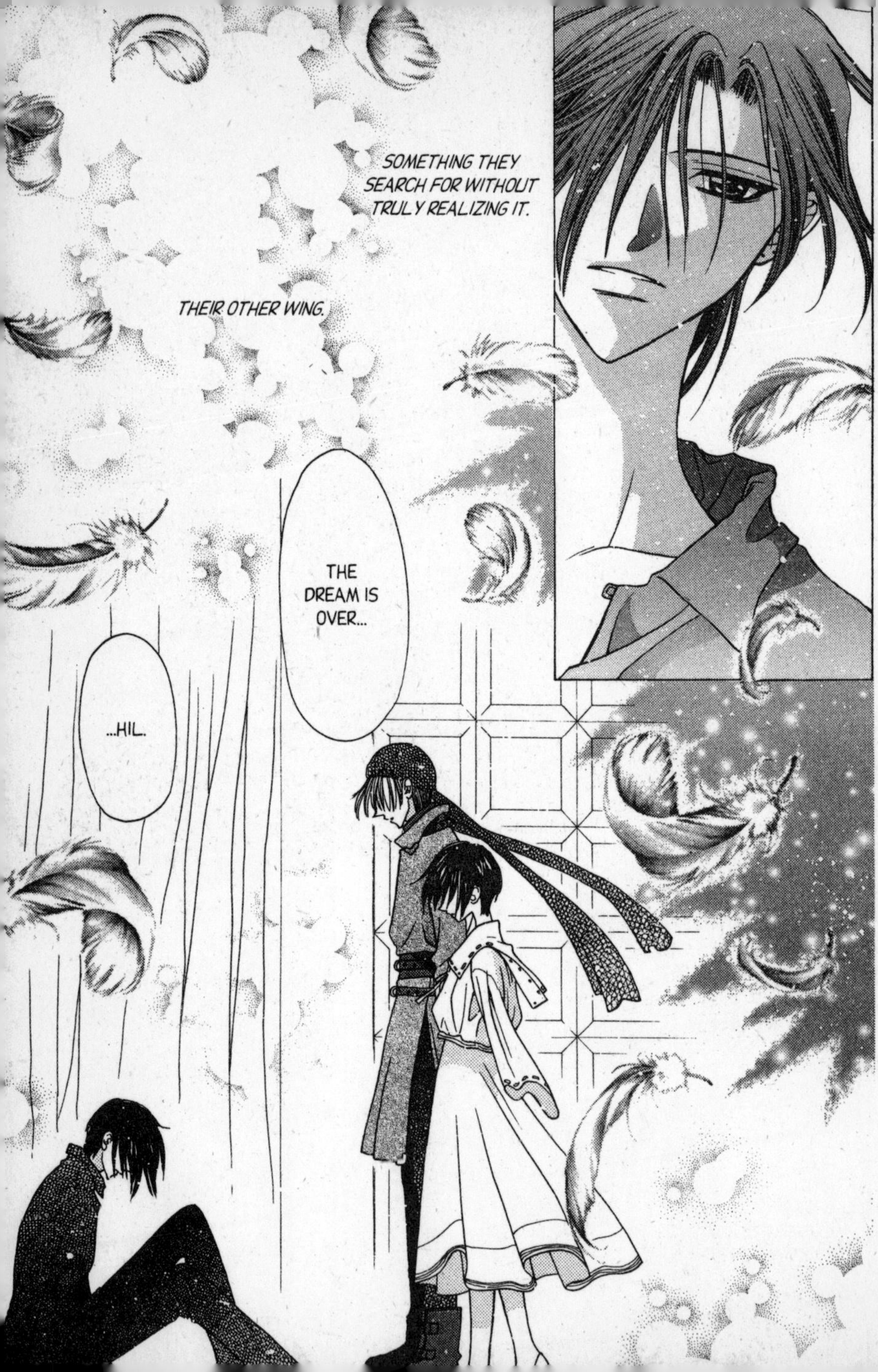
SOMETHING THEY SEARCH FOR WITHOUT TRULY REALIZING IT.
THEIR OTHER WING.
THE DREAM IS OVER...
...HIL.

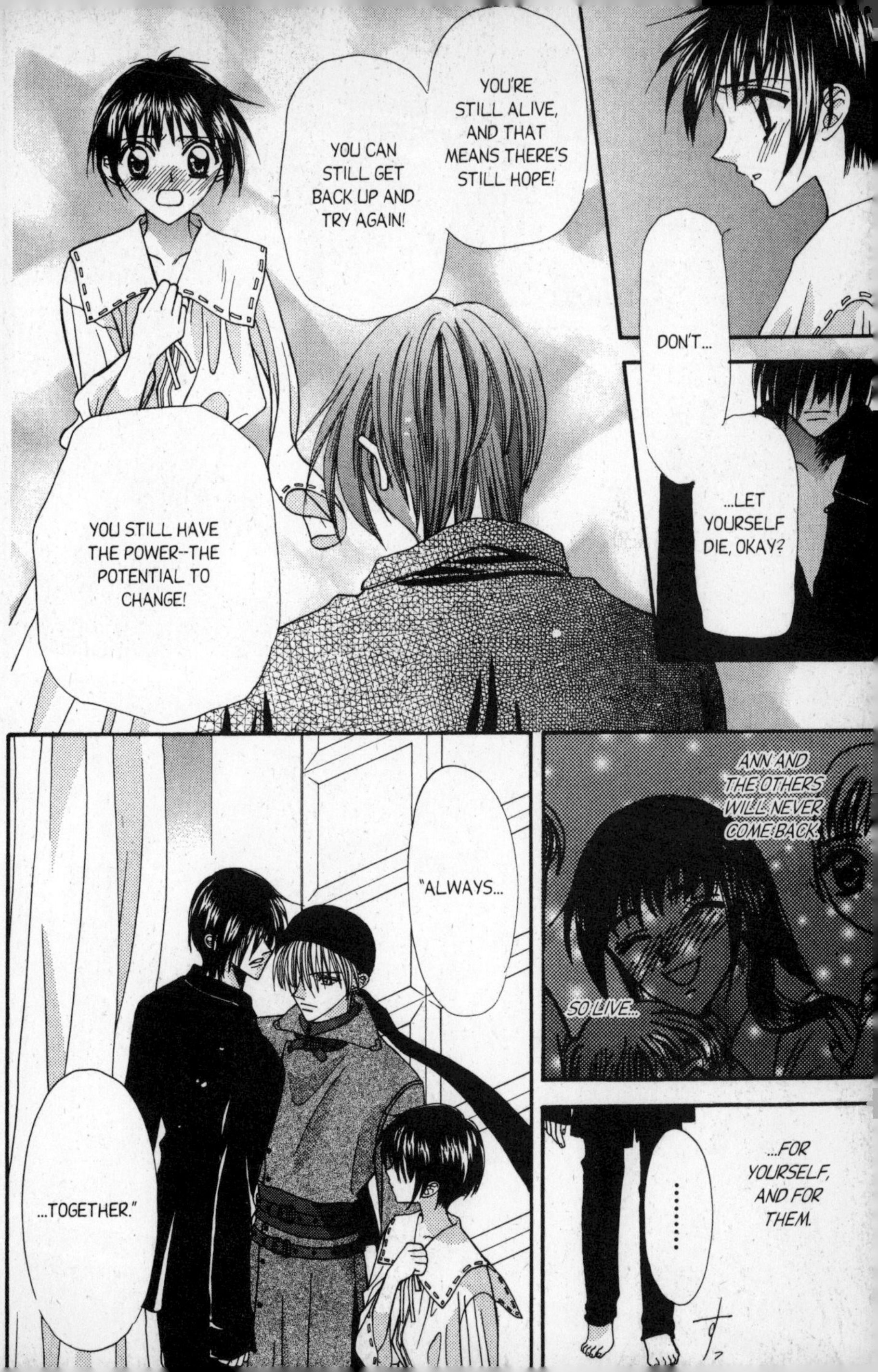
DON'T...
...LET YOURSELF DIE, OKAY?
YOU'RE STILL ALIVE, AND THAT MEANS THERE'S STILL HOPE!
YOU CAN STILL GET BACK UP AND TRY AGAIN!
YOU STILL HAVE THE POWER--THE POTENTIAL TO CHANGE!
ANN AND THE OTHERS WILL NEVER COME BACK.
SO LIVE...
...FOR YOURSELF, AND FOR THEM.
......
"ALWAYS...
...TOGETHER."

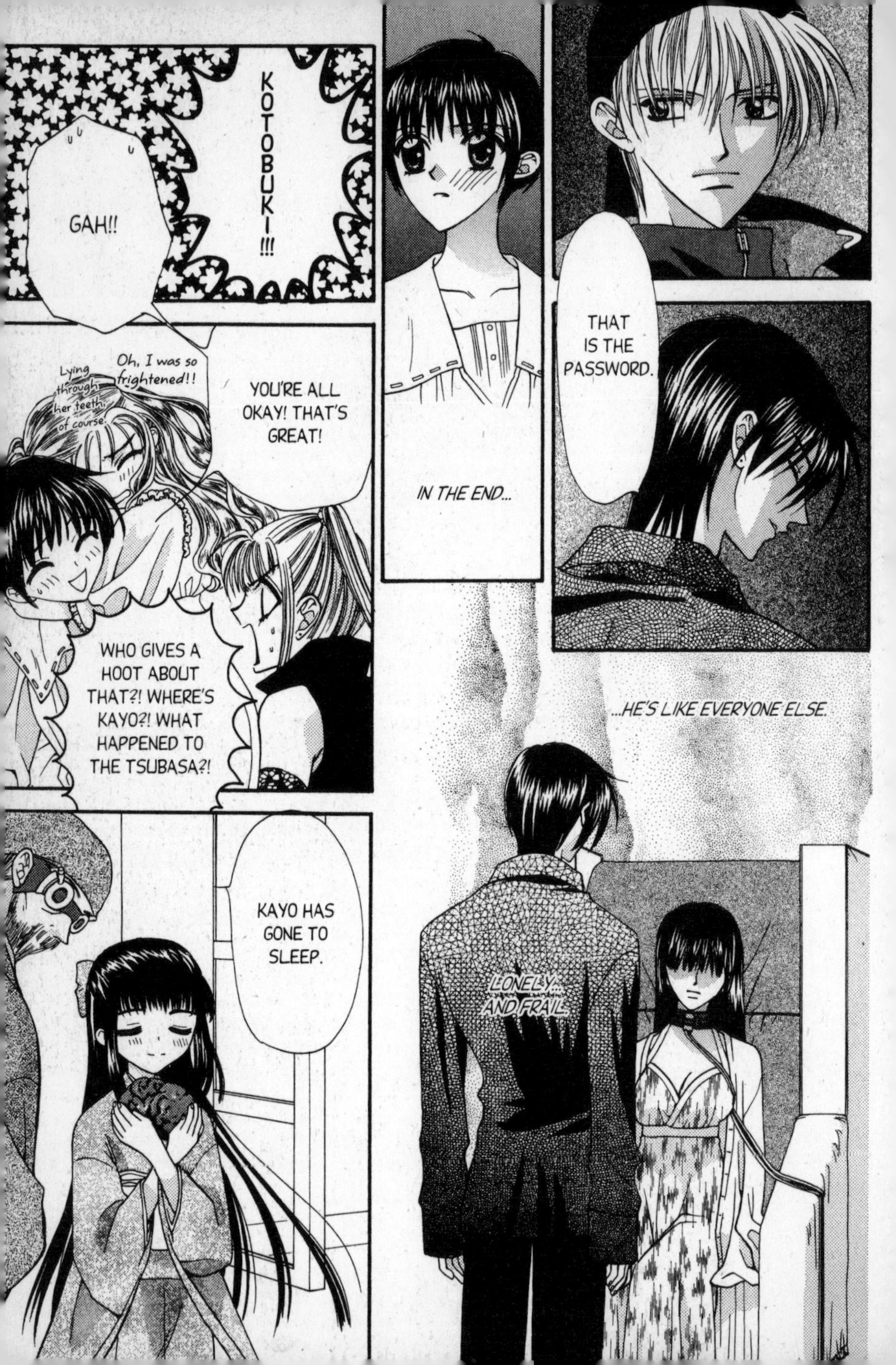
THAT IS THE PASSWORD.
IN THE END...
...HE'S LIKE EVERYONE ELSE.
LONELY... AND FRAIL.
KOTOBUKI!!!
GAH!!
YOU'RE ALL OKAY! THAT'S GREAT!
Oh, I was so frightened!!
Lying through her teeth, of course.
WHO GIVES A HOOT ABOUT THAT?! WHERE'S KAYO?! WHAT HAPPENED TO THE TSUBASA?!
KAYO HAS GONE TO SLEEP.

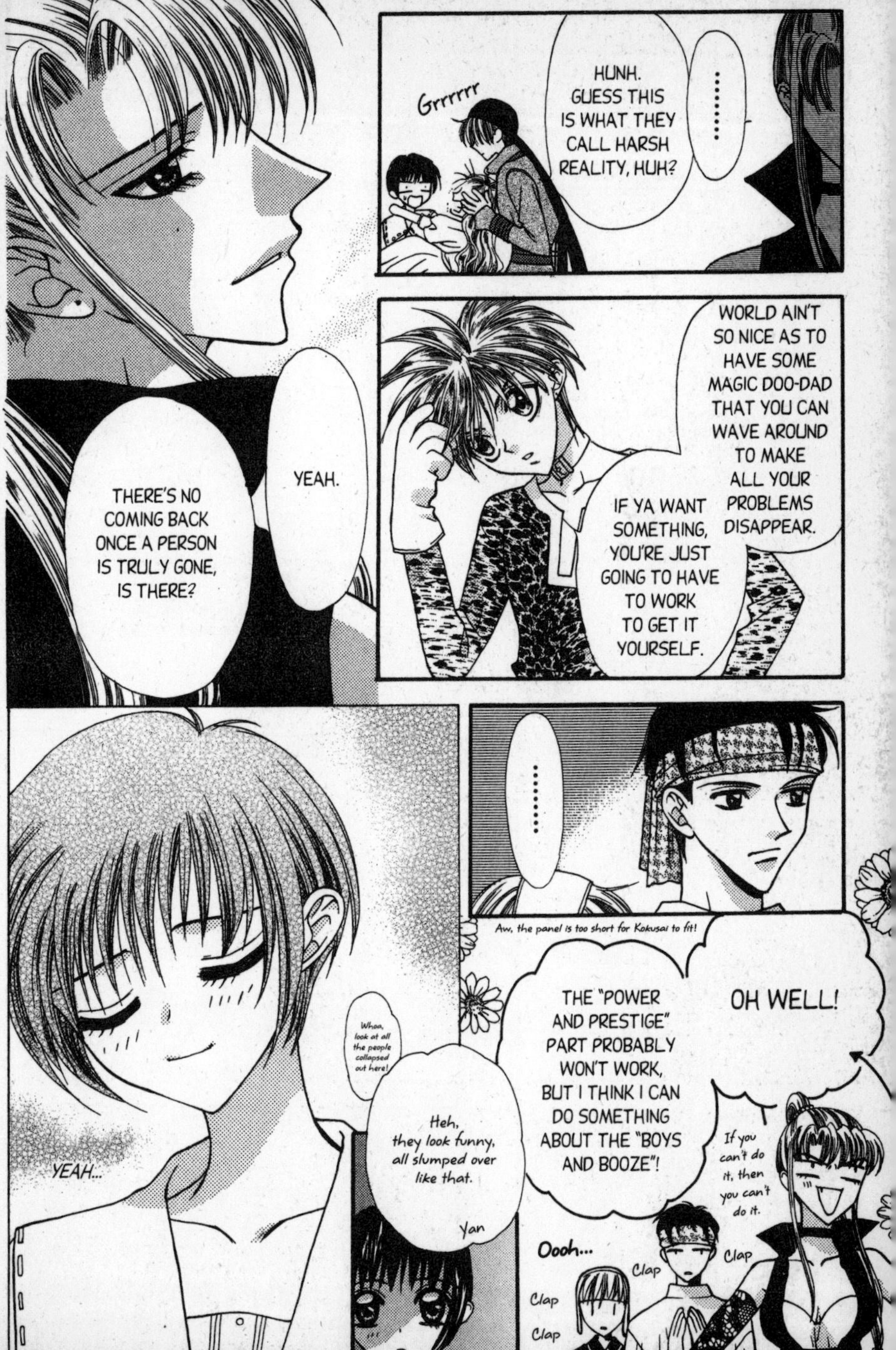
......
HUNH. GUESS THIS IS WHAT THEY CALL HARSH REALITY, HUH?
Grrrrrr
WORLD AIN'T SO NICE AS TO HAVE SOME MAGIC DOO-DAD THAT YOU CAN WAVE AROUND TO MAKE ALL YOUR PROBLEMS DISAPPEAR.
IF YA WANT SOMETHING, YOU'RE JUST GOING TO HAVE TO WORK TO GET IT YOURSELF.
YEAH.
THERE'S NO COMING BACK ONCE A PERSON IS TRULY GONE, IS THERE?
......
Aw, the panel is too short for Kokusai to fit!
OH WELL!
THE "POWER AND PRESTIGE" PART PROBABLY WON'T WORK, BUT I THINK I CAN DO SOMETHING ABOUT THE "BOYS AND BOOZE"!
If you can't do it, then you can't do it.
Clap
Clap
Oooh...
Clap
Clap
Whoa, look at all the people collapsed out here!
Heh, they look funny, all slumped over like that.
Yan
YEAH...

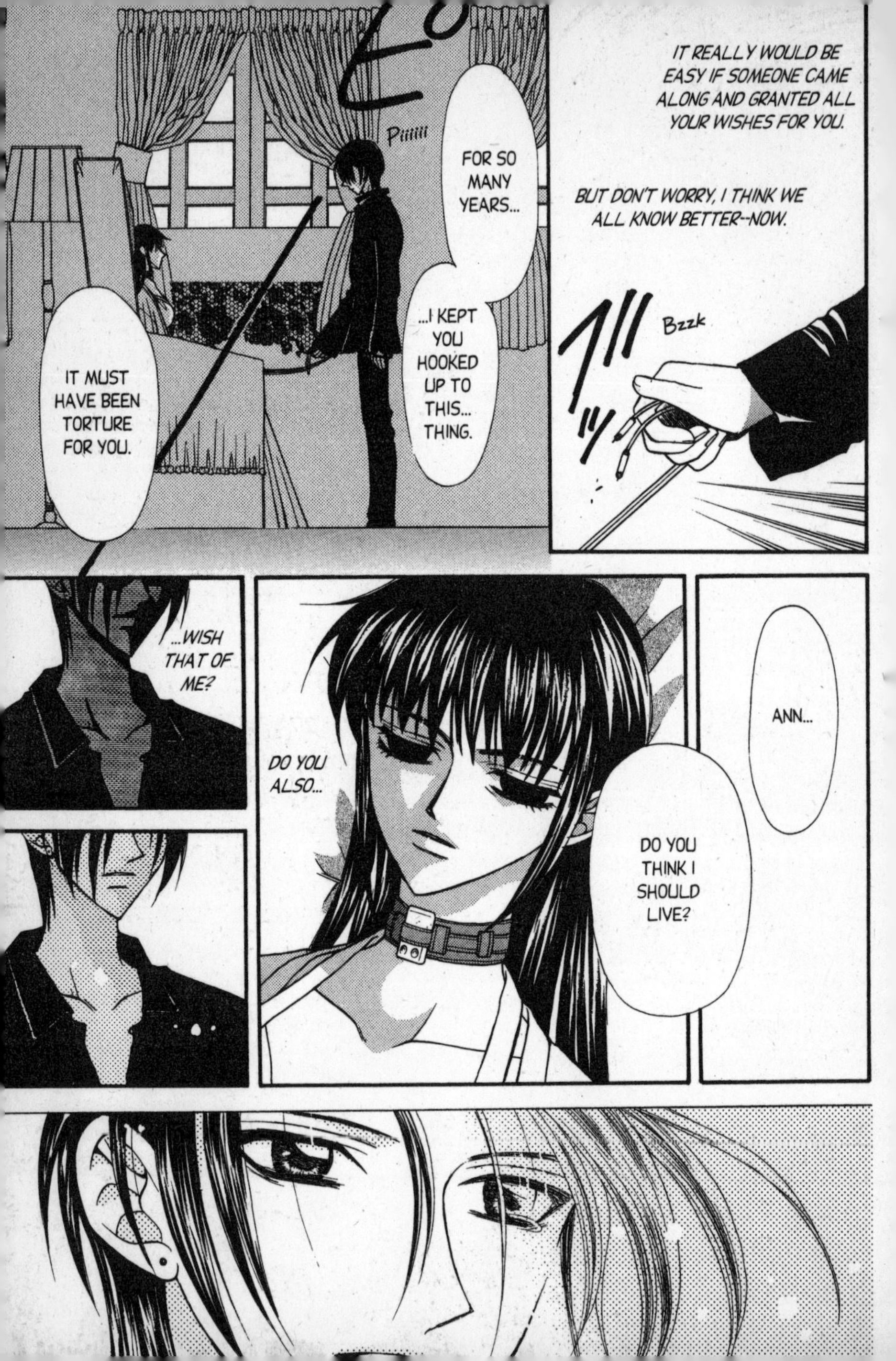
IT REALLY WOULD BE EASY IF SOMEONE CAME ALONG AND GRANTED ALL YOUR WISHES FOR YOU.
BUT DON'T WORRY, I THINK WE ALL KNOW BETTER--NOW.
Bzzk
Piiiii
FOR SO MANY YEARS...
...I KEPT YOU HOOKED UP TO THIS... THING.
IT MUST HAVE BEEN TORTURE FOR YOU.
ANN...
DO YOU THINK I SHOULD LIVE?
DO YOU ALSO...
...WISH THAT OF ME?

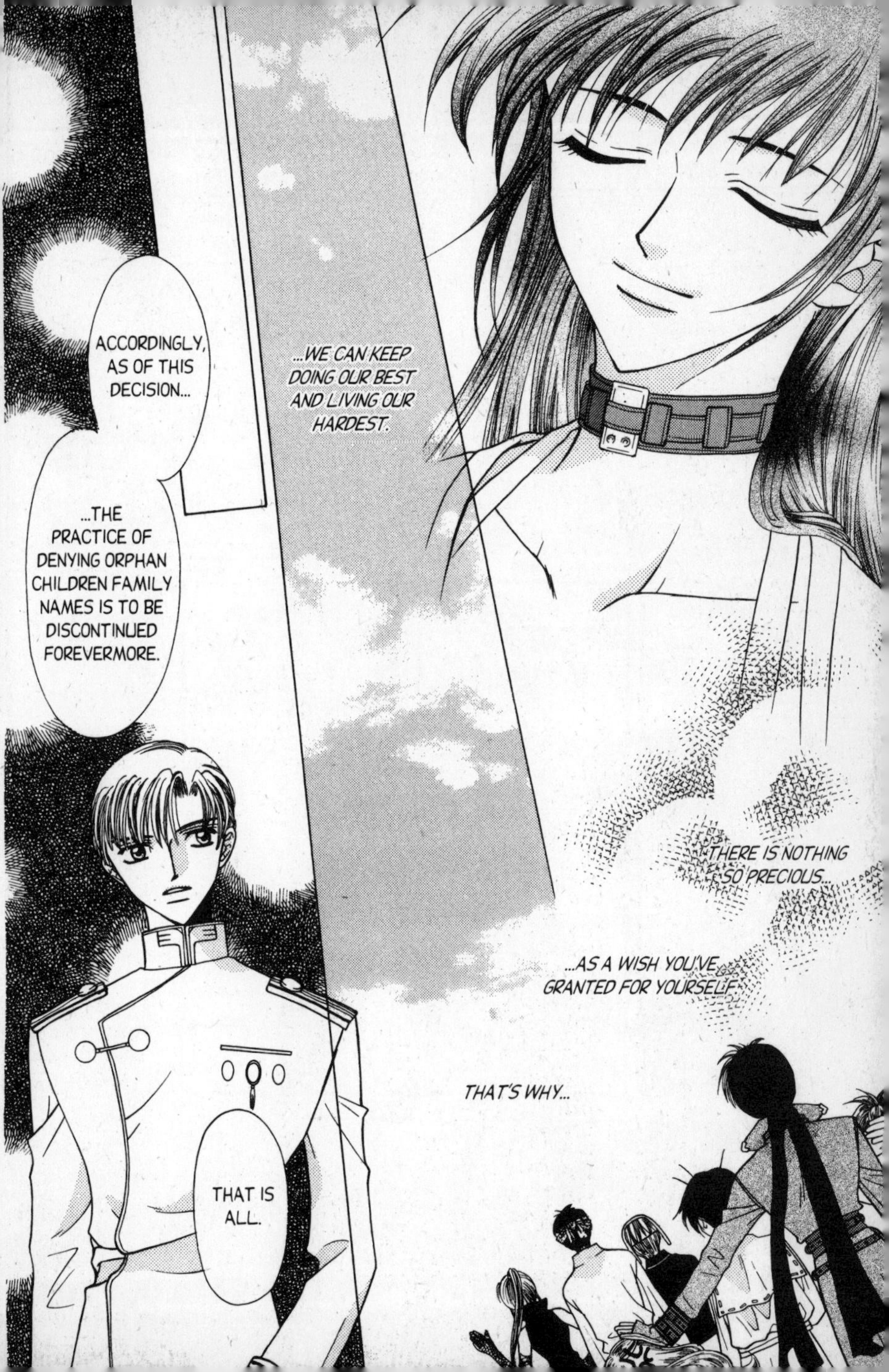
THERE IS NOTHING SO PRECIOUS...
...AS A WISH YOU'VE GRANTED FOR YOURSELF.
THAT'S WHY...
...WE CAN KEEP DOING OUR BEST AND LIVING OUR HARDEST.
ACCORDINGLY, AS OF THIS DECISION...
...THE PRACTICE OF DENYING ORPHAN CHILDREN FAMILY NAMES IS TO BE DISCONTINUED FOREVERMORE.
THAT IS ALL.

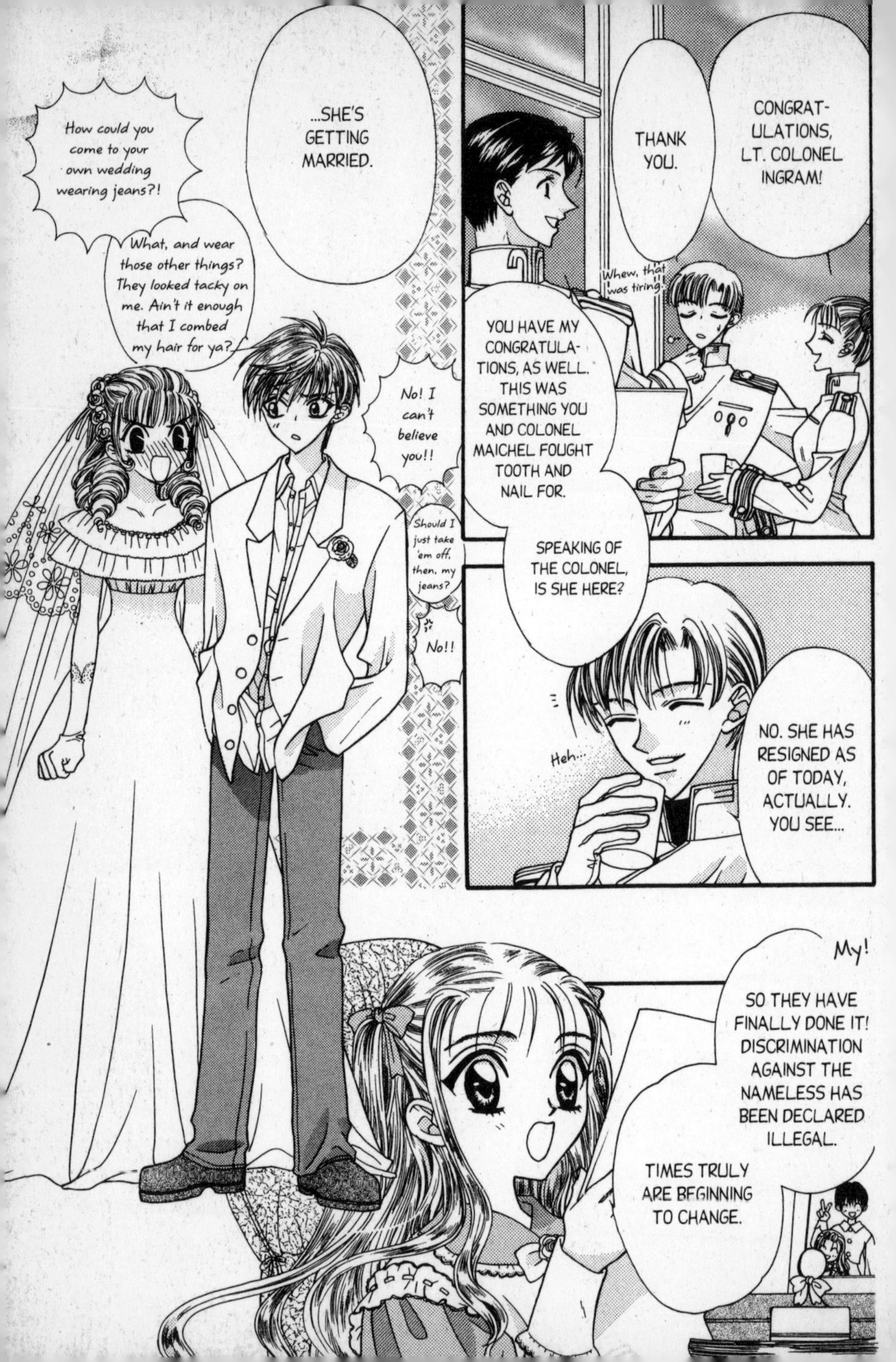
CONGRAT-ULATIONS, LT. COLONEL INGRAM!
THANK YOU.
Whew, that was tiring.
YOU HAVE MY CONGRATULA-TIONS, AS WELL. THIS WAS SOMETHING YOU AND COLONEL MAICHEL FOUGHT TOOTH AND NAIL FOR.
SPEAKING OF THE COLONEL, IS SHE HERE?
NO. SHE HAS RESIGNED AS OF TODAY, ACTUALLY. YOU SEE...
Heh...
My!
SO THEY HAVE FINALLY DONE IT! DISCRIMINATION AGAINST THE NAMELESS HAS BEEN DECLARED ILLEGAL.
TIMES TRULY ARE BEGINNING TO CHANGE.
...SHE'S GETTING MARRIED.
How could you come to your own wedding wearing jeans?!
What, and wear those other things? They looked tacky on me. Ain't it enough that I combed my hair for ya?
No! I can't believe you!!
Should I just take 'em off, then, my jeans?
No!!

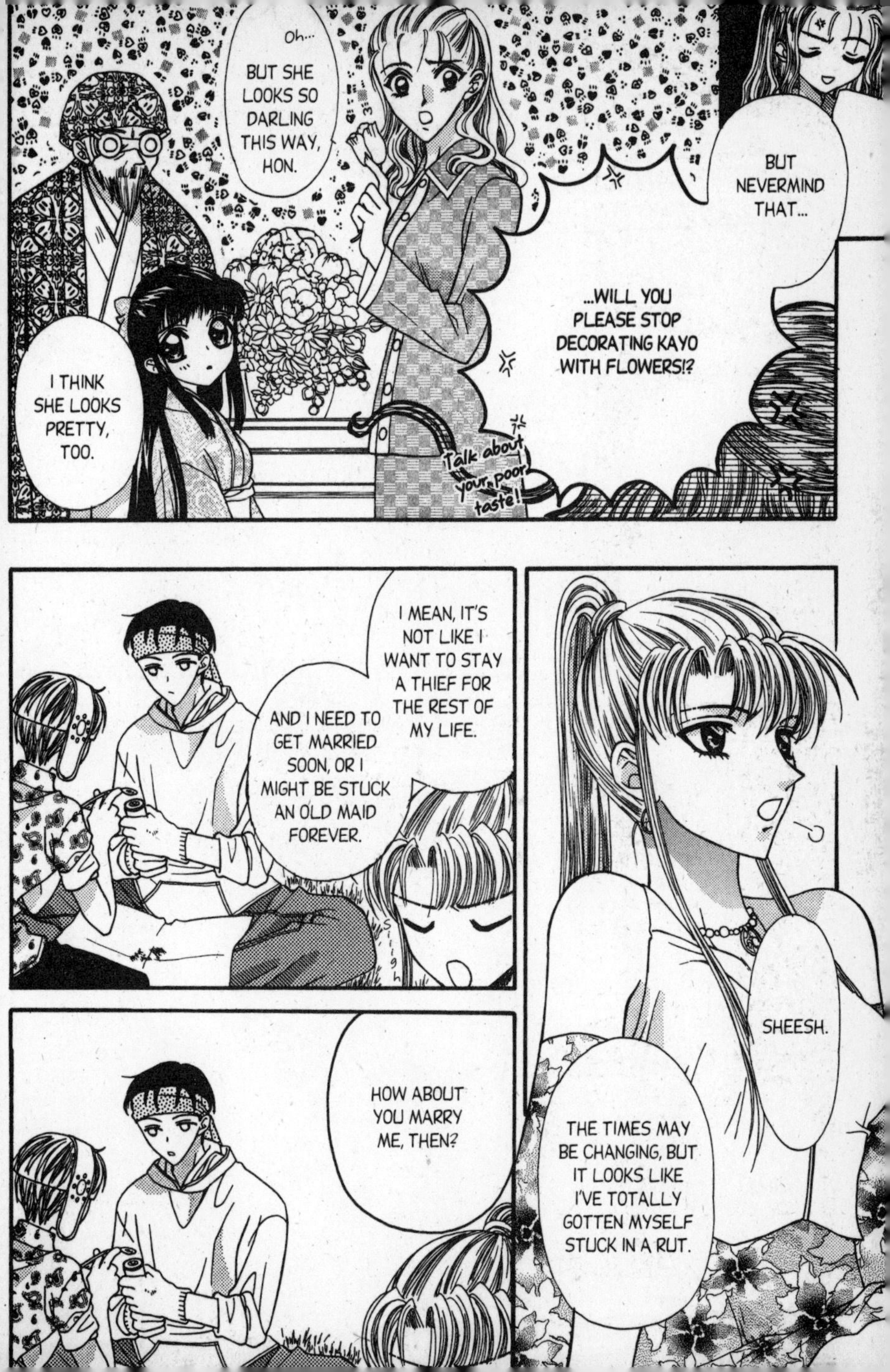
BUT NEVERMIND THAT...
...WILL YOU PLEASE STOP DECORATING KAYO WITH FLOWERS!?
Talk about your poor taste!
Oh...
BUT SHE LOOKS SO DARLING THIS WAY, HON.
I THINK SHE LOOKS PRETTY, TOO.
SHEESH.
THE TIMES MAY BE CHANGING, BUT IT LOOKS LIKE I'VE TOTALLY GOTTEN MYSELF STUCK IN A RUT.
I MEAN, IT'S NOT LIKE I WANT TO STAY A THIEF FOR THE REST OF MY LIFE.
AND I NEED TO GET MARRIED SOON, OR I MIGHT BE STUCK AN OLD MAID FOREVER.
Siiigh
HOW ABOUT YOU MARRY ME, THEN?

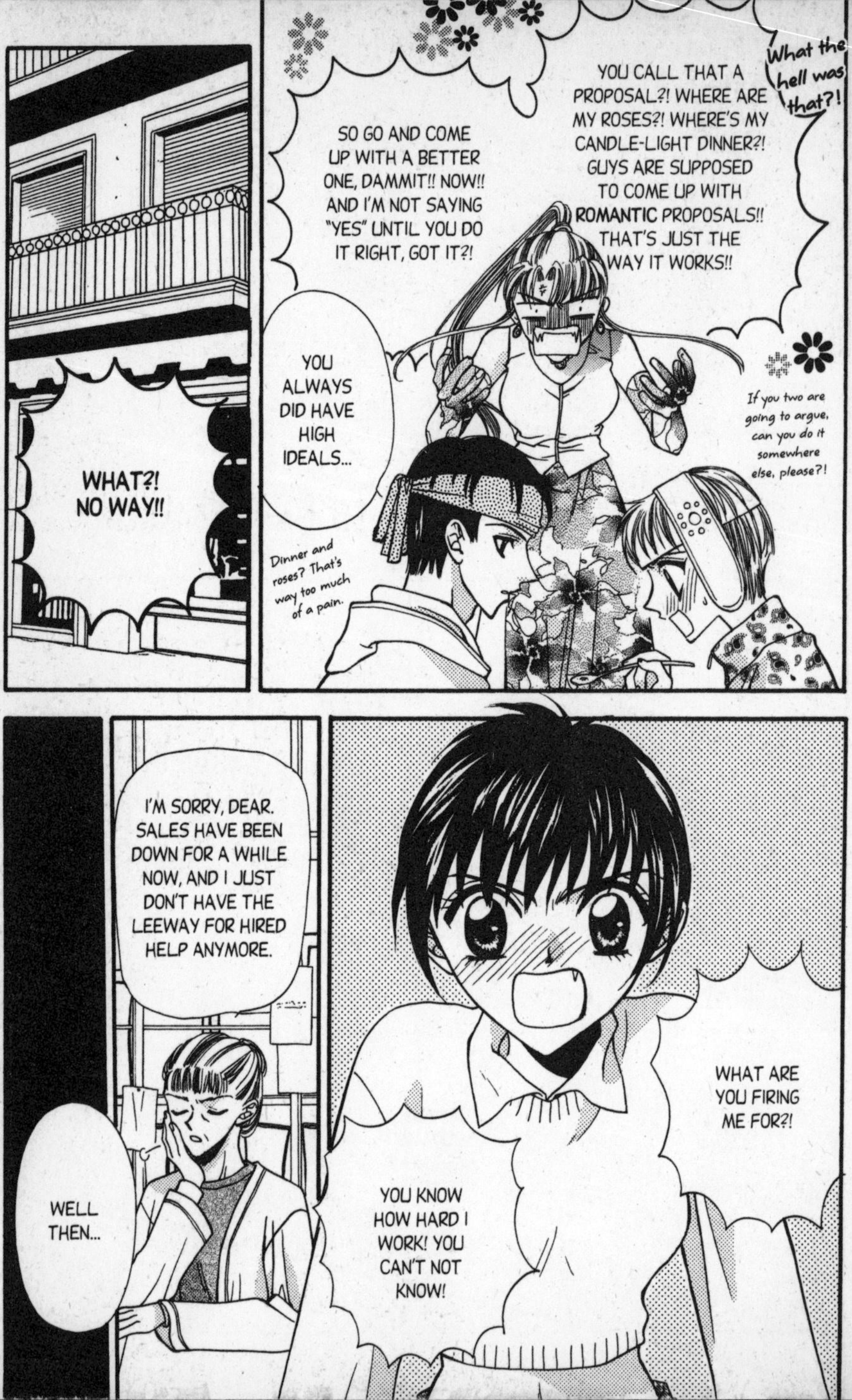
What the hell was that?!
YOU CALL THAT A PROPOSAL?! WHERE ARE MY ROSES?! WHERE'S MY CANDLE-LIGHT DINNER?! GUYS ARE SUPPOSED TO COME UP WITH **ROMANTIC** PROPOSALS!! THAT'S JUST THE WAY IT WORKS!!
SO GO AND COME UP WITH A BETTER ONE, DAMMIT!! NOW!! AND I'M NOT SAYING "YES" UNTIL YOU DO IT RIGHT, GOT IT?!
If you two are going to argue, can you do it somewhere else, please?!
YOU ALWAYS DID HAVE HIGH IDEALS...
Dinner and roses? That's way too much of a pain.
WHAT?! NO WAY!!
WHAT ARE YOU FIRING ME FOR?!
YOU KNOW HOW HARD I WORK! YOU CAN'T NOT KNOW!
I'M SORRY, DEAR. SALES HAVE BEEN DOWN FOR A WHILE NOW, AND I JUST DON'T HAVE THE LEEWAY FOR HIRED HELP ANYMORE.
WELL THEN...

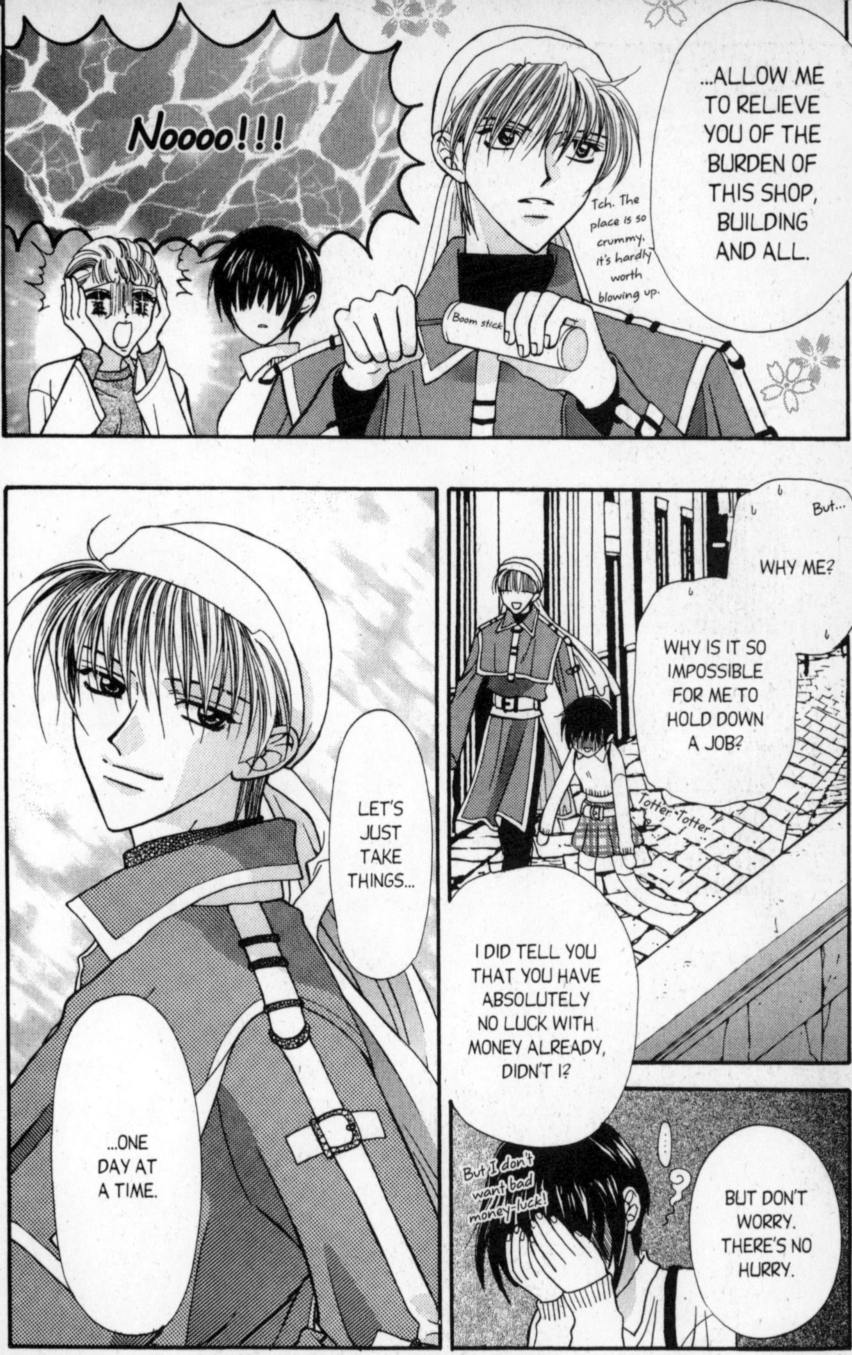
...ALLOW ME TO RELIEVE YOU OF THE BURDEN OF THIS SHOP, BUILDING AND ALL.
Tch. The place is so crummy, it's hardly worth blowing up.
Boom stick
Noooo!!!
But...
WHY ME?
WHY IS IT SO IMPOSSIBLE FOR ME TO HOLD DOWN A JOB?
Totter Totter
I DID TELL YOU THAT YOU HAVE ABSOLUTELY NO LUCK WITH MONEY ALREADY, DIDN'T I?
BUT DON'T WORRY. THERE'S NO HURRY.
...
But I don't want bad money-luck!
LET'S JUST TAKE THINGS...
...ONE DAY AT A TIME.

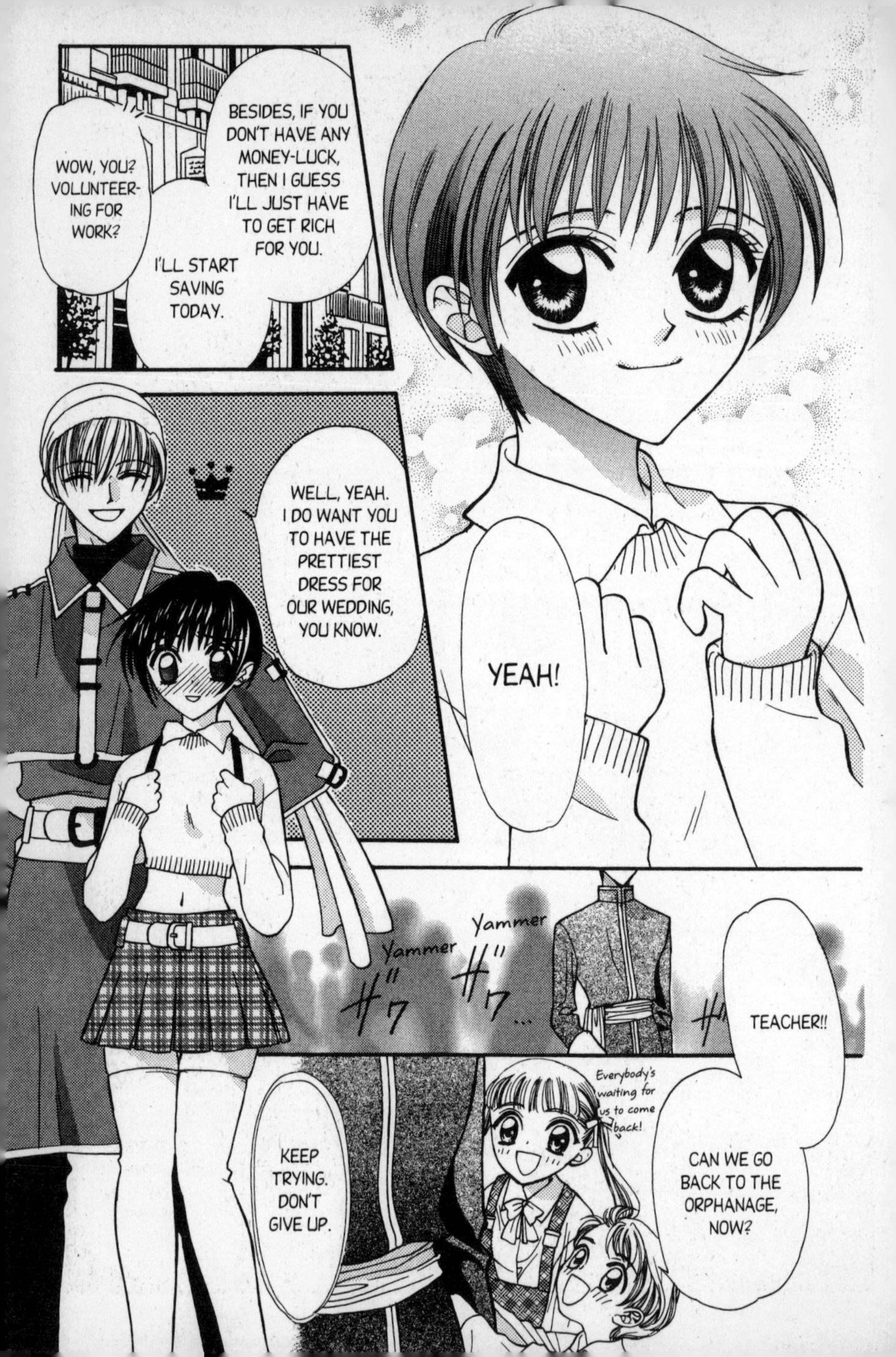

YEAH!
BESIDES, IF YOU DON'T HAVE ANY MONEY-LUCK, THEN I GUESS I'LL JUST HAVE TO GET RICH FOR YOU.
I'LL START SAVING TODAY.
WOW, YOU? VOLUNTEERING FOR WORK?
WELL, YEAH. I DO WANT YOU TO HAVE THE PRETTIEST DRESS FOR OUR WEDDING, YOU KNOW.
TEACHER!!
Yammer
Yammer
CAN WE GO BACK TO THE ORPHANAGE, NOW?
Everybody's waiting for us to come back!
KEEP TRYING. DON'T GIVE UP.

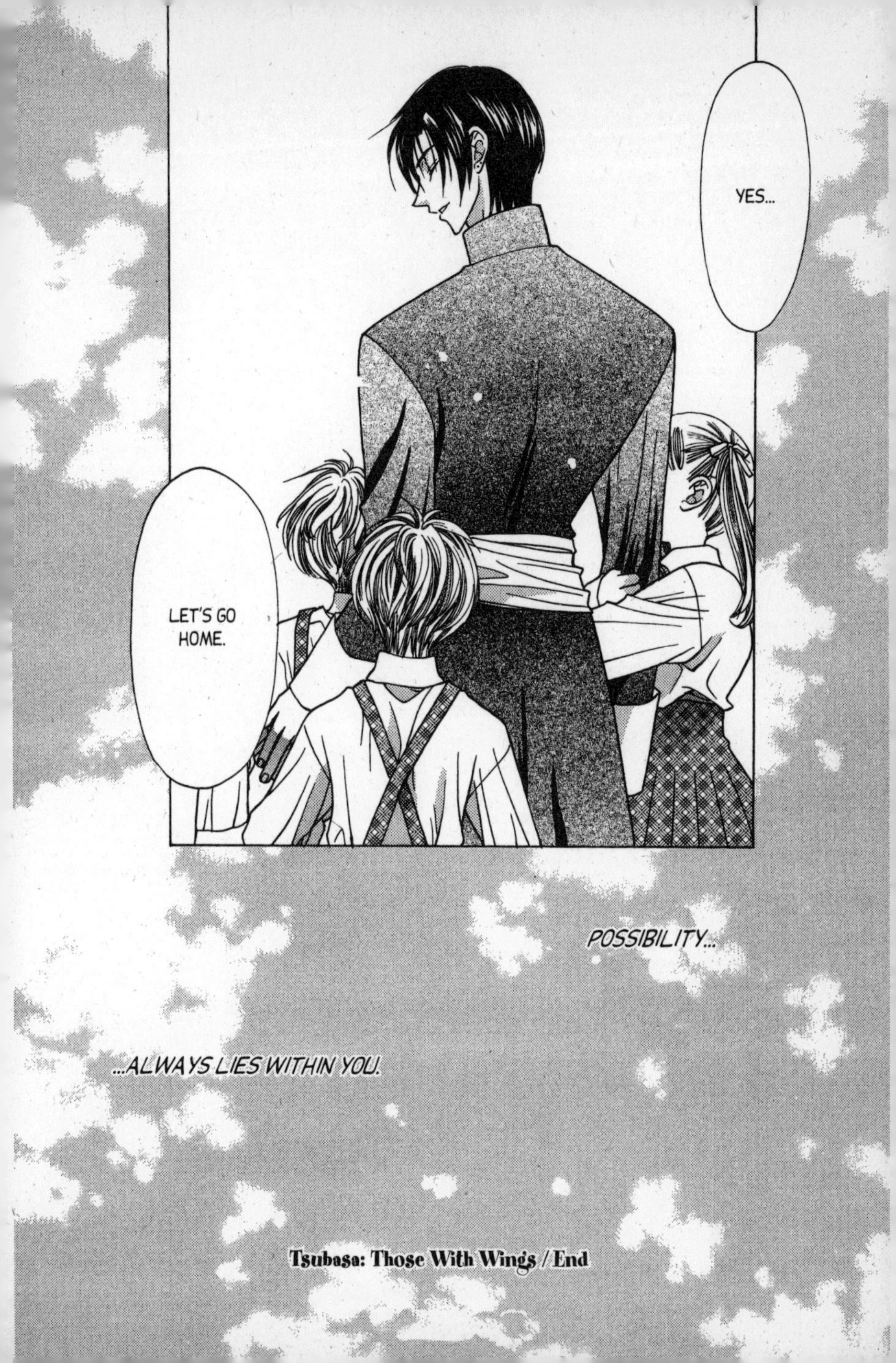
YES...
LET'S GO HOME.
POSSIBILITY...
...ALWAYS LIES WITHIN YOU.
Tsubasa: Those With Wings / End

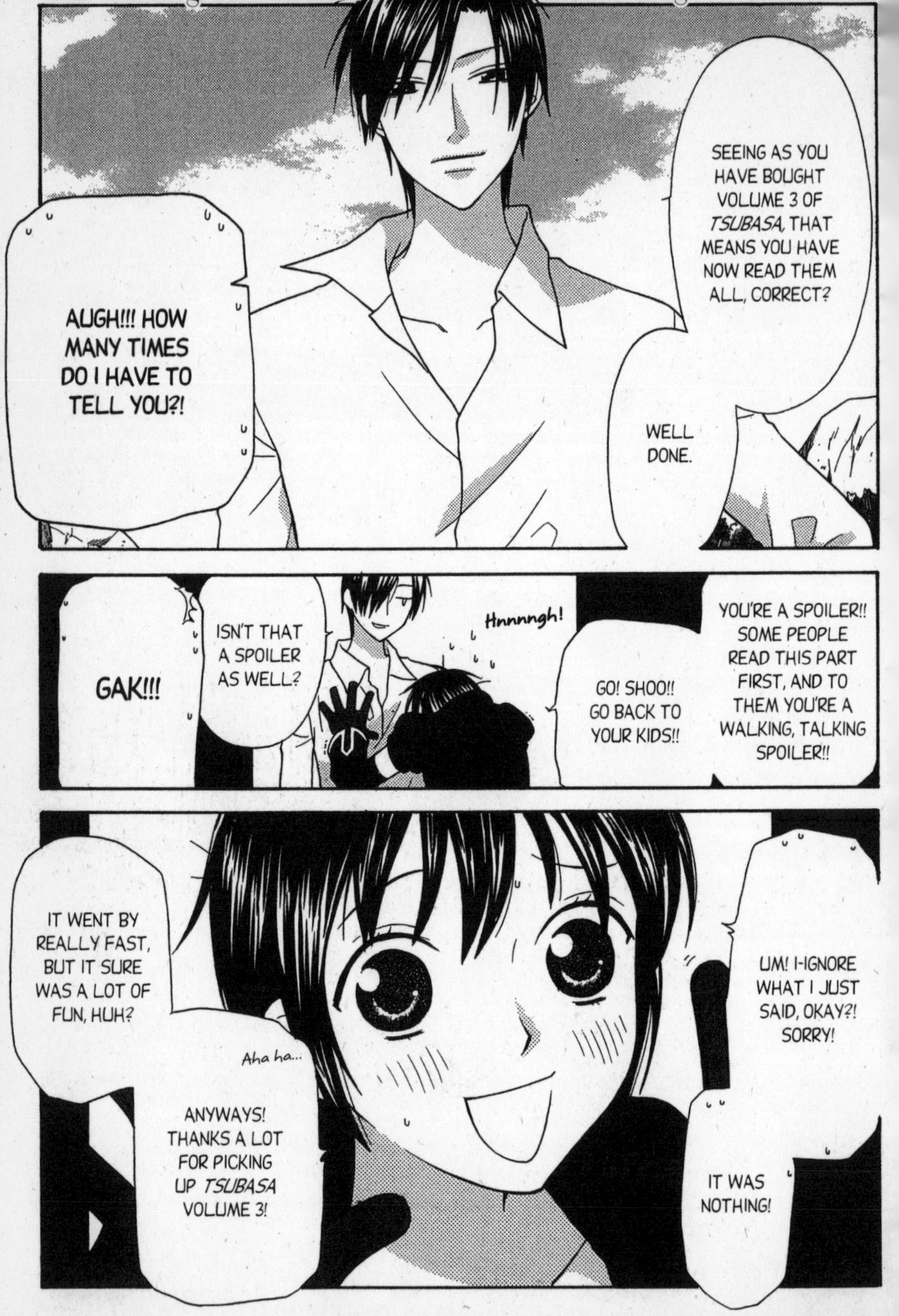
SEEING AS YOU HAVE BOUGHT VOLUME 3 OF *TSUBASA*, THAT MEANS YOU HAVE NOW READ THEM ALL, CORRECT?
WELL DONE.
AUGH!!! HOW MANY TIMES DO I HAVE TO TELL YOU?!
YOU'RE A SPOILER!! SOME PEOPLE READ THIS PART FIRST, AND TO THEM YOU'RE A WALKING, TALKING SPOILER!!
GO! SHOO!! GO BACK TO YOUR KIDS!!
Hnnnngh!
ISN'T THAT A SPOILER AS WELL?
GAK!!!
UM! I-IGNORE WHAT I JUST SAID, OKAY?! SORRY!
IT WENT BY REALLY FAST, BUT IT SURE WAS A LOT OF FUN, HUH?
Aha ha...
ANYWAYS! THANKS A LOT FOR PICKING UP *TSUBASA* VOLUME 3!
IT WAS NOTHING!

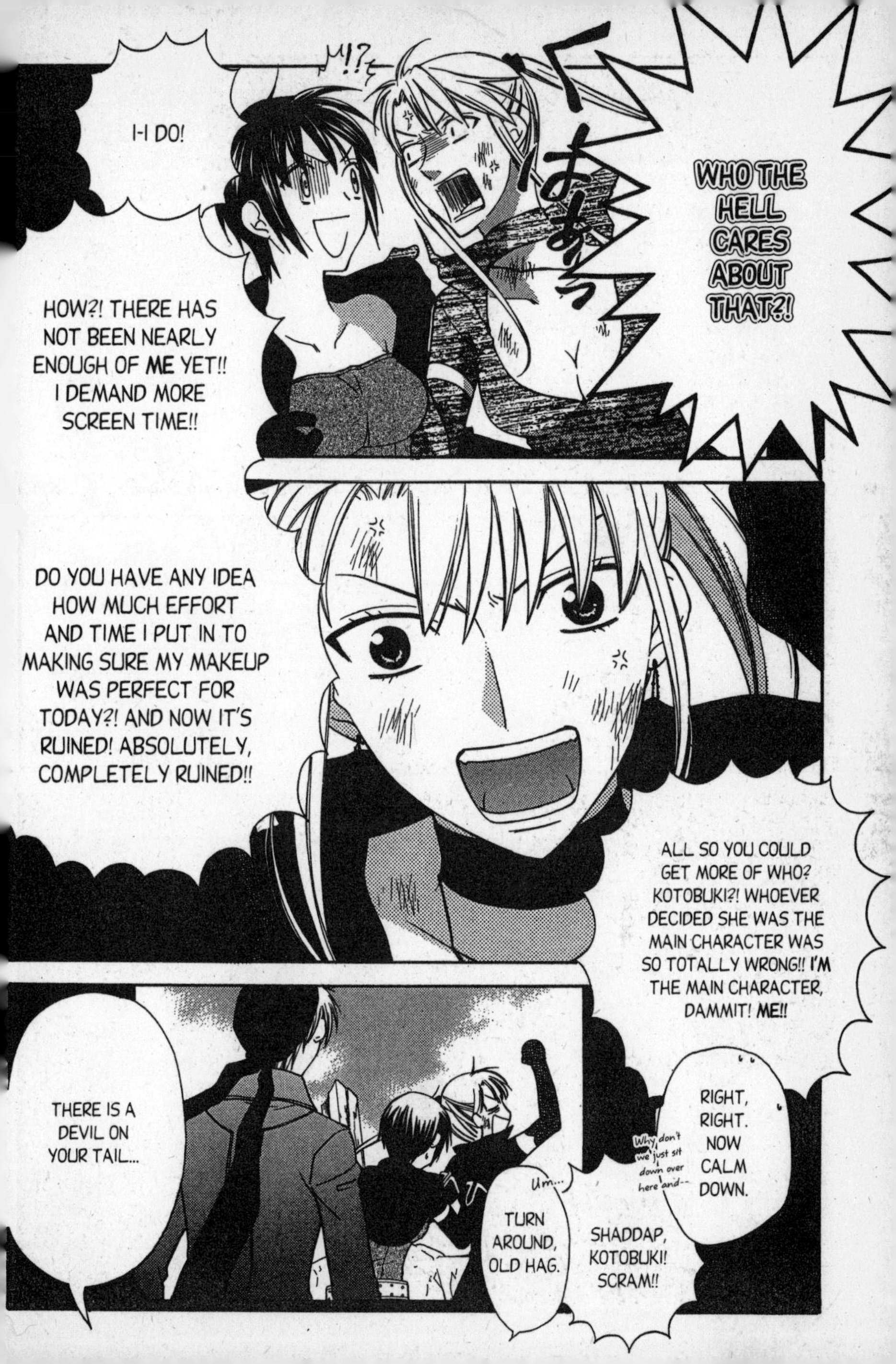
WHO THE HELL CARES ABOUT THAT?!
!?
I-I DO!
HOW?! THERE HAS NOT BEEN NEARLY ENOUGH OF **ME** YET!! I DEMAND MORE SCREEN TIME!!
DO YOU HAVE ANY IDEA HOW MUCH EFFORT AND TIME I PUT IN TO MAKING SURE MY MAKEUP WAS PERFECT FOR TODAY?! AND NOW IT'S RUINED! ABSOLUTELY, COMPLETELY RUINED!!
ALL SO YOU COULD GET MORE OF WHO? KOTOBUKI?! WHOEVER DECIDED SHE WAS THE MAIN CHARACTER WAS SO TOTALLY WRONG!! **I'M** THE MAIN CHARACTER, DAMMIT! **ME!!**
RIGHT, RIGHT. NOW CALM DOWN.
Why don't we just sit down over here and--
SHADDAP, KOTOBUKI! SCRAM!!
Um...
TURN AROUND, OLD HAG.
THERE IS A DEVIL ON YOUR TAIL...

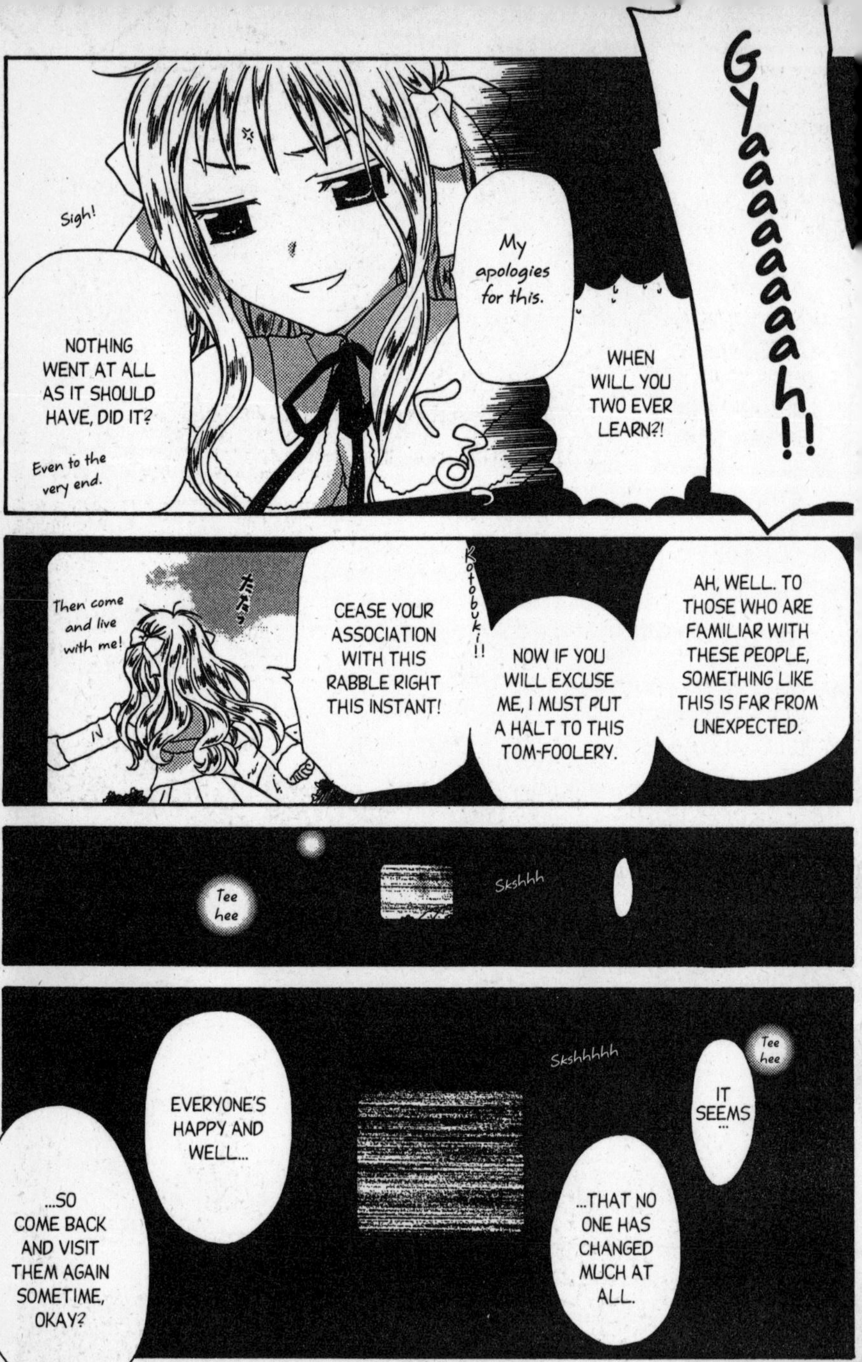
Gyaaaaaaah!!
WHEN WILL YOU TWO EVER LEARN?!
My apologies for this.
Sigh!
NOTHING WENT AT ALL AS IT SHOULD HAVE, DID IT?
Even to the very end.
AH, WELL. TO THOSE WHO ARE FAMILIAR WITH THESE PEOPLE, SOMETHING LIKE THIS IS FAR FROM UNEXPECTED.
NOW IF YOU WILL EXCUSE ME, I MUST PUT A HALT TO THIS TOM-FOOLERY.
Kotobuki!!
CEASE YOUR ASSOCIATION WITH THIS RABBLE RIGHT THIS INSTANT!
たたっ
Then come and live with me!
Skshhh
Tee hee
Tee hee
IT SEEMS...
...THAT NO ONE HAS CHANGED MUCH AT ALL.
Skshhhhh
EVERYONE'S HAPPY AND WELL...
...SO COME BACK AND VISIT THEM AGAIN SOMETIME, OKAY?

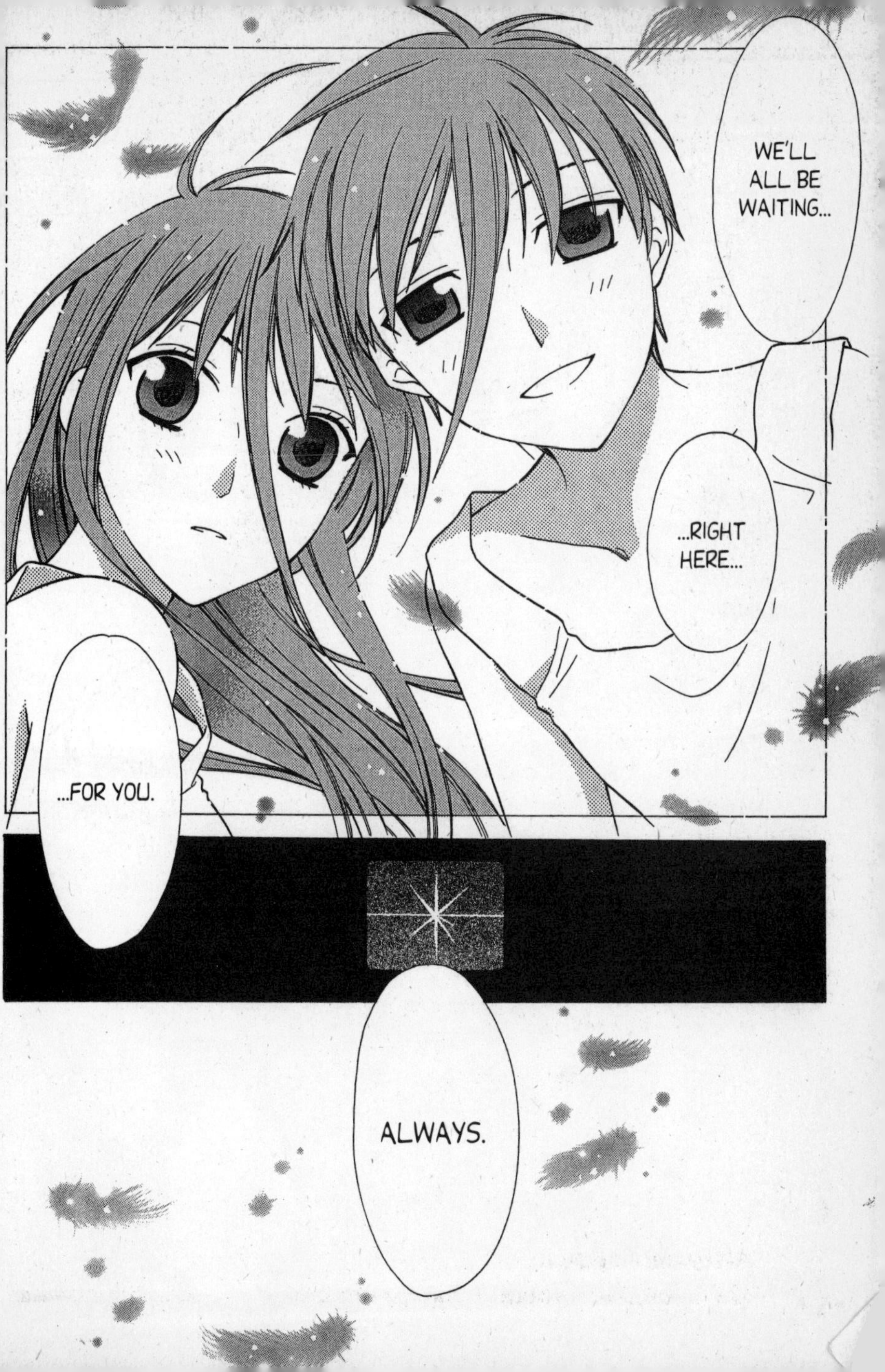
WE'LL ALL BE WAITING...
...RIGHT HERE...
...FOR YOU.
ALWAYS.

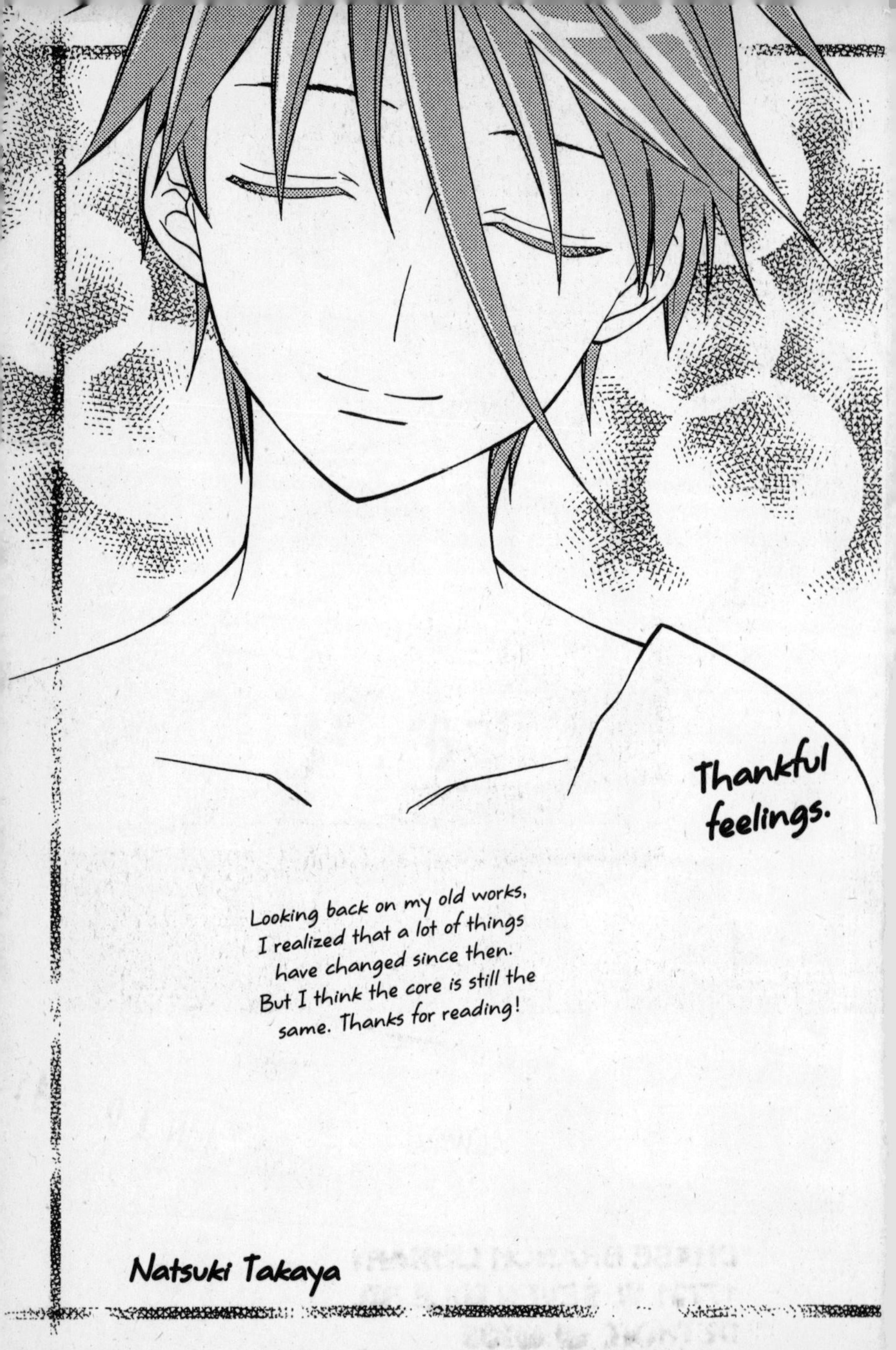
Thankful feelings.
Looking back on my old works, I realized that a lot of things have changed since then. But I think the core is still the same. Thanks for reading!
Natsuki Takaya

STOP!

This is the back of the book. You wouldn't want to spoil a great ending!

This book is printed "manga-style," in the authentic Japanese right-to-left format. Since none of the artwork has been flipped or altered, readers get to experience the story just as the creator intended. You've been asking for it, so TOKYOPOP® delivered: authentic, hot-off-the-press, and far more fun!

1
2
3
4
5
6
7
8
9
10

DIRECTIONS

If this is your first time reading manga-style, here's a quick guide to help you understand how it works.

It's easy... just start in the top right panel and follow the numbers. Have fun, and look for more 100% authentic manga from TOKYOPOP®!

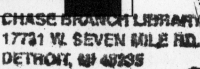